FOUR CHEEKS
TO THE WIND

FOUR CHEEKS
TO THE WIND

The story of a two year transcontinental bicycle ride

Mary Bryant

Mary Bryant

Matador
5 Weir Road
Kibworth Beauchamp
Leicester LE8 0LQ, UK
Tel: (+44) 116 279 2277
Email: books@troubador.co.uk
Web: www.troubador.co.uk/matador

ISBN 978 1848761 292

British Library Cataloguing in Publication Data.
A catalogue record for this book is available from the British Library.

Typeset in 11pt Bembo by Troubador Publishing Ltd, Leicester, UK
Printed and bound in Great Britain by TJ International Ltd, Padstow, Cornwall

Matador is an imprint of Troubador Publishing Ltd

For my mother
Mabel Eaves
who was proud of us for living our dream

and

for my husband
Warren Askew
without whom the trip would never have happened

CONTENTS

'Whatever you do, or dream you can do, begin it. Boldness has genius, power and magic in it. Begin it now.'

Quote from the great German writer
Johann Wolfgang von Goethe

CHAPTER 1

LEAVING ENGLAND

Neither of us can remember when we first decided that we wanted to cycle around the world. What we can remember, however, is that in the middle of a conversation I suddenly turned to Warren and said, 'Shall we cycle round the world one day?'

Warren didn't bat an eyelid at the question. 'Yes, alright,' he replied.

From that moment on, all conversations about the cycle trip began, 'When we cycle round the world . . .'

It was just one of those dreams that people have . . . or was it? Maybe that's how it started, but as time went by we began to discuss the possibilities of cycling round the world, and we started to believe that our dream was one that could become reality. Other people had done it, so why not us? Some things seemed against us. Whilst Warren was fit, enjoyed many outdoor pursuits and could cycle long distances, I was a plodder. Whilst I enjoyed cycling, I didn't like cycling up hills, I didn't like cycling long distances, and I didn't even like cycling fast downhill. I was keen, however, to cycle slowly round the world enjoying each day as it came. I was concerned that I would hold Warren back, but he was adamant that so long as he was on the road cycling, he didn't mind how fast we went or how far we went each day. There would obviously be times, though, when we would have to cycle long distances because accommodation wasn't available. I didn't mind the thought of occasional long days of cycling, and felt certain that as we progressed, my fitness and stamina should improve – maybe I would even lose weight!

Eventually we decided that, if our plan to cycle round the world was to become a reality, we should make some definite plans for the future. We calculated that it would probably take us two years of planning and preparation, so our new year's resolution for the millennium was to aim to be ready to leave England in the spring of 2002, and we began to work towards that date.

We already had bicycles, because we both cycled the short distance to work each day, and had also spent two or three holidays cycling and camping. However, for a world tour we needed special bicycles that were strong, comfortable, easy to maintain and capable of being repaired in any country. Warren was the expert. To me, a bicycle is a thing with two wheels, a saddle and handlebars, so Warren was left to organise our new bicycles. We had frames made to measure by a specialist frame-maker in Newcastle, and we bought the parts separately to have the bicycles made. We chose grey and black for the frames, because we didn't want the bicycles to be too noticeable, and we also had leather saddles fitted. There was a special drag brake on my bike to stop me going down hills too fast. (This brake also proved incredibly useful when parking my bike on a slope, and also stopped people who tried to move my bike). Both bikes had drop handlebars and 27 gears adapted by Warren to cater for low gears. The bikes also had racks to hold five panniers for our large quantity of luggage.

It was an exciting day when we collected the finished bikes, and we proudly stood alongside the sparkling bicycles to have our photos taken. We booked a cycling and camping holiday in Portugal, because we wanted to test how easy it was for the bikes to be taken on a plane. We knew this was something that we would have to do at times on our trip. Maybe it was a mistake with such brand new bikes in pristine condition, because we were so concerned that they would be damaged that we wrapped them in cardboard held together with miles of parcel tape, and said goodbye to the bikes, patting the saddles as they were wheeled from the check-in at Gatwick airport. The bikes, however, arrived unscathed despite our concerns, and we had an excellent practice run cycling along the Algarve coast. We made notes during the holiday of anything we felt we would need to take with us on our long trip, and we found this incredibly useful. We returned back to England even more excited about our world trip, and spent countless weekends on the bikes for the following year.

They say it takes 1,000 miles to break in a leather saddle, and after a three week cycling and camping holiday in Normandy the following year we had achieved this magic figure, and the hard leather saddles had moulded to the shapes of our backsides and were now, at long last, incredibly comfortable, despite their solid and old-fashioned appearance.

We had arranged for our house to be let and handed over to agents. Because we wanted to take our time cycling, we expected to be away on our trip for about three years. We were now in the new year of 2002. Powers of Attorney had been set up, we had sold our car, and we had saved like mad for two years and put the savings into special emergency savings accounts which we could access via the internet. Over the previous year we had been vaccinated against rabies, yellow fever, Japanese encephalitis, typhoid, polio, tetanus, diphtheria, Hepatitis A, Hepatitis B and meningitis.

We were ready to fix an actual date for leaving, and decided that this would be soon after my 58th birthday on 1st June 2002. We were running slightly behind our original schedule, but we decided to hand in our notice to leave our jobs by the end of April. Luck was very much on my side, because my job became redundant, and I was able to leave work at the end of May with a very nice redundancy payment, which would prove useful as a financial cushion when we returned to England. Warren left his job as a prison officer on the same day, and we celebrated early retirement together with our work colleagues in a local pub.

At the beginning of June we left our home town of Reading, saying goodbye to my three children and four grandchildren, and we travelled to Durham to say our goodbyes to Warren's parents and brothers. Then we travelled to Needham Market in Suffolk where my mother and brother lived, and I made last minute plans while staying with my mother to buy travel insurance and ferry tickets for the Channel crossing. Horrified to find that it would cost us £52 for two single fares from Dover to Calais, I booked two cheap day returns for £10 instead. I often wonder if the ferry operators are still waiting for us to return . . .

We checked our bags — we had two large pannier bags on the back, two smaller pannier bags on the front, and on the handlebar was a bag which could be clipped off and carried using a shoulder strap. My mother was amazed at the weight of the bags, convinced that it would be impossible to cycle on the level with them, let alone uphill. We packed and repacked our bags several times to ensure that everything we were carrying was necessary. By the time we left, the weight of Warren's bags was 40kg and the weight of mine was 30kg. These were now very heavy bikes, and would make cycling uphill especially difficult.

We had bought clothes that were lightweight, easy to wash, quick to dry and non-creasing. If we were cold we would wear several layers of lightweight clothes. We had cycling shoes, Teva sandals for cycling in hot weather and flip-flops. Everything that we had bought to take with us had to be as small as possible, as light as possible and preferably have half a dozen uses. We carried with us a good quality tent, pure down sleeping bags, which packed to a very small size in compression bags, saucepans and a frying pan, and a tiny lightweight stove which could use any fuel, such as petrol, paraffin or diesel. We couldn't reduce the weight of some things, such as first aid kits, which were bulky and fairly heavy. As well as the usual plasters and ointment, tablets for headaches, diarrhoea, allergies and sinusitis, we had included courses of antibiotics and a number of syringes in case we were unlucky enough to need injections or treatment in places where we doubted the standards of the hygiene. Other emergency items included a waterproof cover for covering the bikes or making a shelter from the rain, and an expensive ceramic water filter that would make even muddy ditch water suitable for drinking. Toilet bags also bulged with every possible item of toiletry.

Our cutlery bag held titanium spoons and forks, sharp knives, scissors, lighters and matches to light the stove, a Swiss Army penknife, a tiny container of washing up liquid, small containers of salt and pepper, and fold-up utensils for cooking.

We had bought a short-wave radio so we could check what was happening in the world. We knew we would often be away from tourist areas for long periods, so we needed to keep in touch. We also took with us a world atlas in the form of a small book, a present from my mother, so we could plan our route as we travelled.

Cycle tools were obviously necessary but also very heavy. Warren reduced the size and weight of the necessary spanners by sawing off the end he didn't need and making a detachable handle which would give leverage to the shortened spanner heads. He then made a roll-up bag for the tools which opened out with a large square of spare fabric, on which he would be able to place nuts, bolts and screws as he removed them from the bike, so they wouldn't be lost in the grass or dirt – this proved to be an invaluable item.

Our handlebar front pannier bags were likely to be very heavy. These held our valuables, such as our passports and money, but also cameras. We had decided to take with us our Canon SLR cameras, despite the fact that they were very heavy compared with modern tiny digital cameras. The extra lens, a telephoto one, was very heavy as well, but would be a vital accessory for taking photos of people, animals and birds from a distance, to get the most natural shots. I put into my bag a diary and also a tiny dictaphone (another present from my mother) which proved to be the most useful tool I carried – this was for making notes, so that I would remember as much as possible as we travelled on our bicycles to put into my diary at the end of each day.

Finally the day of departure arrived. Despite the heat of the days before, on the 18th June 2002 when we were due to leave England there were thunderstorms overhead. My brother was driving us 140 miles to Dover with our bicycles in the back of a van, so we said our tearful goodbyes to my mother. We didn't know how long it would be before we finished our trip, and knew that mum wouldn't be able to come out to see us somewhere along the route as we hoped some of the family would do. We promised to do a holiday in reverse at some time, and come back to England to see mum and the rest of our families. John took photos of us with mum and our bicycles, and we loaded our precious belongings into the van. As John drove down the road, we waved out of the windows to mum, who stood leaning on her stick at the door of her bungalow.

Lightning flashed several times through the sky as John, Warren and I travelled to the ferry. The boat left on time, with us waving to John as he stood on the dock, but as we approached Calais it began pouring with rain – not a good start for our trip! As soon as the passengers were called to their vehicles we began putting on all of our wet weather gear, and by the time we were ready to disembark, everyone else had vacated the boat and the rain had stopped!

We cycled around the streets of Calais until we found the road to Bologne; we needed to find a campsite or accommodation fairly soon as it was already late in the afternoon. As we approached a campsite a short while later the sun came out. We were on the outskirts of Calais close to Sangatte, famous only for its camps for illegal immigrants. After putting up our tent, we walked onto the beach behind the campsite. The sand and water looked beautiful, so long as we ignored the half dozen ferries sailing close by, and for the first time we felt as though we were on holiday. The planning of the last two years had never seemed quite real – until then it had seemed like a dream. We stood on the beach holding hands and grinned at each other. Our dream holiday had begun . . .

CHAPTER 2

CALAIS TO MARSEILLES, FRANCE

France is twice the size of Britain and is the largest country in Western Europe. France is extraordinary in its diversity – in the north are rolling hills and wild coastline, and in the south are the beaches of the Mediterranean. In between are mountains, vineyards, canyons, rivers and forests. The climate is temperate, apart from the mountainous regions, with a pleasant Mediterranean climate on the south coast.

Our plans were to cycle south avoiding Paris. Capital cities, whilst often interesting and beautiful to visit, are not ideal places for cycling, so we intended to avoid major cities where possible. We hadn't decided at this stage whether to turn left to go over the Alps, or whether to continue cycling south until we reached the Mediterranean. Obviously the latter would be the less hilly route.

We slept well in our tent on that first night despite our excitement at having begun our journey, and in the morning I went for a shower. As I turned off the shower, I heard a man coughing in the next cubicle, then two men speaking in French in the communal area. I was panic-stricken, realising that I must have walked into the men's shower block by mistake. I tried hard not to cough, and stood there waiting until it went quiet. Once I thought everyone had gone I dashed out of the cubicle, but a man was stood there in his trousers having a strip wash at one of the basins. I panicked again, put my head down muttering 'Bonjour' and passed a man as I ran out of the door who said 'Bonjour' cheerfully to me. Checking later I discovered that I hadn't made a mistake, and it was the ladies' shower block that I had been using. However, we discovered as we continued through France that the toilets and showers were often used by both sexes!

We set off along the coast and almost immediately crossed the dotted line shown on our map that indicated that the Channel Tunnel was somewhere deep in the ground below us aiming for England. It was hot and humid with an overcast sky as we cycled uphill, but it was a pleasant surprise as we reached the top to see to our right across the Channel the white cliffs of Dover lit up by the sun, looking extraordinarily close. It would be a long time before we saw our native land again. We turned inland for our first day's cycling. The grass verges and hedgerows were full of scarlet poppies, purple clover and mallow, wild orchids, buttercups, elderflower and white and dark pink wild roses. It was very hilly, and I struggled with the weight of the bike and often had to get off to push. The road was straight, but the hills went up and down like a steep switchback at a fair. We were trying to stay on the smaller roads, but our map was unfortunately not a large enough scale, and we couldn't find the road to Marquise. Eventually we found ourselves forced to go onto a motorway, because the road we had cycled led us to this major road only, but we decided to turn off at the next junction. Cars and lorries were sounding their horns at us, but we kept well over on the hard shoulder. If we had been stopped by police, our lack of French would have been very convincing.

Eventually we found our way back to the country roads, and cycled past fields of corn and barley. Flowering rape and flax made patches of bright yellow and delicate blue in the rolling landscape, and we noticed that peas and sweet corn had recently been planted by the farmers.

We found a campsite halfway through the afternoon, but it was twice as expensive as the one the night before. I felt guilty that we hadn't cycled very far because I was cycling so slowly, so I suggested carrying on even though I was already very tired. That was our first mistake, because we were both tired, the day was uncomfortably humid, and we couldn't find another campsite. By 6pm we were looking for a wild campsite, despite the fact that we were both desperate for a shower. We could find nothing suitable, only forest roads or farmer's fields with crops. Eventually we arrived at Desvres and found a gite. It was not yet officially open for the season, but the lady owner took pity on us and agreed to let us stay in the gite for the night. Of course, it was more expensive than the campsite we had rejected several hours before, but by now we would have paid anything, and we were especially grateful when the owner brought us free tea, coffee, milk and water, and sold us a bottle of French wine for €4.

By the third day of our journey, my hands had swollen and were badly blistered from sunburn, and my face looked as ruddy as an old sailor's. Warren said that I looked as though I had been abroad for three months already, not three days, and I was belatedly wearing cycling gloves to protect my hands from the sun, which was now beating down on us every day. Occasionally it rained, especially in the morning, and enormous worms and slugs left the safety of the grass verges as we cycled past and committed hari kari by trying to cross the sealed road.

We arrived in the small, very pretty town of Montreuil and booked into a picturesque campsite built on several levels surrounded with numerous old walls and archways. We walked hand in hand up the steep cobbled hills and through an ancient archway to the old town, passing old stone houses with roses rambling around the doors. At the top of the hill we discovered a lovely square surrounded by pavement cafés and two impressive churches. Trees amongst flower-filled pots and hanging baskets on lamp posts tastefully decorated the square. Typically French elegant tall town houses had shutters and window boxes full of colour. I had never before seen so many restaurants and cafés in one place, so we decided to walk round the entire square to decide where to eat. There were grills, pubs, cafés, hotels, brasseries, pizzerias, saladeries, restaurants, creperies and bars. We discovered that most of them weren't open at all that day.

'Fermé le jour,' said one hand-written notice (closed today), and numerous cafés had signs up to say that they weren't open on Mondays and Tuesdays, or Tuesdays and Wednesdays, or Wednesdays and Thursdays, or else they had no sign at all, but were clearly closed, the chairs stacked on top of the tables and the doors locked. Plenty of bars were open, but only two restaurants were serving food. However, neither of them opened until 7.30, and it was by then only 6pm. Our stomachs were rumbling. We decided to walk back the way we had come – we had seen a single restaurant that looked expensive. If it opened earlier than 7.15 we were willing to pay for a more expensive meal. Ten minutes later we arrived at the restaurant. The door was open, but there was no sign of customers. I walked in.

'A quelle heure sind sie ouvert?' I asked, immediately realising that I had asked what time he opened half in French and half in German. The waiter understood anyway.

'Sept heures,' he replied.

'Seven o'clock,' I told Warren. 'Let's walk back to the big square and have a look in the shop windows to kill time until 7 o'clock. Then we'll walk slowly back to this restaurant. At least it's on the way back to the campsite.'

Just before 7pm we returned to the restaurant, but as it came into view I gasped.

'I hope 'complet' doesn't mean full,' I said, seeing a notice. Sure enough, when we went into the restaurant to ask for a table for two, the waiter apologised that the restaurant was full – obviously all the local French people had been waiting for 7pm as well, and had rushed into the restaurant and filled it within two minutes of it being opened. We knew now we had to get to the other restaurant 10 minutes walk away, before that opened at 7.15 and was also full. Once more we passed the same shoes and the same clothes in the same shop windows as we hurried along the same cobbled road. We were just in time. Within 10 minutes of sitting down, that restaurant was also full and many potential customers were being turned away. We had a wonderful meal, but found the whole situation quite bizarre. Why were so many restaurants closed, when there was clearly the custom for them? Why did they not open earlier, when customers were obviously waiting to eat? And where had the people gone? It was dark as we returned back to the campsite. Old-fashioned lanterns hanging from elegant coils of metal attached to the city walls were lit, making pools of soft golden light on the cobbles. However, the streets were totally deserted . . .

After we had been cycling for a few days, though I kept it to myself initially, I wondered whether I had bitten off more than I could chew. I was finding the cycling incredibly hard, the bicycle was heavy when travelling up hills, and the weather was hot and humid. However, the encouragement of the French was so uplifting and unexpected, that this often gave me the motivation to try a little harder. One day as we set off after breakfast, we passed an accident on the opposite side of the road. We passed 4 kilometres of traffic jams caused by the accident. People in their stationary cars were tooting as we passed, leaning out of the car windows doing the thumbs up or the 'V' for victory signs; they were whistling, waving, shouting, smiling, laughing – not just one or two of them, but all of them! It was something I could not imagine happening in England, and it really cheered us on. When we reached a hill, nothing would have made me get off and push the bike in front of our audience, and the cheers and shouts became even louder.

We found as we continued our journey through France that sign-posted campsites were often miles away down the side roads, but with no indication of how far – no problem with a car but a serious problem for a tired cyclist! We also found that virtually none of the campsites sold food, so we had to buy food from supermarkets and carry it with us. This proved even more difficult as the weekend approached, because even the large supermarkets were closed on Sunday and Monday, so on Saturdays we had to stock up for three days. Although towns and villages had numerous cafés, these seldom sold food, only coffee or drinks. Often the cafés were in very poor condition, with electricity cables looped around the walls, and usually with a door direct to a very grimy toilet. The prices of drinks in the bars and cafés were exorbitant – it was costing €2.20 (about £1.50) for a very small glass of wine, even though it was possible to buy a bottle of wine in the supermarket for half that price. Beer was even more expensive and coffee, though excellent, was a luxury we could hardly ever afford.

Campsites were of very varying standards, and were mostly quite cheap. However, the price was no indication of the standard, often a cheaper site having better facilities than a more expensive one, but we found the toilets and shower blocks usually left a lot to be desired. Often the toilets were the 'squat' toilets that are so common in Asia, but it was clear from the queues for the one or two 'western' toilets that the French, like us, preferred to sit rather than to squat.

Children in campsites befriended us, clearly fascinated by our bikes. I felt sorry that we didn't speak enough French to converse with them or the people we met, but as we cycled through villages people shouted 'Bonjour' or 'Bon journée' as we passed, and it was a pleasure to be travelling in such a cycle-friendly country where Le Tour de France was the national sport.

We were struggling to speak the language, because very few of the French people that we met spoke English. I was able to speak a few simple phrases in schoolgirl French, but Warren had never leant French and I laughed at his pronunciation. However, he got his own back in later countries – he learnt Italian words quicker than I did, and he surprisingly seemed to understand directions spoken in Japanese! Because I speak more German than French, I found I was confusing the two languages, and I now have incredible admiration for linguists who can switch from one language to another without pausing to think.

If we passed a shop or supermarket in the morning, we often stopped to buy a baguette, cheese or paté, fruit or an almond croissant, and sometimes a bottle of wine. It was too hot to carry milk without refrigeration, but in any event we seldom saw fresh milk in any shop in France. UHT milk was always available, but we began to drink tea and coffee without milk. Butter or margarine melted if we carried them, so we chose creamy Brie, Camembert or my favourite French cheese, creamy blue St Agur, which we could spread onto freshly-baked bread. We liked to stop in the corner of a field for a lunch-time break in the sun to eat our cheese and cakes. Passing motorists sounded their horns and waved, and lying on the grass after such feasts and looking up at the blue sky and the overhanging branches of trees remains a permanent picture in my memory.

Our friends know that food is very important to us, so we always ate well even if we cooked 'at home', as we often did to balance our budget. We became experts at cooking the delicious salmon, chicken or steak which was available in the supermarkets, and accompanied this with new potatoes and fresh vegetables. Tractors so often dropped freshly harvested carrots, peas and leeks onto the road in front of us that we were able to subsidise our meals with this produce – Warren called it 'road kill'! We found it fun and a challenge to be able to cook something really good on our tiny petrol-fuelled stove, but we often had to cook strange things together to save fuel and time. If we cooked pasta one evening, we would throw in a few eggs to boil in the water so we could have hard-boiled eggs for breakfast or lunch the following day.

We found that with only a small portable stove we needed to be innovative and Warren, always good at inventing useful things, designed and made an insulating cover from a piece of foam bedroll. This cover completely enclosed one of our saucepans, and we found that we could bring vegetables to the boil, remove them from the heat and cover the pan. The vegetables continued to cook slowly within the insulated saucepan while we used the stove to cook something else!

It was very exciting when we ate in restaurants, where we were able to sample the delicious French cooking – mussels in Roquefort sauce, mussel soup, superb omelettes whipped up in seconds, and amazing large plates of crudités, an assortment of different salads arranged like the spokes of a wheel on the plate, with egg mayonnaise sitting like a hub in the centre.

In the early days of cycling in France we saw many war memorials and British and Allied cemeteries. The battle of the Somme had taken place in this area. It was so sad and very moving to stop to look at the graves. Almost all of those killed were very young, mostly in their teens and twenties, and many grave-stones simply said 'An unknown soldier'. The cemeteries were enormous and beautifully kept, but the vast numbers of them made us aware of the terrible nature and the atrocities of war. It was also the time of year for poppies, the flower of remembrance, and the hedgerows and fields were scarlet with these beautiful, fragile flowers.

As we continued cycling south, the steep hills of the first few days turned into rolling countryside and arable farming. Most of the corn had been cut, and fields were now full of sunflowers and sweet corn.

We arrived at Peronne, a small pretty town in Picardie with moated walls and a portcullised gateway. We were finding that all of the villages and towns in France had beautiful buildings and churches. In Peronne was a municipal campsite, and this pleased us because municipal sites are always in the centre of the town and are normally of a very high standard. We stayed a couple of days, and as we left we noticed a lone cyclist with his tent. The cycle and tent were clearly English, so we went over to chat and discovered that Norman was also planning to cycle round the world, and had started his journey from England only three days after us. His new bicycle was very similar to ours, as were his camping equipment and his plans. After a long chat we said our goodbyes, and set off south again. Three days later, after puffing and panting as we cycled up the steep hill to a fortressed town, we were greeted by Norman standing and waving to attract our attention, having been sat at a pavement café drinking a beer. This time, after several beers and glasses of wine together, we exchanged e-mail addresses and promised to keep in touch. Norman's was the first address of many that were logged in our diaries during our two year cycling trip.

The weather continued to be hot as we moved into July although, as in England, we could unexpectedly have a downpour of rain. We stopped once at an area commemorating the Great War. Two old tanks were sat on grassy mounds, and there were photographs and stories on display to show what had happened during the war in the area. We sat in the shelter of a bush to have some lunch because it was raining a little, but I felt the hairs on the back of my neck stand on end as I heard a spooky sighing sound. Warren couldn't hear it, and I began to think that I was imagining the sound, but the sound became louder. We went to investigate, and we realised that the sighing was caused by the wind blowing along the gun barrel, and it seemed such a significant noise – the sighs that regret the awful things that happened so long ago, yet still within living memory of some ...

As we travelled further south we left behind the war cemeteries, and after that most of the towns we visited were fortified with very old walls around them, but unfortunately for us these were usually at the top of steep hills, which made for hard cycling.

The first large town we stayed at was Rheims, 150km east of Paris, and we decided to find a guesthouse or small hotel, our first since we had started our cycling. The owner of the very first small hotel we approached was very happy to let us wheel our bikes past reception and into an enclosed area at the back. The room was large and old-fashioned but comfortable and in the centre of the city, and at £17.64 (€25.95) was less than the price for bed and breakfast per person in England. For the first time we had a marvellous choice of restaurants, and found it difficult to choose between Chinese, Indian, Mexican or French, but when we saw a Japanese restaurant we were decided. Afterwards Warren swore that he would never eat cooked salmon or tuna again, because the raw fish in the Japanese restaurant had been so delicious! As we left the restaurant, we were amazed to see that the whole of Rheims had become a big market, with stalls in every street. We wandered round the stalls fascinated, eventually getting lost in the maze of streets.

We often stopped cycling for a break of cakes and coffee now. Delicious apple tarts, tarte tatin, almond croissants or fresh apricots set into enormous wedges of custard tart were far too good to pass – the French certainly know how to make delicious cakes!

We were approaching champagne country, and were beginning our third week of cycling. We were both jubilant and felt that this was our first milestone, because we didn't have to turn north again to return home to work, as we had done on previous cycling holidays. We continued cycling south and our confidence was growing. Although I still harboured quiet doubts about being able to cycle round the world, I now felt certain that I could make it to the south coast of France, and surely that would be an achievement to be proud of. We were very surprised when we found ourselves in Chalon-en-Champagne, which was not on our detailed map. However, we found a four star municipal campsite which was the best we ever found in France. Superb showers with constant free hot water to point onto the back of my aching neck and back, a campsite bar, and the thought of being able to visit one of the champagne houses, were all that was needed to persuade us to stay a few days. The mystery of the missing town on our map was solved the next day, when we discovered that Chalon-en-Champagne was a new name for the town, which had previously been called Chalon-sur-Mer.

Internet cafés were few and far between in France, but in Chalon we found one, and were excited to find several e-mails from friends. Because the lay-out of the keyboard was different from an English keyboard it affected my usually fast typing speed, but we managed to send out several e-mails to friends, and I sent the first of the many newsletters about our trip to a large group of friends and family.

We had hoped to spend an average of £20 per day maximum on this trip, although this was likely to be almost impossible in Western Europe. We were spending £30 a day, even though we were camping most of the time and eating out only occasionally, and we knew it would be even more expensive in the south of France. However, we didn't want to give up our wine and, after all, wine was the only thing in France that was really cheap. We had discovered wine that was quite drinkable for €1 for one litre, and we never again on the whole of our trip found wine cheaper. We hoped, however, that once we got to Asia, our average per day for the whole trip would be reduced to less than £20.

We went out for an evening meal which was a great success, despite a very surly waiter. Warren had chosen Oeufs Gratinée, which we assumed would be a type of egg mayonnaise. The dish arrived piping hot in a shallow dish, and turned out to be a layer of cooked wild mushrooms on which two raw eggs had been dropped. Topped with cheese sauce and baked, the eggs had quickly cooked to perfection, so that when Warren took a spoonful of the browned cheese sauce, the soft egg yolk merged with the cheese sauce and cooked mushrooms to make the most delicious starter ever! (We discovered a long time later that this dish was usually known as eggs 'en cocotte').

The following day two Dutch cyclists arrived at the campsite with two teenage children. We were fascinated to watch them put up three large tents, and wondered how they could possibly manage to carry so much. That was only the beginning. A few minutes later another cycling couple arrived to join them, and then two other couples, and they proceeded to put up enormous canvas tents that looked like marquis, with heavy plastic sheets beneath the tents and with poles like scaffolding poles. We counted 30 guy-ropes and 50 pegs around the tent. The whole group of ten people subsequently pulled out their folding chairs, and also produced a large table for the dining area of one of the tents! We were astounded where the gear could be coming from and decided that they were travelling by tardis rather than by bicycle. As Warren and I sat cooking outside our tent, I could hear behind me the sound of puffing and blowing. Not wishing to appear rude by turning round to look, I asked Warren if they were blowing up mattresses.

'No,' he said, 'It's Ursula – their blow-up companion.' Our sides were aching because we were laughing so much, but when I did look round later one of the women was blowing up a 6 inch thick rubber mattress for each person. They kept producing more and more things – a giant water melon, a litre of yogurt, a wok, enormous tins of brussel sprouts. [A week later we found the same enormous tins of sprouts in a supermarket, and discovered that they were from Belgium. Maybe the Dutch cyclists had been Belgian, after all, and possibly it was the sprouts that propelled them along!] When one woman produced a collapsible footstool as well as a chair, we decided it was time to disappear into our tent, as our mirth was surely going to offend the cyclists if they realised why we were laughing, especially as at that point one of the group began to wash up using a large plastic bowl. The next morning was the final straw, when Warren saw that several of them had walking boots – something we would have liked to have brought, but had decided that they were too heavy and bulky to carry.

Our visit to the champagne house that day was fascinating. Underneath the large elegant house surrounded by high walls were two miles of passages dug into the stone. Apparently the Romans had quarried the chalk which had made the caves. It was dark, cool and smelt musty, and everything had mould on it including the corks in the bottles. We saw bottles of champagne at various stages, some upside down, others at different angles, and we were told that the bottles were turned slightly each day. There weren't many workers there, but most of the work was done by hand. There were magnums and bottles with personalised labels that had been ordered by individuals. The tour finished with several glasses of delicious champagne, and we cycled back to the campsite hoping not to be stopped by a gendarme and breathalysed.

The following day we set off again, worried that the ten Dutch people might overtake us with their heavy loads and show us up. The countryside was lovely with rolling hills, and a beautiful mixture of wild flowers coloured the verges – poppies, massive drifts of purple vetch, tiny little cerise sweet peas and miniature yellow antirrhinums, great banks of camomile, white and deep pink convulvus, purple thistles, yellow spires and delicate blue wild scabious. I was enjoying the day, especially when Warren moved some of my gear onto his bike to make it easier for me, and we arrived at the next campsite in good time.

This was another municipal campsite, but couldn't have been different from the last one. The site was good, with grass pitches edged with hedges to give privacy, but after we'd put up the tent I went to find the toilet and shower block. There were three toilet cubicles, each one filthier than the last. Two children were there waiting for their mother who was in one of the squat toilets. These proved even worse – it was actually impossible to use them without standing in excrement, and it was even on the walls. A check of the shower block showed that there was no hot water anywhere. We couldn't understand it – the cars and caravans on the site were incredibly smart and obviously expensive, and children played on expensive quad bikes and miniature motor bikes. The caravans even had large trailers behind the caravans, which we noticed were plumbed into water as well as electricity. We later found that these trailers housed the kitchen – a sink, water heater, oven, microwave and refrigerator lined one side of the trailer. On the other side was a worktop over a washing machine, tumble dryer and freezer. It made the expression 'everything but the kitchen sink' seem utterly inadequate! It became clear that the site was housing travellers who had their own facilities and were therefore not concerned with the state of the toilet block. We moved on to find another campsite without paying.

It was raining the next day when we arrived at Lac de Der Chantecoq, where we were able to cycle on a sealed cycle-way around the lake. It was Saturday, but there was no-one in sight, and although the lake was obviously man-made it was pretty, with a church standing alone on a peninsular at one end. We found the pretty church had been left empty and unused for many years. The panelled hardwood gothic doors were barred by a locked gate, as were all of the church windows. None of the four faces of the clock in the pretty tower had hands, although the Roman numerals could be clearly seen. A plaque was fixed to the empty church. Translated it said, 'At the foot of this church can be found the village of Champaubert-aux-Bois, swallowed up by the waters of the Lac du Des. 215 inhabitants became exiled from 1969 to 1972.' It was signed by M. Gabriel Thieblemont, who had been the last mayor of the village. The church was on the very edge of the man-made lake, and we thought how sad it was that the local council had not been able to use the church, even if it had been as a small museum to show the former village that now lay at the bottom of the lake. There was no name for the church, which had been built in 1873, almost one century before its village was taken from it.

The next day was warm again, and we cycled through pleasant rolling countryside. When we arrived at the village where we planned to camp we found that the campsite shown on our map was no longer there. The next one was 20 miles further on, so before we set off we filled our water bottles at a green pump in the square. The sky was blue with pretty clouds, but it was very hot and there was no shade. We passed through villages, where families sat in their front gardens round large tables having Sunday lunch. Wine and water was always on the table, and the smell of barbecues made our mouths water. We had a choice of routes at a junction – follow a river across fairly flat ground but with no guarantee of a campsite, or across some hills and valleys but with two campsites shown on the map. We chose the latter, but I became very tired and could feel the sun burning my skin.

We cycled up hills and down again, and were relieved when we arrived at a village where there was a busy café. Having fantasised about a glass of beer, it was wonderful to sit down and be presented with our fantasy. A local lady invited us into her home to see a small museum that she and her family had built, and after that we were on our way again. It was now very late, because we had been cycling all day – our longest day so far. The last few miles to the campsite were downhill – down and down and down, through the dense shade of a forest, so that for the first time that day we felt cold.

The campsite that had been marked on the map was set beside the river. Although it was one of the prettiest sites we ever found in France, it was also by far the cheapest at €3.50 (£2.40). As we put up our tent an English woman came over and offered us a cold beer, which we gratefully accepted as soon as we had showered. We spent the evening chatting to Norman and Gin (Virginia) who travelled extensively in their motorhome, and they had been surprised to see English people cycling in that part of France. Indeed, we seldom saw other English people now. We said goodbye to Norman and Gin in the morning, promising to keep in touch.

Occasionally it was raining when we woke in the morning, and we continued lying in our sleeping bags in the hope that the rain would stop. Before pitching our tent we always checked our compass and, if possible, set up the tent facing east so that the early morning sun (if it appeared!) would have dried our tent by the time we packed it into our bags.

The weather was very changeable, sometimes being unbearably hot, but at least then we could take photographs. We knew that it was going to be very difficult for us to buy souvenirs on this trip unless they were very light in weight so we could send them home, so photographs were likely to be the main reminders of our trip, and already we had taken many. We had decided that the best way to deal with the photographs was to send the films home undeveloped, so that Warren's parents could get them developed for us. This meant that we had to be really organised and keep records of the photos taken, if we were to be able to know in the future exactly where and when photos had been taken. As well as the photos, we sent our maps back to England, because these were a record of where we had cycled and stayed.

At times we cycled along canals, which was incredibly peaceful and quiet after the busy roads. The only noise came from the birds – usually herons or birds of prey – and often a strange, incredibly loud noise came from the plants growing in the canal. We discovered that this noise was made by frogs, but they always disappeared as we approached unless we were especially quiet. We had our first puncture, caused by a small piece of flint, as we cycled along one canal, but at least it was safe to stop to do the necessary repair.

In Langres the municipal campsite was situated within the 7 metre thick walls of a 15th century fortified town on top of a hill. The views of the surrounding countryside were superb from the campsite, and we stood on the walls watching the sun set. A middle-aged couple on a motorbike arrived shortly after us. He was wearing a bright orange jacket and wore a shirt and tie underneath. The jacket was marked 'Royal Mail', so we knew that they were English before we saw the registration of the bike, and we went to chat to them. We were now in our fourth week travelling slowly through France.

We occasionally stopped in pretty villages for coffee, and were surprised how fast the lorries rumbled through the narrow streets. Even the 'convoi exceptionnel' with their exceptionally wide, long or heavy loads, with lights flashing and sometimes preceded by or followed by a warning vehicle, would speed through the narrow streets, despite the very old buildings which surely must have been at risk. However, despite the speed of the traffic, in France we usually felt very safe cycling, because lorries and cars always gave us a wide berth, waiting safely behind us until it was safe to pass on the other side of the road. If a car went very close as it passed, we could almost guarantee that there would be a GB sticker on the back!

We wondered how disabled people fared in France, because there appeared to be no special facilities for them. The kerbs were often incredibly high, and the pavements would narrow suddenly, especially in villages, leaving too narrow a space for pushchairs, let alone wheelchairs or mobility scooters.

One day we arrived at a very small campsite, and a notice on the office indicated that campers should choose their pitch and pay when the office opened for one hour later in the afternoon. We were alone, and as we put up our tent we heard Concorde flying high overhead, a sound that reminded us of 11.30 every morning at home. We chose the only spot of shade, which was under a lone tree, but as the day drew to a close more and more caravans and motorhomes arrived, and we found ourselves surrounded. Warren warned me to get a shower quickly before the rush, as there were only three showers, and he recommended that I go to one on the left which was extra large. As I walked to the showers I could see a couple with towels ahead of me, and in order to get to the best one first I dashed ahead, pulled the door to the shower open and stepped quickly in, locking the door behind me. As I turned I jumped, because there was a man standing there naked with a glass of champagne in each hand. Unable to cover his modesty without spilling the champagne or dropping the glass, he appeared to be speechless as he stared at me.

'Pardon,' I said in French, struggling to unlock the door again.

'That's alright,' he said, so he was obviously English.

I stumbled back out of the shower and straight into the empty cubicle opposite, locking the door behind me with shaking fingers. Only a few seconds later I heard a woman's voice saying 'Hello baby' and giggles (both male and female) coming from the big shower opposite. I don't know if I had put him off, but I didn't feel that they could have had that much fun, because they'd left before

I finished my shower! For the rest of that evening I slunk around the campsite wearing a sunhat in the hope that I'd not be recognised, and praying that I wouldn't hear someone speaking English.

We were now on our way to Dijon. Approaching the city was scary because we were on a ring road which was very busy, but a campsite was fortunately signposted as we approached the city. As in all cities, we had a much wider choice of food, so we chose spicy food, as we had been unable to buy hot spices or chillies to add to our cooking. Dijon was one of our favourite French cities. It's very clean and has many wonderful buildings, with lovely pavement bars and cafés, so we enjoyed sitting and relaxing with a drink in our hands, taking photographs and looking in the shops.

The following day was cooler as we cycled south out of Dijon. We cycled through Dijon's industrial area, and after a few miles we were in Burgundy country. On the outskirts of the villages were ancient wine-presses and other old pieces of wine-making machinery filled with flowers. We passed beautiful chateaux, and vineyards were surrounded with lovely old stone walls topped with pitched roofs made of stone tiles. The temperature had dropped as we arrived in Beaune, a very pretty old town. Beaune was the first town we visited that was alive on a Sunday. It was humming with tourists, with a little road train and a pony and trap to show them the sights. There were lovely narrow roads with cafés and old buildings, towers, steeples, churches and museums. However, the best tourist attractions were the caves, where free tasting of expensive wines was encouraged, and by the time we returned to our tent we were feeling nicely relaxed.

We cycled further south along very quiet, pretty country roads. There were lovely scenes of sunflowers and tall sweet corn – the sweet corn that had been a foot high four weeks ago in northern France was now five feet high and beginning to flower. The fields were full of tall sunflowers, their heavy heads turned towards the sun. It began to rain, so we sheltered in a covered bus stop in a village to eat our bread and cheese for lunch, and we were delighted when the elderly lady in the house opposite opened her front door and ushered us into her large, cosy kitchen so that she could make us a delicious pot of coffee. She spoke no English, and we spoke very little French, but we were pleased to discover how friendly and hospitable the French could be.

After four weeks of cycling, I had expected to be very fit and used to cycling, but although I was now thoroughly enjoying myself, I was still finding it quite hard when we had to cycle uphill, and often suffered with painful hands. (It was not until several years later, still suffering with painful hands and also a painful neck, that I discovered that bones at the base of my thumbs and in the back of my neck were disintegrating with osteo-arthritis, and I eventually had an operation in late 2006 to remove a bone in one hand in the hope of reducing the pain).

Many people we met made comments on how brown we were. As we were now 1,000 kilometres from Calais, we had been on our bikes for several weeks, and already people were amazed that we had cycled so far. We cycled into Lyons and found a hotel in the centre of the city with a garage underneath the building where we could leave our bikes. Most of the tall buildings in the city had superb old cast-iron verandahs, window-boxes, and pelmets to the windows and railings, which we had noticed in many of the French cities. What a shame that so much of the Victorian cast iron was removed from the English cities during the last war.

We didn't carry mobile phones. We hadn't used mobile phones before we left, and it had proved difficult to find a phone that might work in every country, so we had decided not to buy one. However, e-mails from home told us that it was very cold and wet in England. In Lyon it was very hot as we cycled across the river and south again along a road lined with what Warren called 'camouflage trees' – magnificent plane trees with peeling bark displaying patches of greens, browns and beiges on the trunk. Someone was asleep on a bench by the river with his head on a loaf of bread; an artist was painting the river view; a church clock was striking the half hour. South of Lyon centre the Rhone and Saône rivers converged, but a motorway and railway came between us and the river. This area was very industrial, so we were relieved when at last the road became more rural, and we noticed lizards on the sandy path alongside the road. As we approached on our bicycles, the lizards dashed into the crevices of the stone walls edging the vineyards. Every corner of every piece of land was utilised, and vines were planted between houses and almost on the grass verges of the road. We were now cycling alongside the Rhone river again, which was very wide at that point, so it was very pleasant scenery again.

In the next campsite we decided to have an early night and start early the next morning to cycle when it was cooler. Just as we were packing up our gear ready to go to bed, every mum, dad, granny, aunt, uncle and child in the campsite brought their chairs and placed them in lines on the path alongside our tent. It became obvious that this was the boules area, and we had already discovered that everyone in France plays boules when on holiday. The noise of everyone talking, laughing, cackling, shouting and clapping and the loud clicking as the boules hit each other a few inches away from our heads was deafening, but we knew they would soon leave when it got dark. Not a chance – floodlights came on lighting up our tent, and the noise continued until late. We resorted to wearing ear-plugs and eye-masks, necessary items of any traveller's equipment, but the noise was too close and too loud. Eventually the families departed at 11.30pm, and we were finally able to sleep . . .

★ ★ ★

The cycling was very pleasant; it was warm and we were now in the fruit-producing region of France. Neat orchards were full of small trees laden with apples, pears, peaches, nectarines, apricots and plums. There were so many black plums on trees that the heavily-laden branches were bent over touching the ground. Tables set outside the gates of fields sold fruit at ridiculously low prices, and often the farmer or his wife gave us a red-flushed apricot or peach before buying, so that we could have a taste first. For €1 (about 67p) we bought a kilo of white nectarines from one couple, and then they gave us ten of the biggest apricots we'd ever seen 'for the road'.

At this moment two girls cycled past with touring bags. We had noticed them in Lyons, and now they passed us waving as we stopped to buy fruit. When we next caught up with them we found they were German and, of course, spoke excellent English. Their parents had driven them to the Swiss border where they had caught the train to Lyons. Their plan was to cycle from Lyons to Marseilles, following the river south. They were horrified by the amount of luggage we were carrying, until we told them that we hoped to cycle round the world.

We stopped at a supermarket, relieved to get into the air-conditioned coolness of the interior. Half an hour later when we left the supermarket, the bikes were burning hot sitting in the sun, and the temperature had risen to an unbelievable 35°C. I lost the will to go further, which until our stop had seemed possible, so we returned half a mile to a campsite sign which directed us up into the hills, and 3 miles later we found the campsite where we set up our tent in some deep shade. Fortunately most French campsites have plenty of trees to give shade to the tents and caravans. While Warren swam in a small lake formed by a dam across the river next to the campsite, I lay in our hammock eating apricots. I was really enjoying this new lifestyle. Crickets were chirping and very tiny lizards lay in the sun. The campsite had a bar, which was very unusual in France, so cold drinks were also available. We were content.

The next morning as I cooked omelettes for breakfast, it began to rain heavily, so Warren set up a waterproof cover between two trees to enable us to cook and eat underneath the shelter. We decided to cycle only 15 miles to the next large town, where we booked into a forested campsite with very little grass. We were concerned that if it rained again the ground would become very muddy, but at least the tall trees offered some protection from the rain.

After our meal that evening we decided to find a bar to have a drink. Thunder was rumbling in the distance, so we put on our waterproof tops with our shorts and flip-flops. As we visited the nearby marina, rain and hail began, so we hurried to a bar on the first floor. The lightning and thunder were quite frightening, although normally I enjoy thunderstorms. We had just ordered drinks when there was a loud commotion on the metal balcony outside, and everyone came rushing into the bar. Outside there were hailstones as big as golf balls flying down and bouncing all over the balcony and in through the windows. The noise of the hail on the metal was unbelievable, and we turned to the barman to speak, only to discover that all of the bar staff had disappeared. They had rushed outside to move their cars, which we thought was quite strange, until we returned to the campsite to find campers examining the damage to their cars and caravans. Those who had been quick thinking had hurriedly grabbed sleeping bags and duvets to throw onto the cars to protect them, and this bed linen now lay dripping wet and dirty in piles. Those who had not been so quick were now examining the extent of the damage – quite serious dents covered bonnets and roofs of cars, but at least they could sleep that night in their sleeping bags! We were proud to find that our tent was completely unscathed, but knew that it was a tent designed for the most serious of inclement weather, even at high altitudes.

We had now been cycling for over a month, and although we were gradually cycling further distances in a day, I felt that my cycling speed was very poor, especially if there was the slightest hill. However, there was no time limit, so I still hoped that my fitness and strength would improve as time went by. In the meantime, we were both thoroughly enjoying ourselves, and one day Warren suddenly cycled past me with a big grin on his face. It was 9 o'clock on a Monday morning, and as he passed me he was laughing out loud.

'I've just realised – this is the office,' he shouted, pointing at his bike, 'And this is my work!' He waved his arm generally at the road ahead and the surrounding countryside.

I often wondered what the French cyclists thought of us – they were always friendly and shouted 'bonjour' as they flew past us on their skinny bikes with their skinny tyres. They wore matching skin-tight gear (usually red and black) to match their bikes, gloves, shoes and aerodynamic helmets, and there was never a single gram of extra weight on their bikes. We, however, plodded on with five bulging bags each and extra items strapped on the rack behind us; flannels and tea-towels were strapped on top flapping in the wind to dry, and we wore ordinary shorts, shirts and sunhats with Teva sandals! They would never have put a demi-baguette on their bike, let alone the bags of meat, potatoes, bread and eggs that we often carried for the day's meals!

We arrived at Viviers, which we discovered to be a beautiful mediaeval city reminding us of Robin Hood's Bay on the coast of north Yorkshire. Robin Hood's Bay is an ancient picturesque fishing village with a maze of pretty cobbled streets. In Viviers there were similar quaint cobbled streets going uphill in every direction to the ancient cathedral at the top, and very old buildings lined these pretty streets. At the top of the hill by the cathedral was a large statue, and the panoramic views of red-tiled roofs from the top reminded us of the Mediterranean.

We were now close to Avignon, and I was looking forward to seeing 'Le Pont d'Avignon'. We stopped at the top of a hill to see the view of mountains in the distance; there was the aromatic smell of wild lavender beneath our feet. We ate our bread and cheese and some apples picked that day from a tree, and then cycled down the steep hill on the other side. There were more vineyards, birds were singing, crickets were chirping, and sunflowers in the fields looked almost ready for harvesting, the dying petals leaving the enormous drooping seed-heads looking forlorn on their tall stems. Elderberries and blackberries were ripe in the hedgerows; this was very early compared to in England – it was still not yet August. Hills were always in the distance now, junipers and poplars divided fields and vineyards, and several tractors were spraying the vineyards. As we approached Avignon we saw a campsite on the outskirts, and decided to stay there rather than try to find a campsite in the centre. We realised that this was a very good decision when we discovered that a festival was held in Avignon for the arts, theatre and opera for 23 or 24 days every July. We had certainly arrived at the right time! Avignon is a walled city with a maze of streets inside the walls. As we walked through one of the 14 gateways in the city wall into Avignon we discovered that it was full, absolutely full, of tourists and strangely dressed people. There were a lot of American tourists, but we had never seen Americans anywhere else in France. People had pierced faces, strange hairdos, paint and tattoos over their bodies; people were singing in the street and laughing, or standing on boxes shouting. It reminded us of Reading, our home town, during the annual Pop Festival weekend.

In the central square, which was full of cafés, we wandered around watching what was happening. Travelling theatres were drawn to Avignon during this month, and there were people doing drawings, portraits, sketches and caricatures; people with their bodies painted silver or gold were standing still as statues, and actors were doing sketches. There were singers, mediums, people making fancy shapes out of balloons, people on stilts, people dressed up in weird clothes, people playing every type of musical instrument one could think of. A lovely old-fashioned carousel stood in the centre of the square. There were people doing mimes, people on unicycles, people in theatrical masks and fancy dress, rap dancers, tap dancers, jazz bands, groups of people standing in semi-circles watching acts, bands with accordions, cellos and guitars. There was an ethnic man with long hair and a very long beard blowing an even longer wooden tubular instrument and drum; there were henna tattooists, stalls selling jewellery, people playing African musical instruments. The whole town was covered with posters for every type of entertainment, and leaflets were constantly being handed out to advertise comedians, singers, plays, operettas and magicians. Avignon is the cultural centre of France, and the whole town was crazy for almost a whole month. It was a perfect time to visit, but we couldn't imagine what Avignon would be like at any other time of the year.

We went to see the bridge. Every time I thought about it I found myself singing the famous French song that we had been taught as young children in school. No-one had ever bothered to translate the words for us, so we had learnt the song parrot-fashion, and it seemed a shame that at the time, as a young girl, I had never been aware that the song referred to a bridge at Avignon in France. The bridge was immortalised by this song that we all learnt as children:

'Sur le pont d'Avignon, l'on y danse, l'on y danse.
Sur le pont d'Avignon, l'on y danse tous en rond . . .'

★ ★ ★

Pont St. Benezet was built in the 12th century but was reworked in the 15th century, and it was the first bridge built over the Rhone. St. Benezet wasn't actually canonised, but is believed to have been a real person. Apparently in 1177, he was tending his sheep in Viviers when he heard a voice telling him to go to Avignon and build a bridge over the raging torrent of the Rhone. An angel showed him the way, because he had never left his village before, and a cardinal asked him to lift a stone to prove it was God's voice that he had heard. The stone would have required 30 men to lift, but Benezet lifted it and threw it into the Rhone, and it's said that this became the first stone of the bridge. The local people were so enthralled that they raised money to help build the bridge, which was finished in the mid 1180s.

The bridge no longer scans the whole river, but is very photogenic. We decided to get up very early the next morning, as we knew that the bridge would look especially pretty at sunrise. The next morning saw us creeping out of our tents at 4.30am while it was still dark. This was when we found that we were locked into the campsite. The site was surrounded by high fences with large gates, and the pedestrian gate, for which we had a card, wouldn't open. As the sky gradually began to lighten, indicating that sunrise was imminent, we desperately struggled with the strong gate to try to get out. Eventually Warren managed to pick the lock (had he perhaps had advice from one of his 'clients' from his previous job as a prison officer?) and we were free, cycling like mad to get to our chosen spot before the sun rose.

It was all worth while. As the sun rose and hit the bridge, the colour of the grey sandstone turned to golden, and we took a number of very lovely photos, the arches of the bridge mirrored in the still water below. Afterwards we walked through one of the gateways of the city into the maze of cobbled streets to find a café for breakfast and coffee. (Those cobbled streets were very painful for cyclists!) The town was very quiet. The only other people in the streets were the cleaners, cleaning up the papers, the ripped posters, the leaflets and flyers, the cigarette butts, beer cans and bottles left after the parties the night before. Presumably they had to do this every morning during July while the Festival was on.

We were very excited as we left Avignon to continue south, because we knew that it would now be only two days before we reached Marseilles, and we were so looking forward to seeing the sea again after over five weeks of cycling across land from Calais. The road was very busy, and for the first time in France cars were sounding their horns at us to tell us to get out of their way. Unfortunately, the French have large numbers of minor accidents, and the glass is always swept into the gutter where we were cycling. By now we had had a number of punctures, and didn't want to risk cycling where we could see broken glass.

After 15 miles the road became more rural again. The fruit trees had now given way to olive trees, a sure sign of the approaching Mediterranean, and even the breeze as we free-wheeled down hills was hot against us.

On Saturday, 27th July 2002, we achieved two goals – my cycle computer clocked up 1,000 miles (Warren's computer was set to kilometres), and a few miles later we cycled into Marseilles. We had still not seen the sea, despite having cycled up a number of hills, and as we cycled through the busy streets Warren unexpectedly stopped in front of me. The road dipped down into a tunnel, so we switched on our lights and, as we cycled out of the tunnel at the other end, there was the Mediterranean in front of us. 1004 miles from Calais to the Mediterranean! The sea was the most amazingly striking blue, and we stopped to take a photograph of ourselves before cycling on, looking for somewhere to stay. It was very busy, very noisy, cars were sounding their horns, there were numerous lanes and it was rather frightening, but none so much as when we suddenly found ourselves entering a tunnel on a downward hill with traffic alongside and behind us. There was no time and no place to switch on lights; I was ahead and couldn't even see the ground in front of me. There was poor lighting in the tunnel, and there was no sign of light at the end of the tunnel. I knew Warren was immediately behind me; all of a sudden I felt, rather than saw, that I was going uphill, and I struggled to keep up the speed for fear that a vehicle behind might plough into us from behind. With a sigh of relief I saw light ahead and we were out in the open again. We were now passing different ports, and noticed that the cars waiting to board were stacked several feet high with luggage on the top, and we wondered what people were taking home. The ferries were bound for Tunisia, Algeria and Corsica.

Cars disembarking from ferries joined our two lanes from the right, and we found ourselves in the middle of fast flowing traffic, so we were relieved when we eventually got through Marseilles, even though the roads had become very hilly. We hadn't been able to find any of the campsites marked on the map, and the road ahead was going up and up. We were several miles the other side of Marseilles, and now there was only a pass ahead of us, with no chance of any accommodation until we were over the mountain. Warren and I knew that it would be very hard to cycle over the mountain at the end of a hard day's cycling, so we cycled back to the nearest village. However, the only hotel was full, so we had to cycle several miles back to Marseilles. My heart sank as we cycled downhill, knowing that the next day we would have to cycle back the same way again and then over the mountain pass – it was really quite disheartening.

Despite road signs pointing to hotels, we just couldn't find any at all, which seemed extraordinary in such a large city, so we eventually booked a three-bedroomed apartment for the night for €70. For £47 it didn't seem bad value compared to English prices, and at least we could save money by cooking our own food. The air-conditioning and bath were such bliss for my aching legs, shoulders and feet, so we put a bottle of champagne into the fridge, cooked a lovely meal, and celebrated reaching the south coast. Now we could enjoy cycling along the Mediterranean coast to Monaco and Italy . . .

CHAPTER 3

THE MEDITERRANEAN
COAST OF FRANCE

The Côte d'Azure, which includes the French Riviera, is renowned for its expensive resorts where the rich and famous spend their time relaxing on the beaches of the Mediterranean. This well-known coastline stretches from Toulon to the Italian border, interrupted only by the tiny principality of Monaco.

It was 5.30am and still dark when our alarm went off the next morning. We had discussed the day's cycling, and I felt I was able to cycle over the pass without any problem so long as it was not in the heat of the day. We had to get to the pass before the sun hit the road, so we left Marseilles as soon as we had eaten breakfast. We cycled up the long hill for 7½ miles, back along the way we had come the day before. Many cyclists were out on the road. It was a Sunday, and the French love cycling up mountains. The road was superb, with a cycle path the whole of the way up to the top of the mountain (1,072 feet), and French cyclists on their empty racing bikes passed us constantly saying 'Bonjour'. I felt very proud of myself that I cycled the whole way, never getting off to push, and at the top was a lovely spot for wild camping (if only we'd known the day before!), with a glorious view of ranges of mountains behind each other in the background. Next it was downhill again, this time at 35 to 40 miles per hour, although I stopped once to take photos. I imagine I was the only cyclist ever to stop going downhill at that speed just to take a photo! Unfortunately we discovered that the climbing wasn't over, and another mountain was ahead of us. By this time the road was in full sun, so I found it hard going and didn't enjoy it at all. However, we eventually climbed to the top and down again, despite the heat on our backs.

We arrived at a small town, La Ciatot, and there were traffic jams, which reminded us of England. Everyone was heading for the beach, but we just stopped for coffee and cycled past the traffic until we found a campsite. Now that we were on the coast the prices were higher, and the rate was a set price for two people, a car and a tent. There was no reduction for us without a car. We asked for a site with shade, and were shown a tiny site behind a building with no grass. The campsite was very busy and this very small pitch seemed to be the only choice for us. There were walls on two sides of the pitch, which would block any breeze, and the ground was bare of grass and hard. The one redeeming feature of the pitch was that it was surrounded by trees so we would have shade all day so, as shade was paramount, we agreed to pitch our tent there. However, we did notice later that there were small sharp stones under the base of the tent, so we were worried that they could have damaged the fabric.

The sight of the azure blue sea on one side of us, a stall on the campsite selling barbecued chickens, a restaurant and shop selling wine and, finally, good showers, persuaded us to stay a second night. The sites were certainly very different from those inland in France, where not even the smallest shop selling basic food was available. I went for my first swim, but the beach was only a few feet wide and covered with large stones. It was difficult to avoid people as they sunbathed on the very uncomfortable surface. Meanwhile, Warren serviced the bikes, and made friends with another Englishman on the site from whom he borrowed a spanner. Warren returned, full of stories about the Englishman who had told him of his extensive travels, and how, if his car failed its MOT in England, he just drove it abroad and carried on driving until it wouldn't go any further. In this way he had visited Greece and Turkey many decades ago, in cars that were illegal to drive in England. He had also become an international coach driver, just to satisfy his yearning to travel, and had had many interesting experiences, such as having been in a country that had suddenly declared war, so the coach had to be escorted to the border by police. When he heard that we had cycled from England, he was incredulous.

We had a barbecued chicken from the stall holder for our evening meal, which had been basted with herb and garlic oil as it turned on the spit. Accompanied by beautiful new potatoes which had been cooked below the chickens with lardons of bacon, we had the most delicious meal as we sat overlooking the sea. It never ceased to amaze me how quickly I forgot the pain of cycling up the hills once we had enjoyed some lovely food with a bottle of wine. The cicadas started singing in unison as soon as the sun set, and a short while later at 9.30pm they all suddenly stopped. I never discovered how they stopped simultaneously – it was as though they were watching a conductor waving a baton, who had just given the signal to stop.

It was the end of July and the height of the season, so the roads were very busy as we continued cycling. We turned inland in the hope of finding quieter roads. However, the road climbed higher and higher, and we were concerned that we were lost. Warren was ahead of me and out of sight, so halfway up a hill I stopped to check my map again. A man, 70 if he was a day, suddenly stopped behind me, leapt off his bike and came to pore over the map on my front bag. He appeared to be flirting with me, so I explained that 'mon mari' was waiting for me further up the hill. He admired my bike, and put his hands on the saddle as I stood astride the bike. I wasn't sure what he was doing, then realised he was trying to lift the bike to test its weight. He was very impressed when he could only lift it one inch off the ground and said I must be very strong, squeezed my calf muscle with one hand, wished me 'bon journée' and sped off on his bike. I continued my journey at a slower pace, only to find him chatting to Warren in broken English and sign language. He had apparently told Warren I was a good strong woman, and he became quite excited when he saw me arriving!

We approached Toulon, having passed some grim looking flats in an unpleasant slum area, and it was terrifying cycling through the city, because we often had to cross busy lanes. We stopped in the centre of Toulon at 9am for a cup of coffee, and the waiter told us of a cycle route which led from the centre of the city. The cycle route followed the coast for quite a long way, so it was very pleasant, especially as the day was cloudy and therefore cooler than the previous days. The combination of the cooler weather and an early start made for one of the most pleasant day's cycling so far, despite the nerve-wracking main roads of Toulon, so when we passed a very large market near Carqueiranne, we stopped to buy some new shorts and vests for ourselves. As we walked around the enormous market, there was the rumble of thunder in the distance, so it was no surprise when large spots of rain began to fall on us later as we cycled. We continued in the rain; it was still warm, the rain wasn't heavy and cooled us as we cycled. I was wearing a bathing costume with shorts over the top and Teva sandals, so it didn't matter too much if they got wet.

In towns that we passed the cycle paths were often lined with flowering oleander, pampas grass and trees. In other places there were weeds, but they were beautiful weeds – pink valerian intermingled with the vivid royal blue and pink striped convulvus climbing up fences and trees. We passed salt pans on either side of the road at Hyères, and later the cycle path cut through rock, so we guessed it had once been a railway line. There were vineyards in odd places amongst the terracotta-roofed houses, and we decided to call it a day as we cycled into Le Lavendou and found a very quiet campsite. This was our first stop on the Côte d'Azure.

There was an English couple there who visited the same site every year and had got to know the other regulars, all of whom were French. They had been welcomed by the locals and had even been invited to a wedding in France by one of the other families at the site. We had seen weddings virtually every Saturday since we had been cycling in France – rows of cars, every one decorated with bows, drove from the church to the reception, every one sounding their horn.

It was now the first day of August, and we knew that most French and Italians take their summer holidays in August, so it was going to be busy and expensive for us to travel along the coastline at this time. The route was very scenic, up and down hills alongside the coast, with constant glimpses of vivid blue sea and sky, terracotta roofs and white buildings. Going up one hill I nearly jumped out of my skin when a sound behind me like the QE2's foghorn warned me that something big was approaching. It was an enormous circus lorry trailing two trailers the same size as the lorry plus a third smaller trailer behind. It was terrifying to be passed on a small winding hilly road by something so long, and very annoying when he sounded his horn at us and indicated that we should get off the road to allow him to pass. Several other similar-sized lorries with trailers followed behind, and we were amazed that they had chosen this route instead of the auto-route that went in the same direction. Eventually, after numerous more hills up, and a puncture to repair on Warren's bike near the top, we were able to fly downhill again towards St Tropez, where we stopped at a farm that had two fields for campers on the main road. The fields were fairly empty because it was still early, but the farmer's wife warned us not to camp near the road as it was noisy. She also warned us to watch our bags when we went to St Tropez, as there were many pickpockets there. We chose a site in one corner in the shade of three large fig trees, and were able to pick the last few incredibly sweet and delicious figs from the tree.

Warren and I removed our heavy bags and cycled four miles to St. Tropez, and gazed in awe at two fabulous coaches that had been converted to luxury motor homes. In the marina enormous yachts and motor boats were moored, and we marvelled that individuals can be rich enough to own such boats. I bought a post-card to send to my mother – she was enjoying receiving a post card from us every week. Sat on comfortable chairs under an umbrella in the sun, drinking our expensive glasses of wine and admiring the scene and the warmth, we gloated that our friends back home were busy at work.

When we returned to the campsite, the fields were full of tents and caravans. Only one other person had chosen to camp under the fig trees near us. It was a considerable shock, therefore, when I got up early the next day, to speak to a German man whose tent had been slashed open in the night by a thief. His wallet and passports had been stolen as he and his son slept, even though he had put the precious items only a few inches from his head. We discovered that two other tents had also been burgled in the same way, and when we saw the tents with their completely slashed sides we were really worried. We couldn't understand initially why the thief or thieves had chosen the German's tent, because it was surrounded by other tents with no trees or bushes for cover. Our tent, on the other hand, was almost alone and surrounded by fig trees where a thief could have hidden. I was very worried – I told Warren that if I had woken in the night to see a knife cutting through the tent a few inches away from my face, I may never have camped again – it would have been a terribly frightening experience. However, in hot weather we always opened both ends of the outer section of our tent to give the maximum fresh air. Our bikes were lying locked together on the ground, covered with a waterproof cover pegged into the ground, so we were able to keep an eye on our bikes through the ends of the inner tent, which are made from mosquito netting. In the end, we decided that the reason that our tent had not been chosen was because it was open at both ends, and a thief wouldn't have known whether we were looking out from the inner section or, indeed, which end we were sleeping. The German had a tent with only one opening, so it was obvious that any valuables would be kept at the opposite end. The thief could therefore fairly accurately gauge where to cut through the outer and inner tents.

The German was very angry, because he had discovered from the police that there had been a lot of burglaries from the site, and this was presumably why we had all been recommended not to camp near the road, where the thief would probably have struck first. This campsite, unlike most in France, was not surrounded with high fences to stop people coming in. It was difficult to get away from the German – once he realised that I understood his language, he ranted and raved in German about the French and France, saying that he would never go to France again, and that Italy was just as bad!

We set off along the beach road, stopping at a small sandy beach to take photos of our bikes leaning together looking out at the sunrise. Campsites were now much more expensive than they had been in northern France, even though the pitches for the tents were much smaller. The sites were also very crowded now, and the grassy pitches of the north had changed to dirt or stones. We found that everyone (including us now) found the need to define their personal space in the campsites, and that campers became quite territorial. In the campsites further north the pitches were large and well-defined, being enclosed by hedges and trees along the boundaries. Now that there were no such boundaries, people in their caravans brought out tables and chairs as soon as they had parked, so that they could make sure that everyone knew that that piece of space was 'theirs'. Even if they had a motorhome and drove off in it, various pieces of furniture were left to ensure the space remained free for them. A large awning even wider than the caravan, maybe a gazebo and occasionally even a small tent just for cooking were laid out, and we found ourselves hemmed in on both sides with only just enough space for the tent, and nowhere to sit and cook. With our little tent and only two bikes it was very difficult for us to spread our belongings, so we ended up defining our boundaries by putting up a washing line between trees on one side, hanging our clothes on the line even if they were clean and dry. A hammock between trees on the other side ensured we had some space to sit, either as a cooking area or just to relax and read.

Once again I found myself in the men's showers (there were no signs on the doors and no-one was in the shower when I went in). I realised my mistake when I heard the man in the next cubicle singing, but his voice was so beautiful I felt I'd made the right choice. He was singing a song from a French opera. I saw him in the campsite later – he was tiny and rotund with a large moustache, but because he was still singing as he walked along the gravel path I recognised him.

Warren and I went to the local shop to buy food, and we saw a man and woman looking at frozen sweets. Despite the fact that they knew Warren was watching, the man put two frozen ice cream Bounty Bars down the front of his trousers and walked to the till staring at us and daring us to say something. I wished I could have been able to explain to the assistant what the man had done, but knew that my French was insufficient and that any actions to explain might cause confusion. How wonderful it would have been to have made the man sit or stand waiting while the police came – there would have been no need to have searched him!

It was still very hot, so we always rose early and started cycling before the sun rose. At 7am the lay-bys were still full of motorhomes as we passed. There in the lay-bys they had the beaches, the spectacular cliffs and sea views to themselves. Motorhomes are allowed to park in lay-bys in France, so often only use the official campsites for disposing of waste water and for topping up again. We were now cycling up and down the roller-coaster road cut into the side of rocky cliffs which dropped away to our right, where the sea crashed onto craggy rocks and dark red pebbles far below. To our left the cliffs rose vertically above us. It was spectacular scenery.

The south of France was much as we had imagined it to be, especially as it was August. Whilst the scenery between towns was spectacular, the towns were busy, with hordes of people and no space on the beaches between the sunbathers. Cannes was our idea of hell – miles of narrow beach heaving with almost naked people, with cars parked on both sides of the road alongside the beach, and cars holding up traffic trying to park in impossible places. It seemed obligatory for the French (and also the Italians, we discovered later) when doing any difficult manoeuvres such as parking in a space a few centimetres longer than the car, to have a lit cigarette in one hand and to carry on a conversation with a mobile phone held in the other hand. They never thought it necessary to check in the mirror before reversing to see if a cyclist was approaching, nor to check if a cyclist was overtaking their car before opening the car door wide to get out. One day I saw a driver with a mobile phone in his hand reversing onto a pedestrian crossing.

(We weren't sure why the French have pedestrian crossings, because no-one ever stops to allow pedestrians to cross!). He was totally oblivious of the female who stepped off the kerb to cross the road, who was also too engrossed in her mobile telephone conversation to notice the car reversing fast towards her. Fortunately the driver stopped just short of her. How ironic that they both continued their journeys uninjured and oblivious of the near accident!

We cycled through Nice at 8am, and once again it was very frightening trying to cross several lanes of fast moving traffic. Nice reminded me very much of Brighton, with its stony beach and magnificent Regency-style terraced houses. The road from Nice to Monaco is well-known for its beautiful scenery – on our left the cliff rose vertically above us or even sometimes overhung the road, and on our right was a sheer drop down to the sea below. Now and again the road disappeared into a tunnel through the rock, but cyclists were not allowed in the tunnels, and in order to avoid these tunnels we had to cycle up the mountains and over the top of them.

We had been cycling for nearly seven weeks, doing a leisurely average of 25 to 30 miles each day, with occasional days off. We were now looking forward to leaving France and experiencing a different country . . .

CHAPTER 4

MONACO AND ITALY

Monaco is a tiny principality on the south coast of France and is a sovereign state covering only 1.95 sq km. With a population of 30,000, Monaco is most famed for its casino, the Monte Carlo Grand Prix and the port which is always full of fabulous yachts belonging to multi-millionaires.

Italy, with its distinctive boot-shaped peninsula, is a country of beauty. Many people have romantic images of Italy. Most of the land is mountainous, with the Alps dividing the country from France, Switzerland and Austria. With its amazing ancient architecture, beautiful beaches, islands, mountains, forests, four active volcanoes, art galleries, museums, food and wine, Italy has something to offer everyone.

We arrived at a town called Cap d'Ail, which was only 3km from Monte Carlo, so we decided to book a room in a hotel there rather than stay in Monte Carlo, which we knew would be more expensive. Watching television in our room after we had showered, we heard that it was due to rain the next day, so we made an instant decision to cycle to Monte Carlo immediately while the sun was shining, and return to our hotel before it got dark. It was very hot and sticky as we cycled down the steep winding road to Monte Carlo, and I couldn't help but think what a long climb it would be on the way back.

Monte Carlo is a very strange city. There are many beautiful old buildings surrounded by hideous modern blocks beside, below and above them. The whole city is terraced into the mountain, but there is a bizarre beauty about it. I loved the architecture of the old buildings – the lovely stone balconies, the arched windows, and the painted stone. Incredibly impressive boats were in the marina, and we sat and sipped drinks as we watched the world go by. A mini road train went by with tourists in three coaches. The driver slowed to go over a bump in the road, but once he had passed the bump he sped up, so that each coach behind him jumped faster and faster over the bump. Warren roared with laughter – he said that the ladies in the final coach were being tossed in the air so high that their boobs were likely to give them black eyes!

The following day we cycled into Italy clocking 2,000 kilometres. Our plan now was to follow the western coastline of Italy, cycling past Genoa and Rome until we reached Naples. From this point we would travel across land to Brindisi, which is on the 'heel' of Italy, and close to the southernmost point of the Adriatic coast. From Brindisi we wanted to catch a ferry to Greece.

The promised rain had never materialised that day – there were clouds in the sky initially, but soon after we had passed through Monaco and back into France on the other side the clouds disappeared and it was very hot again. Warren had achieved his goal of cycling through the tunnel under the hotel in Monte Carlo through which the Grand Prix racers drive, so he was very happy as we cycled out of Monaco, despite the steep hill that took us back into France. I was very excited about crossing our first border, but it was an incredible anti-climax. Both the French and Italian offices were closed, as well as the now defunct exchange bureau, and there wasn't even anyone there to say 'Buongiorno'. At the very moment that we were crossing the border, a scooter with an Italian driver and female passenger shot between us actually brushing my arm as they passed – this should have been a warning about Italian drivers . . .

The road went through numerous tunnels cut into several mountains, and houses appeared to hang from the mountain sides, some looking dangerously close to toppling off their cliff-side ledges. Their windows looked down several hundred feet to the sea below. Sometimes the railway line was alongside us, and on one occasion as we rested we could feel the rumble of a train passing in a tunnel below us through the mountain, but most of the time the train ran alongside the water. We thought what a lovely train ride it would make, passing through such spectacular scenery.

We arrived at our first Italian town, which was a rather unpleasant surprise when the Italian way of driving became clear. Hordes of scooters overtook at every opportunity, even when a car was approaching them on the opposite side of the road. They swung out dangerously, making cars brake at the last minute, and to find these scooters coming towards us en masse on the wrong side of the road was most unnerving. Sometimes dogs stood between the legs of the driver, their front paws on the handlebars, or the female passenger sat side saddle, her scarves and skirt flying dangerously close to the wheels. If there was no room on the road for the scooters, they drove en masse on the pavement, and it was obvious that scooter drivers felt that traffic lights did not apply to them. We felt the need to learn the Italian words for 'stupid imbecile' as quickly as possible.

We cycled fast downhill as we approached the campsite shown on our map. I was speeding ahead of Warren when I noticed a youth standing in the road with a football. As I passed close by him he kicked the ball straight towards me and I screamed, thinking that the ball was going to hit me. He was obviously deft at football skills and had immediately retrieved the ball with his foot, and he stood in the middle of the road laughing at me as I continued down the hill, still shaking from my shock. However, as I stopped at the entrance to the campsite, Warren drew up alongside me grinning. The youth had been so busy laughing at me that he hadn't seen Warren approaching fast behind him, so Warren applied the brakes violently just as he reached the youth. His brakes always screeched alarmingly, and the lad spun round screaming – the look of horror on his face made it clear that he thought he was about to be run over. It was our turn to laugh.

Now we discovered the problem with Italian campsites. They were much more expensive than French ones, most had fencing and gates around them that would be the envy of many prisons and, whether we paid up front or not, the Italians always insisted on holding our passports until we left, often not allowing us to leave before 8am which was a serious problem for us. They said that the Police needed information from all passports, but our concern was that they never gave us receipts for our passports, nor did they ever keep them secure and safe. Usually the passports sat in a box or in a pile on the counter, where anyone could help themselves if they so wished. The other problem with Italian campsites was that there was no grass. There had been dirt or stones at the ones in southern France – we hadn't seen grass since central France – but here the ground was beautifully paved with bricks. We looked in amazement as the girl showed us where to put the tent.

'But where do we put the tent pegs?' we asked.

'Between the bricks,' was the reply.

I went to see the showers, and rushed back excitedly to tell Warren that there were wonderful modern 'posh' showers. It wasn't until later that we realised that actually they were just very nice, clean, modern showers and toilets, and the doors were aluminium and glass so they weren't rotten and dirty like the French ones. We had obviously become used to the low standard of the toilet and shower facilities in France. I'm sorry, France, but where toilets and showers are concerned, it was like coming out of a third world country and into a western one.

In the late afternoon it began to get very windy; branches were falling around our tent, and dark clouds were hurrying across the sky. We walked to the nearby beach. There was an orange glow just above the headland beyond our bay and, as we watched, the glow expanded to show a line of green. Gradually the beginning of a rainbow began to emerge, even though the rest of the sky around it was very dark. The light began to fade with the setting of the sun, but a ship on the horizon was lit up with the setting sun, and it looked bright and white against the dark sky, like a phantom ship in the distance. It began to rain and the wind began to howl, but we continued to watch because we could see far off lightning illuminating the clouds, which was a very ghostly and extraordinary sight.

An Italian cyclist arrived at the campsite and began to put up his tent next to us, so we chatted to him and he gave us some ideas of interesting places to visit where there were good campsites. Matteo was a young doctor who hoped to specialise in orthopaedics. He loved cycle touring, but said that he had a problem finding like-minded people, so was cycling alone from the Pyrenees to his parents' holiday home in Celle Ligure on the Italian coast. (Whilst the French and Italians love cycle racing, it's very unusual for them to tour on bikes.) We cycled with him for a short distance the following day, but we (or rather, I) were clearly holding him back, because he usually cycled 200km every day. He asked us to phone him when we arrived in Celle Ligure two days later, so that we could meet and have a meal together.

We took a wrong turning and climbed up an incredibly steep hill; I thought it was never going to end. We eventually stopped at the top in the shade of some trees to rest after our exertions and, looking down, could see a cycle path in the distance far below us, completely flat alongside the sea. By the time we had flown down the other side of the hill into the next town, Warren admitted that he had made a mistake reading the map, so we had cycled up a very steep hill unnecessarily. I thought that I was very restrained . . .

Because it was the first week in August, we were now finding that many of the campsites were full, so sometimes we had to cycle much further to find campsites. We had become used to French shops and supermarkets being closed for an hour and a half at lunch-time, although in the south of France they had often stayed open. Now that we were in Italy, the land of the super siesta, shops were usually closed for over four hours at lunch-time, so we had to be very organised with our shopping.

Looking at the map of Italy, one can see that the road follows the coastline. However, as we had found, this doesn't mean that the road is at sea level. A look at a larger scale map gives the clue – the road twists backwards and forwards like a wriggly worm, following the contours of the land and the rocky coastline – up and round, over and down, the roads twist and bend, climb and fall. Pushing hard on my pedals I hoped that round the next bend would be the summit, but often found that the road climbed still further. I stopped frequently to sip drinks of water. Glimpses between the trees showed the sea hundreds of feet below, fishing boats mere specks on the water. Frequent signs indicated the danger of falling rocks from the sheer cliffs above, and houses clung perilously to the same sheer cliffs. At or near the top of the road, or as the road bent back on itself, there would be fantastic views, and because the roads twisted and turned constantly, whichever way we looked there were different views. The bays of azure blue were splashed with flashes of white, where speedboats in the far distance below were shooting through the waves. Minute white triangles showed how far below us were the yachts. The blue sky was dotted with fluffy clouds. Then the road plummeted down again, and we would be met with a blast of air, hot or cool depending on the time of day, as we flew back down the winding roads. Where the road touched sea level again a cluster of houses, bars and cafés huddled together waiting to welcome travellers, and we could easily be tempted to stop and enjoy a delicious Italian coffee whilst admiring the view. The vivid pinks and purples of bougainvillea and the softer colours of flowering oleander added splashes of colour, framing the vivid blue of the sea. We set off again, often cycling through deep, cool tunnels cut into the mountainside. It was certainly a glorious area to be visiting.

We were finding it difficult to get up early in the mornings, because the Italians talked so loudly in their tents or played loud music, often until 3am or 4am. Because the pitches in these expensive Italian campsites were so small, tents were almost touching each other, so voices carried very clearly. We were paying up to €30 (£20) a night for a pitch for our tent, and the tents were so close that our guy ropes were crossing. No wonder it was noisy – we could hear the guy in the next tent breathing, let alone snoring or having a loud conversation with his friends. Even if we shouted at our neighbours in the middle of the night to be quiet (which we often did), the noise would only subside for a short while, until gradually the volume of noise increased again to the original level.

I fell off my bike – well, I didn't fall off exactly. Because my bike has a crossbar to make it as strong as possible, I have to throw my leg over the saddle instead of mounting the bike daintily like a lady. Warren was ahead, but I stopped to take a photo. As I dismounted I overbalanced backwards, and fell onto my bum into the road with the bike on top of me. People came running up asking questions in Italian. I recognised the word 'male' which I knew meant injured, so I just kept saying 'no, ok, gracie' and doing the thumbs up sign. An elderly couple tried to pull my bike off me, but were unable to lift it because of the weight. I felt so stupid, but the only thing hurt was my pride. Thank goodness Warren didn't see – he would have fallen off his bike, laughing!

Neither of us had ever spoken Italian before but, as always, we tried to learn some common words. We found that the Italians, unlike the French, were very keen to speak English and their English was good. Also, having spent six weeks in France, we were finding that we were still thinking in French, and automatically said 'Pardon' to someone instead of 'Scusi'. We constantly tried to speak the language, but it was difficult.

Here's an example of me trying to speak in Italian when doing the shopping. I pointed to the pork chops in the supermarket and said, 'Two, please' in Italian.

The butcher replied in English. 'Of course, which two would you like?'

My English accent was obviously quite excruciating, or else I looked obviously English – I never found out!

We had now been cycling in Italy for a few days, and our first impressions of the difference between France and Italy were quite significant – the toilets and shower blocks in Italy were good quality and beautifully tiled, which was very different from France. Also, in Italy the Italian toilets usually had a cubicle for the disabled, which was something that we had never seen in France. Italian police were very evident strolling the streets, whereas in France we had never seen policemen on foot. Campsites were much more expensive in Italy, being a minimum of €20. Coffee was almost half the price in Italy that it had been in France – two gorgeous cappuccinos, espressos or Americanos cost about €2.60, whereas in France one café au lait cost €2.20 or €2.30. We discovered that bread was sold by the kilo in Italy, so was always weighed before being sold. There was also a lovely choice of different breads, but we especially loved the focaccia which made our fingers oily when we touched it. In France there was only one type of bread – baguettes. We were surprised to discover that some (though not many!) Italians actually stopped at pedestrian crossings – this had never happened in France. In Italy the vegetable shops had the wonderfully-flavoured, giant, knobbly, ugly tomatoes that we had previously bought in Spain, but had never seen in England or in France. We saw a few 'No Smoking' signs in Italy, although most Italians smoked. We never saw a 'No Smoking' sign anywhere in France, and had noticed that most French people smoked as well.

One day we were passed by four Italian cyclists in their matching gear and skinny bikes. However, despite their frequent standing on the pedals, they were not actually going very fast. We had seen this several times – serious Italian cyclists cycled up and down the mountains, but occasionally we saw the 'posing' cyclists with expensive gear but no idea how to cycle properly. I could see Warren was itching to race them, despite the unsuitable match of bicycles, and once they were out of sight Warren put on a spurt.

'I'll see you further up the road,' he called out, and he was gone, complete with 8 stone of bike and baggage!

He crept up behind the cyclists unnoticed, and when they did see him they sped forward but were unable to shake him off, even though his pedalling was much more relaxed than theirs. They slowed behind a parked lorry, but Warren overtook it and sped away. When they finally caught up with him he was waiting casually in a lay-by reading a map, and they all looked with bemusement at his bike, no doubt wondering if he had a hidden engine!

We were now approaching Celle Legura where Matteo had his holiday home. We were stunned by the lovely views ahead once we could see the holiday resort from the high road. There was a large sandy beach, and very pretty colourful houses were in every street of the small town.

We were amazed as we approached the town to see that the balconies, porticos, pillars, shutters, fancy scrolls, panelling, stonework and many of the windows were painted onto very plain houses. Complete with painted shadows to give the effect of depth, it was impossible to tell from a distance that the balconies and beautiful stonework weren't real. The houses were painted green, yellow, pink, rust, peach, cream and red, so were very colourful, and we were eager to take photos of this very pretty town. If the windows of a house were unevenly spaced, an additional window was painted onto the wall, or on the blank end of a house several windows with balconies would be painted. Through the painted stone balustrade of the balconies were dark green wooden shutters, also painted onto the plain wall of the house, and smart stone blocks had been painted on to the corners of the houses. Sometimes friezes and borders several feet high had been painted onto the houses, very similar in style to the classical wallpaper borders that can be bought in England. We discovered that painted houses like these were typical of the area.

When we met Matteo he insisted that we stay with him at his parents' holiday apartment, and he wanted to cook a typical Italian meal for us that evening. We all went shopping. In a delightful small shop selling fresh pasta and fresh pasta sauces, Matteo bought Trofie, freshly-made tiny pieces of pasta which was a type of pasta that we had never seen before, but which Matteo told us was typical of the area. (Four years later we first saw it available in England). Everything in this shop was freshly made each day, and the smells were wonderful. We followed Matteo into many different shops, where he bought focaccia bread, freshly made pesto sauce, soft white local cheese, Bresaola (smoked cured beef), an enormous chunk of parmesan cheese, and finally a large watermelon and a huge bunch of black grapes. He wouldn't let us pay for anything, so we splashed out on some really expensive bottles of wine, and returned to Matteo's parents' apartment up a steep hill with many bags full of shopping.

As Matteo prepared the food, we chatted about cycling, and about the places we had visited. Matteo excelled himself and produced a superb meal which makes our mouths water every time we remember it. We started with Trofie with pesto sauce – Matteo told us that it was not normal to have parmesan on this particular pasta dish, but the pesto sauce was more delicious than any we had ever tasted before. Matteo produced a plate covered with slices of Bresaola, and I was amazed to discover that this was not to share but there was a plateful each. On top of the Bresaola Matteo had sprinkled shaved pieces of parmesan and extra virgin olive oil, and he served it with focaccia that was so oily that our fingers were covered in olive oil as we ate it. We couldn't believe that such a simple dish could be so wonderful. After this course Matteo served the local soft white cheese, and for the fourth course he placed on the table a glass bowl in which sat the enormous bunch of black grapes in cold water with ice cubes. He also served us with large wedges of water melon, so our cheeks became wet as we gnawed at the beautiful red flesh. We drank sparkling white wine and red wine, then tasted some grappa which had been distilled by Matteo's parents from grapes after they had been pressed for wine. Suffice it to say that it was very alcoholic and probably tasted very similar to other home-made distilled drinks such as Irish poteen.

After eating, talking and drinking, it was time to go to bed, and I wondered where we were going to sleep as there didn't appear to be any bedrooms, only a narrow hall, bathroom and the living room which was combined with the kitchen. However, Matteo pulled out a bed hidden in a shallow cupboard in the hall, and two further beds came out of a display unit in the living room, so we were all comfortably catered for and slept well after our delicious meal.

At 7.00 the next morning we cycled into Celle, where we had the usual Italian breakfast of cappuccino and cakes. Matteo wanted to cycle with us for a while 'just for exercise' and he planned to show us a short cut through an old unused railway track. He was a little concerned about one point, though, and kept telling us that there were many galleries, but we couldn't understand what he meant. Matteo's English was very good (though he constantly said it was poor) but we understood when we looked it up in our Italian dictionary – the Italian word for tunnel is 'galleria'. His concern was whether we would be happy to negotiate the unlit tunnels along the old railway track.

The wind was blowing hard as we cycled along the coast and onto the old railway track. It ran alongside the sea, and we were glad of our waterproof clothes, because we were getting wet from the spray of the choppy waves. The tunnels were more difficult to negotiate than I had expected, because the railway track had not been officially converted for bicycles and was covered with large pieces of gravel. Inside the tunnels it was pitch black with water dripping from the ceiling, and the bicycle lights did little to help light our way through the puddles in the loose gravel. However, at least we didn't have the worry of other traffic in the tunnels. Eventually we came out of the last tunnel and said our goodbyes to Matteo, who was now going to return back home.

The rain came suddenly and very heavily. Although we had planned to stay in Genoa, we decided to stop as soon as we could find a campsite, because the rain was torrential. We began to climb a long hill but the rain was beating against us. I had never cycled in such rain and was thoroughly soaked, despite my waterproofs. Rain ran down my neck, my sandals were squelching, rain ran into my cycle helmet and splashed up onto my shorts. I struggled to get up the hill, my eyes smarting as the wind beat the rain onto my face, so that I could hardly see. We reached the top of the hill and began to cycle down the other side braking, because I was nervous of the rushing water that swept across the road from the hillside. We skidded across the road with relief when we saw a campsite, and rang the bell outside the giant electric gates. This was another prison-like campsite surrounded by tall fences and gates. The gate slid noiselessly open, and as we cycled into the site a man came out with an umbrella and immediately spoke in English asking us to follow him to shelter – he had heard us talking together through the intercom at the gate.

We stood dripping in a covered area full of pool tables. Many other people stood there sheltering from the rain, and three Chinese men chatted to us in excellent English. They couldn't believe that anyone would want to be out on bicycles in such weather, or that anyone actually wanted to travel by bicycle. We explained that by cycling we were able to meet the 'real' people in each country, because we often travelled through areas that were not frequented by foreign tourists, but of course really bad weather was an obvious disadvantage when cycling.

When the rain subsided we found a stony pitch that had a small man-made cave alongside it, cut into a cliff that formed one boundary of the campsite. We could use the cave for cooking if the rain began again. When we tried to sleep later that night it was difficult, because the noise in the campsite was unbelievable – loud radios were blaring, footballs were banging on a nearby door, toddlers were screaming, and a boules game was in progress with people cheering and clapping. We eventually fell asleep at 1am, even though the noise had not yet abated.

Despite the noise, we admitted the next day that we were grateful to have arrived at the campsite when we had. It was not until a few days later that we discovered that bad weather had swept across the whole of Europe including Great Britain, and Russia and Austria had been badly affected with considerable damage because of the wind and rain. Apparently the rain in Italy had been just the tail end of the bad weather in Europe, so we had been lucky! However, we dreamt of grass-clad terraces overlooking the sea, and peace and quiet. We knew it would be quiet again in September, when the Italians returned to work. Apparently the major cities, such as Milan, Rome and Florence, were normally quiet in August because so many people flee the humid atmosphere of the cities to go to the more comfortable climate of the sea or mountains.

We cycled through Genoa, and at the next campsite we had to pitch our tent on thick mud. We chatted half in French and half in English to a French couple who were camping next to us, and when they went to bed that night they were in fits of giggles because their blow-up mattress made terrible farting noises every time they moved, so we ended up in fits of giggles as well.

The scenery along the road we were travelling was spectacular, though once again we were cycling up and down roads which clung to the cliffs. When we stopped in towns or villages, the Italians often came up to us and spoke in English.

We were constantly being shook by the hand with words like 'My compliments to you' by complete strangers.

We decided to take a small side road one day, because on our map we could see a campsite marked on the coast, and we loved falling asleep to the sound of waves on the beach. A small town was shown near to the campsite, so we could buy food there if there was no shop or restaurant at the campsite. The road descended steeply, and we found ourselves at the entrance to a tunnel with traffic lights. We drew up behind the one car that was waiting at the light, but were surprised when he switched off his engine. The entrance to the tunnel was arched, and clearly only big enough for one vehicle. Although we had been through many tunnels in this mountainous area of Italy, this was the first that was so narrow. We waited . . . 5 minutes . . . 10 minutes . . . 15 minutes. I pulled out my Italian dictionary, and tried to translate the notice that stood alongside the lights, and discovered that the traffic lights only changed three times an hour. This concerned us how long the tunnel was – our map didn't even show a tunnel. On bicycles, could we get through the tunnel in the allotted time before traffic began to travel in the opposite direction towards us? We had two choices – to carry on through the tunnel and hope for the best, or return up the steep hill and retrace our steps for several miles to join the main road where there were no campsites shown on our map. We chose the former, and prepared our bikes by switching on the dynamos which worked our front halogen lights and switching on the flashing back lights. As we rarely cycled in the dark, it was a long time since we had used our lights. By this time there was a long queue of traffic stretching out of sight behind us. Without warning there was a rumble from within the tunnel, and seconds later cars shot out of the entrance to the tunnel like rabbits bolting from their warren and, one after another, they disappeared up the steep hill behind us.

It was 25 minutes before the lights changed to green, and we nervously followed the car in front of us into the darkness of the tunnel. There were no lights in the tunnel, but the cars lit the way for us, and there was just enough space for them to pass us on the left. Because of the arched shape of the tunnel the wall to our right leant towards us, and we were therefore unable to cycle close to the wall of the tunnel. A long queue of cars slowly passed us, gradually picking up speed, the roar of their engines echoing noisily in the restricted area. Within seconds they had all passed us and we were alone in the tunnel. It was pitch black and eerily quiet, and I couldn't see anything, not even the shape of the tunnel, because my front light was not pointing down to the ground properly. I was terrified, and screamed to Warren behind me that I couldn't see, so he cycled alongside me and warned that we shouldn't stop to adjust the light – we needed to cycle as fast as we possibly could to get out of the tunnel as soon as possible.

Our legs were going round and round faster than ever before in an attempt to get to the end of this nightmare. Suddenly we could hear the rumble of cars approaching, and we knew that more cars had entered the tunnel behind us, so Warren cycled behind me and we prayed that the cars that were speeding towards us would see us in time to move over to pass us. The cars' headlights lit the way ahead for a moment as the cars slowed and passed us, and after that we were alone again in the darkness as the echoes rumbled into the distance. Needless to say, we were relieved to see daylight ahead of us, and we shot into the sunlight, our eyes automatically closing in the bright sunshine.

Our hearts sank as we saw that we were on a stretch of road no more than 30 feet long between two tunnels, with no space at the sides for us to stop for a few minutes. On our left was the sheer rock cliff going upwards, and on our right was the sheer rock cliff going down to the sea far below. We quickly adjusted my light, and shot into the next tunnel. The thought that the traffic lights would change to green and cars might soon be speeding towards us made us fly along. No cars appeared this time, but it was another mile before we shot out into the sunlight again. Here there was a section of road about 50 feet long, but there were traffic lights on this section, and the lights in both directions were now red. A stretch of grass on one side meant that we could move out of the way of the traffic. Two empty cars were already parked in this small section, and a steep path with steps went up and over the mountain away from the sea – there was no way out for us up there. At this point we noticed that there were signs saying 'No bikes, no motorhomes, no caravans, no lorries, no pedestrians'. Why hadn't these signs been at the first entrance to the tunnel? There was no way we would have entered the tunnel if we had seen a sign that said bicycles weren't allowed, and none of the drivers of the cars in the queue had approached us to warn us. We obviously had to go on or go back. We had no way of knowing how much further the tunnel continued, but hoped that the 3 or 4 kilometres that we had already travelled was more than halfway. We were annoyed that our map gave no indication of a tunnel on this road, but we could see that the campsite we were aiming for was not much further – the tunnel must surely end soon.

We stood with our bikes on the grass and waited. After about 10 minutes we could hear rumbling within the tunnel which grew louder and louder, and suddenly cars shot out of the tunnel ahead of us and straight back into the darkness of the tunnel behind us. There was a whistling sound as the cars flew out of the tunnel, and we were aware only of a blur of colours as the sunlight struck the sides of dozens of cars as they sped past us and disappeared again instantly.

From our bags we pulled out extra flashing lights to put on the bikes, because our big concern now was that another queue would have built up at the entrance to the tunnel where we had started, and as soon as our light went green, so would theirs. This time the cars had no idea that there were two cyclists ahead of them, and their speed would have built up by the time they reached us if the tunnel ahead of us was long . . . I was very scared, and although he didn't admit it, I could see that Warren was very concerned as well.

Eventually the light turned to green in our direction, so I cycled to the entrance to the tunnel, but saw lights coming towards me. Either someone had driven against the red lights, or they were travelling much slower than the average Italian. We waited until he had passed and started cycling as fast as we could, praying that no-one else would be as stupid as the last motorist. It seemed only seconds before the rumbling noise began, indicating that cars were approaching us from behind again, and the noise became louder and louder as they drove nearer, the echoes bouncing around us. My heart was beating so fast I thought I might die, and I was terrified that the first car wouldn't see us and would plough into us at speed. All of a sudden there was light behind us, and the relief was intense when the first vehicle slowed down behind us. It made no attempt to pass us, which we thought was strange, and we cycled on and on as fast as we could, our legs spinning the pedals round wildly. The cars behind the first one couldn't see why the first one was going so slowly, so they began to sound their horns, and the echoing noise in the tunnel became deafening as more and more cars joined in. We were going faster and faster now, and I assumed that the road was going slightly downhill (although I couldn't see it) because our speed suddenly increased. It seemed an interminable time that we had been cycling – certainly far longer than in the other tunnels – but in the distance I saw a chink of light to the right. I screamed to Warren that I was going to slow down, because I was scared he wouldn't realise what I was going to do and might cycle into me at speed, but the echoing roar of the cars and their horns made it impossible for me to know if he had heard. I was approaching the opening very fast and shot into it, realising with horror in that very instant that to the right of the road was a sheer drop down into the sea. It was too late to stop, but as the bright sunlight hit me I shot into an open area and screeched to a skidding halt alongside a fence 20 feet from the tunnel, beyond which was the sheer drop to the sea that had concerned me. Warren's front tyre was almost touching my back tyre as he stopped, and we looked back to see the opening in the side of the tunnel, with cars whizzing past it at an amazing speed.

Two men standing nearby ran up to us, shouting and waving their arms wildly, and were indicating that we should get out of the way immediately. As we quickly moved we saw why – two of the cars in the stream unexpectedly detached themselves from the rest and shot through the archway without slowing, braking quickly before they hit the fence where we had been standing. As we looked around we realised with amazement that we were in the campsite that had been shown on our map. The site was only 20 feet deep, but terraces had been cut into the cliff one above the other to form space for cabins, static caravans and tents. To the right and left of the entrance to the campsite were incredibly steep slopes which led to the higher and lower terraces, and caravans were perched on cantilevered 'shelves' wedged between trees. How had they put the caravans there? By crane? How had the crane got there? Presumably not through the tunnel with its restrictions, and there was no other entrance to the campsite – the sea was far below us.

My heartbeat was now gradually returning to normal as Warren and I discussed the very frightening episode that we had just experienced, and we discovered from our cycle computers that the last tunnel had been 4km long (about 2½ miles). The vehicle behind us hadn't overtaken because it was a large van – another prohibited vehicle in the tunnel, and presumably too wide to pass us in the very restricted space. We had a few moments of grave concern when we were told by the campsite reception that there was no room even for a small tent, and none of the cabins or caravans were vacant. However, they must have seen the fear in our faces and taken pity on us, because they led us to a very small stony area alongside the track on one of the higher terraces, where they said we could pitch our tent. Fortunately there was a small shop and restaurant on the site, so we were able to eat that day – there was certainly no chance of us returning to the small town we had seen on the map in order to shop for food!

We found we could walk down the steep slopes between the terraces until we reached the sea, where large boulders and slabs of rock jutted out from the cliffs alongside a small jetty. We took our stove down to the edge of the sea and sat on one of the slabs of rock just above sea level where we cooked our evening meal while watching the sun set beyond the horizon. We went to bed early, because we knew that we not only had another section of tunnel to negotiate, but once past the tunnel we had to cycle over a mountain pass.

I had nightmares that night. Normally the thought of a steep hill, let alone a significant mountain pass, worried me, but all I wanted was to be past the tunnel and out in the open again waiting to start climbing over the mountain pass. The echoing sounds of the tunnel reverberated through my dreams, waking me constantly, so it was with shaking hands that I mounted my cycle at 6.30 the next morning, and stood alongside Warren once more at the entrance to the tunnel.

The traffic lights were red in both directions, and there was no sound within the tunnel. We edged as close to the entrance as we dared to try to look inside, but it was pitch black. The temperature so early in the morning was still cool, but my hands were clammy. The lights changed to green in our favour, and we stood on our pedals and pushed ourselves once more into the tunnel. We had been told by the campsite attendants that there was only another 2km of tunnel, but this information hadn't reassured us. We were going fast and sensed that we were going downhill, when we suddenly heard the unmistakeable distant roar of a motor engine coming towards us. Somebody must have entered the tunnel against the red light! We braked to a skidding halt, chillingly aware that as soon as we stopped our dynamo headlights would begin to fade. However, we were also wearing head torches so, as we flattened ourselves against the damp, cold wall, hugging our bikes to us, we shook our heads hysterically as we faced the vehicle that was rushing towards us. We hoped that the driver of the vehicle could see the small lights that were moving wildly in the tunnel ahead of him, but we were panic-stricken and besides ourselves with fear and apprehension. Within seconds the noise was all around us as the echoes once again bounced off the walls. A light appeared out of nowhere, there was a rush of wind as a motorbike raced past us without slowing, and the echoing noise gradually disappeared into the distance behind us. For a few seconds we stood in the darkness saying nothing, then panic hit us again and we realised that we must get out of this tunnel fast. We flew through the tunnel as though we had wings. Our speed was increasing more and more, because the passageway cut through the rocky tunnel was going down an incline towards sea level. Unexpectedly we saw literally the light at the end of the tunnel, so we made an extra effort and shot out of the tunnel like bats out of hell, out onto a normal road again. The brightness of the sky hurt our eyes as we drew to a halt and looked around, and we hugged each other in relief that the tunnel was finally behind us.

The beach was on our right, so we were now exactly at sea level, but as we turned to look to our left we drew in our breath at how high the mountain pass was. A motorway went through tunnels in the two mountains high above us, and the road stood on giant columns joining the two mountains across a steep valley. The road was so high that it was only a tiny white pencil line against the dark mountains, and we wondered how we could cycle so far, because we knew that the motorway was halfway up the mountain, and we had to get to the top. However, someone up there had been listening to my prayers, because the sun remained hidden behind clouds. For the next five hours, we climbed higher and higher. I stopped frequently for water and a rest, and noticed at 9.30am that my average speed had been 4.2 mph (despite the mad dash through the tunnel!) and that we had actually cycled only 6 miles. Despite the cloudy day I sweated buckets. It was Sunday, so Italian cyclists were cycling up and down the mountain on their skinny, light-weight, unladen bicycles, and they shouted encouragement to us as they passed. We stopped at one point to look down on the motorway. It was now far below us, and the cars on the road were tiny dots in the distance. It seemed impossible that, earlier that morning, we had wondered how we were ever going to cycle so high, but we still had a long way to climb. We finally reached the pass where it showed that we had cycled to an altitude of 2,018 feet, and we continued further uphill for another mile.

The views were spectacular, and we sat and rested before speeding downhill again for several miles, but to our dismay we found that the road began to go uphill again. The sun was out now, and we were very tired from our day's cycling, so it was a relief to turn a corner and look down over a fence to see a campsite with trees and grass. It was the first time in weeks that we had seen grass in a campsite, and we were delighted to find excellent showers and also a washing machine where we could wash our clothes. We had no food apart from our emergency supply of packets of dried pasta with sauce, but we were able to buy some cakes, biscuits and a bottle of wine from the campsite bar which made the meal acceptable. The nearest village with a shop was six kilometres away, but we decided to stay a second night so we could cycle to the village with empty bikes to do some shopping the following day, after we had rested.

We woke several times in the night hearing different noises – a donkey nearby was braying; there was shooting in the woods which we understood was boar hunting; a tent was being erected next to ours and they were hammering pegs into the ground; the couple in the next tent were making love, and talking loudly afterwards (and presumably smoking their Players!); there was the sound of zips and Velcro being ripped open, and people were walking round the side of our tent. When we woke the next morning we discovered that the campsite was full, so there had clearly been a lot of activity in the night erecting tents. The couple in the tent next to us had erected not only a tent with electricity for the television, but a second tall tent with a chimney which housed only the cooker and the food. Although they had arrived late in the evening, after we had gone to bed, they had also put out a table and four chairs with an umbrella set over the table ready for breakfast, ensuring their personal space in the wooded campsite. As we emerged from our tent, both the man and the woman were engrossed in very loud mobile phone conversations.

After the initial 100 yards of uphill cycling, the cycle ride to the village was downhill all the way. We were fascinated in one of the tiny shops to see a customer carry in a basket full of freshly-picked wild mushrooms to sell to the shop-keeper. We had noticed in Italy that the woods were often full of Italians picking wild mushrooms, and I envied them the knowledge of being able to recognise and pick fungi that was safe to eat. It was also interesting to know that anyone could take a wild mushroom to the local pharmacist, who would be happy to identify it. The shop-keeper excitedly held up a perfect clump of wild mushrooms, still attached to a small clod of earth and grass, and the mushrooms were duly displayed on the front of her counter, ready to be admired and bought. I was tempted by some of the mushrooms, but didn't know how to prepare them. The shop-keeper spoke no English, but was excited to find that I wanted more information, and she dashed around the shop collecting items to show me, and with her hands and these items she painted a picture to explain a recipe. I duly bought everything, though the large bunch of parsley was a present from the shop-keeper, and I returned to the campsite, where I pounded the yellow wild mushrooms to a pulp with fresh parsley and garlic, added extra virgin olive oil and white wine, and left the paste for the flavours to amalgamate. We served it later on toast as a starter and it tasted delicious, though we never knew whether this was how it was supposed to be served!

During the afternoon we relaxed in the shade of the trees, but two couples had made friends and were all talking – literally. As Warren and I lay in our hammocks we looked at each other and smiled, knowing that we were both thinking the same thing. Every one of this foursome was talking loudly, and not one of them was listening to what any of the others were saying. I asked Warren if he'd noticed, and he said it was really winding him up, especially as their voices were so loud, but we found this quite typical of many Italians. This was even more noticeable the next morning when we woke early, and the couple next door also emerged from their tent at 7.30am. Instead of whispering as we did, because everyone else was still asleep, they talked loudly at each other so that their voices carried to every other tent in the campsite.

We set off cycling that morning, and noticed from our map that Pisa wasn't far away. We had arranged with my brother to meet him at a campsite there. He wanted to drive across France and Italy, and we planned to put our bikes into his car and drive into the mountains of Tuscany for a holiday together. It was only two days cycle ride to Pisa, but we had eight days in which to do it, so we needed to find somewhere pleasant to stay for a while. We sat in a bar by the harbour in La Spezia with our map spread out on the table, and planned to cycle south-west to find a campsite on the peninsula.

We arrived in Lerici, a very pretty coastal town with lots of character, and we found a campsite which was terraced, which meant that every tent had a view of the bay through the trees. We pitched our tent under the olive trees, and found we could walk down the terraces to the sea and swim in the warm water from the rocks. We saw no English people there, but chatted to the German lads in the tent next to us. The coastline was very pretty – there were rocky bays and inlets, and the colour of the sea ranged from jade green to azure blue and turquoise.

Every day we walked to the centre of the small town, up a hill and down again through ancient steep, stepped paths between the houses. We sat in bars and cafés by the pretty harbour, backed by tree-covered hills with terracotta-roofed houses. Although it was a busy resort, it was very pleasant and relaxed, with lovely restaurants, cafés and shops, although unfortunately there was no internet café to catch up on e-mails. One thing that Italy is famous for is the ice cream. The choice of flavours was quite unbelievable, so we hovered in front of the display at the Gelateria, trying to choose from chocolate, Nutella, tiramisu, hazelnut, liquorice, coffee, milk chocolate, cream, vanilla, cassata, English trifle, banana, strawberry, cherry, pannacotta, coconut, lemon, white chocolate, yogurt, melon, toffee, caramel, rum and raisin, pineapple, mandarin, plum pie, peach, pistachio, mint, raspberry or orange chocolate.

Because the stay in Lerici was costing us an average of £38 per day, double what we hoped would be the average daily cost for the whole trip, we often bought take-away pizzas and sat on a bench by the marina watching the sun set behind the hills. It was beautiful; silhouetted against the pink sky, elegant old-fashioned lamp-posts came to life and shone light down on the pavement, where the foreigners began to set up their stalls selling jewellery, clothes and souvenirs, and entertainers began singing or playing their musical instruments. Sometimes Africans, South Americans or eastern Europeans spread out their wares on sheets on the ground –sunglasses, handbags, clothes, sandals and jewellery – and their pretty children played accordions or pipes, hoping to collect money from passers-by. One evening our attention was drawn to a beautiful dark-skinned black-haired child who was about 6 years old. He was alone, but sat on the marina wall playing an accordion very badly. Alongside him was a plastic cup, and we noticed that children begged their mothers for money to put into his cup. Men walked by chatting without noticing, but their wives passed the boy, stopped and looked back, opened their handbags and gave him some money. Warren took a photo of him and gave him some money, and he noticed that the cup was already full of Euros. The boy suddenly stopped playing and looked up – a man was approaching, who put his finger to his lips and walked straight past him. The boy stood up, took his cup of money and concertina and followed the man at a distance. We saw him later, playing in another part of the town, and a quick look around confirmed that the man (who we assumed and hoped was his father) was there in the background.

No-one bothered us as we sat on the bench watching the world go by – children scooted by on their scooters, Italians walked by shouting into their mobile phones and smoking, couples walked by having loud arguments, the women screaming and the men shouting back – they were totally oblivious of anyone else around, and this was something we never saw in any other country! After our pizza and a glass of wine, we once again returned to the campsite walking up and down the hundreds of steps.

We were ready to move on to Pisa, and were surprised to find that the coastal road was completely flat. There were literally hundreds of cyclists, most of them Italian tourists with rusty bikes in terrible condition, but some of them keen cyclists on fast expensive bikes. We waited at traffic lights, but groups of Italian cyclists sped by, all in red, yellow, blue and green, completely ignoring the lights. I heard Warren talking behind me, and discovered that he was talking to another cyclist, who accompanied us for several miles.

After a while, our new friend said, 'I don't know where we are!'

Warren quickly replied, 'Italy, cycling south – that's all we need to know.'

They both seemed to find it really funny, and laughed so much that they nearly fell off their bikes. We stopped, and Serge introduced himself to us. He was a Belgian barrister from Brussels, was married to an Italian girl and was in the area visiting his in-laws. He treated us to a coffee at a café that we passed, and we chatted about various cycling experiences. Ten years before, Serge told us, he had organised a group of eight to cycle around Scotland. His plans had backfired a little, because he had planned the days carefully, forgetting that the distances on English maps were in miles, not kilometres! He was very interested in our bicycles and the equipment that we carried and, like most Belgians, Serge spoke excellent English. We added Serge's name to our list, and promised to keep in touch.

We continued on our way along the coast, passing Carrara port which was full of enormous pieces of marble and stone, many of them 2 metre cubes or even larger. Giant pieces were strapped onto trailers and were being craned onto enormous ships. This area was famous for shipping the beautiful marbles of Italy, and these giant cubes of marble were delivered all over the world and ended up as magnificent hotel marble floors, wonderful kitchen and bathroom worktops, slabs of marble to cover whole walls or cut into smaller pieces to make marble tiles.

We had been travelling for some time through northern Italy on the road numbered SS1, and had noticed that every kilometre there was a milestone showing a decreasing number – 461, 460, 459, etc. This showed the distance to Rome, and apparently such numbering is on all of the roads that radiate from Rome. There is a well-known saying, 'All roads lead to Rome', and in fact they once did – when Rome was expanding, roads were being built from Rome in every direction. It was interesting to discover that the modern word 'mile' was derived from the Latin 'milia passuum' which meant one thousand paces!

We were not far from Pisa, and the main road had turned inland towards Pisa. The road was lined with trees on either side, and we passed an opening. Sat in a chair in the shade was a sight for sore eyes – a woman, or more likely a transvestite, was sitting there wearing fishnet stockings and a tiny skirt; her hair was a brassy blond and she had bright red lipstick on. She sat on a chair eating grapes, though there was no sign of any transport and it was miles from anywhere.

Warren was behind me, and after we passed he called out to me, 'Was that what I thought it was?' A mile or two further on we saw another woman – definitely a woman this time. She had an enormous bust and most of it was on show in a low-cut skin-tight sweater. She was sat on a chair, again with no sign of transport, presumably waiting for 'clients'. A mile or two further on was a third opening in the trees, and a third woman, looking very much like an average attractive housewife, sat on a tall bar stool alongside her car, her legs crossed to show off her thighs. Clearly this stretch of road was a popular 'meeting place'!

We found the campsite just outside Pisa where we had arranged to meet my brother, and set up our tent underneath some trees, leaving a space for John's vehicle. The campsite was the cheapest for a long time despite the fact that the famous Leaning Tower of Pisa was only half a mile away. We were camped next to a very impressive new shower block, but within an hour forty French teenagers had arrived with backpacks and tents, and were setting up tents beside us with four in each space usually reserved for one tent. It was bedlam, and when I went to the shower block there were teenagers screaming in the showers. We searched the site for a quieter spot, moved our tent and bikes to a corner with a less modern shower block nearby but no sign of the loud teenagers, and sat and waited for John to arrive.

It was exciting to see John again – we had already met so many lovely people on our trip, but we had always hoped that friends and family would come out to see us in different places. John had had an interesting drive to Italy, and had visited familiar places en route where he and his family had previously enjoyed holidays. Our bikes fitted, though with difficulty, into the back of John's four wheel drive car, and we set off to the city to see the famous landmark.

Everyone recognises the Tower of Pisa, but I wondered how many people would recognise it if they saw a photo of the building straightened. Resembling a very ornate wedding cake and built of white marble with numerous narrow arches supported on tall pillars on six of its eight storeys, the tower is indeed a very beautiful building. I felt sure that it might have been a tourist attraction even without its precarious angle. Construction on the famous bell tower began in 1173, but by the time the builders reached the third storey construction stopped. It was clear at that time that the building was already beginning to lean, and specialists are certain that if the building had continued at that time the tower would have fallen down, because the tower had been built on unstable shifting sands. 100 years elapsed before building recommenced, by which time it was fortunate that the underlying soils had consolidated. In order to try to rectify the leaning angle, the upper storeys were built leaning slightly in the opposite direction, but by the time the construction had reached the seventh storey, building once again stopped, probably because of wars. Ninety years elapsed before building began again, and the angle had worsened during that time. It was obvious that the builders were aware of the problem, because workers had corrected the angle in 1370, when the tower was officially completed, by adding six steps from the seventh storey up to the bell chamber's floor on the south side, but only four on the north side.

Numerous attempts have been made since the 19th century to rectify the lean, and in recent decades there was concern that the lean was accelerating and that the tower was finally on the point of toppling over. Because of this, in 1990 the tower was closed to tourists, which caused outrage amongst the local Pisan people who feared the loss of tourist revenue and the resulting impact on the local economy. Work during the latter part of the 20th century and the early part of the 21st century has now hopefully halted the lean, and it is thought that the tower is now safe for another 300 years. The tower when we saw it was surrounded by fencing and a building site, because it had just had more work done to underpin the tower. Despite the pinning, one side of the building was still sunk scarily into the ground, emphasising the considerable angle at which the tower leaned.

We were disappointed that we couldn't see inside the tower. John, who had walked to the top of the tower when he had visited it many decades ago, told us how strange it had felt to be walking up stairs which seemed to suddenly change angles. The tower was surrounded by tourists, and there were many English people around. This was a surprise for us, having seen virtually no English people since we began our trip in June, two months before, but we discovered that airlines were offering extremely cheap deals from England to Pisa, so we assumed that to be the reason for the large number of British tourists.

We set off in John's car towards Florence, and the rain that had been threatening all day started suddenly. Within minutes the roads were flooded, and cars were sheltering at the side of the road because their windscreen wipers couldn't cope with the quantity of rain. Branches of trees were scattered across the roads, and motorbikes and metal stands were blown over with the gusts of wind. It was as though a whirlwind had swept down the road. As quickly as the rain had started it stopped again, and we continued on our way to the beautiful city of Florence, where we found a campsite. At €40 a night it was the most expensive site so far, so we chose to put up the large, two-bedroomed tent which John had borrowed from a friend, otherwise we would have paid double for two tents.

My mother had insisted on supplying John with sufficient money to treat us all to several special meals, so we were pleased to find a lovely restaurant fairly close to the campsite. We drove up a long, steep drive to the restaurant, and sat outside under pretty pointed gazebos with a superb view over the city. We had various starters which we shared – bressaola, which had been introduced to us by Matteo, and mixed toasts with different toppings of grilled cheeses, fish, mushrooms and paté. John had gnocchi, Warren had pasta with truffles, and I had fillet steak with wild mushrooms. Accompanied by a large quantity of Chianti the meal was a great success.

Despite the fact that the campsite was so expensive, we wanted to stay another night so that we could visit Florence. We sat at a pavement café in the city when thunder began to rumble in the distance. There was an incredible crack of lightning, thunder crashed immediately overhead, and café tables and chairs flew into the road as strong gusts of wind blew. Within seconds torrential rain was flooding the road, so we paid quickly and ran to shelter in a shop, waiting until the rain stopped as suddenly as it had started. We walked around Florence admiring the beautiful buildings and churches, and the spectacular panoramic view of the wide river Arno which flows through the city of Florence.

On our return to the campsite we found that because we had left the 'window' open in the cooking area of the tent, water had poured through and filled the seat of John's canvas chair. Water was coming through the outer part of the tent in a number of places, and was even beginning to seep into the inner bedroom sections. We dealt with the problem as best we could, and went to bed that night praying that it wouldn't rain any more. We knew that our own small tent could withstand any such weather, but it was only a small two-man tent. Luck was with us, and we were able to pack away the tent the following morning with the sun shining through the trees.

We drove east, wanting to stay in mountainous areas, because John didn't like hot weather, and we were soon climbing higher. Everything was green, the hills were forested with very few buildings, and we could see several ranges of mountains.

We stopped for wonderful sandwiches of focaccia filled with ham, slices of boiled egg, wild mushrooms and salad. The prices were dramatically lower than we had been paying so far in Italy, so we were pleased that we were now away from the coast and the tourists. We found a pretty terraced campsite run by an Italian family, and chatted to Silvia, the daughter of the owner, who was fascinated with our journey and wanted to be added to the list of people who received our regular newsletters by e-mail.

More rain came and went, but whenever the weather began to clear we marvelled at the amazing scenery. The campsites were now almost empty, because it was the end of August and almost time for the Italians to return to work. The temperature was much cooler in the mountains, so for the first time for months Warren and I were wearing trousers, socks and shoes instead of shorts and sandals. We found another wonderful Italian restaurant, and once again had a meal with money that my mother had sent us. We enjoyed ostrich, fillet steak and lamb, accompanied by delicious grilled Mediterranean vegetables, and afterwards we had the most expensive dessert in the restaurant, a selection of five of their specialities. Everything was delicious, and the waiter brought us complimentary sweet wine to accompany the desserts, and we toasted Mum to thank her for the beautiful meal.

If we were driving past a village or town and saw a market we stopped immediately, because we were all addicted to wandering round market stalls. The Italians' love of wild mushrooms means that they also dry their own porcini mushrooms, which were sold from sacks on stalls. I bought an 'etto' of dried porcini to add to meals cooked on our camping stove, and after some research I discovered that an etto is the informal Italian name for a hectogram, or 100 grams.

Another evening we were in a walled town called Poppi which had magnificent views during the day because, like so many walled cities, it was on the top of a steep hill. It was now evening, and we passed the castle and tower and found a very expensive restaurant which had been converted from wine cellars. There were vaulted brick ceilings and highly-polished floors scattered with rugs. We were earlier than most people – the Italians seldom go to a restaurant before 8pm, and often not until after 9pm – and we chose one of two tables raised on a wooden dais. This was to be the last of the three meals that Mum was paying for us, and the three different pasta dishes that we chose for starters were so delicious that we could hardly wait for the next course. My chosen dish, translated as 'Angler fish pasta', turned out to be pasta with two different sauces, one fresh tomato sauce and one a fresh pesto sauce, poured prettily over the pasta in stripes and decorated with cooked mussels. My starter was followed by veal with figs, while John had the most enormous prawns that I had ever seen, and Warren had a beautiful chicken dish. Unfortunately this superb meal was spoilt, because six Italians arrived, having booked the table next to us, and we could only describe their conversation as shouting, usually all at once! There were times when we couldn't even hear each other speak; this resulted in us declining a dessert and coffee, so we returned to our tent where we drank another bottle of wine before retiring for the night.

The next day we found a supermarket – the first we'd ever seen in Italy – and excitedly pushed our trolley around the aisles choosing food to make a delicious meal on our camp stove for John. Salmon fillets, fresh vegetables, fresh herbs, wild mushrooms in olive oil and pesto sauce. We wanted crème fraîche to make a lovely sauce with the pesto, but couldn't find any sort of cream in the supermarket, so bought mascarpone cheese instead. Of course, we also bought bottles of wine.

A little later in the day we arrived at Arezzo, where there was an outdoor antique market which covered numerous roads and side streets. It was fascinating, but very expensive, and we were interested to see very large items of furniture such as tables and wardrobes for sale, as well as old panelled doors and pieces of architectural salvage. On the way back to the campsite we stopped at a village bar for a drink, which caused quite a stir amongst the locals. They were obviously unused to seeing strangers, let alone foreign strangers, in their village.

After a week of travelling in the mountains, it was time to return to Pisa. Warren and I wanted to set off from the campsite where we had met John, so our cycle route on our map continued uninterrupted by the week's holiday by car. We arrived back in Florence, and booked into a different campsite. That evening we found a Chinese restaurant. We had eaten no Chinese food since we had left England, so it was quite exciting for us to eat something different. The restaurant was very small but it was still early, so we were able to get a table straight away. We ordered several starters to share, because at €3 each (about £2) they seemed very cheap. One sounded very exciting – it was called 'Nubole di Drago Fritte' (the English translation was 'Fried Clouds of Dragon'), so I had to try it. It was rather disappointing to be presented with prawn crackers, but we did think that fried clouds of dragon sounded so much more exotic, exciting and Eastern! At the end of a vast three course meal, which included duck, prawn, chicken and beef dishes, we paid only €45 (£30), and the cheap price for the good food was obviously the reason why, when we left just after 9 o'clock, there was a long queue waiting outside the small restaurant despite the drizzling rain.

The following day was Monday, 2nd September, which was probably the reason for the nightmare traffic that we encountered as we drove through Florence. August had finished, so everyone was going back to work for the first time for a month! We found the internet café we had previously used, and I found eighteen e-mails waiting for us. The most important one was from my son, Julian, and his wife, Lucy, announcing the birth of their first child, my fifth grand-child. Thomas had been born three days before on 29th August 2002.

The weather turned hot again as we approached Pisa for the second time, and our bikes were pulled out of John's car and checked ready for us to begin cycling again for the first time for over a week. We said our goodbyes to John, and as we cycled over the river we could see the leaning tower to our left standing above the other buildings. John planned to drive back to England very slowly, enjoying another week's holiday on the way.

It was good to be back on our bikes – the cycling was flat, but we didn't want to go far for this first day. We arrived at Marina di Pisa, only 11 miles from Pisa. It was a seaside resort, but we were amazed that the beach was completely empty – not a tourist in sight. The Italians had gone back to work, and we had the resort to ourselves! The difference from one week before was unbelievable. We had the same experience when we found a campsite and realised that we were the only guests. It was also very cheap compared to previous sites – we assumed that this was because it was now out of season.

There was a distant rumbling in the sky as we left the next morning, and thunder had rumbled throughout the night. We cycled through Liverno, a massive port, past endless containers waiting to be shipped, and past embarking points for ferries. We passed the ancient port walls of the old naval base as we entered the town, and alongside their fishing boats the fishermen were selling their catch direct to the public. Boxes of silvery, pink-tinged fish looked very tempting and a box full of octopus was a mass of entwined tangled tentacles.

We wanted to continue on the SS1 to Roma, but we were not allowed on it because it went into a long tunnel after which it became a motorway. We had to navigate smaller roads, and ended up getting lost amongst estates of enormous houses in roads lined with very tall elegant conifer trees and flowering oleanders. After 32 miles we decided that we'd had enough when we found a campsite, and pitched our tent under low-growing young pines in a fairly busy campsite alongside a beach. We had just showered when we noticed that the wind had suddenly picked up and was gusting in all directions. We had heard thunder rumbling in the distance, and had experienced before that a dramatic change of weather was often preceded by sudden gusts of wind. We immediately began to put up a shelter, so that we had somewhere dry to cook outside. We put everything inside the tent, but noticed that no-one else was bothering to do anything. People were still lying on the beach, or wandering around unconcernedly. Washing was still hanging on lines, chairs and tables were laid out in the open ready for meals and people were still sitting listening to radios when a few large spots of rain warned everyone that it might rain. Within seconds the heavens opened, a fierce wind began to blow, thunder cracked and lightning flashed overhead, and we sat in our tent watching everyone panic, running around hammering extra pegs into the ground to stop their tents being blown down. They were running in and out of their tents and caravans to collect washing that was blowing crazily in the wind, and to pull to safety all items not pegged down that were in danger of blowing away or of being spoilt in the rain. The tent opposite us remained with the outer coverings open so that the interior began to flood; a kitchen roll on the picnic table rolled crazily then became soggy, and the towels on the line ripped off in the wind, becoming muddy on the now soaking wet ground. Obviously the occupants had gone out for the day. The queues were unbelievable that evening to go to the campsite restaurant – obviously very few people were prepared to cook inside their tents or caravans, and no-one else had a cooking shelter like us. We were comfortable cooking under our shelter – maybe it was because we were English, and used to wet weather!

We noticed that our tent was beginning to die – it had been a very expensive tent, but was now many years old, and the bottom of the sleeping area was no longer fully water-tight, possibly as a result of pitching the tent on gravel. We knew that we could get it repaired by the manufacturer, but this was impossible while we were travelling – we needed a replacement while it was being repaired. We decided to hang on in the hope that we wouldn't encounter too much rain – in view of later experiences, this was very wishful thinking . . .

★ ★ ★

The scenery had changed. We had been used to coastal roads, either promenades on the sea front in towns, or cliff roads high above the sea. Now we were a mile or two inland; in the distance to our left were mountains topped with clouds, and in front of them and to our right were fields full of sweet corn, vegetables or tomatoes. The fields were very tiny, some as small as allotments. The autostrada, the SS1, ran parallel to our road a few hundred yards to our right. When we found a campsite we appeared to be the only guests, and the swimming pool had already been emptied because August had passed, even though the weather was still hot most of the time! It poured with rain in the night, and the thunder was so loud that we could feel the ground trembling beneath our heads as we lay in our tent. At least it drowned out the noise of loud music from the campsite owner's house.

Our next campsite at Follonica was expensive and not as good as usual, but it had a view of Elba. The tiny island of Cerboli stood between Elba and the mainland, a very small dark grey shape outlined against the large pale grey shape of Elba in the distance. We treated ourselves to a meal out, and shared a starter of wonderful mussels cooked with garlic, herbs and lemon, which was served with bread to soak up the wonderful liquor. Relaxing after two more courses, a carafe of wine and an excellent Italian coffee, Warren announced, 'This is the life!'

The fields were newly ploughed as we cycled on the next morning. The sunflowers, which had looked so bright and cheerful a few weeks ago, now looked very sad and forlorn with their dark brown dead heads hanging on dying stalks. There were masses of wild flowers – miniature antirrhinums, which were primrose yellow with golden yellow centres, pink star-like flowers, blue daisies, mauve vetch, tall yellow spires of flowers and miniature cerise wild sweet peas. Trucks passed us, laden with mountainous piles of black grapes.

We reached a road that led to the bay, where we struggled initially against the wind. From here we could see Orbetello, which would have been an island over 2000 feet high except for the fact that it was joined to the mainland with three spits about 7km long. These three spits formed two large sea lakes within them, and there were campsites and buildings on the spits. The island and spits formed a natural wide bay, and here the sea was a mass of colour with surf-boards being pulled by kites at least 20 feet across, which looked like giant Alice bands or crescents in the sky. As we turned a corner the wind hit us from behind and we sped along. We decided to cycle along one spit to the island, and to return via a different spit. There were so many trees on either side of the road that we couldn't see the sea or the lake, but we returned through a forest on the spit which was very pleasant.

Very few Italians spoke English in this area, but they took a great interest in our bikes. Because they often wanted to know how far we had travelled, we were now learning numbers in Italian, and one man's face was a picture when we said that we had cycled 'duo mille otto cente kilometres' (2,800km) and he turned to shout at his friends so that they could come and congratulate us! Along the coast many of the campsites were now closed, even though it was only 10th September and still very hot, and we had the beaches and bars to ourselves. In one deserted bar I noticed a bottle of Cointreau on the shelf, so I was able to have a glass of my favourite liqueur, which was the first since I had left England.

One day I was pushing my bike up a hill in a residential area, and as I turned a corner a dog in its compound threw itself at the fence towards me barking. I felt safe, because a wire fence was between me and the dog, but I decided to take the opportunity to check the dog-dazer that we had bought for our trip. Dogs can be a big problem for cyclists, and because of our concern that we might be attacked or chased by dogs we had bought a dog-dazer each. As the dog continued to throw itself at the fence, snarling and growling, I pointed the dog-dazer at it and pressed the button once. The result was instant and very satisfying. The dog literally fell backwards, and retreated quickly to the furthest end of his compound, and he didn't return to the fence even when I walked away. (A dog-dazer works simply by emitting a high-pitched sound too high for a human to hear, and it doesn't harm the animal in any way).

We decided to stay in a hotel as we couldn't find a campsite, but to keep the cost down we cooked in the room on the marble floor with the window open. This worked well, and we cooked a meal of fried turkey escalopes with tiny new potatoes, porcini mushrooms and globe artichokes, which was accompanied by a mixed salad. Eggs had been boiled in the water with the potatoes, so we had egg sandwiches for lunch the next day as well!

The signs were now saying only 30km to Rome, but we planned to avoid the city itself, having visited it several years before. We didn't like the idea of cycling in Rome – the traffic in that wonderful city is scary in a car, let alone a bicycle. The weather was now very changeable. It was the middle of September, but was often hot and humid, so we tried not to camp near rivers or lakes because of the mosquitoes.

One evening we treated ourselves to a special four-course meal. I didn't understand what the starters were, so the waitress grabbed my hand and led me to the counter to show me the bowls of different delicious foods. We had risotto with scampi and cream, a pizza, verdura (roasted Mediterranean vegetables), veal in lemon sauce, tiramisu and marsala wine. Although the restaurant was empty when we walked in, after an hour it was full – the Italians always eat very late, probably because they have been asleep all afternoon. I was fascinated by the people on the tables around us. At the next table a couple sat with their fat son aged about 12, and he literally leapt on every course that was put onto the table – oysters, mussels, chicken, pizza, vegetables; on the corner table was a girl of about 10 years old, whose mother cut up her food into tiny pieces as though she was a toddler – this reminded me that in France we had often seen 5 year-olds with dummies in their mouths!

The following day I stood outside a shop looking after the bikes while Warren tried to buy a map. A man aged about 60 came up and spoke Italian to me, holding my arm in a too friendly manner.

'Non parlo Italiano,' I said, pulling my arm away from him.

He replied in English, presumably recognising my awful accent. 'What is your state?' he asked.

I was about to say I was fine when I realised he was asking my country, and when I told him I was from England he shook my hand but wouldn't let go, and kept telling me how pleased he was to meet me. He called to his friend and said how brave I was and what a wonderful person I was and did I have a husband? His friend smiled weakly and the look on his face said, 'Why doesn't the old devil leave women alone?'

At one of our visits to an internet café I found an e-mail from Norman, the Englishman we had met in France who was also cycling round the world. I had e-mailed him from Florence to say, 'We're in Florence at the moment.'

I received a reply from him. 'I'm in Florence now,' he said, but it was a week later, and we had long since left Florence! Sometimes when we heard from him he was behind us (he had spent quite a long time sampling wines in France!), and at others he had overtaken us, but because Warren and I didn't carry mobile phones we were never up-to-date with where Norman was. We hoped to meet up again somewhere, some time.

In one campsite I went to the loo in the middle of the night and noticed that there was an English tent pitched nearby with an English bicycle stood alongside. We both thought it was Norman, but in the morning it was Mikey who emerged from his tent. He was English and came from Suffolk. He had become bored with commuting to London and had decided to try cycling. He had bought himself a tent and a bike, never having camped or cycled before, and had set off alone through northern and eastern Europe. He was finding camping in Italy the most expensive country so far, so was looking forward to getting to France. However, he was horrified when we told him that there were another 1000 miles to cycle through France before getting back to England – he had zigzagged through a lot of smaller countries, so had notched up many more countries than us. After chatting over breakfast we said our goodbyes, adding Mikey's address to our list.

We stopped at a bar in a garage to have breakfast, but doughnuts were all that were available, as well as the always available coffee. Men came into the bar still half-asleep, ordered coffee (one-third of a tiny cup of very strong espresso), drank it in one shot, snapped themselves upright with the caffeine shock, slapped the money down on the counter and left, ready for the day's work. As we sat there a tanker came into the forecourt to refuel the station and was pumping the fuel into the open manholes. An Italian came into the forecourt, parked four feet from the open manhole, got out and lit a cigarette. He stood there smoking for several minutes as he refuelled his car. No-one told him to extinguish the cigarette, but Warren and I were both ready to dive behind the bar!

We were now approaching the area around Naples, and wanted to turn east to cross Italy north of Naples, as we planned to cycle across to the Adriatic coast to catch a ferry to Greece. We were now cycling through seedy towns and grim industrial areas with some farmland in between. Occasionally a tractor passed us, piled high with tobacco leaves, and the plants could be seen in the fields, standing 6 feet high but with all the leaves stripped from the base. Alongside houses were metal-framed buildings with polythene roofs, under which long strips of yellowed leaves were drying. At times the sweet smell of dried tobacco wafted across the road, and the smell took me instantly back to a childhood memory. When my brother and I were very young, my parents moved house. Instead of a front room we had a general shop selling everything. My mother ran the shop, and she kept packets of pipe tobacco in a large glass jar. As a child I used to open the top just to sniff the amazing aroma of tobacco which had wonderful names like 'Old Shag' and 'A1'. How strange that I hate the smell of tobacco burning, but I love the smell of fresh tobacco.

Now that we were travelling inland we knew that it was unlikely that we would find campsites, so we needed to move faster between towns and stay in hotels. However, we were finding it difficult to find accommodation, as most of the hotels were already closed for the season. The first hotel we found was at a very busy junction where five major roads met. There were no traffic lights or roundabouts and no lines on the road to denote priority. There were a few pedestrian crossings which everyone ignored, and it was pure chaos trying to cross the road in any direction. We chose the 'economy' room at the hotel, which meant we had no television and no air conditioning, but the room was large and our bikes had been safely locked at the back of the hotel, guarded by a barking German shepherd dog. The restaurant in the hotel was closed because it was out of season, and there were no bars, restaurants or cafés in the vicinity. It was a very industrial area, but we found a supermarket, so with a few provisions we were able to cook a decent meal in our room.

The next day's cycling was horrible, and we had difficulty finding our way through the industrial areas, seedy towns and small areas of farmland in between. We cycled on and on, unable to find a hotel. It was hot and dusty, my arms, neck, back and knees ached, and my sinusitis was seriously painful. Warren wasn't enjoying it either. Only one amusing incident cheered us. As I stood outside a shop with the bikes while Warren was inside, a very tall, skinny cyclist passed wearing lycra gear to match his bike. He was watching our bikes so hard that he nearly hit a parked car. He wobbled and straightened himself, continued to look at the bikes and nearly hit me. It was obvious that, despite the expensive bike and clothes, he was actually no good at cycling at all. Warren and I cycled along the pavement, because the road was blocked with traffic, and further along the road we saw him again. He was sat on his bike leaning against a lamp post with his feet still clipped into the pedals; he was looking around to check who was admiring him. He was actually posing!

As we approached he decided to shoot ahead of us, but as he tried to turn right into a side road he fell off his bike. His cleats were obviously too tight because he couldn't get his left foot out of the pedal so, with his left leg still attached to the fallen bike he tried to right himself. His right foot in its specialised shoe couldn't grip the sealed road, and he kept doing the splits as his foot slid across the road. His long arms and legs were shooting everywhere, and it was so funny that I wished I had a video camera to record it. We stood waiting for the poser to sort himself and his bike out, and noticed that the passengers in a car waiting in the side road were laughing hysterically at the scene. As we cycled on we heard the bike crashing to the ground again!

After a few hours of cycling we tried to find a hotel away from the main road. People had directed us to hotels which we eventually found were closed, and we were constantly retracing our route, so we had wasted a great deal of time. After 50 miles we eventually found a large hotel which was half way up a mountain and quite a long way out of our way. They didn't take credit cards, and we had only just enough cash to pay for one night and for a meal. The hotel said they would cook us a meal, but we had to wait until 8.30pm, which for us was quite an ordeal. It was a set meal with no choice, but it was very good. However, it seemed bizarre to be sitting alone in one corner of an enormous banqueting hall – we were the only guests in the hotel, although the following day there was to be a wedding reception in the hall.

When we reached our room we found that I had left behind at the last hotel a pair of padded cycling gloves, and as it wasn't possible to buy such gloves in Italy, and we were both suffering with pressure on the hands Warren decided that he would return the 50 miles to the hotel the next day, getting some cash from an ATM on the way, while I remained at the hotel to rest.

Warren set off very early the next morning with an empty bike, and said he was looking forward to a fast ride, despite the busy roads he knew he had to cycle. I found a computer shop in the nearby village and asked if there was an internet café anywhere; I was amazed that the lady stood up and offered me her chair. She charged me very little for an hour's typing, gave me a cup of coffee, and we chatted. This was hard work, because she and her husband spoke no English and I spoke only a few words of Italian, but we used the dictionary and I told them about my new grandson and showed them photos that Julian had put on a website. When I returned to the hotel, Warren had already returned. He was looking very flustered, and explained what had happened.

He had arrived at reception. The receptionist's pretty daughter was working there part-time, and was very keen to practise her English.

She said to Warren, 'You want kiss?'

Warren was a bit taken aback to say the least, and didn't want to offend her by saying 'no' outright, so said nothing, but she was clearly waiting for a reply, so he shook his head, backing away.

She looked confused, and held up our hotel room keys and said, 'You don't want kiss?'

Warren, utterly relieved, quickly said 'Yes,' snatched the keys from her hand and rushed out of reception . . .

We had some serious hill climbing to do as we continued, and even Warren sometimes had to get off his bike to push. One 7 mile climb got steeper and steeper as we got higher, and heavy lorries from the nearby quarries were struggling to get up the hill in bottom gear. We could hear them rumbling up the hill a mile behind us. At the top of the hill was a bar, so we just fell into it and asked for 'due cappuccino'. The girl spoke no English, but we were able to converse in German, and she told us that if we waited five minutes there would be fresh 'cornettos' (croissants). Sure enough, five minutes later she bore in a tray of steaming croissants filled with marmalade, and she joined us at the table and helped us to eat them all! Visiting the toilet behind the kitchen afterwards, Warren said he had shared it with a rat, but we felt too embarrassed to tell the girl, who had been so kind to us.

From the bar it was eight miles of freewheeling down a long hill to the next large town. It was a very busy town full of shoppers, and we nervously cycled through the heavy traffic until we found a hotel that was open. This was a four star hotel and, to us on a budget, incredibly expensive. They reduced the cost of the €110 room to €78, so we decided to indulge ourselves for a change. We luxuriated in a bubble bath, and enjoyed using the soft fluffy towels instead of the usual giant tea towels that are available in Italian hotels. We made the mistake of having a rest before we went out to visit the shops – the heavy traffic we had earlier encountered had disappeared, the shops were closed despite the fact that it was 1.30pm on a Saturday, and there were virtually no people in the streets either. It was like a ghost town. We had forgotten that everything closes in Italy for four hours from lunch time, and we wondered where the shop assistants went during that period. By 6pm the town was busy again, with groups of people standing around or sitting in bars, presumably waiting for 8pm when the restaurants opened.

At the breakfast buffet the next morning we ate as much as we could, and filled our bags with bananas and boiled eggs for the journey. We had finally left the seediness of Naples' industrial area behind us, and it was enjoyable cycling in the country again. It was lovely to see the fields and trees after the very busy seaside resorts. There were now signs of autumn in Italy. Golden leaves were beginning to float down from the trees, sweet chestnuts, walnuts and hazelnuts littered the roads and pavements, and the prickly outer shells of the chestnuts were crushed in the roads by cars, looking like tiny squashed hedgehogs. People were gathering the nuts in buckets and bags to take home. In one village the pavements had been covered with a layer of nuts outside each house, presumably to dry them, so that pedestrians were forced to walk on the road!

As we continued east the scenery became very rural. We were continually cycling uphill as we had to cross the Apennines, a mountain range that runs north to south like a backbone throughout Italy. We were looking forward to getting to the top and cycling down the other side. The weather deteriorated dramatically, and rain poured down the road like a river – we were cycling uphill through water and against the wind. We had to shelter under bridges and in tunnels through the mountains, and we were very cold and wet. The wind was funnelled through the tunnel, and the echoing noise of the cars as they raced through the tunnels was unbearable, reminding us of our earlier terrifying experience in a tunnel. The sky was black and thunder rumbled overhead, but we knew we had to continue so that we could find accommodation.

Eventually we reached the top of the mountain and cycled downhill for several miles. We found ourselves on a beautiful plateau, surrounded by mountains. For a short while the sun came out, and it was a wonderful rural, peaceful scene. The only sound was the tinkling of the bells round the cows' necks as they grazed in the lush green fields – the scenery seemed to be too perfect to be real. We had to cycle up another mountain to get out of the plateau, and as we cycled down the other side we could see the rain coming towards us from the south. Almost immediately we were engulfed in the deluge. There was very little visibility with such dense rain, and the mountain ahead disappeared in the torrents of rain. Once again we had to shelter under a bridge.

The only hotel we could find had closed for the season the day before we arrived, and eventually we realised that we were going to have to camp wild. We found a site of deserted holiday wooden bungalows and cycled around to check that no-one was there. We found a vandalised bungalow with no doors or windows, and I checked it out, thinking that it might be better to put the tent up inside the building out of the rain. However, it was clear from the dirty mattress on the floor, and the second mattress stuffed into one of the glassless windows, that a tramp had been using the bungalow, so we instead chose a grassy patch nearby to pitch our tent.

We discovered that the waterproof covers on our pannier bags had not been able to cope with the constant rain, and our bags were very wet, as were the contents. We hung the wet items in the vandalised bungalow to try to dry them out. As we lay in the tent reading, hoping that the torrential rain would stop long enough for us to cook some food, I felt a wet patch beneath my mattress. Horrified, we discovered that the base of the tent was leaking badly, the grassy patch was beginning to look like a paddling pool, and we were going to be flooded out. There was no other choice – it was now dark, but in the pouring rain we dashed backwards and forwards taking the contents of the tent into the vandalised bungalow, sniffing in disgust at the unpleasant smell inside. The toilet and wash basin lay on the floor, having been ripped from the wall. Bin liners full of old clothes, broken furniture, broken glass from the windows and pieces of wood cluttered the floor. We put up more clothes lines and hung all of our wet gear, the outer of the tent and our soaking wet pannier bags onto the lines, and cleared a space on the wooden floor to set up the inner part of our tent where we planned to sleep. I prayed that the tramp wouldn't arrive. The lack of glass in the windows and the open doorway meant that the gear on the clothes lines flapped loudly all night in the high winds, and we didn't need a light because the lightning flashed constantly throughout the night. Thunder crashed overhead so loud that the whole building shook. It was so cold that we were tempted to build a fire, but because the bungalow was made of wood we decided it would be too dangerous. However, we were able to light our stove, which roared into action and soon warmed us as we sat around it. In the middle of the night there was a deafening crash inside the room; I woke instantly from my disturbed sleep and shot upright in bed, my heart racing. Warren discovered that one of our bags had fallen from the line in the wind and had crashed to the wooden floor, so we tried to settle back to sleep.

The amount of rain that came down that night was unbelievable, and the lightning and thunder didn't stop. I had nightmares that the bad weather would continue the following day and we would be holed up there for days without food. In one nightmare we were floating down the mountain still inside the wooden cabin because the whole area had been flooded. However, the morning came with no rain, some blue sky and the sun trying to shine.

Most of the journey that day was downhill – with a very slight gradient we could cycle at 20 mph without effort. The scenery was wooded and agricultural. Stubble in the fields had been burnt, and there were steep wooded hills and mountains to the sides of us, with fields ploughed on what looked like impossible slopes. Villages sat on the mountain tops with painted buildings contrasting against the blue sky. The roads were edged with trees, the breeze making the leaves drop in our path. Cyclamen carpeted the woods, their leafless delicate little pink flowers peeping through the bare earth. The rivers we crossed were running fast and were brown with the soil that had been churned up with the storm. Broken branches and debris were further evidence of the storm. At one point there was a long panoramic view to our left of hills. At the top of each hill stood a windmill, and concrete irrigation canals ran alongside fields for kilometres, designed to carry vast quantities of water down the slopes for farmers to water their fields. We cycled amongst rolling countryside with the mountains in the distance, and there were small farms with patchwork fields.

As we steered onto the straight run down to Cerignola there were vineyards and olive groves lining the road. The vines were planted differently than in France. They were taller and the vines joined each other across the top, so it was like a roof with bunches of grapes hanging down, so the workers could work underneath to harvest the grapes. Orange and lemon trees stood in gardens. The sun shone, it became hot again, the scenery was lovely, quiet and rural, and life was wonderful again! How different it made us feel because the sun was shining! We had effortlessly cycled 70 miles that day!

A few days later we were cross with the Italians, because the passenger in a passing car had thrown the contents of a bottle of water at us and we were soaked. Minutes later a car tried to run us off the road deliberately. We stopped at a bar, still trying to dry out from the first incident, when a car with several youths stopped outside. The driver passed me on the way into the bar, and I felt nervous at the way he kept looking at me. Warren came out of the bar after a few minutes; he was grinning and was very excited that the youth in the car had invited us to his father's workshop to see a 'wooden bike'. I felt nervous about this, but Warren was adamant that we should go. We followed the car on our bikes for a mile or two across the town and began to wonder if it was a wind-up; the passengers were constantly looking out of the windows to check that we were still following the car, and if we lagged behind the car slowed down to walking speed for us to catch up. I kept voicing my concerns to Warren (when I could catch him up!), but eventually we followed the car into a side street and then into a deserted area with garages, where the car stopped and all of the youths jumped out of the car. We both stood astride our bicycles, unable to turn the heavy bikes quickly ready to flee, and we were immediately surrounded by the youths. I was convinced that we were about to be mugged, especially when the driver put his arm across Warren's shoulders and indicated that we should follow them through an alleyway. Two of the passengers brought up the rear, and my heart was pounding as I walked through the alleyway following the others.

As we emerged from the alleyway we found ourselves in a modern housing estate, and it was with incredible relief that I saw a few people in the street. However, my concerns rose again as the six of us walked down an incline to a basement garage below a house, but the garage door opened into a workshop, where Danielli's father, a skilled cabinet maker, was intricately carving a piece of ebony wood at his work bench. Now that I realised we weren't going to be mugged I could relax, and Danielli proudly introduced us to his father. When we saw his work, we were incredibly impressed. Danielli's father showed us several bicycles that he had made almost entirely of wood including the handlebars, saddle, spokes, frame, mudguards, lights, rack and bike stands. Only the Campagnola gears, light bulbs and tyres weren't wooden. They were works of art, but could be cycled. Danielli also showed us with pride the tall cabinet his father was making out of solid mahogany with inlay; it had curved and carved doors and drawers, and was a definite antique of the future. After taking photographs, Danielli led us back out of the town and directed us onto the right road again, so after meeting Danielli and his father we felt happier with the Italians again, and were sorry to have mistrusted him initially!

We cycled past the salt pans, where the reflection of the sky made the water look pink and mauve, and later that day Warren and I arrived at the coast again – we had finally arrived at the Adriatic on the east coast of Italy. We found a campsite that appeared to have closed, but the owner agreed, for a substantial fee, to allow us to camp on the beach. There were miles of sand in both directions, but we were the only people on the beach. We were so concerned about our leaking tent that we pitched it on an open building on the sand which had a marble floor and a roof supported by columns. Although it was late September it was still beautifully warm, so we took advantage of the empty beach to go skinny dipping in the sea, and afterwards sat on the stunning beach and watched a 360° sunset with pink, red and orange in the sky whichever way we looked. Sunset was followed by a lunar rise, a big yellow ball of a moon rising from the horizon partly obscured by the clouds. We went to bed listening to the waves lapping on the beach a few feet away – it was good to be by the sea again . . .

I don't know if the Italians have more deaths from road accidents than in

England, but we constantly saw memorials to young people at the side of the roads. We often saw slabs of marble engraved with a picture and the date of birth and death of the deceased, and the memorial was usually decorated with plastic flowers. Judging from our experiences in Italy (we had been almost knocked off our bikes many times) we felt that the Italians were terrible drivers. Just as in France, they reversed without looking; they turned out of junctions with mobile phones in their hands, deep in conversation; they seldom appeared to think before making a manoeuvre, and they frequently opened car doors without checking the road behind. In large towns in Italy it was quite terrifying to cycle. We discovered that red lights have a different meaning in Italy – as soon as the traffic light turns to red, it means accelerate as fast as you can to get across the junction before the traffic in the opposite direction moves forward. Three cars can probably get through red lights in this way. As the drivers also move forward before the green light goes on, this can cause a problem with traffic colliding. Scooters don't need to take any notice of traffic lights at all; they can go up one-way streets the wrong way, and drive on pavements between pedestrians. Children, babies and dogs should be carried in front of the scooter driver, and helmets must be worn on the back of the head with straps left flapping undone.

We arrived in a town called Trani but lost our way. A crowd of people came round the corner into the quiet street where we were. Warren stopped and one of the crowd asked where we were from. She was obviously a tour guide with a group of about 20 people, and she spoke excellent English. Since leaving Pisa we had encountered very few Italians who spoke English. When we told her we had cycled from England, she clapped her hands in the air to draw attention to herself, and translated to the group what we had said. There were shouts of 'bravi' from the audience and everyone clapped. Warren and I stood there grinning stupidly, as she asked more and more questions, each time translating and waiting for the clapping to subside before asking another question.

'How long had we been travelling?' 'How many kilometres had we done?' 'How many kilometres did we do in a day?' 'Where were we going?' 'How long did we intend to continue travelling?' As she translated our answers to the waiting crowd there would be murmurs of approval, more shouts and loud clapping. Next there were questions from the 'audience'.

'Do you wash?' asked one.

'Sometimes,' I replied, but wondered how the translation would be taken – probably not in the jokey way I had intended, I suspected.

'How did we wash our clothes?' one woman asked ... Our favourite method was to put our clothes with washing powder and water into a bin liner which we sealed into a ball and kicked around the shower for a while, but we felt that this was difficult to explain, so we answered that many campsites had washing machines. We didn't bother to explain that our own washing line was usually fixed between trees as soon as we had chosen our camp site. The questions continued for a few minutes until we were allowed to continue on our way, and we left to shouts of 'bye-bye, ciau, arrivederci, goodbye, buon voyagio'.

The weather had changed – once the sun set the temperature dropped dramatically, and it often rained. However, most days it was still pleasantly warm to cycle. Most of the grapes had been harvested, though we occasionally saw workers picking black grapes by the roadside. The bunches were bigger than any I had ever seen, and all we could hear was the snip, snip, snip as the workers cut the bunches with their scissors, dropped the bunches into buckets over their shoulders, and threw the contents of the bucket into a trailer. The fields had been ploughed and newly planted with artichokes and brassica, and there were many olive and fig trees.

Now that we were on the east coast we decided to investigate a ferry crossing to Albania, just the other side of the Adriatic sea. However, we found that we needed a visa which was only available in Rome, so decided instead to continue cycling south-east down the coast until we reached Brindisi, which is situated in the 'heel' of Italy, where we would take the ferry to Corfu. I did some calculations – we had now been away from home 99 days, during which time 27 days we had rested. Of the rest of the days we had cycled an average of only 30.72 miles per day, which is a very short distance by most cyclists' standards. We had cycled 2,357 miles. It was time to leave Italy . . .

CHAPTER 5

GREECE AND THE GREEK ISLANDS

Greece consists of about 2,000 islands although many of these are uninhabited. Most of the country is mountainous but, with its typical Mediterranean climate, the beaches and the islands form the main tourist attractions. However, travelling through Greece is like travelling through time, with the ancient archaeological ruins being a testament to Greece's former glory.

It was 28th September 2002 when we embarked on the ferry to Corfu. By the time we had tied our bicycles to the side of the lower deck and gone up the stairs to the main part of the boat, the ferry was already under way. It would be eight hours before the boat docked in Corfu, so it was likely to be dark when we arrived. We were tired, so looked for somewhere to sleep. We went into the cinema which was dimly lit, and it appeared to be empty apart from bags and back-packs, but we stumbled over people who were asleep on the floor between the seats. We joined them and slept a little, cuddled together for warmth, but our feet got colder and colder, so we went up on deck for a walk.

The ferry was moving south, parallel to the Albanian coast, which looked mountainous and inhospitable. The mountains were rocky, and only a few roads could be seen, zigzagging up the mountains, which were topped with clouds. We could see no sign of houses or villages. Maybe it was fortunate that we hadn't travelled to Albania after all!

When we arrived at Kerkira in Corfu we had a problem getting our bikes out, because they had been blocked in by enormous lorries which were not disembarking until the ferry reached the mainland, its next stop. None of the men working on the boat would help us, but Warren managed to free my bicycle and told me to cycle down the ramp to the quayside while he struggled to remove his bike. Warren was the last to leave the ferry, and I was horrified as I stood on the quayside and saw the ramp beginning to rise, because Warren hadn't left the boat. I tried to shout above the noise of the ferry, but as I did so Warren appeared at the entrance and cycled fast down the slowly-rising ramp. My heart was in my mouth as I saw that the end of the ramp was already at least a foot above the ground as he approached it, but he put on a spurt of speed and bent low over his handlebars. Warren and the bike, heavy with pannier bags, dropped from ramp to quayside safely, to a round of applause and cheers from a crowd standing nearby. There was no way that I would have attempted such a jump, so it was lucky that he had managed to get my bicycle out first.

There were two hotels on the quayside. The first hotel refused to accommodate our bikes, but the second was happy to put them in a locked store-room. There we found another bicycle, which Warren immediately recognised it as Norman's. We had caught up with each other at last! We had missed each other and passed each other so many times, but now we could chat about our experiences. We left a message for Norman at reception, and received a phone call from him at 11pm. It wasn't until the morning when we went to meet him at breakfast that we realised it had actually been midnight – the time in Greece was an hour different from France and Italy. We talked and talked, not leaving the breakfast table until mid-day.

Norman had been in Corfu for one day, so he took us to explore the area. Corfu was a culture shock – after travelling for so long in non-tourist areas, it was extraordinary to see somewhere so clearly geared to English people. Notice boards outside shops and tourist offices were in English, restaurant menus were in English, and English people were everywhere. We decided to leave the town and cycle around Corfu with Norman for a few days.

The views were spectacular as we cycled along the coast. There were constant signs to our right saying 'To the beach' in English, but the roads were down impossible gradients, and I felt nervous to be cycling alongside dramatic drops from the road to the sea far below. We turned off the coastal road and cycled down a long, narrow zigzagging road until we reached a tiny picturesque village nestling in a small bay by the sea. We were immediately accosted by a Greek man who ran out to offer us accommodation for a couple of days. Settled into our new two-bedroomed apartment, we later went to a bar which had been recommended to Norman by a friend, so the barman immediately bought us all drinks on the house!

We went on to a taverna, and this was our first experience on this trip of the wonderful Greek food – Saganaki (fried cheese), stuffed peppers, ratatouille, sardines, kleftico and a large quantity of wine. That night Warren had his first upset tummy of the trip, but he had drunk Corfu tap water before we had been warned that although water elsewhere in Greece is safe to drink, it isn't in Corfu.

Gerald Durrell, the famous author, once lived on Corfu, so we visited the house where he had lived and discovered that it was now a restaurant. After mussels in garlic sauce, mushrooms in cream sauce, stuffed aubergine, chicken in ouzo and swordfish in garlic, we all announced that we were looking forward to eating our way through Greece!

We sat at a bar having breakfast the next morning, where we pretended not to be English as we listened to a Yorkshire couple behind us grumbling that the Greeks didn't know how to make a proper cup of tea! We stayed in the village relaxing for a few days, before deciding to return to Kerkira so that we could continue our journey to the Greek mainland. After a laborious climb back up the zigzagging hill, we cycled into Kerkira and found a different hotel for one night. Although we were not in the centre of the town, we had a stunning view of the fort in the sea with the mountains of Albania beyond. The coast of Albania was incredibly close – far closer than the Greek mainland. Now that we were back in a tourist area the prices were much higher – a litre of wine was €11.50 in Corfu, whereas it had been €3 in Italy.

We needed to get to the non-tourist areas again to reduce our budget, but we also knew that we had to get to the Greek islands as quickly as possible, because many of the ferries stop at the end of October, and it was now 3rd October – we had to cycle across the Greek mainland to Athens before we could get a ferry to any of the Aegean islands. As we checked the ferry times to Patra on the Greek mainland, we met a Dutch couple, Bert and Marianne, who had taken a year off work to cycle, and we chatted to them for a while. Their bikes were typically Dutch, with the upright seating position that was so different from English touring bikes with drop handlebars. That evening Norman, Warren and I pushed our bikes onto the ferry at 10.30 for a night crossing to the Greek mainland. We hadn't booked a cabin, so made our way to the deck where we laid out our thin self-inflating mattresses and sleeping bags. The stars were out, there was no sign of rain and, apart from the constant rumbling of the boat and the breeze on our faces, we were extremely comfortable. Eight hours later, at 6.30am, the boat docked at Patras on the Greek mainland, and we said goodbye to our new Dutch friends who intended to stay on the ferry until they reached Kefalonia, one of the Ionian islands on the west of the Greek mainland.

It was still dark but I was hungry, and Warren, Norman and I eventually found a café selling wonderful cakes and pastries. This was my first experience of spanakopita (or spanakotyropita) – flaky pastry encasing spinach, feta cheese and ultra thin slices of potato, which was delicious.

We cycled towards Athens with the Gulf of Corinth on our left. Whilst this area, the Peloponnese, is part of the Greek mainland, it's separated from the rest of the mainland by the Gulf of Corinth and the 6km long Corinth Canal, which was hewn out of the rock to allow large ships to pass through, and effectively makes the Peloponnese a large island.

Mountains soared above us to our right and more mountains were on the other side of the gulf – we were told that this was a popular ski-ing destination for the locals in winter. The hills went gently up and down, but the beach was far below us on our left. The water was the clearest we'd seen so far, and rocks on the sea-bed way out to sea could be clearly seen through the deep aqua blue water. The weather was now much warmer than it had been in Italy.

We found a hotel run by a Greek man married to an English girl. It wasn't cheap, especially considering we were nowhere near any tourist area, but we were tired after not having a proper night's sleep on the ferry. Here a dog befriended us, following us backwards and forwards as we went for walks, and sitting patiently waiting for us while we ate at the local restaurant. Warren and Norman called him 'Wellard' and he turned out to be the first of many dogs that become our temporary pets as we travelled. As with most of these dogs, they had at some time been mistreated. This was obvious, because if we picked up a stick to throw for him to retrieve, Wellard was clearly frightened and cowered and cried, his ears flattened and his tail no longer wagging – in his experience sticks were for beating dogs.

Several football teams from Moldova and Liechtenstein had invaded our hotel, and in the morning they had eaten everything on the breakfast buffet. We set off on our bicycles, saying goodbye to Wellard, who was waiting outside the reception doors for us. Further along this stretch of coastline we were able to find two or three campsites, which were almost empty apart from a few Germans and Dutch in their caravans. Most of the campsites had a bar, so we could pitch our tents between the bar and the beach and eat in the local small restaurants, and the prices of the campsites were now incredibly low.

We seemed to be spending a lot of our time eating and drinking, and were thoroughly enjoying Greek food. In fact, as we ate our lunch we seemed to be planning what and where we would eat in the evening, but we made the excuse that we needed the nutrition as we were using up so much energy cycling in the heat! The Greek wine could be quite good and we were now paying on average €3 or even less (about £2), but this was for half a kilo. This seemed to be a strange measure for liquid, but appeared to equate to half a litre. Occasionally it tasted pretty awful – one rosé wine we chose tasted like pink paraffin! – so it was a bit hit and miss. The restaurants away from the cities all had their own home-made wine, some good and some bad. Then there was retsina, the local Greek wine which is flavoured with pine resin (known as the Greek wine of the gods). However, as pine is a 'flavour' usually reserved in England for toilet cleaners, we didn't enjoy this particular type of wine, so decided to leave it for the Greek gods. Warren and Norman enjoyed Greek coffee, which was always served with a glass of iced water. Instant coffee never appeared to be available and, although I know that one shouldn't drink the sludge-like sediment at the bottom of a cup of Greek coffee, I always seemed to end up with the gritty sludge in my mouth. However, frappé was available everywhere, so I enjoyed this delicious iced coffee instead.

Very few people spoke English in this part of Greece and the menus were only in Greek as well, so we struggled to learn the basics of Greek. The fact that the Greek word for 'yes' sounds like 'no' in English and the word for 'no' sounds like 'ok' in English is confusing to start with, and we had to learn that a triangle is pronounced as 'th', 'b' is 'v', 'p' is 'r', and this was without the other extraordinary looking symbols! However, we all much preferred this to the tourist areas where everyone automatically spoke English, as in Corfu.

We continued our journey across the mainland, the weather becoming hotter and hotter. A lorry passed us. It had an open back, and a saddled horse stood in the back, which seemed rather strange. At another point in the road we could see ahead of us a motor scooter driving very slowly and erratically. A barrel was strapped onto the back of the scooter. As we approached (yes, we were cycling faster than the motor scooter!) we could hear the driver singing, and he was weaving backwards and forwards across the road. We assumed that he was drunk, and as we cycled past Warren took a photo of him, but he just laughed and called out 'Hello my friends' in a slurred voice. We had visions of him stopping at lay-bys for refreshments, where he would lie on the ground with his mouth beneath the tap of the barrel!

There were still olive trees and fig trees, but we also noticed that every garden and spare piece of land had orange, lemon or lime trees. Occasionally we'd see a pomegranate tree, its pink, orange or red fruits looking quite startling amongst the leaves. Everywhere there were unfinished houses; often a flat downstairs would be lived in, whilst the upstairs was still a shell, or even vice versa! Red or ochre tiled roofs topped white or cream painted stone houses, and logs were usually stacked neatly against the sides of the houses. In the background were the wooded mountains, and occasional cypress trees stood erect against the skyline. Bougainvillea was everywhere, and I had never seen so many different colours – dark red, scarlet, orange, pale pink, deep pink, white, cream, orange, yellow, lilac and white – and familiar pyracantha laden with berries looked quite incongruous alongside the exotic-looking bougainvillea.

We continued to follow the coast, and at Kiato we saw a building being built of two feet thick slabs of marble. It was an extension to a Greek orthodox church, and a crane was trying to place a carved marble plinth on top of marble pillars. A Greek priest was directing the operation, but when we stopped to watch and take photographs, he came to talk to us, and he proudly showed us inside his church, which was full of amazing mosaic pictures in gold and bright colours.

When we searched later that evening for somewhere to eat, we found a restaurant with a notice stating that English was spoken. Inside the vast interior was only one person eating, and he was the owner. His English was poor, but obviously much better than our Greek, but there was no menu. He asked us if we liked fish, and when we all nodded enthusiastically he smiled and disappeared into his kitchen. He returned with a pitcher of home-made rosé wine, and bowls of garlicky mashed potato and spicy cheese, both of which we had often been served as a dip. After we had finished these starters he produced saganaki, delicious fried cheese served with a wedge of lemon, after which he placed a magnificent tureen of fish soup on the table which appeared to have every type of sea food in it. This was a complete meal already, but the owner was now in full flow and had probably not had any guests for days. Pork fillets and barbecued swordfish were placed before us, together with a plate of Greek salad large enough for six people. With 2½ litres of wine between us, some liqueurs and coffee, we pronounced the meal the best yet. The meal for the three of us was €75 or £50 – not cheap for people like us on a budget, but definitely a feast fit for a king!

At Korinthos we had to cross onto a different part of the mainland. Here the mainland had been made into an island in 1893 by a deep canal cut into the rock. In ancient times boats and ships had been carried overland on wheels rather than take the long route round the mainland by ship. As early as 600 BC the Greeks had thought of building a canal, but didn't have the technology. Twenty-three years after Suez this 6 kilometre long canal was built. Rather than installing locks to go up and over the hills, the canal was cut down to sea level, so the canal is dominated by 100 metre sheer rock walls on either side, even though it is only 25 metres wide. 12,000 ships a year now take this important short cut from the Adriatic to Athens, but it isn't wide enough for super tankers. We cycled across the bridge looking down the amazing distance to the sea below, and stopped to take photographs before continuing on our journey to Athens. Now that we had passed Korinthos, we were cycling with the Aegean sea on our right.

One day we had cycled so far in the heat that I was beginning to feel faint, but still we hadn't seen a hotel. It was a relief to eventually find two hotels opposite each other on a deserted bay. The better hotel was unbelievably expensive, despite the fact that the hotel appeared to have no guests there and it was out of season. We tried the hotel opposite, but were dismayed at how seedy it was. The manager spoke English, but it was most disconcerting that he smelled so strongly of alcohol. He offered us a room each at €20 a room – good value for Warren and me sharing, but more expensive for Norman on his own. However, beggars can't be choosers, and we accepted. We were worried about our bikes, especially as the owner refused to allow us to put them in the rooms. We didn't trust him, so chained them up outside, but decided we would sneak them up to our rooms later. We began to get even more worried when the manager knocked on our bedroom door.

'My friend,' he said, 'I am worried about your bikes. There are many thieves here. I will put them in my office.'

We declined his offer, but he came back twice more to try to persuade us to change our minds. Where were these thieves? We had seen no-one in the area at all except the staff at each of the two hotels! We had paid the manager in cash, but he claimed not to have change and told us he would pay us later. As we suspected, when we returned later he claimed not to know what we were talking about, and his English suddenly became less fluent! However, Warren insisted in a fairly intimidating way and eventually got his money.

I was also concerned about the enormous gilt-framed mirror on the wall in this otherwise very poorly-furnished room, and Norman said his room was the same and he had the same concerns – were they perhaps two-way mirrors? We tried our keys in each other's doors and found that each key fitted every door on the landing . . .

We returned early to our rooms after eating out, and crept past the manager in his office who was playing cards and drinking with friends. We quietly carried the bikes up the two flights of stairs and into our rooms. There was very little room to move, but we wedged the door shut with our bikes and, as we began to fall asleep, our fears were confirmed. We heard a click, which was the unmistakeable sound of a key turning in the lock, and in the dim light we saw the door handle turning. The door gave a little as it was pushed, but because of the bikes wedging the door it wouldn't open. Warren shouted, asking who was there.

'Oh, hello my friend,' replied the manager. 'Are you alright?'

When Warren replied he went away. The manager had presumably taken the opportunity to try to steal from our room – he must have thought that we were still out because our bikes weren't chained up outside. Despite very little sleep, we left at dawn the next morning, desperate to get away, and I was just grateful that I hadn't been in that scary place on my own.

The closer we got to Athens the bigger the boats were in the sea to our right. There were many giant tankers, and we were passing industrial areas, boat menders' yards with massive boats in dry docks, and oil installations. There were now several lanes in both directions and the traffic was very heavy. We were less than 30 miles from Athens, and the cycling was hot and dusty with road-works the whole way. There were big lorries and massive cement mixers everywhere, and the road was white with cement dust. With the sun reflecting from the white road we found it difficult to see properly. The Greeks were building roads and motorways into Athens ready for the Olympics in 2004. It was very busy and there was no hard shoulder, but occasionally there was space at the side of the road, so we could rest for a few minutes. There was a long drop down to the sea, but we noticed that the whole of the side of the mountain was covered with rough concrete which had solidified around the trees and down the cliff in waves, totally obliterating the grass and shrubs. As we stood there, a giant concrete mixer stopped alongside us, and discharged its excess concrete over the trees a few yards from us. We were amazed that the workers were allowed to destroy the countryside in such a way.

As we approached Athens we had to cross five lanes to get to the left because the road divided into two roads, and this was absolutely terrifying. Even Warren said he needed a coffee to settle his shaking hands. We stopped frequently to rest, and arrived in the centre of Athens at noon, where we bought a street map and were able to find clean, basic rooms with bathrooms and air-conditioning that weren't too expensive.

This was the first capital city that Warren and I had visited on this trip, and we obviously wanted to do the tourist thing while we were in Athens and visit the Acropolis, so once we had found a café to have lunch we all set off. We were very impressed with the underground in Athens, which was very clean, had stainless steel waste bins, and was beautifully tiled. We wished that the London underground was as impressive, but we discovered that the Athens system had only been opened the year before. The London underground system was 137 years older than the Athens underground – maybe after 137 years the system in Athens would also look shabby!

The Acropolis in Athens is on a flat-topped rock which rises 150 metres (490 ft) above sea level, and is one of the most recognisable monuments of the world. Standing proudly on the top of the hill, the Acropolis can be seen from most of the side streets in the city. The Athenians worshipped their gods in the temples at the Acropolis and it was always a sacred place for ancient Athenians, but the first habitation dates from the Neolithic period. The temples were destroyed or burned several times in ancient times, but the Parthenon and other main buildings that we see today were built by Pericles in the 5th century BC. Even in its state of ruin, the Parthenon is imposing and breath-taking in its beauty, with its lines of tall, elegant columns. Unfortunately when we visited the Parthenon it was being renovated, presumably in readiness for the Olympics, and was surrounded by scaffolding which would obviously spoil our photos. A walk around the Parthenon showed different views of Athens stretching out endlessly below. It was beautiful.

Athens was upgrading everything ready for the 2004 Olympics. In every street was a building site, so this was not the best time to be visiting the Greek capital. However, the marble pavements and steps were magnificent, and we were impressed as we walked around the town.

The food in the capital was definitely not as exciting as the more local food that we had been experiencing in rural Greece. We also couldn't understand why 19 out of 20 toilets in Greek cafés had no locks. Most of them had doors that didn't shut properly either, and often they opened outwards, so it wasn't even possible to wedge the door shut with a foot! In one café I had to climb over beer crates which were balanced precariously on the steps of the spiral staircase which led to the toilet. At the top was a squat toilet (no door at all this time!), but it had been set into a high step so that it was at sitting level. A bottle of washing up liquid with the label removed stood by the washbasin.

The three of us visited the bar next to the hotel for a beer, and found that after the first drink we were not allowed to buy any more, as the barman and the locals wanted to treat us. We spent a pleasant evening chatting to them, but the ouzo was a mistake, and we all woke the next morning feeling decidedly delicate!

Warren and I decided to look at the map and make our plans for visiting the Greek islands, and Norman planned to do the same separately. In this way we wouldn't be influencing each other, and would probably be going our separate ways for a while again. We all knew that once we started island-hopping, we would be cycling less than we had so far been doing, but we were all looking forward to this break from cycling. Warren and I planned to visit a number of islands, ending in Rhodes, from where we could catch a ferry to Marmeris in Turkey. It was now 11th October – we wanted to spend a month visiting the Greek islands before we caught the ferry to Turkey. Our current plan (though plans are made to be changed!) was that we would cycle north to Istanbul, where we needed to get a visa for India and catch a plane to Bombay. Unfortunately the situation in Iraq, Iran, Afghanistan and Pakistan made it impossible for us to even consider cycling overland to India.

We tried to book our chosen ferry tickets. We all planned to catch the same ferry, but Warren and I wanted to visit Syros first, while Norman planned to continue on the ferry for another hour to Paros. However, we found that the ticket office had sold out of tickets from Piraeus, the port near Athens, because there were general elections at the weekend, and the Greek people had to return to their homes on the islands to vote. We visited a few more ticket offices, and finally found one that had a few tickets available, but we had to pay for the more expensive business class.

Our new friends in the bar next to the hotel waved goodbye to us as we set off on the cycle ride from Athens. We had to cycle seven miles to the port of Pyraeus, and it was a hot, dusty, busy road. However, one incident stands out – the three of us were cycling behind each other and a taxi driver joined our lane. He drove very close to Warren, obviously expecting him to stop or get out of his way. However, Warren's 'trick' when cars came too close was to flick their wing mirror, which made a loud noise inside the car, so that the driver would think he'd hit something and move away. Warren did this, but the wing mirror flew off as he flicked it and it bounced straight through the open window into the passenger's lap! The passenger, not knowing what it was or where it had come from, was throwing the wing mirror up and down like a hot potato! Norman, who was just behind Warren, was roaring with laughter so much that he had to stop. Needless to say, Warren shot ahead quickly between the cars to get out of reach of the shocked and possibly irate taxi driver!

We disembarked from the ferry at Syros and said goodbye to Norman. We followed the sign to 'rooms' up a picturesquely steep stepped back street, and found a basic room which had air conditioning, a fridge and a balcony which overlooked the town and the port. At €18 it was cheap, and we looked forward to seeing sunsets from our balcony.

The following day the weather changed; thunder rumbled and lightning lit the darkened sky, and soon it was pouring with rain, flooding our balcony. We could hardly see across the harbour because of the rain, and the beautiful stepped side streets became spectacular waterfalls in minutes. We walked through the rain to get breakfast, and gradually the rain eased and a few glimmers of blue showed in the sky. However, the clouds had dropped so low that the houses higher up the hill had disappeared from view.

After two days in Syros we went by ferry to Mikonos, stopping briefly at Tinos on the way. Mikonos was very pretty but touristy and expensive. It had the most expensive coffee in Europe at €3.50 (over £2 a cup) – more than the cost of half a kilo of wine!

In Mikonos we had a few days of very windy weather, and most of the ferries were cancelled. We wanted to go to Delos, an island considered sacred by the ancient Greeks. It was uninhabited now, and was about half an hour's ferry ride away, though we discovered that the ferry was a small fishing boat! When we arrived at the quayside to catch the ferry, local fishermen were standing at a long marble counter selling their catch of the morning. Three pelicans, one white, one beige and one pink, sat there expectantly, waiting for their breakfast.

The ferry left for Delos on time, but the windy weather caused the boat to rock up and down and roll sideways as well. Not being a very good sailor, I needed to stand outside, gripping tightly to anything solid, but each time the boat rolled to one side substantial waves washed across the deck and over our feet. On two occasions, a green-faced passenger from inside the boat rushed up the steps to stagger to the rail to be sick.

It was windy and rather cool on Delos. First inhabited in 3,000 BC, the Greeks had built temples, sanctuaries and statues on this sacred land, which was complete with an amphi-theatre; this had once been the centre of worship and the capital city of the Aegean islands. Columns, plinths, porticos, ruins of small houses and stone walls stood everywhere. There were statues of lions, carved friezes on marble, mosaic floors and giant mortars made from marble and granite for grinding corn. The ground was littered with broken pieces of terracotta pots, and the small museum was very impressive.

After our trip to Delos the weather improved, and the temperature was averaging 24°C, even though it was now mid October. We continued to Naxos, stopping at Paros on the way. The ferry was a catamaran, so had no space to put bikes inside. After a few minutes at sea, the catamaran tipped so far on its side that I thought it was going to flip over; everyone screamed, and everything untethered shot from one side of the boat to the other. The rope holding our bikes snapped and our bikes were thrown across the deck, but fortunately they weren't damaged. We were the last to leave the ferry, and were approached by a man who offered us accommodation for €15 a night. The room was so cheap that we went to look, and were pleased to see that as well as a double room with bathroom and a small kitchen area, there was a television, air conditioning, and a tiny garden with table and chairs. Our new landlord gave us some soapy water in a bucket, and switched on a hose, so we were able to clean the salt water from our bikes as well.

I thought Naxos one of the prettiest islands, with wonderful quaint back streets in the old town. Its jumble of old houses were joined by crazy-paved slate paths with steps going up and down to the white-painted houses. Geraniums and flowers made splashes of colour on the balconies. Some of Greece's many cats sat on the white steps or prowled the arched alleyways, and there wasn't a tourist to be seen.

As we sat eating in one of the cafés, Warren suddenly jumped up and rushed over to a couple who were passing. I wondered what he was doing, until he returned with them to our table. It was Mick and Sarah, a couple we knew from our home town of Reading! We knew that they had moved permanently to Greece, but didn't know where. We heard that Jack, a mutual friend of theirs and ours, had left Naxos only a few days before. What a small world!

We were finding it very easy to get cheap accommodation everywhere we went. The locals always waited for the ferry to arrive, all clamouring at the tourists that their rooms were the best and the cheapest, some carrying photos to prove it. As there were so few tourists at this time of year, by the time we disembarked (always last, because we had to collect our bikes), the locals knew that we were their last chance. We were finding that we could have double rooms with small kitchen and bathroom for less than the cost of a site to pitch a tent in Italy. This was very encouraging, as our budget had been badly hit in Europe so far.

From Naxos we booked a ferry to Amorgos, a less well-known island and likely to be much quieter. This island has had cars only since 1985 – before that time donkeys had been the only form of transport. We understood that there were still numerous donkeys being used in this way, and they were probably the best form of transport in the narrow streets of the towns.

We were shocked when we went to catch the ferry to Amorgos. We queued to get on one of the large ferries, but were told that it was not our boat, and were directed to a very small ancient, rusty local boat. There was room for one lorry in the hold, and as well as a lorry waiting to embark there were boxes and crates of everything you could think of – toilet cisterns, planks of wood, crates of beer, vine plants, sacks of potatoes, bags of cement, slabs of marble, boxes of groceries, barrels of oil. We had been told that the ferry took 3 hours, but in fact it took almost 6 hours and visited four tiny islands (Schinoussa, Iraklia, Kouffinisia and Donoussa) before reaching our destination. At each tiny island about 20 people were waiting on the jetty with their vans and trucks. They ran into the hold before the ramp was properly down, and then ran in and out of the boat carrying boxes and crates, overloading their tiny vans with the goods. More produce was put onto the ferry, and by the time the ferry had begun to move away from the island again, the jetty was empty again, the vans having moved slowly back up and over the hill to the villages. At one island the ramp at the back of the ferry wouldn't open, which was a considerable concern as it was the only way out for passengers, vehicles and our bikes. We were delayed for half an hour while the crew tried to fix it. There was the sound of violent hammering from inside the boat as the crew struck the door again and again, until it was eventually forced open. The islanders all thought it highly amusing, but it gave us a few concerns as to the seaworthiness of the boat.

There was no food available on the boat, and because we had been told that the ferry would take three hours we hadn't brought any supplies with us, so we were getting very hungry. We decided to try the coffee – the crew member put a spoonful of unnamed coffee powder, some water and sugar into a plastic cup and frothed it in a blender before adding evaporated milk and boiling water. Maybe it was because we were so hungry, but it actually tasted delicious!

None of the crew spoke English, but as the ferry left Kouffinisia we asked if we were now going to Amorgas. We understood from him that there was one more stop. We assumed we were going to Keros, which was on the way to Amorgos, but our compasses showed us that we were travelling north-east, and soon all islands disappeared. We realised that we must be going to Donoussa, as this was the only island to the north-east, though it was certainly out of the way for a route from Naxos to Amorgas. It was also 28km away, and even further back south to Amorgos in the south-east.

By the time we reached Amorgos it was dark, and we had seen a wonderful sunset at sea. We were horrified to find that there appeared to be no sign of life and there were no lights, apart from one at the end of the jetty. How would we find accommodation if there was no-one there? It was a relief when we discovered that there had been a power cut on the island, and there were 3 or 4 people standing in the shadows. In the pitch black we followed one of the locals in her car to a tiny resort of cottages. These were owned by her sister, who welcomed us with a big hug, cooked us a wonderful meal, and showed us to a neat small room where we could stay.

It wasn't until the following day that we discovered that we had landed at a different port from the one we wanted, and we needed to travel to the south of the island to catch our next ferry. The place was quiet, even deserted, and our hearts sank as we looked at the map and realised that we would have to cycle over a mountain 1,475 feet high in order to travel the 20 kilometre to the southern port. We made enquiries about other forms of transport in the village, and also asked our landlady. There were no ferries from this port, we were told by our landlady, and she tried to persuade us to stay with her longer, saying that the mountain road was far too steep to cycle. However, we had no choice – we had to cycle over the mountain.

Our landlady took a real liking to Warren. She was a lovely lady, but very big. Every time she was near him she would pat his head or rub his shoulders, or even lay her head on his shoulder. Warren said threateningly to me, 'Don't leave me on my own with her!' and he wasn't amused when I fell about laughing. She came to give me a big kiss when we left, and had her arms out to hug and kiss Warren, but he dived into the garden and was gone.

The going was incredibly tough as the climb over the mountains began, and we both frequently needed to push our bikes. We hoped that a kind truck driver might offer us a lift, but we saw only half a dozen vehicles in the next 2½ hours to Chora, the first signs of civilisation. The natural stone in Amorgos is slate, and the beautiful rust and blue-grey stone was clearly evident along the roads through the mountains where they had cut back the rock to build the road. The views were stunning as we climbed higher and higher, and we were grateful for a strong wind to cool us. However, as we zigzagged up the mountains, the wind was sometimes against us. The only life we saw were herds of goats blocking the roads, with bells around their necks on leather straps, and they scattered as we approached, surprised to see other forms of life on the mountain. The strong wind whistled through the telegraph wires, making a very eerie sound. There was no other noise apart from the tinkling of the goats' bells. The one good thing was that we had spectacular views of the whole of that side of the island from our high vantage point, but as we looked down hundreds of feet to the sea, pushing our bikes up the steep s-bends over the mountain, we saw in the distance a ferry leaving the northern port that we had just left and going towards the southern port. We were incredibly cross that our landlady had told us that there was no ferry

– we now realised that we could have hopped onto a ferry for a journey lasting 20 minutes instead of spending 4 hours in the heat cycling 1,475 feet up and over the mountain!

We stopped at Chora, which was a pretty town in the centre of Amorgos. From here it was downhill all the way. Chora stood nearly 400 metres above sea level, with views of both the east and west coasts of Amorgos. At least a dozen churches were dotted around the village, and there were beautiful shaded squares and narrow lanes along which we wandered. We stopped at one of the tavernas in the village to have a well-earned sandwich and ice cold frappé, before cycling off again and shooting downwards past the terraced fields and the five windmills outlined against the sky on the edge of the coast. The hairpin bends were incredibly steep, and the port came quickly closer and closer.

When we arrived we checked the ferry times, and realised that we would have to spend three more days in Amorgos. However, there was more life in this port, and Warren was able to strike a deal with one of the locals, so we paid €35 for three nights (about £24). The room was over a restaurant, which was convenient, but was approached via a dirty metal staircase, past the owner's room with open door and permanently unmade bed, and along a smelly corridor with shabby, cheap, faded pictures hanging at all angles. Around the corner was a grim communal kitchen with broken marble table and bottled gas stove, but we knew we wouldn't use that. Our room had a balcony, and looked out over a neighbouring garden with chickens. The room was in much better condition than the rest of the house, and had a large modern fan and a clean bed.

There were yachts moored in the harbour, and in the evenings several groups of English people arrived from the yachts to have meals at the local restaurants. We knew they were English, even though we hadn't spoken to them, because they brought with them their own bottles of HP sauce! The cafés and restaurants were unpretentious, but we had had some superb simply-cooked meals, including the usual vast quantities of delicious barbecued lamb chops, served with chips and Greek salad. In one café we watched television with the locals, and were interested to see that they were watching the Greek version of Ready Steady Cook, which we had also seen in Italy.

Before we left Amorgos we wanted to visit the famous Monastery of Panayia Khozoviotissa which clings to a cliff on the east coast a few kilometres from Chora. We waited for a bus to take us back up to Chora, and the driver arrived ten minutes after the due time, unlocking the bus and loading it with boxes of groceries before allowing anyone to enter. The journey back up the zigzagging hairpin bends took only ten minutes, the driver and the Greek occupants crossing themselves every time we passed a church or shrine.

We began walking. There were eight or nine old windmills on the ridge of the hill overlooking the sea, and we could see both the east and west coastlines from that height. After a while we began to climb down towards the east coast, the road snaking backwards and forwards around the bends. The water in the bay below was a clear, cool, pale jade green. An English couple from the bus walked with us, and we saw a Swedish girl from Stockholm who we had seen four times, the first time on the long boat trip to Amorgos. Eventually we were back down at sea level, and looking along the coast we could see the pure white monastery which appeared to be clinging like a limpet to the cliff over 360 metres above the level of the sea. We began to climb the hundreds of rust and grey slate steps going up to the monastery, and when we arrived in the small garden of the monastery we climbed the white steps and went through the tiny entrance door. We could see very little initially, because it was so dark compared with the brightness of the white steps in the sunshine, but we found ourselves in a small chapel no more than 2 metres wide. Before being allowed up the next flight of stairs we had to ensure that we were dressed suitably, and could borrow gowns if we wished. Women had to wear skirts and cover their arms. We went up further flights of uneven steep white steps. The space was cramped, because the white painted wall to our right, which was part of the actual cliff, leaned inwards. Each flight of steps led into narrow rooms, and we were invited with another couple into a room with table and chairs. Here we were all offered Turkish delight, a glass of water and a glass of liqueur. We were then led through a low marble doorway and up another flight of stone steps to the tiny church at the top of the monastery, where silver and gold ornate candelabra hung, and gilt-painted icons were on display. We noticed that gifts had been left by people – watches, rosaries, rings, even wedding bands.

We couldn't imagine how this magnificent monastery had been built so far above the sea. It was only five metres wide at its widest part, though it had 50 rooms over eight floors, all connected by narrow staircases which were carved into the rock. The monastery had been built in the 11th century, but now there were only three monks left, and the view from their rooms were of wild rocky cliffs plunging down to the dramatic jade sea far below, and the distant silhouettes of other Greek islands on the horizon.

We left the monastery, blinking and screwing up our eyes in the hot bright sunlight, and stroked the tiny kittens that played on the steps. Now we decided that it was time to move to another island. Looking at the map, we had decided to travel to Astipalea, which we imagined would be another quiet island. It was obviously not a popular destination, because the only ferry we could book was at 1.15am. We were surprised when, unlike the last ferry, the boat that arrived was the Blue Star Naxos, the Greek Island's newest and biggest ferry, with banks of escalators from the vehicle deck to the upper decks, decks full of cabins, and shops and restaurants on the main deck. Needless to say, at that time of the morning everything was closed, but the most extraordinary thing was that, apart from the crew, we appeared to be alone on the boat – we never saw another passenger on this massive ship!

I want you to picture the scene . . . we went up on deck; the sea was dead calm, the winds of the previous days having abated. There was a full moon and the night was dead, dead still with the moon shimmering off the still sea. It was eerie and spooky.

The boat arrived at Astipalea dead on time, and we stood on the vehicle deck with our bikes, waiting for the giant ramp to lower, so we could have our first sight of Astipalea. It was still dark, and this was the boat's final destination. No other foot passengers were present on the boat, but there was one vehicle on the ferry, a red van, waiting to disembark. We stood by the red van as the ramp slowly went down. There was no sound apart from the creaking of the ramp until it finally clanked into position on the jetty. We could see very little – the jetty was poorly lit and everything was black. However, as the van began to edge forward in front of us there was a dreadful wailing sound from the quayside which became louder and louder, and we could see as we cycled slowly forward that there were 12 women dressed in black standing in the back of a truck; they were screaming and wailing and clinging to each other.

It was at this stage that we realised that the red van alongside us was carrying a coffin, obviously bringing someone home for burial. There had therefore been two other passengers travelling with us on that enormous boat, one of whom was dead!

It was 4am, so there was no point in looking for accommodation. We found a closed office on the quayside, put our mattresses on the floor of the doorway, crept into our sleeping bags and were instantly asleep. We were woken by a lorry emptying dustbins nearby, so we crept out to find somewhere to eat. Amazingly we found, on this incredibly quiet island, a seedy bar run by a red-haired English girl, who had stayed on the island after falling in love with a local man. After breakfast we found a woman who was willing to open up the small hotel that she had closed the previous month, so that we could have a room. We discovered that most of the life on this island was 'at the Chora', and the locals always pointed to the top of a steep hill. Because we could find no restaurants, shops or a post office, we realised that we were going to have to go to 'the Chora' (the name usually given to the most important town or village of any Greek island).

After following the hundreds of steps up the hill we saw windmills perched on a ridge with views of the sea in both directions. We found a restaurant, and watched the restaurant owner through a hatch as he cooked our meal, a cigarette hanging out of his mouth. The meal was superb. He gave us some of his wonderful home-made bread drizzled with green olive oil and served it with olive tapenade, so we could eat this with our drinks as we waited. We had the most delicious salads as starters, and my starters were followed by pork loin pieces in hot mustard sauce. Warren chose grilled lamb chops, and was shocked to be asked did he want a kilo!

'No,' said Warren. 'Half a kilo is fine.'

After Astipalea we took the ferry to Kalymnos, and were surprised to find that the port was the largest we had seen so far on the islands. We made friends with a lady who had several apartments, and we chose one of her apartments designed for eight people, which cost us only €15 a night (£10). How nice it would have been if loads of friends and family could have come out to join us. We stayed in Kalymnos several days, enjoying a leisurely bike ride to the opposite side of the island, where the smell of wild thyme, rosemary, lavender and sage filled the air as the sun warmed the plants between the rocks.

Every morning we went to the bakery to buy fresh bread. I noticed that the women were handling rolls and loaves and turning them over, discarding one for an identical neighbouring one – completely the opposite of in Italy, where everyone had to put on disposable polythene gloves before handling fruit, vegetables or bread in any shop.

Every time we bumped into Ipapanti, our landlady in Kalymnos, she gave us hugs and kissed us, and she seemed genuinely upset when it was time for us to leave. We took the ferry to Kos, one of the more well-known and larger islands. The clocks had been put back an hour the day before, and as we waited early in the morning for the ferry to arrive, the sun rose and bathed the white buildings in a peachy golden glow. We tied our bikes in the hold of the boat, which we noticed smelled strongly of fish, and we arrived at Kos two hours later. As usual there were people waiting at the quayside offering rooms to tourists, even though it was now well past the tourist season. We chose a room with a balcony with a lovely view of Turkey across the sea.

We went immediately to find breakfast. The bars and restaurants on the beach were all vying for our attention, offering free sun loungers. This was when we discovered that in the next day or two most of them would be closing for the season, despite the fact that it was now beautifully hot, 28°C, with not a cloud in the sky. It was 28th October. As we bought food from a small supermarket later, we noticed that once we had passed the shelves, the owners were emptying the tins and packets into bin liners, ready to remove them from the shop which was closing the next day. Most of the owners returned to their homes on the mainland for the winter. We had planned to visit Symi, but if a large island like Kos was closing down, a quiet island like Symi was probably closed down already, and it might have been impossible to find accommodation. We decided to stay four days in Kos, and then travel to Rhodes, our last Greek island. We had ordered a new tent from England to replace our leaking one, so planned to stay in Rhodes waiting for the tent to arrive by post.

We went for a meal and found a wonderful Greek restaurant run by a family. Mother cooked the food and spoke no English, but her son was the waiter and spoke a little. He recommended many dishes to us, every one of which was superb. A group of four local people enjoying themselves at the next table raised their glasses to each other – I could see that a glass on the table was going to be knocked over, and it crashed to the floor and smashed on the tiles. They all laughed and said 'cheers' and 'happy birthday' in English. They saw me grinning, and one asked where I was from.

'England,' I said.

He raised his glass to me. 'I think you are really pretty,' he said.

'I think you are really drunk,' I replied, laughing. He initially denied this but eventually conceded that he may be a little drunk. We continued our meal, and the waiter brought a third ½ litre of wine, which we hadn't ordered. He nodded to the other table, to indicate that they had paid for it, so we raised our glasses to them and said 'Efharesto' (thank you) and 'Yamos' (cheers).

We were enjoying our time in Greece immensely. The Greeks were friendly, though we often got the feeling that they assumed all tourists were incredibly rich, and their friendliness was perhaps to get a sale. We thought that the food was wonderful, and if we could find a 'real' Greek restaurant not frequented by the tourists we were especially happy.

What were our favourite foods? Piles of crispy whitebait, barbecued fresh fish caught that day (swordfish, bream, snapper or octopus), sweet roasted peppers stuffed with feta cheese, dusted with flour and fried, giant butter beans cooked in a herb, onion and tomato sauce, dolmades (vine leaves stuffed with rice), fried aubergine or courgette fritters, meat balls, tzatziki, taramasalata, Greek salad, spicy cheese dip, aubergine dip, tuna salad, pumpkin flowers stuffed with feta, dipped in batter and deep-fried, fried chickpea balls, not to mention kebabs, piles of barbecued lamb chops and every one of the gorgeous traditional Greek stews like stifado and kleftiko, and the most well-known Greek dish of all, moussaka. We also loved the freshly-baked Greek bread.

One day in Kos we went to find a restaurant at the back of the town. I had earlier spoken to the owner who had lovingly described how he made the best stifado, and we were determined to try it that evening. We got lost in the maze of tiny streets, but eventually found the restaurant. However, it was only 7pm and the restaurant was closed, probably not due to open for another hour. There were several other restaurants nearby, but none had tables inside and the wind that evening was very cold. We eventually found ourselves back in one of the main tourist squares where there were many restaurants, but virtually all had pictures of the meals on show outside. As a matter of principle we always avoided these restaurants, in the belief that they would be full of English tourists – we preferred the more authentic Greek restaurants.

The Greeks were very keen to attract tourists to their cafés and restaurants, so often translated their menus into English. Some of the translations made for amusing reading, and we smiled as we read that 'roast biff' or roost chicken' was available, or 'jacked potatoes', 'frigid fish' or 'octopus balls'.

We allowed ourselves to be persuaded by the owner of a restaurant in the square to eat at his restaurant, despite the pictures of food. The main reason we agreed was that his restaurant had tables outside surrounded by temporary polythene walls, keeping out the cold wind. We initially sat in a corner but it was draughty, so we made the mistake of moving to a table surrounded by other people. Behind Warren was a table with eight English tourists and to his right was a table with two tourists.

We had others around us, but the women on these two tables obviously knew each other and were talking across our table in loud raucous voices –

'Ennit windy? Can't grumble though. We've 'ad some lovely wevver.'

'Apparently Essex 'as 'ad some 'orrible windy wevver. Our pa'io in Chelmsford is awl knocked abart an' it was really strong, wonnit Dave?' (turning to husband).

'We're flying back to Stansted toni'. Ar Andrew 'ates flying so we go on a ni' fli'. If the kids are 'appy we're 'appy, ent we?'

Ar Andrew, a plump 5 year old boy in football strip on the big table, pressed his face against his mother's ample bosom, and his grandmother, equally well-endowed with a tight low-necked t-shirt to emphasise her curves, explained as she nodded to her husband holding up a camera. 'Ar Andrew 'ates 'aving 'is pho'o took'. She added, ''E finks e's David Beckham but only when 'e plays for England, not that Man Uni'ed.'

Grandmother continued non-stop. 'We've go' a barf in ar apar'ment. I love a barf, me. I don't need much wa'er, but when I ge' in it's full up to 'ere' (indicating her chin). At this point there were raucous screams of laughter from the large ladies on both tables. The lady on the smaller table managed to get a few words in.

'We've go' a pool a' ar place but the wa'er's cold so I won' go in. ''E (nodding to husband) goes in but e's 'ard'. She scratched her arms. 'Cor blimey, these mosqui'o bi'es are 'orrible. They don' arf itch.'

'I know,' replied Andrew's grandmother, 'My bum's covered with 'em an' awl.'

Warren and I didn't say anything, and we tried hard not to look at each other for fear of getting uncontrolled giggles. We noticed that the English couple on the table to Warren's left had also become extremely quiet, and were also keeping their heads down.

The people from the big table got up and left. It was noticeable that all the ladies had ample bosoms exposed and wore tiny short denim skirts exposing their equally ample thighs.

Our meal arrived. 'Efharesto,' (thank you) we both said.

'Parakolo,' (you're welcome) said the waiter. There was a loud whisper from the woman to Warren's right.

'What did they say?' she asked her husband.

'Oh, it's Greek,' he said knowledgeably.

We finished our mediocre meal in record time and dashed through the blustery streets laughing, until we reached the Greek café we'd been to the night before. There we were welcomed with open arms as though we were old friends. It was quiet and cosy, with four other customers sat watching Greek television. We sat in a quiet corner, and enjoyed a jug of wine before retiring to bed . . .

We went for a cycle ride one day in Kos, and as we sat in a café having a cool drink we saw a couple passing on their very upright bikes. We instantly recognised them as Bert and Marianne, the Dutch couple whom we had met in Corfu, so we finished our drinks, dashed to our bikes, and finally caught up with them a mile down the road.

They had travelled a completely different route from us, having crossed to Turkey from Samos, a Greek island further north, cycled 225km in Turkey and back to Greece via Kos. The Turkish mainland is very close to the eastern Greek islands, and can be seen from most of the islands quite clearly.

As we cycled that day with Bert and Marianne we passed women in black skirts and headscarves harvesting olives. We rang our cycle bells to attract their attention, and they waved to us, calling 'hello'. They used small plastic rakes like children's toys to pull the olives off the branches onto the plastic sheet on the ground. These were the first pickings from the olive tree, which made the prized extra virgin olive oil. The Greeks then had to wait for the rain to come in early November, because the rain plumped up the olives to make them suitable for eating. By the third week of November (depending on the weather) those olives were ready for picking. Hand picking produces the best fruits, but often the trees are shaken to drop the ripe olives onto the nets below. If there was too much rain it was a problem, because the mud damages the dropped olives. We understood that Greek housewives split their olives and put them into water before eating, but if they wanted to keep them longer they put them in salt water with oil and vinegar.

Virtually every small garden owned at least one olive tree, and each family takes their olives to the factory, which is open only during the olive picking period. We discovered that this co-operative method was popular throughout the olive growing countries. The factory keeps a percentage of the oil as payment.

The by-products, the stones and the crushed pulp, also belong to the factory. 'Stones oil' could be made from crushed stones, and the pulp used as fertiliser.

We cycled past a beautifully restored small amphitheatre, and a sunken communal bath was surrounded by ruined buildings and a stunning mosaic floor. There were ancient stone roads clearly showing the indents from the carriage wheels that had passed over the road two thousand years before. Thousands of pieces of ancient carved marble lay on the ground amongst fallen columns. We walked along the stone road, thousands of years old, touched the carved letters and sat in the sunken bath. As with so many of the ancient sites in Greece, they are so common that there was not even a sign to indicate this beautiful archaeological site. After spending some time with Bert and Marianne we once again said our goodbyes, promising to keep in touch by e-mail.

We went to our regular café for a last meal before leaving Kos, and had another fantastic meal with the locals. Our waiter recommended some of his mother's favourite dishes, so we had pumpkin blossoms stuffed with feta and fried with a golden crust, fava (creamed butter beans), chickpea balls, stuffed peppers, and pork in a sauce with caramelised onions.

Our next stop was Rhodes. We left Kos early in the morning of 1st November, and the ferry travelled south between Kos and around the Turkish peninsular. We travelled close to Turkey most of the way, and could see the white dots of houses on the sides of the mountains, with roads zigzagging up the mountains. The boat made its way between two other Greek islands, Tilos and Symi, towards the impressive harbour at Rhodes. Behind us we could still see the peninsulas of Turkey, like fingers stretching out from the Turkish mainland. Four hours after leaving Kos we arrived at Rhodes.

The harbour was a shock, with the biggest ocean-going liners we had ever seen. They looked like skyscrapers, and clearly wouldn't have fitted into any of the harbours of the islands we had so far visited. Rhodes was also a shock, the accommodation being much more expensive than the previous islands we had visited, and because it was now so late in the season there was no-one waiting on the jetty to offer us accommodation. We cycled around in circles, not really knowing which way to go, but we finally decided to stay at a youth hostel in Rhodes Old Town which someone recommended. The old town is a walled city 500 years old, with a maze of quaint, narrow, cobbled streets. Lost in the maze of streets, we were poring over a street map when a girl on a motor scooter asked in perfect English if she could help. It turned out that Celia was actually English but lived in Rhodes, and we followed her on our bicycles through the narrow streets until we arrived at the entrance to the youth hostel, and promised to meet her and her friends later at their favourite bar.

The hostel was very pleasant – only three other people were staying there, all of them young back-packers, but they were in the main building. We had a double room with private bathroom off an inner courtyard, and we could sit outside our room and have our breakfast in the courtyard under the shade of a vine-clad pergola. If we were in the town at lunchtime, we often had our lunch in the courtyard. We bought dolmades (stuffed vine leaves) and fresh bread, picked a lemon from the tree in the courtyard to squeeze over the dolmades, and dunked our bread in the delicious green oil and lemon sauce. A glass of wine to accompany it was, of course, obligatory! The cost of this accommodation was about £12.80 per night, much more than we had become accustomed to paying in Greece, but every traveller that we met agreed that Rhodes is definitely one of the more expensive islands. We now had to wait for our tent to arrive by post, after which we would catch the ferry to Turkey for the next leg of our journey.

Two days later, as we walked to the shops, we once again bumped into Bert and Marianne! They had just arrived in Rhodes and, like us, had had difficulty in finding suitable accommodation. We recommended the second en-suite room in the courtyard, and later returned to find them already installed in their room.

For the first time on this trip we hired a car for the day to explore the island of Rhodes – it was lucky we didn't cycle that day, because for the second time only since we had been in Greece it rained. There was a sudden darkening of the sky, a heavy thunderstorm immediately flooded the roads and then the sun was out again!

Our tent hadn't arrived after a week, and we were concerned that the ferries to Turkey were being reduced dramatically, and the Greek ferry was due to stop very shortly. We needed to move on before we were stranded in Greece for the winter! We were now cooking most meals for ourselves, because so many of the restaurants were closed. Only the tiny food shops for the locals remained open. However, it was very obvious if a large boat had docked at the harbour. Suddenly every shop was open again, their wares spilling out onto the cobbled streets outside, and the restaurants were open to serve food and wine. We couldn't understand what had happened when we saw this the first time, but then we saw the hordes of well-dressed tourists walking en masse up the street from the cruise liner. Dressed in blazers and smart trousers, elegant dresses and high heels, and dripping with jewellery, these tourists were clearly from a cruise liner and not the back-packers or package tourists that were more commonly seen – they crowded into the shops buying souvenirs, filled the chairs which had only an hour before been set outside the restaurants, and clearly brought a lot of money to the island each time the ship docked. As soon as the ship left the harbour, the shops and restaurants again put up their shutters, and the owners disappeared to goodness knows where until the next ship arrived!

Finally our new tent arrived, our old tent was returned to the manufacturer for repairs, and we were ready to buy tickets for the ferry to Turkey. No boats were leaving any of the Aegean islands that day – there was bad weather all over Europe, and apparently Athens had seen hailstones as big as tennis balls. In parts of Athens the floods were waist-high, and one person had drowned. All flights from Athens airport had been cancelled, and it was apparently the fourth time that year that Athens had seen serious floods. The rain was pounding down in Rhodes, the wind was blowing a gale, and there was thunder and lightning; streams were running down the cobbled streets in the old walled town, and we watched locals putting sandbags in front of their doors. The waves were rolling in, and there were numerous white caps on the dark sea.

No-one could say when the next ferry would leave – every ferry had been cancelled for two days because of the bad weather. Eventually we were told that the ferry might leave early the next morning, but it was the last Greek ferry to run to Turkey that year, and there was no guarantee that the captain would allow us to put the bikes on. We just had to wait and see what he said.

The rain continued throughout the night, accompanied by more thunder and lightning, and by morning the courtyard outside our room was flooded and water was beginning to seep into our room. I was concerned how rough the sea might be, so wasn't sure whether I hoped that the ferry would leave or not!

The ferry stood in the harbour, and a crowd of us stood waiting alongside. No-one was allowed on board until the captain had decided whether it was safe to set off. Eventually it was decided that the ferry would run, the winds of the previous days having finally abated. The captain was happy to take our bikes on board, and the catamaran took only one hour to reach Marmeris in Turkey.

We had been very lazy in Greece and hadn't cycled much since we had started island-hopping. Any cycle rides had tended to be only for a day out. We had now cycled 2,740 miles (4,400km), and were looking forward to proper cycling again in Turkey, although we knew that there were some mountain passes to cycle over on our way north to Istanbul. If we felt like a change we could hop onto one of the ferries that loop up the Turkish coast and do part of the journey by boat . . .

CHAPTER 6

TURKEY

Turkey is well-known as being partly European and partly Asian; the population is predominantly Muslim. Bordering the Black Sea in the north, the Mediterranean in the south and the Aegean Sea in the west, Turkey has a very long coastline, 6,000 kilometres of it facing the Mediterranean, much of which is given over to tourism. Turkey is bordered by eight countries – Bulgaria, Greece, Georgia, Armenia, Azerbaijan, Iran, Iraq and Syria. A vast country, Turkey's climate ranges from the temperate Mediterranean climate in the south to a harsh, arid climate inland. A large plateau rises east towards the mountains, where winter temperatures can reach minus 45°C.

We arrived in Marmeris in south-west Turkey on the 9th November, and it rained for two days, so we spent those two wet days sightseeing and visiting the local shops. We found a room in a small hotel with a very pleasant owner, who chatted with us in excellent English and recommended some very good places to eat and visit. We appeared to be the only guests in the hotel, so he gave us a separate double room where we could lock our bikes out of the way!

We bought postcards to send home, but found that if we bought the stamps from the shops rather than the post office, the shop owners charged double in order to make some extra profit. We enjoyed visiting the carpet shops, and one shop owner showed us how he repaired antique rugs and carpets, dyeing the pieces of wool or silk himself with vegetable dyes to get the exact match. He told us how he regularly visited London to visit a friend who had a carpet warehouse, and he taught his friend's employees how to repair the very valuable old carpets, many 150 to 200 years old.

As we wandered around the shops, we noticed the men who delivered Turkish tea to the shops for the staff and customers. They rushed past us swinging silver trays, suspended on three arms. The small tulip-shaped glasses of tea stood on silver saucers but, despite the fact that they always dashed between pedestrians, none of the tea was spilt. No milk was available, of course, but there was always plenty of sugar. The Turks were incredibly friendly, and in Marmeris most of them spoke very good English. We chatted to many of them, because they were eager to talk to us, and they told us that they learnt English in the hope of being able to leave the country, as there were so few jobs available in Turkey. However, in the meantime if their English was good they could work in the tourist areas, where they could earn reasonable money compared to the non-tourist parts of Turkey.

After over four months of using the Euro, we now had to get used to the Turkish Lira, a very different currency! At that time there were 2,191,400 Turkish Lira to the English pound, so we had assumed that the television contest, 'Who wants to be a millionaire?' would not be very popular in Turkey! How wrong we were! We had seen 'Who Wants to be a Millionaire?' on televisions in bars and hotel rooms in France, Italy and Greece and, apart from the language, it was identical to the English version – same music, same studio setting, same chairs, same stairs, even the same standard phrases, such as '. . . but we don't want to give you that!' They had adjusted the prizes for the Turkish version of the popular quiz show, but the top price was very much smaller than the £1,000,000 that was possible in England.

On the third day the rain lessened, and we started cycling. We found it hard after so little cycling in Greece, especially as we had two mountains to cross in the first two days. We climbed higher and higher, and gradually the sea and the harbour became smaller in the distance below us, but there was the haunting sound of calls to prayer which echoed up the valley. The view of the fields and sea below us surrounded by the mountains was spectacular, and as we went higher we could see another higher range of mountains that were capped with snow ahead of us. We stopped at a restaurant that had dramatic views of the sea and mountains, and then we cycled on, the lorries groaning up the hills behind us in bottom gear, struggling (as we were) to get up the incline.

I noticed something I thought was odd – forsythia bushes, which flower early in the spring in England at the same time as the daffodils, were out in flower alongside pyracanthas full of berries and deciduous trees with their autumn colours. There were clear signs of autumn everywhere, and we knew we had to cycle north as quickly as we could, in order to avoid the cold winter that could soon be upon us. We had been warned that otherwise we could be trapped by snow before we reached Istanbul.

The mountains were covered with pines and deciduous trees, and when we got to the top of the mountain and began to cycle downhill again, there were grassy areas and streams. It was all very pleasant, and we were delighted to see how green Turkey was compared with Greece.

We hadn't seen any accommodation, so when we saw a village below us set by an estuary we decided to visit it. The village was tucked out of the way, a holiday resort at the mouth of a river with a beautiful backdrop of mountains. It had a tiny harbour facing west and was very rural. Cats, dogs, cockerels, hens, ducks and geese roamed the streets at will, and it was incredibly peaceful. We found a fabulous luxury apartment owned by an Austrian woman at the bargain price of £8 a night. She spoke no English, but I was able to speak to her in German. She showed us to a nearby classy fish restaurant and introduced us to the owner, who produced an amazing meal for us. Numerous starters included tzatziki, spicy cheese dip, chilli dip, aubergines, houmous, spring rolls and Russian salad; each dish was beautifully presented and served with toasted pitta bread. The owner produced a large sea bass for each of us served with salad. Including two glasses of wine, free liqueurs and Turkish coffee the total cost was 22,500,000 Turkish Lira (exactly £9!). As we left the restaurant, the waiter stood at the door with what looked like a plastic bottle of washing up liquid. He indicated to us to put out our hands, and he squeezed some lemon-scented water onto our hands, which was to clean our hands. We found that this was a custom often practised in Turkey.

We wanted to stay longer, especially when we saw the amazing sunsets across the harbour, but we knew that we couldn't afford to stop at this stage, and needed to continue cycling north. However, one day we plan to go back there.

We found the Turkish people to be incredibly kind, generous and helpful; the food was good, and because the economy was bad and the Turkish Lira was very weak, this made everything very cheap for us. This was a bonus, since our budget had been badly hit travelling across Europe for five months.

We continued cycling – we still had another mountain to cross, and the second one was worse than the first – we had to cycle uphill for 10 miles. The road zigzagged back and forth, and I often pushed my bike. The countryside, however, was so beautiful that we didn't mind. A man standing in a stream picking watercress stood up to wave as we passed; toothless old men on their bikes grinned at us; battered cars packed with youths sounded their horns and waved; lorry drivers gave us the thumbs up as they passed.

We turned a corner and had to stop abruptly, because a car had stopped in the middle of the road. In front of the car were two wild looking dogs growling at the driver of the car. The dogs turned their attention to us as I stopped behind Warren, so Warren bent down to pick up a stone and I did the same. Suddenly another car turned the corner behind us and his brakes screeched as he skidded past me, crashing violently into the first car. My heart was in my mouth as the car was shunted several feet forward with the impact, but both cars just missed Warren. We left quickly, but the dogs had left even faster!

Eventually we got to the top of the mountain, and freewheeled down a short way onto a plateau. A north-west wind was against us, and we were getting quite cold, so we needed to find accommodation soon. When we reached the next small town we found a room at a hotel, but for more than the price we'd paid the night before for a beautifully-furnished three-roomed apartment with television, we were now in a run-down hotel room with cheap carpet, disgusting furniture, curtains that didn't meet, missing light bulbs, a cupboard full of cobwebs, and an ancient bathroom with an electric shower above the toilet, with a dangerous-looking electric socket just underneath the shower.

Since we had left England we had often encountered this type of shower room, which at that time we had never seen in England. The 'wet room' is now popular in some modern English properties, but the wet rooms that we had seen so far in hotels in France, Italy, Greece and now Turkey (and throughout Asia as well) were not very practical. The toilet was usually situated at the far end of the fully tiled room, and the shower would be on one of the walls nearer to the door. This always meant that once someone had used the shower, anyone using the toilet had to walk across wet floors to reach the toilet, and the toilet seat would often be wet. Throughout Europe we had found electric sockets were often situated within reach of the shower, which we found pretty scary.

We continued on our way. We often sat in one of the very basic cafés having a glass of tea; the cafés were frequented by farm-workers and poor people, who took an interest in us and our bikes. Often when we came to pay, we discovered that someone had already paid for us and had already left, or the owner insisted on treating us. If we stopped at a junction to look at our map, someone would run over and insist on us taking a water melon or a bag of oranges without accepting any payment. Despite the fact that our bikes were already over-loaded, we accepted gratefully, saying 'thank you' in Turkish, and ate the goodies as soon as we were out of sight in order to lessen the weight on the bikes!

We were finding plenty of internet cafés, even where there were no tourists, because the local children used the computers to play games. I was regularly sending newsletters to a group of family and friends, so that they could experience second hand the journey that we were making.

The first thing we had noticed about Turkey was that it was so green. We had expected it to be like Greece, looking quite barren, because the eastern Greek islands and the west coast of Turkey are so close. It was therefore a very pleasant surprise to see that instead of mountains covered in rock or scrub, the mountains were covered with trees, both conifers and deciduous, and the scenery was beautiful. There were also large areas of grass by the roadside, something we hadn't seen since France, and the countryside was full of growing crops, again something we hadn't seen much since France. Sweetcorn was being harvested, and fields of okra looked strange with green fruit at the top of tall golden stems. There were cabbages, cauliflowers, chillies, tomatoes and broccoli. We passed cotton fields where the cotton was being picked by the Kurd workers, who camped in their makeshift polythene tents by the fields. The tractors passed us on their way to the cotton factories with their trailers piled dangerously high with giant sacks of the soft cotton wool balls, and on top sat the workers who always waved excitedly to us as they passed.

The other common crop was the olive, and it was fascinating to learn how versatile the olive tree is. It's not uncommon for an olive tree to live for over 1,000 years, and trees are known that are 2,500 years old. We had already learnt in Greece that the first olives are picked in early November for the first pressing to make extra virgin olive oil. Because rain had already fallen, the olives were now plump and ready to pick for eating. We passed families every day who were picking the olives. Covers were spread over the ground while the young men climbed the trees to shake the branches. A horse or donkey usually stood nearby; a baby often played on a rug close by, and children ran excitedly around sorting the fallen leaves from the olives. The women put the olives into the sacks which were loaded onto the waiting animal or vehicle, and the branches were cut and taken to the factory to process into soap, so none of the tree was wasted!

We passed a magnificent white and purple marble building which was being built, and I was just pulling out my dictaphone to make a comment when a soldier standing guard jumped in front of us with his hand up to make us stop. As he had a rifle slung over his shoulder we did stop – he looked very young, but quite officious. We didn't understand what he was saying, and he looked a bit nonplussed. He called someone over, and one of the builders walked to us with a laden trowel in his hand. A passing older man also stopped. We could understand from odd words and actions that the last two were asking where we were going and where we'd been, and the soldier was looking from one to another as Warren described our journey. He obviously didn't want to be left out of the conversation.

'Passport!' he snapped.

Warren ignored him, describing with a waving arm the two mountains that we had crossed. The two men laughed, doing cycling actions and patting their thighs, so the soldier began to join in the laughter. The old man, who had simply been a passer-by, waved and wished us luck as he continued his journey, and we cycled off with the soldier waving his rifle and the builder waving his now empty trowel.

One day I had had a serious problem with my tyre, which appeared to be disintegrating, so I could only cycle very slowly in case the tyre blew completely. The road was undulating, but eventually we arrived at a village which was at the top of an unbelievably steep hill. As soon as we stopped alongside the tiny market, everyone left their stalls and stood watching us. Those who could speak English talked to us, but a barber who spoke excellent English closed his shop so that he could lead us through the streets to a tiny bicycle shop. We were followed by a crowd of about twenty people, who stood outside in the street as our new friend spoke to the bicycle shop owner. He produced an ancient second-hand tyre that was the right size. It cost the grand sum of 10p, and a crowd five deep stood around Warren as he fitted the new tyre. The barber invited us to go for a cup of tea, and the crowd led us through the streets, people stopping to watch and calling out to our new friend. Some young girls came to talk to us to practice their English. They were only aged about 12, but one ran off and returned with a present for me which she had just bought; it was beautifully wrapped in paper with coloured string with a matching bow. I couldn't believe it – it was a framed picture of a Turkish mountain scene, and the girl seemed very proud when I asked her to stand with me for a photograph, proudly holding the picture in front of us.

There was no accommodation in this town, but we were assured by the barber that it was all downhill to the next large town. However, after the initial fast downhill run we began to climb up steep hills again, and we knew we wouldn't make it to the town before dark. We found an area of waste ground near some houses, where we decided to put up our tent, and we asked someone if we could have some water. The man didn't speak English, but he and his wife made it clear that they didn't want us to camp, and they invited us into their house. They gave us beds for the night, and shared their evening meal and breakfast with us and their two young teenage children, but they wouldn't take money. The meals were spent sitting on the floor on cushions around a large tray which had been raised several inches off the floor. The cloth on the table was extended into our laps, so that we used the cloth to catch any crumbs, and after the meal the whole cloth and contents were scooped away to the kitchen. There were many plates of food, which included yogurt, meat in oil, fried cabbage with chilli, hard-boiled eggs and olives, with plenty of bread. When water was brought to the table we all shared the same glass. We spent the evening trying to talk each other's language from dictionaries, and we each showed photographs of our families. We took photos of all of us, and promised to send them a photograph once it had been developed in England. They showed us to the concreted bathroom which had a large hole in the floor for the water to drain, and they were obviously very proud to own an electric shower, which was on a wall alongside the squat toilet. It was very cold in the morning when it was time to go, and we felt quite choked as we said goodbye to our new friends.

Everyone shouted 'hello' as we cycled past – children, people working in the fields, and even police in passing police cars sounded their horns, slowed down, waved and shouted 'hello'! In the tourist areas most people spoke some English, but everyone seemed to have been taught the same things when learning the language.

'Hello. How are you? Where are you from?' they would say in quick succession.

We obviously answered that we were from England, and often had some extraordinary responses.

'Ah – David Beckham,' was a common reply, but twice we had the response 'Lovely jubbly'!

Then they would say, 'My name is ***. What is your name?' and 'How old are you?'

In the areas away from the tourists English was not often spoken, so we were learning a lot of basic Turkish words. However, the older Turkish men often spoke German, because the Turks for many decades have traditionally been employed in Germany for manual labour, so once again my knowledge of German came in useful.

Food was cheap, and at lunch-time we often had delicious lentil soup, which cost 1 million Turkish Lira (40p). A large lidded plastic container always stood on the table filled with chunks of fresh bread, and we could help ourselves to as much as we wanted. A glass of delicious Turkish tea was 10p to 40p, depending on how touristy the place was; in an ordinary café the most expensive meal was about £1.40, a can of beer in a supermarket was 30p and sometimes could be as cheap in a bar. Warren and I were horrified to discover later that we had eaten, by accident, 'turnspit bowel spleen', which is meat wrapped around with yards of tubes (intestines) to hold it together and cooked over a spit, cut up and served in bread. We thought it was a joint of meat with fat on the outside being spit-roasted, but discovered on eating the snack that we had to keep picking pieces of tube from our mouths! Never mind – we both survived the experience, and apart from this incident the food continued to be excellent and very cheap.

Unfortunately wine was not easily available, but could occasionally be bought for about £3 for a decent bottle. Luxury 4 star hotels cost us £16 pounds for a double room and cheaper hotels were available from about £8. Even cheaper accommodation was available in small guest houses (or pansiyons), the cheapest having been £1.40 for both of us! We were pleased that at last we were spending less. However, we knew when we planned the trip that our costs had to be averaged over the expensive European countries and the cheaper Asian countries.

When we started cycling in Turkey we found that the early mornings were very cool, so we dressed in several layers which we could remove as the day warmed up. For 2 or 3 hours in the middle of the day we were cycling in shorts and vests. Gradually, however, the days became cooler, and central heating in the hotels was much appreciated in the evenings. We knew as the days went by and we moved into December that it would get much colder, especially as we were travelling north to Istanbul. We had even been told that there was the danger of snow, so we were very eager to get to Istanbul as quickly as possible to avoid the possibility of getting stuck in snow with our bikes!

We passed fields where ploughs were being pulled by horses; square bee-hives were set in long rows, and occasionally a tiny shack stood amongst them. As we approached Milas, we passed herds of large, long-haired, curly-horned goats being driven along the road by groups of gypsies, and soon we were on a serious downhill run to Milas.

The towns were often interesting, especially the less touristy ones. There were fascinating shops full of copper pans for everyday use, ironmongers with old-fashioned tools like scythes, butchers with curtains of linked sausages covering the pavement side of the windows, carpet shops galore selling old and new rugs, barbers on every corner and jewellers on every other corner full of gold. Warren had a shave a few times in the barbers, and he swore that a shave with a cut-throat razor gave him the best shave ever. It also cost only 60p, but always took a long time because included were a face and head massage and sometimes a face pack! During a shave, the Turkish barbers also trimmed nasal hairs if necessary and removed hairs in the ears by singeing them with a flaming cotton bud that had been dipped in alcohol!

We could never resist the markets, and the display of vegetables and fruit on show in the Turkish markets was spectacular. Everything was perfect and beautifully presented and displayed – tomatoes of the same size stacked in piles, every one just perfectly ripe, the biggest cabbages we had ever seen and perfect cauliflowers and broccoli, leeks with not a gram of waste on them, aubergines – white or purple, round and long, shiny and plump. Giant mounds of chillies, from the tiny Thai ultra-hot chillies and bonnet peppers, to the very large mildly spicy red, yellow and green chillies that are wonderful stuffed. Beautifully sweet oranges, blood oranges, satsumas and lemons were stacked in mounds. Everything was locally grown and brought by the farmer to the market, and everything was incredibly cheap.

Because we were travelling up the west coast we often stayed in fishing towns or villages and it was interesting to see the fishing boats arriving with their catch and selling the fish immediately to the locals. It was extraordinary to see that the local cats knew the boats and began to congregate on the quayside as soon as a fishing boat came into sight on the horizon, and by the time the boat arrived there would be as many as 24 cats waiting hopefully for a dropped fish!

In one town we had to buy a washbasin plug so that we could wash some clothes in our hotel bathroom. We found a shop with a washbasin outside, so assumed it to be a plumber's merchant. We pointed to the opening in the bottom of the washbasin, and the assistant nodded excitedly and disappeared into the depths of the shop, only to return with a plastic u-bend! Endless gesticulations and drawings later, he produced a choice of two rubber plugs, and we paid him 1,000,000 Turkish Lira (40p). By this stage, however, a group of interested locals had congregated, and two of them pulled up chairs and insisted we sat down. Two of the older men spoke a little German, and one spoke a few words of English. We were told that tea had been ordered, and shortly afterwards it was delivered on a silver tray and presented to us. There were only two cups – no-one else was drinking. As we sat drinking our tea, eight people stood around talking to us. Several of our new friends escorted us down the street, while the rest stood and waved as we left the shop.

The drinking of tea in Turkey is a ritual. Whilst Turkish coffee is perhaps more famous, it is actually black tea that the Turkish drink, any time, any place, and tea is constantly offered to customers in shops, even though they are strangers. The accepting of a glass of tea in a shop shouldn't make one feel obliged to buy. The Turks are just very generous people. In the shops no-one appears to make their own tea. There is always a little shop somewhere in every village or town that is there just to make this delicious tea and deliver it in the pretty tulip-shaped glasses on silver platters to anywhere in the village or town. Each shop has a buzzer outside which, when pressed, indicates the number of glasses of tea that the shop requires to be delivered. Warren and I once followed the cables up and down trees, across pavements and fronts of shops, until it reached a tiny back-street room where men rushed in and out with their trays making deliveries.

If we wanted a cup of tea we went to a tea-house. Even the tiniest village would have several. In the villages they tended to be large rooms brightly lit with neon lights and massive windows. The chairs and tables were always very basic, the floor tiled and the walls painted, and although the tea-houses didn't look very inviting they were always full of men (never women!), and the air was always thick with smoke. Even if it was bitterly cold outside, it was likely to be very hot in the tea-room, because a wood-burning stove always stood in the centre of the room, and the heat would hit us as we walked into the room. It was clear from the way the flue was attached by wires to screws in the ceiling that the boiler was temporary and would be removed once the warm weather returned. The men sat around, seemingly all day, playing cards, backgammon and reading newspapers, and we were always definitely the centre of attention when we walked in! No food appeared to be available in these tea-houses, and the only drink available was . . . tea! Turkish tea is grown on the eastern Black Sea coast, where the mild climate and fertile soil suit such a crop. Spelt 'çay' and pronounced 'chai', the delicious black tea in such a place usually cost about 5p or 6p a glass. In one village, we sat for a while drinking 6 glasses of tea and paid with a one million lira note (40p), leaving the change of a 100,000 lira note as a tip. The elderly lady running the tea-house ran out with this note thinking we had forgotten it. When we said she could keep it she was embarrassingly grateful. The note was worth 4p, and from her reaction we assumed that she had never had a tip before!

There were always plenty of cafés selling food in non-tourist towns, but these were extremely basic, and it was obvious from the décor, the hurried service and the fact that many people sat with their hats and coats on, that food was just fuel and not something to be enjoyed and savoured. However, the food was good. Kebabs made from chicken or spicy mince with rice and salad was a common meal for about 80p, and soup was always available, usually lentil and often deliciously flavoured with fresh mint. Sometimes available was a lovely yogurt, mint and rice soup, not to be confused with the other white soup which was made from tripe! Bars and classy restaurants were usually only to be found in areas frequented by tourists.

Since we had been in Turkey, the Turks had been celebrating Ramadan (called 'Ramazan' in Turkey) and the fast was due to finish on 5th December when there would be celebrations and three days of public holiday. We were told that we were lucky not to have been cycling in eastern Turkey where the Muslims were much stricter and all cafés and restaurants would have been closed during daylight hours. An announcement from the minaret loudspeakers on the mosques was made each day at 5pm when it got dark to tell everyone that food could now be eaten. As the Muslims only fasted during daylight hours, the minute the announcement had been made the cafés were full of people eager to eat. During the early hours of the morning, at any time from 2.30am to 4am, drummers walked slowly round the streets of the towns banging muffled drums to wake people. This was to ensure that they had time to prepare food, eat breakfast and pray before daylight came. At 5.30am the loudspeakers from the minarets announced the call to prayers, and if our hotel was close to a mosque this was unbelievably loud, waking us with a start!

We were finding the cycling quite difficult because the roads didn't have good surfaces. Whilst the roads were sealed, the tarmac was set with large pieces of gravel which jarred every bone as we cycled, but was especially painful on the wrists. This was on the roads in good repair, but when we got to poorly kept roads we really suffered.

We found a campsite marked on our map, and decided to camp – so far in Turkey we had only stayed in hotels, which were extremely cheap. The campsite was next to a beautiful lake backed by mountains, and as we flew down a hill on our bikes we could see the lake below us. We turned along a dirt road to the campsite, which was next to a dilapidated olive-pressing factory. No-one else was camping – it was 15th November, so hardly the camping season. By 3.30 in the afternoon it was already cold, so we needed to set up our tent quickly in the eucalyptus woods beside the lake.

A large flock of geese flew over the lake and landed on the beach beside us. Warren was as happy as a sand-boy, because he could collect dead wood and make a fire on the beach to keep us warm. We searched for the showers, but the doors were broken, the hoses broken, there was only cold water and the squat toilets, like other ones in Turkey we'd seen, had no flush but only a tap with a jug. However, having paid only £1.60 for the night, we didn't feel we could complain!

When we woke in the morning the view had changed – the mountains on the other side of the lake had disappeared into the mist, and we looked out on what appeared to be the sea with the horizon in the far distance.

Before we left the campsite, we noticed that men had arrived at the broken down shack to do olive pressing, so we asked if we could see round the olive-pressing factory. Outside the door stood sacks packed full of olives, each one labelled with a name. The owner showed us round – he spoke no English, but we were fascinated to see the green and black olives being weighed before being shovelled into a concreted hole in the ground outside the factory, where an Archimedes screw carried them up into the building. There the olives were minced to a pulp and dropped down a tube into an enormous tub on wheels. This was pushed by two men to the other side of the dark room, where one person took a bucketful at a time and poured it into an envelope made of hessian which was as thick as a doormat and about 20 inches square. A second man stacked these filled envelopes into a pile onto a press, and the oil began to seep out of the hessian envelopes even before the press was put into action. The press pushed down until no more oil could be squeezed out, and the golden oil poured into a wooden vat below the floor on which the men stood. It looked as though it needed to be strained before being used, and the hygiene in the factory definitely wouldn't have come up to EU standards!

We climbed another mountain as we left that morning, and everything was shrouded in mist. I had to take my glasses off, because I couldn't see through the misty lenses. As we climbed higher the sun came out, until at 11am it was very hot. As we flew down the other side of the mountain we found we were on a plain surrounded by mountains on all sides. The fields were full of cotton plants, which looked dead but had little balls of soft cotton attached to the open seedpod. These cotton-wool balls are called 'bolls'. Picking cotton isn't a pleasant job – when picking the cotton the bolls open up to expose very sharp needles on the tip of each hull, so fingers bleed doing such a job. Workers were filling enormous sacks over 6 feet high with the soft white cotton bolls. We stopped to take photos, and the workers waved as they stood inside the sacks, jumping up and down to compress the cotton. As we cycled along, we could see little balls of cotton everywhere, caught in the grass and bushes by the roadside. We later passed cotton factories, where the large sacks of cotton were stacked in mountains on the concrete, waiting to be processed. Pieces of soft cotton peeped from the seams of tightly-packed sacks which were stacked precariously high on tractors, waiting to be unloaded.

Later in the day we passed two marble cutting factories, the first cutting white marble, and the second cutting dark red marble. The marble was stacked in giant slices waiting to be transported. As I struggled behind Warren cycling up a hill, a farmer passing on his tractor indicated that I could hang on to his tractor and he would pull me up the hill, but I declined, picturing myself being pulled under the wheels of the tractor if I didn't hold on properly!

We were now approaching Selçuk, where John the Baptist is alleged to be buried. Selçuk is the nearest town to Ephesus, and as we approached the main road a girl in her garden stood and waved to us.

'Come and have a coffee,' she called out.

We were surprised to hear English, even though we knew that Selçuk was popular with back-packers, so we cycled over to meet her and her friend. She was Greek, married to a Turk, which was very surprising considering how the Greeks and Turks usually hate each other. The girl with her was Joy, an Australian who spent a lot of time in Turkey and spoke the language fluently. They were making gösleme (Turkish pancakes) on an open fire and stuffing them with spinach and cheese, baked aubergine, onion and tomato. We stayed so long, eating pancakes and drinking coffee, that it was nearly dark when we left, but Joy had recommended a guest-house that was run by her Greek friend's brother. The rooms were old-fashioned, but the atmosphere was wonderful. The food was cooked by Maria, the owner's mother, and was fantastic. Wine was available to buy, and we spent several evenings discussing travel with people from many different countries who were staying there. An Australian couple, Tony and Lynne, gave us their e-mail address and invited us to stay with them in eastern Australia when we got there.

We spent a day exploring Ephesus, which we thought was a very special place to visit – many consider it to be the best preserved ancient city in the world. It had been a city in biblical times, and I marvelled that I was walking along roads in a city that had been mentioned in the Bible, and that St. Paul had written at length to the people of that ancient city. We walked up the steps of the amphi-theatre, admired the narrow streets leading to the private terraced houses on the hill, and were impressed with the stadium, the fountains, temples and baths. We were amazed at the extent of the terracotta pipes half-buried in the ground which had been part of the central heating system thousands of years before, but even more impressive were the rows of communal latrines. As we sat side by side on these public lavatories, we learnt that in the early days water had run continually below these marble seats to remove the waste. There was originally a fountain in the large square room, and the seats all round would have been covered by a wooden roof supported by marble columns. It must have been a sociable place – there were no cubicles, the men sitting side by side on the shaped holes cut out of the long marble seat. An interesting anecdote is that wealthy men caught short while they were in town would send their slave ahead of them to warm up the seat!

My favourite building was a magnificent library, which was built in the 2nd century, and once held thousands of scrolls. A fire many centuries ago damaged the library, but the façade was undamaged and still stands today, two high storeys of elegant columns and arches. Ephesus was probably the epitome of ancient architecture, but we now felt we had seen enough amphi-theatres and ruins to last a lifetime, having seen so many in Greece as well.

We continued our journey north. Two men passed us on small motorcycles, the backs of their vehicles laden high with branches for firewood. They drove past us at bicycle speed to say 'Merhabah' (hello), giving us enormous grins, before accelerating away. Like most Turkish men they had enormous bushy black moustaches, and when they smiled they had beautiful even white teeth.

We were surprised at breakfast in a hotel one morning to find a Turkish man also eating. As Ramadan was not yet over, we never saw local people eating during daylight hours. The waiter laid the table for the three of us, placing the cutlery neatly on three sheets of newspaper which acted as place mats. Our fellow guest spoke in German to us – he was Turkish but was married to a German girl, and they had a six-year old son. However, he had returned home to his mother in Turkey for a few months because he was suffering from stress and exhaustion. Because he was ill he had special dispensation to eat during daylight hours throughout Ramadan.

'My stress and exhaustion,' he said in German, 'Is because in Europe it is all work, eat, sleep, work, eat, sleep, and I couldn't cope with this and it made me ill.'

I made sympathetic noises and translated his words to Warren.

He continued, 'Now I have had three months of recuperation in Turkey without my wife and son, I plan to return to Germany. I will get a job, and then I will be able to apply for a German passport. This is much better than a Turkish one, because I will be free to travel without visas.'

It appeared that the main reason for this man returning to Germany was not to see his wife and son, but to make sure that he could get the German passport that he so coveted. I wondered how long his marriage would last once he had acquired it. It also made me realise that in poorer Asian countries the people often envy westerners our lives of apparent luxury, but what they don't realise is that we have to work hard for it and that our lives are often very stressful as a result. This man obviously wanted the luxury of a German passport, but he wasn't happy to work hard like a German to get it. We had noticed that it was usually the women in the poorer countries who worked the hardest, while men seemed to sit around a lot talking, drinking and smoking.

We arrived at Izmir, the third largest city in Turkey after Istanbul and the capital, Ankara. A city of 3 million people, Izmir has palm-lined promenades, and avenues and green parks are set in sweeping curves along a circular bay. Izmir has an exceptionally mild climate and many fine hotels as well as a busy commercial and industrial centre. However, we found ourselves in a rather seedy area, but were very pleased because there were rows of cycle shops along one of the roads – we desperately needed to replace our tyres. We had now cycled 3,000 miles (4,700km) and our tyres were clearly reaching the end of their life. We booked into a hotel which was very cheap – less than £5 for the room for the night. However, when the toilet was flushed the water poured from the cistern onto the floor, and we found that our windows didn't shut properly.

We had a problem finding suitable tyres, because the most popular were thick knobbly mountain bike tyres, whereas we wanted our tyres to be as slick as possible for the smoothest, easiest ride on sealed roads. We eventually bought the most expensive tyres we could find that seemed suitable, but the four tyres only cost 35,000,000 Turkish Lira (about £16), and were clearly not good quality – it was even impossible to balance them perfectly because of the imperfections. However, they would have to do until we could find something better.

While we were in a large city we tried to buy anti-malarial tablets which we needed to begin taking one week before we flew to India. We visited three pharmacies, and although none of them could speak English they understood what we were asking for. However, when they looked up in their medical books the name of the drugs that we were requesting, we discovered that there were no anti-malarial drugs available anywhere in Turkey. We were flabbergasted, and realised that we would have to arrive in India and buy tablets there, and hope that we didn't get bitten by any malaria-carrying mosquitoes before our tablets took effect.

We were finding it very cheap to travel in Turkey, rooms often costing us only £3 or £4, and simple but delicious meals often costing less than £2 for the two of us. However, while we were in towns we were finding that we often had disturbed sleep, and this wasn't because of the extremely hard Turkish pillows. We could hear the drummer walking the streets at 4am and after that the muezzin announced the call to prayers over the loudspeakers from the minarets of the mosques at 5am, 6am and 7am. One night after the drummer had gone past our window at 4am, we heard people talking loudly in the echoing marble staircase of the hotel. Someone began to knock constantly on a nearby door. The knocking stopped, after which a phone rang constantly in the room next to ours. Then the knocking began again. Obviously the inhabitant of the next room was dead or dead to the world. At one stage I was going to open my door and say 'Sshh', but the knocking suddenly stopped. However, doors continued to be banged, and it sounded as if the inhabitant of the room above us was moving furniture. This had happened before, and we wondered if people moved their beds across the marble floor to make space for praying.

There were still pleasant rural scenes between the towns, and although it was now the end of November we often had pleasantly warm days for cycling. Olive trees were abundant, and fields of tall okra shone golden yellow in the sun. Sweet corn had just been harvested, and we saw many more fields of cotton.

In Bergama we stayed at a small hotel close to a spectacular mosque with elegant tall white towers with blue roofs. I chatted to the owner of the hotel, and admired the flowers in the hotel garden that had been planted into Roman urns. The urns turned out to be genuine Roman ones, and he told me that every house near the Acropolis in the town had two or three Roman urns in the garden! We visited the giant market in the town, amazed at the prices of the superb fruits and vegetables. 3 kilos of windfall apples cost only 4p, and 4 kilos of potatoes or onions were 40p.

We checked our e-mails one day to find one from Norman. He was ahead of us in Ayvalik, but was planning to stay there a few days, so we guessed that we would be able to catch up with him and cycle together again for a while. By this time I was suffering very badly with a painful neck and wrist, both problems caused by the cycling. Warren tried to ease the problem by raising my handlebars, so I felt as though I was cycling an old-fashioned 'sit-up-and-beg' bike. However, it did help the problem, especially when he wrapped the handlebars in yellow foam rubber to cushion my wrists from painful jarring.

We eventually arrived in Ayvalik, and met Norman in the square where he was drinking a glass of tea, so we booked into the same luxury hotel that he was in, and agreed to continue together to Istanbul, which was still about 400 miles away.

Warren, Norman and I were cycling together when I saw in the distance above the trees a rather splendid mosque which I announced I wanted to visit. We cycled round and round through the trees and couldn't find it initially, but we eventually came across it in the middle of an olive grove. It was under construction, though the dome and minarets which we had seen above the trees were virtually complete. We were lucky enough to find there a man who (from bits of Turkish and hand signals) we gathered had donated the land and was actually paying for the building of the mosque as well. He was incredibly proud of the beautiful mosque and showed us round. I was even allowed through the main door, through which women would never be allowed once the mosque was completed. He produced plans from a bag hanging on a nail, and these were a delight in themselves. Sketches of the proposed mosque were shown in detail from every angle, all on one length of paper which was many metres long.

Odd pieces of wood had been nailed together to a very great height to form scaffolding inside the mosque, and it certainly didn't look at all safe! We took photos of this generous gentleman in front of a notice which bore his name and explained in Turkish that he had donated the land and paid for the mosque. As we left he shook my hand and picked two olives from a tree to give to me. I understood that this was an indication of respect. However, Warren and Norman were quite taken aback to get, as well as a handshake, a kiss on both cheeks! It's normal in Turkey to see old men walking arm in arm in the street, or men kissing as they meet.

Warren, Norman and I cycled north up the west coast of Turkey, and just before we reached Cannarkale we turned off to visit Troy, the famous ancient city. For centuries the fascinating story involving the destruction of the prosperous city of Troy in a long war fought over the legendary beauty, Helen, was thought to be fiction from Greek mythology. The story, told by Homer in the Iliad, was regarded as just a myth until the ruins of the city were found in western Turkey in the mid-19th century. Troy is a city which existed over 4,000 years ago, and was considered to be the centre of ancient civilizations. For a long period Troy (or Ilium, as it was called at that time) was to the Heathen world what Jerusalem is now to the Christians – a sacred city which attracted many pilgrims. Today the romantic story of Helen and the Trojan horse still draws many tourists and archaeologists to the site, but there's not a great deal now to be seen apart from ruins of the ancient walls and roads. It was fascinating to see that Troy is a city of layers – city after city has been built on top of the previous ruins – cities destroyed either by fire, wars or earthquakes. The first Troy was an early settlement with a wall built of small stones and clay, its date being about 3000 BC. A replica of the famous Trojan horse which enabled the final conquering of the city now stands on the site, and we took typical tourist photographs of us looking out of the tiny windows high up in the wooden horse. The setting was spectacular, giving wonderful views of the sea and the high cliffs of the Gallipoli peninsular beyond.

We continued towards Cannarkale, 20 miles away, but the going was slow. The rain came down steadily and it was very cold, and there were long hills which I found difficult. We were now fully dressed in waterproof clothing. We stopped at a restaurant on top of a hill, and were the only customers. A coat-stand was pulled towards a boiler, so we could hang our wet coats on it to dry while we had a cup of tea. A lady was making dolma, the Turkish equivalent of the Greek dolmades. She sat at the table next to us filling vine leaves with a delicious-smelling mixture of rice, lemon, parsley, tomatoes and dill. She nipped off the stem, nimbly tucked the sides of the leaves in and rolled them up into a neat roll. She passed us some to try, served with a dollop of yogurt as well as a wedge of lemon to squeeze over. Stuffed peppers were brought in and put on the stove where the pan bubbled away, the steam from the pan mingling with the steam rising from our wet coats as they dried in the heat. We imagined that there would be a stunning view from the restaurant on a fine day, but the mist and the rain outside totally obliterated everything.

We were relieved to arrive at Cannarkale, and decided we wanted a bit of luxury and warmth after the day's cold cycling, but our luxurious room soon looked messy once we had hung up a number of washing lines to dry out our wet bags and clothes. We went to a local café for a meal, but it was one of the few disappointing meals in Turkey – my tuna was cold and didn't taste like tuna, and the stuffed peppers to go with it were only luke warm. Norman asked for sea bass, but didn't think it was sea bass, and Warren was convinced that his chicken wasn't actually chicken, but we couldn't think what else it could be ...

The following day we washed loads of clothes, so our room looked just as bad as it had the day before, and I went to the internet café while Warren and Norman explored the town. It was very slow typing, because there are two different letter 'i's' in the Turkish language, one with a dot above and one without. They have two different pronounciations, but the 'i' in the normal place on the keyboard was the wrong one. If I sent an e-mail with the wrong 'i' my e-mails when they were received were like gobbledegook, every 'i' having been changed to a capital Y with an accent! Every keyboard in each country so far had been different, each country having its preferred favourite letters in the centre of the keyboard.

At Cannarkale we had to take a half hour ferry to cross the entrance to the Sea of Marmara, and we were now travelling north-east and would soon turn east to Istanbul with the Sea of Marmara on our right. We had a north-easterly wind against us and it was raining hard again. However, in our favour was the fact that the sealed road was smooth, and the road mostly flat. The scenery initially was reminiscent of Scotland, and it felt as though we were cycling alongside a loch. The scenery became more green and rolling with fewer mountains as we headed towards Gallipolli.

Gallipolli was one of the Allies' great disasters in World War One. Allied leaders, including Winston Churchill and Lord Kitchener, scoured their maps. The Dardenelles Strait leading from the Mediterranean to Istanbul caught their eye – a successful attack in that area would open a sea lane to the Russians through the Black Sea, and provide a base for attacking the Central Powers through what Churchill described as the 'soft underbelly of Europe'. This would also divert enemy attention from the Western Front.

At 4.30am on 25th April 1915, Australian and New Zealand troops, together with Irish, French and British forces landed at Gallipolli, and attacks and counter attacks took place over the next eight months. Reports vary, but it is believed that between 100,000 to 200,000 Allied soldiers died during the battles at Gallipolli, with a similar number of deaths sustained by the Turkish armies who were defending their country. Another quarter of a million were wounded.

As well as heavy war casualties, by the end of November 1915 torrential rain in the area drowned 100 Anzac soldiers in the trenches, then there were ferocious blizzards with driving snow, and hundreds more men froze to death waist deep in the trenches. Deadlock on the beaches persisted, and the whole offensive was finally called off in December and it was arranged for the troops to be evacuated. By mid December, eight months after the attack began, a massive operation had taken place over a period of two weeks to evacuate 83,000 troops plus horses, donkeys, artillery and vehicles.

The landing place became known as Anzac Cove, deriving its name from the initial letters of the Australian and New Zealand Army Corps (ANZAC). 10,000 Australians and Kiwis visit Gallipolli every year on 25th April to attend the Anzac dawn service held on the Gallipolli peninsular, and to visit the battlefields and the war graves of their relatives.

Despite the sad reminder of the area, the scenery was pretty; it was a shame the weather was so bad. A number of dogs ran barking towards us, so we had our dog-dazers at the ready, but two puppies about 6 months old detached themselves from the group of dogs and followed behind us for several miles, wanting to make friends.

It was now 8th December, and the weather was getting very cold. To make matters worse, I had cramps in my tummy, and was feeling decidedly unwell – I wondered if that dubious meal at Cannarkale was the cause? It looked as though I was getting my first upset tummy of the trip – perhaps not so bad considering we had been travelling now for six months. We stopped for some lunch, but I couldn't eat much, and was beginning to feel weak, possibly from lack of food. I was also still suffering with pains in my wrists and neck, so was beginning to feel like a hypochondriac.

The countryside was rolling and green and very pretty, rather like Ireland. Fields were vivid emerald green, even on that constantly dark day. The hills became steeper, and I got off to push my bike, while Warren and Norman forged ahead, and once again I was offered a lift by a passing tractor, this time filled with women who had been working in the fields. They waved until they were out of view over the top of the hill. We were very high at that point and the views were spectacular, but now we had to go down to the coast again, and we flew down the hills and up again, freewheeling up the hills because of the high speed we were reaching, and the road continued like a switchback until the final freezing cold fast descent just as the sun set to our right, a glorious golden glow setting off the silhouettes of trees on the hills in the west.

The first hotel we visited had no bathroom – rather a problem with my tummy – so we found a strange hotel with rooms that appeared to be damp and unheated, but at least had en suite bathrooms. We went to a restaurant for a meal, but it was a mistake for me to eat. Emerging from the squalid squat toilet at the back of the restaurant, I decided I would have to eat dry biscuits or toast and water until I was feeling better.

When we arrived in a small place called Sarkoy, we realised that we weren't making the progress that we had hoped, because we had been staying in places waiting for the weather to improve. Also, sometimes the rain or wind was so bad against us that we hadn't been able to cycle as far as expected. Accommodation in Sarkoy was very poor, and there was only one basic café where food could be bought. The waiter was very nice, but he kept on his white woolly hat and a big scarf, because it was very cold in the café.

We left Sarkoy but were struggling to cycle 3 or 4 mph on the flat because the driving wind against us was so strong. We stopped at a tea-house in a village and I chatted to two men in German. When I told them where we were going they were horrified, saying that the road ahead was 'schrecklich' (dreadful) and even a car couldn't get through. It was beautiful, they said, but only for walking, and not on a cold, wet day. They suggested that we travel to Istanbul by bus.

We returned the 5 miles we had struggled (now going at 16mph without effort because the wind was behind us!) and knew that the only other way out of Sarkov was the way we had come, and there was no way I wanted to cycle up those steep hills on such a cold, wet, windy day, especially with me feeling so ill. We decided to catch a bus to Tekirdag, the next big town about 52 miles away. Unfortunately, we discovered that it was a public holiday because Ramadan had just finished, and as it was traditional for everyone to go to see their relatives at that time (particularly for young people to visit elderly relatives) the buses were full. It would have cost us 2 million lira each on a bus (80p) for the 52 mile journey, but instead we had to try to get two taxis for the three of us, three bikes and 15 pannier bags. The taxi company wanted 100 million lira (£40) which was a massive amount for Turkey, but the thought of staying another night in that very dismal town persuaded us to agree the price. The back seats were put down in an estate car taxi, and two men began putting our bags and bikes in the back. We were concerned when we saw that they were trying to put Norman's bike in as well, because it was obvious that we needed two taxis, and we had assumed that the agreed price was for two taxis – once the back seats had been put down, there was only one passenger seat left available. As it was, I would have to sit on Warren's lap for the 52 mile journey. Where did they think Norman could sit? How could three bikes and 15 large cycle pannier bags fit into the back? They suggested that two of us take the bus, while they took the third by taxi, but the charge would still be the same as already quoted! Arguments ensued, because when we said it was obvious that we needed two taxis they wanted to charge us double the original price. They beckoned us into their office, where they asked us to sit down while eight other taxi drivers stood or sat around smoking. We kept asking if there was a problem, and they said 'no problem' (international words!), but they passed me a telephone to speak to one of their bosses in German. After that they asked Norman to speak to someone else on the telephone, but as that person didn't speak English and Norman didn't speak Turkish, it certainly seemed like a waste of time.

Warren jumped up, saying, 'I like pantomimes, but now I'm getting bored,' and he went out into the rain and began to pull our bags back out of the taxi. Norman and I went to help, and the taxi drivers panicked when they saw this, and everyone suddenly agreed that we could have two taxis after all for the agreed price.

We arrived in our taxis at Tekirdag to see the waves crashing violently onto the harbour wall, and the locals were all huddled into their thick grey coats and scarves to keep out the wind. Facing the sea was an impressive-looking hotel. We looked at each other and nodded – whatever the price we were going to stay there. We were soon settled into our luxurious hotel rooms which had cost us only £12 per night for a double room.

We were very cold as we went out to find a restaurant, and as we left the restaurant I noticed that my thermometer had dropped to 2°C. The wind was bitterly cold coming from the north east – it felt as though it was coming straight from Siberia. On the television in the hotel bedroom that night they were showing snow drifts 10 feet high, floods and gales, but unfortunately, not being able to understand Turkish, we couldn't work out where in Turkey this was. We knew that in eastern Turkey it is always very much colder, and we knew that the temperature there was already minus 15°C.

I was becoming concerned that we might find ourselves stranded somewhere small (such as the last town) and that there would be no transport running because of the deep snow. We had bought warm woolly hats, scarves and gloves in an attempt to keep warm. When we had a flurry of snow the next day, I felt it was a warning which we shouldn't ignore, and I tried to persuade Norman and Warren that we should take a bus with our bikes to Istanbul, which was 90 miles further to the east. Initially they weren't keen, but each time we turned a corner the freezing cold wind hit us in the face, and they eventually agreed that we should go by bus. This decision proved to be a good one. We got on the bus the next day; snow fell thickly for the whole of the journey and we saw no hotels along the way. We were sat opposite the doors, and because the bus stopped so frequently we froze on one side with blasts of icy air hitting us each time the door was opened. The pretty scenery had vanished and had been replaced by a sprawl of newly-built houses, mostly unfinished, in fields with no paths or roads. This went on for miles, with no sign of town centres, shops, hotels or cafés. Thank goodness we weren't cycling. There was 140km of such scenery, getting busier and more built up as we approached Istanbul.

As we unloaded our bikes from the bus at the bus station, we were standing in one foot of slush and snow. And so we arrived in Istanbul – a city of 10 million people, and the only city in the world that bridges two continents, Europe and Asia.

We assumed that hotels would now be much more expensive in a major city such as Istanbul, but decided to splash out on something really expensive for a couple of days. We needed to stay in Istanbul at least a week while we waited for our Indian visas to be approved, so we could look for somewhere less expensive after two days of luxury. A minibus took the three of us to the centre of Istanbul, promising to take us to a 'very good but very reasonable' hotel. The taxi driver dashed into the hotel as soon as he arrived, while his co-driver ran round to begin pulling our bikes out of the back of the bus. The hotel manager came to greet us, but was unwilling to commit to telling us how much the rooms were until we had all come into the reception. We refused, realising suddenly that we were being taken for tourists and the mini bus driver was waiting for a cut of the inflated hotel charges. The manager eventually quoted us 120 million lira for a double room. This was five times the amount we had paid for nice hotels in other towns, and we were certain we could find ourselves a better deal. Sure enough, a nearby four star hotel offered us a double room for 62 million lira per night for a double room, so we were amazed that for less than £25 in the centre of Istanbul we had a luxurious double room with deep carpets, thick velvet curtains and a beautiful bathroom.

Warren and I fell in love with Istanbul, even though we generally prefer the rural areas to the cities. The Grand Bazaar was my favourite – the forerunner of the big shopping centres but first built in 1461! The present building was built in 1894 and has 5,000 shops spread out in a giant labyrinth of small streets and passages, which are mostly arranged according to their trade. The atmosphere was very colourful and eastern. There were brightly-coloured fabrics on bales stacked to the ceiling in shops that looked like caves; beautiful coloured glass lights hung in abundance outside shops, and fabulous Turkish carpets made of silk or wool were stacked high in the numerous carpet shops. There were shops full of colourful sweets, shops with sparkly costumes for belly-dancing, and leather shops galore full of coats, bags and other goods. Cafés were full of low tables and cushions on the floor; jewellery shops were full of the most fabulous oriental jewellery in gold and silver studded with diamonds, gems and precious stones. Beautiful handmade jewellery sold in one shop was copied from ancient designs up to 5,000 years old. The copper and brass shops had an amazing array of objects and souvenirs, such as brass samovars and copper jugs. There was an antique section in the middle of the Bazaar which was a treasure trove of objects such as icons, old coins, embroidery, porcelain, ornate silver tea services, weapons and objets d'art. Everything was full of colour, and the ornately painted ceiling above each street or passageway was domed and supported by giant pillars.

Of course, we were instantly recognisable as tourists because we didn't wear grey overcoats, and as we passed every shop we were called to see their goods.

'Would you like to buy a leather jacket?'

'Please come and see my carpets – you don't have to buy.'

'Please come and have a glass of tea with me and I will show you just two carpets.'

There were beautiful buildings to see in Istanbul, especially the magnificent mosques and churches; there were tea-rooms and coffee-rooms to sit and have a drink; we ate our gösleme, delicious large pancakes cooked on a convex dry pan and stuffed with cheese, spinach and chillies as we watched the locals smoke the water pipes (sometimes called hubble bubble pipes). There are so many beautiful mosques in Istanbul, but our favourite was The Blue Mosque, an incredibly elegant building built in 1617. It's named the Blue Mosque because it is decorated inside with 21,000 17th Century Iznik tiles, but is also gilded and painted in stencil designs in matching colours. Most interiors we saw were absolutely awe-inspiring, and photographs could never truly show the magnificence of the decorations. The Topkapi Palace, a former residence of Ottoman rulers, but now a museum, houses an absolutely priceless collection of Chinese and Japanese porcelain, mostly 14th century Ming. There are also rooms with jewels of the Treasury, a famous 86 carat diamond, jewel-studded ornaments to go in turbans and jewel-studded weapons and armour. There were also many museums to visit in Istanbul, displaying carpets, mosaics, Islamic art, ceramics and archaeology.

We either walked or used the tram to travel around the city, having left our bicycles in our hotel. We walked to the Bosphorus to see the sun set, and watched men on fishing boats at the Golden Horn who were frying the fish they had caught that day. They sold the fried fish fillets in baguettes with raw sliced onions, lemon juice and salad, leaning precariously over the side of the rocking boat to hand the baguettes to customers on the quayside. For 60p it was truly a delicious snack, but the wind was so strong that the boats rocked violently on the waves, flames shooting several feet in the air as hot oil splashed over the giant frying pans onto the hot coals beneath.

After two days we had moved from our luxury hotel to a much cheaper one, which was still very central and very clean. For a double room including breakfast, Warren and I were now paying less than £14, which we considered excellent value for a room in the centre of a tourist city. We even had a radiator in the bathroom, which was luxury indeed compared with what we had been used to! We stayed there for several days, and were fascinated to see that every other day the hotel filled up with people from Macedonia, Slovenia, Croatia, Albania, Yugoslavia, Russia and other eastern European countries. Every time we returned to the hotel we would find the landings and the reception full of stacks of clothes and other items, which the guests were packing into giant black plastic bags or boxes. It was extraordinary to see them jumping on the clothes to compact them into the strong plastic bags, after which they sealed the bags with yards of parcel tape and then sucked out the air with a vacuum cleaner to make the parcels as small as possible! Sometimes there were things that wouldn't pack neatly, so a few shop window dummies stood with the parcels, tied together in naked abandon, looking at us with strange expressions, their fingers pointing unconcernedly at the ceiling. We discovered that these people regularly arrived in Istanbul, stayed for two days while they bought anything that they could sell back home, and disappeared again, leaving the hotel empty for another day or two. We had noticed that signs in shop windows in the back streets were often in Russian as well as Turkish and English.

The early morning call to prayers hadn't been a problem since we had arrived in Istanbul, so it was annoying to be woken at 5am one morning when several dozen eastern Europeans arrived at the hotel. They were obviously wide awake, having just arrived, and seemed oblivious to the fact that other occupants in the hotel might still be asleep. The small lift was near our room, and we could hear it going up and down, up and down, depositing new guests on our landing. Other guests were walking up the stairs, talking and laughing as they passed our room. Doors were banging and people were shouting. It was quite extraordinary. Warren and I had got up early to leave before dawn many times, but we had always crept around whispering quietly so that we didn't disturb anyone. Finally I got out of bed and opened the door, saying 'Sshhh' loudly to the noisy crowd. They stopped instantly, looking surprised and sheepish for a second. Five seconds later they were making just as much noise. In the morning, when we went down for our breakfast at 9am as usual, there was no food left, because the new guests had eaten it all!

It was very cold in Istanbul, and we were wearing all of our clothes at the same time – a summer vest, a t-shirt, a long-sleeved shirt, a fleece jacket and a waterproof jacket, together with two pairs of trousers. Cycling shoes are not waterproof, so we were wearing polythene bags over our socks inside our shoes, to keep our feet dry and warm. We bought woolly hats, scarves and gloves, which we intended to leave behind once we left Istanbul. Although Istanbul is on the same latitude as Naples, it is much colder because of the prevailing north winds.

When we woke to find everything blanketed with snow one morning, we knew we had to leave Istanbul soon. However, it was wonderful to see the mosques adorned with a coating of white snow, and we hurried out to take photographs.

We became used to being approached by locals wanting to sell us their goods. In an attempt to make them go away, we sometimes attempted to sell our gloves or hat to the salesmen, which really confused them.

Another ploy by one person was to say, 'Give me a minute and I will change your life.' (No, I don't know what he was selling!)

Warren confused him by stopping and looking at his watch. 'Ten seconds are gone already,' he said. Fifty seconds later Warren announced, 'You've failed!' and they both laughed, enjoying the banter.

Regularly we were approached outside our hotel by the same man trying to sell us a leather jacket, and he often followed us for some distance refusing to give up. When he followed us the third time, the conversation went like this:

'Would you like a leather jacket?' He walked alongside us holding up a leather jacket.

'No, thank you.'

'Very cheap – only 50 euros.' (Or dollars, but never pounds or Turkish lira!)

'No, thank you – I don't want a jacket.' We continued walking at a brisk pace and the man with the leather jacket ran to keep up.

'It's very good quality and very good price.'

'No thank you – I don't like leather.'

'How much do you want to pay?'

'I don't want to pay anything; I don't want a leather jacket, thank you.'

'It's only 50 euros and very good quality.'

At this point Warren stopped walking, looked at the man and said, 'That's much too cheap. It should be 1,000 euros.'

The man looked confused, so I added to his confusion by saying, 'No, 1 million euros.'

The man hesitated, realised we were joking, laughed, patted Warren on the back, shook his hand and left quite happily.

We passed a tea house which had a special room for smoking water pipes. The room was full of men smoking, and I decided to take a photo. I opened the door, and although I don't normally like the smell of tobacco burning, the most delightful smell of herbs and tobacco filled the smoky room. The water pipes stood on the floor, and a man was walking around the room filling the open containers at the top of the pipes with red hot burning charcoal. The gentle sound of water bubbling filled the air, as the men sucked the smoke through the cooling water in the pipe. I indicated that I was about to take a photo, but no-one took any notice of me. The camera flashed through the haze, and I quickly retreated.

We went to look for the Egyptian Bazaar mentioned in my guide book, and found it near the Golden Horn. Turkish delight and nutty toffee were displayed on counters, and dried mushrooms were hanging like bells on strings with other dried vegetables and chillies. Shops sold fabrics, meat, fruit and nuts. Outside one shop stood silver foil-covered tea-chests full of loose tea leaves. A man passed by, pushing a trolley with a giant brass samovar from which he dispensed tea into plastic cups. As we walked back to the hotel, we saw that one street was full of shops selling safes and scales of all types, and the next street was full of shops displaying sewing machines. There was an area of tiny shops with ironmongery, another with camera shops and also a street of shops selling fur pelts. In one street every window displayed naked window dummies, so it was the actual dummies that were for sale, and another street was lined with nothing but shops full of fabulous lights – wall lights, ceiling lights, table lamps, desk lamps and garden lights. There were streets of cycle shops, wedding dress shops, world-wide courier offices, and streets full of shops selling electrical tools. We thought it was an excellent idea to keep everything together in this way – if you wanted to compare prices you didn't need to run backwards and forwards across the city to different shops!

It was nearly Christmas, and we had achieved our aim of avoiding the three month period of commercialism that always precedes Christmas back home. We had seen nothing of Christmas in Turkey apart from one Father Christmas model in a shop window and one small decorated Christmas tree outside a restaurant in Istanbul. There were no Christmas cards available, no panicking people rushing round in their lunch hour, and no people telling us in mid-September that they'd finished their Christmas shopping and had wrapped all their presents! I found it hard to find cards suitable to send to my mother and to my children, Mandi, Julian and Sarah, but eventually found some cards showing lovely old prints of Istanbul, and thought that they would at least look different on their mantelpieces amongst the Christmas cards. Warren also sent a card to Jean and Steven, his parents, and to his brothers, and our Christmas shopping was complete!

We had hoped to be in Goa (a Christian state in India) for Christmas, but time was running out. We now had our Indian visas safely stamped into our passports, although it had taken three visits to the embassy on the other side of the city to sort it out. We went to book flights to Mumbai (formerly Bombay), but found that all flights to Mumbai before Christmas were booked. We were cold and we were looking forward to the warmth of India now, so Warren and I booked a flight to Delhi instead, hoping that we could get an internal flight or train to Goa from Delhi so we could still be there for Christmas. Norman was remaining in Istanbul for a few more days, waiting for a new credit card to arrive, so we said our goodbyes once again. We had loved Turkey, but now it was time to visit a different country.

On 20th December, Warren and I left the hotel and flagged down a taxi to take us to the airport. It was not until the third taxi that a driver would agree to take our bikes, but of course we had to pay a vastly inflated fare. Large flakes of snow were falling on the icy streets as we left the centre of Istanbul. Our plane was delayed, but eventually we boarded a plane to Bahrein, putting our bicycles on a plane for the first time on our trip. At Bahrein we had a seven hour wait, the plane apparently having been delayed because of fog at Delhi. We looked at each other in amazement. Fog? In Delhi? This didn't sound promising!

After a miserable wait at Bahrein airport, we eventually left for the three hour flight to Delhi, arriving at 9am. It was still foggy and it was only 12°C, but we had arrived! There had been some concern at immigration that our completed forms didn't show the name of the hotel where we were to stay. We tried to explain that we hadn't yet booked one, but they told us next time to ensure that the form was correctly completed. We learnt from our mistake – after that incident, if requested to complete this information we always inserted the name of any hotel which we took from a guide book. Now all we had to do was find a hotel in this vast city . . .

CHAPTER 7

NORTH INDIA, GOA, KARNATAKA AND KERALA

India is a vast country divided into 25 states. There are 23 official languages, although Hindi and English are the official languages of communication for the government. The different areas of India are diverse, ranging from the mighty Himalayan mountains in the north that form the border with China, to the flat Ganges basin and the three great oceans that bound the west, south and east coasts of India. Many of the coastlines boast beautiful beaches. The main religion is Hinduism, although there are areas where Islam and Christianity are dominant.

North India

The journey from Istanbul to Delhi had lasted 13 hours, so we felt shattered by the time we reached Delhi. Our bikes were battered and had obviously been thrown around, but there was no serious damage. We had been lucky not to be charged for excess baggage, because we were well over our weight limit with the bikes, but fortunately the girl at the check-in desk hadn't weighed the bikes, only our bags.

We went to a hotel reservation counter at the airport and the Indian girl was very helpful and booked us into a 4 star hotel – we were surprised that it was so expensive compared with what we had been used to in Istanbul, but at 2,750 rupees (about £37) it appeared to be one of the cheapest hotels on her list. She warned us to insist that the taxi driver took us to that hotel, because she said he would try to take us to another one where he could get 50% commission which would be added to our bill. (In retrospect I suspect that she received commission from our booking, and it was this that made the hotel so expensive). She told us that taxi drivers say the hotel is full, has been burned down, or use any excuse.

She was right, and the taxi driver said all of these things, trying to persuade us to go to a hotel of his choice. We said we had to go to that hotel because we'd left a message for a friend to join us there. We were given the third degree about who the friend was, where he was coming from, what flight he was arriving on. When the taxi driver couldn't make us change our mind he stopped to pick up someone else, who then started the persuasion technique/third degree all over again. Next they wanted to phone the hotel and check us in themselves so they could get commission. Then they said they couldn't find the hotel. It was such hard work that in the end I said I was very tired, I just needed to get to the hotel to sleep, and if they couldn't find the hotel we had booked we would find another taxi. They gave up trying to persuade us to go to another hotel and took us to the one we had booked. Our hotel room was very pleasant but, despite the fact that the hotel was classified as 4 star, the stairs and corridors were very shabby, and the lift wasn't working. When we reached our floor we noticed that the doors to the lift were open; however, the lift wasn't there – only a gaping hole down to the basement three floors below!

Here's a typical entry from a guide book. '*Delhi is daunting for most new arrivals to the city and India. Exhausted from a long journey, most people find the harrassing of the beggars and touts too much, especially as they're also trying to manoeuvre past cows and rickshaws and deal with obnoxious smells, insufferable noise and pollution at the same time….Many decide that Delhi (and therefore India) is just too much and book the next flight home.*'

This is how we felt – Delhi, with its population of 17 million, was just too vast and too crowded. We didn't like at all. It was just so much hassle. We know there are poor people and this can be very distressing, but they wouldn't leave us alone which was horrible. If our taxi stopped in traffic, the beggars (often children) were in the midst of the horrendous traffic tapping at the window or waving the stumps of their arms (with most of the arm missing) through the glass. All we could do was wait for the taxi to move on. If we were on the pavement they tapped us on the shoulder and put their hand out for money. If we said 'No, sorry,' and continued to talk they continued to tap our arms and talk non-stop (sometimes in Hindi, sometimes in English). If we walked away they followed, virtually tripping us up. None of them took 'no' for an answer, so the harassing we had encountered in Istanbul was absolutely nothing compared with Delhi. If we gave anyone money, we were immediately surrounded by a dozen others with their hands out, so it was a 'no win' situation.

We noticed that, despite the cold nights in Delhi, whole families slept on the pavement, the only privacy for them being a sheet draped from a fence to form a tent-like structure. There were roads where we didn't like to walk at night because the pavements were covered on both sides with these sleeping families.

They didn't even have anything under them to protect them from the cold pavement. Women breast-fed their babies sitting on the pavement, and half-naked children played in the gutter despite the busy roads. We wondered what happened to these poor people when it rained. We just wanted to move on, away from the city.

We then made a big mistake and went into a travel agent/tourist information office. We asked about plane tickets to Mumbai or Goa, and were amazed that the price was almost as much as the Istanbul to Delhi flight. We were told that internal flights were very expensive. We didn't check, but with hindsight we suspect that he was lying. A train to Goa took 38 hours, which meant that we would have been travelling over Christmas day, and we didn't want to do that. So he made a suggestion, which we thought about and decided to accept – it was expensive, but we decided it would be our Christmas treat. We booked a car and driver to take us to Jaipur in Rajasthan to see the sights, and after that we would travel to Agra in Uttar Pradesh to see the Taj Mahal on Christmas day. From Agra we would catch a train to Goa arriving in time for the new year. Delhi, Jaipur and Agra are approximately 140 miles apart in a triangle shape and are known as 'The Golden Triangle'. The travel agent had asked where we were staying, so knew approximately how much we were paying for a hotel. He showed us brochures, and we chose expensive hotels for India (2,200 rupees each) and paid over £200 in cash for the whole trip, which is a fortune in India. We did have some concerns about whether we had done the right thing, but the agent delivered our train tickets (from Agra to Goa) to us that evening, and our driver turned up the next morning.

With our bikes strapped to the top of our driver's car we set off for Jaipur, 5 or 6 hours away. We set off through the chaotic traffic of Delhi – horns were continually sounding, cars swerving and slamming on brakes and rushing at people or bicycles. On the outskirts of Delhi there were people everywhere with overloaded bikes, rickshaws and motor scooters. Camels pulling long trailers added to the chaos, and cows wandered unconcernedly into the traffic to reach the lush plants on the central reservation. Whole families with babies were camped at the sides of the road, and someone was sleeping on a narrow wall. The roundabouts were pretty, but were protected from cows with fences.

As we left Delhi the land was flat and divided into fields which looked green and fertile. Corn, mustard and rape were growing, and occasionally there were kilns with tall chimneys where bricks were being made from the clay soil. We passed a woman carrying hay in a fabric parcel tied with string. The package was on the woman's head and was so enormous that it stuck out about 3 feet on either side and looked like a haystack on top of her head. A herd of sheep passed on the wrong side of the dual carriageway, causing chaos and confusion, and motor scooters also went the wrong way. Dozens of camels went past pulling large loads on trailers. Women were working in the field in their beautiful saris; a group of boys played cricket on a patch of bare earth, using a piece of wood for a bat; two people were carrying piles of leafy branches on their heads that were so large that they looked like they had masses of shaggy green hair.

We passed low brick scruffy buildings interspersed with houses made of scrap pieces of wood, polythene and corrugated iron. Sheep, goats, camels, dogs, monkeys and pigs roamed freely, beside and on the road. Cars passed with people hanging on the outside of every door as well as inside. A full bus passed with six people sitting on the roof rack. Outside the cafés we passed there were not only chairs set out but also beds without mattresses. People sat cross-legged on the springs, chatting. Tractors pulled trailers so loaded with hay that it hung down on either side almost to the ground.

It became hillier as we approached Jaipur. The traffic was even more chaotic than in Delhi. There were large numbers of elephants in the midst of the traffic, their ears colourfully painted, and camels pulled trailers looking disdainfully down their noses at everyone. Thousands of tiny scooter taxis (designed for two people but usually carrying many more) dashed between other vehicles, and people riding cycle rickshaws and bicycles took their lives into their hands as they stood on the pedals to try to manoeuvre their way through the traffic. Pedestrians dashed between vehicles with no apparent regard for safety; a man walked across the road between the vehicles carrying a long home-made bamboo ladder. Cows ambled slowly along in the middle of the road secure in the knowledge that, because they were sacred, no vehicle would dare to bump them. Several pigs and dogs ran amok as horns sounded at them, and a small puppy, looking lost, ran along the centre of the road, dashing between the vehicles. Horns blared, people shouted, elephants trumpeted, camels spat and traffic was almost at a standstill.

Our worst fears were confirmed when we arrived at the hotel where we had been promised that a reservation had been made. It was full and they had no reservation for us. The next hotel we were taken to was not very pleasant, and it was unlikely that a room there would have cost 2,200 rupees. Various phone calls were made to the travel agent, but it was obvious we were not in a good bargaining position, as we were not going to return to Delhi. We liked our driver and suspected that he was not in on the scam because he had been inconvenienced himself by the change of plans, so we knew we just had to make the most of it.

At long last we managed to buy the anti-malarial tablets that we needed, and sufficient tablets for a 4 month period cost us only £12, less than the cost of anti-malarial tablets bought in England for a two week holiday. We had been getting paranoid every time we saw a mosquito, knowing that we weren't protected, so that was now one worry off our minds.

Jaipur is the capital of Rajasthan and is known as the Pink City because it was built of pink stucco to resemble red sandstone. Pink is the colour of hospitality. We visited the palace where the Maharajah still lives. We were surrounded by girls in their beautiful saris and men in turbans, so it seemed extraordinary to suddenly hear Christmas songs being played. In a courtyard within the palace we could hear 'I'm dreaming of a white Christmas' and George Michael's 'Last Christmas'. Beside an enormous Christmas tree stood a black midget dressed as Father Christmas! Three Indian teenage girls dressed in saris passed us, one of them saying indignantly, 'But Santa isn't black!'

We had been impressed with the beautiful rugs in Turkey, but they paled into insignificance alongside the ones in that palace. The most magnificent Kashmir carpets dating back to 1600 were on show, and the two biggest carpets in the world, nearly 400 years old, were also on view. In a glass case were unbelievably detailed tiny pictures with fine and delicate details that had been painted with one eye-lash from a camel, and intricate writing could be seen with a magnifying glass on a single grain of rice. In the grounds a man was walking with bare feet and wearing only a loin cloth. He was covered with ashes, and his hair and beard were matted, as though they hadn't been washed or combed for years.

We went on to see the Amber Fort, made of white marble and red sandstone. Elephants slowly walked up the hill carrying tourists to the fort, and we marvelled at the intricate carvings and the exquisite paintings on the walls, and the beautiful carved ivory shutters that covered the open windows.

The day we left Jaipur I phoned my mother. It was Christmas Eve and her 84th birthday, and she was thrilled to hear from us. She was experiencing our journey second-hand, receiving the postcards that we sent every week, and enjoying showing all her visitors the line of cards on her mantelpiece.

Once again in the car we passed tumbledown shacks on either side of the road, where donkeys, camels, dogs, pigs, chickens, cows and bulls rummaged in the rubbish dumps trying to find food, and men sat around fires sleeping while women carried pots and heavy loads on their heads. The camels had massive feet and they plodded slowly along the road pulling their trailers. One driver was asleep on top of his enormous load, while the camel continued in a straight line.

The fields became greener, and in one very green field we saw a line of women working, the amazingly vivid colours of their saris dazzlingly bright in the sun – cerise, shocking pink, royal blue, turquoise, electric blue, luminous orange (the most popular), lime green, sharp lemon, scarlet, crimson, emerald and golden yellow – a kaleidoscope of colours. Not for the Indian women the soft pale colours that suit the pale western colouring – they looked magnificent with their black plaited hair and dark skin in these wonderful colours. We passed an area where men chipped away at marble and stone, and the road was lined with beautifully-carved statues. Camel dung was stacked everywhere, having been flattened into plate-shaped discs and left to dry, ready to use as fuel.

The room in the hotel that had been booked for us in Agra was obviously not a 2,200 rupee one, but when we enquired the price of the room from the hotel staff they all clammed up and refused to give us a price. Clearly they were used to ripping off tourists. We bought ourselves a guide book, and we found a warning about travel agents in Delhi dedicated to ripping off tourists – apparently hundreds of complaints are received by the guide books every year! We should have bought the book before India, but we had so far not used a travel guide on our trip because we had concerns about the extra weight. Now it seemed to be a well worth addition to our heavily laden bikes.

The Taj Mahal is probably the most famous building in the world, and was built by the Mughal emperor Shah Jahan, who was grief-stricken when his third wife, Mumtaz Mahal, died during the birth of their 14th child. Construction of the mausoleum in memory of his wife began soon after her death in 1631. A work force of 20,000 skilled craftsmen from Asia and Europe completed the mausoleum in 1648, and the surrounding buildings and gardens were finished five years later. Over 1,000 elephants were used to transport the building materials during construction.

On Christmas Day we woke early and walked to the Taj Mahal, having been told that sunrise was the best time to see it. It was dark and very foggy and the street lights weren't working, so it was quite spooky as we walked through the trees trying to find our way, especially when monkeys jumped out in front of us. We experienced our first racial discrimination when we looked at the board with the prices. Warren and I and a few other foreigners had to pay 750 rupees (£10) each, but the sign clearly said that for Indians the price was only 10 rupees! A handful of us stood there, cameras at the ready, waiting for the sun to rise behind the magnificent building – we had been told that it would be a magical moment.

The sun didn't rise behind the Taj Mahal that day. We saw a faint outline of the building as the darkness began to lift before the fog began to enshroud it completely, and we watched the Taj Mahal disappear from the bottom up in the fog. We took photos quickly before the fog wholly enveloped the famous outline, and afterwards all we could do was walk around and inside the building to look at the detail of the marble up close. It was breath-taking in its beauty, and we stroked the cold translucent marble and marvelled that the Emperor had loved his wife so much that he had created this awesome mausoleum in her memory. Every part of the polished white marble walls is inlaid with coloured marble, jasper and jade; the work is extremely detailed with stylised delicate vines, flowers and fruits. In the inner chamber the white marble is inlaid with precious and semi-precious gemstones, such as sapphire, carnelian, turquoise, lapis lazuli and crystal – in all 28 different types of precious and semi-precious stones were gathered from many parts of the world to adorn this memorial to Mumtaz Mahal.

Everyone had to take off their shoes to enter the mausoleum, and the icy cold marble on our bare feet made us shiver. It was still very cold two hours later; the fog was still thick and we were shivering, so we returned to our hotel. There we were told that the best view of the Taj Mahal was from the hotel roof, so later in the afternoon we were able to see the sun shining on the white marble of the Taj Mahal, and we took some lovely photographs using the telescopic lens on our camera.

We were tired after our early start to visit the Taj Mahal, so went to have a rest in our room. When we woke later we realised that Sharma, our driver, might be wondering where we were. We dressed quickly and hurried to the hotel car park, but neither Sharma nor the car were at the hotel, and none of the staff could tell us where he was. We spent an anxious hour wondering if he had done a runner with our bicycles locked onto the roof of his car, but he eventually returned and suggested that he take us early to the station where we would catch the train to Goa.

We weren't looking forward to the 38 hour journey on the train, and we sat for several hours on the platform with our hearts sinking lower and lower. I told Warren that I was finding India depressing, despite having seen some wonderful things, and I didn't know how I'd be able to handle the travelling if it continued to be the same throughout India. Warren told me that he felt the same, and had written it in his diary the day before. He had also spent the last four days wondering if our bikes would be there in the mornings or when we came out of the palaces or forts that we had visited. We were thinking of cutting our trip in India short, and it was a shame when we had looked forward to India so much. We hoped things would get better.

It was noisy and dirty on the platform, and there were still beggars tapping our shoulders. As we sat on the platform watching, we found the sights around us unbelievable. There was 1st class, 2nd class, 3rd class and goodness knows what class, but the people in the bottom class of carriage were herded in like cattle – the trains looked like the ones taking the Jews to Auschwitz! As the trains drove out of the station, the doors were still open with people sitting in the doorways, and there were people hanging out of the train still trying to get on. We even saw one of these people climb up over the top of people's shoulders to get in! Hordes of people crossed the lines, jumping down from the platform and climbing up the other side, rather than take the longer but safer way over the bridge. One of them was a badly crippled man, who struggled to walk barefooted with his crutch, his legs giving way badly beneath him with every step, so that with every step his knees touched the ground. Because he was so slow he was forced to stop as a train pulled into the station in front of him, and he then made his way the length of a coach struggling over the rough chunks of stone, his feet and stick constantly slipping. He managed to drag himself up the ladder to the open door of the train. At the top he was unable for several minutes to get in, because the doorway was blocked with people sitting on the floor, but he ended up actually clambering over the top of them before disappearing from view. At no time did anyone try to help him.

However, there were also sights that were wonderful to see, such as the six Indian women who walked past in a line through the crowds sitting cross-legged on the platform. They were wearing vivid coloured saris, and each was carrying a massive bundle on their head wrapped in a large length of fabric which was tied in a knot on the top. Unfortunately I couldn't get my camera out quickly enough to take a photo, but it is a colourful memory that I will always remember. Monkeys played on the motor scooters that were standing on the platform, and jumped up and down on the boxes and packages that were stacked so high that they looked in danger of toppling. Dogs slept on the packages despite the constant noise.

The first problem we had encountered on showing our tickets was that our bikes hadn't been booked onto the train – the agent had promised to do this for us but had conned us once again. We had therefore been advised to pay the porters to take our bikes onto the train, otherwise the bikes would have to follow 3 days later. We were obviously not prepared to allow this. The train was an hour late, and there was pandemonium as people pushed and shoved their way in front of us to try to get onto the train. The noise was appalling, though it all quietened down in our carriage once the train was under way, and our fellow travellers, all Indian, were very nice. An Indian woman, no bigger than a child, slept between the two toilets. I had to step across her head to get into the toilet, and she was fast asleep with nothing between her and the cold metal floor except the clothes she was wrapped in. When I later went again to the toilet (simply a large hole in the floor!), she appeared to have left, leaving only her clothes, a bundle of rags, on the floor by the toilet. Closer inspection revealed that she was still inside the clothes, her head completely covered. It seemed impossible that an adult human being could be inside this pathetic bundle of rags, and in such a horrible position by the toilets, next to the moving part of the floor where the two carriages joined. The two carriage doors were wide open, so it must have been very cold, and I also thought it was incredibly dangerous and wondered how many Indian people fall out of trains?

When a ticket inspector arrived he told us that we only had one bed booked, and that we needed to pay 2,300 rupees (over £30 pounds and the price of a good Indian bike!) to keep our bikes in the compartment. We cursed the travel agent who had supplied the tickets, and decided we would have to pay without argument when the ticket collector returned, but strangely he never came back, and no-one else asked us for the money. We managed to acquire the upper bunk so we had a bed each, and no-one ever told us to move. It was very cold that first night in the train, and we ended up having to open up our bags to get our sleeping bags out. The carriage seats folded down into beds, converting the carriage into a dormitory. The lights dimmed and everyone prepared to sleep, but we noticed that most people had chained their bags to solid objects or to themselves, which made us very nervous about our numerous belongings. We spent the journey suffering awful headaches, and we began to wonder why we had put ourselves through such a trauma when we could be living comfortable lives at home!

In the midst of all our suffering, there were glimmers of hope. We had been concerned what food would be available, so had bought some strange looking sandwiches at Delhi station. However, a railway employee regularly came round asking if we wanted to order food. We ordered a vegetable thali each, and when the meal arrived we were amazed to be handed a tray of different curries, with a chappati and a sealed container of water – the cost of this delicious meal was 36 rupees, less than 50p. As the train arrived at each station, sellers on the platform rushed to the train the second it stopped to provide tea and food to the passengers, and ran alongside the moving train as it set off again, pushing a paper cup of tea through the bars at the window in exchange for a few rupees.

It was lucky that Warren decided to ask the last ticket collector what time the train arrived in Goa, because by now we had been travelling for well over 30 hours. The train was called the Goa Express, which was a misnomer considering the train took a total of 38 hours to travel the 2,000 kilometres! However, we were now told that our carriage would be de-linked from the rest of the train in the next hour as it wasn't going to Goa, but its final stop would be in another state before Goa. Although the word 'Goa' was written on our tickets, they were apparently for a station 120 miles east of Goa's border – how we wished we could have gone back to Delhi just to see that agent again!

The ticket inspector said we needed to move to the front part of the train if we wanted to go to Goa, so we had to move all of our gear (10 cycle panniers, 2 bikes, and a few other bags that we strap on the back of the bikes) to another compartment. We had to walk backwards and forwards through 3 carriages to do this, and the ticket inspector stopped at the end of a compartment near the toilets, where he requested two Indian men to get out of their beds so that they could be given to us. Our previous compartment had been fine, but here the smell of urine was overpowering, despite the fact that the nearby doors remained open. It was at this point that we were told that we had to pay excess fare to Goa. This was the final straw, but we had no choice but to pay it – fortunately the excess was less than £3, but we were so annoyed to think that we had been thoroughly conned and could do nothing about it.

I sat reading the travel guide as we approached Goa, and noticed that the last but one stop in Goa, Margao, was only 8 miles from a beach. We decided that we would get off at Margao, but several Indians tried to dissuade us, as there was only a three minute stop at that station. However, we were determined now that the end of the 38 hour journey was in sight. It was a panic trying to get everything out of the train in the three minutes that the train stopped, and some western travellers helped us by throwing our last bags out to us as the train moved out of the station again. Suddenly the train had gone and we were stood on the platform surrounded by our bags and bikes. We put the bags on the bikes and set off towards Colva Beach in South Goa, cycling for the first time for nearly three weeks. It was warm now, much warmer than it had been in northern India. We could see no road signs, so we followed our compass west to reach the coast. Although it was hot, and we were very tired, smelly and dirty from the long train ride, the cycle ride was wonderfully therapeutic. We hadn't cycled for so long and we felt at home again, now we were on our bikes. There were palm trees everywhere which gave us shade, and our headaches began to ease and we felt much happier – what bliss after the chaos of Delhi, Jaipur and Agra! As we cycled into Colva Beach we passed a small Punjabi restaurant, and decided to stop for breakfast. After a superb Indian breakfast of puri bhaji with lassi, a yogurt drink, we knew that we were going to enjoy it there. (A puri is a deep-fried flat bread which has been rolled out into small circles of dough. When fried in hot oil the puri puffs up with air like a small balloon. Puris are commonly served as a breakfast or lunch dish in many parts of India. Served with the puris is a bhaji, a fairly dry mild potato curry, which is also often served with a spicy pickle on the side. To eat this meal, pieces of puri are torn off and are used like a spoon to scoop up the bhaji and pickle.)

Christmas and New Year are the peak season in Goa and the most expensive and busiest period, so we were concerned whether we would find accommodation. The first hotel we approached was full, but the owner phoned someone else and led us by motor scooter to our new accommodation, which was run by Moira, a Scotswoman from Aberdeen.

The room was basic but very pleasant, with a giant bed, table and chairs, and a separate private shower room. There were mosquito nets at the window, an enormous fan kept the room cool, and we had a balcony with table and chairs in the shade. It was not a hotel, but four cottages in a garden set behind the shops in the main street. It was convenient for everything, but was pleasantly quiet. There were more tables and chairs under the trees, and for 300 rupees a night (£4) we felt we had a bargain, and suddenly we could see that we might be able to live within our budget for the first time since we started the trip. We had a rest, sorted out a pile of washing to give to Lolita, the young Indian girl who worked for Moira, and set off to explore Colva Beach. Warren kissed me and told me he loved me – we both suddenly felt human again after several stressful days. We knew now we were going to enjoy India after all ...

Moira recommended one restaurant for steaks which she thought were better than Aberdeen Angus, and she was right – the beef was from a bullock, not the sacred cow, and we enjoyed these tender steaks stuffed with mussels or with peppered sauce if we decided we wanted a western meal for a change. However, we continued to prefer the wonderful Indian food, even at breakfast time. As is usual for coastal resorts, fish was always available in Goa, and swordfish, tuna, giant prawns, kingfish and any other fish caught that day were displayed outside the restaurants. Being a former Portuguese colony, Goa makes its own wine, a cross between red wine and port selling for less than £1 a bottle in the restaurants. Wine is generally not readily available in other Indian states, but the Indian beer is good.

I went to one of the many internet cafés to e-mail home, and was very pleased to find that for the first time since we had left England the keyboard was the same as in England – I could now type fast again.

Goa

A former Portuguese colony, Goa was renowned for many years as a place for travellers to 'hang out'. It has now become one of the most popular holiday destinations from UK, being more westernised than the rest of India, but with the guarantee of sun, sand and sea. Facing the warm Arabian Sea, Goa's palm-lined white sand beaches stretch for 75 miles. There are many old Christian churches and cathedrals built by the Portuguese, festivals to watch, markets to visit and wonderful local food.

I was floating on my back in the warm waters of the Arabian Sea, looking up at the blue sky dotted with tiny clouds and feeling small waves ripple under me. If I raised my head and looked towards the beach I could see the white sand and the palm trees beyond. I thought, 'This is what I had in mind when we first talked about cycling round the world!'

We had visited Goa in 1999 and enjoyed it, and now we found it very difficult to move on from Goa. We stayed more than two weeks in Colva Beach, and felt at times that we would end up like Moira, the Scottish lady who ran the cottages where we were staying. She had arrived in Goa 11 years earlier and had never gone back to Scotland apart from brief visits!

We had a wonderful New Year celebration – for £2 each we had bought tickets to a local restaurant. A long table was groaning under the weight of the buffet – pakoras and king prawns, samosas and poppadoms, freshly baked naans coated with melted butter, tandoori dishes including whole fish caught that day, chicken xacuti and vindaloo (both traditional Goan dishes), prawn curries, fish curries, delicious vegetable, lentil and rice dishes. We could eat as much as we wanted, and there was live music all night. There were as many Indians as Europeans celebrating, and we toasted in the new year together.

For those who have never been to Goa, the state is naturally divided into North Goa and South Goa by a river. There are lovely resorts in both, and although Goa is the smallest state in India it has 100 kilometres of continuous white sand. The beaches are dotted with the local fishing boats, so sometimes we rose early to watch the fishermen bringing in their catch on a morning.

Colva Beach is in south Goa; there are more Indian tourists than European, although there are plenty of English people around. Virtually everyone speaks English, so language isn't a problem. There are also many ex-patriots in Goa, and an extraordinary number of people who go to Goa for several months during the winter, which is the best time to be in Goa and definitely the best time to be away from England. Most ex-pats move away from Goa when the monsoons, which circle round India, reach Goa on 1st June. By moving to Chennai in east India (previously called Madras) or to somewhere like Greece or Portugal for a few months, the ex-pats can enjoy wonderful weather year round.

There was one ex-pat who we often saw in our breakfast restaurant. Each morning he bought his liquid breakfast − a tumbler full of neat brandy one day, two tumblers full of brandy the next. He told us in a slurred voice that he was celebrating his mother's birthday that day, and said that he hoped she was watching him from 'up there' as he pointed to the sky. The Indian waiters stood in a group fascinated to watch him leaving the restaurant. He walked very slowly up the path as he left, each foot carefully testing the ground in front of him before he put his weight on it, and he kept his arms outstretched to balance himself.

Another Englishman who we met had just spent the last three weeks of his three month holiday in Goa having daily visits to the dentist − not a perfect way to spend a holiday, perhaps! His teeth had been crowned and capped and bridges had been put in, and when we met him his treatment was almost finished. He certainly had a mouth full of beautiful teeth, but because of the recent treatment he was unable to open his mouth fully to show us. His treatment, which would cost thousands of pounds in England, had cost him only £300, so many English people go to Goa for the excellent medical, optical or dental treatment, paying a fraction of the cost in England.

Medication and tablets are also very cheap in India. When Warren went into a chemist in Goa, the chemist lowered his voice and leaned across the counter.

'Would you be interested in some Viagra, sir?' he asked Warren.

Warren shook his head in surprise, but it appears that some people buy such things to sell at a profit when they get back to England!

We met a woman from Lancashire who had been visiting Goa for several months each winter since her husband had died. At Mumbai airport she was trying to find a taxi to take her to her hotel. She was besieged by Indians fighting to take her suitcases (to get a tip for carrying them), but at last she got into a taxi. Instead of taking her to the hotel she had named, the taxi driver stopped and began to carry her cases into an awful place which she described as 'like a brothel'. He had probably never met such a forceful lady before – she grabbed him by the collar and shouted at him to take her to a smart hotel she could see lit up in the distance. When he arrived there she dragged him into the reception and told the staff what he'd done, and they promptly took him outside and beat him up!

We heard a story about an Englishman who was electrocuted and so badly burned that he had to stay in Goa several months to recover. We listened to the story with increasing sympathy, until we discovered that he had been 'caught short' on the way home from an evening of drinking, and had relieved himself against the side of a transformer, electrocuting himself!

As we walked along the beach in Colva, Warren and I were often approached by Indian families, or groups of young Indian people or couples, asking if they could have their photo taken with us. We found this terribly strange at first – it's a bit like being a famous film star – but I suppose it's not that different from us taking the photos of Indian people who we think look different and interesting. We were obviously a bit of a novelty in India. One young man approached me.

'What is your name?' he asked.

'Mary,' I replied.

His face lit up with excitement. 'I too am Christian,' was his response.

There were many Christian signs and names in Goa. There was the 'Infant Jesus Mini Supermarket'; notices on coaches, cars and taxis said 'Jesus protect our way', 'Jesus Christ' or 'Praise the Lord'; fishing boats were often called 'The Infant Jesus' or similar, and the local bus company was called 'Amchi Jesus Bus Travels Goa'! However, whilst Christianity seems to predominate in Goa, many other religions were evident as well. In restaurants pictures of Jesus often hung on the wall alongside shrines to Hindu gods.

We always went to the beach just before sunset, when the beach filled with Indian people, families, couples and children. We never saw Indian tourists on the beach at any other time. The sight of the colourful saris was amazing, but even more amazing was the fact that the girls and women went into the water fully clothed, even with their dupattas on (the long flowing scarf bit) and sometimes even with their leather sandals on. They didn't mind getting wet and submerging completely, their long black plaits swinging heavily behind them. The women stayed together playing and splashing and taking photos of each other, even taking their cameras and video cameras into the water, so we wondered how the photos turned out! We took beautiful photos of women in saris walking on the wet sand, the colours of their saris reflecting in the water. The men were not as strict when it came to undressing. They stripped to their underwear to go into the water, and we thought it strange that they were happy to be seen in their wet y-fronts and vests, especially as it was clear that very few Indians are able to swim,

The Indian people were always very friendly – they always said 'good morning' or 'hello' or 'goodnight' as we passed, or if it was obvious we were going back to our cottage for the night they called out 'good dreams', which I thought was rather nice. They didn't pressurise us to buy from their stalls in the unpleasant way that the people did in the cities.

For me, the Indian women wearing their beautiful saris epitomise India. The Indian women have such superb posture, probably because they carry heavy weights such as pots of water or logs for firewood on their heads. They look beautiful in the wonderful clashing colours of their saris. However, although very beautiful garments, they also seem very impractical garments in which to work, especially as average saris are 5 to 6 yards long, and can be up to 9 yards long. Women wear them doing the washing, cleaning and cooking, working in the fields or even wearing them as they labour on the roads, carrying the stones in large pans on their heads. They even run up ladders in their saris carrying piles of bricks on their heads to build houses. It was seldom that we saw men doing labouring – this is work for women in India.

However, saris are very dangerous on bikes, motorbikes and scooters. I saw one lady trying to disentangle her dupatta from the cog of her bicycle, which had floated into the chain and was wrapped around the wheel. Women always sat side-saddle on the backs of scooters or pushbikes, the skirts of their saris and their dupattas flying out behind them. Moira told us a very sad story of a young couple who, the day after they were married, went out on his Royal Enfield motorbike. Her sari caught in the wheel, causing an accident. She was killed instantly and he had to have his leg amputated as a result of the accident.

On to a less sad story – Lolita was a very sweet Indian girl who worked at the cottages where we were staying, but she didn't speak very good English. One day I asked her for some toilet paper for our bathroom, but she didn't understand. I found myself doing the actions before I realised how undignified I must look, but still she didn't understand. This was probably because Indians don't use toilet paper – they use their left hand, and always have a jug sitting on the floor of the toilet under a tap. Whilst toilet paper is readily available in Goa, it is only for the tourists, so we had to make sure that we stocked up before we left Goa, just in case!

Connected to this last paragraph, I watched a group of young Indian men at a restaurant one evening, and it was very obvious that they were only allowed to use their right hand for eating. With their left hands in their lap, it looked very awkward as they tore naans with one hand and used that piece of naan in the right hand only to scoop up the curry. I expect the Indians think we are disgustingly dirty to use both hands during eating!

There was another incident in a restaurant that I found interesting. A couple came into the restaurant, and she was wearing a black burqa, the Muslim garment that exposes only the hands and has slits for the eyes. I was fascinated to see how she would eat – would she have a straw that went up under the fabric? Would she raise the fabric to put a fork to her mouth? I was relieved to see that once the food arrived she removed the lower part of the veil to expose a very pretty face with gold ear-rings, so she was able to eat normally.

Whilst we know that many Indians speak some English, it did seem strange to hear Indians sometimes conversing together in shops in English. We realised that this was because there are so many Indian languages, but English is the common language. As well as Hindi, Bengali, Gujariti, Kashmiri, Punjabi, Tamil and Urdu, there are many other recognised official languages, and 18 different languages are written on every banknote. English is the official administrative language, although Hindi (spoken by 20% of the population) is the official language of the Indian Government.

It was strange to be cycling on the left side of the road again after so many months in Europe. On our rides we saw corn spread out on woven raffia mats drying in the sun, with women shuffling through it with their bare feet to turn it. We saw the fields being ploughed by bullocks pulling wooden ploughs, and women in their saris working in the vivid green paddy fields. On the side of the road thousands of small fish were laid out on nets to dry; these would be made into fertiliser. Some fish is dried for human consumption, and this type of fish could be seen in a special section of the fish market. Dried fish has an awful smell, unlike fresh fish, and it reminded me of when I once decided to try Bombay Duck in an Indian restaurant in England. (No, I don't know why Indian dried fish is called Bombay Duck!) The waiter returned to the table to tell me that the Indian restaurants in England were no longer able to obtain it, because the Health and Safety people had banned the import of it from India because of the unhygienic way in which it was prepared. If it was the same fish we saw at the side of the road drying, I can understand why . . .

We cycled one day to Margao to visit the fish market – baby hammerhead sharks were laid on marble slabs, alongside the most enormous prawns and the biggest mussels I had ever seen in pretty turquoise or jade-edged shells. The women trying to sell their wares constantly called us over, hoping that we might buy some of their wares. Their buckets were full of small fish, which were bought by the locals to make fish curry. On the marble stalls were swordfish, tuna, red snapper, kingfish, pomfret, sea bass, salmon, mackerel, lobster, calamari and crab. In an empty marble trough two men were fast asleep, and outside the new market building cows, chickens, dogs and cats foraged in the rubbish for food to eat. Buzzards were circling in the sky above and occasionally swooped down towards the rubbish heaps, making the animals scatter in all directions. The temperature was well over 30°C, so the smell was quite overpowering.

As we cycled back to Colva beach we stopped to buy a coconut from a stall in the shade of some palm trees. While her husband slept in the dirt beside the coconuts, the woman deftly swung a machete and sliced the top from one of the green coconuts. She passed the coconut to me with a straw, and I began to drink the delicious, refreshing, mildly coconut-flavoured liquid while she chopped a second coconut for Warren. When we had finished, she chopped the coconut fully open, and in seconds had made a spoon from a small section of the shell. She handed this to me, and indicated that I should eat the jelly-like coconut inside, which was delicious! This gel is the unripe coconut meat, and is also delicious on fruit salads instead of cream. If the coconut is left on the tree to ripen there is less liquid, and the ripe coconuts are cut in half and left to dry in the sun for one day. The shells are then separated from the nut and the coconut is left to dry for two more days, by which time the coconut is then ready to grate for curries or desserts, and is sold in the markets for about 20 rupees per kilogramme.

The small Punjabi restaurant where we had enjoyed our first breakfast had become our regular for breakfasts. I found it quite amusing one day, as we ate puri bhaji and aloo paratha (a pancake stuffed with mild potato curry), that an Indian gentleman opposite us was having porridge and fried egg on toast coated with tomato ketchup for his breakfast. We always sat for ages at our table outside the restaurant watching the world go by. A wooden cart with colourful wooden wheels pulled by two oxen with painted horns was driven past by its owner. A temple elephant was led past by its trainer and encouraged to do simple tricks. If a tourist so much as lifted his or her camera, the trainer was instantly by their side demanding 50 rupees, a phenomenal amount by Indian standards. Herds of cows wandered by, blocking the traffic. Pigs and chickens snuffled in the rubbish thrown on the verges, and children also sorted through the rubbish hoping to find something useful that they could sell. In the garden of the house next door, an Indian lady ran her own laundry. There was the constant thud as she thrashed the washing onto a solid concrete block in the middle of her garden, and her washing lines were always full of immaculately clean bed linen.

On a street corner there was often a cart carrying a large heavy machine. This was a sugar cane juice extractor. The raw sugar cane was pushed through heavy rollers about 10 times until all the juice was extracted. Lime or lemon juice was added to counteract the very sweet taste, and a tumbler full was sold for 5 rupees (about 6p). The bright green liquid had a strange, though not unpleasant, 'green' taste which was quite refreshing.

As we cycled, Indians shouted out 'nice bikes' as we passed. They constantly asked us how much the bikes were worth, but as our bikes had cost more than 60 times the price of the most expensive bike available in India, we didn't feel we could tell them. We were also often approached on the beach and asked how much our cameras had cost. Such outspoken curiosity concerned us and made us grip the camera rather tightly; we usually said we'd just borrowed it, it wasn't ours, and we didn't know how much it had cost. We found throughout Asia that personal questions that would have been considered rude in England were quite normal.

Most Indians have bicycles, but there are only three styles of bikes available in India. The most common is the Hero bicycle, a traditional Indian 'sit up and beg' 1940s style of bike, made of heavy steel and with no gears. The manufacturers, Hero Cycles of Punjab are in fact the world's largest manufacturer of bicycles, and in 2006 the Hero Group celebrated its Golden Jubilee year and announced sales of over 15 million motorcycles and over 100 million bicycles. The second type of bicycle available in India is a mountain bike made of heavy steel with no gears, but finally there is the 'crème de la crème' heavy mountain bike with five gears. We never saw an Indian riding such a bike – these mountain bikes appeared to be available only on hire to tourists. The cheapest of the cheap bicycles available in England would be considered wonderful compared to anything available in India. Bicycles came in one standard colour – brown. They had brown handlebars, brown mudguards, brown wheel rims and spokes and brown chain – everything brown from rust and dust! The bicycles would clunk and grind and click along the road, the Indians obviously not realising that it's far easier to ride a bike that has been well-maintained. They rang their bells constantly as they cycled, and as we passed they would smile and say 'Good morning, madam, Good morning, sir.' There was seldom one person on a bike, but if there was no passenger on the back or on the crossbar, there would certainly be a mountain of baggage in front and behind them.

India is a strange mixture of old and new. As we cycled, we passed a bullock cart driven by a man in a lungi (a sort of sarong) wrapped round his waist. The cart overtook men and women who were laboriously digging ditches with hand-made picks and shovels, and the women were carrying away the dirt and stones in large containers on their heads. Massive wooden rolls full of fibre optic cables stood to one side of the road ready to be laid in these ditches. [In July 2008, The Guardian reported that BT planned to spend £1.5bn to install fibre optic cables in the UK, which would be capable of much faster speeds for the internet service providers than the current copper-based phone lines. This was 5 years after we saw the same cables being installed in India!]

Walking home on the night of 5th and 6th January we noticed that it was a new moon – were any of our friends looking at the new moon back home, we wondered? The extraordinary thing was that it wasn't facing to the right or to the left, as we see it in England, but looked exactly like a big smile. We had noticed that the constellations were difficult to recognise, because they're upside down or on their sides compared to their positions in England, and when there was a full moon, we noticed that the man in the moon was on his side!

We loved to wander along the beach, stopping at one of our favourite bars for a banana or pineapple lassi, a delicious drink made from yogurt (known as curd in India) blended with fresh fruit. On the beach was an area of thatched huts where the local fishermen lived. The women sat outside, baking and sewing, while their children played in the sand. We assumed that in the monsoon season the huts would be demolished by the rain and the fierce waves, so that the huts were rebuilt every year, but we didn't know where the locals moved to during that time.

We decided one day to take the bus to the nearby town, but when the bus arrived it was completely full. Despite this dozens more locals pushed their way onto the bus, but we decided to wait for the next one. Another bus soon arrived, nearly empty, and we congratulated ourselves on our decision as we found ourselves two seats next to the exit.

However, at each of the next bus stops there appeared to be a crowd waiting to embark, and it was only a few minutes before every seat was full and there were standing passengers squashed together like sardines in a tin. Talking of sardines, the lady who stood alongside Warren was holding onto the rail in front of Warren's face. Hanging from her hand was a clear plastic bag full of small fish, their dead eyes hypnotising Warren as the bag swung to and fro with the movement of the bus.

The bus driver sped along the road, his hand permanently on the horn as he overtook everything ahead of him. If he needed to stop at a bus stop he allowed only a few seconds for passengers to disembark or for new passengers to get onto the bus before speeding off again without any signals.

The exit door in front of us was wide open, and this allowed at least six more passengers to stand on the steps, some of them hanging out of the bus. Suddenly there was a warning shout from the driver, and the bus conductor, who stood on the bottom step, began to push and shove everyone further into the over-crowded bus. Once there was space he just managed to push the door shut before we passed a stationary police car. The second we had passed, the door was opened once more, so that everyone could breathe again and hang back out of the doorway. As we approached a river, we noticed that the driver threw a garland of flowers through his open window into the water as an offering to the gods.

We were relieved when we arrived at the bus station, and we remained seated while everyone pushed and shoved to leave the bus — not for the Indians the British tradition of queuing or waiting their turn! We counted the number of passengers as they passed through the exit, and were amazed when we counted 76 passengers, even though there were only 23 seats!

Before we left Colva Beach we bought clothes which we considered suitable for India. Whilst tourists could wear shorts or strappy vests or dresses in Colva Beach, I knew that once we reached areas not frequented by tourists I would need to cover up my arms and legs more. However, we never threw away anything if we could think of a use for it. An old pair of stretchy trousers was discarded, but a strip of leg made a cover to protect our guide book while it was in the pannier bag, and the zipped pockets were cut out to form small zipped soft protective bags. The excess fabric from a pair of Indian trousers bought and shortened into three-quarter length for cycling was kept for cleaning the bicycle chains.

Eventually the time came for us to leave Goa, and we left early in the morning and took a small road not shown on our map. We passed shops still shuttered up, but they had colourful hand-painted red shutters with a picture of a well-known brand of chocolate, suggesting that we 'take a break'. We took a ferry across a river, wading through the shallow water carrying our bikes to the small boat, and after that the scenery became very jungle-like. We passed a stunning temple set amongst massive palm trees. The hills were very steep and it was incredibly hot. Indian roads do not have many signposts, and Indian maps are notoriously inaccurate, so at one stage when the road divided we asked an Indian gentleman where we were and which road we needed to take.

'This is Iliaria,' he said with pride in his voice.

'Iliaria?' we repeated, looking at the map to see where it was.

'Yes,' he said. 'Very Iliaria.'

'Oh,' we said, suddenly understanding what he meant. 'Yes, it is a very hilly area.'

Monkeys swung through the trees, calling 'oo, oo, oo' as they played and ran across the road in front of us. There were palmolive trees laden with vast bunches of golden palm olives alongside a perfect green cricket pitch where a game was in progress. It looked very British with the pavilion in the background. We reached the top of the hills and there was a wonderful view, though hazy, of a crescent of beach in the distance and mountains beyond. We cycled on along roads shaded by tall palms, past temples, and across bridges where we could see the women below washing clothes in the river and thrashing the wet clothes against the boulders. We passed a lorry, the driver lying underneath on a blanket, resting in the shade. Motorbikes slowed down and drove alongside us to ask us where we were from.

We stayed in a small town where we were clearly the only westerners. We had noticed in northern India, and were now reminded again that Indians like to spit, especially early in the mornings. Through the walls between bedrooms we could hear the horrible sound that they made in their throats before they spat, and every café had a washbasin in the corner. We learnt not to sit near the washbasin, because the Indians liked to spit in it as well as wash their hands, and it definitely put us off our food. Even women spat in the street and we wondered why spitting is so prevalent in eastern countries – we had already noticed it in Turkey. We had also noticed many pretty Karnatakan women of lower caste had spoilt their looks because their teeth were stained dark red. They looked as if they'd been in a fight and their gums were bleeding, but this staining was the result of chewing betel leaves and betel nut (which should properly be referred to as arecu nut). The practice of chewing betel leaves is a stimulant, and chewing arecu nuts wrapped in betel leaves is an addictive past-time which is very common throughout Asia.

As we wandered round the market in the afternoon, women grabbed our hands to pull us to their stalls, wanting us to take photographs – this was unusual, because on the whole Indian women were quite shy compared to the men. We bought some stainless steel cups from one of the many shops that sell nothing but stainless steel kitchen ware. (Interestingly, the very basic cafés always used stainless steel plates and cups, but the more expensive restaurants used plastic!) The stainless steel plates, bowls and cups were sold by the kilo, so every time we asked a price they had to weigh the item first before answering.

We passed a shop full of ancient blenders, possibly second-hand, though Indian advertisements always showed new ones which looked as though they'd come straight out of the 1950s or 60s. Warren commented that it was amazing how this third world country used other countries' abandoned moulds to continue making appliances, and certainly the beautiful Royal Enfield motorbikes that the Indians continue to manufacture look vintage as soon as they are made.

We knew when we had reached Karnataka, because there was a border control. A policeman asked Warren where he was going, so Warren said 'Karnataka, that way,' and pointed ahead – a stupid answer to a very stupid question! And so we cycled into Karnataka, the next state . . .

Karnataka

Whilst Goa is a very tiny state with coastline along its entire length, Karnataka is a large state which sweeps north-east of Goa but has only a relatively small coastline south of Goa. Karnataka is a major producer of coffee and spices and produces the majority of India's silk. Its capital, Bangalore, has become the IT centre of India and is one of India's fastest growing cities.

We intended to cycle down the coast road, and because Karnataka had only a short coastline, this meant that it wouldn't take long to cycle through Karnataka into Kerala.

We arrived in Ankola on market day. It was very busy and we obviously caused a stir and stood out like a couple of sore thumbs. Warren tried to take some photos, but was mobbed. Everyone stood very close just looking at him, saying nothing – it didn't embarrass them at all. It was immediately noticeable in Karnataka that a lot of women wore long green dresses with almost halter-like necklines, so that their shoulders and backs were completely bare. This type of dress was a surprise, because Indian women are very strict in their clothing and never expose their shoulders, but we understood that the women wearing these dresses were from a lower caste.

We had our breakfast in a little café where there were more flies than I've ever seen in my life, and we both hoped that our stomachs would survive! They couldn't make tea for us without milk, because the strong tea was already mixed in the urn with hot milk and vast amounts of sugar. We continued on our way. We passed some salt pans, and an office standing alongside proudly announced that it was the 'Office of the Inspector of Salt' – how the Indians love titles!

There were some very holy places in Karnataka, and it was extraordinary how many men went on pilgrimages by four-wheel drive! These vehicles passed us, full of Indian men, with their luggage on the roof. Orange flags flew from the car (orange is considered a very holy colour) and usually there was a picture of a favourite Hindu god in the window. The cars took these men, never women, to various holy places where they stayed to pray and wash in the holy waters, after which they would be driven to the next holy town. We had always imagined that pilgrimages were made on foot, taking many weeks or months to visit such places, but now we knew better.

One of the towns that we visited was Gokarna, which is one of the popular pilgrims' resorts and has many Hindu temples. Enormous chariots, as high as three storey houses, with wooden wheels that were taller than a man, stood outside one of these temples. These chariots were made of wood and were carved with animals, and were bedecked with bunting and flags at the top. They were dragged by dozens of men through the streets during festivals.

We found the bathing tanks at these holy towns fascinating – they looked like outdoor swimming pools, with steps at different intervals down into the water. Sometimes there were covered shady areas on the perimeter of the pool. At the ghats (the steps) pilgrims bathed themselves in the holy water, but also the local women went there to wash clothes. Although the water always looked incredibly dirty, they soaked their clothes in the water, rubbed them with soap, and thrashed the clothes hard against the concrete steps in order to beat the dirt out of the clothes. The final result was always surprisingly good, but clothes didn't last long with such treatment! A group of beautiful Indian girls were brushing each other's hair after washing themselves in the bathing tank. I indicated that I wanted to take a photo of them, but they shook their heads shyly and turned away.

Cows ambled past us as we stood at the edge of the ghats, and a man suddenly tapped Warren on the shoulder and beckoned him to follow. We hesitated, but he was insistent that we follow him to see a temple in a cave, and a German girl introduced herself to us, saying that she had been following him for some time and he had been showing her the sights. We joined the two of them, and began to climb a hill, finally entering a cave which had been made into a temple. Before entering the cave our guide, who was a Brahmin, removed his shirt because he had to enter the temple bare-chested. It was apparently a very sacred place, and obviously ancient. In an alcove a rough pillar had been carved out of stone to form a sacred linga, a phallic symbol which is worshipped by the Hindus. Our guide asked us for a 'donation' to give to the gods and to leave at the shrine. When we continued to the top of the hill, we could see Om Beach far below us, two perfect crescents of sand separated by a rocky outcrop and one of Gokarna's five famous beaches. An 'om' is a spiritual symbol shaped like the number 3, and the beach was so named because it took the shape of this symbol.

It was in Gokarna that we noticed that most of the Indian men wore what looked like large tea-towels around their waists. The usual men's dress in Karnataka and Kerala consists of a long-sleeved shirt with the cuffs rolled up. The shirts are often striped, and look more suited to working in the city (London, that is!) than to standing around in a dusty Indian village, but beneath this the man wears a type of sarong tied round his waist. If the sarong is coloured it's called a lungi and this is the most popular wear in south India. If it's white with a stripe round the bottom, it's called a mundu and is worn extensively in Kerala. The lungi or mundu reaches almost to the ground, and it was common to see the man walking around holding the corners, looking as though he was about to curtsey. It was even more common to see the garment worn short, when the man lifted the hem, folded it to his waist or hips over the top of his shirt, and tied it very loosely in front. As he talked to his friends he would play with the mundu or lungi constantly. First of all the lungi was tied up so that it was short and above his knees, then he loosened it and dropped it halfway down, still holding one corner, then he pulled it up again. When he walked the garment needed to be retied constantly as it was always only loosely tied at the front. When sitting or when entering a house, the garment had to be dropped to full length. When the men rode a bike or scooter, the lungi or mundu was tied up so that it didn't catch in the wheel. Trousers are very seldom seen in the south of India, and we never saw an Indian wearing shorts or jeans in these areas.

Being such a holy town, there were also many Sadhus in Gokarna. Many wore the orange robes that we had already seen in other parts of India, but some were naked or nearly naked, with ashes painted on their body and their hair a mass of dreadlocks. The Sadhu tradition has a long history, not only in Hinduism but in other religions as well, and a Sadhu renounces worldly ties in the hope of gaining a higher value of life. Usually Sadhus live in society but are detached from society's pleasures. They are dedicated to achieving liberation through meditation and contemplation of God, and most people will have heard of the extraordinary feats that Sadhus have endured, such as standing for 17 years, staying in the same place for more than two decades, crawling hundreds of miles and many similar efforts, in their quest to attain liberation.

As we walked through the crowds in Gokarna one day we heard some singing behind us and turned to see what was happening. A group of men were jogging through the street singing loudly and cheerfully. The first man was carrying sticks and brushwood high above his head, and the rest of the group were carrying a stretcher full of flowers as they jogged. I quickly took a photo, but as they passed I noticed that the flower-covered stretcher contained a body, although only the face was visible. I felt mortified that I had unintentionally taken a photo of a funeral.

Because Gokarna was popular with backpackers and travellers, we were able to exchange the two paperback books that we had finished reading for two more second hand books. We never disposed of books during the whole of the time that we travelled, even though they were heavy to carry, because it was almost impossible to buy English paperbacks. However, everywhere that backpackers travelled (often in the hotels and hostels themselves) there was always the facility to exchange books. Sometimes we read books that we might otherwise not have considered reading, simply because they were the only ones available, but we found some very interesting books because of this.

The night before we left Gokarna we were woken at about 4am by someone hammering very loudly; there was also a sawing sound and then the sound of a drill, all in the kitchen which was next to us on the ground floor. Indian voices were raised outside our room, echoing down the corridor. This continued for over half an hour, so Warren dressed and charged into the kitchen.

'Who's in charge?' he shouted.

There were five men in there, but they acted like little children as soon as Warren shouted, all starting to slink out of the door with their heads down, and no-one wanting to take responsibility. It turned out that the drilling sound had been the blender running on the counter next to our wall, but we never found out what the other noises were. We discovered at that time (and this was reconfirmed to us every time we ever raised a complaint in India) that managers and people in responsible positions lie and argue with customers, rather than ever admit responsibility and apologise. The manager told Warren that 'some of your people' (meaning westerners) had arrived in the night and wanted food, but the register showed no-one arriving after us; as the Indians are fanatical about keeping these enormous books up to date, this proved that the manager was lying. However, there was never any advantage in continuing such arguments in India – it was always a no-win situation!

We continued our journey through Karnataka, and in one town we were fascinated to see men sitting by the roadside working. One man was making flip-flops from old lorry tyres. As we stopped to watch, he offered to resole the flip-flops that we were wearing. As new flip-flops in India cost only a few rupees we declined, but it was impressive to see how things are recycled and repaired time and time again before anything is actually thrown away. A man alongside him was cutting shapes out of old oil cans to make kitchenware. Hand-made ladles, colanders, containers with lids and dishes were stacked at his side, and it was difficult to believe that a short while ago they had been old oil cans. He sat with a pile of cut metal circles between his feet, while he smashed a heavy hammer onto the centre to form bowl shapes. I held my breath every time the hammer fell, because his feet were only an inch or two away, but his aim was always exact and I could see no sign of scars or damage to his feet.

We booked into a hotel on the main road one day, and it wasn't until we had settled into our first floor room and looked at the view from the window that we saw a massive statue of Lord Shiva (the Hindu god with four arms) towering above the trees in the distance. This was Murdeshwar, but we could find no record of it in any of our guide books. We locked the hotel room with our padlock (Indian hotels always supplied their own padlocks to lock hotel bedroom doors, but we preferred to use our own for security), and jumped onto our bag-less cycles. Unused to the light weight of our bikes we wobbled initially, but we had soon cycled the three miles to the coast, guided by the Lord Shiva statue towering above the trees.

We arrived at the beach to find the huge statue sitting proudly on a peninsular, the people on the beach below tiny dots in comparison. At 123 feet in height and apparently the world's tallest idol of Lord Shiva, it took nearly two years to build at a cost of 10 million rupees, and is positioned so that the sun shines directly on it, making it appear sparkling. The waves rolled into the two bays on either side of it. However, the most fascinating thing about the place was the party-like atmosphere – everywhere there were stalls selling trinkets, food, toys and cold drinks, and balloons and bunting criss-crossed the road. It was rather like India's equivalent of England's Blackpool, but for us was really interesting. There were literally thousands of people there, but we were the only westerners, so once again we found it difficult to move without being surrounded by Indians asking us questions, touching our bikes, ringing the bells, and pointing to the strange tyres which were very slick compared with the knobbly tyres they preferred.

Something we found quite disconcerting in India was the fact that men hold hands. They walked along, young or old, holding hands with another man, their fingers linked together. If they stood talking, they would stroke the other man's hands gently. This was purely a friendly gesture, because in India homosexuality is illegal, and any man claiming to be homosexual would be disowned by his family, as it is considered so shameful. Occasionally we saw women holding hands or walking with arms linked, but this wasn't common. However, we never saw an Indian man and woman holding hands, linking arms or showing any affection towards each other, and at all functions, festivals or meetings that we attended the men and women were always segregated, the women and children together on one side and the men on the other. We wondered what the Indians thought of western tourist couples who walked along hand in hand.

It never ceased to amaze us that the Indians slept everywhere in India, whatever the time of day. Wherever we went there was someone asleep, and often in the noisiest or most unlikely places. On the pavement in Delhi, with traffic hooting and roaring by, whole families slept. On a brick wall only 12 inches wide a man slept with a plastic carrier bag under his head. In a shop a woman was fast asleep in the corner with dresses hanging above her. On the way into a restaurant someone was asleep in the passageway. On the station platform numerous people slept in the most awkward places, such as on boxes or coils of rope. Under a tree a builder slept with his head on a brick, and we often saw lorry drivers asleep under their lorries in the shade. And this was during the day, not at night!

Now that we were cycling in India, we were finding the rules of the road quite frightening. One of the most terrifying aspects of cycling in India is the very poor level of road safety everywhere. This lack of safety involves every element of the road – the actual road-worthiness of vehicles, especially large vehicles such as buses and lorries; the way the Indians drive, especially bus drivers; the apparent lack of understanding of what manoeuvres might be dangerous; the total disregard by drivers of large vehicles for anyone else on the road – it almost seemed to us as cyclists that the bus driver's aim for the day was to hit or kill at least one cyclist.

There didn't appear to be any law to ensure the road-worthiness of vehicles, or if there was no-one attempted to enforce such a law. Vehicles such as buses and lorries were always dangerously overloaded, but this was considered the norm. Lorries had loads which overhung the sides, back and front of the trucks, often not properly secured, and often causing the lorry to tilt dangerously to one side. As cyclists we didn't dare to overtake such vehicles if they were stationary without giving them a very wide berth, for fear the load could fall.

Small vehicles, even cycles, were always loaded so precariously with oversized packages for the size of the vehicle that it was obvious that accidents must be common. We saw cyclists with packages loaded so high that you couldn't see the cyclist from the back – this seriously impaired the stability of a bike. We couldn't understand why they didn't have panniers or containers at either side of the wheels as we had, which ensured that the load was as low as possible to ensure stability. We saw a motor scooter with a passenger who was carrying a full-sized door in front of him upright on the seat – an obviously unstable load. Even a large sheet of glass, obviously a very dangerous load, was carried by one motor scooter passenger, the sides of the glass protruding on either side of the scooter as it swerved between traffic.

We saw bicycles with passengers on the crossbar or rear rack more often than bicycles with just the cyclist; we often saw motor scooters with three adults on them and motorbikes with families of four was common; we even saw a family of five on a motorbike. The Indians are encouraged by the manufacturers to have female passengers riding side-saddle (this is now banned in Europe as it is dangerous), because they design bikes with special steps for the two feet on the left side.

In the big cities – Delhi, Agra, Jaipur, Mumbai, Chennai and Kolkata, rickshaws abound. These are three-wheeled bicycles with no gears, and they have room for two small passengers at the back. The drivers are always very skinny with legs like sticks that don't look strong enough to cycle heavy loads. They always stand on the pedals to get them moving, and the rickshaws look difficult and heavy to pedal even when empty and on the flat. We were told in Agra that the charge for sightseeing in a pedal rickshaw was 5 rupees an hour, and we saw very heavy weights put into these rickshaws, with unbelievable loads such as long planks of wood, sheets of glass, doors, and sometimes there were as many as four passengers on these vehicles, the third and fourth passengers hanging on the back while the driver struggled to move forward.

In the smaller towns and villages, the auto rickshaws (or tuk-tuks as they are known) are more common than taxis. Lines of them could always be seen waiting by the side of the road. The auto rickshaw is a 3-wheel vehicle with one wheel at the front with a very small motor scooter engine and motor scooter handlebars. The driver sits on a small bench seat in the middle of the vehicle, and there's a narrow uncomfortable seat behind him for two people. In practice, the auto rickshaw carries a limitless number of people, and we saw up to a dozen adults and children in one of these tiny vehicles. They look as if they'd tip when they hit the large potholes, and they struggle to get up hills, even with moderate loads. The cover over the top is fabric, and they usually have no door or sometimes curtains. The average price for a 1km ride is 3 to 5 rupees (about 5p). Most of the auto rickshaws are painted yellow and black and look quite endearing. We thought they would be great (with doors and heating!) in English towns, because they take up little space when parking and can manoeuvre easily through traffic.

We also sometimes saw similar types of vehicles that had been made into trucks for carrying goods rather than passengers, and these were similar to the Piaggio vehicles that we had seen in Italy.

In the town all the auto rickshaws were parked together, all the hand-painted lorries were parked together, all the white ambassador taxis were parked together, and all the grey jeeps (another form of taxi) were parked together. This was the case however small the town.

Not only the public forms of transport were constantly overloaded – we heard of a Mini Moke that crashed with forty people in it. We don't know if they were trying to get into the Guinness Book of Records, but the driver should have been considered criminally insane to have driven under such circumstances.

The tyres on buses and lorries often looked as though they were ready to burst. It was not unusual to see bald tyres with patches of canvas showing and chunks of rubber missing. As we cycled, we noticed the parts of buses and lorries that had dropped off the vehicles – it was a concern to see large nuts and bolts still covered in oil and grease at the side of the road. It was even more disturbing to see men hand-making enormous leaf springs to repair lorries and buses at the side of roads. The buses bounced alarmingly as they drove past, as if they had no shock absorbers.

It was quite common to see a chassis being driven along the road, the driver sitting on a makeshift seat made from old wooden pallets. The chassis comes from the massive Indian company, Tata – it was very rare to see any other make of vehicle on India's roads. These chassis are taken to the coachbuilders at the side of the road, where wooden bodies are hand-built onto the chassis. Before a European company can sell a bus or lorry, the vehicles have to be crash-tested to check the safety of such vehicles before selling them for public conveyance. Presumably there is no such testing in India if each body is made individually by hand.

All Indian drivers, but especially bus and lorry drivers, drive far too fast for the condition and type of roads. Indian drivers consider that it is their right to push anyone else off the road if their vehicle is bigger than the other one. Indeed, the guide books say that the law of the road is 'Might is right', meaning that the bigger the vehicle the more right to the road they have. They show no courtesy whatsoever and would rather drive straight into a cyclist than slow down or stop for them. We were often cycling along the road when a bus coming in the opposite direction turned onto our side of the road to overtake someone. He would drive straight at us with his hand on the horn and his foot on the accelerator, waiting for us to dive into the dirt or the ditch alongside the road. Of course we always did dive for cover – if we hadn't, we could have been mown down by the large vehicle to become another death statistic on India's roads.

The horn was used constantly and this was encouraged. We even saw drivers who were learning to drive using the horn. Every lorry in India has a sign on the back saying 'Sound horn OK' or 'Sound horn please'. This means that every time anyone overtakes they sound the horn. We therefore took little notice of horns sounding because the noise was constant, but on one occasion when a horn sounded behind us Warren fortunately turned to look. Two buses were heading towards us at speed side by side, one overtaking the other. Coming towards us in the opposite direction was a lorry. Not one of the three vehicles applied the brake; they all kept their feet on the accelerator. We dived into the dirt at the side of the road and left them to swerve violently to avoid each other, all this at speed with overloaded vehicles. This sounds crazy but was normal driving in India. Whilst the Indians are lovely people, once they are behind the wheel of a vehicle they are unbelievably rude.

Quite often we saw signs warning of accident spots. These were always on a blind bend or the brow of a hill, and every driver should know that one should never overtake at these places. However, the Indian driver appears to have no conception of the danger involved in such a manoeuvre, and the number of lorries and buses we saw upside down at the bottom of embankments by bends bears testimony to this fact. If we were cycling fast down a winding hill, we had to brake at every corner in case some crazy bus or lorry driver had decided to overtake on that blind bend and was coming up the hill straight towards us on the wrong side of the road. Crazily, bus stops were often situated on the brow of a hill, forcing vehicles to overtake at blind spots.

No-one ever looked in the mirror or used indicators when driving, and often they didn't even have a mirror. Many times we overtook a stationary bus and the driver suddenly drove off, leaving us trapped between the bus and oncoming traffic in the middle of the road. We were convinced that bus and lorry companies employed a man to stick his hand out of the window, because it was cheaper than fitting mirrors and indicators that needed maintenance. Interestingly, in many western countries, the law is that the larger vehicles give way to the smaller, and it is the same in the ocean – steam gives way to sail. The Indians would definitely be horrified by such a law!

Whenever an accident occurred, and we saw the aftermaths of many, the damaged vehicle would immediately be surrounded by people standing and staring but doing nothing to help the poor injured or trapped people. A Danish couple we met saw a bus on its side, having just been in an accident. Everyone was standing around chatting and laughing, even though people were still trapped inside with no-one to help them. We found this a very strange and difficult attitude to understand – wouldn't they want to be helped if they were the ones trapped or injured?

Despite the fact that it was dangerous to be on the roads in India, we were now thoroughly enjoying ourselves. We felt safer being on bikes on the road than being in Indian buses. Having talked to travellers who used the Indian buses to make their way round India, it appeared that most of them had their hearts in their mouths for the whole journey, and the constant sound of the driver sounding his horn meant that it was not even possible to sleep!

We had noticed when we were in Goa that the milestones were alternately in Hindi and in English. (Maybe we should call them kilometre stones, because distance is measured in kilometres in India). Once we reached Kerala they were alternately in Malayalam, Kerala's local language, and Hindi, with occasional large road signs showing English as well.

We were now cycling through areas where tourists seldom visited, and this was very obvious from the reactions of the locals as we arrived in a village or town. If we had grown green heads and had aerials sticking out of our heads, we could not have been more objects of curiosity to the locals! The Indians are very friendly and always waved as we passed. Now that we were in Karnataka everyone shouted 'Hi' rather than the 'Allo' of Goa. Now we noticed that they ran into a shop or house as we passed to call their friends and family, who would run out to stare at us and point as we went by. If we stopped, we were immediately mobbed and surrounded by people. This could be quite disconcerting, because often they didn't speak English and just stood very close to us staring. They didn't even talk to each other making comments. If we parked the bikes outside a café, a crowd immediately gathered around the bikes and another crowd stood watching us eat. One day we went into a café, and as I sat down with my back to the window and door I noticed that the room had suddenly darkened. I turned to look, and through the large window and door all I could see were faces peering in, totally blocking out the light. The owner asked us where we were from. He was one of the few people we met who spoke English in this area. As we ate our meal, there was a constant stream of locals coming in to speak to him. We didn't understand what he was saying, but the word 'England' came up every time, so they were obviously coming in just to ask him where we were from. From the look of pride on his face as he saw us to the door and waved goodbye to us, he probably talked about the occasion for days afterwards!

Children especially were fascinated by us. I stopped once to take a photo of hundreds of Muslim children walking along the road to school very early in the morning, as Warren cycled a short way ahead. The children were aged about 6 or 7, and the boys looked very sweet in their little white pill-box hats and the girls looked beautiful in their white scarves pinned tightly under their chins. As I stopped, I was immediately surrounded by 30 or 40 screaming little boys.

'What is your name? What is your name?' they shouted.

As I tried to take a photo of the children walking down the road the boys jumped up and down trying to get into the photo. However, as I turned the camera towards a group of girls who had stood back watching quietly, they immediately turned their backs and began to walk quickly away. This was very noticeable generally in India – the women and girls seldom wanted photographs taken, but the boys and men constantly asked to have theirs taken. As I cycled off, the little boys ran alongside chasing me. Warren tells me that he took two photos of me cycling along the road looking like the Pied Piper, with numerous little boys running behind me!

The Indians often asked, 'From what nation are you coming?' They understood the answer 'England' but people we met from places like Norway, Denmark, France or Israel said that it was obvious that the locals had never heard of these countries.

Now we were in a completely non-tourist area food was incredibly cheap. Breakfast in a roadside café, where food was cooked quickly and put on our plates piping hot, usually cost about 20 rupees (26p) for both of us. We had noticed that as we cycled further south, the style of breakfast was changing – normally the mild potato curry remained the same or similar, but the 'bread' with which it was eaten was different.

One day we were having breakfast in a dark shack, accompanied by local men (women never had breakfast in such places, but the cafés were always busy with men). A Sadhu sat opposite us, his eyes constantly turning to us in amazement. No-one spoke English. Warren suddenly jumped up, his camera in his hand, and all eyes turned to him. Warren put the camera on top of a sack of rice facing all of us, switched on the timer and sat down again. Everyone looked at the camera as the warning flash bleeped on and off for 10 seconds waiting to take the photo, but unfortunately the Sadhu couldn't control his curiosity, jumped up and looked closer at the camera, just as it flashed and took a photo! However, we do now have a photo of us with a number of men in a breakfast shack looking at the camera with their mouths open in astonishment!

Another small café that we went into for breakfast was empty apart from a lady wearing a sari. She was presumably the wife of the owner, because she disappeared into a back room as soon as she saw us, and her husband appeared quickly and shook Warren warmly by the hand to welcome him. He seemed relieved when we asked for puri bhaji and lassi, and hurried to get it. We sat facing the road. A man walked past leading a cow with a colourful blanket tied over the hump on its back. It was fascinating watching this different world go by; Warren said how he loved our breakfasts in these places, and I agreed. The food was always delicious and unbelievably cheap. Three cows arrived and tried to walk into the back of the café, but the owner quickly arrived to give them each an idli (a white rice cake eaten in the southern part of India for breakfast), and after their breakfast they happily turned and went on their way. This café was obviously part of their regular early morning route!

We continued on our way up and down hills, and at the top of a hill we saw the sea. Although we had been travelling parallel to the coast for many miles, this was the first view of the sea from the road for some time. We therefore decided to take a turning to the right that day to see what we could find. We cycled along a dirt track until we reached sand dunes and palm trees. We could immediately smell the unpleasant aroma of dried fish, and as we walked past the bushes onto the beach we found a beautiful kilometre long white sand beach covered with small silver fish. Just a few yards away, women were raking piles of fish to spread them out, and a fishing boat was at that moment surfing the waves to land on the beach. We chatted to a man supervising who spoke English, who told us that half of the fish would be used as fertiliser and the other half as chicken feed. After taking a few photographs, everyone stood waving goodbye to us as we returned to the main road.

Stalls beside the road cooked the most delicious foods, which often served as a quick lunch if we were still travelling, although we always tried to stop cycling before noon when the sun was at its hottest. We had hesitated before trying the food on the stalls, but were rewarded by discovering the most delicious snacks. They were usually deep-fried balls which could be held in the hand and eaten – creamy mildly-spiced potato bhaji encased in batter, spicy vegetable burgers, mashed potato with vegetables covered in breadcrumbs and fried, the most delicious onion bhajis we had ever tasted, and banana or pineapple fritters. They cost 2 rupees each and a glass of tea was always available for about the same price. We also discovered that many of the small stalls by the roadside sold the most amazing omelettes, which were great for a quick lunch. Two eggs were whisked with finely chopped onion and a little chilli and cooked in front of us in a wok. Such omelettes were excellent, and seemed to be identical wherever we went. The charge for such an omelette was approximately 6p – I never saw fresh eggs for sale, but wondered how much they cost if an omelette was so cheap! If we wanted fruit, we bought a large ripe pineapple for 18 rupees (just over 20p), a coconut for 10 rupees, some of the delicious tiny sweet thin-skinned bananas at 1 rupee each, or we could have a half pint glass of blended fruit for 10 rupees. We always asked for black tea while we were in India, as we couldn't get used to the Indian tea which is made with half a glass of boiled milk added to very sweet, strong tea.

As we travelled further south we discovered a wonderful south Indian breakfast dish called Masala Dosa, which consists of an enormous pancake about

18" diameter made of chickpea or rice flour, which is incredibly light and melts in the mouth. This is filled with mildly spiced potato curry, and served with three different sauces and sometimes pickle as well. At a cost of 10 rupees it was often too much to eat for breakfast, and even in the tourist areas was not likely to be more than 15 or 20 rupees (26p). Desperate to try to cook this dish at home I eventually found a recipe, but was disappointed to discover that the cheap cost in India belied the many hours of preparation that the dish required.

Whenever we sat in a café or restaurant, the waiter immediately brought a glass or stainless steel beaker of water, though we never risked drinking it. Every café and restaurant had a wash area, usually a washbasin actually in the café, but in a very small roadside café it was often just a washing up bowl full of water standing on concrete blocks in the dirt outside the café. A wash area was necessary because food is only eaten by the Indians with the right hand. However, they sometimes gave us a spoon, guessing that as tourists we were not used to eating their way, but we certainly had no problem eating with our fingers if no cutlery was available. We also noticed that in many of these non-tourist cafés that we frequented the Indians were given squares of banana leaf which served as a plate, which was ideal as a disposable, bio-degradable piece of crockery, but often the waiter automatically gave us plates.

We got up as always one morning while it was still dark, and by the time we were outside the hotel and on our bikes it was close to sunrise. As we passed over one of the many long bridges across the estuaries there was a ball of red sun rising in the sky over the backwaters to our left. Fishermen in their dug-out canoes were outlined against the crimson red water, and the palm trees were outlined against the lightening sky. As we passed through a small town, a man with wild eyes, wild hair and wearing only a loin cloth, jumped out in front of me. He had a horrible rasping voice as he spoke, but I couldn't understand what he was saying. I swerved around him, but couldn't understand why I could still hear that voice further down the road.

Warren suddenly passed me, standing on his pedals and shouting, 'Get a move on – the wild man is chasing us!' and I turned to see that he was close behind me, shouting all the time. We had been chased by wild dogs and by monkeys, but never before by a wild man!

We arrived in Mangalore, and decided to stay overnight and cycle into Kerala the next day. The first hotel took 15 minutes to tell us that they had no rooms, and the second didn't initially want bikes in the bedroom, although they eventually agreed. It was an expensive room, but we were too tired to look further. We washed some clothes and left them hanging on our makeshift washing line under the fan while we went for lunch, and Warren spent a couple of hours doing a repair on one of the bikes before we went to bed.

At 6.15 the next morning we got up, but at 6.30 the telephone rang. The hotel employee announced that this was my early morning call. I was confused.

'I didn't request an early morning call,' I said.

Five minutes later the phone rang again, asking if we wanted tea or coffee. When I said 'no' they asked what time we were leaving. I was annoyed. 'When we're ready,' I said.

A minute later the phone rang again. I was too annoyed to answer it, so Warren did. They wanted to know what time we were leaving. Although we had intended leaving very shortly, Warren replied '10 o'clock,' at which they said that someone was waiting to move into our room. Warren was furious. In Indian hotels there is no set time to leave – it is always 24 hours after you arrived. As we had arrived just before noon the day before, we were entitled to stay in the room until noon that day. We went down to reception. The employees and managers were waiting for us, and they all began shouting at us when we complained. The gentleman who was waiting for his room was sat in reception, and he decided to speak.

'I think the English couple have a point,' he said.

The manager was furious; he turned to the gentleman, pointed his finger at him and shouted at the top of his voice, 'Be quiet!'

It was hilarious. The manager was now shouting in Warren's face and was stabbing his finger at him, and I thought it time to intervene.

I went up to the manager and touched him on the arm. 'Don't poke Warren,' I said.

The manager's face was an unbelievable picture as he spun round to see that a woman had dared speak up to him – I thought he was going to have a heart attack, his face went so purple, and he immediately threatened to call the police.

'Good,' we both said. 'Please phone them straight away.'

Needless to say, they didn't. We got nowhere, apart from the pleasure of winding up the very unpleasant manager of the hotel, and as a childish, spiteful gesture we threw the key to the room in a ditch a mile down the road.

We approached a busy roundabout in the centre of Mangalore that morning, and as the buses drove round the roundabout we noticed that they were leaning at a serious angle to the left. This was because there were so many people on the buses (including numerous school children), that many of them had to stand on the steps, hanging on the outside of the two doors. The slightest accident to the front or right-hand side of the bus would have caused the bus to tip onto its left side, crushing to death all of those people hanging on the outside and steps of the bus, but no-one seemed concerned.

We knew we were approaching Kerala when we approached a road block. Lorries were queued up on both sides of the road waiting for the police to check

Turkey
Mary sitting on a 2,000 year old loo. (The Roman latrines at Ephesus)

India
An overcrowded tuk-tuk in Agra, North India

Vietnam *(left)*
Most Vietnamese carry baskets balanced at each end of a bamboo pole
Japan *(right)*
Warren paying the bill at a restaurant in Ouchi

Laos
Warren repairing his bike, watched by the usual audience

India
Happy children always surrounded us whenever we stopped

Myanmar *(left)*
Children rest in front of Buddha, Schwe Dagon temple, Yangon
Cambodia *(right)*
Asians can sleep anywhere, any time! Phnom Penh

Turkey
Mary and Warren on the steps of The Library, Ephesus

India
Women and children work together building the roads, Goa

Vietnam
A betel-nut chewing mother is teased by her daughter

Cambodia *(left)*
One of the many faces of the Bayon Temple, Angkor Wat
Vietnam *(right)*
A Vietnamese lady is surprised to see Mary cycling past

Cambodia
Warren cycling ahead on the main road to Siem Reap

India
Women in their traditional clothes, Karnatika

Laos
Putting our bikes on the ferry to cross the mile-wide Mekong River

Myanmar
Young boys look after the water buffaloes

Myanmar
Four ladies go shopping together in Lake Inle

India
If we stopped for a break, we were immediately surrounded by school children

Myanmar
Stupas on the edge of Lake Inle

their loads. The sign by the barrier said 'Sales Tax Check Post', so presumably there were different taxes in different states. We cycled past the lorries in the queue, and the police lifted the barrier and waved us on.

Kerala

A long narrow state which hugs the western coastline and reaches almost to the southern tip of India, Kerala has become almost as popular as Goa as a holiday destination for relaxing holidays in the sun. It is lush, green and fertile, with dense forests and serene backwaters, tea-growing hills, numerous spice, coffee and cashew nut plantations, national parks with elephants and tigers, and palm tree lined golden beaches. Whilst the main religion is Hinduism, there is a large Muslim population in Kerala.

We knew we would spend some time cycling in Kerala before we reached Tamil Nadu, because Kerala's coastline is 590km long. We had also looked at our map of the world and noticed that there were flights from Kerala to the Maldives or to Sri Lanka, so it seemed a good idea to check out the prices and the possibilities of travelling to one of those places before we continued our cycling in India.

We stayed in a small town called Kumbla, and we walked along the dirt at the side of the road looking for somewhere to have lunch. No-one in the café we found spoke any English, so we went into the kitchen to see what was on offer. The concrete kitchen was dark, and the only light was from a really hot fire that was burning in a grate. Hanging over the fire was a cast iron pot of delicious-smelling food. In the corner of the room was a giant granite pestle and mortar that had been converted to electric; it was spinning round making the masala paste for Masala Dosa for breakfast the next day. We pointed to the food in the cast iron pot and nodded, and within minutes we were enjoying another wonderful Indian meal.

In the evening we looked for a restaurant that served beer with the meal. These are often difficult to find (as they were in the non-tourist areas of Turkey), so eventually we had to ask. We discovered that the nearest place that alcohol was sold was 14 kilometres away! The following day in the next town we asked in a restaurant if they had beer. The waiter looked very shocked, and told us that it was illegal to drink alcohol in public places in Kerala. This was indeed a set-back! However, the waiter leant over and spoke in a whisper. Apparently in a nearby street there was a shop that sold alcohol if we wanted to drink it privately in our hotel, although we needed to check first that our hotel would allow it. We had noticed that many of the hotels had notices saying 'Liquor forbidden' or 'Alcohol is not permitted', but regardless of any notices, we decided to buy a bottle of wine to take back to our hotel to drink on our balcony.

After our meal we crossed the road and turned into the street indicated by the waiter. The street was dark, but dozens of men were walking down it towards a light at the end. As we followed the crowds and approached the light, we could see that there was a building that looked like a factory unit, and a queue was waiting to be served at a counter. Metal rails either side of the queue ensured that no-one jumped the queue. We were 19th in the queue, but there were taxis, motorbikes and groups of men waiting to one side. I was the only woman. Above the long counter was a sign saying 'Alcohol injures your health', but clearly none of us were going to take any notice of that! We had to pay one man for a bottle of wine and he wrote down what we wished to purchase on a scrap of paper torn from a newspaper. We walked two yards along the counter and handed the scrap of newspaper to the second man, who searched high and low until he found one very dusty bottle of wine. Everyone else was buying the hard stuff – very cheap Indian whisky, rum and brandy. We were handed a different hand-written ticket by the second man, who handed the bottle to someone further along the counter. We had to walk another two yards to this third man, who took our ticket and handed us our bottle of wine, and finally we moved down the queue with our bottle of wine to a fourth man, who wrapped our bottle with great deliberation in a sheet from an Indian newspaper, carefully sellotaping the paper in place. We had discovered already the need by Indians each to do their own job, and to us it seemed extraordinary. On a previous occasion in a pharmacy we had asked for an item, but our assistant stood looking around the shop and appeared not to know where to find it. We could see it on a shelf within arm's reach behind the counter and pointed it out to him, but he shook his head – it wasn't his job to remove it from the shelf, and he stood and waited until the man whose job it was had finished helping someone else. This man removed it from the shelf and handed it to our assistant to hand to us!

We walked quickly back to our hotel, feeling the need to keep the bottle hidden, laughing like a couple of school kids. In front of us an Indian man staggered up the road absolutely drunk. He obviously wasn't keen on carrying his bottle home, so had downed the contents beside the shop!

Occasionally we found bars in big towns, but they were extremely seedy, usually very dark, and were mostly in obscure and difficult to find places. They were always full of Indian men drinking brandy, rum or whisky – sometimes whole bottles! The intention for an Indian man visiting a bar is to get drunk as quickly as possible, and once this has been achieved he leaves. We visited such bars on two or three occasions, mainly for the experience. In the time that it took us to drink a Kingfisher beer between us, maybe diluted with lemonade for me, Indian men came in and drank whole bottles of cheap whisky or brandy as they stood at the bar, and then staggered back into the street again. Women were clearly not expected to visit such places, and the barman often tried to dissuade me from going into the bar. I certainly wouldn't have wanted to visit such a place on my own, but Warren always made it clear that we both intended to stay for a drink. Warren and I spent a long time discussing the merits of the ban on drinking alcohol in public and the obvious need of many Indian men to drink purely to get drunk, compared with the relaxed attitude to alcohol in countries such as France, where drinking wine is a pleasant and sociable accompaniment to meal-times, and children are introduced to wine diluted with water from an early age.

We also discovered while we were in Kerala that it was illegal to smoke in public, and it was also illegal to play cards. We saw illicit card games being played by men in groups under the palm trees, and since our cycling trip there has been a total ban in India on smoking in public.

Naturally, the tourist areas of Kerala wouldn't get many tourists if no alcohol was available, so 'special tea' is available on menus in these places. If the special tea costs 5 rupees, it will be tea. However, if it seems rather expensive for tea, the teapot or mug will be full of beer! We were amazed the first time we were served beer in a teapot, the froth pouring out of the spout. It seemed rather extreme when everyone, including the police, was aware of the scam, but it seems a blind eye is often turned by the police in the tourist areas, so long as there is no drunkenness.

Many of the Indian hotels are called 'tourist homes'. These are designed for the Indian tourist and are basic, usually reasonably clean but incredibly cheap. We stayed in one such hotel, which looked more like a block of flats. Indeed, we discovered that there were many permanent residents in our hotel, and we chatted to a lovely girl called Nalini, who lived with her husband and 8 year old daughter, Angeli, in a room similar to ours. There was hardly room for the bed for her daughter, because a small kitchen had been built in the corner of the bedroom, and off the room was a bathroom like ours with squat toilet and shower.

Nalini sat on the narrow balcony which ran along the back of the hotel joining the rooms. She was gutting fish with a sharp curved blade, and she intended cooking fish curry (the most common meal in that part of the world) for their dinner that evening. I was fascinated, and sat watching her while we talked. Later that day her daughter arrived to tell us something, but she spoke only a few words of English, but Nalini then appeared with a meal, because she wanted to share her fish curry with us. We sat and ate it, and she was thrilled that it wasn't too hot and spicy for our taste, and Warren and I marvelled once again how it was that such obviously poor people wanted to share their meals with us. I took a photo of her sat on the balcony, and promised that I would send her a copy of the photograph (which I did), and Nalini was clearly thrilled at the thought.

As I walked out of our bathroom after using the toilet later that day, my flip flops slipped on the wet floor and I crashed onto my back across the tiled step leading into the bedroom. I was in agony, and Warren rushed to my aid, concerned that I might have seriously injured myself. I survived, but was covered with bruises on my back, arms and legs for a long time, so I was always ultra careful after that when using the 'wet rooms' that were so common throughout Asia and much of Europe.

We cycled on, passing many marble works where I was fascinated by one particular marble that was patterned in alternating stripes of baby pink and pale blue. We marvelled at a football stadium that we passed, where the tiered grandstand for everyone to sit was hand-made by strapping pieces of bamboo together.

In one village we watched an old lady struggle to carry a 50 kg sack, so a young man with her helped to lift it onto her head. He then walked along the road with her as she slowly walked, bent double with the heavy load. She passed several small boys in cubs' uniforms, who stood waiting at a bus stand. On the outskirts of the village felled palm trees were laid in a wood yard. Men were chipping away the bark by hand, and once sawn the beautiful flecked dark and golden hardwood would be made into bowls and polished. We noticed as we passed through this Muslim area that there were magnificent modern houses set in the shade of coconut palms in walled grounds with massive wrought-iron gates.

We stopped in a small town and had to ask the way, but we were immediately surrounded by a dozen young men on motorbikes and bicycles. When asked his name, Warren replied 'John' – we had discovered that no-one could understand or pronounce the name 'Warren' so this seemed simpler. However, on this occasion one of the men followed us on his motorbike, producing an exercise book and asking for our autographs. I looked over Warren's shoulder as he signed the name 'John Johnson' and wondered what our new Indian friend was going to do with the autograph!

We met a waiter in a very tiny village who spoke excellent English and, unlike most Indians, he could also read a map. He pored over our map and marked a number of places that he could recommend, especially a lovely beach resort in Muzhapilangadu (which we always later called 'My Happy Land', a similar-sounding name!) As we left the village we went to the post office to send films home to Jean and Steven, Warren's parents. They always had the films developed for us, because we couldn't carry the photos on our bikes. There was only one customer in the post office when we entered, but once it was obvious that we were sending a parcel to England people seemed to appear from nowhere, and we were soon surrounded. None of them spoke English, and we assumed that this was the first time a parcel had been sent abroad, so we did have some concerns whether the parcel would be delivered safely to England. However, the parcel arrived within a few days – we were always impressed with the postal service in India! The one thing we had always been warned was to ensure that the postage stamps were franked in front of us; the temptation to remove the stamps which could be resold for a personal profit might have been too great for some post office employees.

We would never have found Muzhapilangadu if we hadn't been determined to find it after the waiter's recommendation. Eventually Warren stopped to ask a policeman the way.

'And what is your good name?' asked the policeman, as he continued to direct traffic in the middle of the road.

'John,' replied Warren, and bid him goodbye. We waited at a level crossing while an extremely long train passed. Pedestrians and cyclists crawled under the closed gates to cross the line before the train passed, even when they could see the train approaching. Dozens of motorbikes were lined up across the road in front of the gates on both sides of the railway line, waiting to surge forward the second the gates began to lift, so it was utter chaos once the train had passed.

We discovered that the only entrance to the beach resort in My Happy Land was from the beach itself, so we had to cycle for a mile along the beach, a wide expanse of sand. In a coconut grove alongside the beach stood five small cottages with woven palm leaf walls and thatched roofs. At 500 rupees a night (about £6) these were very expensive compared to what we had so far experienced, but obviously the delightful setting accounted for the high price. Even more expensive was a pair of semi-detached cottages, but these were brand new and more substantially built. We finally agreed 1000 rupees for two nights in one of the new rooms, which had a lovely shower room and a well-furnished newly-painted bedroom. Within minutes, Warren had strung hammocks between the trees, and we were relaxing comfortably when I saw an unusual sight.

'Warren,' I said. 'There are two white people coming this way!'

Brian, an Englishman, was walking towards us with his Norwegian girlfriend, Ingeborg, and it was so long since we had seen any other white people that they must have wondered why we were gaping at them with our mouths open. As we chatted to them we were even more amazed to discover that Warren and Brian knew many of the same people. Brian had once been a representative for a company selling windsurfing equipment, at a time when Warren had been working as an Outward Bound instructor at Kielder Reservoir, a massive man-made lake in Northumberland. As the afternoon wore on the other occupants of the resort appeared. Louise was from Australia, and had fallen in love with Kerala. She planned to return every year, teaching English in a convent. A Danish couple arrived later with their two adopted Indian children aged 13 and 11. They had brought the children to see the country and culture of their birth, but so far the children had been unimpressed and were eager to return to their home in Denmark.

The meal that evening was prepared by Rajesh, the manager, and was delicious. We all sat together at one long table, eating wonderful Indian food and enjoying the stories that everyone told of their experiences in India. Rajesh had also broken the law and supplied us with beer, which we had ordered before he went shopping at the nearby town! Candles were ready for the power cut – in Kerala everyone had a one hour power cut each evening, and for that area it was from 7pm until 8pm. Each week the power cut was one hour later, and this continued for the whole of the time that we were in Kerala.

We stayed for many days, walking along the beach early in the mornings, swimming in the warm sea, climbing over the rocks or just relaxing in one of the nearby coves. We chatted to local 16-year old schoolgirls; their school uniform was a very pale lilac salwar kameez, the loose tunic top worn over drawstring trousers that many younger Indian girls wear in preference to saris. They stood thigh deep in the sea holding up a camera, asking if they could take a photo of some of them with us. We obliged, and also took photos of them with our own camera. We walked back along the sand and, taking a short cut through the trees, found a smouldering bonfire which we later discovered was the local crematorium. Local women were digging as usual in the sand as the tide went out. They located small humps in the sand and, with a dessert spoon, a knife or their fingers, dug down an inch or two and pulled out a small shell. Each woman left the beach with heavy bags full of the shell fish, ready to be cooked for a delicious free evening meal.

A group of young Indian schoolchildren arrived at the beach one day, and Rajesh allowed them to use the shady grass area in the resort to have their packed lunches. However, when he saw that they were throwing paper plates down on the ground he supplied them with a box for the rubbish. They duly put their rubbish into the box, but once it was full they took it to the beach a few yards away and just emptied it onto the sand. We couldn't understand why the Indians had so little concern about rubbish around them; places that westerners frequented were kept much tidier, but only because the locals knew that westerners expected this.

One evening we walked onto the pitch black beach to look at the stars. Fishermen were swimming out with their nets – we could just make out their shapes as our eyes became accustomed to the dark. Brian warned us afterwards that we should use a torch at night because there were snakes and toads in the area. Later we found on our bedroom wall the biggest spider I'd ever seen – it was the size of the palm of my hand and its eyes shone like cats' eyes when I shone the torch on it; there was a distinct thud as it fell to the floor and I literally heard it scuttling away. Despite everyone's assurances that this type of spider was harmless, I began to feel nervous about creepy-crawlies, especially when a beetle later landed on my bare chest as I lay in bed.

We hired Krishna to take us on a backwater trip. The backwaters of Kerala are beautiful – wide open rivers of sea water lined with palm trees meandering peacefully around islands. Local men were dredging shellfish, boys were swimming, and women on islands were hanging up their washing or making rope from coconut fibre. Krishna poled us in his large heavy boat, and told us proudly how he used it to mine sand. He looked as though he should have retired 20 years earlier – he was stick thin but must have been very strong to do such work. We saw the sand-mining boats where men stood in the water shovelling wet sand from the bottom of the rivers into their boats. As they poled their boats along, the tops of the hulls were only just above the level of the water because of the heavy load. Islands were newly planted with tiny mangrove plantations, a project by the Kerala Forest Department. Tiny silver fish jumped out of the water and skimmed the surface, and colourful birds flew from tree to tree, sometimes diving into the water to catch fish.

Rajesh told us about a religious festival that was held once a year in a village nearby; it was due to take place the following day, so Warren and I decided to cycle there, though we were unsure what to expect. The village was in the middle of nowhere, and we constantly stopped to ask locals for directions. Eventually we found the village celebrating with hundreds of people from other villages. We were the only westerners there, so it was wonderful to be present at such an important festival. As usual, all of the women stood to one side with the children, while the men stood together on the other side. Twenty-nine men representing gods were dressed in the most amazing outfits, wearing enormous wooden frames round their bodies and giant wooden fan-shaped head-dresses painted in vivid colours. Everything, including their bodies, was brightly painted red, orange and yellow, and they wore wooden masks with moveable large jaws, rather like a Donald Duck beak. Their painted stomachs protruded from their costumes, so I felt certain that they must have been specially chosen because most Indian men are very thin. Drummers played frenetically, and it was clear that the atmosphere was building up towards the climax of the day, when the 29 men would walk through the red-hot embers of a fire that was burning to one side of the clearing. Two men walked either side of each of the 29 men, holding their hands to support them; the wooden head-dresses and body frames were obviously very heavy and difficult to manoeuvre, but it was also clear that the 29 men were all heavily drugged.

Warren stood amongst these men as they stood dancing to the beat of the drums, taking close-up photographs of the amazing scene, but he jumped a mile when all 29 men suddenly leapt into the air shouting. We noticed that we were often of more interest than the highly-decorated men, and many of the Indian men were taking photographs of us, which we thought was extraordinary. We didn't want to see the finale, so left before they walked through the embers, but we found out later that these 29 men always take drugs on the day of the festival 'but only until 7pm' – it was considered acceptable to take drugs if it was for religious purposes. We were thrilled that we'd been able to see the festival, which had been a genuine local celebration and not something planned for tourists.

It was time to leave this paradise. We said our goodbyes to our new friends, and Brian and Ingeborg gave us a toilet roll – what a relief! We had almost run out of toilet paper, and it was impossible to buy in non-tourist areas. Now we had sufficient until we reached one of the popular tourist resorts of Kerala.

We set off on our cycles early one morning, cycling through the coconut groves until we reached the road. We stopped on a bridge to watch dozens of men in shallow circular coracles woven from branches pulling in their fishing nets. The sun rose behind them.

We passed through Mahé, one of the four small pockets of India that used to belong to France, and which are now owned by the Union Territory of Pondicherry. Mahé is only 9 square kilometres, the smallest of these four unconnected districts. The biggest advantage of these districts is that, unlike the states surrounding them, they are allowed to sell alcohol without restriction. There was only one street, but we understood that there were 37 liquor shops in Mahé. We passed through at 8.30am on that Sunday morning, and every liquor shop was open, although the shutters were down on every other shop. Passing lorry drivers were queuing to buy alcohol before driving back into dry Kerala a few yards further along the road!

We turned away from the main road at a small crossroads to cycle towards the sea, and found ourselves cycling through the winding roads of a village. We attracted a great deal of attention, and I doubt that the villagers had ever seen Europeans there before. We stopped when the road came to an end beside the beach, and we were immediately surrounded by children who were screaming to attract our attention. Men and women stood closely around us, occasionally saying 'hello', and I counted at least 50 people around us. The bravest of our audience leant forward when we weren't looking to ring our bells or to touch our pannier bags, but jumped back in horror when we turned. We tried to take photos of them, but the children were so excited that they were jumping up and down in an attempt to be at the front of every photo. A man walked by with large shallow baskets at both ends of a bamboo pole – the children excitedly showed us the baskets, which were full of freshly caught fish lying on chunks of ice.

Later that day we booked into a 3 star hotel in a small town. We hadn't seen stars on hotels since the large cities, so were very pleasantly surprised when we were able to have a superb room with bathroom for less than £5 for the night. It was February, and as we were travelling further south the temperature was rising above 30°C and it was becoming more humid, so an air-conditioned room would be a welcome luxury for a change.

I sat reading the personal ads in The Hindu in the reception area. Unlike most Indian newspapers, this one is written in English, so it was interesting to discover that many parents were advertising for a groom for their daughter or a bride for their son. The father's profession was always stated, and the required bride or groom always had to be 'fair, beautiful and slim'. Fair skin appears to be very important to people in all Asian countries and if a man or woman is fair, meaning a light Indian colour, they would generally be described as beautiful, regardless of other features. No other requirements were made in any of the ads apart from the request that a prospective groom should be 'stable', and there was usually a request for a horoscope and a photo. It is apparently very important for Indian parents that a couple's horoscopes match well before a marriage can be arranged.

The hotel was being used for a conference and dozens of men, all in smart striped shirts and white mundus, walked past me in reception carrying their briefcases. As with many of the more expensive Indian hotels, we had been asked to pay a deposit. When we asked what the deposit was for, we were told it was in case we stole the sheets! (Maybe some Indians made them into mundus!) We collected our return of deposit the next morning and set off again.

There didn't appear to be much countryside any more, so it was less pleasant cycling, and we were finding more and more road works. We were diverted along poorly-maintained side roads full of pot-holes, and when we tried to book a hotel in a town we found that, because of a school festival, all hotels were booked. This meant that we had a long day of cycling ahead of us before we were likely to find accommodation.

We stopped in a classy hotel in the town to have a banana milkshake and continued, but both of us soon began to feel sick. How extraordinary – we had eaten Indian meals in cafés that looked decidedly dirty and had never suffered a moment's illness, but as soon as we had a European treat in a more expensive location we were suffering. Warren was suffering particularly badly. He was constantly being sick at the side of the road, and it was obvious that we needed to find accommodation as soon as possible.

We cycled alongside a long sandy estuary, where men were washing themselves and women were washing clothes. Bullocks were led to the edge of the river to drink. The nearby town didn't look very inviting, and we couldn't initially find any accommodation. Plenty of small establishments were labelled

'Hotel', but in India this often denotes a small café without accommodation. We searched for a tourist home and found a seedy, not too clean establishment where we were offered a room with en suite shower room for 125 rupees – less than £2 for the night. It was laughable that they requested us to pay an extra 75 rupees to be returned when we left – there was certainly nothing of any value in the room to steal! I felt fine and was feeling hungry, but Warren didn't want to eat. However, he felt well enough after a shower and a rest to accompany me, and I was glad of it when we went out into the dark town. The few cafés that were open looked awful, but outside a shop stood a man with a wok and frying pan on a gas burner. I asked him for an omelette, and he expertly whisked two eggs with finely sliced onion, salt and green chilli, and cooked me a delicious fluffy omelette for only 8p! We returned to our hotel. It was a shock to see the room at night – two curtain-less windows on different walls allowed the light from the street to stream in. Warren fixed up our waterproof camouflage cover to block most of the light and we slept soundly.

We were now finding that we were travelling from seedy town to seedy town, and we never saw any westerners in any of these places. At one hotel we were told that only a de luxe room was available for 500 rupees, so I said I would look at it while Warren stayed with the bikes in the extremely squalid reception area. The bedroom was large but not luxurious in any way, and didn't even have a television which was common in the better rooms in Indian hotels. I returned to reception to find Warren talking to four young men. I shook my head to indicate that the room was not good.

'We've had better rooms for 200 rupees,' I said, and Warren laughingly replied that the young men had just told him that the most expensive room in the hotel was 200 rupees. The young men were incredibly angry that the hotel was trying to stitch us up, and they were concerned that it would give us a bad view of India, but we assured them that this hadn't happened before, and we still loved India. We left the reception, leaving the four men arguing in loud voices with the receptionist. The employees of the hotel next door were friendly and helpful, offered us a very pleasant en suite room with television for 180 rupees, and told us that there was a 24 hour service for tea or coffee – we only had to ring the bell!

Eating in a restaurant later that day we found the Indians actually turning their chairs to watch us eating. However, I was more fascinated by the way the Indians ate than they were by me. A woman was with her husband; they mixed the rice and curry on the stainless steel plate so vigorously with their fingers that food scattered all over the table. She pressed and moulded curry-soaked rice into balls so that she could pop the food easily into her mouth. However, the whole of her right hand, palm and fingers were covered in rice, and curry sauce and rice had squeezed through her fingers to the outside of her hand. A man on the table in front of me squeezed the rice and curry into a ball in the same way. As he held the ball in his hand while he talked to his friends, the curry sauce from the squeezed ball dripped between his fingers onto the table. Everyone used their left hand to lift the glass of water, and after eating each person stood with their right hand held aloft and walked to the wash basin in the corner of the restaurant. There they washed their hands, usually without soap. This procedure was always accompanied by the disgusting loud sound of phlegm being brought up to the mouth to spit into the wash basin. We asked for a spoon to eat our meal (we never saw forks being used) and spoons were always brought to us without any hesitation.

Only a few days later we were held up in a traffic jam because of a religious festival, and when we passed the traffic to get to the front of the queue, we found a procession of young men with pots on their heads full of leaves. They all looked dazed and glassy-eyed, so we assumed that they'd been taking drugs. One young man was being carried aloft by four friends. He was laid out flat on their arms, and was writhing as if in agony and his head was lolling, so he had obviously had even more of the magic mushrooms or whatever it was they had been taking!

I had found a mention in our guide book of an island just north of Kochi in Kerala, so we turned right and crossed the causeway to the small island, stopping to watch the fishermen throwing their circular nets. Wipin Island is long and narrow, running parallel to the mainland, with the causeway running from the mainland to the centre of the island. As we cycled along the palm-lined road of the island we noticed a raised platform made of bamboo, on which sat several Europeans. A row of four cottages with corrugated roofs stood in the garden. We slowed down, and a young Indian man approached us to say that if we wanted accommodation two English girls were just about to leave, and we could have their room as soon as it had been cleaned. We joined the other travellers on the platform, and could see now that it had been built so that there was a superb view of the sea and the fishermen in their boats a few yards away – high sand dunes otherwise blocked the view from the garden. The two English girls who were leaving were waiting for a taxi to collect them, and they were full of praise for the tiny resort and for Vipin, the young Indian man we had just met.

There was no town nearby, but for just pure relaxing, swimming in the sea or sunbathing it was perfect. We swam in the sea while dolphins played in the water only a few yards away. We could hear and see the waves from the porch of our hut, and we put up our hammocks between two palm trees where there was a lovely soft breeze. We intended to stay two nights, then stayed another two nights and then another two ... we had to go in the end, but it was difficult. Like the resort in My Happy Land, although this resort was run by an Indian, only westerners stayed there, and at breakfast and in the evenings we sat eating together, chatting, having a beer and exchanging experiences. One of the other travellers played his flute in the next cottage, which was a beautiful haunting sound, especially combined with the sound of the rolling waves. One night it rained, the gentle noise of the drops pattering on the corrugated tin roof above us which lulled us to sleep.

Vipin's mother cooked amazing food for us, and was happy to prepare anything we requested. For breakfast we had mouth-watering Keralan pancakes stuffed with fresh coconut, sugar, chopped cashew nuts and sliced bananas, all grown locally and served with black tea flavoured with cardamom pods. We had an incredibly delicious starter called Gobi Manchurian, and a dessert called Payasam (Kheer in northern India) which is a type of rice pudding, though it was apparently sometimes made with vermicelli noodles. Flavoured with cardamom, saffron, pistachios, almonds, cashew nuts and dried fruit, it was a delicious end to a wonderful dinner.

The four huts were constantly full; as soon as one couple moved out the room was filled by someone else. There were two Frenchmen who spent several months every year in India, buying goods which they exported to France in containers, so that they could sell the goods in their local markets for the rest of the year. There was an Englishman who was a doctor who had been doing voluntary work in India, but now his wife had come out to join him for a month's holiday before they returned to England. There was a Scottish girl and her boyfriend, a Dutch couple and two Australian girls. So many people, so many interesting stories . . .

From the southernmost tip of Wipin Island we took the 15 minute ferry to Kochi (previously called Cochin). We bought tickets from a man standing on the jetty – they cost us 1 rupee each for the 15 minute ferry crossing. We walked three steps to the boat, where a second man requested the tickets, tore each one in half and dropped the pieces on the jetty. He stood ankle deep in pieces of paper.

As we stepped onto the boat, Warren bet me a tenner that they didn't have enough life jackets for everyone.

'Bet you a million pounds they don't have any!' I replied.

Kochi was initially a shock, because it was full of westerners. There were postcards in the shops, and we hadn't seen any for weeks – we had bought a stock at the last tourist town so that we had enough to send our parents every week. We were also finally able to buy toilet paper in the shops which was fortunate, because we had been on strict rations with our last toilet roll. Prices were three times what we had been paying because we were now in a tourist area, though anyone arriving direct from Europe would have thought it very cheap.

We liked Kochi immensely – more than any of the other larger towns we had visited in India. Kochi and Ernakalum are twin cities, forming one of India's largest ports which has been used for centuries for exporting spices. Kochi is the old city; Ernakalum lies inland across the large natural harbour and is a modern city. We took the ferry from Kochi, where we were staying, to Ernakalum. The ferries crossed between the twin cities every few minutes and cost 2½ rupees for the 15 minute trip (about 3p). The ferry was packed with local people going to work. We found Ernakalum to be a large town jam-packed with noisy traffic, and the streets were full of shops, banks and offices. It was clearly not a tourist town, despite the fact that its twin city was very much so.

We wandered along the busy pavements, looking into the shop windows and occasionally wandering into the shops. There were many shops selling saris, with dazzling arrays of vivid coloured silks in their windows. We went inside one shop, and were immediately welcomed and led to an area where a white covered double mattress was surrounded by low stools. Sitting on the stools were a middle-aged lady and her daughter. The shop assistant picked an orange sari, edged with gold embroidery and fine tassels. She dramatically threw the sari across the mattress holding one end, so that the sari rolled out over the white fabric. The ladies fingered the edge of the fabric, while the assistant pulled out another sari, this time kingfisher blue, and threw it alongside the orange one. The blue sari was followed by a lime green sari, and the assistant continued choosing and displaying saris in this way until the white mattress was completely covered with lengths of gorgeous silks of every possible colour, the bright light above picking out the gold and silver threads of the embroidery that adorned the fabrics.

Whilst I think that saris look wonderful on Indian women, I'm not certain that they suit Europeans, so decided to buy for myself a salwar kameez as a souvenir to send home. A salwar kameez, which many young Indian girls prefer to saris, consists of three pieces – a short-sleeved dress or tunic, usually thigh length with slits up the sides, a pair of simple trousers which are one-size and shapeless but tie at the waist and taper down the leg to the ankle, and a dupatta, a matching shawl which is usually draped round the front of the neck and hangs down the back. I bought a pack – embroidered fabric to make into a tunic, a dupiatta already made from finer embroidered fabric with tassels at each end, and plain matching fabric for the trousers. I chose a stunning emerald fabric embroidered with gold for 396 rupees (just over £5) and for another 100 rupees a tailor made it up for me that afternoon before we returned to Kochi.

Kochi is quieter than Ernakalum, but has interesting old buildings and a beach where Chinese fishing nets have been built into the water. Each Chinese net is a massive construction which looks like an enormous four-legged spider made of branches roped together. It has a square net hanging beneath it, each corner attached to one of the four legs, with the centre of the net pulled up to form a cone when the net is out of the water. The whole construction is mounted on the end of a huge 'A' frame which lowers the net into the water. Rocks are suspended on ropes at the opposite end and these are the counter-weights. The construction is always built on stilts in the water, and is operated by a minimum of four men, who haul on the ropes to reveal the catch (nowadays very poor), and the fish are then scooped out with a net on a long stick. These Chinese fishing nets are everywhere in south Kerala – on the beaches, the rivers and in the backwaters, and are a result of Chinese influence on the region many centuries ago. The fishing nets made wonderful silhouettes for sunset or sunrise pictures. Alongside the nets on the beach picturesque multi-coloured striped fishing boats landed to unload their catch of tuna.

We were interested by the trees that lined the promenade, which had exotic flowers and enormous bean-like seed pods, so we took photographs in the hope that we could later identify the tree. An Indian man approached us.

'The seeds from these trees are used for growthing of the hair,' he told us. As most Indians have beautiful thick wavy hair we could only assume that the 'growthing' medicine worked!

As in all Indian coastal regions the Keralans eat a lot of fish, and we loved to watch the different ways that they fished. As well as the Chinese nets, some Keralans used circular nets which they swung round their heads as they stood in their small boats, throwing the weighted nets into the water in a perfect circle on top of any shoals of fish that were swimming past. They quickly hauled in the nets which had closed around the fish. There were also fishermen who waded a few yards out into the shallow sea, and laid nets early every morning. They returned a few hours later to collect any fish caught in the nets. There were also large fishing boats, carved out of solid wood, and more than a dozen men rowed each boat out to sea, where they dropped their nets in the hope of a good catch.

There is an area in Kochi called Jew Town, where the Jews used to store, sell and export the many spices grown in Kerala. There are still many spice shops there, and we walked past the shops we inhaled the aroma of coriander, ginger, cloves, cinnamon, star anise, mace, cumin seeds and aniseed. Also in Jew Town are the antique shops; these were a complete surprise for us, and we spent a lot of time exploring these wonderful shops, most the size of warehouses or emporiums. Many of them stocked reclaimed architectural items, and these particularly fascinated us – delicate antique cast-iron or wooden spiral staircases; magnificent carved and panelled doors which they made into stunning dining tables or coffee tables; incredibly elegant wide, shallow brass or bronze antique Indian cooking pots, now being used to make fish ponds for the conservatory or containers for the garden; complete oriental gazebos for the garden; solid rosewood or teak columns which could be used to make fabulous four-poster beds. There were wooden boxes, carved or inlaid with brass, ivory or mother-of-pearl stacked to the ceiling of a warehouse in every size from money box or jewellery box to massive blanket chests carved out of camphor wood. When the lids were lifted from these camphor wood chests the pleasant smell of the wood reached our nostrils. Of course, compared to England the prices were incredibly low, so we were tempted to fill a container to send back to England, but obviously the cost of shipping and of any customs duty payable as the goods entered England might have been prohibitive. However, I have to say we were very tempted . . .

We took a rickshaw back to our hotel, and the driver asked us if we would like to visit a special shop. He told us that he was given a point for a t-shirt for every customer that he brought to the shop. We were tired, but he was pleasant, so we agreed. We admired the beautifully made new rosewood and teak furniture, obviously made for the European market, and the taxi driver excitedly told us on the way home that he now had 7 of his 10 points to get his t-shirt!

As we cycled further south we noticed men painting the hoardings which were set up alongside the road in the fields. I think it is quite well known that in India many of the advertising posters, including the massive hoardings, are hand-painted. It was fascinating to see enormous long lengths of bamboo roughly tied together to form scaffolding which leant on a giant hoarding with no apparent fixing. It looked precarious, but a man was sat on one of the horizontal pieces of bamboo with his paint tin and his brushes, carefully painting the enormous advertisement. Sometimes the advertisement was for milk, and showed a picture of a beautiful plump black and white cow, very English-looking and quite unlike the bony Indian cows. It might be a picture of Wills' Scissors filter cigarettes, or Good Knight mosquito coils. Surprisingly, considering the Indian view on exposing bare flesh, there was often a picture of a woman in bra and panties advertising underwear 'for your melodious moods', or advertisements for insurance companies, the most popular being the Prudential, my previous employer!

Every poster, every end wall of houses, every garden wall, every shop sign, every road sign was hand-painted, and this probably accounted for the frequent different spellings for town names – each artist used his own spelling! We saw Wipin Island spelt as Wypen, Wippin, and Wypeen on four different signs within a few miles of each other. Maps often showed a different spelling again – it was most confusing. However, I found it quite endearing to see that everyone spelt English words in the way they thought it should be spelt – menus in restaurants offered 'Chinees' or even 'Chainees' dishes. Oringe, Choclat, Watermilon, Temtassion and Delite were all on the same ice cream menu, and a business card from a tailor described the fabrics that he sold – 'Pour cottan, pour silk, leenan and rayan'! Large notices by the roadside often advertised 'two wheelar servising'.

We passed Christian churches so full of worshippers that people were even standing outside singing hymns, and it wasn't even a Sunday. We missed the turning to the National Highway, so found our way blocked by a small river. However, there were three small boats tied together with planks to make a platform, so we stood on the planks with our bikes with two motorbikes and their drivers and were ferried across. Going in the opposite direction was a tuk-tuk on a similar ferry! There was no charge for the service, and a few minutes later we rejoined the main highway.

We were travelling along a dual carriageway, and every few hundred yards were signs to encourage safe driving. We considered these to be token gestures only, judging by the dreadful standards of driving in India, and some of the notices didn't make sense. Others were so desperate to rhyme that they were pathetic. 'Left is right' said one. 'Speed thrills but kills' said another. They went on and on – 'Rash causes Crash', 'Accidents are not accidental', 'Hurry causes worry', 'Stop accidents before they stop you', 'Dim and bright – do it right', 'Do not mix drink with drive', 'With a little care accidents rare', 'He who kills time commits suicide', 'Safety has no margin for error', 'Never be absent-minded; ever be safety-minded', 'Time is precious but life is more', 'Two wheels for two – not too many'. This last one made me laugh – it was common to see whole families on small motorbikes; indeed, it was rare to see less than two people on a bicycle, and we had never seen vehicles more unsafely overloaded than in India.

We constantly had to swerve on the dual carriageway to avoid large steaming heaps of elephant droppings – we had seen many temple elephants in the past weeks as we cycled through Kerala. The elephants were mostly used for special religious occasions and festivals, and we had seen them dressed up in their finery – gold head-dresses which fitted over the top of their head and down between the eyes to the tusks. The sides of these metal head-dresses were decorated with brightly coloured baubles, and one or two young men always sat on top of the elephant holding aloft coloured parasols on very long handles. It looked very impressive to see a line of such elephants, but we were concerned that each elephant always had three of its legs shackled with chains looped together, and we had heard that the temple elephants in India were often ill-treated. The previous year we had seen hundreds of elephants in the wild on holiday in Africa, so it made us very sad to think of these beautiful, usually gentle creatures being restrained. (Whilst Warren and I had been wild camping in the bush in Botswana with a guide the previous year, we had learnt that if wild elephants came too close to our tent all we had to do was clap our hands sharply. The elephant would simply turn round and go away, and this even worked for small herds of elephants – how could anyone ill-treat such a wonderful animal?) We read a few weeks later in The Hindu newspaper that a trainer had been attacked by his elephant and killed, and the elephant hadn't allowed anyone near the dead trainer for several hours. The paper reported that ill treatment by the trainer was the cause for the attack – it was a case of the elephant getting his own back, but no doubt the elephant was destroyed because of his final act.

We arrived at Allapey where we intended to spend a lazy day travelling south on a boat through the backwaters to Kollam. There were mostly western travellers on the ferry, possibly because the price of the tickets was prohibitive for Indians (but maybe they were allowed on the boat at a reduced price!). Our bikes were strapped to the railings of the boat, and we travelled along canals, waterways and across lakes, seeing life at the riverside. Small houses were dotted alongside the palm-fringed waterways, and we constantly saw women washing clothes at the edge of the river, children washing and playing in the water beside them. Keralan houseboats cruised passed us. The houseboats looked oriental rather than Indian. They had coconut palm leaf roofs which curved up and down in the most spectacular and elegant way, and raised flaps at the sides protected the glassless windows to give shade. On the banks of one canal these houseboats were being made – each one was a different shape, with hooded 'eyebrows' over the openings for windows and doors, and wings were added to give shade. Some had verandahs at the top, again protected with roofs to give shade.

In many places we saw coconut fibre being prepared and spun to make string and rope. The coconut palm is a fascinating tree which has so many uses, and is as important to the Asian countries as the olive tree is to the Mediterranean countries. A coconut is protected by two outer layers, a fibrous yellow-green husk around a hard brown shell. Inside the hard shell is a third layer, the coconut meat, and inside that a central cavity containing watery coconut milk. The younger a coconut is the softer the meat will be, the more liquid it will have and the better it will be for drinking. As the coconut ages the milk is absorbed and the coconut meat firms. Coconuts bought at the supermarket in this country are brown and hard with fibrous hair, because the outer husk has already been removed.

The unripe coconut supplies refreshing milk and coconut 'gel' and the ripe coconut is dried and grated to be used in cooking. The fibre is used to make string, rope, brushes, mats and mattress stuffing. Dead leaves of palm are soaked to make them supple, and they are woven to form a fabric which can be used for roofs and fences. Coconut oil is obviously made from coconuts, and is the most commonly used oil in India. Coconut toddy is an alcoholic brew made by the locals by tapping the buds of a coconut flower whilst it is still on the tree. Yeast present in the sweet sap ferments the sugar changing it into alcohol. The liquid when removed is not alcoholic initially, but becomes more alcoholic each day. In our experience it smelt and tasted like old socks!

We watched the heavy wooden boats, hand-carved from solid wood, poled along the waterways laden with straw, coconuts and other goods. The same boats were used as tiny ferries for locals to cross the rivers. The boats, designed for 3 or 4 fishermen, carried 15 or more standing passengers, many of whom were holding their bicycles beside them as well!

We passed schools where the children stopped their chanting as we passed, and ran to the banks of the canals shouting 'One pen, one pen,' hoping that we would throw them the pens that they loved. We came to an open area of water, where there were dozens of Chinese fishing nets, and our ferry passed through an avenue of these massive nets, which looked like abandoned cranes at a dock.

The sun began to set behind the palm trees, and shortly afterwards we arrived at Kollam in the dark. After the chaos of trying to disembark from the boat and fighting our way through the hordes of Indian taxi drivers offering us lifts, we cycled to the rather dismal town to find a hotel.

Back on the road the following morning we had a delicious breakfast of appams (pancakes made of rice flour served with curry sauce) and black tea. The tea was served in a glass with a spare glass alongside. There were two reasons for the spare glass – to cool the tea, and also to drain off the tea leaves. At a total cost of 6 rupees for the two of us (8p) it was the cheapest breakfast so far! We were aiming for Varkala, which was 15km off the main road – we knew it to be a haunt of western travellers, and had heard that it had a beautiful beach.

As we approached Varkala we were lucky enough to bump into Patrick along the road. Patrick was an American from Wisconsin, and told us that the house where he was living had a spare room. We followed his directions, and found a brand new house set amongst the trees, where the owner offered us a lovely room for 300 rupees (£4) a night. We put up our mosquito net over the bed so we could leave the windows wide open at night to get plenty of fresh cool night air.

Suddenly, there were more British, Americans, Australians, Germans, Danes, Swedes and French than there were Indians, and although we had always enjoyed meeting the locals and chatting to them, it was wonderful to speak to westerners again and not to feel different from everyone around us. We could exchange experiences, discuss places to visit, and simply relax. We met Helen, an English girl who had been living in California, who had decided to cycle round India alone. I thought she was incredibly brave to travel alone and she had certainly had some interesting experiences.

On one occasion cycling through India, Helen had been followed by an Indian man in his thirties. He was pleasant, polite and well-spoken, but for several days while Helen was cycling he had followed behind her on his motorbike. No doubt he had fallen for Helen, a pretty blond-haired confident girl, who was certainly very different from any Indian girls that he would know. When she stopped for the night at a hotel he would also book his own room. On one occasion Helen had stopped cycling to take photos of some young children in a field looking after cows. She spoke to the children, but they didn't understand her. Her admirer approached, and she asked him to speak to them. He was horrified, and refused to speak to these children, because they were of a lower caste than him! Helen was eventually able to get rid of her follower, but this story warns of problems that could exist, especially for girls travelling alone in out-of-the-way places.

The sandy beach at Varkala was beneath a steep cliff, and there was quite a lot of surf as the waves came rolling in. At the top of the cliff was a walk where all the restaurants, bars, tailors' shops and souvenir shops were situated. There was also an Ayurvedic clinic, where I booked myself in for a massage to ease my aching neck and arms. At 6 o'clock every evening, we sat in a restaurant on the cliff top overlooking the glorious beach, watching the sun set through the palm trees. On the beach the fishermen were pulling in their fishing lines, with the help of numerous western travellers. We drank our beer from large china mugs or small china teacups, which we poured from a teapot. However, if we were at the back of the restaurant out of sight of passers by, we were allowed to keep a bottle of beer hidden under the table. We passed a couple of westerners on the cliff top path, watching a plane make a double vapour trail in the sky as the sun began to set.

'I think it's a meteorite,' said one in awe.

Warren and I grinned at each other, and out of earshot Warren whispered to me, 'I thought Heathrow was an airport, but maybe it's a meteorite launching station!'

Varkala was very clean, because an American traveller had taken it upon himself to tidy up the beach and cliff top and install waste bins. The local council were trying to get him deported because he had shown them up, but we felt that this was very short-sighted of them. Litter is unfortunately one of the things that spoils India (though we have to say that we saw a lot of rubbish in many of the Greek islands as well). In towns and villages there was always a tarmac road with a dirt area between the road and shops for pedestrians. This area was usually covered with empty glass and plastic bottles, metal bottle tops, broken flip-flops, pieces of coconut shells, paper, polythene bags, cigarette cartons, pieces of newspaper, strips of fabric (from the many tailors), paper and cardboard. Any vegetable waste was quickly eaten by the rummaging cows, dogs, chickens and crows, and we often saw the cows eating the cardboard as well. When we once returned ice-cream tubs to the shop to be binned, the owner angrily took them, crossed the road and threw them onto the ground. After having a take-away from a street stall, we returned the newspaper wrapping to the stall-holder, but he simply threw it on the ground alongside his stall! As the Indians are fanatical about sweeping their own little piece of dirt in front of their shop or house, we found this total lack of concern about litter very difficult to understand.

While we were in Varkala we were told about Kumali, an Indian lady who liked to cook meals in her own kitchen for travellers. We went to see her to give her notice that we would like lunch the next day, and she turned out to be the most amazing, lovely motherly lady, who hugged us as soon as she met us; she was clearly thrilled to be cooking for us. For our lunch the next day she made eight different vegetable dishes for us to eat with rice and poppadoms. On a banana leaf she placed in turn curries made from carrot, beetroot, unripe papaya, bananas, okra, potato, lentils and drumsticks. (The latter is a very fibrous long vegetable which tastes similar to asparagus – the flesh is scraped out with the teeth and the fibrous outer covering is discarded.) We ate in a covered porch surrounded by black and white family photos on the wall, including two photos of deceased relatives in their coffins surrounded by flowers and family. The food was different from anything we had tasted before, and we enjoyed a wonderful meal for a small cost, after which Kumali delighted in showing us her garden where she grew cashew nuts, jackfruit, breadfruit, tamarind, papayas, coconuts, aubergines, chillies, and other vegetables. She was also very proud to show us her new kitchen, where she cooked mainly on a log fire in the corner of the granite worktop. She was nervous to use the new gas hob, because a new gas bottle would cost her 300 rupees, she told us!

Kumali kept chickens, and when she discovered that she had three fresh, still warm eggs, she wanted to cook an omelette for us immediately, even though we were full to bursting! She also kept a cow which produced fresh milk for her, and a man came to milk it every day for her at a cost of 200 rupees per month (£2.50). (Interestingly, India produces more milk than any other country in the world). She wanted it to have another calf – if the calf was female she would keep it, but if it was male it would be sold for meat. Cows, of course, are sacred, so are never eaten by Hindus. It was meeting local people like Kumali that made travelling so interesting.

We had such a wonderful meal with Kumali that we booked to have breakfast at her house one morning, and she cooked a typical Keralan dish called puttu, which is made from wheat or rice flour, salt and water. This mixture is put into a cylindrical puttu cooker alternated with grated coconut, and is steamed for a few minutes. The swiss roll shaped puttu is removed, and crumbled over the plate or banana leaf and served with savoury or sweet accompaniments. Kumali wanted us to try both, so we had it first with mung beans and afterwards with banana and sugar, and both were delicious.

Warren cut my hair for me, and he was by now my official hairdresser – those who know him will find it hard to believe, but he became very competent. It all began when I had a 50 rupee (67p) haircut in Varkalla. The hairdresser left me with an uneven fringe, and insufficient hair had been cut from the back. It may be because the scissors she was using looked like wallpaper scissors, and they certainly weren't very sharp. There was no mirror for me to watch the cutting process, but it was clear that the Indian girl cutting my hair was unused to short hair. Warren had been watching the whole process.

'I could do better than that,' he said, so I handed him my hairdressing scissors (I regularly cut his hair), and risked it. He snipped away confidently, leaving me with such a professional-looking short haircut that several of our new friends complimented me. I was impressed.

The last evening before we left Varkalla, we returned to our room to see that in the ground floor room below us several Indians were laying coloured powders onto the marble floor. There was a square of blue powder, and two men were painstakingly making neat circles inside each other with white powder within the square. They spent several hours working on the design, adding ornate details around the corners and within the circles. It looked quite beautiful. We asked what they were doing, and a man who we thought was possibly a holy man said it was for the gods, so it was obviously going to be for a Hindu ceremony.

I was woken at 2am by the sound of firecrackers and chanting, so I went to see what was happening. There was a fire burning in the middle of the ground floor room, the holy man was chanting, and women were sat throwing flower petals into the fire and on the floor alongside a pair of enormous brass candlesticks. Numerous people sat around inside and outside the room, and a man was asleep on the floor in the doorway. I returned to bed, but the ringing of a bell in the room below us kept me awake. In the morning I went again to investigate. The room was empty, but the fire was still smouldering on the marble floor; leaves and rubbish had been swept into a pile, and two stainless steel pots and dozens of stainless steel cups stood to one side alongside the candlesticks. Apparently a relative of the owner of the house had died, and this ceremony took place in every house connected with the deceased.

While we were relaxing in Varkalla we had an opportunity to look at our world map to try to plan where we would go when we left India. We had decided to travel to Myanmar, formerly known as Burma, and knew that we would have to fly into that country – no tourists were allowed to cross the border. We decided to travel up the east coast of India to Kolkata (formerly Calcutta), where we would go to the Burmese consulate to get a visa and fly to Yangon in the south of Myanmar. That was the simplest part of the planning. We also wanted to visit Vietnam, Laos and Cambodia, but visa restrictions for each of those countries made it very difficult for us to plan. The visas for each country lasted only one month, but some of these visas could only be obtained at the embassies in Bangkok. It was occasionally possible to get visas at certain land borders, but we had to plan our journey carefully because border rules could be changed without notice. It was incredibly complicated trying to plan a trip that would allow us to visit all three of these countries in Indo China. Because we were cycling we would obviously take longer to get through each country than someone using public transport, so sometimes the visa didn't allow us enough time for the route we wanted to take. However, it was clear that we needed to start the trip from Bangkok.

The next leg of our journey should have been simple but was made very complicated by Sri Lankan airlines. From Varkalla it was not far to Thiruvananthapuram (previously called Trivandrum, which was definitely easier to pronounce!) where there was an international airport, and Warren and I discussed whether to fly to the Maldives or to Sri Lanka. I wanted to go to the Maldives, despite the fact that there would be little opportunity to cycle, but we discovered that the Maldives were not suitable for the independent traveller unless he or she had plenty of money – there were no cheap places to stay. The Maldives was way out of our budget, even though the flight itself was very cheap, so we decided to fly to Sri Lanka for two weeks, after which we planned to return to India to continue our cycling.

We booked a return flight to Colombo, the capital of Sri Lanka, but were told that the flight was always overbooked, so we wouldn't know until the day before whether or not our booking could be confirmed. We therefore had to cycle to Thiruvananthapurum to be ready for the flight without actually being sure that we would have a flight! It was quite comforting as we arrived in the town to see words and initials in non-tourist towns that seem so familiar to us in England. The head post office was marked GPO, just as it used to be in England, and outside the local hospital were the letters ENT (ear, nose and throat). One hospital we passed was advertising itself as a 'multy speciality hospital' (sic), and I wondered if this made it a general hospital?

We phoned the travel agent to get confirmation of the flight but were told that we were 'on the waiting list' for the flight, and that was the only way they sold tickets. (They hadn't, of course, told us that when we booked the tickets). Every phone call was the same – phone later, phone tomorrow morning, phone tomorrow afternoon, or else the office was closed and all we got was the answer phone. We phoned Sri Lankan Airlines, who told us that we could only fly to Colombo if there was a cancellation; however, they assured us that they were able to confirm our return flights! We were thoroughly confused and frustrated. We began to think that we weren't going to fly to Sri Lanka, when our hotel receptionist called us to say that the travel agent had just phoned to say that our tickets were confirmed.

The next morning we were up at 5.30 and had to cycle along roads which weren't signposted despite the fact that they were leading to an international airport. When we arrived at the airport building the armed guards wouldn't allow anyone in the building until 7am, so we spent the time preparing our bikes and bags for the flight. We had decided to pack all of our eight large pannier bags into two large cheap holdalls which we had purchased in an Indian market. There was no way we could lock them, so we tied them round with string. We did this to a large audience of Indians who were standing behind a barrier presumably waiting for arrivals. When we checked in we found that our bags were probably the smartest of any of the others being checked in – most of the Indians were checking in cardboard boxes tied with string! Problems began when we were told that we had excess baggage. This was annoying, because we'd checked first with the airline before booking the tickets and had been told that the bikes wouldn't be charged for. Eventually the officials agreed to waive part of the excess fee, but as we went to pay the reduced fee, someone chased after us to tell us that we didn't need to pay after all!

We made the mistake of leaving our cutlery bag in our hand luggage, and it contained a couple of sharp knives and some scissors, as well as our titanium cutlery, a gas lighter, special matches that light even when wet, folding cooking tools, miniature salt and pepper pots and many other invaluable bits and pieces. They confiscated the whole bag, saying that we could collect it at Colombo, but when we asked for a receipt they said that they never gave one. Before getting onto the plane, all the passengers had to walk onto the tarmac to a vast pile of luggage and identify their own suitcases. It was total pandemonium as people fell over bags and luggage searching for their own possessions. It struck us as very odd, because it gave ample opportunity for anyone to remove a knife or other weapon from their already checked in luggage. As we walked up the steps to the aeroplane we chatted to an Englishman. He told us that they'd found some nail scissors in his hand luggage and were going to confiscate them.

'Well, I'm obviously not going to kill anyone with them, am I?' he had said.

'Oh, alright then,' they said, and handed the scissors back to him!

The flight was only 45 minutes, so within a very short time our plane was descending to Colombo airport. We had made it to Sri Lanka after all!

CHAPTER 8

SRI LANKA

Suspended like a teardrop in the Indian Ocean off the south-eastern tip of India, Sri Lanka is a typically tropical island. Although the island is only 269 miles/433km north to south and 151 miles/244km east to west (about the size of Ireland or Tasmania), it has two monsoons a year, which means that the north-east and the south-west regions of the island have dry seasons at different times. The centre of the island is mountainous, luxuriously wooded and cold, but the coastline is mostly flat. The first Sinhalese people are thought to have originated from north India. They represent 74% of the population, speak Sinhala and are predominantly Buddhist. Tamils, the second largest group, constituting 18% of the population, originated from south India. They live in the north of Sri Lanka, speak Tamil and are mostly Hindu.

It was the end of February when we landed in Sri Lanka's Colombo airport, and the first surprise was the fact that we had to add half an hour to our watches, as Sri Lanka was 6 hours ahead of Great Britain, whereas India was only five and a half.

In the baggage reclamation area our worst fears were confirmed when we were told that they knew nothing about our cutlery bag. Our hopes were dashed even further when they asked for our receipt, and told us that we should have asked for one! We knew there was no hope of replacing most of the items in the bag and they were very important to us, so we decided to wait until the next plane arrived the following day, so the airport official promised to telex Thiruvananthapuram airport requesting that our belongings be put on the next plane. Suffice it to say that we spent the first two days of our holiday in Sri Lanka staying near to the airport, making numerous frustrating phone calls to the airport, and waiting to see if the one plane each day would arrive with our belongings. On the second day we received good news, and Warren made a mad dash to the airport before it closed for the day. He was handed the bag intact, and we were able to continue our journey.

Whilst the central mountainous region is very interesting to visit with its forests, waterfalls, rice, rubber, fruit and tea plantations, we had booked only two weeks in Sri Lanka, so had insufficient time to visit the whole island. Cycling up mountains takes a lot of time, so we chose to cycle north a little to Negombo, and then back down the west coast to the southernmost point of Sri Lanka. Along this coast are the finest beaches in the island, many of them popular for surfing.

We noticed immediately that Sri Lanka appeared to be far more westernised than India. There were very few women in saris or men in lungis. Women wore trousers or long or calf-length skirts with short-sleeved tops, and men wore trousers, shorts or jeans. We couldn't recall ever seeing an Indian in shorts or jeans apart from in Goa, and only one or two women in western dress. The cars were far more sophisticated as well. Most of them were expensive Japanese models – Toyota, Nissan, Mazda and Mitsubishi, whereas the vehicles with few exceptions in India were made by Tata, the massive Indian company. We even saw an articulated lorry, something we'd never seen in India. There were proper pavements and kerbs, even in some of the villages, and in the busy towns there were plenty of police directing traffic to allow people across the road – almost unheard of in India.

We saw Sri Lankans on racing bikes, wearing lycra shorts and gear, and locals out jogging – the first since we had left Italy. Women sat side-saddle on the crossbars of bicycles holding babies or tiny children in their arms and holding an umbrella aloft to give them shade. In India the women always sat on the rack at the back of the bicycle, their saris floating in the wheels. Helmets were worn by motor-cyclists and passengers – a rarity in India – and we saw enough Dutch cyclists in Sri Lanka for a local to call out to us 'Hello Holland' as we passed!

Although still very cheap compared with England, the prices in Sri Lanka were double India's prices, and accommodation cost more than double. 10% was often added to the bills for restaurants and hotels, and this came as a shock to us. Beer was about the same price as in India, but we saw European wine for the first time since we had left Europe, though it was comparatively expensive. Alcohol was freely available, unlike most of India. We understood, however, that the Buddhists weren't allowed to drink alcohol on the night of a full moon, so at that time restaurants disguised alcohol in the same way as in Kerala, serving it in cups and mugs!

Our first breakfast was a little daunting. We stopped in a small local café at the side of the road, and found that the food looked very different from in India. In a glass cabinet, sitting on a sheet of newspaper were mounds of noodles about 3" in diameter and a similar height. These were called 'string hoppers' and were eaten with dhal (lentil curry). The pile of noodles was in fact made up of a number of disks of tangled noodles stacked on top of each other. There was no alternative food, so we chose the string hoppers, but because the waiter picked them up with his bare hands and because there were flies buzzing around inside the glass cabinet, we removed the top and bottom layers of noodles and left them uneaten on our plate. Tea was served in pretty china cups and saucers, and we found this to be the case throughout Sri Lanka. The string hoppers were delicious and the dhal was excellent, and we found it consistently good in Sri Lanka. However, after we had finished our meal, the waiter picked up the disks of noodles left on our plates, and threw them back on top of another pile in the glass cabinet, ready for the next customer! We were pleased to find later that this wasn't the usual standard of hygiene, and often enjoyed a popular Singhalese breakfast of dhal with a whole newly-baked loaf of bread chopped into chunks to 'dunk' into the curry. The only bread we ever saw in India was chappati or naans.

Food was generally more westernised than in India. Though we tried hard to find local food, it was sometimes difficult because the areas we were visiting were so geared to tourists, so we often found ourselves eating steaks, spaghetti bolognaise, pizzas, prawn cocktails and other western dishes, simply because there was no other choice. For us, though, eating the local food with the local people was a very important part of our travelling.

Having first travelled north of the airport, we had now turned south again and had to cycle through Colombo, the capital of Sri Lanka. Soldiers stood behind sandbags near every important official building with their machine guns at the ready. In 2002 a cease-fire had been agreed and the Tamil Tigers and the Sri Lankan government were tolerating each other, but it was clear that despite the truce the government were not taking any chances. Once we left Colombo we saw no more soldiers.

The road and the railway followed the coast, criss-crossing each other, and as we cycled south we had the shade of trees from the east but to the west we had spectacular views of the beaches. The beaches in Sri Lanka are beautiful – long stretches of sand fringed with coconut palms, with white-tipped surf rolling in onto empty beaches. Flat-bottomed fishing boats carved from solid wood with 45° angled ends stood side by side on the sand, alongside very narrow boats with an outrigger on one side. These boats were too narrow for anyone to sit in, so the fishermen sat on a plank fixed on the top.

We found it interesting to watch the strange way the south Sinhalese fishermen caught their fish – each fisherman sat on a stilt embedded into the sand in the shallow surf. The stilt was a simple sturdy branch from a tree, usually with a tiny platform added for them to perch on. They wrapped one leg round the stilt and sat with their line in the surf, waiting patiently for the fish to bite. However, if they saw a tourist taking a photo, they immediately jumped off the stilt, ran through the water, across the beach and onto the road, where they put out their hand and asked for 30 Sri Lankan rupees (about 18p). Clearly tourism produced more income than fishing – many Sinhalese would consider 30 rupees a good income for a day's work!

We noticed from the road signs that the Sinhalese language was incredibly beautiful, with rounded curly letters that looked more like art than the alphabet. Certain areas that we passed were popular tourist destinations, where we met English, German and French tourists. We stayed in guest houses or hotels, always with attached bathrooms, but on one occasion we were waylaid by a local woman as we left the second hotel that had told us they were full.

'One room,' she said, pointing to the house next door. We followed her into the house. Her living room looked pleasant, but the bedroom she showed us looked shabby despite the fact it was not well lit. However, we were hot, tired and dusty from a few hours' cycling, and were desperate for a shower, so we agreed to stay for one night. Only when we pulled back the curtains did we see the rubbish on the floor, one corner of which she'd swept as she stood talking to us; the furniture was thick with dust and the net curtains were filthy. I later found a pair of men's pants on the floor and, thinking they were Warren's I threw them into his open bag nearby. It's lucky I mentioned it to him as I did it, because there was a shout of horror.

'They're not MINE!'

The enormous shower room at least had a good shower, though the cracked wash basin was not a pretty sight first thing in the morning. However, the overgrown back garden, full of elegant apricot amaryllis flowers which were now growing wild amongst the weeds, led straight onto the stunning beach at Mirissa. The beach was a crescent of white sand protected at one end by a palm-covered headland and at the other end by Parrot Rock, an 'almost' island where we could paddle across the sandbank and climb up onto the grass-covered rocks. This was our favourite place for watching the sun set across the bay, while the surf rolled in and crashed onto the rocks below us.

We moved to a hotel three doors away the next morning, where we had a pleasant clean room with a lovely bathroom, but we could still wander through the garden onto the beach to sit at one of the beach cafés for a drink or a meal, watching the steep rolling waves hammering the sand. At virtually every hotel in Sri Lanka we could hear the waves rolling onto the beach as we lay in our bed at night, because the road followed the coastline so closely.

Interestingly, most of the guest houses and hotels stated 'Foreigners only' on their signs. Whilst we consider this discriminatory, the Indians and Sinhalese appear to have no problems being prejudiced in this way. Foreigners are preferred because the Sinhalese and Indians can ask them for more money than the locals. In India, for example, there are two prices for the same train tickets –

the official price for a foreigner buying a train ticket is double what an Indian would pay.

We saw some interesting wild life in Sri Lanka. Monitor lizards up to four feet long basked on rocks in the sun only a few feet from our table at lunchtime; the biggest hermit crabs we'd ever seen appeared to be happy travelling long distances from the beach, and even tried to cross the busy road. We saw the same lovely birds that we had seen in India – kingfishers, bee-eaters, cattle egret and storks. One morning we watched dozens of enormous bats with wing spans of over one metre swooping high over tall trees above the road as we began our early morning cycling, and we realised that these were Indian flying foxes, the largest of all bats. We also often saw pretty little squirrels with striped backs in the trees between towns.

We noticed that the locals in Sri Lanka made coconut toddy, which was also popular in India. Toddy trees are not allowed to bear fruit. The toddy tappers scale up the trees to tap the juice – the opened flowers are bent over and tied, and sap starts to drip out into a half coconut shell that has been placed to catch it. Every morning and evening the toddy tapper climbs from flower to flower, changing the full shells for empty ones. One palm yields an average of 270 litres annually, and a good tapper can get a month's sap from one flower. Toddy can be boiled down to make jaggery, a type of brown sugar, and fermented and distilled toddy becomes Arrack, a honey-coloured alcoholic drink. Vinegar was also a by-product of distillation.

Again, we saw many uses for the coconut palm. The ekel broom is made from the tough mid-rib of the coconut leaf – the rib is split open to expose the long, strong, wiry bristles inside that form the brush. The brooms are made into the style we know as besom or witches' brooms, though in Sri Lanka they are usually used without handles. Bowls were made from polished coconut shells. We discovered that it is ritually significant for a baby's first solid food to be rice cooked in coconut milk, and this is also served at weddings. The bud of the coconut can also be pickled and eaten.

We saw heavy rain on a number of occasions in the evenings or during the night in Sri Lanka, usually following a few hours of overcast skies and extra high humidity, but we couldn't get a consistent answer from the locals whether this was usual or not. Whilst the climate is complex because of the two monsoons, all literature we read indicated that rain started in the south and west (where we were) in May – it was only March at that time.

One day as we were cycling, we saw a sign saying 'To a beautiful Buddhist temple', so we turned off to find it. Two novice monks, aged 14 and 17, clothed in dark red robes sat beside the sacred bodhi tree (Ficus Religiosa). This is a type of fig tree and is considered sacred by both Hindus and Buddhists, and is often found in Buddhist monasteries and Hindu temples. The bodhi tree in this monastery was so old that the ancient large branches had been propped up with lengths of wood to stop them breaking. Around the tree was a cement walkway, so that the monks could walk round and round the tree.

The banyan tree (Ficus Benghalensis) is another sacred tree, and is a giant tree common in India and Sri Lanka. It starts out life as an epiphyte, a plant that is supported by another plant but doesn't need it for nutrition. As it grows, it produces aerial roots that hang down from the horizontal branches and take root where they touch the ground. These thick strong roots hang like a curtain, and eventually grow to look like tree trunks – these can create a forest on their own, and form a virtual wall of wood. There is a famous banyan tree near Poona in India which is said to measure half a mile around its perimeter and is capable of sheltering 2,000 people! The tree is considered so sacred that only in dire need would anyone pick its leaves or damage it, and a pilgrimage to a sacred banyan is equal to 12 years of sacrifice.

The novice monks invited us to look at the temple interior. A monk with shaved head in orange robes accompanied us, and opened the doors with a massive ornate solid brass key. Inside the temple was a central shrine where a large golden Buddha statue sat, together with statues of other Buddha images around it, reclining and sitting in prayer. A circular walkway ran around this central shrine, and from the walls leaned colourfully painted statues of gods, monks, women and fishermen. In side rooms off this central walkway were other colourful scenes full of statues, again painted in brilliant colours. It was like a glimpse of a theatrical scene through the theatre curtains. In front of various small shrines around the walkway were the heads of flowers such as frangipani and marigolds, which were offerings to Buddha. The walls of the interior of the bell-shaped temple, which had apparently taken one man five months to paint, were also covered with paintings of various scenes, one of which included Adam's Peak.

Adam's Peak, the second highest mountain in Sri Lanka (2,224m) is said to be the very place where Adam first set foot on earth – and there's a huge footprint on the peak to prove it. However, Buddhists believe that it's Buddha's footprint, visiting an island halfway to paradise, and Hindus believe that it's the footprint of Lord Shiva, a Hindu god. Some believe it to be that of St. Thomas the apostle, who visited south India after Christ's death. Whichever legend you wish to believe, Adam's Peak has been a major pilgrimage destination for many religions for over 1,000 years, and as many as 20,000 pilgrims climb the mountain on a night with the full moon to arrive at the top to wait for sunrise.

The island of Sri Lanka is almost joined to India by a series of sandbanks and islets called Adam's Bridge. According to Hindu legend, these are the stepping stones created and used by Hanuman, the god of devotion, to rescue Sitar, his beautiful wife, from the clutches of the evil demon, Rawana, King of Lanka.

We spent a lot of our time at Hikkaduwa beach, enjoying a relaxing holiday. Hikkaduwa is a package holiday destination, so there were many Europeans there. We sat at a beach bar that belonged to one of the large hotels, and chatted to an English couple. We found the prices in the bar very expensive, especially as they charged an extra 10% service and also another 10% for Service and Goods Tax (the equivalent of our VAT). We discovered from this couple that it was usual for the package holiday hotels to charge 20% on top of all advertised prices to cover these two taxes, but the waiter would still expect a tip because none of that money went to him! The English couple, however, thought the prices very cheap, but that was of course compared to England. We recommended to them the lovely café we had found where we had the most delicious breakfasts for only a few Sri Lankan rupees and no 20% added, but they were horrified at the thought of eating foreign food. They had never eaten anywhere except in their own hotel. We found this extraordinary.

In one of the small resorts we stopped at a mask centre to see the famous Kolam masks. The carver and his brother had been taught by their father, and on permanent display were 18 black and dark red masks which their father had made in 1946 for the medicine man to heal the local people. Each mask was different, each was grotesque, and each was designed to treat a specific illness. However, the new masks which the brothers had made to sell were beautiful, painted in dark autumn colours unlike the garish masks we had seen in tourist shops. Each design had a different meaning – a mask with flames for harmony, a peacock for good luck or a cobra for protection. They were made from a very soft, lightweight wood which the brothers told us was Strychnos Nux-Vomica, an Asian evergreen known as the Poison Nut Tree. The masks are worn in Kolam, a traditional musical dance drama of rural Sri Lanka. The idea in wearing a mask is to hide the person's real identity, so that they project a different character or personality, and the masks often represent deities and demons. Kolam is similar to an opera, having a theme and a series of episodes enacted by dancers wearing masks to present the story.

We cycled further south. When we reached the southernmost tip of Sri Lanka, which is even further south than India, we were amazed to be told that there was no further land until Antarctica!

After a thoroughly enjoyable two weeks, it was time to return to India and we had to phone the airline once again for confirmation. The girl couldn't find Warren's name at first and kept putting us on hold, but eventually she was able to confirm his ticket. However, she was adamant that my name wasn't on the list and asked if I was called by any other name.

'Sometimes I call her Squidgybum,' Warren was tempted to say, but realised she would probably want to know how it was spelt! All was finally confirmed.

That afternoon I realised that it was Warren's birthday, and felt really guilty that I had forgotten, although sometimes we didn't even know what month it was, let alone what date! As it was a special occasion, we went to an expensive restaurant frequented by Westerners and treated ourselves to a bottle of French wine which cost us far more than it would have cost in England. There was a group of Indians at the next table, and they were making valiant efforts to use the cutlery laid out on the table. Mostly they just used a spoon for the curry, but two men used a knife and fork, both in the wrong hands, each held like a dagger. They were clearly struggling to use the unfamiliar eating utensils, and it reminded us of how most westerners struggled when using chopsticks!

A few days later we flew back to Thiruvananthapurum.

CHAPTER 9

SOUTH INDIA TO KOLKATA

We realised immediately that we were back in India when a small crowd surrounded us in the airport to watch as we put together our bicycles, and repaired the damage done by the airline. Whilst we had been in Sri Lanka we hadn't experienced the stares, the crowds around us or the feeling that we were somehow different. As we cycled out of the airport and down the road, children called to us and waved, and we almost felt as though we had come home, it was all so familiar to us.

We didn't have far to cycle, but we were tired after a very early start that morning, so we were grateful after a break for a samosa and a cup of tea to cycle down the hill into Kovalam in south Kerala. Kovalam is the main tourist package destination for Kerala, so we knew that there would be a lot of Europeans, mostly British and German. We planned to stay there for four days before setting off to the next state, Tamil Nadu.

The first thing we noticed about Kovalam was that we were constantly interrupted and harassed by locals trying to sell sarongs, sandals, fruit, large boxes of cigarettes, carved stone ornaments, delicate paintings on skeleton leaves, brushes, jewellery and sunglasses. If we ignored them because we were talking they just continued to interrupt us. If we said politely, 'No, thank you', they kept telling us 'Very cheap price', as though it was only the price that was stopping us saying yes. We hadn't experienced this before in any part of India.

Although not as cheap as the non-tourist areas, it was noticeable that we were back to Indian prices. However, we were also back to dry Kerala, so with our tandoori barracuda that evening we had bottles of beer that had to be hidden on the sand under the table! Men in Black II was showing in the restaurant that evening so we decided to watch it, but it had obviously been filmed with a video camera in a cinema because the silhouette of a person passing in front of the camera frequently obliterated the film!

It was 30°C at 8am as we walked along the beach to a café for breakfast the next morning. Indians were pushing out their fishing boats, pulling in nets and sitting mending nets, and women in saris were standing in the sea refreshing themselves after the night's sleep. We found a small café at the end of the beach by the lighthouse which was clearly intended for Indians, but it sold the Indian breakfasts that we loved. We were also not harrassed by anyone trying to sell souvenirs, but as soon as I began to write my diary an elderly Indian gentleman at the next table kept asking if he could have my pen. As we sat in the café we watched the fishermen with their unusual boats. They were made of several pieces of solid wood which fitted together like a jigsaw to make a banana-shaped boat on which they stood or sat astride. Knobs on the ends enabled these boats to be carried, though they were so heavy that the boat was usually dismantled at the water's edge so that one person could carry the boat piece by piece back up the beach. The paddle was made from a piece of bamboo split lengthwise, which didn't look very efficient. An Indian lady walked by with an enormous fish in a giant bowl on her head, its head and tail sticking up in the air. Several men walked by with giant blocks of ice on their head, rolled cloths protecting their heads.

Later that day there were scores of Indians on the beach – apparently there had been a strike in Trivandrum, so the locals had decided to go to the seaside for the day. There were no women, only men, and the beach was full of men holding hands walking along, jumping in the waves and standing talking. They stood staring at any European women sunbathing, so police and lifeguards tried to move them on, but this was almost impossible because there were so many of them. One Indian pretended to take a photo of his friend, but a girl in a bikini stood behind his friend – the next minute a policeman had grabbed the camera and pulled out the film to ruin it.

We went to an internet café to get away from the crowded beach, and discovered that my son, Julian, had now set up a photo website, so we were able for the first time to see some of the thousands of photos that we had already taken and sent home for developing. A long e-mail had arrived from my mother, and I replied to tell her how proud of her I was that in her eighties she was able to use the typing skills that she had last used as a secretary at an aeroplane factory during the war. After typing the e-mail, complete with address and date as in a letter, my brother John had helped my mother to send it.

After masala peanuts with a drink that evening, we had an unusual salad of crispy fried green lentils with chopped green pepper, banana, cucumber and coriander which was delicious. This was followed by sail fish, which is related to the marlin. It's a large fish with black skin, with a long spear extending from its snout and an enormous sail-like fin on top. We finished the meal with chikku, a fresh fruit that looks like a small brown potato about the size of a kiwi fruit. (It's called sapporti in Malayalam, the local language). Inside the chikku is soft segmented brown flesh with large black seeds; it's extremely sweet and the texture of very ripe pears. We found it quite a pleasant taste and unlike any fruit we'd tried before. As we sat eating, we could see lightning flashing across the horizon, lighting up the clouds. We were leaving early the next morning, so hoped it wouldn't be raining.

It was still dark but already hot as we walked along the sea front the next morning. Waiters were sleeping on the restaurant tables, covered only with the table cloths that would probably be replaced on the tables for breakfast! The fronts of the restaurants were open, so there was a breeze from the sea which would keep away the mosquitoes. After cycling up the hill out of Kovalam we stopped at a roadside café and had two delicious appams each. Thick rice pancakes, mild vegetable curry and a spicy vegetable burger with two cups of tea cost us 17p, so already we were away from the tourist trap!

We passed many new banana plantations, but the road soon became very busy and horns were constantly being sounded, which was quite a shock after our last cycle ride on the quieter roads of Sri Lanka. We passed a line of lorries on both sides of the road which indicated that we were close to the Tamil Nadu border, but as we approached the police just waved us through.

Tamil Nadu

Tamil Nadu is the home of the Tamils. It is a large state with 1000km of coastline on the east facing the Bay of Bengal. It is most well-known for its huge temples and its intricate rock carvings, and there are many ancient sites frequented by pilgrims, especially at Kanyakumari at the southernmost tip of India, where three oceans meet. The climate ranges from the tropical climate of the fishing villages on the coast to the cooler climate of the hill stations. Chennai (Madras) in the north is Tamil Nadu's capital.

We were now aiming towards Kanyakumari, India's 'Land's End'. We were again travelling in areas where tourists are not often seen, so would once again be experiencing the 'real' India. After that we planned to travel to north-east India, possibly catching a train to Kolkata, where we needed to complete our plans for the south-east Asia part of our trip. We had hoped to fly to the north of India from Chennai, so that we could do some cycling along the Ganges, but it had proved to be almost impossible – there were no direct flights, the cost was prohibitive, and the journey involved both a plane and trains. We therefore decided to leave the Ganges for another trip. We also knew that we were going to arrive in South East Asia when the temperature was very hot and humid, so we couldn't delay staying in India too long.

We passed plenty of wine shops and there were bars attached to family restaurants, so it was obvious that Tamil Nadu was different from Kerala in that respect. Buses passed us, spewing out exhaust fumes as we cycled over a long, narrow bridge with a river far below. Women were pounding clothes onto smooth boulders in the river to clean them, and the bank below us was covered with brightly coloured sheets, saris and lungis, spread out on the ground to dry.

The temperature rose steeply, so we stopped in a small town to spend the night. As we walked around the town after booking into a hotel, it was obvious from the stares that very few, if any, westerners ever stopped at the town. Prices were now very different from touristy Kovalam, and we enjoyed two thalis with an assortment of curries, rice, chapattis and poppadoms for 67p. Nobody spoke English, but that didn't bother us. As we returned to the hotel the heavens opened, and we arrived back at our room soaking wet from the sudden downpour of rain.

We were woken from our sleep during the night by a tapping on the door, which I initially assumed to be at a neighbouring room. Then the doorbell rang – it's normal in India for hotel rooms to have doorbells. We sat up in bed wondering who it was and what time it was, when hammering started on the door.

'What's going on?' I called out, as Warren wrapped a sarong around his waist and walked to the door. The knocking became very loud, and as Warren switched on the light, we could see the door bending with the force of the banging. I sat up in bed under the mosquito net, covered only with a sarong, and could see as Warren opened the door that a policeman with three pips on his shoulder stood there. An audience also stood behind him.

'What's the matter?' asked Warren.

'I just wanted to check who you were,' said the policeman. 'It's alright, sir,' he added, preparing to leave.

'It's not alright!' shouted Warren angrily. 'Why have you woken us at 1.45 in the morning?' A common reaction to complaints or any form of emotion in India is laughter, and at Warren's angry retort they all began to laugh. Warren, normally a very cool, calm and laid-back person, became even angrier.

'Don't laugh at me!' he shouted. 'Tell me why you've woken me in the middle of the night for nothing.'

'I just needed to check who you were,' repeated the policeman.

'And who are all of these people?' asked Warren, counting. 'There are 16 of them – are they all policemen?'

'Yes,' said the policeman with the three pips. We didn't believe this – one was the hotel manager, and only six of the men wore police uniforms. Warren began to shout even louder at him.

'Is this what you usually do in this town? Wake people up in the middle of the night? You haven't checked anything.' He turned to the hotel manager who was standing at the back of the crowd. 'I want my money back.'

'Passport,' said the policeman, hesitatingly.

'You're only asking now for a passport because I've told you that you haven't checked anything,' said Warren, and with that he slammed the door in the policeman's face with such a bang that it ensured that everyone in the hotel was now awake if they hadn't been already, and he came back into the room, his face like thunder. There was a final angry kick on our bedroom door, but we could hear the police retreating down the stairs. We looked through the window as the policemen returned to their two vehicles in the road outside – we were amazed to see that one was the sort of vehicle that takes policemen to riots, and we wondered who they had been expecting to find in our bedroom! We could hear arguing amongst them, though we couldn't understand what they were saying. We went back to bed, and heard nothing more, but found it difficult to get back to sleep. (And no, we never found out what it was all about, either . . .)

The next day we continued our journey 30 or 40 miles to the southern-most tip of India. The scenery was spectacular, with newly-planted banana plantations, coconut groves, paddy fields and ponds (called 'tanks' in India) covered with stunning double pink water-lilies, all backed by strange-shaped mountains in the distance to our left. We stopped often – the advantage of cycling was that we could stop instantly if we want to take photos, whereas in a bus, car or train, the view was past as soon as it was seen. Music blared out loudly in every village that we passed, despite the fact that it was still only 7am. We had breakfast in a small café, and it was the first time that we had seen a woman in such a place. She sat her beautiful toddler son on the table beside us, and fed him rice with her fingers, rolling the rice into small balls which she popped into his mouth. He couldn't take his eyes off us as he ate, and his mother was very happy when we indicated that we wanted to take a photo of both of them.

Lines of lorries were parked at the side of the road, waiting for their drivers. Every lorry was dangerously overloaded with hay which even overhung the driver's cab, making the lorries look as though they had shaggy haircuts. A man waved to us from a river as we passed above him on a bridge. He was covered in soap lather from head to toe, but he was fully clothed despite the lather! On the bank a small naked child was also covered with soap lather, and his mother had a bucket of river water poised above him ready to rinse off the bubbles. Every village had several ponds with water-lilies, and vivid crimson dragonflies hovered over the bright pink flowers. Children played cricket in a planted field – they had cleared a 'run' by trampling down the plants. It was an idyllic spot with mountains beyond.

After such a lovely ride, the town of Kanyakumari on the southernmost tip of India was a disappointment – we found it a depressing town with stalls and shops selling cheap plastic jewellery, toys, shells and coral, souvenirs, pictures of gods and flip flops. However, undoubtedly no Indians would ever agree with us on that point, because Kanyakumari is considered such a holy place. We had noticed that holy places in India seemed to be Indian versions of those English seaside towns which were popular several decades ago, where there were 'kiss-me-quick' hats, amusement arcades and cheap souvenir shops. Touts constantly put sunglasses or jewellery in front of our faces trying to sell them, chasing us down the street when we said 'no, thank you'.

We considered ourselves lucky to find a hotel room that had a spectacular view looking away from the town. We could see mountains in the distance, the coast to our right, windmills, a stunning church very much like an English cathedral, and a bathing tank with ghats (a holy place for bathing and washing clothes) in the foreground.

At Kanyakumari three great oceans meet – the Indian Ocean to the south, the Arabian Sea to the west, and the Bay of Bengal to the east. As in the south of Sri Lanka, there was no more land to the south until one reached Antarctica, apart from two tiny rocky islands only 400 metres offshore. On one of these islands is the Vivekananda Rock Memorial, dedicated to an Indian philosopher, and on the other is a giant statue. All who seek mystical enlightenment come to meditate here, and the rock is besieged by tourists from across the world. Queues of Indians waited to board the 8 rupee ferry which would take them to these islands, but despite the short distance we thought that the rusting ancient boats looked as though they might sink before reaching their destination, especially as they were also desperately overcrowded.

At our hotel we were surprised to meet another cycling couple. John and Cazz (Catherine) were from Australia, and were cycling in the opposite direction to us. We therefore arranged to meet for a meal that evening, taking with us our maps and diaries. We discussed the places that we had visited, and we all came away with information about places that we hoped to visit in the near future.

There were many disabled people in Kanyakumari – a man with skeletal legs that bowed inwards to enormous knees and out again to club feet; a woman with fingers missing on her hands, presumably from leprosy; a woman whose right foot bent under so far that she walked on the upper of her foot; a man whose shin bones were so disfigured that his legs were triangular in shape; people with no legs, people on the ground with useless bone-thin legs, people with elephantiasis, which we understood was a mosquito-carried disease. The disabilities were very distressing to see – 5% of India's population is disabled, but in Kanyakumari there were more than we had ever seen before.

We passed one of the many temples. A man sat on the ground hand-sewing soles onto a pair of shoes. Several men dressed in orange robes who had been sitting in the shade smoking all day were now lined up outside the temple with their begging bowls in front of them. It was nearly sunset, so it was a busy time for pilgrims to visit the temple. We watched the sun setting, and even the sky in the east was red from the reflection of the sun as it sank below the horizon.

We decided to travel by train up the north-east coast to Chengalpattu, about 40 miles south of Chennai, and from there we hoped to cycle to Mamallapurum on the coast. For the last few weeks the weather had been incredibly hot – it was already 25°C by 7.30am, but rose quickly to the mid-thirties with high humidity. We always started cycling at dawn in order to avoid the heat of the day. We usually stopped after half an hour for breakfast at a café; we had cold drink breaks and photo stops on the way, and hoped to stop cycling by 11am, by which time we were dusty, sticky and desperate for a cool shower. We knew that as we continued our travels into South East Asia, the temperature and humidity would be higher, so we now felt that we needed to move on quickly, having spent several months already in India. The best time for visiting South East Asia is November to February, but on a trip like ours it was impossible to visit every country at the best time, and already it was the 19th March 2003.

Buying a train ticket in India is an experience in itself. We queued behind two other people, but found that others constantly moved past us by sneaking up the side. Initially we were too polite to say anything, but eventually we got fed up – obviously the British habit of queuing hadn't rubbed off on the Indians. Eventually we decided to politely speak to one elderly Indian gentleman who kept edging in front of us.

'Excuse me,' Warren said. 'Can you please move to the back of the queue.'

'I was not trying to enter the queue,' said the gentleman, as he sidled back behind us. He subsequently sent his wife to try to push her way in front of us. Because it took so long to deal with each person, we needed to stop these queue-jumpers. Warren had by now perfected a method to block queue-jumpers which seemed to work. With his elbow pointing towards the queue-jumper's face and his strategically-placed foot on their bare or flip flop clad feet, he cast a warm smile at the Indian Railway employee.

'Oh, terribly sorry – was that your foot?' he added, turning to the queue-jumper, but quickly turning again with a smile to the man at the kiosk.

The Railway employee was delighted to have a happy customer ...

There was a choice of seven different types of seats that could be booked, numerous combinations of seats or sleepers, 1st or 2nd class, air-conditioned or non-air-conditioned, two-tier sleeper or three-tier sleeper (and this was without the 'cattle truck' carriages that carried the Indians who couldn't afford these seats). We had to complete a large form, giving not only the names of the departure station and the destination, but also our ages, passport numbers and home address. Once this had been completed, the railway employee completed another form in triplicate, using old large pieces of carbon paper, checking and rechecking the position of the carbon before eventually beginning to write very slowly. After another half an hour we had our tickets, but we still had to book our bikes in separately the next morning before we caught the train.

When we woke the next morning, the television in our room was full of reports that USA had started bombing Baghdad, which was awful news though not unexpected. Everyone seemed to be saying that it would be a brief war, but we thought people always said that at the beginning of every war, didn't they?

At 11.30am we went to the station. People were lying on the filthy concrete floor, completely oblivious to the dirt, even though there were empty chairs nearby. A herd of seven goats wandered through the lobby and onto the platform, but no-one took any notice. In the upper class waiting room people were asleep on the tables and the floor, and a woman sat on the floor eating rice and curry which she mixed with her right hand on a banana leaf which was laid on a sheet of newspaper in the dirt.

We prepared our bikes for the journey, protecting them with a large quantity of cardboard which we taped round and round. Next we had to queue to book our bicycles onto the train. After completing an A3-sized form, the lady handed me back the form and asked me to 'write the names of the bikes on the form'. Resisting the temptation to write 'Adam and Eve', I wrote 'Dave Yates', the name on the bikes and the name of the man who had built the frames for us. At this point she asked us to call the porter. We eventually found him, and he examined the bikes. After calling three other people for reinforcements, he announced that the locks had to be removed, as they couldn't carry the bikes and needed to wheel them. I said they were easy to carry (we had removed the heavy bags), and I walked up and down carrying one bike, to show them that even a woman could easily carry the bikes, but I couldn't shame them into changing their minds. The railway employee behind the counter filled in some more forms, after which she asked us to call the porter again. He supplied us with two pieces of cardboard torn from a box, on which we had to write our details (with our own pen) and stick them onto the bikes (with our own parcel tape). He borrowed our pen to complete some more forms, and eventually confirmed to the lady behind the counter that she could continue with her form-filling. This she did, very laboriously, with constant referrals to people behind her. Finally she asked us for 142 rupees (less than £2) and gave us our receipt. We had finished the forms and we now had the tickets for our bikes, but it had taken a total of one and a half hours to get tickets for ourselves and our bikes!

When the train arrived, the porters discovered that the bikes still couldn't be wheeled, because we had clamped the brakes on underneath the protective cardboard to ensure that they didn't roll around inside the guard van. They refused to take the bikes to the train, because they had to carry them.

'No problem,' we said. 'We'll do it ourselves.'

At this they changed their minds, realising that they would lose the chance of a tip. They carried the bikes 10 yards to the end of the train and put them in the guard van, then stood with their hands out waiting for their tip. We were carrying the difficult load – ten bicycle pannier bags with a total weight of about 55 kg – easy to carry on a bicycle, but very difficult and awkward to carry by hand. They didn't offer to carry the bags because they could see that they were heavy and awkward. However, Warren put one of the bags he was carrying into one porter's arms and asked them to help us – if we had to pay them, they could at least do some work. They found a porter's trolley, so it was easy for the two of them to push the trolley along the platform by the train. We walked and walked and walked – have you ever seen how long these Indian trains are? We realised that our carriage must be at least one kilometre from the end of the train where our bicycles were. We eventually found the carriage with our names printed on the form which had been stuck to the outside of the train window, and we handed the porters their tip. I think it must be standard for them to try to extricate even more money from passengers by looking glumly at the money in the palm of their hand hand and poking it with one finger, as though to say 'What's this I've been given?'

We had met a few western cyclists in India and Sri Lanka, and many of them jumped on and off buses, boats and trains, missing sections that might be difficult or boring to cycle. However with all the gear that we had, it was not so easy. If we were cycling in India or south-east Asia alone, we would have needed very little baggage and clothing, and could have taken a special nylon bicycle bag for journeys on planes, trains or buses. The wheels could be removed from the bikes and everything dropped into the bag, which can be carried by a shoulder strap. However, because our journey involved such different continents and countries, over such a long period of time, our baggage was much more considerable.

As we had anticipated, the air conditioning in our carriage was a little cool, but we settled down for the 13 hour, 950 kilometre journey. After a while we discovered from another passenger that the train only stopped at Chengalpattu for two minutes; this was a concern, because we had to collect our bikes from the guard van as well as unload our bags. Did we have time to run from our carriage to the end of the train before it left our station, still with our bikes on it? Warren practised at the next big station – it took him several minutes to sprint from our carriage to the guard van, dodging people, boxes, suitcases and food trolleys, so we had to make plans . . .

We woke at 5am for the 5.10 arrival time, but found that the train was running half an hour late. We stacked our luggage by the door ready for me to unload it onto the platform, and Warren attempted to walk through the train towards the rear. Several doors were locked, so he woke a carriage attendant, who was very helpful, despite having been woken from a deep sleep. Warren told me afterwards that he was glad that we had the air-conditioned carriage. The smell in the 'local' carriage was disgusting, and Warren even saw a woman holding a small child in front of her as he defecated on the floor of the corridor outside the toilet!

The train arrived at Chengalpattu and I anxiously unloaded the bags onto the platform – I couldn't see the rear of the train because of the curve of the platform, so I sat on my bags and waited for Warren to wheel the bikes back to me. The train began to pull out of the station. I watched a beautiful sunrise, unfortunately spoilt by a row of goods wagons stood at another platform. The time ticked by, and I began to be concerned where Warren was. No-one else was at this very end of the station. I was on my own. It was quiet. It was hot. There was a disgusting smell of urine from the tracks. The sun rose higher. Had Warren been unable to get off the train and passed me on his way to Chennai? It should only have taken him 15 minutes to remove the protective cardboard and walk the length of the platform to me.

Suddenly he came into sight, but my heart sank when I saw that he wasn't wheeling the bikes. What had happened? He was followed by two porters. He was fuming so much that I could almost see the steam coming out of his ears. He told me that the bikes had been removed from the train at an earlier station and had been put on another train. He didn't know why and he didn't know where they were – we had to go to see the station master. The porters had followed Warren, knowing that there were bags to carry (and a tip to follow!), so we followed them across the rails and onto the next platform, ignoring the safety of the bridge, across the next rails, and so on until we reached the main platform of the station.

We tried to complain to the various railway employees but, as always when a complaint is made in India, everyone lied in the same transparent way that a child does. It's never their fault and they would do anything to get out of being blamed. Customer service is an expression that they don't understand, and this is very frustrating for the westerner. Our bikes had been in the parcel carriage of the train, but we were now told that there were no parcel deliveries to Chengalpattu. Then we were told there would be a parcel delivery later that day, but when questioned about the first reply, the Indians shuffled their feet, looked at the floor and went quiet. They said luggage never stayed on the train with the passenger, but we had been assured at the outset that it would. They said the bikes weren't labelled for Chengalpattu, but the cardboard notices had been put on by ourselves, and anyway, these people had never seen the bikes or the notices, so how could they know? They muttered about the parcel office and about broad gauge and narrow gauge trains. Eventually it transpired that, because our train was due to stop at a different platform from the parcel office, all parcels had been removed to another train which would arrive later in the day, so that they wouldn't have to carry parcels further than the width of the platform! Our bikes had obviously been removed with the other parcels. We were assured that a train would arrive with our bikes at 7.30am, though after the previous answers to our questions it was difficult to believe. We had an anxious two hour wait, by which time it would be very hot for cycling – that was, if our bikes actually turned up.

They did. However, a motor-bike had fallen onto Warren's bike causing damage which, fortunately, Warren would be able to repair. It hadn't occurred to anyone that a motor-bike should be tied inside a moving train. When Warren complained they laughed as usual, which made Warren very angry. In that part of the world it is not considered the done thing to show emotions, so there was shock and horror when Warren began to shout at them, and they began sidling out of the door, eyes to the ground, desperate to escape from the mad Englishman.

We asked to see the station master, and he at least was sympathetic though not much help. He insisted on giving us both a small cup of coffee, which came with boiled milk and at least three spoonfuls of sugar. Warren likes espresso – strong, no milk, no sugar – so it was especially painful for him to drink it! We eventually decided to give up trying to get compensation and continue on our way to Mamallapuram, 20 miles away, so we prepared to set off on our bicycles. Warren unzipped one of the legs of his trousers which would convert them into shorts, and the crowd that always stood around us watching our every move went deadly quiet as they saw what he was doing. He removed the lower part of his trouser leg and began to unzip the other one. Every head craned forward with mouths open as they watched him do the same with the second leg. They just couldn't believe what he had done!

India's a strange place – you hate it and want to get on the first plane home, and afterwards everything changes and it's wonderful again and you love it. The journey to Mamallapuram was lovely – children waved; cyclists chatted alongside us; we passed numerous bullock carts, and the bullocks had different-coloured horns to denote their owners. Women were busy in the paddy fields but turned to wave to us, and we passed through villages with colourful markets and skyscraper temples. Girls were threading beautiful flower heads onto string to make necklaces to be hung around statues, pictures of gods or in taxis. Tiny flowers and flower buds were in their hair, hanging prettily on strings. Men stood at their market stalls selling colourful fruit. We passed mud huts with coconut palm leaf thatched roofs, where the sound of their televisions and mobile phones reached us as we cycled past.

We stopped to take a photograph of a particularly colourful bullock cart, and as soon as we stopped crowds of school children ran up to us screaming and laughing. I took photos of the children – the girls were pretty with braided loops in their hair and flowers around the braids. As I took a photo of them a man suddenly appeared and began to strike one of the young girls hard across her face. I was shocked and shouted at him to stop, but as I was stood astride my bike and holding a camera, I couldn't move quickly. Warren rushed over and grabbed the man's arm to stop him hitting the girl, and pushed him across the road – the man was incredibly skinny, so was no match for Warren. However, a young man standing nearby looked concerned and hooked his forefingers together as he spoke to us in his own language – this sign indicated that the man was a relative of the young girl, and we realised that he was possibly her father. Warren was concerned that he had intervened, although his response had been automatic – it was a different culture, he said, and he shouldn't have done it. However, I didn't like to think that it was acceptable for the man to hit the girl even if he was her father, but we were concerned what might happen to her later. The girl cheered up after the man had slunk away and didn't seem concerned, and the whole group ran alongside us as we set off again, waving goodbye.

In a village that we passed, grains of rice had been spread across the road so that vehicles 'threshed' the grain as they drove over it. As we continued the road became very open, rather like an African road, and it was very hot with no shade, so we were relieved when we approached Mamallapurum on the east coast. Everywhere was the sound of hammers and chisels on stone, sanding and angle grinding, as carvings of everything from enormous statues down to beautiful small pendants were being made of stone, alabaster, granite and marble. We passed men sitting in the shade of trees, carving massive pestles and mortars from large chunks of granite by the roadside. It was an interesting town, and is one of the two main places in India where stone carving is done, Agra being the other.

I went to an internet café to catch up with the news from our friends. A sign said 'Don't spit in the surrounding area. Use dustbin'! As I typed I noticed that flecks of black were dropping on me. I looked up, and immediately behind me was a man standing on a desk removing the 5 feet wide window.

I leapt up with great concern, shouting, 'It's not safe for me to be here.'

'No problem,' said the internet café owner. 'There are four men.'

Yes, there were, but only one was holding the large window. The other three men stood watching from the pavement, and certainly wouldn't have leapt to catch a giant pane of glass to stop it falling on me. However, none of them could understand my concern at all – they were completely bewildered by my attitude, but they certainly also wouldn't have had insurance to cover public liability!

As well as new carvings being made by the locals, there were also ancient carvings in Mamallapurum. On the beach stand 7th century carved temples and caves, ravaged for millenia by wind and sea, and this area is now a World Heritage site. There are stone carvings of animals and gods – a lion, a hump-backed bullock and a life-sized elephant, gods in repose, standing goddesses, rain gods, sun gods. The whole area was hidden in the sand until the British excavated the site 200 years ago, and 'new' ruins are still being discovered. There is also a massive 30m by 12m rock face called Arjuna's Penance, which is covered with carvings of gods, demi-gods, men, divine creatures, animals, birds and fable characters. Arjuna's Penance is the world's largest bas-relief. To the right of Arjuna's Penance sit a pair of carved monkeys on a rock, one picking fleas out of the other's head, and a gigantic natural ball-shaped rock called Krishna's Butterball rests precariously high up a slope on a narrow rock base, apparently defying even elephants to shift it.

Warren and I fell in love with a large green granite carved Dog of Fo (sometimes called a Chinese Lion – pairs always stand guarding the entrance to Buddhist temples), which we eventually decided to buy and ship home. It was incredibly expensive by Indian standards (£140), but the quality of the carving was outstanding. Parts of the Dog of Fo had been polished to a smooth, shiny black surface, contrasting with the dull green of the unpolished granite, and it was grotesquely beautiful. A ball had been carved inside the lion's mouth, so that if we poked a finger between the lion's teeth we could roll the ball inside its mouth, and at the sides of the lion was intricate open carving. Sending a parcel was another experience that, as always in India, involved a lot of bureaucracy and time. Our carved lion was wrapped with bubble-wrap and paper shavings and packed into a made-to-measure plywood box lined with polystyrene. The box was then taken to a tailor – a 'parcel-stitching wallah' is usually situated near large Post Offices – who made a tight-fitting bag in cheap white linen which was hand-stitched to fit perfectly round the box. Every stitched seam was sealed with sealing wax and a seal was pressed into it. The charge for stitching these bags was usually only a few rupees. When Warren collected the parcel (now weighing nearly 20kg) from the tailor, we had concerns whether or not we had the correct parcel, because the tailor had three similar-sized boxes wrapped in linen. How did he know which one was ours? He spoke little English, and couldn't understand Warren's concerns. We could only wait and hope that the parcel, when it reached England in two to three months' time, was the right one, especially as we had enclosed a number of our own pieces of clothing which we had used to help wrap the carved Dog of Fo! Special customs forms had to be completed in duplicate; one form was glued onto the parcel and the second was stitched onto the fabric. It cost us the equivalent of £37 to send the parcel to England.

Every evening at 6pm before going out for our evening meal we took our radio up onto the roof garden of our hotel, where we ate pineapples or papayas while watching the sun set and listening to the latest news on Iraq. Because Mamallapurum is a popular town for western travellers, it is also full of wonderful restaurants and cafés which serve the locally caught fish and other delicious Indian dishes, so we thoroughly enjoyed ourselves. We were amazed when we bumped once again into Helen from California, and arranged after a meal together to meet up when we all reached Bangkok.

We left Mamallapurum in the afternoon, but even before we had left the town Warren had a puncture. We stopped in a shady side lane to do the repair, and were entertained by two monkeys playing alongside us. It was lovely as we cycled through the countryside again – rural scenes of people working in the fields, cutting the rice, laying it on the roads and sifting the grains from the chaff.

From Chengalpattu we had another long train journey to Kolkata, this time lasting 32 hours. We felt we were ready for anything this time, but arriving back at Chengalpattu station with our train tickets in our hand, we were told that they couldn't book cycles onto the train at that station! As the station master himself had told us to come at 6pm to book our cycles, Warren headed off to find him; the station master pulled strings and phoned earlier stations, asking them to ensure that there was space left in the parcel van for two bikes. The parcel manager was not happy to have his authority over-ruled in this way, so took as long as possible to sort this out for us and was extremely rude as well. He logged details of the bikes in a vast ledger, writing in one column that the bikes weighed 40 kg each. Warren hotly disputed this – even together they wouldn't weigh that much – but the parcel manager showed us in his official printed book that the weight of one bike, any bike, was 40 kg! The whole process took one and a half hours, during which time we were surrounded by a group of men staring at us and our bikes. The locals seldom asked questions, but one man was especially brave.

Pointing at the bikes, he asked, 'Gears?'

In a country where five gears is the ultimate in luxury, we could never tell them that our bikes had 27 gears, so we just nodded and said, 'Yes'.

As we waited for our train, several rush hour trains arrived. It was worse than the London underground – people were standing packed into the trains as tightly as possible. Every door was open and people were literally bulging out of the doors, hanging on desperately to anything they could reach. Even before the train had stopped they had jumped down the three feet onto the track or onto the platform, and hordes of people crossed the tracks – nobody used the bridge.

Of course, our train was going to arrive at the furthest platform, so we carried our 10 pannier bags across the bridge – not for us the railway tracks! When the train arrived Warren went with a porter and the bikes to the guard van, while I loaded the bags into the compartment. The train began to move, and still Warren hadn't arrived; once again I was worried that we had been separated, and that I was now on my way to Kolkata alone! Eventually he joined me – there had been a problem opening the guard van. Twenty people had joined Warren and the porter to bang on the door, but the guard had been so fast asleep that he hadn't heard. Eventually someone had to be found who could unlock the doors from the inside. Warren discovered once the doors were opened that there were three completely empty parcel vans, which made nonsense of any concerns that there wouldn't be room for our bikes! We had covered the bikes in cardboard, and on the cardboard had written in very large letters that the bicycles should not be removed from the train until Kolkata, so we hoped not to have a repeat of the last journey. It was already dark when we got on the train, so we enjoyed one of the cheap set meals, ordered from and delivered by the special waiters dealing with train food, before settling down for a good night's sleep.

As well as the disconcerting way that the Indians chained their luggage to themselves on the train, there were also notices on the wall warning not to take food from fellow passengers. The notices explained that it may be drugged, and one could wake up with a headache but no luggage or wallet! The train was almost empty, so we spent a pleasant day after our first night on the train, watching the scenery passing us. The scenery was now very flat – enormous paddy fields, some with rice but most already harvested, filled the view as far as the eye could see. Whenever we passed patches of water we could see groups of people, mostly men who were obviously dhobi wallahs, washing clothes at the sides of rivers, banging the wet clothes on big boulders or even pieces of concrete to loosen the dirt. Saris were laid out on the scrubby grass to dry, the long lengths of fabric making a wonderfully colourful picture. Some clothes lines were erected, but these were not as popular as the bushes for laying out the washed clothes. The 'express' train was travelling incredibly slowly, but unfortunately was still travelling too fast to take decent photos. As we travelled further north we could see hills and mountains far to the west, with occasional glimpses of the sea to our right. Every time we passed a level crossing there were people waiting to cross the line, and amongst them were cycle rickshaws, the first we'd seen since visiting the cities in the north of India.

It was very cool in the train and with the tinted windows it seemed like a dull day. However, a visit to the loo, where there was no air conditioning, showed it to be very hot, even at 5pm when the sun had set. We discovered from a passing Indian Railways employee that the train arrived in Kolkata at 4.15am, not 10pm as we had originally been told, so we would be on the train for more than 38 hours. We had another night to spend on the train, but one advantage was that we would save the cost of one night's accommodation!

After a second night of travelling, the train arrived at 3.30am at Kolkata, but we had to spend an hour waiting while the three now full parcel vans were emptied. As they threw the parcels onto the platform we thought about our Dog of Fo, and wondered if it would arrive intact in England. (We were right to worry. It was not until many weeks later that we heard that our carved granite Dog of Fo had arrived at my brother's – yes, it was the right parcel but sadly, despite the careful packing, there had been a lot of damage to the delicately carved sides...)

West Bengal

Kolkata, the capital of West Bengal, is situated in the north-east of India. The state is long and narrow, running from the delta of the Ganges River in the Bay of Bengal, through the Ganges plain to the Himalayas and Darjeeling. South of Kolkata is a large delta which is the home to the endangered Royal Bengal tiger. Kolkata is probably most well-known because of Mother Theresa and the work that she did for the poor people of that city.

As we left Kolkata station at 4.30am it was still dark; people were sleeping on the pavement lying on cardboard, sacks, rags or on nothing at all, and they were fast asleep despite the noise of the already incredibly busy traffic and the street lighting. Most of them had a rag over their face as protection against mosquitoes. We didn't want to cycle through such heavy traffic, so we began to walk pushing our bikes. It was impossible to walk on the 'pavements' (dirt at the side of the road) because of the sleeping bodies, so we walked in the road. Further down the road several tents had been made from tying pieces of fabric, sacking and polythene to walls and railings, and through the ends we could see whole families with children and babies sleeping, sometimes under makeshift mosquito nets.

Because we had our travel guide we knew where we wanted to go, and as we walked it became light and people began to wake. Piles of rubbish had been swept into heaps, and amazingly people slept alongside them despite the stench. Men were cycling tricycles designed to carry goods. Most of these tricycles were full of massive steel pipes from a steel-works nearby, and the pipes protruded at the front, back and sides of the flimsy vehicles. The cyclists were standing on the pedals, straining to turn the cranks, and the trikes were clearly very heavy to manoeuvre. There were numerous rickshaws pulled by old, thin men, who looked far too weak to run along the road with two or more passengers behind them. Kolkata is the one remaining city in India that has these types of rickshaws. Other cities have cycle rickshaws and the auto-rickshaws I've described before, but in this city the men had to run pulling the passengers behind them. We walked 3½ miles and eventually arrived in a backpacking area and managed to find a reasonably-priced hotel room. It was rather dingy and not as good a standard as we had been used to, but there was a television as well as an en-suite bathroom.

The next morning we left our hotel early in the morning, and walked through the side streets to the Myanmar consulate so that we could book our visas. It had poured with rain in the night and the roads were flooded, and at times we had to paddle ankle deep through muddy puddles. I wondered what had happened to those people who had been sleeping on the pavement. Everyone knows that Kolkata is renowned for its slums, mostly because of Mother Theresa's work, but it was a shock when we saw how many people lived in squalor. However, 'lived' was possibly not the best word – 'existed' would definitely have been a more suitable word. People were preparing food on the pavements where they had slept; they were pumping water from the hand pumps on the pavement into whole goats' skins, the legs still attached; tiny, dark, dingy food shops were heating up woks full of oil to fry puris and samosas; the mangiest dogs I'd ever seen still slept in the gutters; tired, stick-thin old men prepared their rickshaws ready to pull passengers through the dirty, noisy, crowded Kolkata streets; adults and children tugged at our clothes as we passed and put their hands to their mouths in the typical Indian manner of begging for food; people were washing clothes on the pavement next to the pump, rubbing the clothes against the kerbstone; washed clothes, rags and sheets (still dirty) hung from pieces of string tied to the buildings, or were laid on the ground to dry; children and adults defecated and urinated in the street without any concern about who might be watching; rubbish was being swept into piles, where it stayed rotting for days; children played half-naked in the streets, stopping to stare as we walked past; a man still slept on the pavement, no covers under or over him, his head on a step, one leg four times the size of the other with elephantiasis, a common ailment in the poorer areas of India; a woman breastfed her baby, covering herself and the baby with her sari as she sat on the pavement; a man suffering with leprosy sat on the side of the road with arms outstretched as we passed. He had no hands or feet. This was the depressing side of the big cities of India.

We couldn't find the Myanmar consulate, and none of the Indians we asked were able to help us. We passed one consulate that looked very impressive and different from the other run-down consulates in that area – it was the Russian consulate. Massive white walls were topped with rolls of razor wire, and three Indian soldiers stood outside the gate. We approached the soldiers to see if they could help us. The three soldiers all spoke at once in very halting English.

'One at a time,' said Warren.

The soldiers all looked at their watches and told us the time in unison. We gave up, and went into the consulate, where two Russian women were very helpful, writing down the new address of the Myanmar consulate. We were so impressed that we decided to go to Russia on our next trip …

As we walked through the back streets we saw dozens of rickshaws piled together, grass and weeds growing amongst them. Despite the fact that they had been dumped there because they were no longer usable, the rickshaws still looked charming with their beautifully hand-painted decorations. We pulled out our cameras to take photos, but were moved on by security guards.

Later we walked through more side streets in Kolkata. Shutters had been removed and small shops had opened on the pavements. Most of them were no bigger than cupboards with room only for the owner to sit cross-legged behind his goods. Tailors sat at their treadle sewing machines; book shops had opened with rows of second-hand books; shops were busy selling sweets, crisps and Coco Cola, and cafés and telephone booths were now open. A butcher sat cross-legged on the counter beside a pig's head – there was no room in his cupboard-sized shop for him to move. We passed railings lining the road which were covered with clean washing. Nearby stood a stall covered with cloth, on which stood a pile of ironed clothes and an ancient iron filled with coals – this was the laundry-man's patch. Colourful stalls were now packed along the kerbside, and business was brisk. Three men sat on the pavement outside the court-house with their ancient Remington typewriters, typing official letters for local people for a few rupees at a time. Shoe-shine boys with hand-made wooden boxes were shining shoes using Wren, Kiwi and Cherry Blossom wax polish. Barbers were sitting cross-legged on the pavement shaving men sat in front of them. The side streets were full of stalls selling delicious-smelling food – noodles, chappatis with curry, pieces of chicken on sticks, barbecued corn on the cob. Cashew nuts grown locally were being fried in dry spices, and samosas and banana fritters were being deep-fried. Masala tea was being sold in tiny terracotta cups, which were smashed as soon as the tea was drunk; chai, hot, milky and very sweet, was sold in glasses at every other stall. Men approached us offering bags for sale, sunglasses, umbrellas, hand-made puppets, children's toys and hand-made leather sandals. Markets had opened up in every other street. Flower heads on strings hung from the stalls above piles of different fruits. Women in beautiful saris and men in smart trousers walked the streets. The streets were full of colour and optimism – the total opposite of the streets that we had seen a few hours earlier.

We were still enjoying the Indian food and hadn't tired of it at all. We had found a small café in a side street that sold half a tray of rice with two vegetable curry dishes for 10 rupees (13p), so we frequented this café for breakfast and lunch, which meant that we had sufficient funds left to splash out for our evening meals. In one of the smart shopping areas near the airline office we found an air-conditioned Italian coffee shop frequented by wealthy Indians and travellers, where we enjoyed amazing iced coffees. Nearby was a Suttons Seed office, and newsagents displayed English and American magazines for 50 rupees that would have cost £2 or £3 in England. As we walked along the road a fire engine drove by very slowly, with a fireman standing on the outside pulling a rope to ring the bell. It was very hot and humid, and the sky was overcast, so we decided to take a taxi, but three refused us as they didn't know the road we were asking for. We considered taking the metro, but I was concerned that we might be expected to hang out of the open doorway in the tunnel. We continued walking.

As we left our hotel the next morning, three women were working on the road with their shovels. One bare-footed woman stood up to her ankles in dry cement, and another used her bare hands to mix it with the sand. A rickshaw driver followed us through several streets, running beside us muttering in Bengali, despite us constantly telling him that we didn't want to use a rickshaw. When we left our breakfast café he was still waiting for us. We passed a number of buildings that had once been beautiful – obviously Victorian and built by the British, with ornate cast-iron spiral staircases, balcony railings and giant brackets supporting the balconies. Now they were slums and in terrible disrepair.

We walked towards the river. The traffic as always was heavy, noisy and belching exhaust fumes. A motor cyclist had been involved in an accident in the middle of this chaos and was struggling to get up and pick up his bike, but traffic continued to swerve around him sounding their horns, and three policemen stood on the pavement watching! Strangely, the motor cyclists wore crash helmets in Kolkata, but they looked like World War II German soldiers' helmets! We saw a double-decker bus that had been 'butchered' – the lower front of a damaged bus had been chopped off to make space to fit it behind a lorry cab, so people sat hunched over with very much reduced head space in this strange articulated vehicle. Dozens of buses, one behind the other, stood in the traffic jams, so we preferred to walk despite the heat. By the end of each day our feet showed the marks of our flip flops in the dirt on our feet, and it was obviously very unhealthy living in Kolkata judging by the fact that whenever we blew our noses the tissue was black!

We passed numerous police in riot gear. Their shields were made of bamboo, and they were wearing what looked like cricket pads on their shins. They all jumped out of a bus labelled 'Calcutta Police – Rapid Action Force'. The traffic was slowed as a procession of hundreds of men walked along the road carrying banners, demonstrating against Blair and Bush going to war in Iraq.

We arrived at the Hugli River, a wide tributary of the Ganges. Pleasant walks were alongside the river, despite industry being on both banks, but in places there were disgusting smells – hardly surprising, seeing the rubbish tip alongside the river and the line of men standing urinating on the bank of the river. Magnificent bridges spanned the wide river, and there were boats similar to Chinese junks propelled with large paddles at the rear.

On our last day in Kolkata we visited the Queen Victoria Memorial, built between 1906 and 1921 as a memorial to Queen Victoria who also had the title of Empress of India. It's a majestic white marble building surrounded by magnificent gardens and, unlike most other monuments of British Imperialism in India, it has been well maintained.

We at last had our Myanmar visas, which had taken a few days to arrange, and we had managed to change our last remaining rupees into US dollars, the currency most useful in Myanmar. We decided to take a taxi to the airport because the plane left very early in the morning. We had so far cycled a total of 4,386 miles, 1,095 miles of which had been in India.

It was 3rd April, and the taxi arrived on time to take us to the airport. I noticed as we travelled that, as usual, the taxi-driver's speedometer didn't work. We passed an Indian who had dozens of plucked chickens hanging by their feet from the handlebars of his bicycle; two men slept together on the bare springs of a single bed on the pavement; we passed buses and trams that were falling apart, full of rust and with chunks of metal missing and bald tyres. We went along a dual-carriageway where people were just waking from their sleep on the pavement, and we noticed that their washing was hanging along the central reservation. We were also surprised to pass a western girl cycling alone, and some time later she arrived at the airport. This was Martina, a German girl, and she was flying to Yangon on the same plane as us.

In order to reduce the possible cost of excess baggage, we were carrying everything we could as hand baggage in two large, heavy pannier bags. Despite this we had to pay 2,310 rupees excess baggage (about £30). The bags we were carrying were completely emptied and checked thoroughly by airport security.

'What's this?' the security officer asked.

'A water filter,' I replied.

'A what?' she said.

'A filter for water.'

She still didn't understand. 'What's this?' she asked, turning to the next item.

'A radio,' I said.

'Does it have batteries?'

'Yes,' I replied.

'So if I press this button it will go on?'

'Yes.'

She did. It didn't. She abandoned the radio and rummaged through my bag. 'What's this?'

'A ground-sheet for the tent.'

'A what?'

'A sheet to go under the tent.'

Her face looked completely blank; she probably didn't know what a tent was. 'What's this?'

'A bicycle pump.'

'What's it for?'

'For pumping up bicycles,' said Warren quickly. He was beginning to get annoyed as well, but fortunately the official had missed the sarcasm in his answer. And so it went on – 'A hammock – for hanging between trees'... 'A clothes line – to hang up washing' ... 'Clothes pegs' ... 'Malaria tablets'... 'A cooking stove'... 'Sauce-pans.'

Later we had to identify our luggage before they put it into the plane. Our bikes were standing on the tarmac with Martina's alongside.

'These two bikes are ours,' said Warren, pointing.

'Three bikes,' said the official.

'No, two bikes – these two,' replied Warren.

'Three bikes,' said the official again.

'No, two,' said Warren, slowly counting under his breath to ten. 'One, two – THESE two.'

The flight was delayed, but eventually everyone was sat on the plane waiting for take-off. After revving the engines a few times the pilot's voice announced, 'This is your pilot speaking from the flight deck.'

Warren whispered, 'We'd be worried if he was speaking from the departure lounge!'

'We have a problem,' continued the pilot. 'It appears that the wheels have sunk into the tarmac and we can't move, and we need everyone to get off the plane, please.'

There was initially laughter because we thought the pilot was joking, and then a groan from all of us as we realised that he wasn't. We wondered if we were going to have to give the plane a push. As we filed off the plane we could see that the wheels had completely disappeared into the tarmac. Unfortunately the 'Photography Prohibited' sign we had passed on our way to the plane meant that we couldn't take a photo. We were starving, but had no rupees left to buy food. It was 12.30 before each passenger was given a dry cheese sandwich, a piece of cake and a coffee. Three more hours passed; we had to go through all of the security checks again, and eventually we took off and waved goodbye to India.

The plane seemed to be almost full of Buddhist monks, and we were entertained by reading Indian newspapers. There were several articles about Severe Acute Respiratory Syndrome (SARS), a previously unknown deadly respiratory disease which had hit many areas of Asia, and which was a viral infection spread like the common cold. Within a matter of weeks since its emergence in November 2002, the epidemic had spread to 37 countries around the world, and the fatality rate was almost 10%.

The Hindu newspaper told us that India was not taking the recent SARS outbreak seriously. The paper said, 'Indian health officials think there's no need to worry. The disease is not very fatal.'

The Hindustan Times said, 'Avoiding panic seems paramount. We have no cases in India and anyway, the mortality rate is only 4%.' In another section of the same newspaper it referred to a confirmed case of SARS in Calcutta.

We landed one and a half hours later in Yangon, Myanmar.

CHAPTER 10

MYANMAR

Myanmar, formerly called Burma until 1989, is situated between Thailand and Bangladesh, with India and China touching its northern borders. To the north-east, the famous Mekong River divides Myanmar from Laos. Myanmar has miles of coastline and beautiful islands on the west to the Bay of Bengal and the Andaman Sea. The centre of the country has extensive plains and wide rivers, but mountains divide the border of Myanmar and Thailand to the east. The Himalayan mountains rise to the north between Myanmar and Tibet. Ancient religious sites, including Bagan with its 1,000 year old temples, the colonial-era architecture of Yangon (formerly Rangoon) from the days when Burma was a British colony, the serene Lake Inle with its floating villages and the ancient royal city of Mandalay all combine to make Myanmar a fascinating place to visit.

We wouldn't have been allowed to cycle into Myanmar. Tourists are allowed to visit only certain areas of the country, and the four main tourist areas are Yangon (formerly Rangoon), the capital; Mandalay, the former capital when the British took over; Bagan, a deserted city of ancient temples considered one of the wonders of Asia, and Lake Inle, a cooler retreat set in the mountains. As cyclists we planned to visit areas between these points that are not usually visited by tourists, where we would be able to see how the local people lived. We were excited as the plane circled before landing; the sun was glinting on numerous golden bell-shaped temples, and we realised that this country already looked different from any others that we had yet visited.

At Yangon airport all foreigners had to purchase US$200 worth each of Foreign Exchange Certificates (FECs), despite the fact that the local currency was the kyat (pronounced 'chat'). These could be used as dollars in hotels in tourist areas, where prices were always quoted in US dollars. FECs had to be paid for in dollars or pounds sterling, but the exchange rate was not as good as the usual dollar exchange rate, so the fewer we had to buy the better for us. As we didn't think we'd need US$400 for the two weeks that we intended to stay in Myanmar, we asked if we could buy $200 worth between us.

'Come closer,' said the girl, bending her head towards the metal grill.

Warren couldn't understand, because he could hear her perfectly well, but now she was whispering. He leant forward.

'Do you have a $10 present for me?' she asked.

The penny dropped. We had read in the travel guides about the 'presents' which expedite a lot of official administration in Myanmar, so we agreed to give her a present and the deal was done. Despite the cost of the present we still had a better deal by reducing the amount of FECs that we had to purchase.

We collected our bikes and began to put them together again ready for cycling, and Martina did the same. She had been cycling alone in India, and was planning to do the same in Myanmar. Warren lent Martina a spanner to fit her pedals; hers had been confiscated by customs in Kolkata, and they had promised that it would be returned to her on arrival in Yangon. No-one knew anything about it, Martina told us, so she was now going to have to stay in Yangon waiting in the hope that her spanner would eventually be sent to her on a later plane – she was having the same experience that we had in Sri Lanka! As we straightened our handlebars, pumped up our tyres, replaced pedals and put on the pannier bags, an official came to ask if we were ready to leave. The airport was waiting to close, he told us, and the three of us were the only ones left!

We said goodbye to Martina, promising to keep in touch, and set off for Yangon, 13km away. The Burmese have driven on the right side of the road since 1974, although most of their cars are still right-hand drive, which we thought was very confusing, and they also still measure in miles rather than kilometres. The road was excellent; it was lined with beautiful golden Buddhist temples, and a stunning golden archway bridged the 6-lane road welcoming us to Yangon. The temperature was 39°C and very humid, so we splashed out $20 per night for an air-conditioned room with satellite television in a very nice centrally-located hotel. A few yards away from the hotel was a major roundabout, built around Sule Paya, a 200 year-old Buddhist temple. Around the base of the temple were small shops, but the temple rose 48 metres, golden and bell-shaped, and could be seen from all the roads that radiated from the roundabout. At night the temple was superbly and subtly lit, so that it appeared that the light was shining from within the golden bell.

In the morning we went to the small dining room in the hotel for our breakfast.

'Eggs?' asked the young lad serving breakfast.

We had ordered a Burmese breakfast with the proprietor the night before, but when we explained this to our waiter he didn't understand.

'Eggs?' he repeated. It was obviously the only English word he knew.

We finally realised that we'd have to accept the western breakfast. After eggs, toast and cereals, the proprietor suddenly appeared, and was horrified to see that we had the wrong breakfast. She dashed into the kitchen and reappeared with large bowls of noodle soup, the Burmese breakfast, which she placed in front of us. We didn't have the heart to refuse, so waded through the delicious soup before staggering out into the sunshine with decidedly bloated stomachs.

The streets were lined with food vendors; tiny tables and even tinier, child-sized stools with seats only 8" x 5" covered the pavements. Here we could eat a tasty meal for about 300 kyats (25p), and a kettle full of Chinese tea stood on every table for customers to help themselves free of charge. One concern, however, was that the cups were never washed. Each customer poured a little tea into the handle-less cup, swilled it around and poured it onto the pavement, before pouring himself a fresh cup of tea. Because of this and the real concern about SARS and other diseases, we immediately bought our own cups!

In a back street we found a man sitting on the kerb in front of a wok full of oil over a fire. He was deep frying tempura; we handed him 30 kyats, about 2p, and he gave us a small bunch of watercress (or something similar) and thinly-sliced potatoes and aubergines, which he had dipped in batter and fried. He also handed us a delicious chilli relish to dip the vegetables. We asked for more, they were so delicious, but when his friend arrived just as we were having a third helping, he suddenly announced that the price was 200 kyats. He had obviously been charging us the local price instead of the tourist price! As in all the tourist areas of South East Asia and India there are two prices – one for the locals and one for the 'rich' tourists.

Food in Myanmar was excellent – Chinese, Indian and Thai flavours all influence the cuisine, and there were also fast food establishments in Yangon selling burgers, pizzas, sandwiches, doughnuts and good coffee. Burmese curries are the mildest in Asia and rice is the staple diet, but noodles are usually eaten at breakfast and mid-day, although there was a choice of Burmese or western breakfast at the tourist hotels. We discovered when ordering soup that it would be served in a massive 1 litre bowl, enough for the two of us, so for lunches we often chose delicious Thai, egg noodle or vegetable soup.

The cycle rickshaws were different in Myanmar from India. The Burmese men ride a normal bicycle with a side-car bolted onto the right hand side of the bike. Two passengers sit with their backs to each other, one facing forward and the other back, and the seats are very narrow, designed for the tiny Burmese hips and bottoms. As in India, it was not unusual to see overloaded bikes, with the poor cyclist carrying families of four in his side-car, and we noticed that the Burmese keep dogs as pets and look after them, unlike the Indians who mostly have a fear of dogs.

For the first time in many months we saw modern supermarkets, even selling

Australian wine, though at prices double the price of wine in England! However, most of the shops were small, and in the evenings the pavements were lined so tightly with stalls that there was hardly room for pedestrians to pass.

We were surprised to see these signs of westernisation, because we had understood that Myanmar was not as westernised as other parts of south-east Asia. However, we were also aware that there were no ATMs and no credit card facilities, so we had to rely on a supply of US dollars; there were also no internet cafés, so we would be out of touch with anyone back home during our stay.

The Burmese, like the Indians, are very slim, and the women looked very elegant in long tight-fitting skirts and matching fitted short-sleeved blouses. The men wore longyis, a length of fabric about 2m long sewn into a tube. The longyi is wrapped around the waist to form an inverted pleat at the front to make a full-length skirt. The men's longyis were always checked or striped in smart masculine colours. We noticed that the Burmese men, unlike Indian men, had tattoos, often in squares like the pattern on a giraffe's skin covering the arms and over the chest. We understood that these tattoos were designed to ward off evil spirits.

Women sometimes wore longyis instead of skirts, but they chose brightly-coloured or floral designs, and theirs were tied to one side, which looked like a wrap-over skirt. Women and children often had their faces painted with a white or yellow chalk-like paste, usually painted in a design on the cheeks which was applied with a shaped sponge in a circular, leaf, square or triangular design. This fragrant paste is called thanakha, and is derived from the bark of a local tree, and is used to give protection from the sun. Thanakha in its natural state is for sale on stalls as small logs, and the bark is ground into a powder with water on a circular flat stone before applying to the face. Burmese women believe that it removes acne, gives smooth skin and lightens the skin (of great importance throughout Asia) as well as acting as a sun block.

We went to see Shwe Dagon Pagoda in Yangon, which we had seen on its hilltop site from the plane as we approached the airport. This pagoda is the most sacred and largest Buddhist temple in Myanmar. On the way we passed many churches – Baptist, English Methodist, Catholic, and we also noticed that a mosque and Hindu temple stood close to the Buddhist temple in the centre of Yangon. Acacia trees were flowering alongside the road, covered with masses of golden yellow flowers.

The southern entrance to Shwe Dagon Pagoda is incredibly impressive, being guarded by a pair of giant Dogs of Fo (sometimes called lion dogs or Chinese dogs). These awesome Dogs of Fo are magnificent cream and gold ferocious mythical creatures about 40 feet tall, standing either side of an ornate gold-leafed building that covers the very wide flight of stairs which rises to the pagoda. The main part of the pagoda is a 100 metre high golden bell-shaped building which glinted in the sunlight. The top of the spire is encrusted with over 5,000 diamonds and 2,000 other precious and semi-precious stones. The building is surrounded by niches with Buddha images and numerous golden stupas, and is absolutely spectacular on its own, but surrounding it are roads of marble and 82 other buildings, each one different. All are very oriental in design, with multiple-tiered curved roofs, carved teak and ornate finials, and gilded and painted rust, dark green and white. In each building were shrines – images of Buddha were standing, sitting, lying or reclining, on their own or in groups. Some were enormous, some small, some gilded, others marble with painted faces. Gold, marble and Burmese teak was everywhere.

An enormous ornately cast bronze bell stood in a special building. The British had tried to take the bell during the days of the Empire, but they accidentally dropped it into the Yangon River. When they couldn't recover it, they gave it back to the Burmese! The Burmese later re-floated it using vast quantities of bamboo.

We couldn't stop taking photographs; everything was just overwhelming. Buddhist monks with shaved heads, wearing dark red robes and carrying matching umbrellas or parasols with bamboo handles, were walking barefoot or kneeling in prayer. We also had to remove our flip-flops, and the marble was so hot that it was burning our feet! We dashed from shadow to shadow to try to keep cool. Families sat in the pagodas and tiny children slept in the shade of the temples. Boys as young as five were dressed in Buddhist monk robes – all Burmese men are expected to take up temporary monastic residence twice in their lives, once between the ages of 5 and 15 and again after the age of 20, and it's considered an honour to a family when one of its sons takes up the robe and bowl.

We considered that the US$5 entrance fee per person to visit these wonderful buildings was well worthwhile, and seeing this pagoda and its surroundings was a breath-taking experience. Interestingly, we saw no other westerners at the Shwe Dagon Pagoda.

We also visited one of the lakes in Yangon, where a splendid reproduction of a royal barge had been built as a floating restaurant and hotel. Two massive golden swans supported a stunning building with tiers of oriental roofs, the swans' tails forming an impressive towering entrance to the restaurant.

We sat and planned our cycle trip to Bagan and Mandalay, with the intention of flying the 450 miles back from Mandalay to Yangon for our onward flight to Bangkok. We set off early the next morning. We cycled past a man carrying 12 cane chairs on two large diameter bamboo poles over his shoulders. He was followed by a young boy carrying four chairs in the same way. Dozens of small pick-up trucks passed us. These were the local equivalent of buses, each one with at least six, but often as many as twelve people standing on the back step hanging on for dear life, because the truck was already packed as full as a rush hour London tube train. Another truck passed us later with 10 people sitting on the roof-rack. This was probably one of the 8 hour journeys that the small pick-up trucks run – too long to hang on at the back! As we cycled out of Yangon there were miles of fences made out of tank tracks left behind by the British and recycled by the locals.

At a roadside café where we stopped for lunch, I asked where the toilet was. The waitress took a key from a hook and led me out of the back of the café, past an abandoned bus, across a field and between two large houses on stilts to a tiny building on stilts with steep steps, which she unlocked. This was the loo! Beneath the squat toilet was a pipe directed down to the ground. She waited for me, and after locking the door again she led me back to the restaurant. There she handed me a bowl of water and some soap. To dry my hands she pulled a length of paper from the toilet roll that sat on our table covered by its special plastic holder; every table in every restaurant in Myanmar had a similar toilet roll, to be used as serviettes.

It was 26 miles before the scenery became rural, but there were no pretty or interesting views. We were very hot and stopped outside a café to buy a cold drink, but we hesitated because it looked so busy. People looked out of the windows and beckoned us in and, as we hesitated, a lady came out and led us into the café, ushering us to a table that had been hurriedly vacated. We looked around and saw that everyone was wearing their best clothes, and that a pile of presents stood on a table, and it was at that moment that we realised that we had gate-crashed a wedding! The lady spoke a little English, and told us that she was the wedding supervisor; she insisted that we join them and that the wedding couple would be very proud if we did so, and she brought plates with triangles of Madeira cake and bowls of strawberry ice cream.

'Ice cleam,' she said, smiling. She was the only one there who spoke any English. As soon as one bowl was emptied another bowl of ice cream was put in front of us, but after the third we declined any more. The bride in her traditional pink dress and the groom wanted a photo of us with them, and we stood in our sweaty vests and shorts to have our photos taken before we left.

I shook hands with the wedding supervisor to say thank you and goodbye. Whoops! – only as I dropped my hand did I notice that her left hand had been touching her right elbow as we shook hands – a sign of deep respect. I should have reciprocated and done the same, but was able to do so when shaking hands with the bride and groom. (How would we manage without the guide books to advise and warn us of such things?) All the guests and the bride and groom left the building with us, and stood in the middle of the road waving goodbye until we were out of sight.

Shortly afterwards, we passed a child's funeral. Music was blaring out of loudspeakers, and two men led the procession carrying a gong between them on a bamboo pole on their shoulders, banging the gong every few steps. The carriage holding the tiny blue-painted coffin was made of bamboo and covered in flowers, and was pulled on ropes by two lines of young people. Behind the carriage were dozens of people on bicycles and people in bicycle rickshaws, umbrellas raised to protect them from the blazing sun.

It had been very noticeable in Yangon that the Burmese enjoy chewing betel nut, because many men and even women (especially older women) had the distinctive dark red, stained teeth and mouth that results from chewing this nut. Worse still, the pavements and roads were covered with permanent dark red spittle stains because spitting is common in Asia even amongst women. Getting a smile from a betel user was a pretty scary experience! Now, however, I had an even scarier experience. As I cycled along the road a lorry passed me and I felt water on my face and arms. As I looked down I saw red spots of liquid on my arms and bike and realised that I'd been spat on, though probably not deliberately. The worst was that I felt a spot of liquid on my lip, and I immediately thought of the SARS epidemic and all the horrible Asian diseases that I might catch, and had to stop to wash my face with water from my water bottle. My cap was also spattered with tiny spots of red.

Because of the intense heat we had planned to cycle short trips with plenty of breaks, starting at 6am and stopping at 10am or even earlier. It was not to be – the towns shown on our map turned out to be very basic villages with no accommodation, and we had to cycle on and on for many hours before we found a small town with accommodation. By this time it was late afternoon; the cycling had been unbelievably exhausting in the heat, and the tarmac was melting in the heat, so that our tyres were sticking to the road like glue. As always when cycling, we were exposed to the open sun, often with no trees to give us shade. The temperature had risen to an unbelievable 40°C (over 100° F) and the humidity was the highest we had ever experienced.

We had clearly been spoilt in India, where very cheap but decent accommodation with private bathrooms had always been available along the road, even away from the tourist areas. In this small town the only accommodation was a dirty, small room with a pig sty outside the window – this cost us far more than a decent room with bathroom in India, and it's better that I don't describe the toilet down the corridor, or the kitchen that was attached to the adjoining restaurant! The 'shower room' that we had to share with several other people was a tiny dark concrete room with a concrete tank full of water – the water had to be scooped up with a bowl so that we could sluice it over our bodies. We had no choice but to pay US$14 for the room, not a lot less than the air-conditioned room in Yangon, and the proprietor obviously knew that he could charge what he liked as there was nowhere else to stay. The hotel owner wore a lungyi with a vest over his fat stomach, exposing numerous tattoos, and he stood with a cigarette hanging from his mouth as he took our order for a meal that evening.

We could see from our map that towns of the size that we were in became further apart, and there was no guarantee that there would be any accommodation in the next few days; even this filthy guest-house was better than none. Whilst long distances wouldn't have been a problem in cooler weather when we could have used our tent and not been so desperate for a shower, it was foolish to continue in the extreme heat and humidity, so we decided to take a train with our bikes to Bagan and then on to Mandalay.

We made enquiries at the local train station that evening, where they had clearly never seen westerners before. We were invited into the station master's office to sit down, and crowds of people looked in at us through the door and windows. Our bicycles were again considered great curiosities, as in India, and a crowd stood around the bikes. The station master spoke a little English.

'Yes,' he said. 'There is a train at midnight tonight to Bagan.' He gave us a price for upper class (higher than 1st class, with a sleeper). It was the equivalent of £2, which seemed far too cheap for a 400 mile journey, even in Myanmar.

'What time does it arrive?' we asked.

'Late,' was the reply.

I re-phrased the question. 'How many hours on the train?'

He wrote down the answer. 'Late.'

I tried again. '6 hours? 12 hours? 24 hours?' I asked hopefully.

He consulted with another station official, and replied, 'We have no information.'

We were concerned. If they had no information, how did they know what time it arrived at their station? Would we leave our room in the middle of the night, only to wait in vain for a train to appear? Then we had another problem – they wouldn't accept dollars, even though officially in Myanmar all foreigners must pay for train and plane fares in US dollars. Obviously in this town away from the tourist cities they hadn't heard of the official rule. We had insufficient kyats, so we knew we had no choice now but to cycle the 50 miles back to Yangon in the heat the next day.

We had a restless night. We doubted the cleanliness of the mattress, but had covered it with our sarongs rather than sleep on the bed linen supplied. There were no curtains, so we had fixed our waterproof cover to the window for privacy. Throughout the night there was a crunching sound beneath our bed, and Warren finally flashed his torch and looked over the edge of the bed. A startled gecko stared at the sudden light, a giant cockroach protruding from its mouth. It was obviously finding plenty of food in this establishment!

We left the next morning at 6am. It was already 25°C, even though there was a fairly thick mist. We were quickly covered in a fine film of water, but it was still warm. I had to remove my spectacles, as they were covered with a foggy haze and I couldn't see. Out of the mist ahead of us appeared a single file line of 20 Buddhist monks, each carrying a large, black bowl. They were graded in size, the tallest monk at the front, with the tiny 5-year-olds at the back. They were identically dressed in dark red robes, with shaved heads and flip-flops on their feet. They were visiting shops and homes to collect food in their bowls from their donors.

A few miles further on a bullock cart came out of a side road shrouded in mist. Two bullocks pulled the cart, which was driven by a man wearing a pith helmet made of narrow strips of bamboo. Clumps of bamboos, giant in circumference and height, grew alongside the road on either side of him. The sound of jingling bells approaching warned us of the five horses and traps that suddenly appeared from the opposite direction, and disappeared again into the mist behind us. The only modern vehicles were the large Chinese lorries travelling in the opposite direction on their way back to China, only a few hundred miles north.

It remained misty until 7.30am, when the sun burned off the mist, and the temperature rose dramatically. We passed through villages, where people waved. At a bus stop stood yesterday's bride, who pointed us out to her friends. As we waved enthusiastically, her face beamed and she jumped up and down waving and screaming. A bus went by; along its side a piece of string had been tied, and hundreds of dead chickens and ducks had been tied by their feet along the length of the bus.

The journey was very difficult, especially as we had still not recovered from the journey the day before, and also hadn't slept well. As we finally arrived back in Yangon city, we stopped at Aroma, an air-conditioned café that sold wonderful iced cappuccino, and we lingered there in the cool air making our drinks last as long as possible. It was only another mile to go, so we opened the café door to the sauna-like heat outside and pushed our bikes back onto the road. The city was busy, but the roads were well-marked and organised, with many traffic lights, so we arrived safely back at our hotel, to the surprise of the staff who welcomed us back with open arms as if we were old friends!

We spent two more days in Yangon, while we organised flights to Mandalay and Lake Inle, back to Yangon and on to Bangkok. This was easier said than done, because even the airlines wouldn't accept credit cards. The only way we could get money was to buy more Foreign Exchange Certificates. We therefore had to queue with other foreigners at the special counter of the Foreign Trade bank where we could use our credit cards to buy more FECs to pay for the flights. We had taken plenty of US dollars with us to Myanmar, but hadn't taken enough to pay for several unexpected flights. However, the delay gave us time to enjoy more of Yangon.

We sat one evening having a delicious meal in a friendly café and bar. Warren suddenly nudged me, pointing to the floor below the neighbouring table. There was a hole in the floorboards, and out of the hole peeped a rat, its nose and whiskers trembling. It suddenly made a dash to another table, grabbed a crumb of bread and shot back to safety down the hole. We were then entertained for the next half hour throwing peanuts onto the floor, and watching the rat shoot backwards and forwards, its quivering nose constantly peeping out of the hole, ready to make the next dash for food!

The Burmese people are lovely – very friendly and helpful, and always smiling. The girls are very pretty, and have beautiful shiny black hair, usually worn tied back or plaited and hanging down to waist or even knees. Warren thought that the lovely condition of their hair was probably due to their offal diet – strolling through the streets that evening, when the temperature had dropped to 32°C, we noticed that most food vendors in one street had piles of heart, tripe, liver and other unrecognisable parts of animals, prepared and ready to cook! We stuck to rice, noodles, vegetables and chicken, though Warren said he was willing to try the fried crickets.

Our friendly hotel was happy to lock away our bikes and most of our bags free of charge, so we were now able to travel lightly with a small backpack each, and U Myint Aung took us in his taxi to the airport a few days later.

Our flight to Mandalay was a bumpy one in a small propeller plane. Mandalay is the second largest city in Myanmar with 500,000 people, and is only 200 miles south of the Chinese border. Like Yangon, the city is built in a grid-style layout and has many beautiful temples, pagodas and monasteries to visit. It is also surrounded by ancient towns, some in the mountains, which can be visited by road or river. Visits to the stunning pagodas and monasteries, built of white marble and carved teak, sometimes painted, but often gilded, made our stay in Mandalay very enjoyable, and we were able to watch Buddha images being carved from marble, teak being ornately carved, temple walls being gilded with gold leaf, and intricate embroidery being sewn by young girls. The culmination of our stay in Mandalay was a bare-foot walk up the 662 steps to the top of Mandalay Hill to see the sun setting, 230 metres above the rest of the city. The view of the city, with its 2 kilometre square palace wall and wide moat just below the hill, the massive Ayeyarwady river in the distance, and the dozens of golden buildings shining in the light of the setting sun, was stunning.

A Buddhist monk had joined us on our walk up the steps, asking if he could chat to us to practise his already excellent English. After he left us another

Burmese man joined us, but he was as rude as the Buddhist monk had been charming. He said he thought I was a man, probably because I had such short hair, and Burmese women always have beautiful long hair. He also asked how old I was, and when I replied he said that I was too old to be walking up the steps. He asked Warren how many men he had killed, and later told us we must be very rich to be doing this trip. We just wanted him to disappear.

From Mandalay we caught a nine hour ferry down the Ayeyarwady River to Bagan. We were relieved when we saw the ferry, with its air-conditioned rooms and comfortable reclining seats. There were only a few passengers, and all of us were westerners who had paid US$16 per ticket, a massive amount by Burmese standards, but well worthwhile when we saw the alternative local ferries, which were rusting boats packed to overflowing with people, packages and bicycles. After a relaxing day's journey on the river, we were excited to notice that there were large numbers of old temples on the eastern river bank. Some were set amongst trees, some in the open, many in large groups, some were red brick, some white marble with gold leaf, some bell-shaped and some tiered. All were beautiful. We were approaching Bagan . . .

Bagan's period of grandeur began in 1057, when the King brought 30 elephant-loads of Buddhist scriptures on marble tablets back to Bagan after conquering another kingdom. He also brought back artists, artisans and monks. Over the next two centuries, magnificent buildings were erected in Bagan, but Myanmar's economy began to decline in the 13th Century, partly due to the vast amounts of money and labour poured into the building of Bagan. By that time there were 13,000 monuments, but in 1287 Bagan was ransacked and was never rebuilt. A major earthquake in 1975 caused a lot of damage to the remaining temples, but most of the remaining temples have now been restored or reconstructed, and there are now 2,500 temples in an area only 4 miles square. Along every road, in every direction are temples, all of them almost 1,000 years old. Most of them are built of brick with ornamental brickwork doorways and archways. The larger temples are made of marble and have the traditional golden bell-shaped domes, and these temples have massive six feet thick brick walls surrounding them. In one of the temples was a 92 feet long reclining Buddha, and many of the standing, reclining or sitting Buddhas were 30 or 40 feet high. Some of the temples had the original hand-painted interior walls, and one had the original glazed terracotta tiles around the outside of the building. Remedial work was being done on one temple, and it was interesting to see that rough timber work was made from solid teak, and scaffolding was made from bamboo, with cleverly intertwined diagonal bamboo steps.

We visited a number of the temples by taxi, and ended at sunset at a temple with steep steps up its side. Whilst I have a fear of heights, I considered it worth the climb – the view across the plain was unbelievable, with hundreds of temples, white, gold and red brick, dotted across the landscape in every direction, the setting sun giving the whole vista a wonderful soft glow.

From Bagan we flew to Heho, and travelled 3 kilometres by taxi to Lake Inle. In the distance on either side of us were mountains; paddy fields were green with growing rice, and were edged with rows of banana palms. Workers wearing Chinese-style coolie hats worked in the paddy fields, water buffalo were knee-deep in water pulling ploughs, and long flat-bottomed boats travelled along canals which criss-crossed the fields. Bamboo houses on stilts lined the roads, and tiny thatched buildings nestled amongst the paddy fields. The temperature was a few degrees cooler than we had been used to, and for the first time the breeze from the open car window wasn't oven-hot. However, every time we passed through a village we had to shut the windows, because we were visiting Lake Inle during the Water Festival, the Buddhist New Year, which meant that for five days the local youths were allowed to throw water over everybody. A little squirt of water might have been acceptable, but two young local girls in a rickshaw in front of our taxi were clearly very miserable, having had buckets of water poured on top of their heads, and hoses directed at them.

When we booked into our room, the bathroom tiles were cool to our bare feet for the first time in Myanmar, and our thermometers registered a comfortable 29°C. We were now well above sea level in the mountains, so looked forward to a relaxing few days in the slightly cooler climate. We had found a wonderful hotel run by two sisters, who cooked lovely food for us for breakfast and evening meals.

We found it difficult to know how much to pay.

'Pay how much you want,' they always said, but the food was so delicious that we were always happy to pay more than average, and perhaps the sisters realised this. On one occasion I complimented one of the sisters on her lovely green tomato salad with peanut dressing, so the following day she called me to watch as she made it. I had never realised that green tomatoes were edible without cooking, so it was amazing to discover how delicious they were.

We hired bicycles for a day at a cost of 50p each, but the heavy bikes were terrifying to ride when we were so used to our lighter bikes with many gears and excellent brakes. As we cycled down the road two youths stood with buckets of water which they threw straight into our faces. Fortunately we had packed our cameras in waterproof bags just in case, but it was difficult to take photos without risking water damage to our cameras.

We teamed up with four other travellers the next day. Christina, Juanita and Juanita were from Columbia, and Todd was from Durban, South Africa. Todd worked in London for 6 months of the year as an accountant on contract work, so that he had sufficient money to travel the other six months of every year. We hired one of the long solid teak motor boats with a driver for a day, and it sped down the canals into the vast lake. Through the early morning mist we saw the local fishermen, with their strange cone-shaped nets, and their extraordinary method of manoeuvring the boats, standing with one leg wrapped round the guiding pole. There were villages on stilts in this massive lake, with 'streets' and 'side streets' of water, rickety bamboo bridges crossing the 'streets', and water taxis passing us with women in coolie hats or with oriental parasols. In the shallower areas there were paddy fields surrounded by rough walls of mud. Occasionally we passed a bar, café or shop on stilts, where the purchases were being loaded into boats. There were floating gardens where, amongst other things, tomatoes and orchids grew, and a floating market. We wondered where the children played, until we saw tiny children in boats, managing them very well with the paddles.

On a distant shore, set against the mountains, we could see numerous white spires surrounding a pagoda. These spires are sacred monuments and are called 'stupas'. Stupas were originally built to cover relics of Buddha; they have symbolic meanings, and they often form part of a temple's structure. We disembarked and found a crowd of children by the monastery, who we assumed to be orphans. They were initially very camera-shy, but once Christina and one of the Juanitas had shown them photographs of themselves on their digital cameras, they crowded around, their mouths open with amazement, wonder and disbelief.

We watched Chinese silk being hand-woven on very basic bamboo looms; we saw Burmese cigarettes being handmade, and pure Burmese silver from the mountains being beaten into bowls, and afterwards boiled with tamarind seeds, a natural acid, to polish them. We saw the 30 feet long solid teak long-boats being made. It took four men one month to make the basic boat, which would be sold for US$800. There were apparently 10 boat-builders around Lake Inle. Everywhere we visited, we were welcomed with Chinese tea and home-made biscuits. We stopped for lunch at a café on stilts, and visited a monastery on stilts. We saw many more of the hard-working water buffalo near or on the banks of the lake. These creatures, although fierce-looking with their large curved horns, seemed incredibly docile, and tiny children used them like climbing frames. The children jumped on and off the buffaloes, and even hung on their tails, but the buffaloes just continued grazing. Boys 5 or 6 years old had the job of riding the water buffaloes along the paths and through the water to the grazing or working areas.

As the sun began to set we returned to our hotel, travelling along a narrow canal where boats whizzed past us in the opposite direction carrying gangs of boys throwing water. They scooped it up from the canal in bowls and threw it over every boat that passed, so we were soaking wet by the time we returned back to our rooms. Once the sun had set, however, no-one was allowed to throw water again until the following morning, so we were safe for a few hours!

Shopping in a market one evening, we discovered the strange measuring system in Myanmar. Rice, small fruits and nuts are sold in volume rather than weight. The standard measure is a bu (a condensed milk can); 8 bu equals a pyi (one small rice basket), and 16 pyi equals a tin (one jute sack). All liquids are sold by the imperial gallon, except milk, which is sold by the viss (3.6 lb or 1.6kg). Cloth is still sold by the yard, short distances are measured by furlongs, but long distances in miles – certainly as complicated as the old British Imperial measuring and weighing systems!

Our days at Lake Inle were lovely – another magical place in Myanmar. We spent a relaxing time, but for those who wanted to be more energetic there were treks into the mountains to see the hill tribes and, as well as the Water Festival, we had celebrated the New Year and Buddha's birthday while we were at Lake Inle. It was strange enough to be wished 'Happy New Year' in the middle of April, but even stranger to realise that the year was now 2546 BE (Buddhist Era).

We were sorry to leave Lake Inle, but set off in a taxi at 7am to go to the airport. Before leaving the village our taxi driver stopped to fill up with petrol. Two men with lit cigarettes in their mouths poured five gallons of petrol into a drum on legs from a large container, and they carried this with petrol-soaked hands to the car, where they managed to pour most of the petrol into the tank of the car with the aid of a funnel and tube! There were few other cars on the road, and none as empty as our Toyota people carrier taxi, but it was clearly the local rush hour, as we made our way slowly out of the small town. Between villages the roads were full of people – crowds of them were walking, men pulling heavily-laden handcarts, men carrying long flexible saws or tools over their shoulders, women with babies or toddlers strapped on their backs, ponies and traps, hundreds of cyclists, men carrying bamboo poles with baskets on each end, rickshaws carrying women or monks holding umbrellas aloft, Buddhist monks walking, most of them carrying their lunch in stainless steel tiffins. Pick-up trucks were overloaded with people; two-wheeled trailers pulled by rotovators each carried about 20 people who were clinging to each other for safety, and many people walked with giant parcels on their heads. Blossom was beginning to fall from the large flowering jacaranda trees, so there were circular carpets of purple below them. A strange tree had blood-red dahlia-like flowers adorning its leafless branches, and orange, red, pink and purple bougainvilleas climbed into the trees and flowered high in the branches. Once we were away from the villages we travelled faster along the mountain road to the airport, where we flew back to Yangon to pick up our bicycles and bags.

We booked a taxi to take us to the airport, but when the taxi arrived the driver refused to carry our bikes, even though he had an estate car which could easily accommodate them. He eventually agreed for an extra charge, and we were hindered by a passer-by who wanted to help load the bikes, and who subsequently asked for money for doing so! On the way to the airport the taxi driver muttered that it was illegal for Warren to sit in the back with the bikes, and that the police could stop him and fine him. We couldn't help but marvel that any taxi driver in Myanmar would say this, despite the fact that taxis were usually over-laden carrying dozens of local people – the taxi driver was obviously hoping for a large tip!

At the airport we were told that we had 31kg more baggage than was allowed, so we had to pay excess baggage.

'But I will only charge you US$34 for 10 kg excess,' said the girl.

We handed over our credit card, but the girl was taken aback.

'We have no facilities for credit cards in the airport,' she said. 'Do you not have kyats?'

She was surprised that we had no kyats, but why would we if we were now leaving the country? Kyats would certainly be of no use anywhere else in the world. We shook our heads.

'Then I will take US dollars,' she replied.

We told her that we had none, though this wasn't quite the truth. She shrugged her shoulders, and waived the fee. It was lucky she hadn't weighed our hand baggage, because we were also carrying 24 kg more than the allowed 7 kg each.

Numerous people on the plane were wearing face masks, but we didn't know whether these were to protect other people because they had visited SARS-infected countries or whether they were to protect themselves. The plane was more than half empty – none of the seats in the 4-seat deep centre aisle were occupied, so we would have been annoyed to have paid excess baggage.

Just over one hour later we arrived at Bangkok in Thailand.

CHAPTER 11

THAILAND

Thailand is a large tropical country, comparable in size to France, which lies in the centre of south-east Asia, bordered by Myanmar in the north and west, Laos and Cambodia to the east, and Malaysia to the south. Dozens of lush tropical islands line the western coastline in the Andaman Sea and the eastern coastline in the Gulf of Thailand. The northern region has mountains, forests and fertile valleys and the fertile plain in the centre of the country is one of the main rice-growing areas in the world. Known as Siam until 1939, Thailand has become the most popular tourist destination in south-east Asia, and tourism is therefore its main industry. Diverse elements, including crisp mountain scenery, exotic hill tribes, forests worked by elephants, colourful festivals, ancient cities, exquisite temples, islands with stunning palm-fringed beaches and coral reefs teeming with colourful marine life, floating markets, delicious highly-spiced cuisine and friendly people contribute to Thailand's popularity.

Thailand was the ninth country we had visited on our trip. As we entered the arrivals lounge, we were concerned to see an official pointing a hand gun at each person's head, but we were told that this was a special type of thermometer which could check if anyone had a fever – there were obviously great concerns about the spread of SARS. We realised that we were back to some sort of civilisation when we saw the ATMs! A taxi wanted 1000 baht to take us to the city centre, but we were certain we could do better. An air-conditioned coach took us to 'Backpacker-land' for 100 baht each. Bangkok was very hot – so hot and humid that the slightest exertion reduced us to balls of sweat. We knew that April was supposed to be the worst month of the year to visit Bangkok, but despite that there were still plenty of travellers around when we arrived in Khao San Road. Bangkok is one of the major destinations for backpackers and, whether as part of a world trip or a visit to Asia, most backpackers will visit Bangkok. The Khao San Road area was alive with cafés, bars and restaurants, almost all with large flat-screened televisions to attract westerners, selling good coffee, iced or hot, and western food and beer as well as local food and beer. The fact that we had been given a glass of wine on the flight (our first wine since Goa!) had told us that Thailand was going to be more westernised than India or Myanmar. We were surprised to notice that vehicles were driven on the left in Thailand.

The streets were full of small shops, some of them air-conditioned. Souvenir shops, cafés, stalls selling food, stalls selling everything you can think of, new and second-hand book-shops and stalls with plenty of English novels and guide books, good quality rucksacks at bargain prices, clothes at ridiculous prices, and internet cafés were everywhere. There was even a Boots the Chemist amongst the shops, a dog lying asleep in front of the entrance, trying to catch the cool air-conditioned breeze as it escaped under the closed glass doors. Stalls were cooking chicken satay, fried noodles and soup, and restaurants were barbecuing fish and chicken breasts outside on the street. The smells were wonderful. Once the sun had set, old VW campers converted into mobile bars parked in the streets, their signs showing more than 100 different cocktails available. Tables and chairs were set up around the vans, and business was brisk.

We decided that we liked Bangkok, although we realised that it wasn't the real Thailand that we would see once we started cycling. However, we thought that Bangkok was definitely a fun place to be for a short time. We used one of the many internet cafés to contact Helen from California to arrange to meet in Bangkok, but we had a reply from her to say that she had already left Bangkok and had flown to Mexico City in South America.

Our previous plans had been to fly from Bangkok to Hanoi in Vietnam, cycle through Vietnam to Laos and Cambodia, south through Thailand to Malaysia and Singapore and then through various islands in Indonesia. However, we knew from travellers going in the opposite direction that Cambodia was even hotter than Myanmar, and we felt that south-east Asia would be more enjoyable if we arrived in November, when it was cooler, and we could therefore take more time exploring it. Another concern was the SARS epidemic. We knew that a visit to Vietnam or Singapore at this time, both badly hit by the disease, would make entry to other countries such as Australia difficult. We had already been required to complete special SARS forms on entry to Myanmar and Thailand confirming that we hadn't visited certain countries – people living in Hong Kong, where the epidemic had started, were no longer allowed to travel, in an attempt to contain the outbreak.

We decided to review our plans, in view of the fact that south-east Asia was far too hot to begin cycling in April, and we looked on our world map for somewhere cooler to visit. Our eyes alighted on Australia; it was autumn there, so would be much cooler. We could return to south-east Asia later in the year when the temperature was cooler.

We decided to visit Tasmania first which, being in the south, was the coolest part of the country. In a few weeks' time, Tasmania might be too cold for cycling, but by that time we would be cycling north up the east coast, following the sun. Later we hoped to visit Western Australia. However, as always, plans could be changed if we decided to go elsewhere. We had already arranged to visit Japan in October, and after that planned to arrive back in south-east Asia in November 2003, when the weather would be more suitable for cycling. We had to keep our fingers crossed that the SARS problem would be over by that time.

We spent most of the day at the Australian embassy, where we had problems getting a visa because we had visited Asia. If we had wanted to stay in Australia less than three months we could have obtained an instant visa with our flight ticket without attending an embassy, but the six months visa that we wanted meant that we needed to attend the embassy and complete a multi-page questionaire. The staff at the embassy were concerned that we may have contracted tuberculosis on our travels through Asia, and wanted us to have chest x-rays. We eventually persuaded them that we were unlikely to be able to cycle if we had TB, but we had to sign a disclaimer because we were choosing not to have the recommended x-rays!

We went shopping, treating ourselves to a wide-angled lens for our SLR camera, so that we could take even better landscape photographs. We sent home a dozen films to be developed, because we hadn't felt confident with the postal system in Myanmar. Our concerns proved correct – my mother never received any of the postcards that we sent from Myanmar. We bought our tickets to Australia, going to the ATM to collect cash to avoid being charged 3% for using our credit cards. When we explained to the travel agent that it was not normal in western countries to pay this charge, he argued heatedly that this was impossible – everywhere in the world passed this charge to the customer, he insisted.

It poured with rain later that evening, and lightning lit the sky as we scurried back to our hotel after visiting the mobile bar for a refreshing gin and tonic. We had one more day before we caught our flight to Australia, so we visited one of the famous colourful floating markets in Thailand, where locals sold fruit and vegetables, cooked noodles, souvenirs and clothes from their boats on the canal.

We caught the shuttle bus to the airport; there were as many as 10 lanes at times, some lanes splitting to go onto the fly-overs. We were amused to see a very small motorbike go past with the passenger sitting backwards. He was holding the handles of a large sack trolley which rolled along the road behind the motorbike with a large television strapped to it! We passed names that were so familiar – Burger King, MacDonalds, KFC, Pizza Hut, and there were ads on giant hoardings next to the fly-over for Mitsubishi, Sony, Canon, Sanyo, Panasonic and Hitachi. We hadn't seen these familiar names for so long.

Australian airlines usually insist on bikes being boxed, and we were told that we had to pay 700 baht for two boxes. However, our bikes just wouldn't fit into them. If we removed the wheels the luggage racks would still protrude, and where could the wheels go? The check-in assistant finally allowed the bikes onto the plane without boxes, but we had to sign disclaimers in case there was any damage caused to the bikes en route. We discovered afterwards that British Airways and Qantas passengers shared the plane with two different flight numbers, and if we had been British Airways passengers instead of Qantas passengers there would have been no requirement for the bikes to be boxed!

Our flight from Bangkok was due to land in Sydney, where we had to catch a flight to Melbourne and then another to Hobart, the capital of Tasmania. On the plane we put our watches forward three hours to Melbourne time, and celebrated with a glass of delicious Australian wine as we flew across the equator. We had a nine hour flight ahead of us, but my neck was painful in the restricted position of the seat, and I couldn't sleep.

Sydney was grey and very overcast, which was disappointing. Our onward flight to Melbourne was so late that there was a danger that we might miss our flight from Melbourne to Hobart. At Melbourne airport we ran along miles of corridors, but our bicycles were the last to arrive at baggage reclaim. The Australians are so strict about quarantine that we were told that the bicycle tyres would have to be washed before they could be allowed into the country (in case there was contaminated dirt on them!), so our flight to Hobart left without us. We asked to be booked onto the next available flight to Tasmania, which was to Launceston in the north of the island, rather than to the capital of Hobart. No problem – we'd cycle round the island from a different point. It was raining in Melbourne when we left the mainland, and we arrived in Launceston, Tasmania on 27th April 2003.

CHAPTER 12

AUSTRALIA

Australia is a huge country with very few people. It is one and a half times the size of Europe, but only 19 million people live in Australia, most of them in the charming coastal cities – this is one third of the population of Great Britain! From the mountains of the south-east and Tasmania, where snow falls in winter, to the flat, dry, inhospitable and remote inland region with its salt lakes and scant vegetation; from the tropical area in the north to the rugged magnificent scenery of the north-west 'final frontier'; from the superb surfing beaches on the Pacific Ocean in the east to the magnificent beaches on the Indian Ocean in the west, Australia is a country of variety and natural beauty.

Tasmania

At the airport we experienced the first of many kindnesses from Australian people. I asked a girl where she had found her trolley, and she showed me where to get one. However, I needed $3 to release it, and I only had the $50 notes I had just collected from the ATM. She rummaged in her purse and gave me the money, insisting I took it. I was overwhelmed.

We found a room at a pub, where we were given white fluffy towels, and the sheets were the whitest and crispest I'd seen in a long time. There was no en suite bathroom; this was the first time on this trip we'd had no private bathroom, but we were the only people staying at the pub, so it wasn't a problem. We had drinks in the bar – the wine was wonderful after nothing decent since Italy, and we went to bed and slept for 14 hours, waking at 10am the next morning.

Tasmania was a surprise to us; although we had heard it was lovely, we hadn't expected it to be so beautiful, and we both fell in love with the island. Tasmania is the only island state in Australia, and is very much a holiday isle. We had arrived in Launceston, which was named after the English town in Cornwall, but is pronounced as it is spelt, rather than 'Lornston' as we say in England. Amazingly, it is also on the river Tamar, again obviously named by someone to remind them of back home. Launceston has wide hilly tree-lined streets, and is full of elegant Victorian houses, very reminiscent of England, with beautiful cast-iron Victorian railings and balconies. As well as the typically Australian eucalyptus trees, there were also olive trees, reminding us of the Mediterranean, and also birch trees and roses, reminding us of England. Because it was now autumn, the colours on the trees were also very beautiful. The streets were very clean, and everyone was so friendly and eager to talk that it was sometimes difficult to get away!

'G'day,' 'Goodonya' and 'No worries' were expressions we heard constantly.

We discovered quickly the Australians' need to abbreviate everything. Potatoes were 'taters' or 'spuds' and even a tin of potatoes was labelled as 'Tiny Taters'! The supermarket aisle with vegetables was labelled 'Veggies' and Tasmania was 'Tasi' to everyone, just as Australia was 'Oz'. We discovered later that virtually every town and city in Australia had an abbreviated name. We also discovered the Australians' sense of humour, and laughed at the sign in the back of a van parked in the main road.

'You don't like my driving? – e-mail dontgiveash★★@gof★★★yourself.com'!

Tasmania is an island a bit smaller than Ireland, and has a variety of different types of scenery. In the north near Launceston we were amazed by the scenery of green rolling hills full of trees, cows and sheep, which was so like England. The north coast has lovely beaches, and the road runs alongside the beaches for much of the way. The west of Tasmania is very wild and rugged, with few towns, many of which are the original mining towns. There are the most amazing sand dunes, just mountains of sand for miles and miles, and there are rainforests full of magnificent trees and tree ferns. In the central part of Tasmania is Cradle Mountain and the Lake District – within the Cradle Mountain and Lake District area alone there are 5 mountain ranges, World Heritage areas, 56 mountains, 18 rivers plus their tributaries, more than 2,000 kilometres of walking tracks, 275 kilometres of beaches, 2 canyons, National Parks and 3 extensive cave systems. In fact, over one-third of the state of Tasmania is actually National Park, which shows what a wonderful island it is for anyone who likes natural beauty. The west, east and central areas reminded us very much of the west coast of Scotland. Hobart, the capital, is a lovely city surrounded by hills and overlooked by Mount Wellington, which often had its top covered with clouds. We visited the lovely harbour area of Hobart with its great restaurants, cafés and bars. North and south of Hobart are wonderful beaches and islands, considered the best in Tasmania.

There had apparently recently been a serious drought in Tasmania and the Australian mainland. A man we chatted to at Sydney airport told us of a reservoir that had been made by flooding a valley and town. Because of the drought, the level of the water in the reservoir had fallen so low that a few weeks earlier the roofs of the houses were just visible above the water, and eventually there was just a stream of water running down the high street! The longed-for rain had begun just before we arrived, making Tasmania green again overnight.

Everywhere in Tasmania there were hills – lots of them. We will definitely go back to Tasmania one day because we loved it so much, but for me the non-stop, often very steep hills were very hard indeed on a bicycle.

Obviously the fact that the island is hilly is one of the reasons that makes it so beautiful – the views were often breathtaking from the tops of the hills or mountains, but so many of the out-of-the-way places that we would have liked to visit were a long way down poor roads to the coast which were dead ends, meaning that we would have to cycle all the way back up again to the main road. This is the main disadvantage of cycling; maybe next time we can hire a motor-home!

Despite the fact that so much of the scenery reminded us of England and Scotland, there were always animals and birds to remind us that we were in a very different country. As we cycled, we often disturbed flocks of brilliantly coloured parrots that flew upwards in an amazing splash of colour.

It was often fairly cold during the day, but there was always the most beautiful blue sky, with wisps of white clouds; at night the sky was full of stars, right down to the horizon, and we'd never seen the Milky Way so stunningly clear – it was a broad band across the sky. Presumably the clarity is the result of no pollution in that part of the world.

We wanted to cycle around Tasi, but there were virtually no roads in the south or in the north-west of the island, and the road going across the southern part of the island from the west to east coast crosses National Park wilderness. As there was nowhere to stay on this isolated stretch of road which would take us days to cycle, we decided that we would take the bus from Queenstown on the west of Tasi to Hobart in the east.

We decided to circumnavigate Tasi in an anti-clockwise direction, so left Launceston heading west. Our bicycle computers almost immediately indicated that we had cycled 5,000 miles/8,000 kilometres since leaving England. It had been raining, so we had on our wet weather gear, and the long hill out of Launceston was a very unfortunate start for our first day's cycling for so long!

I was suddenly struck by something odd.

'What's the sun doing over there – it's in the north!' I called out to Warren.

We realised, of course, that because we were now in the southern hemisphere, although the sun still rises and sets in the east and west, it goes a different direction in between. The cool, dark rooms in Australia are the south rooms, not the north rooms as we are used to in England – it was obvious when we thought about it! The other phenomenon that we had heard about and had now seen was the 'coriollis effect' – the fact that in the southern hemisphere water going down plug holes swirls in the opposite direction to the northern hemisphere, and whirlpools are affected in the same way. Vines too are influenced by coriollis – if you look at vines, they always coil upwards in the same spiral direction. In the northern hemisphere they go one way, and in the southern hemisphere they go the opposite. Amazingly, on the equator they can go either way!

Because prices of accommodation were now much more expensive than Asia (approximately Australian $55 a night, over £20), we decided that we needed to start camping again, something we hadn't done since Europe. At our first Australian campsite (the Australians call them caravan parks) we discovered that the campsites had campers' kitchens, usually covered, but sometimes indoors, with free electric griddle plates – the Aussie version of a barbecue. Sometimes toasters, kettles, microwaves, fridges, televisions and log fires were also supplied. We noticed that these electric griddles for barbecuing were also at the public picnic sites or in popular areas for anyone to use free of charge, which we thought a wonderful idea.

We woke to vivid blue skies; as we cycled we were amazed by the stunning views – green rolling fields, trees, mountains in the distance, sheep and cows, and trees in autumn colours. It was so picturesque and so English! We were now wearing cycling helmets, because they were compulsory in Australia although, ironically, the roads in Tasmania were more traffic-free than any other country in which we'd cycled so far. The temperature didn't rise above 15°C all day, so we were wearing shoes, trousers and layers of t-shirts and shirts for the first time since Turkey in December. Everyone was so friendly, stopping their cars to chat to us, and by the end of the first day we had received two offers of accommodation in people's homes if we needed a bed for the night. Australia so far had been a surprise – it hadn't even been a country that we'd been yearning to visit, but we were enjoying it immensely.

'Australia is wonderful,' said Warren, as we cycled along the quiet roads. 'I love the people and I love this country. I'm going to emigrate!'

I felt the same. How could we have fallen in love with the place so quickly?

We were very cold in the tent at Deloraine the next night and couldn't get warm. When the morning came we discovered that it was minus 1°C; we scraped thick ice off the tent and huddled shivering as we ate our fried egg sandwiches for breakfast. Well, we couldn't complain, could we? We had wanted cooler weather! Our four camping neighbours were wearing thick woolly hats and coats, but we didn't have proper cold weather gear. By 10am it was 8°C and it was 12°C by noon. We decided that we would have to stop camping until we reached a warmer part of Australia, so after that our budget was blown. We booked on-site caravans which had all facilities, including television and heating, so we were now able to spend the evenings watching television whilst sipping a glass of Australian wine – very civilized! A nice touch was that there was usually complimentary tea, coffee, sugar and milk in the caravans as well. These caravans were costing us between $30 and $50 a night. However, we cooked our own food most nights to eke out our budget.

It wasn't possible to buy wine in supermarkets in Tasmania. When we couldn't find the wine section in the first supermarket we visited, I asked the checkout girl where the wine was, and the look of horror on her face told me that I'd put my foot in it. I apologised profusely, explaining that in England every supermarket sold wine, and a customer overhearing me said that there were plans afoot to change the law so that supermarkets could sell alcohol, but many people were against the idea. The checkout girl obviously thought we were raging alcoholics to expect wine in a supermarket, and we discovered that we had to go to a 'Bottle Shop'. These were often attached to a pub or a hotel, but in bigger towns there would be a drive-in Bottle Shop with two fast lanes and one 'browser' lane. These shops always had a walk-in cold store stocked with cartons of beer, ready to go and ready to drink. We heard a discussion later on radio with a man who was vehemently opposed to the new proposals of selling alcohol in supermarkets. His argument was that housewives might buy a bottle of wine or beer on impulse when she didn't really need or want it, and this could lead to alcoholism . . .

After Deloraine we turned north towards the coast to Devonport, by-passing Sheffield. There was a strong cold wind against us – I could feel it whistling in my ears and stinging my cheeks. We travelled west along the coast for a couple of days, through Ulverston and Penguin and on to Somerset, the beach on our right for most of the way. The side of the road had been planted with flowers and shrubs – geraniums, cannas, allium, marigolds, nasturtiums and daisies, which looked lovely with the sea beyond. We stopped at coffee shops and cafés for breaks, and in caravan parks each night. We chatted to the locals and the late tourists, mostly from the mainland, who recommended endless places for us to visit. At one coffee shop we ordered chicken burgers for lunch to try to warm up. I hadn't expected the chips that accompanied it, let alone two slices of bacon, a thick slice of cheese, beetroot, tomato, cucumber, lettuce and an egg on top of the chicken burger! This was when we discovered that burgers or filled bread rolls in Australia are rarely served without beetroot, an ingredient we found rather strange as an essential ingredient.

At Burnie we stopped to take a photo of ourselves under a signpost that said 'Eiffel Tower, Paris 17,040km' – we had only cycled 8,000 of those kilometres! At our campsite that evening we met two Australian girls, Rachel and Shellie, who were also cycling. They came from Victoria, and had chosen Tasmania for their first ever cycling and camping holiday.

We turned south and took the road inland towards Strahan (pronounced 'Strawn') on the west coast. It was a beautiful day again, and we immediately began to climb steeply. The hedgerows were full of rosehips, berries and autumn leaves, and after a while we looked back and could see the sea spread out in the distance way below us. We were now used to seeing a lot of wild life – unfortunately, because most of Tasi's wild life is nocturnal, the animals we saw were usually dead by the roadside – wallabies, wombats looking like cuddly teddy bears, bottlebrush-tailed possums and Tasmanian devils, an animal which we had both assumed to be mythical until now. We were cycling towards the wilder part of Tasi, and there were very few houses, but those that we saw had lovely gardens, with dahlias and fuchsias in abundance and large geraniums still flowering. Cotoneaster and pyracanthas were covered in berries, red and yellow hot pokers were in flower and hydrangea bushes were covered with giant heads of flowers. The scenery changed from rolling hills and fields to forests of conifers and eucalyptus trees. Magnificent tall tree ferns covered the ground below the trees. Areas of forest had been cut, and giant logging trucks continually passed us, sometimes empty with their 12-wheeled trailers stacked on top of the tractor unit, and sometimes with the trailer piled high with massive tree trunks stretched between tractor unit and trailer.

Suddenly we were flying down dark, shaded roads, round and round the s-bends, averaging 25 to 30 mph free-wheeling. I stopped several times to add extra layers of clothing, and after a few miles of travelling non-stop downhill we were at the bottom of Hellyer Gorge, with a similar hill to cycle back up again on the other side of the gorge. We had only cycled 30 miles that day but, apart from the final dash down to the gorge, it had all been uphill, so we planned to camp wild in the gorge that night. There was a picnic area with tables and chairs and, despite the fact that we were miles from anywhere, there was a block of flush toilets complete with soft toilet paper! A river rushed by a few yards away, and we walked through the cool temperate rainforest, marvelling at the trees, thick with green moss, the giant tree ferns towering over us and the birds.

We were very cold that night, and it was the last time we camped in a tent whilst we were in Tasi. It was minus 2°C in the gorge when we woke, so we quickly made our breakfast of porridge and hot chocolate before setting off again. Because we were at the bottom of a gorge, a layer of cold air had dropped to the bottom where we were camping. At least we had no ice on the tent, because we had set up our tent underneath the trees for protection. We had been warned of the awful hills to come by a group who had stopped at the picnic area the afternoon before, but now we were grateful to have a hill to climb that morning to warm us up. After an hour of cycling uphill, it was 5°C and we were very hot, but we were still climbing up, round and round the s-bends. It wasn't as bad as I had expected – just a long, slow slog in bottom gear going up and up and up, and round and round the bends, with no views because of the tall trees lining the road. Tree ferns and man ferns lined the roads, often down embankments below us, so we could see the full beauty of the ferns from above – the circles of fronds were 18 feet in diameter. We often heard water running, and there were waterfalls of icy water running over mossy rocks down to the road, after which the water shot under the road and continued on its way down the hill.

We cycled for almost 5 miles before we reached a flat stretch of road – we had cycled uphill solidly for over an hour, so we were warm again! The road continued up and down through the forest, through areas of new eucalyptus trees recently planted, the blue-silver foliage contrasting with the white trunks of the trees. There were natural forests with many different trees and ferns, bracken, mossy logs and spiky grasses. In open areas, small plants with white, pink or coral berries were growing. After nearly 3 hours we had cycled only 20 kilometres. A sign at a junction showed that we had another 40km to go to our destination, but a hotel was 7km away if we turned right. We were already tired, especially as we hadn't slept well the night before, so we opted for the hotel, even though we would have to retrace our journey for 7km the next day.

The hotel was an old pub in a village at an altitude of 600m (just under 2,000ft), and a coach load of white-haired elderly people were enjoying lunch in the dining room. They soon left and we were left with the village to ourselves. There was the pub/hotel in the village and also the general store/café/service station, where we had sat and ordered a meal as we arrived in the village – the sausage, egg and chips had been brought to us by the man who had just served petrol to another customer! Apart from these two buildings, there were several closed down shops and a few houses. In the hotel we were shown to a comfortable room full of elegant Edwardian mahogany furniture and a high bed, and the windows overlooked a tall waterfall, the pride of the village, with a view of forests undulating into the distance. There was no en-suite bathroom, but down the corridor from our hotel room was an enormous bathroom where I ran a hot bath, my first since Italy. The water ran hot, brown and steaming from the tap, but despite the colour I luxuriated in the water. It reminded me of a holiday cottage where we had stayed in the Outer Hebrides, where the water was equally brown – not because of any problem with the water, but because the water was naturally filtered through peat.

The water was piping hot, and four large bulbs on the ceiling heated the room, so I eventually got out of the bath looking like a boiled lobster. However, I was warm again – such bliss after the night before! The bar to the hotel filled up that evening as we enjoyed a pleasant meal, so the hotel was obviously the centre of the village. As we ate next to the log fire the door opened, and Rachel and Shelley walked in. It was already dark and very cold; they had chosen not to spend the night in the gorge as we had, but like us had been enticed along the side road because of the promise of a hotel nearby.

In the morning the four of us, the only residents, had to make our own breakfast in the vast hotel kitchen, which was rather bizarre. We set off before Rachel and Shelley, waving goodbye. It was slightly warmer now, 4°C, but foggy. We passed streams, trees, mountains and grasses like pampas. Again we were climbing, and the sky became blue again once the fog cleared. After 690m (2,240ft), we cycled downhill past a beautiful lake to our destination town, which had a population of 250. The place was dead and had no accommodation; every time we turned a corner we expected to see tumbleweed rolling down the road, so we decided to go on to Rosebery, a bigger town. In the café where we had lunch a tanker driver told us it would take 2 or 3 hours.

'You're winding us up,' I said. 'It's only 16 kilometres.'

'Yeh,' he said, 'but you have to go over that mountain.'

We turned to look where he was pointing, and our hearts sank. The hill was so steep that we had to push our bikes, but we saw stunning mountain views on the way. At the top we put on all of our clothes for the cold descent, and flew down into Rosebery, an old mining town.

Again it was a very quiet place with scores of 'For Sale' signs on the shops, although our caravan park was surrounded by lovely mountain ranges on three sides. Unfortunately the massive local mine, a considerable eyesore, was on the fourth, but this mine dominates both the town and the local economy, and buckets on lines snaked across the road and mountains leading from the mine. Formerly mining gold, silver, lead, zinc and copper, the mine now produces mostly zinc. The caravan park owner told us that there weren't any cafés in the town, but he had made an arrangement with the miners' mess – we could have a 3 course meal there for $10 (just over £4) if we wanted, and we could take a bottle of wine with us to drink there.

It sounded good to us, so we went to join the miners. The food was good and plentiful, and the canteen was presided over by a woman who was there, it seemed, to make sure that plates were fully laden. There was a choice of main course.

'I'll have the fish,' said Warren, when he reached the front of the queue. She put one large piece on the plate and lifted the last piece from the fryer.

'Do you want two pieces?' she asked. Warren was tempted, but didn't want to appear greedy.

'Someone else in the queue might want fish,' he said.

'Well, they'll have to bladdy wait then, won't they?' she said, slapping the second piece of fish on the plate. As there was no more room for the chips and vegetables, she piled these onto a second plate! As we sat down we were once more joined by Rachel and Shelley – since there was very little choice of accommodation, it was hardly surprising that we kept staying at the same places!

The next day we had only 20 miles to cycle, but it was my least favourite day. The hills went constantly up and down; there just didn't appear to be any flat stretches of road in Tasmania. The hills were so steep we were pushing the bikes up each hill, taking about half an hour each time, but it would take only two minutes to cycle fast down the other side, before getting off to push them up the next hill. It was hard work – one of those days when I wondered why I had wanted to cycle round the world! The views were of miles of undulating forest – we could see nothing else.

As we cycled into Zeehan, our destination for the day, we could see tall plumes of smoke in the sky, and realised as we approached that they were burning off strips of land to protect the local forests from accidental forest fires. We had to cycle across Pea Soup Creek Bridge in smoke so thick that I couldn't see my bicycle wheel, which was terrifying. Later in the day the sky turned red with the smoke particles obliterating the sun, which looked really spooky, and that evening we saw our first live wallaby in the campsite. The wallaby was unconcerned that we were approaching, and bounced slowly away into the bushes as we came very close.

The following day it was raining heavily, so we decided to have a lazy day without cycling. Rachel and Shelley were once again in the same caravan park, but they decided to cycle on, because they had limited time off work in which to complete their cycling holiday. We waved goodbye to them as they cycled off in the pouring rain, and our paths never crossed again. We visited the local museum which gave the history of the mining communities in the area; gold, silver, tin, lead, copper, ores, minerals and gems have all been mined in Tasi, and several mines still remain in the western part of the island.

We cycled on to Strahan on the coast the following day. Despite the cold, the sun was shining and the sky was blue, and the scenery was very much like Scotland – green hills with mountains in the distance, gorse bushes, heather and conifers. We arrived at the west coast, and stopped to explore the dunes – mountains of sand going up and down for miles towards the sea. As we cycled into Strahan a small seaplane landed in the harbour, having taken tourists to see the beautiful views from the air.

We booked ourselves and our bikes onto the Abt train to Queenstown, as we had heard that this tourist steam train had been recently restored and carried visitors through virgin rainforests, gorges, past rivers and waterfalls, over 40 bridges and through dense forest. It would also save us cycling up another mountain!

The Abt railway was opened in 1896, and was considered a miracle feat of engineering at the time. Queenstown is 22 miles inland, and was isolated from the rest of Tasmania at the time; only the mule trains could navigate the terrain. Queenstown is the mining centre of the west coast of Tasmania, and is surrounded by wilderness and some of the most ancient rainforest systems in the world. In order for the copper mining in Queenstown to be profitable, it had to be possible to get the copper ingots to Strahan port. The land was too steep for a normal railway, so a 'rack and pinion' railway was built over the rugged terrain to ensure that the train could negotiate the 1-in-16 and 1-in-20 hills. It cost £216,000 to build, which was more than half the total cost of establishing the Queenstown copper industry, and many people were convinced that the train wouldn't be able to negotiate the hills and would slide back into the King River. The railway was built by hand using picks and wheelbarrows. Not even dynamite was used, as there was no-one experienced in using it. The railway provided the only link with the rest of the world for the people who lived along its route until the 1930s, long after other roads had been built in Tasmania. Queenstown remained landlocked, surrounded by its circle of bare hills, until a winding road connected it across the hills and mountains to the capital of Hobart.

The men who built the railway had to cut through mountains, dense forests, flooded rivers and steep gorges up to 500 feet deep. They had to haul logs up rapids to build timber bridges, one of them a quarter of a mile long. Suddenly the company's money ran out before the railway was completed, and it seemed likely that the company would go out of business. However, a rich seam of silver was unexpectedly discovered, the company survived, and the railway was completed.

We boarded the train which set off with a dog in hot pursuit, barking. We passed through the rugged wilderness of rain forests, thick with protected trees and man ferns, past gem mines, gold mines, across and alongside rivers, brown with the minerals in the ground. Local trees included the famous Tasmanian Huon pine, a wood so full of oil that it could lie on the forest floor for centuries and still be useable. Myrtle trees and Blackheart Sassafras were trees that were also highly valued because of their beautiful dark red and striped woods which could be lovingly crafted into individual pieces of furniture.

Queenstown seemed very dead when we arrived there, and we cycled around looking for a caravan park. We thought the town was very gloomy; the surrounding hills were totally bare, having been stripped of timber to fire the local copper smelters, and there was an air of depression. By chance we saw a Tasiline bus, and asked the driver when the next bus was to Hobart. He was about to leave on the four hour journey, he told us, and the next bus was not until two days later. Not wanting to spend two days in Queenstown we jumped quickly on the bus, and our bikes were stored in the trailer behind. As the bus slowly made its way up the 99 bends hewn out of the bare rock leading out of Queenstown, we were relieved not to be on our bikes, and for the next 240 kilometres there wasn't a straight stretch of road. We passed massive lakes, gorse, mountains and forests before darkness fell. Halfway to Hobart, in the middle of nowhere, we were all asked to get out – we had to swap buses, because the drivers only drove halfway and then back again! Our original bus drove off with its new passengers, and our new bus driver turned the ignition. There was a groan as the engine tried to turn, but the driver couldn't start the bus.

'Everybody out and push,' he said. Everyone laughed nervously.

'You think I'm joking?' he asked.

We realised he wasn't, and all of us had to get out and bump start a 52-seater bus in the middle of nowhere in the dark. Fortunately it started immediately; we jumped back on the bus in relief, and were off again. Our half-joking requests for a discount were ignored by the driver.

For anyone who, like me, suffers from travel sickness on buses, the journey was pure hell. The cardinal rule of 'keep your eyes on the road ahead' was impossible to follow, as the bus turned almost 180 degree turns up and down the hills, and anyway, much of the journey was in darkness. Four hours, two dead wallabies and three near misses later, we arrived in Hobart, Tasmania's capital, where we booked into a very clean and pleasant backpackers' hostel.

Hobart is the capital of Tasmania on the east coast, and appears to be 'the place to be' in Tasi. More modern than Launceston, the second largest city, it has a smart harbour area lined with cafés, restaurants and bars, but like everywhere in Tasi was very quiet at that time of year. The city spreads out a long way, and houses can be seen climbing up the hills on all sides around the large shopping area in Hobart. Mount Wellington looks down over the city, often with a cloud obscuring the top.

We spent several days in the backpackers' hostel, chatting to different people. Hiro was from Tokyo, staying with his girlfriend who was working in Tasi teaching Japanese. He had decided to try cycling, never having done any before, and was now keen to cycle in New Zealand. There was also a Dutch cyclist, and an American cyclist from Chicago on a recumbent bike, so we weren't the only crazy people! One of the cyclists gave us her no longer needed Australian guide for cyclists. In it we read that we should wear 'knicks' (the Australian term for padded lycra shorts) and that '...baby nappy rash creams also guard against chafing – apply liberally around the crotch area before riding' – what a horrible thought! We had opted to break in leather saddles before we left England, and had never suffered from any such problems despite wearing normal shorts and trousers – maybe a good saddle should have been recommended instead of nappy cream!

Having heard about the wonderful beaches on the east coast, we first cycled south from Hobart to visit Bruny Island. The east coast of Tasmania is hilly, though not as severely as the west coast, and the views are lovely. On our left were areas of water that looked like lakes and islands, but were actually part of the Derwent and Huon River estuaries. We cycled through Kingston and Margate and on to Snug, where we booked into a very pretty caravan site with views across the water and islands. We saw numerous oyster beds which are common around Tasmania, and we were excited to see many of the white wallabies in the caravan park which we were told were quite common in that part of Tasmania.

We asked the caravan park owner how far it was to the Bruny Island ferry.

'It's only five minutes,' he said.

In Australia, distances are always quoted in minutes, hours or even days. We hadn't yet found a formula to convert the minutes to kilometres or to minutes on a bike, but one hour later (yes, it was mostly uphill!) we arrived at Kettering just in time to catch the ferry to Bruny Island. It was the most beautiful day of our 38 days in Tasmania. The colours in the sky ranged from turquoise to deep blue, the sun was shining, and there were white clouds to contrast the blues. Kettering looked stunning in the sunshine, with sailing ships moored in the harbour, and the becalmed sea looked like a blue mirror. We looked forward to a coffee when we got off the ferry half an hour later, but a sign saying 'Café – 30km' warned us that we had a while to wait. It was lucky that we were prepared as usual, and had brought our sandwiches and water! There was a steep climb out of the small harbour, and the views were so spectacular looking across the sea to other parts of the island that I kept stopping to take photos and admire the view.

Bruny was beautiful – in every direction was a different view across the sea, either of the mainland or of one of Bruny's peninsulars. The day became quite hot which, with so many hills to climb, made us grateful not to have arrived in Tasi mid-summer. We cycled off the road and sat looking out to sea at a wonderful view just like the west coast of Scotland. As we boiled water to make soup and coffee for lunch a plumber arrived in his van, a little taken aback to find someone in his favourite isolated lunchtime spot at that time of year. We chatted for ages, admiring the view and, despite the fact that he had travelled extensively, he said he wouldn't want to live anywhere in the world except Tasmania. However, like so many locals we spoke to, he loved Tasi best in winter when the tourists had gone home. He told us that Bruny Island's population of 500 swelled to 5,000 at Christmas time, the main summer holiday period, and our small lunchtime spot would be full of tents at that time. Once again we left with recommendations of places to visit.

We arrived at the 'neck' of Bruny Island, effectively a causeway joining two islands, and 236 steps led up to a look-out platform where we could admire the spectacular views. To our east was a crescent of perfect sand with rolling waves. There was no sign of any people, but it was apparently a popular haunt of the small Tasmanian fairy penguins. Looking north or south we could see the length of the causeway with beaches and sea on both sides.

We arrived in Adventure Bay and booked into a caravan park.

'G'dayfrit,' said the old gardener, and we agreed – it was a good day for anything. As soon as dusk arrived, so did the white wallabies, and they allowed us to approach fairly close. Later that night Warren was standing in the dark, looking up and admiring the stars, when he heard a strange sound.

'Boing! boing! boing!'

He looked down to see the white shape of a wallaby bouncing straight towards him. He stood very still, and the wallaby stopped just in front of him, as though suddenly aware there was an obstacle, and then bounced round him.

'Boing! boing!' and the wallaby disappeared into the darkness behind Warren.

In the 19th century, Bruny Island had been a busy whaling area with four whaling stations, and the whalers almost made the Southern Right whale extinct by the indiscriminate killing of breeding females and baby whales. The next morning we walked through the woods where we saw the remains of a whaling station, but the day was now overcast and it began to rain. As we dashed to the caravan to get out of the rain we saw the gardener again.

'G'dayfrit,' he said.

'Er – yes,' we replied, as lightning lit the dark sky overhead, and we wondered exactly what it was a good day for!

The following morning as we sat in the caravan having breakfast, a pair of stunning parrots preened themselves in the bush outside our window. They had green breasts, red and yellow heads and blue tails – very exotic and very different from any of the British birds that we were used to.

Now that we had seen Bruny Island, we had to cycle north again to Hobart via the ferry. The weather was overcast, so we were glad we'd seen Bruny Island in such beautiful weather on the first day. As we cycled, parrots and exotic birds flew up alongside us from the roadside bushes, and I stopped to look at a dead Tasmanian devil in the centre of the road – even in death it looked evil, its lips still pulled back in a snarl, exposing sharp teeth.

On the road back to Hobart we missed the turning that took us on the hilly coast road, and instead found ourselves on a dual carriageway that cut several miles off our journey. However, it also went up and over a mountain, and the road went very slowly uphill for many miles, culminating in a steep descent down into Hobart. From the top of the hill we could see the vast sprawl of Hobart, a city built on many hills, and the harbour beyond it with the Tasman Bridge spanning the estuary of the Derwent River. When Warren saw the descent ahead of him, he beamed from ear to ear, bent over the handlebars and shot off ahead of me. He topped his record so far, reaching 81.5 kilometres an hour, which is over 50 mph – no wonder the policeman in his car had slowed alongside him, pointing frantically to the speedometer on his dashboard!

That evening we went for a cheap Cambodian meal, and went to the Bottle Shop to buy a bottle of wine to take with us. We chose a bottle of Jacob's Creek wine; at $10 a bottle (£4.20), Australian wine was not much cheaper than in England, although it was possible to buy 4 litre boxes of cheap wine, boxes of wine in Australia being called 'casks'. Most of the restaurants in Australia were BYO or 'Bring Your Own', which is an idea we'd like to see much more in England, bearing in mind the high price of wine back home. Sometimes corkage was charged, but only 50c to $1.50 per bottle. The man serving us in the Bottle Shop commented on our bikes.

'They're no good,' he said. 'You can't get a crate of beer on one of them – I'd get a trailer for the beer if I was you.' He was serious, too . . .

The next day we left Hobart and set off across the Tasman Bridge. It was very unpleasant – the wind nearly blew us off our bikes as we crossed, because the cycle lane was a narrow unprotected pathway; the cars were on a level below us, protected from the wind by a wall!

Once we had turned off the dual carriageway towards Richmond it became very rural. We passed vineyards and orchards, hills and mountains, all alive with autumn colours, and the hedgerows were full of rose hips above self-seeded clumps of golden rape. Richmond is a pretty town, famous for its stone bridge built by convicts in 1823. As this bridge is the oldest bridge in Australia, it made us realise how new Australia is! There were pretty old churches and a famous gaol; I was eager to visit Richmond as my elder daughter, Mandi, had married her Australian husband there. Unfortunately the weather was overcast again, and rain set in overnight.

After Richmond, we cycled north-east towards Orford and the east coast, and once again found ourselves climbing up and down hills. Several rainbows in the distance were an indication of the changeable weather. At the top of one hill was a sign showing that we'd just climbed Bust-Me-Gall Hill – the altitude was 1,102 feet. After a few miles we approached Break-me-neck Hill, fortunately downhill this time, and Warren's face once again lit up at the thought of a fast downhill ride. Twenty-six miles after setting out, we found our first café and had a break for coffee, after which we cycled up and down the hills again, following a stream which rushed over boulders through the forest. The stream grew bigger until it was a substantial river meeting the sea at Orford. No accommodation was available there, so we travelled on another 9 kilometres to Triabunna.

Now we were travelling north up the east coast to Coles Bay, a tourist resort in Tasmania. It was cold, but there were still lovely blue skies. We were passed constantly by massive logging trucks again, taking the logs to the saw mills. The whoosh of air from a speeding logging truck going in the opposite direction could stop us dead on our bicycles, especially when going slowly uphill, so we were watchful for them coming.

We passed lakes with pelicans and black swans, and we were high up looking down over the bays and beaches to our right. The landscape opened up, and across the sea were mountains and islands, again reminding us of the west coast of Scotland. We arrived at Swansea, Glamorgan, and booked into a caravan park which had lovely views of the beach and sea.

The next day's trip was frustrating – imagine a capital 'A' with a rounded top. Swansea is at the bottom left point, and Coles Bay is at the bottom right point. The horizontal line of the 'A' is Nine Mile Beach, but it stops short of joining the right hand side because of a strip of water 50 metres wide. Sometimes, if he feels in the mood, a man will take walkers or cyclists in his 12 feet dinghy across this narrow strip of water, which saves cycling 60 kilometres around the top of the letter 'A'. We phoned the boatman, keeping all fingers crossed, but he wasn't in the mood to give us a lift. What a shame – the road alongside Nine Mile Beach is probably the only flat stretch of road in Tasmania, so we missed that too, having to cycle the long way round. I felt I needed a break from the difficult hilly cycling because it was causing me considerable pain in my neck, wrists and hands.

We cycled past ponds and ditches noisy with the sound of frogs, and past lagoons, creeks and rivulets full of birdlife. Parrots flew from bushes as we passed, and the sun shone as we cycled into beautiful Coles Bay.

The next day we paid $3.50 each to go into the National Park, and cycled through forests with views of the sea and mountains in the distance. The mountains are pink and red granite, so look especially spectacular at dawn or sunset, when their colour is accentuated. We left our bikes and began to climb up steps of granite, logs and wood through the forest. We were surprised to see a wallaby sat alongside the path, and it allowed us to come really close. Giant pink granite boulders lay under the trees, reminding us of the pink granite boulders on the beaches of north Brittany. We admired the amazing patterns and colours of the striped bark of the eucalyptus trees, and beyond and between the trees we had glimpses of the sea far below. At the top of the path, which was a pass between mountains, a lookout had been built to view Wineglass Bay – a perfect circular bay of stunning blue sea, edged on one side with a crescent of white sand, surrounded by mountains and backed by lakes. We later watched the sunset from the beach by the caravan park, and saw the setting sun light up the Hazards, a range of red granite mountains across the sea.

The next day was warm, and we set off in a hired sea-kayak to see the scenery from another angle. It was beautiful on the water – the reflection of the red granite mountains in the mirror-like sea was fabulous, and once again we marvelled at how like Scotland it was. Having missed our annual sea-kayaking holiday in the west coast of Scotland the previous year because we were about to start our cycling trip, it was especially nice to be able to do some sea-kayaking again, if only for a few hours this time.

Bicheno was 25 miles north up the coast, and was our destination for the next day, and for once it was an easy ride without the need for a break. It was a cool 9°C, but sunny with blue skies. The Australians have a great sense of humour – on a gate that we passed was a hand-painted sign, saying 'Pedigree Pony Poo – $1 per bag'!

In Bicheno, after booking into a caravan park, we chatted to locals as we drank our coffee, and after two hours we had had two offers of free accommodation if we wanted to stay longer. We discovered from the locals that many of them had a number of part-time jobs, because of the shortage of work in Tasmania. One man we spoke to was a qualified engineer, but he worked making pizzas for two evenings, packed crayfish for export to China one day a week, erected fences when he could get the work, and drove a water lorry for filling swimming pools. We were told to visit the English couple who had just emigrated from England and settled in Tasmania, having bought the local shop, and we discovered that the business that they had bought was now flourishing. The BBC had filmed them for a series on television about emigration.

On our way out of Bicheno we went to the rocky beach to see if we could see the penguins that had settled there, but again they were elusive. Apparently the best time to see them is at sunrise. However, as we had been lucky enough on holiday in 2001 to have sat for several hours on Boulders Beach near Cape Town, South Africa, amongst 3,000 tiny jackass penguins as they played, dived, swam and strutted inquisitively around us, we weren't too disappointed.

On our trip to Scamander, further north, we turned off to investigate one of the many free camping areas, and were very impressed to find a lovely wooded area of several acres, next to a stunning sandy beach, where anyone could camp free of charge for up to a month at a time. Log cabin toilets were dotted around in the trees, and the few people camping there had log fires burning. A converted bus and a couple of motorhomes were enjoying their free stay.

We had been recommended to go over Elephant Pass to St. Mary's, where there was a café selling Australia's best pancakes, and this was also the route recommended by the guide books. However, locals warned us that the hill was frighteningly steep for bicycles, and they recommended a newer road that had been built around the mountain hugging the coastline.

It was now the end of May, the middle of winter in Australia, and at St. Helens we booked a bus to take us west across land back to Launceston. We went through Cleveland, Epping Forest and Perth, and booked into the same pub again in Launceston. We spent a few days resting after our 610 miles of cycling in Tasmania. I visited an osteopath in the hope that he could ease the pain in my neck and wrists, and I celebrated my 59th birthday on 1st June.

A few days later we caught a local bus to take us to the ferry in Devonport, a journey which took 1¼ hours. We were the only passengers but the driver, a cheerful joking person, didn't stop talking the whole way. He had previously been a tour guide and had a vast knowledge of Tasmania, so we discovered during the journey that 260,000 tons of potatoes are produced in Tasi every year, 90% of them are made into chips, and Tasi supplies the whole of Australia with potatoes. In November and December the fields are full of pink poppies grown to produce medication, and they are processed by two large pharmaceutical factories in Tasi. There are 190,000 people living in Hobart and 90,000 in Launceston, and the colour of the rivers is due to tannin dyed by plants. He ended the journey by informing us that the Bass Strait was one of the roughest stretches of water in the world. As we were about to cross it on a 10 hour ferry, this was not something I really wanted to know ...

We boarded the boat, and were delighted to find that we had been allocated a 4-berth cabin with en-suite shower and toilet which no-one else was sharing, even though we had only paid for two lounger chairs in the salon. We had no idea if it was a mistake or whether they had deliberately upgraded us, but we were certainly pleased, especially as the enormous ferry rocked and rolled its way across the Bass Strait. We were en route to Australia's mainland for the next leg of our journey.

Victoria

The ferry from Tasmania arrived at Melbourne at 7am and it was still dark. We set off on our bikes, following the bike path to the east, which hugged the bay so that the sea was on our right the whole way. The cycle path was lined with mature palm trees. We were on our way to meet Helene, who had offered us a bed for the night. John and Cazz, who we had met cycling in Kanyakumari in southern India, were her daughter and son-in-law, and Helene had offered us accommodation even though she hadn't met us, although through frequent e-mails we felt that we already knew each other.

The sun rose over Melbourne as we continued our journey past beautiful houses overlooking the sea. We passed the Brighton Royal Yacht Club and the Sandringham Croquet Club. It all seemed more English than England! Joggers were out in force, and cyclists were on their way to work, and we followed the excellent bike path past very large, obviously expensive houses until we reached Black Rock, where Helene lived.

We had got to know Helene from e-mails only, but felt at home with her straight away. Helene was English and was originally from St. Albans, but had married an Australian and had lived in Australia for decades. She took us by car into Melbourne, a wonderful city, to see the sights. Melbourne is a lovely combination of old, new and ultra-modern buildings. Wide roads were lined with trees full of golden autumn leaves, and the Victorian buildings with their ornate cast-iron balconies and railings fascinated us. As always in Australia, the pavements were full of very attractive cafés, bars and restaurants. Open areas, the Yarra river, and plenty of grass and trees gave the centre of the city a very welcoming feel. We had lunch in Kensington, and in the evening after a very civilised gin and tonic, we took our bottles of wine to a Thai restaurant in Hampton. The early settlers certainly went to a lot of trouble to make themselves feel at home when they named the areas where they lived!

We left Black Rock the following day and cycled just a few miles to Dingley Village, another lovely suburb of Melbourne. We flew along, helped by a strong wind behind us, and arrived in front of an imposing neo-Georgian house with a columned porch. Here we were to stay with Marie and Ken, who we had also not yet met. We had met Marie's sister and brother-in-law, Helen and Rob, in Zimbabwe on holiday in October 2001. They had taken a photo of us with Victoria Falls in the background, and when we later met again at the bar by the hotel swimming pool, we exchanged e-mail addresses. Rob and Helen had been receiving the newsletters that I had been writing about our journey, and Helen had been passing them to all of her family.

Marie was Helen's sister, and she and Ken had offered us accommodation in Melbourne, and they were incredibly welcoming when we arrived. Warren was fascinated by the electronics and gadgets that Ken had. For all Ken's hi-fi gear, he had originally had twelve remote controls, but these had now been amalgamated into one, and they were having a problem knowing how to work it because it was new! Ken could work the heating, the air conditioning, the spray for the garden, the lights and everything else when he was away from home by dialling certain numbers into his mobile phone. We also discovered that Ken had built the house himself, and had also helped to build houses for each of his children. We felt quite overwhelmed by the magnificence of the house, and Ken joked that we could put our tent up in the garden if it made us feel more at home!

Once more we had a wonderful time, and we were introduced to many different members of the family, sons, daughters and sisters, who all told us they were enjoying our newsletters. Marie and Ken took us to see other sights in the area, so we were being thoroughly spoiled.

It was enjoyable to have home-cooked food after so long travelling, and Marie's salmon patties were so delicious that I had to ask for the recipe. Warren loved Ken's plumbed in coffee machine – at the press of a button the machine ground the coffee beans, filled automatically with the relevant amount of water and made whatever type of coffee that had been requested – espresso, cappuccino, latté, Americano! We stayed with Ken and Marie for several days, going out for a final meal with them, where we were introduced to a wonderful Australian dish – Oysters Kilpatrick. For each person a dozen oysters in half shells were sat on a plate of rock salt, and the oysters had been sprinkled with pieces of bacon and drizzled with a sauce made primarily with Worcestershire sauce before being grilled until the bacon was crispy – Ken's favourite starter, and very delicious!

By the time we left Marie and Ken we felt like we were old friends; it didn't seem possible that we hadn't met them until only a few days before! We were now on our way to meet Helen and Rob, who we had met in Zimbabwe. We had to cycle through Melbourne, one of the largest cities in the world in size but very cycle-friendly. We passed through distinctly different areas of the city, fortunately quiet as it was Sunday, and noticed areas with Greek, Turkish and Middle Eastern restaurants, where halal butchers were busy, alongside local mosques. We cycled alongside trams, but found it annoying to have to keep stopping at tram stops for passengers to alight. After Kalkalla we were cycling through more rural areas, with pasture land and rolling hills, but the scenery was not very exciting.

We travelled directly north towards Mulwala, near Yarrawonga on the Murray River, where Helen and Rob lived. We had been invited to stay with them in one of their holiday units. The family was horrified that we planned to cycle to Yarrawonga, even though for us it was not a long cycle ride. It was going to take us six days to cycle averaging 50km per day, but for cars it was a three hour drive. Helen was insistent that she came to pick us up, but we eventually agreed on a compromise – she was going to meet us half way.

On the first night we ran out of daylight on the freeway, not having found accommodation, so we decided to camp at a rest area just off the freeway. Not only was there grass and trees for a good site for our tent, but also a decent toilet block and a caravan selling food and drinks, so we spent a comfortable and warm night in our tent for the first time for a long time. A tanker carrying manure was parked in the truck area. It had a large printed sign on the back.

'It may be shit to you, but to me it's my bread and butter!' – that Australian sense of humour again.

We turned off the freeway the following day so that I could phone Julian, my son, to wish him a happy birthday. The public phone cut me off after I had spoken to Julian's answer phone for only a few seconds, and I was very annoyed because the machine had eaten the last of my change. However, when I phoned Julian again the following day he was laughing about my earlier call. Although I thought I had been cut off, Julian could still hear me, so his answer phone was full of me cursing the public phone for cutting me off.

We continued cycling for a further two days until we met Helen and Uncle Jack, so we had the unaccustomed luxury of travelling by car, with our bikes in the trailer. Mulwala (population 1,500) and Yarrawonga (4,600) are side by side, only 2½ miles apart. One is in Victoria and the other in New South Wales, and the two towns are divided by the Murray River. They are both popular holiday destinations as the climate is usually good, and Lake Mulwala offers all types of water sports and boating activities in the summer. Cycling along the cycle paths and through the reserves around the lake we saw an amazing amount of birdlife. Pelicans sat with their cavernous beaks full of fish, and at dusk the trees were full of white cockatoos (called 'cockies' by the locals), so that the trees looked as though they were covered with white flowers.

The locals often had to cross the bridge that divided Victoria from New South Wales to go shopping. We noticed on the bridge that there were signs warning that any fruit or vegetables had to be left at the side of the road rather than be carried into the other state, and we wondered how people managed this! The Australians are very strict at airports and don't allow any form of food to be carried into the country. However, it was a surprise to see that food could not be carried between states, and also that tractors and similar vehicles were banned from crossing the border in case there was contaminated dirt lodged in their tyres!

Helen and Rob gave us our own self-contained holiday unit next to their house – it was out of season and was therefore empty. Again we met more of the family; Helen and Rob have six children, and Marie and Ken have four children, so it was a very large family. We did a bit of money-laundering while we were at Helen and Rob's – we discovered when taking the washing out of our machine that Warren had left a $50 note in his trouser pocket! Thank goodness the brightly coloured Australian bank-notes are plastic (something the Australians didn't like when they were introduced) – the money, which always looked brand new and clean, looked just the same when it came out of the hot wash!

It was good to be able to visit a decent bicycle shop to buy some spares, and we found it strange to hear the shop assistant referring to 'Mitchies' (Michelin tyres) and 'Campy' (Campagnola gears)! Even official signs outside the cafés announced that they were 'Open for brekkie', mushrooms in the supermarket were labelled 'mushies' and 'sunnies' were on sale in the optician's.

One evening Helen took us to her golf club where we saw kangaroos, including twin 'joeys', gathering beneath the trees and on the grass at dusk. We were excited, as these were the first kangaroos we had seen since we arrived in Australia – there are no kangaroos in Tasmania, only wallabies. Tiny round buildings set amongst the trees were toilets – obviously on a 45-hole golf course it would be too far to go back to the club-house! The location was amazing, and we watched the sun setting above the trees with the colours reflected in the lake.

We assumed that crime was very low in the area, because people happily left their car running, with doors open and a handbag on the seat, while they popped into a nearby house or shop to chat to someone – something we would unfortunately not consider doing back home in England. Front doors were often left unlocked, and Helen and Rob had even left their back door open whilst they went on holiday for two weeks, so that their dog could run in and out of the house to visit Uncle Jack or Luke, their son, who lived in holiday units at the back of the house!

While we were staying in Mulwala, a representative from the local paper came to interview us and take photos of us with our bikes, so we felt like celebrities, and later in the week when visiting the local pub with Helen and Rob for a meal, Norm, the pub manager, announced to everyone that we were there, having cycled from England, so we got a round of applause from the locals!

Because we regularly sent newsletters back to our friends and family in England we constantly needed to find internet cafés on our travels. Now that we were in Australia we found that internet cafés were very expensive at $10 or $12 per hour. If we stayed in any village or town for more than a day we were able to book one hour at the local library, which was free of charge, but we were finding the cost of internet cafés and also the cost of postage to send films back home the most expensive so far.

We had a lovely relaxing time at Helen and Rob's, but eventually announced that we planned to cycle to Albury, 100 kilometres away, on our way to Sydney. Helen wouldn't hear of it, again considering it too far to cycle, despite our insistence that long distance cycling was what we did! Helen insisted on driving us to her daughter's house in Albury, because it was only an hour's drive, she said. She drove us along the scenic route, so we were able to visit Ned Kelly's old 'stamping grounds', visiting Helen's brother-in-law en route so that we could see the enormous new house he was building for his family. We passed through Beechworth, which was a very pretty old gold-mining town, with many quaint Victorian buildings. The scenery from there to Albury was stunning – very green and hilly, with valleys, gorges and waterfalls, and the sun shone on the weeping willows and highlighted the brilliant yellow autumnal colours. When we arrived in Albury, Helen drove us to her daughter's house, where we were once again invited to stay.

Kirsty, Helen's daughter, and her husband Ian had two tiny daughters, and we were fascinated to see that Kirsty and Ian were also building their own new house. Luke, one of Helen's sons, had also been building his own house in Mulwala, and it was interesting to see the wooden frame with the brick outer skin, which was so different from English house construction, but so quick and easy to construct. Kirsty and Ian's house was built on a slope, one side of the house being built on stilts which was topped with a massive decked area, so the family could walk out from the living areas to enjoy the lovely views across the hill. The passage to the family bathroom included not only a guest bathroom but also a 'powder room' which was to be used by guests and by Kirsty and Ian's daughters when they grew up. I could see that Warren was itching to pick up a hammer and start helping!

Far more people in Australia build their own houses than in England; the houses are generally bigger than their English counterparts and are mostly bungalows, though the Australians don't call them that – a one storey house is simply called 'a house' and a two-storey house is 'a two-storey house'. However, two-storey houses are quite uncommon. On the outside of the house's wooden frame goes the insulation and then a brick skin or weatherboarding is added. The houses are often built on concrete slabs, and sometimes have a metal frame, which is an advantage if termites are common in the area. Most Australian houses have corrugated tin roofs, which seems very strange to us in England, but the roofs actually look fine, and the tin roofs were often coloured. Some houses had tiled roofs, but we assumed that the lack of tiled and slate roofs in Australia meant that clay and slate were materials that were fairly scarce.

Most of the houses we saw had large walk-in pantries, and the kitchens always had islands of units with sinks and hobs to separate the kitchen area from the living area. The interiors of the houses were always much larger than we expected from the outside, with massive open living areas and usually four very large bedrooms. We were also envious of the sundecks and gardens which always included the 'barbie' and usually a swimming pool.

So that night, once again, we were lucky to enjoy the wonderful Australian hospitality with Kirsty and Ian and their daughters, and once again came away with a recipe to remind us of our cycling trip, this time for Kirsty's delicious Mexican starter.

In the morning we set off for Albury station, only 1km away. The pretty Victorian railway station was exactly like Victorian stations in English small towns and villages – an absolute picture. Here we had to pack our bikes into boxes for the train journey, and soon the train left Albury station for the 8 hour journey to Sydney. We had noticed from weather reports that Sydney was always several degrees warmer than Melbourne, and the further north we travelled the warmer it would get, even though winter was now setting in. Because Australia is so vast, it was impossible for us to cycle all the time before our visas ran out, so we were planning to jump sections by travelling on planes, trains, buses or cars. It made sense, therefore, to jump this section and begin cycling north from Sydney, though we planned first to cycle south to the famous Bondi beach – how could Warren, a keen surfer, miss that one?

It was dark as the train arrived at Sydney, and the vast platform area reminded us strongly of main London stations. However, as we cycled out of the station, we gasped at the view – gazing up we saw nothing but skyscrapers, and as we cycled further up the street, a monorail train went past one floor above us. We grinned as we realised that we had arrived in Sydney exactly one year to the day that we had set off from Dover on our cycling trip – it was 18th June, 2003. We had to go out that night to celebrate ...

New South Wales

We stayed in Sydney for a few days to see the sights. We were in a backpackers' hostel in a double en-suite room on the 8th floor, so it was lucky they had a lift for our bikes! However, at $85 per night it was almost twice what we had been used to paying. For the first time in Australia, though, the internet cafés were cheap and plentiful. Now we were in Sydney the price had dropped from $10 or $12 per hour to $2 per hour or even $1 per hour through the night, if I had wanted to sit in front of the computer between 9pm and 9am!

Although Warren and I prefer rural areas to cities, Sydney was fun and interesting with lots to see and loads of photographs to take. Sydney has a monorail system, and it's strange to see a train come out of a building one floor above the pavement, shoot across the street and round the corner, and we thought the double-decker trains for commuting were a great idea. As in all major cities, there was a good choice of restaurants of different nationalities – Indian, Chinese, Thai, Mexican, Japanese and Italian. There were also numerous cafés and bars, and obviously plenty of shops. In larger Australian towns or cities the shops, department stores and shopping arcades were so like the ones in England that we often forgot that we were in a foreign country!

We visited the tourist areas, taking arty photographs of Sydney Opera House and the sun setting behind the Harbour Bridge. We must have looked efficient (or maybe it was the expensive cameras we were carrying!), because we were constantly being asked to take photographs of foreign couples with their own cameras.

After a few days in Sydney we travelled south to the famous surfing area of Sydney, Bondi Beach. We booked into another backpackers' hostel, but found it a little disconcerting that not only the knife and the tin opener, but also the benches, kettle and toaster were chained to the walls in the communal kitchen!

We relaxed at the beach, although it was very quiet at that time of year. Everyone was in the mountains ski-ing, because the Australian ski-ing season was in full swing during June. We admired a wall by the beach covered with very elaborate and artistic graffiti and paintings, and we realised it must have been a 'wall of remembrance', because there were paintings and names of people with their dates of birth and death.

'Keep riding the eternal wave,' we read, so we assumed that these people who had died were all surfers, and had possibly even been killed in surfing accidents.

As we walked back to the hostel one day we noticed massive clumps of small beetles on the trunks of trees. They were squashed together and on top of each other as if for companionship, and were noticeable because of their amazing colours – orange, red, electric blue and emerald, many of the colours iridescent, and each one multi-coloured. We discovered later that these were bugs, not beetles, called Scutiphora pedicellata and were native to eastern Australia. Because of their beautiful colours and irridenscence, these bugs had the common name of Jewel Bugs or Metallic Shield Bugs.

Because the ride out of Sydney to Bondi had been so scary in the heavy traffic, we chose to leave Bondi on a Sunday, because we had to ride straight through the middle of Sydney and onto the freeway on the north side. We hoped that there would be less traffic in the city on that day. We found our way across the city fairly easily, and we were again amazed by the contrast of old and new buildings. A pretty 19th century public house stood on the corner of a block, whilst behind and around it towered dozens of skyscrapers filling the whole block, the sun dazzlingly bright on the glass walls of these monstrous buildings.

We couldn't find our way onto Sydney Harbour Bridge, which we needed to cross, so two cyclists on mountain bikes kindly showed us a short cut. They cycled fast round corners and across wide pavements, as we struggled with our heavily-laden bikes to keep up with them. We shot past the crowds admiring the Opera House, its huge billowing sails hovering above the harbour water. We passed a Scottish regiment outside a church, complete with kilts and playing bagpipes, but we couldn't stop to take photographs, because our cycling guides were still dashing ahead.

Fortunately there was a cycle path over the Harbour Bridge, and here our guides left us to return to their friends. Our only view was to the west, away from the Opera House and the city, because the railway line and the road traffic lanes to our right blocked our views of the city. However, we wanted a photographic souvenir, so we stopped a security officer walking along the cycle lane and asked him to take a photo of us on our bikes with the ironwork of the bridge above us.

We cycled onto the Pacific Highway, which hugs the east coast of New South Wales. This was our first experience of not so considerate drivers in Australia. We had been impressed with the courtesy and patience given to us by drivers in Tasmania, but now was a different story. There was heavy traffic travelling north of Sydney; maybe they were day-trippers because it was a lovely day. Although the road was mostly two lanes, it sometimes narrowed to one lane. Car drivers were sounding their horns at us if they couldn't overtake us, and we wondered what they wanted us to do – push our bikes onto the grass to let them pass, perhaps?

After a while, if a car sounded its horn, we stopped in front of them and looked round, smiling at them.

'Did you want something?' we'd call innocently.

It seemed to work well and the drivers became quiet and embarrassed, rather than enraged. Warren crossed a long uphill traffic junction ahead of me, and the traffic lights changed to red when he was halfway across, after he had passed one of the two wide left-hand turnings. I stopped at the traffic lights, but the driver of the car behind me drove fast onto the junction despite the red light against her, and started sounding her horn at Warren – she obviously wanted to quickly turn left at the second junction, and Warren was in her way. I saw her car stop, so I knew that Warren had stopped in front of her, and his voice rang out quite clearly.

'What do you want me to do? Do I look like ****ing Harry Potter?'

Something that disconcerted us was that we often saw crosses by the roadside where people had been killed in accidents. Names and dates were always on the crosses, and they were usually surrounded by artificial flowers. We had seen this in other countries, but it seemed more common in Australia. We weren't sure if that meant that there were more accidents or just a different attitude to them. A very sad sight one day was a line of five crosses with a different name on each.

Whenever possible we tried to take an alternative road from the Pacific Highway, because the road was very busy with large trucks. (We had now learnt to call them trucks, rather than lorries!) Unfortunately, although the Pacific Highway hugs the coastline, it was seldom that we could actually see the sea, but occasionally we walked through the paths across the dunes to see the stunning beaches, which were mostly empty at that time of year. There was always miles of sand and, beyond it, massive rolling waves ideal for surfing. One beach was called Seven Mile Beach for obvious reasons, and there wasn't a single person on that massive expanse of beautiful white sand.

We went over Mooney Mooney Bridge, and even Warren wouldn't go near the edge because it was so far down to the water. We discovered later that it was the highest road bridge in the southern hemisphere, and the water at high tide was 75 metres below the bridge! It was apparently a very popular site for suicides, so the locals were petitioning to have a higher fence built to stop people throwing themselves over the side. We were both glad when we had crossed the 480 metre span, and we continued up and down hills enjoying the views. We were looking down over wooded valleys in both directions, and there were lakes and inlets to our right. I stopped at one time to admire and photograph some amazing flowers in the shade under the trees. Each flower looked like a giant amaryllis on a stalk 10 to 12 feet high. On some of the stalks were dark red flowers bigger than a football, and on other stalks giant seedpods towered above the strap-like leaves.

We passed towns with familiar names – Swansea, Newcastle, Hexham, Stroud and Gloucester, interspersed with fascinating Aboriginal names like Dungog, Tuggalong and Coolongolook, and the even more extraordinary double Aboriginal names like Way Way, Kangy Angy Creek and Kurri Kurri.

We were still trying to understand distances in Australia, because very few people knew the distance in kilometres. Our questions about distances were always answered in the same way.

'It's a 3 hour drive,' or

'It's only 10 minutes away.'

The Pacific Highway was lined with massive hoardings advertising Kentucky Fried Chicken, MacDonalds, BP Gas stations, seaside resorts, and the signs always stated the distance to their establishment in minutes, from 5 minutes to 180 minutes. I began to check the distances to find the formula to calculate to kilometres, but found that the times shown had been calculated using speeds ranging from 31 kph to 100 kph! However, we had now discovered that if someone told us that a town was 3 or 3½ hours away, this was for us a week's cycling, based on us cycling approximately 50 kilometres a day. 5 minutes away was half an hour's cycling, and 30 minutes away was probably a day's cycle ride.

By this time we were setting off at 9am each morning, and we usually cycled for three or four hours. However, we always stopped for coffee, which often took a while because people usually wanted to chat! We also stopped for lunch breaks, and there might be other short 'comfort' breaks and photo stops. We usually arrived at our destination by 2pm or 3pm with plenty of time to find accommodation and explore the town.

One of the biggest problems for us travelling in Australia was that it didn't feel like a foreign country – this was obviously one of the main reasons that makes Australia a popular choice for emigration, but a bit disconcerting for us in the middle of a foreign trip. What was it that made Australia so familiar, and what obvious differences were there? . . .

First of all, there was the obvious familiarity of the language – we no longer needed to speak slowly and carefully without idioms, slang or complicated sentences. The Australians understood everything we said and we could understand them! The Australians even had complaints about similar things to us in England, tax and pensions being popular grumbles. With up to 9% stamp duty on house purchases (the amounts varied from state to state), in England we should consider ourselves lucky! We discovered also that everyone who works has to complete a tax return in Australia, although the point of completing it is usually to receive a tax rebate, not to pay tax! The tax returns must have been simple to complete, because we saw advertisements for tax returns to be professionally completed, and the fee was only $55 (£22) – a tiny fraction of the cost that accountants charge in England. We discovered that we were better off in England in another respect – if in England we qualified for a state pension we would get it once we reached retirement age. In Australia someone might qualify for a state pension, but that pension would be reduced for every bit of income received from other sources, such as personal and company pensions. The pension could even be reduced because of the amount of money someone had in savings and investments. Anyone in Australia who has a decent superannuation or personal pension, or has saved money during their working lifetime may therefore get no state pension at all in Australia. Some of the 'ten pound pommies' who emigrated to Australia from England in the past had qualified for small English state pensions as well as Australian ones, because they had worked in both countries. However, the Australian pension was reduced because of the English one. This wouldn't happen to an Australian living in England, or it doesn't at the moment, but don't tell the politicians . . .

The roads seemed much the same as in England. We were cycling on the left and, surprisingly, we noticed that we had cycled more on the left during our trip than on the right. The scenery often didn't look foreign in Australia. There were no golden temples, no elephants, no Buddhist monks walking in single file, no people in saris or other national costume, no bullock carts, no overloaded buses or bikes, no women carrying water containers or firewood on their heads, not even any men wearing hats with corks on strings – just familiar-looking cars, bikes, taxis and buses. The main exceptions were the massive trucks, and the high proportion of very large four wheel drive vehicles on the roads. Some of these 4WD vehicles even had 'snorkels' up the side to enable the vehicle to drive through deep water or in very dusty conditions, but heavy bull bars were standard. On Australian roads we also saw a lot of caravans, which appeared to be far more popular than motorhomes. Some were 'off-road' caravans with high ground clearance and stronger suspension, but most were 'pop-tops', where the caravan roof dropped down to lower the profile of the caravan to around the same height as a 4WD vehicle, to make it more aerodynamic for long distance towing.

In the southern part of Australia the winter climate is similar to England's climate, though not so cold and wet. As it was exclusively settled by people from Britain, albeit some of them reluctantly, they have spent the last 200 years trying to make it as much like Britain as possible. They named everywhere with British names, built Victorian buildings as much like those at home as possible, brought British farming methods, deciduous trees, introduced British pests such as rabbits and foxes, and even introduced blackberries and other weeds which made it look just like England!

There was grass by the roadside, and we often saw pastures full of cows. Presumably Australia looks very much more foreign in the scorching hot summer when the grass turns completely brown, and obviously if we travelled to the outback, further inland, the scenery would be very different. Whilst some people do cycle inland, we felt that its very remoteness would make cycling an unpleasant and dangerous experience. The trees lining the roads were eucalyptus, eucalyptus and eucalyptus which, although not common in England are certainly not unknown. We saw forests of eucalyptus where the trunks and branches were black from fire damage, but the leaves had grown again, and the damaged black bark had dropped off to reveal the new white trunks beneath. We passed banana plantations; open-bottomed tin foil bags covered the bunches of bananas to ripen them. However, shortly after the plantations the road was lined with woods again followed by an immaculate golf course, and it was almost as though the banana plantations had been a figment of our imagination!

Because I'm interested in plants, I noticed that the plants in gardens were different from those at home. Giant poinsettias, so familiar to us at Christmas time as house plants, grew to 12 feet tall with flowers as big as dinner plates. Cream as well as red poinsettias were all in flower in Australian gardens at that time, camellias were flowering, and hibiscus bushes were stunning with red, cream, apricot or pink flowers. Orange trees were loaded with fruit, and I was surprised to learn that they fruit twice a year, and that the winter crop which we were seeing was much sweeter if frost touched them. Now we were travelling further north, we were seeing more palm trees in the popular resorts, and monkey puzzle trees were also very popular in the caravan parks.

The caravan parks varied tremendously in quality, some cabins being decidedly shabby without heaters, even though it was very cool during the night. We needed to leave the hob on throughout the night to keep warm. These cabins were not necessarily cheap, but others that were cheaper surprised us with their luxury. Many had cabins that were obviously privately owned, and we smiled when we saw one named 'Didubringabeeralong', imitating the Aboriginal names.

In supermarkets such as Woolworths or Safeways the shelves were full of familiar things. Heinz beans came with a choice of 10 different sauces as well as the tomato sauce familiar to us in England, and brands of butter and margarine, tea and coffee, packets, tins and jars of food, soaps and cleaners were all familiar items in the same brands as 'back home'. Australia was the first country where we had seen sliced bread on the shop shelves since we had left England! The biggest difference food-wise was maybe the quantity of jars of beetroot on the shelves.

There were no big developments of private houses as in England – any 'estates' of houses were a collection of individually built or self-built houses, all built in the construction that I've already described.

The birds in Australia were very different, very vocal and very colourful. As we cycled through the wooded areas, we often heard the whistling or strange singing noises of birds. It was a pleasure for us to have flocks of parrots flying over us when we were cycling past trees. To look up and see the colours was amazing – Warren commented that it was 'as though a child had painted each finger with different colours and had finger-painted the sky'. There was a small tree next to our raised cabin porch at one caravan park, and the stunning red flowers on the bush by our porch were obviously the parrots' favourite food. These red-beaked parrots, with their purple-blue heads, pale and bright green backs, red and blue breasts with splashes of yellow, were almost camouflaged in the green bush with bright red bottle-brush shaped flowers, as they did somersaults and acrobatics, hanging upside down on branches to reach the red flowers with their beaks. We were able to stand six feet away watching them and photographing them. We discovered that the flowers were called Callistenom, but on another bush were similar flowers with petals that had delicately hooked ends, and these were called Grevillea. Another extraordinary flowering bush that was common in these Australian caravan parks was the Banksia, which had cone or candle shaped flowers made up of hundreds of tiny flowers, and these were also very popular with the birds. The Banksia was named after the botanist Sir Joseph Banks who sailed with Captain Cook on his first great voyage, and he introduced many Australian plants to Europe. It must have been incredibly exciting for him to discover the fantastic variety of previously unknown plantds!

At another caravan park there were six kookaburras who regularly sat on the railings of our porch or on the tree next to it, and they even sometimes sat on our bikes, not being the slightest concerned when we came close to take photographs. They were my favourites, because they looked so cute – puffed up, fluffy, fat birds with strange beaks. Their heads and fronts are pale coffee colour with a chocolate-coloured stripe running horizontally backwards from their dark eyes, making them look as though they are wearing masks! Above the beak running up to the top of their heads is a mottled brown and coffee stripe. Around the back of the neck is a dark patch, usually triangular but sometimes almost a horizontal stripe. Their backs are chocolate brown, and on their wings are light patches of very pale blue. Their fairly short tails are horizontally striped coffee and chocolate, and the long beak is strangely rounded at the bottom. They would dive from the rooftops or branches straight into the ground, presumably for insects as they are carnivorous birds. About the size of an owl, the kookaburra also looks similar in flight to an owl but is actually a type of large woodpecker, and it reminded me of a rhyme I'd learnt as a small child:

Ha-ha-ha. He-he-he.
Kookaburra sits in the old gum tree.
Very merry king of the bush is he.
Laugh, kookaburra, laugh, kookaburra.
Gay your life must be.
Ha-ha-ha. He-he-he.

We discovered that there were two more verses, which I had never heard before:

Kookaburra sits in the old gum tree
Eating all the gum drops he can see.
Stop, kookaburra! Stop, kookaburra!
Leave some there for me!

Kookaburra sits in the old gum tree
Counting all the monkeys he can see.
Stop, Kookaburra! Stop, Kookaburra!
That's not a monkey, that's me!

The rhyme had meant nothing to me when I'd learnt it – I didn't know at that age what a gum tree was, let alone a kookaburra, but here they both were. To hear dozens of them in the eucalyptus or gum trees at dusk was quite unbelievable and, yes, it did sound like fiendish laughter! Warren had never heard the rhyme, nor had most English people I spoke to, but I and my small class-mates had learnt it at primary school. It was lovely to recall the rhyme that I'd learnt more than fifty years before, and extraordinary how the sight of these fascinating birds had immediately brought back that memory.

Every time we passed a lake or any sort of water there were pelicans. They seemed very lazy birds, mostly sitting, sleeping, preening or floating on the water. It was seldom that we saw them fishing, but when they flew through the air they looked like prehistoric birds. It was also extraordinary how they liked to sit for hours on top of telegraph poles or street lights.

Australia is very clean – it was good to see someone go out of their way to put their cigarette butt into a bin instead of throwing it onto the pavement as smokers do in England. There were many advertisements at that time on television, on buses and posters, saying 'Don't be a tosser', meaning don't toss rubbish on the ground. There was one television ad where a girl at the bus stop dropped her cigarette butt hoping no-one would notice, but a lad saw it, picked it up and dropped it into her shopping bag – something I've always wanted to do! In Melbourne if someone dropped a lit cigarette butt they had an instant fine of $200, and for an unlit cigarette butt on the pavement it was a fine of $100.

At one campsite we met a lovely lady. She was in her 70s, and for the last seven years had been travelling around Australia in her motorhome, visiting her children who lived in different parts of the country. She said she couldn't imagine living in a house surrounded by other houses any more, and she loved the travelling. Also, she said, her children didn't get fed up with her, because she never outstayed her welcome!

We arrived at Coffs Harbour and tried to book into a cabin at a caravan park. Everywhere was full because there were University Sports that week, so we had to book a pitch for our tent. Rather than cook by our tent in the crowded caravan park, we went out for a meal at the Hogs Breath Café and arrived back in the dark and put our bikes to bed. We locked them together and cabled them to the trunk of a small weeping tree very close to our tent, and covered them completely with our basha – an ex-army lightweight camouflage waterproof cover with straps and eyelets for tying it down. The bikes were virtually invisible in the shade under the tree, and we went to bed and slept well, hearing nothing untoward.

There was a horrified shout from Warren the next morning when he woke to find our bikes uncovered, the waterproof cover and Warren's saddle bag having been stolen. In the stolen bag were bicycle tools, a spare inner tube, a puncture repair kit and tyre levers, chain oil and brushes for cleaning the bikes. When we reported the loss to the caravan park reception they just shrugged their shoulders.

'It happens all the time,' they said. 'It was probably students.'

We thought this unlikely, suspecting rather the very unpleasant and unhelpful night security staff, who had been patrolling the grounds through the night. However, we obviously couldn't say this.

We were relieved that we still had our bikes – we had found it impossible to insure our bikes for the journey, so if the bikes had been stolen our journey would have come to a complete halt, and we felt sure that the expensive lock had been the deterrent. When we booked a cabin, caravan or hotel room we always put the bikes inside so they were well protected; we would have to be even more vigilant now. We spent the day searching the shops for replacements to the stolen items, and decided we would leave Coffs Harbour as soon as we had done so. However, even before we had left the caravan park we found we had a puncture, so it was obviously not a good day for us!

We were still finding that every time we stopped at a café for a cup of coffee or at a supermarket to buy food, people stopped to ask us about our bikes and our journey, so the bikes were a wonderful introduction for a conversation. Despite the fact that the long discussions with the locals delayed our progress, we preferred to stop and chat and to get to know them. One day as I walked out of a shop a girl smiled at me and said hello, and I admired her beautiful boxer puppy. She told me that her partner had recently died but, 7 months ago, when he knew that he was dying, he had bought her the boxer pup so that she would have company when he was gone – such a lovely but sad story.

One day when we stopped for coffee the lady serving us asked where we were heading. She told us that we had to cycle over a mountain to reach Kempsey, but that we shouldn't stay there as it was very rough. It was full of Aborigines, she told us, and we would almost certainly have something stolen. She made it sound like a dump, but we had already noticed that very few Australians had anything good to say about Aborigines, and the Aborigines, unlike coloured people in England, did not appear to be integrated with the white Australians at all. We hadn't yet seen any Aborigines, so were interested to get to Kempsey. We finally arrived there to find it looked fine, and there were some very expensive caravan parks there. However, we saw no sign of any Aborigines, which was disappointing.

We stopped at a rest area, and I changed into my sandals for the first time in Australia – it was getting warmer! These rest areas, often in the middle of nowhere, always had toilets – often they flushed, but more often they were dry composting toilets. These were built high with stairs to the room with the loo; don't look down the hole if you don't like heights! Soft toilet paper was always in abundance, despite the long distance to any town, and we always thought how dreadful English public toilets were in comparison.

The days were now pleasantly warm, about 25°C, even though it was the middle of winter, but we were finding wearing cycle helmets fairly uncomfortable for long distance cycling. Also, because we were travelling north, and would continue to do so for some time, the sun was in our eyes most of the time while we were cycling. This was a problem. Because we were forced to wear helmets, we couldn't wear a cap which would have shaded our faces from the sun. It seemed as though the wearing of helmets for us was more than a nuisance – it was definitely dangerous, because we couldn't see properly with the sun in our eyes. We intended to cycle north until we reached Brisbane; after that we would decide how to continue, because we knew we couldn't cycle the full distance to Cairns in Queensland in the time that we had available to us.

As we cycled further north on the main road, we saw a beautiful white temple standing proudly on the hill ahead of us overlooking Woolgoolga. We discovered that this was a Sikh temple, and that the community of Sikhs in Woolgoolga was the largest number of Sikhs anywhere outside Punjab in India. We found a caravan park conveniently situated between the shops and the beach, and booked into a cabin for two nights.

We immediately made friends with Alan and Di, our neighbours in the next cabin. We arranged to go out together for a meal that evening, and they told us about their 14-year old son, who had just found a lump. A scan had been done which showed more lumps, but the report was in such medical jargon that they couldn't understand it. Their son had said if he was going to die, could he go snowboarding for eight weeks, and they had agreed that he could go. Their other two sons said it wasn't fair. They'd rather go snowboarding for 8 weeks and then die as well, they said! The doctor had asked them if their son had been scratched by a cat, because a disease called 'Cat Scratch Disease' (honestly!) could produce the same symptoms that their son had. Di said to the doctor that perhaps in that case their son should have a cat scan, but the doctor's face hadn't cracked! Incredibly this son was not really a son at all – he had asked if he could come to live with them, because his step mother didn't want him. Despite their assertions that they were a horrible family and he wouldn't like living with them he had just moved in, and now they always referred to 'our three boys'. What lovely people, and what a laugh we had with them.

We soon met and chatted to quite a few other people in this friendly place, including an Indian physiotherapist with whom we reminisced about those wonderful Indian breakfasts! It was quite like England in that many of the shops were run by Indians, and we were determined to have an Indian meal while we were there. Australia must have more different nationalities than any other country in the world – apart from the large numbers of English, Scottish and Irish that we had met, there were vast numbers of Italians, Greeks and Turks, and the number of Vietnamese was increasing all the time. We met Cambodians, South Africans, Germans, Dutch, Americans, Japanese, Thai, Malaysians and Chinese, and these were only a small number of the different nationalities living in Australia.

We didn't leave Woolgoolga as quickly as we had anticipated. After two days we decided to stay another couple of nights, because we liked it so much. The days had been warm, and the moonlit walks along the nearby beach had been wonderful.

The only cabin available for the next few days was a disabled cabin, so we moved into it on the third day. The long ramp meant that we could cycle the bikes straight into the cabin, and the extra wide passage to the bedroom, designed for a wheelchair, left room to store the bikes. We had the biggest bathroom we'd had to date in a cabin; the only disadvantage were the extra low worktops in the kitchen. Every morning birds whistling tunes woke us gently, and at dusk every day flocks of parrots and lorikeets descended on the trees in the caravan park. After we had been in Woolgoolga, locally known as Woopi, for a few days, we decided we liked it so much we would stay for two weeks – it was time we have a holiday again . . .

It was usually cool in the mornings, but became warmer as the sun rose higher, shining in a beautiful blue sky. It was July, and therefore the middle of winter in Australia. As soon as the afternoon was halfway through it begin to cool again, and once the sun had set the temperature dropped dramatically.

Our cabin was only 50 yards from the beach, so we could hear the waves at night, and we could use the free covered electric barbecues on the beach to have a 'barbie'. Sometimes the covered table area was decorated with ribbons and balloons, and groups arrived to have a party on the beach to celebrate someone's birthday. A few yards in the opposite direction were the shops, cafés and restaurants, so everything was very convenient. Several times we took the steep walk to the headland, where children flew their kites in the wind, and we watched the whales doing acrobatics and spouting water. Both humpback and Southern Right whales can be seen off the east, south and west coasts of Australia. In autumn they travel north to warmer waters to mate and give birth, and in spring they return south again. Humpbacks are the most visible and acrobatic, but the Southern Right whales swim slowly and are easy to approach. This is why they were called the 'right' whales by the whaling industry in the 19th century, because they were the right – in other words, easy – whales to catch. The right whales were so decimated because of the whaling industry that early last century their numbers had dropped from 100,000 to just a few hundred, making them an endangered species. They are now beginning to thrive again. If only the whales knew how lucky they were to be born in this century and not the 19th!

We woke on the first Saturday in Woolgoolga to find a local fête setting up stalls nearby, and if it hadn't been for the parrots in the trees we would have thought we were back in England again. A man wearing a kangaroo leather hat sat playing a guitar singing country and western songs, and the fête was bustling with locals and tourists. We bought a bag of 10 sweet and juicy navel oranges of mixed sizes for $2 picked from the lady's own tree. We also bought a wonderful home-made banana cake, but declined the bag of 10 hard avocados for $2 because they needed several days to ripen, and were too heavy to carry on the bikes.

One vegetable that was very popular in Australia but rarely cooked in England was the pumpkin, but maybe that's an American influence. Pumpkin was a popular vegetable for roasting, and pumpkin soup was the most common soup in cafés and was always absolutely delicious. In England we only see whole pumpkins for sale in the shops during October, and we know that most English people throw away the delicious flesh after Halloween. We couldn't understand why pumpkins aren't available in England after 31st October, when they are so easy to grow. In Australia, segments of pumpkin were always available in the shops, and I imagine the same applies to America.

The area around Woolgoolga is called The Banana Coast, and most of the banana plantations are owned by Indians living in and around Woolgoolga. The scenery was therefore beginning to seem 'foreign' again. Apparently Woolgoolga is the furthest south in Australia where bananas can be grown, and also the furthest north where apples can be grown, so there is an overlap of climates in this area. There is also a massive blueberry plantation a few kilometres away, again owned and run by Indians.

We met a retired couple in the caravan park, Jungle and Keitha.

'Why are you called Jungle?' I asked him.

'Because I'm like a jungle – thick and dense,' he said, roaring with laughter so much that his flat cap nodded up and down. It had apparently been a nickname since school days and had stuck – even his wife called him 'Jung'. Jungle and Keitha spent ten weeks in Woolgoolga every winter, travelling with their caravan from their much cooler home town in Victoria.

Jungle and Keitha took us in their car to Bellingen, a pretty town 60km back the way we had cycled with a large market once a month; here we were able to wander round the market, listen to the local bands, and taste some of the unusual local fruits. The weird-looking custard apple with its green, knobbly skin looks like it came from another planet. It actually originated from South America, but grows very well in the tropical areas of Australia, and we discovered delightedly that the fruit of the custard apple is the same texture and taste as stewed apple and custard – extraordinary! We also tasted lemonade lemons, which look exactly like a normal lemon but are sweeter, and are used by the Australians to make delicious lemonade.

Jungle and Keitha took us another 30km up into the mountains. We arrived in Dorrigo, where we were able to admire the waterfalls and visit a rainforest on a plateau. We walked along a 'sky walk', a wooden platform built high above the top canopy of the trees where we could see the superb panoramic view across the forest between the mountains to the sea. Because of the altitude, the terrain, the heavy rainfall in that area and the superb volcanic soil, there was a large area of virgin rainforest which we were keen to explore, so we booked a guide in order to learn about the plants and wild life.

As we entered the cool, dark rainforest, the first thing that we saw was a dark blue bird with a beautiful sheen on its feathers. It was a male Satin Bowerbird, and it was surrounded by blue items – plastic water bottle tops, pen tops, pieces of foil, a clothes peg and a blue straw, as well as blue flowers and berries. The Satin Bowerbird collects anything that is blue in an attempt to attract the female, and this beautiful bird, its feathers just like navy blue shiny satin as its name suggests, continued to build its bower as we watched quietly. The bower is the male's dancing platform – an elaborate arch-shaped structure made of shaped twigs, which is designed to enhance its song and dance routine to attract the female. Amazingly the dancing platform is always built facing north to south.

We walked further through the rainforest on a designated path, brush turkeys walking past us scratching in the leaves for grubs. The sound of the whip bird, its call as it name suggests, echoed through the forest. Vines the thickness of small tree trunks hung down, twisting around each other in knots, ferns carpeted the ground, and tree ferns and walking stick palm trees grew between the taller trees. The walking stick palm tree could be uprooted with its ball root to make a walking stick complete with handle. It was damp, dark and cool in the deeply shaded area under the trees. Trees soared skywards, their canopies high above us. The lower canopy was 30 metres above us, with a higher canopy 45 metres up out of our sight. We saw the candlestick vine, which twisted round and round other trunks, its berries suitable for eating, unlike most fruits in the rainforest. The Yellow Carabeen trees had massive buttresses like old churches, to help support their unbelievable size, and they were probably 400 to 500 years old. I thought that the most fascinating plant was the Strangle Vine, a type of fig which takes centuries to fully entwine and then smother the 30m to 45m high tree it has chosen as its host. It gradually strangles the tree by restricting its growth because the trunk is unable to expand. Eventually, over centuries, the host tree decays within the outer casing of the vine trunks, leaving the Strangle Vine standing like a hollow pipe of twisted trunks – the hollow centre is the space where the massive host tree once stood. The vine reaches from the ground to the canopy, its enormous roots snaking out into the undergrowth for support. We were able to peer through a gap between the vine trunks to see the hollow interior and, looking up, could just see daylight many metres above, where the Strangling Fig reached the top of the canopy and the light far above us. It was like looking up a tall factory chimney and seeing a speck of light a long, long way above. The plants in this rain forest were called 'living fossils', because they were the same plants that grew millions of years ago, and a fossil of maidenhair fern 300 to 400 million years old had recently been found in the area.

On the journey back to the caravan park we went through banana plantations, all of them built on steep hillsides. We were able to buy large bags of bananas for one dollar from stalls by the roadside, and we had to drop the dollar into a pipe above the stall. We laughed as we heard it rolling through the pipe down the hillside to the house far below. Amongst the banana palms were very old avocado trees laden with fruit, although the green fruit didn't show up well against the green leaves. Apparently avocados never ripen on the tree. They are picked and then take seven days to ripen. As we returned along the highway, we were excited to see dozens of kangaroos in open areas by the roadside. It was late afternoon, the time when these nocturnal creatures usually appear, and it was the first time that we'd seen kangaroos since Yarrawonga Golf Club with Helen!

In Woolgoolga we were very lazy, walking along the beach and occasionally having a swim, but our favourite walk was the quiet stretch along the eastern side of the bay. We walked across the sand to the rocks that nestled below the cliffs. The usual seagulls had been joined by two ibis, and they pecked in the sand with their elegant long black beaks, their reflections mirrored upside down in the wet sand. Wild flowers nestled in the rocks by the edge of the beach. There were coral-coloured flowers hanging like umbrellas from tall stems, blue flowers forming fluffy heads like ageratum, pink and yellow flowers similar to miniature hydrangea, and even miniature poinsettia. Creeping along the sand next to the rocks was a succulent-leafed plant with small daisy-like flowers. As we walked further away from the sandy beach and onto the rocks we were alone except for the birds, and we found that the plants became more tropical. There were wild pineapple shrubs and trees, some growing out of rock crevices, some rooted into the sand. We hadn't seen these plants since Sri Lanka, and many of them had the pineapple-like fruits which we had been told were not suitable for human consumption. The leaves were large, sharp and pointed, and aerial roots dropped vertically from the branches into the sandy soil, forming caverns behind the curtain of roots. Amongst the rocks and pebbles we found dozens of sponges that had been washed up by the waves – long, tubular sponges, cup-shaped sponges and the more familiar sponges that we use in the bath. Rock pools, seaweed, tiny succulent plants, shells and pebbles were in abundance, and small Banksia trees sprouted from ledges on the cliff beside us. Several times we saw a sea eagle soaring overhead, and it often settled on a branch at the top of a tree above the cliff, its shape clearly outlined against the sky. As we walked on we could hear the sound of the whip bird, its call sounding exactly like the crack of a whip. Often we saw whales or schools of dolphins playing out in the bay, and we would sit on the rocks to watch.

During the evenings if we stayed in our cabins we sometimes watched television, and it certainly didn't seem much different from at home. English programmes like The Bill were shown almost every day, as well as Police Camera Action, Parkinson, a new cooking series of Jamie Oliver's, Birds of a Feather, Monarch of the Glen, A Country Practice and many other familiar programmes. There were Australian versions of Wheel of Fortune, Catch Phrase, The Price is Right, Big Brother, Ground Force and Who Wants to be a Millionaire? Other familiar programmes, including American and Australian programmes such as The Simpsons, M★A★S★H, Friends, Frasier, Opra Winfrey, Malcolm in the Middle, Home and Away and Neighbours ensured that we felt like we were back home instead of in a foreign country!

Shopping for food in Woolgoolga was easy as the shops were so close to the caravan park. We found it strange that in Australia prices were quoted with odd cents, which were always rounded up or down to the nearest 5 cents. We found that if the total came to, say $4.66, the price was rounded up to $4.70. However, if we broke off a couple of garlic cloves (they were sold by the kilo) and added these to our shopping, the price was $4.74, which was rounded down to $4.70. In other words, the garlic was free! This may sound penny-pinching, but we were on a budget!

We eventually left Woolgoolga, saying our goodbyes to Jungle, Keitha and our new friends. We felt like celebrities as we posed for several people to take photographs of us, and we set off, waving goodbye. We passed an Indian restaurant, which had two life-sized statues of elephants standing either side of the entrance, and then we passed the Sikh temple. Shortly afterwards we saw a sign on the main road saying 'Wild horses for 10km', but we didn't see any. We had 64km to cycle to Grafton, our next stop, and because we hadn't cycled for two weeks we both ached badly when we got there. Grafton is named as a historic town, and we did see one building that had been built about 1900, but apart from that it didn't seem historic to us at all! Australians were always amazed if we told them that our own house back home was that age, but of course Victorian houses in England are extremely common.

As we cycled north, we saw a pile of maps and a road atlas of Australia lying in the wet grass by the roadside in the middle of nowhere. Being the scroungers that we were, and always watching our budget, we stopped to collect them, and dried them out in front of the fan heater as soon as we booked into our next cabin. What a find! We now had a $20 road atlas with some handwritten notes to show the good caravan parks, and various highlighted sections to show the routes that someone had taken. But why had the maps been thrown out of the car? The first two pages gave us the vital clue – these pages showed a map of the whole of Australia, with the coastal road marked with pink highlighter. The owners of the map had travelled the whole of the 14,000km (nearly 9,000 miles) around Australia – we could picture them throwing the atlas out of the window once they finally reached home again. What a vast country, and another reminder to us that we could only cycle small sections of Australia. We ripped out the pages that we felt might be useful, and threw away the rest – far too heavy a load for us on our bikes!

On the main highway the newer parts of the road had been planted on either side with wattle, a native Australian small flowering tree and the Australian floral emblem. The wattles, or acacia pycnantha to give the wattle its true name, were now coming into flower, and the trees were covered with rich golden-yellow mimosa-like fluffy flowers, which contrasted beautifully with the glossy dark green delicate foliage. Australia even had a Wattle Day, which was celebrated on 1st September of each year. We could cycle for miles with nothing but golden flowers on either side of us, and the sun on the trees made the colour even more stunning.

We were still cycling north along the Pacific Highway, and occasionally we were able to take a side road, which made a pleasant change from the speeding traffic. After a while the scenery became more rural, and we were approaching the area where sugar cane is grown. A stiff breeze had picked up, though it was behind us, and the sound as it rustled through the sugar canes was lovely. Occasionally amongst the sugar cane was a clearing with a neat lawn and a very large, modern house, presumably owned by the sugar cane farmers. Deep verandahs surrounded these houses, and in the shade of the verandahs were sofas and armchairs, waiting for the farmer and his family to return home to relax. Horses grazed in the adjoining paddocks. We also passed stud farms breeding the Brahman cow, which is the humpbacked cow that is familiar in India, and is apparently becoming popular in northern Australia.

Bags of macadamia nuts stood on tables at the farm gates – they were $3 for a kilogramme. We were told that the farmers waited for the nuts to fall from the trees, which were then gathered from the ground by machine. The nuts were sent to China to be shelled, and returned to Australia where they were sold for $20 for a kilo. On these back roads we often had to take a ferry across the rivers. These were free and took only a few minutes, giving us an opportunity to chat to locals as we waited for the ferry to come and get us. We still had the luxury of occasional rest areas in the middle of nowhere, furnished with tables and chairs and a block of toilets.

We had been trying to buy saddle oil for our leather saddles, but it was only sold in large quantities. When Warren saw a homestead with two horses in the neighbouring field he knocked on the door and asked if we could buy a small quantity of saddle oil. They were happy to fill a small container for us, but refused to take any payment for it.

'Where's you's from?' they asked, as they chatted to us. We had noticed the day before that the locals had a very rural accent.

Shortly afterwards three dogs shot out from a farm and began chasing us, and it was really frightening as they ran alongside my bike barking and snarling. However, I was able to get my dog dazer out and point it at them. Initially nothing happened as I pressed the button, but suddenly they fell backwards as if hitting an invisible brick wall, and we shot away on our bikes unscathed, so we were pleased to see how efficiently the dog dazer worked.

We passed through MacLean, where lovely Victorian shops with cast iron-clad verandahs lined the streets. There were obviously a lot of Scots living in MacLean – as we cycled out of the town along the main road, we noticed that the bottom 5 feet of every telegraph pole for miles was painted with a different tartan, and each had a written sign to say which tartan it was and what family used that tartan. The poles were set against the sugar canes on our right, but lined the river on our left.

We arrived at Yamba, which is a small, pretty coastal town. We booked into our cabin, one of a row of tiny brick-built terraced houses, and made friends with Jim and Robyn who were staying next door. They made us promise to contact them when we crossed the Queensland border, so we could spend a night at their home. In the morning Warren shook me awake, whispering urgently that there was a caravan standing outside our door. In my half-awake state I had misheard – it was a kangaroo. I leapt out of bed, and the kangaroo kept an eye on us as we took photos and watched it, even allowing us to follow it around the caravan park.

It didn't seem concerned by our presence even though we were only a few feet away at times. At one point it turned the corner of our building, only its back and long, strong tail showing as it hid round the corner. I was closely following and stood and waited, and several times its head peered back round the corner, peeping just as a child would to see if I was still watching! The caravan park owners told us that two kangaroos had adopted the caravan park, and often came into the park from the surrounding bush. Sometimes they even hopped straight over the entrance barrier and across the children's sandpit, leaving their distinctive footprints in the sand. This kangaroo was a female, and the large bulge in her tummy indicated that she was carrying a joey in her pouch.

In Yamba we cycled along a wide sea wall, built about half a mile long going straight out to sea. At the end, sitting on a rock only six feet from us was a young sea eagle, its talons firmly gripping the remains of a fish it was eating, and fending off several seagulls that were eager to steal whatever bits they could. A couple watching the sea eagle told us they had seen it arrive with the fish, nearly a foot long, and it had spent half an hour tearing chunks off the fish until now only the head remained. We watched for a while and took photos, pleased to see such a magnificent bird at close quarters.

Later in the afternoon we walked along a farm lane, where we were told we might see hundreds of kangaroos as dusk fell. We chatted to the farmer, who introduced us to his favourite heifer, Champion, who had a beautiful auburn coat and was only six months old. The farmer had raised the heifer by hand when his mother had died in the drought.

'Come on, baby – head-butt daddy!' he called to the heifer, as he crawled across the paddock on his hands and knees!

I don't know how I had imagined Australian farmers, but this was certainly not what I had expected! He then cupped his mouth with his hands and shouted, whereupon dozens of cows and the biggest bull I'd ever seen stampeded across the fields with a week old heifer in desperate pursuit, unable to keep up. They charged up to the farmer and he gave them all a treat of molasses, cut an apple into segments and fed the bull, scratching the tight black curls on its forehead. I wondered how he managed when it was time for the animals to be slaughtered.

'You're welcome to go across my fields if you want to see the kangaroos over there,' he said, nodding to the trees in the distance.

'No – don't worry,' we said, eyeing the big black bull. 'We'll go up the lane.'

As we walked back, having seen the kangaroos only in the distance, we heard a shout and turned to see our farmer friend waving to us from his tractor as it careered across the field chasing a dozen kangaroos. The kangaroos were leaping high in the air as they charged across the field in a line in front of the tractor. They shot through and over the fence without slowing, jumped across the lane just in front of us, and bounded off into the distance across the paddocks on the other side. The farmer waved goodbye to us and returned to his farm, having succeeded in giving us a close up view of these extraordinary animals in action!

It was then that we noticed the two tall, leafless trees in the field alongside us, each topped with a giant bird's nest, lit up by the setting sun. Standing proudly astride one of the nests was an eagle, and we were excited to be able to take photos with a close-up lens before returning back to our cabin.

It was now the end of July. The temperature was gradually rising, despite the fact that it was still the middle of winter. However, it was still cool in the mornings when we set off cycling, so we wore several layers of clothing, removing one layer at a time as the temperature rose throughout the day. We were travelling north towards the hotter part of Australia, which meant we were chasing the sun, so we were looking forward to warmer days. When we watched the weather forecast on television, we saw that Cairns and Darwin in the north were 32°C, Brisbane, which is half down the east coast, was 25°C, Sydney, halfway between Brisbane and the south coast was 20°C. Melbourne, on the south coast was 15°C and Tasmania, the furthest south, was 10°C. Inland was much cooler, and Canberra, only just over 100 kilometres inland and 250 kilometres south-west of Sydney, was freezing at night and only 12°C during the day. It was amusing to hear the weather presenter say that there would be 'fair dinkum rain' meaning a lot of rain was on the way!

We passed an area where they had begun growing coffee beans in 1982, and we spoke to the man and his sister who had started the project. They had set up a co-operative, so that local people could own a few trees each. The bushes produce lovely white blossom and sweet fruit that looks very much like red cherries. Because pruning is necessary but means losing the next year's harvest, pruning is carried out on alternate rows. Inside the 'cherries' are the beans, which have to be fermented in a big tank and dried in the sun. Eventually 7 kg of picked fruit becomes 1 kg of coffee beans.

At times we cycled past areas that had been burnt, where stunted, gnarled trees with strange clam-like open seed pods grew. Amongst them were elegant long grasses on black trunks up to 2 feet tall, the fine grasses waving in the breeze and cascading around the trunk like a Roman Candle firework. Banksia, bracken, heather and small eucalyptus trees grew amongst blackened trunks of dead trees which hadn't survived the bush fires, and these dead trees often gave support to climbing plants. We passed sugar factories with high chimneys, and there was a sweet, sickly smell in the air from the processing of the sugar cane. Pretty 19th century wooden churches stood outside villages.

We were cycling towards Byron Bay along a cycle path beside the beaches early one morning. On top of one of the headlands we suddenly stopped because we could see dolphins surfing. It was a magical moment – three of them side by side, perfectly spaced and perfectly synchronized, their identical dark shapes clearly showing through the face of the wave before it crested, moved diagonally across the wave with far more skill and beauty than any human surfer. Although we had only just begun our journey, we stopped at a nearby beach café for a coffee, so that we could watch the dolphins playing. At times they suddenly flew up into the air through the top of the wave, but eventually they tired of the game and swam back out to sea. As we continued our journey that morning past the various bays, we often saw dolphins playing in the waves.

Byron Bay is the most easterly point of Australia and a backpackers' paradise, but we didn't like it. Our next stop was to be Mullumbimby, very close to Byron Bay, to meet Tony and Lynne, the Australians we had met in Turkey the previous December.

There were plenty of pubs in Byron Bay, but buying a beer in a pub in Australia can be confusing, because each state has different names for the varying sizes of glasses. The most common sizes were 200 ml, 285 ml and 425 ml, but Tasmania also had a 10 ounce size. Different names for different sizes of glasses depended on which state you were in (the Australian state, not one's intoxicated state!). The glass could be called a butcher, a glass, a beer, a pot, a pony, a bobbie, a seven, a schooner, a handle, a middy or a 10 ounce. Finally, in some states the 425 ml glass was called a pint, but English tourists expecting a pint should beware – 425 ml is 15 fluid ounces, only three-quarters of the English pint!

When we arrived in Byron Bay we went to one of the caravan parks as usual to book a cabin, and were amazed that the daily rent was almost double the usual price that we paid. We questioned the price.

'Welcome to Byron Bay,' said the girl. She told us that the prices went up every year; that they would escalate dramatically when the current cabins were ripped down to be replaced soon, and that all four of Byron Bay's caravan parks were owned by the Council, so prices were the same in every caravan park. The council wouldn't allow anyone else to open a caravan park, as they might then have some competition! The caravan parks even charged a surcharge if someone stayed only one night – something we'd never seen before.

We had no choice but to pay, but discovered that the cabin was very shabby, had no en-suite shower-room despite being the most expensive cabin we'd rented in Australia, and the television didn't work properly. When we asked the office for a fan heater, we were told that they didn't supply them, even though they were sat in their office with their own heater on! Heaters were necessary in the evenings and early mornings at that time of year, even if it was hot during the day, and this was the only cabin we had ever rented in Australia where a heater was not supplied. When the maintenance man called to fix the television, he kept up a running commentary grumbling about the caravan park. We were horrified by what he told us.

'The cabins are past their sell-by date and unmaintainable,' he told us grimly. 'This television is really ancient. I'll have to bodge the wiring to get it to work!'

We wandered along the beaches which, like all other beaches on this coastline, were lovely. However, they were full of hippies and scruffy people selling shell jewellery. Car parks were full of very scruffy motorhomes – a sure sign of backpackers – and one was covered with artistic poses of women's bums with the sign 'Just bumming around' painted on the back.

Whilst there were a lot of very nice restaurants, cafés and bars in Byron Bay, it was the only place in Australia that we saw filthy public toilets, and the only place we heard drunken shouting through the night. Because of the high cost of the cabin, we decided to cook 'at home' to eke out our budget. As it got dark I began to prepare the meal while Warren showered in the communal shower block. Suddenly the lights, television and hob went out, leaving the cabin in darkness, and I was left without any power. Warren returned from the shower block to say that he had been in the shower, put his hand on the tap to turn it off, and had received an electric shock. At the same time all the lights in the shower block were flickering, although power stayed on in the communal areas. He was obviously very shaken, and had immediately dashed out of the cubicle because he was standing on the wet floor, a very dangerous situation.

We reported the problem but were without power for two hours, whilst two electricians dashed around the site trying to find the problem, because all the cabins were without power. They eventually came to our cabin to check our shower, thinking that Warren had received a shock in our en-suite shower. When Warren told them that we didn't have an en-suite shower, and that he had received an electric shock in the communal block they exchanged very worried glances.

'Christ,' said one of them, 'I hope no-one's lying dead in there,' and with that they ran to the shower block, which was still being used by other guests!

Eventually power was restored, and the girl from the office came to apologise and said they would give us a rebate the next day. As we left the cabin in the morning on our bikes, we noticed that they were digging up all of the concrete paths around the shower block, still searching for the electrical fault. We were surprised to receive a rebate of $60 (£24), which was far more than we had expected. They handed a blank form to Warren asking him to sign it.

'We'll fill it in later,' the receptionist said.

We realised as we cycled out of Byron Bay that the blank form and the $60 rebate had been to cover the electric shock that Warren had received, and not to cover the inconvenience of having no power for two hours – they were scared we might sue! We were just glad to get away from Byron Bay …

We cycled a short way to Brunswick Heads where we had arranged to meet Tony and Lynne. We walked around the Saturday market and bumped into Robyn and Jim who we'd met several days earlier. They hugged us like old friends and gave us some fruit from their fruit stall. We met Tony and Lynne and, after a relaxing leisurely lunch under a jacaranda tree at the local pub, they put our bikes in their van and drove us to their house which nestled in heavily rolling countryside a few miles inland.

The house was full of interesting artefacts from their travels abroad and in Australia, including some beautiful Aboriginal art, but their 5 acre garden, which included some rainforest, fascinated us the most. Massive ferns, thick bamboos with bar code stripes, mature trees and even a Strangle Fig vine were in the garden. Koalas regularly visited the giant eucalyptus trees and wallabies also visited the garden. Unfortunately, like so many Australian animals, the koala is nocturnal, but we could clearly see the punctures and claw marks on the concrete-smooth trunks of some of the gum trees, where the koalas had climbed them.

I was woken the next morning by a sound similar to monkeys chattering, but then recognised the sound of kookaburras laughing in the trees. Bird life was abundant in this beautiful Garden of Eden. Exploring the garden, we discovered that Tony and Lynne were virtually self-sufficient so far as fruits were concerned. In the garden were five different citrus trees, apples, bananas, custard apples, macadamia nuts, mangoes, paw-paws, guavas, a peacot tree (a cross between a peach and an apricot), rose apples, avocados and passion-fruit vines. As well as the fruit trees, there was a vegetable garden with silver beet, chillies, peppers, herbs and strawberries.

Sitting on the verandah which stretched the length of the house at first floor level we could look over the garden and the forest, and it was a wonderful place to relax for a weekend before we continued our travels up the east coast towards Brisbane.

We continued cycling, stopping at caravan parks, walking on the almost deserted beaches of New South Wales, and eating out or in, depending on our budget for the day. Sometimes we ate at the RSL or the local Bowls Club for a cheap, substantial meal. Returned Services League of Australia has clubs in many towns, usually very comfortably and tastefully decorated and furnished, and non-members like us were always welcome free of charge. We once had a Works Burger (as in 'the works'). This included a burger in a bun with cheese, pineapple, bacon, egg, tomato, cucumber, fried onion, lettuce and, of course, the inevitable beetroot. Served with chips at a cost of $6.50 (£2.40) there was no room for pudding, but we could afford a bottle of wine! Bowls is very popular in Australia, and most towns have Bowls Clubs similar to the RSL clubs, and we had a lovely three course meal one Sunday at a cost of only $10. On the table next to us were

Mr and Mrs Very Fat, with their young teenage children, Master and Miss Very Fat. We couldn't believe the size of them all; even the children had double chins, and the daughter couldn't have been more than 13. All had second helpings of the creamy soup plus rolls and butter, and all had double portions of pudding. We had noticed that there was quite a lot of obesity in Australia – more than in UK, but not as bad as USA.

We found the Australian need to abbreviate everything quite strange, especially when place names were abbreviated. Brisbane became Brissy, Launceston was Launy, Rockhampton became Rocky, and these abbreviated names were used quite readily on television and radio. Other common abbreviations were Salvo (the Salvation Army), pokies were everywhere (poker machines or gaming machines), and someone once told me that they worked in the morning and someone else worked in the 'arvo'. Warren and I stood in a bus queue, and I commented that there was a delicious smell of food.

'It's a roast chook,' said the couple standing behind us, holding up a Woolworth's bag with a hot roasted chicken in it and, sure enough, signs outside shops constantly announced that 'Hot Chooks' were being spit-roasted.

As we cycled we passed local schools, sometimes with an official sign outside announcing that it was a 'Kiss and Drop' area. We passed almost empty beaches where there were sometimes people fishing. The Australians are very keen fishermen, and 4WD vehicles often had special containers by the bumper. The handles of the long rods slotted into these containers, and the rods stretched back over the top of the vehicle. Almost all small shops that sold food also sold bait for fishing, but I didn't really like the idea of these maggots being near food . . .

Queensland

We had cycled along the Tweed Coast, had now crossed the border into Queensland, and were heading up the famous Gold Coast. The beaches were just as lovely as the ones in New South Wales that we had seen, but now the towns were very urbanised. I saw in the distance across a bay a peninsula which I assumed to be Brisbane, because the buildings were high and dense, but it turned out to be Surfers Paradise. Tall blocks of different shapes and sizes dominated the far horizon, and in the misty distance they looked like tall blocks of stone standing on end – an overcrowded Stonehenge.

We passed through towns and suburbs with names like Palm Beach, Mermaid Beach and Miami – indeed, it reminded us of Florida. Each suburb was more built up than the last, until we reached Surfers Paradise. Anyone who likes skyscrapers would like Surfers Paradise – there were tall skyscrapers, round ones, fat ones, white ones, coloured ones, glass ones. Some skyscrapers had views of the sea, some of the river and some of the freeway. The waves rolled onto miles of sand, still almost empty at that time of year, but undoubtedly in summer it would be as packed as Cannes had been when we had cycled through it the previous August.

The last part of the journey to Brisbane was difficult, because at this stage the Pacific Highway became a freeway, on which bicycles were banned. No other roads were shown on the map, but we were assured that service roads ran alongside the freeway. However, these roads were not signposted, and we often had to retrace our route having taken a wrong turning. The temperature had risen quite dramatically; it was now 27°C in Queensland, but that was nothing compared to the heat-wave in Europe that we had been hearing about. Now that we were in Queensland it reminded us what one Australian had said to Warren in a conversation.

'There are only two states to be in during winter – Queensland or pissed!'

At one stage I was struggling up a hill in the heat when a magpie dive-bombed me three times, each time making loud clicking noises above my head. I was very frightened and didn't want to stop cycling, remembering Alfred Hitchcock's frightening film, 'The Birds'. I can't imagine what passing drivers thought, seeing me cycling uphill waving my arms frantically and shouting at a bird that had now retired to a telegraph wire! I also had no idea why a magpie should do such a thing. Interestingly, when I checked the internet to see how common such an occurrence was, there were many instances of cyclists being dive-bombed by crows and magpies, every one in Australia! It was incredibly hot as we continued cycling up and down the hills of the service road alongside the level freeway for the cars, until we arrived at the outskirts of Brisbane.

We booked into a caravan park in one of the suburbs. From Brisbane we planned to drive to Cairns, having already cycled 1302km (805 miles) from Sydney to Brisbane, and it was a further 1700km to Cairns in northern Queensland. We had to pick up the car in the city centre, so we took the bus and were very impressed to find that the buses in Brisbane ran on flyovers alongside and above the freeway. These bus-ways were for buses only, so there were no traffic jams, and along these routes were bus stops similar to railway stations without the raised platforms. Behind the bus stops were large parking areas where cars could park free of charge. 13km and 10 minutes later, including a speedy change of buses in an ultra-modern multi-level bus terminus, we were in Brisbane city centre.

We were able to find a travel agent to book us a flight home to England so that we could visit our families. What we wanted was a return flight flying from Cairns to England, but flying back to Perth in Western Australia in just over a year's time. This was a complicated series of flights, and finally we paid $7,169

(£2,867!) for flights for both of us at the end of August in three weeks time. We would fly from Cairns to Hong Kong, where we would stay for 27 hours. It was now early August 2003, and only one month earlier the World Health Organisation had announced that the SARS epidemic, which had started in Hong Kong, had at last been contained, so it was now safe for us to go there. From Hong Kong we would take a flight to Heathrow, spend a month in England, and then fly from Heathrow to Tokyo to continue our cycling. After several weeks in Tokyo we would fly to Bangkok, and finally (after cycling through Thailand, Vietnam, Laos, Cambodia, Malaysia, Singapore and Indonesia) we would catch the final leg of our flights from Bali to Perth. This last flight was booked for September 2004, a year ahead, because after visiting Indonesia we hoped to see the spectacularly colourful floral display of the wild spring flowers in Western Australia. We had never expected to particularly like Australia but had fallen in love with it, and wanted to spend some time cycling in the south-west of Australia. From there we wanted to fly to New Zealand, on to Fiji and after that we planned to fly to the States and cycle from west to east before finally returning home to England. These plans meant that our cycling trip was likely to last almost 4 years.

Brisbane is another open, clean, pleasant city with attractive old buildings amongst the modern ones and pleasant street cafés. Freeways had been built over the edge of the river away from the buildings, and these flyovers intertwined in loops at junctions so that cars could speed in and out of the city. We put the bicycles into the back of the hired car, joined the freeway, and were soon driving north towards Cairns.

Winter is the best time to visit Cairns or Darwin, the two main northern cities in Australia. The temperature in these northern cities is always hot, but in winter it's hot and dry, whilst in summer it's hot and wet and unbearably humid. We had been told that, although there were some lovely beaches just north of Brisbane on the Sunshine Coast, after that there were hundreds of miles of sugar cane and fairly boring scenery.

It was a two day journey from Brisbane to Cairns, we were told, but that would have meant 18 hours of non-stop driving. There was only one lane on the Bruce Highway, large trucks were common and there were some speed restrictions. We decided to do the trip over seven days. We were glad, as we travelled, that we had chosen this section to drive, rather than cycle. There were long distances where there was very little to see and no accommodation – the scenery was just bush with occasional mountain ranges in the distance. Signs warned us to 'Break the drive and stay alive – rest area 75km ahead' or 'Driver fatigue crash zone next 150km'. Other signs said 'Rest or R.I.P.' or 'Don't sleep and drive'. Cycling such long distances with no change of scenery would have been a nightmare.

We had been warned about the tail-gating trucks. However, when you are travelling at 100km per hour and see one of these monsters through your rear window, with only its radiator and solid bull-bar showing because it's so close, it's pretty terrifying, and there is a great temptation to break the speed limit just to get away from it. All we could do was hope for a steep hill, where the truck would lose speed and where an overtaking lane might allow us to pass another vehicle so that they would have the tailgater behind them when he caught up again (and he always did!)

The ute is probably the most common type of vehicle on the Australian roads, and at that time was only just becoming popular in England. Apparently in 1932 a farmer's wife complained to Ford that she and her husband needed a car that could carry her to church on Sundays and carry pigs to market on Mondays, so Ford designed the first Ford Coupé Utility, abbreviated by the Aussies to 'ute'. Half car, half open truck, such vehicles range from a completely utilitarian vehicle, obviously designed for use by farmers or tradesmen, to a vehicle combining the front of a stylish car with a smart panelled open-topped back, sometimes with roll bars. On this type of vehicle the car section can have two or four seats. Some utes are four wheel drive, many have tarpaulin covers (always called 'tarps' in Australia) covering the truck section, but the utilitarian utes all seemed to have at least one dog in the back, sometimes chained and sometimes loose. As the utes passed us on our bikes, the dogs always stood up and barked at us. We discussed whether we thought every ute was supplied with a dog, and could imagine the ute salesman asking the final question as he completed the order form.

'And what colour dog would you like with that, sir?'

In one area we passed, there were orchards of mango trees with neat heads of long ovate glossy leaves and racemes of flower buds forming. Another area had vast fields of tomatoes, as far as the eye could see. However, the main crop was sugar cane, and it is in Queensland that virtually all of Australia's sugar is produced, and it is one of their main exports, producing $1 billion for the Australian economy at that time. Australian sugar is exported to Canada, China, Japan, Korea, Malaysia, New Zealand, Russia, Singapore, Taiwan and USA, and is Australia's second largest crop after wheat.

Most of the sugar cane in Australia is grown north of the Tropic of Capricorn, and Queensland has the perfect climate. Sugar cane grows to a maximum height of 4 metres, with pampas-like white or pinky-purple plumes waving in the breeze above the spiky green leaves. The fields were in different stages of growth, and we were told that after harvesting new growth shoots through the soil again, and a plant can be harvested four times before being dug up and the field rested. However, the cane takes 12 to 16 months to grow before it is ready for harvesting. In some areas it's possible to harvest canes green, leaving the left over cuttings to form a mulch to keep in moisture and stop the growth of weeds. In other areas the cane is burnt to remove the leaves and weeds. The harvested cane is chopped into small lengths called billets, which are loaded into wire bins and taken by rail or road to the mill. The billets have to be at the mill within 16 hours of harvesting.

Sugar cane was first planted in Australia in the 18th century, but in the post war years many Europeans, especially Italians, came to Australia to work in the sugar cane industry. Narrow gauge railway tracks were laid between the sugar cane fields and the road, and also criss-crossed the fields, so that the harvested crop could be delivered as quickly as possible to the local sugar mills for processing. We saw railway trucks like cages on wheels lined up beside fields, sometimes empty, sometimes full. Sugar mills dotted the landscape, their tall chimneys belching white and dark brown smoke into the sky. Interestingly, the expended cane fibre remaining after processing provides nearly all the fuel required to power the mills, and is also used to manufacture paper and garden mulches.

We passed through Rockhampton, and were excited to be crossing that imaginary line called the Tropic of Capricorn. This part of the coast was called the Capricorn Coast. Two days later we passed the Whitsunday Islands, so named when Captain Cook discovered them on 3rd June 1770. They are the tips of underwater mountains, and have stunning white beaches and clear water. However, they appear to be predominantly geared to expensive package holidays, or one can charter a yacht or take a helicopter trip to see the islands. Our budget didn't stretch to any of these options, so we continued on up the coast.

The day before we were due to reach Townsville, the town suffered an earthquake measuring 4.7 on the Richter scale. Further tremors were anticipated, but we experienced none, and there was no damage in the town and no casualties.

It was noticeable when we got out of our air-conditioned car at the end of each day how much hotter the temperature was becoming as we travelled north. Now we were checking our cabins for fans or air conditioning instead of a heater, and for the first time in Australia we were constantly in shorts and flip-flops. We saw coconut palms for the first time – there were plenty of palm trees further south, but not coconut palms.

We noticed our map had a double warning. There was a sign on one section saying 'Warning – Crocodiles'. A second sign warned, 'Never swim when you see this sign'. We felt that the second warning was definitely superfluous!

We decided to drive inland to the Atherton Tableland, a plateau 1,000 metres high, south-west of Cairns. This area is beautiful, with very lush pastures and pockets of rainforest, volcanic lakes, waterfalls and gorges. In one of these rainforests, we saw the Curtain Tree, a 500 year old Strangle Fig Vine which had been growing up its host tree; the host tree had fallen into another tree, and was supported by it at an angle of 45°. The vine's aerial roots had dropped vertically to earth instead of down the trunk of the host tree, forming an impressive triangular 'curtain' of roots from the 50 metre high sloping tree.

From the Tableland we drove steeply down to sea level again on an incredibly winding road back to the Bruce Highway. We had driven 2,000 kilometres, and were now in Cairns. We booked into a caravan park full of shaded lanes with cabins nestling under the palm trees, and returned the car to the hire company.

Our plans were set – our flights to Hong Kong were booked for 30th August. Now all we had to do was enjoy Cairns and the surrounding area, and the first stop was to book a boat trip to see the Great Barrier Reef . . .

Cairns is a pleasant city with wide streets, although to us it seemed far more like a small town than a city. The population of Cairns is about 120,000, whereas we came from Reading, a town with a population of over 200,000. The Australians were always amazed that for such a large place we didn't call Reading a city! Like all Australian towns and cities, Cairns has plenty of street cafés to enjoy al fresco coffees or meals. Cairns was the only town we visited where we saw Aborigines, but unfortunately the sight of Aboriginal men and women staggering drunk along the street mid-morning confirmed what many people had told us about the problems associated with alcoholism within the Aboriginal community.

From Cairns we booked a boat trip to visit the Great Barrier Reef. 2,000 kilometres of reef stretches from Bundaberg in southern Queensland to just south of Papua New Guinea, an area larger than Great Britain and Ireland combined. The reef is at its closest to Cairns, but the Ocean Spirit, our beautiful catamaran with sails, still took two hours to reach Oyster Reef, 16 nautical miles out to sea. The Great Barrier Reef is actually made up of 3,000 separate reefs, and there are 400 different types of coral and 1,500 species of fish, as well as thousands of types of molluscs, crustaceans and bivalves, such as clams, oysters, sea urchins, starfish, sea cucumbers, crabs and shrimps. The sky was blue and the sun was burning, even at 8.30am, and it was obvious that there were going to be some very bright pink bodies by the end of the day. The colour of the sea was stunning, ranging from the palest turquoise blue to a deep jade green, and in the bright sunshine the water sparkled and was crystal clear, so that we could easily see the bottom of the ocean.

We were offered the opportunity to try scuba diving free of charge, and out of the boat full of people only five of us accepted. Warren and I knew that, even if we enjoyed the diving, our budget wouldn't stretch to the extra cost of the full guided tour underwater afterwards, but it was an excellent chance to try it out without cost. I found the experience too claustrophobic, especially with the spooky, echoey sound of my own breathing underwater, but Warren enjoyed it and would love to do more of this expensive past-time. We switched to snorkels, and swam in the water, which was only 7 metres deep despite the fact that we were so far out to sea. The sights beneath us were unbelievable, and we pointed excitedly at the different types of coral, blue starfish, sponges, fish of every colour, and giant clams with their large 'mouths' opening and shutting to filter the water. The reef is home to more different types of marine life than anywhere else in the world, and the kaleidoscope of colours and diversity of shapes has to be seen to be believed. Fish were swimming around us, unconcerned by humans in the water, and occasionally they nibbled our outstretched fingers. Unfortunately, we didn't see the turtles, dugongs or stingrays which frequent the area, but everything we saw was amazing, although the colours of the coral are not as brilliant in the daytime as at night with lights. I was glad I was wearing a wetsuit – the water temperature of 24°C felt cool despite it, but it also protected my back and legs from the sun as I swam on the surface of the water looking down at the reef.

After a wonderful lunch of chicken, prawns and delicious salads provided on the boat, we moved on to Upolu Cay. A cay is a tiny sandy island on the outer reef that has been formed out of reef which is permanently above water. The exposed reef dies and gradually the reef is broken down into fine pure white sand, and vegetation grows on the larger cays. You know the cartoons of desert islands with one palm tree? Well, that was Upolu Cay, except there was one sun umbrella instead of the palm tree! The cay was an island no more than 30 to 40 feet in diameter in the middle of the ocean with virtually nothing else in sight in any direction except the horizon, but it proved to be a superb base from which to do more snorkelling.

When we returned to the catamaran, one kilogram of raw fish was thrown over the side, and enormous fish called 'spangled emperors' rushed to the surface to gobble the food. They looked good enough to eat, but fishing is not allowed on the Great Barrier Reef, and even feeding the fish is only allowed under very strict conditions, so that the natural food chain is not affected.

On the way back to Cairns harbour we were served with tea and cake, and a complimentary glass of champagne made the day perfect as we chatted to our new friends. We arrived back in time to see the sun set as we approached the harbour.

We set off the next day to cycle north to Port Douglas, a former fishing village. It was a shock to be cycling in the heat again. It was 27°C at 10.30am, and later rose to over 30°C, but it was very humid. We had only been travelling for one hour when we noticed the Skyway station, from which a cable-car carried passengers up and over the rainforest-covered mountains. Having already seen and enjoyed rainforests, we decided against the fairly expensive cable-car. However, next to it was an Aboriginal Cultural Park, where we could learn about the history of the Aborigines, their spiritual and traditional beliefs, see traditional dancing, be taught boomerang and spear throwing, listen to an Aborigine explaining how to make and play a didgeridoo, and listen to another talk on how nuts and berries in the rainforest can be used as food and medicines. It was a fascinating place to visit with a combination of film, indoor and outdoor theatre, and one-to-one chats with Aborigines, so it was many hours before we continued our journey.

We noticed that now we were in the tropical north of Australia the trees were much more reminiscent of India – exquisite white and yellow wax-like flowers covered the leafless branches of frangipani trees, and the road was edged with strange little stubby palm trees. Their trunks were black, probably from bush fire damage, and were patterned as if covered in netting. Termite mounds were dotted between and against the trees. The dark green glossy leaves on trees lining the road set off stunning orange-scarlet flowers, and other trees had very narrow, one foot long seed pods hanging from the branches.

We arrived at Palm Cove, clearly a very expensive resort full of expensive hotels, expensive bars, expensive restaurants and expensive boutiques. Rolls Royces stood outside one of the hotels ready to ferry guests along the brick-paved road which was lined with massive melaleucas, the biggest and oldest gum or eucalyptus trees in Australia. They were certainly the most impressive eucalyptus trees that we had ever seen. We examined one, and found that the texture of its trunk was soft and warm like polystyrene, whereas other gum trees we had seen had trunks that looked like stone or marble and felt cold and hard to the touch. We had a coffee as we sat overlooking the beach, after which we moved on to find a caravan park where we could afford to stay – Palm Cove was obviously out of our price range!

The next day we had approximately 50 kilometres to cycle along a fairly desolate stretch of road, with no places for refreshment until we reached Port Douglas. Fortunately the sky was covered with cloud, which meant the temperature was lower than usual, although it was still humid. The beaches were immediately to our right – long, empty, sandy beaches far superior to the one in expensive Palm Cove, and on our left were rainforest-covered mountains, the clouds obscuring the tops.

It was a fairly narrow road, and the coaches taking people on trips to the north came dangerously close to us. After climbing a long hill we arrived at a viewing point called Rex Outlook about halfway to Port Douglas, so we pulled over for a rest and to admire the view. An old VW motorhome stood in the lay-by, and a man sat on a folding chair alongside it. We said 'hello' and he nodded but, unlike most Australians, he didn't strike up a conversation. As Warren made an adjustment to his bike, I wandered over to chat to him. It was immediately clear that he had a problem speaking, either to say the words or perhaps to recall the words he needed, and he patted his right cheek with his left hand and said 'stroke' to explain his problem; his right arm hung limply by his side. We chatted for a few minutes, and when he tried to say something but failed, he beckoned me to the back of the van to show me the open engine and an empty, rusted fuel can standing on the ground next to the van.

He shook the can and repeated, 'Stupid, stupid,' and I realised that he had run out of fuel. I asked him how long he'd been there.

'Tomorrow,' he said hesitatingly, and I assumed he meant 'Yesterday'. He saw my hesitation.

'Two days,' he said quickly.

I called Warren over, and the man patted his chest and said 'Barry' to introduce himself. We had only ¼ litre of petrol for cooking – obviously no use to Barry, so we offered to take his petrol can with us to Port Douglas and send it back to him full of petrol with a vehicle travelling back south. We knew it would be some distance before we reached a service station, and it would be too far for us to return on our bikes.

Barry patted his empty pockets. 'No money,' he said.

We now understood why he'd been there so long. He had a problem communicating, and if he had managed to ask for petrol from a passer by he couldn't pay for it. He also explained that he wouldn't leave the motorhome – it contained everything he owned, and inside the motorhome we saw a mattress on the floor with a kettle standing alongside. Looking at the condition of the motorhome, we felt it likely that it didn't even lock. However, we knew exactly how he felt – everything we needed was on our bikes, and we certainly wouldn't have left them anywhere either.

Barry asked 'English?' pointing to us, and we nodded. His face beamed. 'Shropshire,' he said, patting his chest again. Barry, like so many people we'd met in Australia, originated from England, and he seemed delighted to meet fellow countrymen. We told Barry we'd buy him petrol, and I thought he was going to burst into tears and hug us, and he kept repeating, 'You're the best.' We asked if he had food and water, and he said 'Yes.' At that moment a car full of tourists pulled up to admire the view, and we cycled off waving to Barry, the rusty fuel can strapped to the back of Warren's bike.

Warren and I clearly had the same idea in our minds as we finally reached the service station in Port Douglas. As well as filling the fuel can we bought him a bag of groceries – basics of bread, butter, water and eggs and a few luxuries. We started accosting every driver who called at the service station, and the third driver, a bare-footed woman in her 30s, said she was driving south and was happy to deliver the goods to Barry. We hope everything was delivered to him – we often wondered how he was, and we both said it just emphasised how grateful we should be for our health.

At Port Douglas we found a pleasant caravan park and booked a cabin for a week – we were going to relax again! Trees and palms shaded the cabins and verandahs, and I found it fascinating to see how many trees and plants were dependent on each other. In crevices in the trees, plants had seeded and sent their roots snaking down the trunk to the ground and their stems up amongst the trees' branches. The branches and roots of the second plant were entwined by a smaller vine, and different types of ferns had seeded and grown in the pockets of soil in the crevices and rough bark of the trees. Strings of tiny round succulent leaves hung from the branches like strings of beads, attached by tiny roots that had embedded themselves into the bark. In this northern part of Queensland there was the widest variety of palm trees that I'd ever seen – clumps of palms with trunks similar to bamboo; palms with trunks with bulbous bases and some with bulbous tops; palms with bottle-shaped trunks, palms with silver trunks, smooth trunks, rough trunks, hairy trunks; short, chubby, bulbous palms, palms with fan-shaped leaves, palms that looked like giant pineapples, coconut palms, palm-olive palms and walking stick palms. There are in fact over 60 species of palm trees in Queensland, half of which grow in the rainforests.

Port Douglas, once a small fishing village, is now a very pleasant, laid-back town with many lovely restaurants and shops. A very expensive hotel complex was built in Port Douglas, and helicopters were always waiting on the helipads alongside the hotel. At almost $700 per night for a room with a lagoon view, this hotel was definitely out of our league, especially when an air-conditioned en-suite cabin in a local caravan park was one-tenth of that price! Postcards showed Port Douglas' famous sandy beach, Four Mile Beach, which is backed by palm trees but, unlike so many beaches that we had seen, was always full of people. Even at dawn the beach was busy with joggers. Unlike the beaches further south in New South Wales, the beach was not a surfing beach and was therefore suitable for swimming. However, the beaches in northern Queensland have stinger nets to provide small areas for swimming safe from the lethal box jellyfish, which is common in the summer season from November to April. Notices warned of the stingers, and vinegar in plastic bottles stood alongside the notices for initial emergency treatment of the stings before being rushed to hospital.

Alongside the estuary in Port Douglas we saw the mangrove swamps, where the mangrove trees with their strange arching roots burrowed down into the mud and sea water. Apparently the excess salt water is expelled by the mangrove through the leaves, and a lick of a leaf will confirm this. However, knowing that estuarine crocodiles (better known in Australia as salt water crocodiles or 'salties') could be found in this type of habitat, we decided not to venture too close to the water to do any leaf-licking, especially as salties can grow up to 7 metres in length! The mangrove tree also sends up snorkels, little roots that protrude vertically out of the mud and water, to help it to breathe in this unlikely environment.

Retired couples in Australia have a very nice way of life travelling with their caravans. We chatted to many of them; they migrated north during the winter from the cooler southern states where they lived, and when the weather became too humid in the north they travelled back to their homes for the summer. Most caravans began moving south on 1st September, which is the first day of spring in Australia. One couple we met were from Adelaide, where at that time (August) the average temperature was 13°C. Every year they took 10 days driving slowly to Port Douglas with their caravan, where they stayed for three months. Very comfortable, semi-permanent sites are erected by these people in the caravan parks, with carports to give shade for the car, and awnings at the side of the caravan to give extra room for freezers, bikes, fishing rods and other storage. Some caravan sites had en-suite facilities, where the caravan was parked alongside a small private toilet and shower block, and almost all caravan sites had a concrete area alongside the caravan parking space, where the table and chairs could be set out on the flat surface beneath a canopy.

The Australian caravan parks were beautifully planted with palms and other trees to give plenty of shade. Even the cabins were well-shaded. Indeed, we had seen sites well-planted with trees ever since we had left England, and it is only in England where we have seen sites which are merely fields with no shade at all. Although England is not renowned for its sunshine, it can be unpleasantly hot in a caravan or tent on a sunny day if there is no shade.

There wasn't much point in cycling further north, because the sealed road runs out a few miles north of Port Douglas, becoming a dirt track. Eventually it was time to cycle back to Cairns, where we would catch our plane to Hong Kong. As we cycled out of Port Douglas, the cycle path took us past the old town cemetery, and we were fascinated to read some of the inscriptions on the ornate gravestones that we could see over the hedge.

"...who met his death by cruel and treacherous murder..." said one gravestone dated 1885, and "...killed by blacks in the 23rd year of his life..." said another. It was interesting to read the words that would never be written these days, and it made us realise the problems that faced both the indigenous people of Australia and the early settlers at that time.

We cycled back along the Captain Cook Highway south towards Cairns. The wind, which had almost always been southerly, was now against us, but we had been told that the winds change in spring to north-easterly warm winds. We passed the lay-by where we had met Barry with his motorhome, but there was now no sign of him.

We stayed overnight in a caravan park halfway along the highway. The caravan park owner chatted, commenting on what a beautiful ride it was on the Cairns to Port Douglas road. I agreed, but told her that unfortunately it was also a dangerous road for cyclists.

'Oh yes,' she said, 'It would be. I remember several times travelling along that road when cyclists were in front of me, and traffic was coming in the opposite direction, and I had to pass very close to the cyclists.'

I don't think she even noticed my gaping mouth, as I tried not to say the words, 'Didn't it occur to you to wait until the traffic had passed, so that you could pass the cyclist safely with plenty of space?' I didn't say them; she just didn't understand, and it occurred to us that there must be plenty of other people out there who also didn't understand!

That night we sat in the local diner next to the caravan park having a plate of fish and chips. Fish and chips are just as popular in Australia as in England but, dare I say it, the quality was usually better. Australian fish and chip shops had a different choice of fish from in England – sea perch, barramundi, flake (a type of shark), whiting, sea salmon, dory, Nile perch, mackerel and hoki were usually on the menu, as well as calamari, scallops, mussels and oysters. Our favourites were barramundi and flake. We sat at one of the tables to eat our meal; the fish and chips were served with large wedges of lemon rather than the malt vinegar that is obligatory in England. A delicious side salad accompanied it, and a dessert followed. With a bottle of wine that we had bought in the neighbouring bottle shop, we had a very economical but delicious meal for $17 (less than £7).

The weather changed in the last three days of our time in Australia; the sky was completely overcast and it rained several times. This didn't stop us taking cycle rides around the town, where we saw children in the school playground wearing the distinctive Aussie school uniforms – shorts in bottle green, white t-shirt with green stripe down the side and green Aussie wide-brimmed hat. We thought the uniforms neat and practical for the hot Australian weather. Many of the houses we passed in that northern part of Queensland were built on stilts, in order that any breeze could blow below the house to keep it cooler. We understood that most of the houses in the Northern Territory were built in the same way. We noticed, as in England, that there were plenty of veterinary surgeons, and advertisements for the RSPCA were common.

It was time to get our bicycles packed ready for the flight. Australian Airlines had insisted this time that our bicycles were packed into boxes, so we had asked a local bicycle shop to supply us with larger boxes than those supplied by the airlines – they didn't charge for them either! However, putting bikes into boxes makes them very heavy and awkward to handle, as the boxes need to be lifted – they can't be wheeled along. We had also noticed that bikes in boxes were thrown into the hold of the plane, whereas bikes unwrapped were pushed up the ramp. We weren't sure yet what we could do with the bikes when we arrived in Hong Kong. Hopefully we could book them straight onto the next flight to Heathrow the following day, but if not we would have to store them at the airport. The worst scenario of all was if we had to take them with us to the hotel – something we didn't want to do in such a busy city.

We could see from our bicycle computers that we had cycled 2,805km or 1,740 miles in Australia, and we had cycled a total of 10,000km or 6,250 miles since we had left England. We had had a total of 9 punctures, and were on our third set of tyres, having bought new ones in Sydney. We knew that we were going to miss Australia and our new friends, and we planned to come back one day to see them again ...

CHAPTER 13

HONG KONG AND ENGLAND

Hong Kong comprises of more than 260 islands facing the South China Sea. From 1842 it was a dependent territory of the United Kingdom, but was transferred back to the People's Republic of China in 1997. Hong Kong's climate is sub-tropical and prone to monsoons. Hong Kong, a global centre of trade, is one of the most densely populated areas in the world. Despite its reputation of being intensely urbanised, Hong Kong has made an effort to promote a green environment, and there is undeveloped hilly and mountainous terrain with 40% of its area reserved as country parks and nature reserves. Hong Kong continues to follow the tradition of common law as established by British colonial rule, and the education system roughly follows the United Kingdom's system.

We arrived at Cairns airport and duly checked in, as always holding our breath and keeping our fingers crossed that we wouldn't be charged excess baggage. It must have been obvious to the girl who checked us in that if our bags alone weighed 35 kg (we were allowed 20 kg each), with two bikes in boxes we had excess baggage. We also carried far more than the 7 kg that is allowed as hand baggage, in order to reduce the weight of the bags weighed. However, she just stuck stickers onto our luggage and our bikes and allowed us through with a cheerful 'G'day'.

The flight was wonderful. After several very dull days with rain, the sun had finally appeared, and as we took off we had stunning views of Cairns and the coastline of Queensland from the air, and as we reached 22,000 feet the clouds looked like white dumplings below us hovering over the blue sea. Even though we were so high, we could see the ripples of waves on the sea, which made it look like a woven bright blue cloth, and occasionally we could see a distinct line across the ocean where the colour suddenly changed to dark blue, indicating a shelf where the ocean suddenly became deeper. We flew above an island, its coastline edged with sand, passed over another island with a town on the mouth of a river, where brown water discoloured the blue sea as the river carried its muddy water out of the estuary. On another island roofs of houses sparkled in the sun, a river snaked backwards and forwards through the hills, and lakes reflected the sun like mirrors. Tiny rivers sparkled like tinsel thrown on the ground, and the green island below us looked as though it was carved from jade. We were flying over the Philippines.

As we approached Hong Kong airport we had magnificent aerial views of the city and harbour in Hong Kong Island. Skyscraper flats were built in clumps of identical buildings very close together, and we could see that the city was very large. We were able to take some wonderful photographs of Hong Kong from the air. As we entered the main part of the airport building, the first shop we saw was W.H. Smith, the English newsagents, which made us feel quite at home!

We were in Hong Kong for only 27 hours, and certainly didn't want to cycle in such a big city, but we were unable to check in our luggage for the flight the following day. We arranged for the bikes to be left at the left luggage office, and we caught a train which links the airport with the city. Although it was now dark, the heat was intense and very humid. I had previously checked on the internet the weather forecast for Hong Kong, and was rather concerned to see that from April onwards the weather became hotter and more humid, until by September one could expect typhoons − today was 30th August. The average top daily temperature at that time of year, according to the internet, was 31°C, but it was 33°C even at 9pm as we approached the centre of Hong Kong. The roads were busy; beautiful, old-fashioned, narrow trams in different colours shot past with people leaning out of the glass-less windows; double-decker buses and expensive cars filled the roads. Skyscrapers of all shapes, sizes and colours rose above us, the restaurants and shops were busy, and side streets were full of colourful neon signs. We found our hotel, which we had pre-booked with our flight tickets, and were delighted to find we had been upgraded to a beautiful suite which had a bedroom with a king-sized bed, a living room and a lovely bathroom. We were on the 19th floor, but buildings around us still towered much higher, and the trams and buses way below us looked like children's toys. We hurried back out into the humid evening to explore and to have a meal, as we didn't want to waste any of the little time that we had in this amazing city.

In the time we had available it was impossible to visit some of the areas of Hong Kong that we wanted to see, such as Aberdeen in the south of Hong Kong Island, where sampans could be seen. We decided, therefore, that we would walk around the streets in order to see and experience as much as possible of one area, and we set off the next morning in the ever-increasing humid heat. It was already 35°C just after breakfast, and when I took out my camera to take a photo I couldn't see anything because the lens was covered with condensation, the camera having been taken from our air-conditioned room into the steamy heat outside.

We took dozens of photos. The pavements were full of people, and every other person crossing the road was talking into a mobile phone. Bamboo scaffolding was used (as in India and other parts of Asia), but here it rose to 60 floors high, and was tied with the plastic tape usually used for parcelling crates.

The roads went up and down steps, and we often had glimpses of Victoria Peak between the side streets, a popular high point for seeing the magnificent views of the whole of Hong Kong. We passed streets which specialised in different shops – one street had camera shops, another street had shops selling ancient maps, prints and paintings, and picture-framing shops rubbed shoulders with beauty salons and spas. Further on were streets of linens, silks, crafts and antiques, and then we passed through a steep side street where soups and teas, noodles and pastries were being sold from stalls. We walked along streets of stalls filled with meat; ducks and geese, brown with marinade, hung from hooks, as well as superb pieces of pork, chicken and other meats. The produce in the fish shops was very fresh – the fish were still flapping their tails and opening their mouths as they lay on the marble slabs, and baby turtles, lobsters, prawns and crabs were all alive, waiting to be sold.

We passed the Central Police Station, a huge grey building built in 1864 which reminded us of Hong Kong's colonial heritage, and then we were in an area full of restaurants offering every type of international cuisine. We hopped onto the Central/Mid-levels escalator, the world's longest covered escalator at 800 metres long, linking the Central district with the Mid-level, half-way up to Victoria Peak. It takes 20 minutes to travel from one end to another, and there were 29 entry and exit points. We jumped off and walked downhill to Hollywood Road, where a traditional Chinese temple stands. There were many people there, some tourists but mostly Chinese people, and inside the air was thick with plumes of aromatic smoke from the incense sticks that are said to carry prayers to the spirit world. A bronze bell dated 1847 and Imperial sedan chairs made in 1862 again reflected this city's colonial historical roots.

Back in the intense heat of the day it was now 37°C, and we kept crossing to the shady side of the street for some respite from the wet heat. We walked along streets full of china shops, antiques, curios and collectibles. Many of the items in the windows were very expensive, but side streets had stalls set up on the steps of the hill, where smaller and less expensive souvenirs could be bought. We could see that Hong Kong was unfortunately not a cheap place to shop. Statues of Buddha, snuff and perfume bottles, carved jade, Chinese furniture and a host of other items covered the stalls and the steps along the street.

We entered Ko Shing Street, commonly known as Herbal Medicine Street, which is the wholesale centre of Hong Kong's thriving herbal medicine scene. Herbal tortoise jelly, deer antlers, dried giant sea-slugs and sea-worms were displayed beside dried seahorses, octopus, mushrooms, mussels, fish, animal's tongues, leaves and roots, animal skins and backbones. Incongruously a bowl of tiny dried rosebuds stood between the giant sea-slugs and sea-worms. As we passed air-conditioned shops the waft of cool air was very refreshing, and it was tempting to go inside just to cool off. We entered Wing Lok Street, commonly known as Gingseng and Bird's Nest Street because of the shops that have been established there for more than half a century.

We suddenly found ourselves back on the main road, the vehicles driving on the left and the skyscrapers shading the streets. Our necks ached as we looked up at the buildings, and an advert for Terminator 3 covered the whole side of a multi-storey building. As I looked up, a window suddenly opened in the middle of Arnold Schwarzenegger's body, and a face emerged at the open window! In one square, circles of people were holding hands and singing hymns (it was Sunday), and in a side street the singing was accompanied by tambourines. Although the majority of Hong Kong residents are Buddhist, there are also many Christians, both Protestant and Catholic. Hundreds of women sat in the shade of buildings and parks, all with table-cloths laid out for picnic lunches, but we found it strange to note that there were no men amongst them.

Eventually it was time for us to return to the coolness of our hotel to have a final shower before making our way back to the airport for our evening flight. We were flying with British Airways, and our worst fears were confirmed when we checked in.

'I think I'll weigh your bikes,' the girl said.

She was the first to do so, even though we had been on many flights since we had started our cycling trip. The bikes were still in boxes, though this was not required by British Airways, and Warren followed her to the outsize weighing machine where he attempted to surreptitiously lift the boxes with his foot to reduce the weight. Despite this, she announced that we had 43 kg excess baggage, and we had to pay 9,750 Hong Kong dollars. A few taps on my calculator showed this to be over £800! We couldn't believe it – it was more than the cost of the flight for one person. We begged, we argued, we tried to reason. In our previous flights only one other airline had ever charged us excess baggage, and that was only £33 by India Airlines. We pleaded, I cried, we made reasoned arguments, and the charge gradually reduced over the next 45 minutes. At £340 we realised we were not going to get the price reduced any further, so we had to pay up. The cost of our trip home had increased dramatically. Although we appreciate that we're lucky not to have incurred these costs before, we felt it ironical that it was a British flight that had charged us on our way home.

The flight was not as comfortable as the Australian Airline flight, despite the fact that, to try to placate us, the check-in girl had upgraded us to wider seats with more leg-room. (We felt, however, that we had paid for them!) Thirteen hours later we were relieved to arrive at Heathrow, and we stood waiting for our baggage to arrive on the carousel. The carousel had no luggage on it yet, but as it went round it was full of rubbish – large broken pieces of plastic, broken boxes, polythene bags, torn labels, pieces of cardboard, a plastic clothes hanger. I had never seen rubbish like this before in any airport in the world, and I wondered what our fellow Chinese passengers thought, especially as this was their first impression of England.

Once past customs I dashed to the ATM to stock up on English money. This was how we always collected the local currency when we arrived in a new country, so that we had money to pay for taxis, buses or trains into the city – a much easier way than cashing in travellers' cheques or changing currencies. The first machine was 'temporarily out of service', so I asked a security guard if there were more ATMs. I followed his directions and found two more ATMs side by side, one of which was unable to pay cash, and the other was out of service. Other people were also trying to get money, so we asked again and found that if we went to Departures there were two more machines. I left Warren with our trolleys, wondering what I would have done if I had been alone. Another girl accompanied me, but halfway there she gave up as it was such a long way; eventually I found two more ATMs. I couldn't believe it when I found that these two machines were also out of service. Several people hovered nearby holding their credit and debit cards and wondering where to get money. I pitied the foreigners arriving in England for the first time, discovering that they were unable to obtain English money.

I grumbled to an English couple standing alongside me. 'There are five ATMs in this terminal, and none of them are able to give me money. I've been travelling for 14 months in 10 different countries, and this is the first time I've been unable to get cash.'

'Welcome to England,' they said …

England

We had left Hong Kong on Sunday, 31st August, 2003 and arrived in England on Monday, 1st September. The next day we heard on the radio and television that Hong Kong was closing down awaiting a 100 mph typhoon. The stock market had closed and shops and schools had shut down, and a number of people in mainland China had already died as a result of the typhoon …

On our arrival at Heathrow from Hong Kong we were met by my brother, John. As he drove us from Heathrow airport towards Suffolk where he and my mother lived, we noticed that the fields were golden from recently harvested corn. The sun was shining and the sky was blue, although it was not the intense blue that we had become used to in Australia. England was still revelling in a long period of good weather, but the ultra-hot, humid weather of Hong Kong and Queensland had been replaced with pleasant summer days.

I told John I was starving, and he said that if I could wait a while we could go to a transport café that he knew in Suffolk. We agreed, as Warren and I love good transport cafés, and eventually John drew up outside a shack on a dual carriageway. Several large lorries stood outside. I led the way, and approached the girl behind the counter.

'Hello,' I said, smiling, waiting for the 'Hello, how are you?' and the general chit-chat that we had become used to in Australia. She was polite enough, but just took our order without any further chat. The food, however, was copious and beautifully-cooked – two sausages, two eggs, two lean pieces of bacon, tomatoes, mushrooms, a slice of fried bread and what appeared to be half a large tin of baked beans each – an 'Aussie brekky'! To accompany the meal were nine slices of bread and butter between the three of us, and a mug of tea each. Not bad for £3.95 each! With stomachs no longer rumbling, we drove on until we arrived at Needham Market, where my mother lived.

We stayed in Needham Market with my mother. It was lovely to see her after so long, and she was looking very well. Warren and I were both tired after the flights, so went to bed early, but strangely by 4am we were both wide awake, so we decided to get up. Mum was up as well, so we had the earliest breakfast ever, but by 10am it felt like late afternoon! The following day we were still feeling jet-lagged, but a few days of rest and some gardening in Mum's garden sorted us out.

After a few days we drove to Pinner in Middlesex, having borrowed a car from my brother's fleet of hire cars. In Pinner we stayed with Warren's youngest brother, Heath, and his wife, Corinne. Their son, Jake, had grown out of all recognition, having been only a few months old when we had left on our trip. The next day we travelled on to my home town of Reading, where we planned to stay with my son, Julian, and daughter-in-law, Lucy. Here I met my one year old grandson, Thomas, for the first time – he had been born in August while we were in Italy. We visited my elder daughter, Mandi, and her Australian husband, Mark. We discussed Tasmania at length, as this was Mark's home, and was also where Mandi and Mark had married a couple of years earlier. My grand-daughters, Charlie and Vikki, now aged 18 and 17, were even more grown up than when we had seen them last. We saw my younger daughter, Sarah, and her partner Kevin. They had moved since we had left England, so we were looking forward to seeing their new house just outside Reading. We heard about the plans that they had for it, and we envied them the rural position with the golden cornfield at the end of the long, mature garden. Sarah and Kevin's children, 11-year old Sam and 10-year old Liam, came home from school, and they had both grown tall since we had last seen them 15 months before.

We rushed from one venue to another, trying to visit as many friends and ex-work colleagues as possible, and caught up with the local news. We fitted in several rather unexciting appointments, such as dental check-ups, visits to the doctors to have booster jabs for Japanese Encephalitis and visits to the opticians to get new spectacles.

We travelled north to Durham, where Warren's family live. Here we stayed with Jean and Steven, Warren's parents, who had been looking after our affairs while we were away. We saw Blair and Tracy, Warren's brother and sister-in-law, and were amazed to see how their daughters, Taimar and Bryoni, had grown. We also saw Shane, another of Warren's brothers, with his new wife, Loui – they had recently returned from their honeymoon in Mexico and looked tanned and healthy.

Eventually we drove back to Needham Market to stay with my mother again, and Warren and I had to sort out everything before we left England again to fly to Tokyo. John had offered to take us to the airport, and we were keeping our fingers crossed that we wouldn't have to pay excess baggage again, although unfortunately we were already booked with British Airways to fly to Tokyo. We had whittled our gear down to the absolute minimum, leaving it with Mum, in the hope that if we were charged, it would not be as expensive as the last time. We felt bitter to discover on the internet that if we had been carrying golf clubs instead of bicycles, these would have been charged at 50% of the normal excess baggage rates. It certainly didn't seem fair.

The weather had been very kind to us throughout the month that we had spent in England, and Warren had managed to stay in shorts and sandals the whole time. It had been lovely to see family and friends again, but now we were itching to get back into our saddles. Yoko had promised to meet us at Tokyo airport. We were very much looking forward to visiting Japan.

CHAPTER 14

JAPAN

Located in the Pacific Ocean, Japan consists of a chain of thousands of islands over 3,000km long. Because of its length the climate varies greatly from north to south. There are four major islands, the main one being about the size of Great Britain. More than 80% of Japan is mountainous, but 75% of the 126,000,000 population live in a few very densely populated areas. The far northern and southern islands of Japan are very sparsely populated and have near wilderness scenery. Japan experiences many earthquakes, and there are over 40 active volcanoes throughout Japan.

Seasons follow the same pattern as in England, but there are big differences between north and south. Heavy snow can be falling in the north of Japan, while the south will have tropical sunshine. In winter there are huge snowfalls on the western side of Japan nearest to Siberia, and Tokyo has very cold average winter temperatures. In summer there is high humidity throughout most of Japan. The spring and autumn seasons are mild, rainfall is low and the climate pleasant. Japan is famous for the cherry blossom in spring and stunning autumnal colours in autumn.

It's extraordinary that Japan, in the middle of Asia and surrounded by China, Taiwan, Russia and south-east Asia, has such a successful economy, but this is due to the industriousness of the Japanese. Within 50 years Japan has changed from a defeated nation with a devastated economy to the world's largest creditor nation and a leader in technology – a very rich, important and powerful country.

On Monday, 29th September 2003, my brother gave us a lift back to Heathrow airport. It was early and we had over three hours before our flight, but already a queue snaked backwards and forwards between barriers for checking in. We asked a British Airways attendant what we should do with the bikes.

'Check in at number 61,' he said, pointing to a far distant counter.

It turned out to be the customer service section for British Airways, who promptly and efficiently checked in our bikes and bags, and phoned someone to get two seats allocated for us on the aircraft. We were through without any mention of excess baggage, and we hurried to the departures area quickly before they could change their minds. Each of us was carrying hand baggage weighing over 15 kg (a maximum of 7 kg is allowed, but hand baggage is rarely weighed), and we placed the bags on the conveyor belt to go through the x-ray machine. As always, the machine stopped and reversed a few times, so that the officer could look more closely at the strange shapes in our bags. The bags held pots and pans, heavy bicycle d–locks and pedals (removed from the bikes to reduce the weight of the bicycles in case they were weighed!), heavy guide books for Japan and South East Asia, toilet bags with shampoos, and anything else we could pack in to reduce the weight of the luggage put in the hold. Unlike most times we'd flown, they didn't want us to open and empty the bags, even though these items were clearly rather unusual as hand baggage, and we were allowed through security without any problems. We finally felt that we could breathe again, and went to have a coffee.

As we sat in the café I was fascinated to watch a man in a machine that lifted him high in the air outside the window, and lifted him close to the windscreen of the British Airways aeroplane parked very close to our building. He washed the windscreen with a rag on a stick, while another man in overalls sat in the pilot's seat pointing to the dirty bits of the window still needing cleaning. I smiled to myself, because it reminded me of the silly film 'Airplane', where a passenger noticed a man outside cleaning the windows during a flight.

An announcement came over the loudspeaker system for a final call to Mr and Mrs X, who needed to hurry to gate number 6 as the plane was waiting to depart. Five minutes later, another final call was announced for the same people, and another five minutes after that a final, final, final call was announced. Where do these people, who have obviously already checked in, disappear to? What are they doing? Where have they gone?

It is 9,500km (5,500 miles) to Tokyo from London. The plane left half an hour late, but the pilot assured us that he could make up the time, and that they had put extra fuel on board in order to do this. At 2.15pm we took off, and very shortly afterwards were flying over Windsor, with a superb aerial view of Windsor Castle. Then we were flying over the estuary of the Thames and out across the sea, and not long afterwards we were looking down over the tiny patchwork fields of northern Denmark, with its lakes and rivers. After crossing the sea again, we passed directly over Gothenburg in Sweden, and even though we were 31,000 feet up we could clearly see the massive roads curving through the forests; the plane's route took us over enormous lakes until we reached the east coast of Sweden. We travelled over Finland, north of Helsinki, and across northern Russia but at this point, after our first glimpse of Russia, clouds far below us obscured our view of the ground. The sun set as we flew high over Moscow.

We had a tiny bottle of wine each before our meal, and the stewardess offered us another bottle each to accompany our meal.

'Is one enough?' she asked us.

Warren, being polite, said 'Yes, thank you.'

I wasn't so polite, and said 'No', so we both got a second bottle. Looking around I saw that we were the only ones with two bottles each. Why had she asked us, I wondered? Did we look like we were desperate for a drink, or were we the only ones cheeky enough to say one wasn't enough?

We tried to sleep, but I failed miserably, and spent most of the night reading a book. The flight to Tokyo takes 11½ hours, so was due to arrive at 1.10am English time. However, the time in Tokyo would be 9.10am, so we were going to lose 8 hours – a whole night's sleep. In the dim light of the plane as most other passengers slept, I watched the television screen on the back of the seat in front of me, following the route we were taking. We crossed the western Siberian lowlands, and the outside temperature at 35,000 feet was an unbelievable minus 62°C. We travelled over the Paton and Aldan Plateaux and across Siberia as the plane headed towards Tokyo. As the sun rose, we saw lakes way below us on the plateaux. The Siberian landscape was bleak and flat, and the lakes had long 'fingers' of water spreading from the central lakes. These 'fingers' were feather-shaped, water spreading into the hollows of the bleak landscape. As the sun rose we passed over bleak, grey mountains as far as the eye could see. The rising sun cast sharp black shadows on the western side of the mountains, making a very lunar-like landscape. This type of landscape continued for an hour of the flight, and occasionally I could see clouds lying at the bottom of valleys. There were no roads, no sign of houses or habitation and no trees.

Suddenly a coast-line appeared; we crossed the Sea of Japan, and shortly afterwards the islands of Japan appeared below us. Some islands were wooded, some were hilly or mountainous, and on some islands we could see rivers and houses surrounded by small patchwork fields. The plane reached the east coast of Japan and we could see Tokyo below us, and there beyond it the majestic sight of Mount Fuji. A few minutes later we had landed in Tokyo.

We had previously met Yoko when she lived for six months in England; she was waiting for us, and quickly whisked us away in her car. The temperature was 25°C, and it was a beautiful sunny day. Tokyo airport is 60 kilometres from the city, so we were lucky to have her help. We passed Tokyo Disneyland and saw Mount Fuji again in the distance from the main highway. We arrived at Yoko's house, which has the same typical Japanese or Scandinavian look that has become so desirable in England. There were pale wooden floors, a glass sloping roof covered with thin bamboo blinds, and rooms divided with wood-framed sliding walls lined with paper. A spiral staircase went up to a bedroom area, with windows looking onto the living area below as well as to the outside.

We were shown how to work the television; it was amazing, because if a film or the news had 'sub-voices', a press of the button on the remote control changed the voices from Japanese to English, which was really useful for us! The washing machine was also very different from what we had been used to – it took only a few minutes to wash and spin clothes, having automatically weighed the clothes and filled the machine with sufficient water for that amount. If necessary, just one item of clothing could be economically washed – something that European washing machine manufacturers should perhaps investigate.

We were incredibly tired from our journey, and Yoko suggested that we had a bath before resting. Japanese baths are shorter than English ones, but very deep (about thigh-high), and the surrounding area in the bathroom is always tiled, with gutters edging the whole of the bathroom. Sitting on a tiny plastic stool we first washed ourselves with soap and then had a shower. Once showered, we climbed into the clean bath water, which remained clean for the next person. Yoko and Nobuho had a 'talking' bath which we found fascinating. It simply needed a button to be pressed in the bathroom or in the kitchen, and the bath would automatically fill with water of the chosen pre-set temperature. When the bath was full, a little tune sang out in the living area, and a voice announced that the bath was ready! The water was level with the top of the bath, so that when I got into the bath, water gushed over the edge in all directions, but Yoko assured me that this was no problem – the bathroom was designed to have water pouring all over it. It was a very relaxing bath, and a thermostatic control ensured that the temperature of the water remained constant – the water was very hot and the level of the water came almost up to my shoulders sitting upright.

The Japanese toilets also fascinated us. They were never located in the same room as the bath as this would be considered dirty, but they looked very similar to a modern English toilet. However, the top of the ceramic cistern behind the toilet on the wall was shaped like a washbasin and had an open plug-hole; a curved pipe with a spout pointed down over the plug-hole which fed into the cistern. When the toilet was flushed, the water ran out of this 'tap' so that there was fresh water to wash hands, and the used water ran into the cistern to fill it up. We felt that such a space-saving toilet and wash-basin would be useful in the small rooms of modern English houses, but it was also water-saving – ideal for those of us who live in areas of England that constantly have hosepipe bans and requests to save water! When the light was switched on, the fan came on in the toilet, which doesn't sound unusual. However, I suspected that the fan was also activated by sitting on the toilet, and I tested and confirmed this by creeping into the toilet with the light off one day! Most Japanese toilet seats were also heated. Yoko's toilet could also be converted to a bidet by switches alongside the toilet, another space-saving idea.

We felt groggy, jet-lagged and tired, and had an early night, and after a delicious Japanese breakfast of soup, rice and salad the next morning, we went with Yoko to the nearby city centre by bus, and caught a train to Tokyo. This is when we discovered that virtually everyone in Japan falls asleep in trains, buses or anywhere that they sit for a few minutes, such as in a queue. We thought it was probably because the Japanese work so hard that when they sit down they fall asleep! Yoko was on her way to work, but had arranged for us to meet her brother-in-law, Kunito, who was to show us around Tokyo that day.

Kunito was an excellent guide – we went with him to a museum, and next to it was the Sumo wrestling stadium (pronounced 'smo' in Japanese). We could see that something exciting was happening, because there were so many people around, and several enormous sumo wrestlers in what looked like dressing gowns were going in and out on bicycles. Bearing in mind the size of the wrestlers, I felt sorry for the bicycles! It appeared that, although the sumo wrestling didn't normally take place during October, for that day only there was a charity match. Tickets are notoriously difficult to buy, people booking them weeks ahead, and they are also very expensive. We were therefore unbelievably lucky that a lady was trying to sell three tickets that she no longer needed, and only wanted 1,000 yen (pronounced 'en') each for the 5,000 yen tickets, which was the equivalent of nearly £30 each.

When we walked into the sumo wrestling stadium, we saw that the whole area around the wrestling ring (the dohyo) was tiered, so that each tier was one step higher than the tier in front. Each tier was divided by low railings into areas big enough for four people, and four large cushions were arranged on the floor. Because of this layout, everyone had a good view. Most people were sitting on the cushions eating their lunch from plastic containers whilst waiting for the wrestling to start, and a Japanese group played music on traditional Japanese instruments.

The basic rules of sumo are simple: the wrestler who first touches the floor with something other than the sole of his foot or leaves the 15 feet diameter ring before his opponent, loses. The fights themselves usually last only a few seconds and in rare cases up to one minute.

The most fascinating thing is the wrestler's gigantic size, and the reason for this is based on a scientific principle – the heavier the fighter, the lower his centre of gravity and therefore the more difficult it is for a rival to force him out of the ring. To ensure this, the wrestler has an elaborate rice-based diet. For breakfast, he is served chanko – a fat-rich stew comprising pork, eggs, cabbage and bean sprouts. After training, he has lunch followed by a nap. This is followed by dinner. This process is based on the principle that heavy eating followed by sleep results in weight gain, so the champions can weigh over 250 kg (more than 40 stone)!

Though the wrestlers look obese, they are incredibly strong. They wear only a wide belt with a strip between their legs which can be grasped by the opponent and used to lever their opponent out of the ring.

There are 70 ways of beating an opponent listed by the Sumo Association, including such common ones as *uwatenage* (over-arm throw) and *shitatenage* (under-arm throw), but few methods of attack are banned. Wrestlers are allowed to trip or slap with an open hand, but eye-gouging, hair-pulling and hitting with a closed fist are not permitted and would result in forfeiting the bout.

A sumo wrestling match is accompanied by a lot of traditional ceremony. The marching-in of the wrestlers was in itself a formal ritual, each wrestler being accompanied by two assistants, one walking in front and the other behind. The referee was clad in a magnificent kimono and wore a strange black hat which was tied under the chin. After performing a series of opening rituals, the contest began as the two sumo wrestlers walked into the ring, eyeing up each other as they stood with their massive bodies leaning forward, stamping their feet and throwing handfuls of salt into the sandy ring to cleanse it. The wrestling ring was a raised clay platform with rope half buried in the clay to outline the ring.

Eventually the wrestlers flew at each other and after a few seconds one was pushed over the rope circle. This procedure continued with 16 wrestlers fighting each other until the final knockout, when an amateur was pronounced the winner, much to the delight of the audience. After the knockout, we enjoyed the spectacle of five tiny sumo wrestlers no older than 5 years old, together trying to push over an enormous professional. Everyone laughed to watch this spectacle, because he appeared to be immoveable, but he finally allowed himself to be pushed over the rope, despite the fact that he had previously pushed each child to one side with the gentle push of a hand. So the children won, and the audience clapped enthusiastically.

More sight-seeing ensued after a lovely lunch, when Michiyo, Kunito's wife, joined us, and after a perfect day we went back to Yoko's home with them, where Yoko prepared for us a wonderful Japanese meal. There was a selection of raw fish – octopus, sea bream, tuna and salmon eggs. We took sheets of seaweed paper (nori) and, with our chopsticks, placed sticky rice and pickles on the nori with a piece of raw fish and a little wasabi (hot, green horseradish paste). This was like a home-made sushi, which we dipped into a mixture of soy sauce and lemon juice, and ate with dishes of salad. It was delicious, and although we know that to most English people the thought of raw fish is distasteful, we thought that most people would enjoy it if they tried it. Obviously it is very important that the fish is very fresh and of good quality, and Japanese housewives are very particular in ensuring this. Warren's favourite was sea bream, and mine was tuna and salmon, but back home I had always enjoyed smoked salmon which is, of course, raw fish.

The cost of living in Japan is very high, with house prices even higher than in the south of England. However, we found that some things, such as technology, electrical goods, cars, cameras and films were much cheaper than in England. Eating out was also expensive, as were hotels and guesthouses. One very surprising thing, however, was that despite the very advanced technology in Japan, the Japanese pay for virtually everything by cash, and therefore always carry large amounts of cash. We felt that this was quite dangerous, but crime was apparently very low in Japan. The ATMs in Japan, apart from a few in the major cities, did not accept international credit or debit cards, which was a considerable problem for us. Outside Tokyo and major cities even very large shops, supermarkets and hotels did not accept credit cards for payment of goods. The other problem for us was the lack of internet cafés, though the reason for this was probably because most Japanese people had a computer of their own at home.

Yoko was very good to us in those first days before we set off on our bicycles, making different meals every day so that we would know what to expect, know how to eat the food, and what the food tasted like. She told us that it was possible to buy reasonably priced food at a ramen restaurant, which sold noodle dishes, and that a set meal was likely to cost about £5; she pointed out such restaurants to us so that we would know what to look for. The set meal at a ramen restaurant consisted of an enormous bowl of soup with a bowl of rice mixed with mushrooms or other vegetables, accompanied by a small plate of tempura, stuffed dumplings or something similar with soy sauce for dipping. Japanese pickles always accompany meals, pickled radish being the most common, but also plums and sometimes pickled baby artichoke buds, which Warren and I particularly loved.

Evening meals at Yoko's house were often cooked at the table, a very popular way of eating in Japan. One day on the table was a special cooker with a teflon-covered top with round indents about 1½ inches across. This cooker made a meal called Takoyaki – Yoko poured a batter mixture into the indents on top of pieces of shrimp, octopus and onion, and as the batter cooked, each one was turned round to form a perfect ball enclosing the fish. The balls were picked up with chopsticks and dipped into sauce before eating. Salads and bowls of rice accompanied the meal.

Every Japanese house had an electric rice cooker, and Yoko told us the story of when she went to Italy to visit friends. Her friends asked her if she would bring them an electric rice cooker, and she filled it with packets of rice and various powdered foods. When she reached Italy, customs wanted to know what it was, but when they saw the cooker's round shape and the powder inside it, they were convinced it was a bomb. They marched Yoko off to a side room, holding her by the arms. They analysed some of the powders and only then were they convinced that the machine, with its timer and powders inside, was actually for cooking!

Another meal that Yoko and Nobuho cooked at the table was Sukiyaki, where thin slices of beef and vegetables such as Chinese leaves, leeks, leaves that looked like camomile and many different types of mushrooms were cooked in a mixture of soy sauce, sake (Japanese rice wine) and water. As each piece cooked, we could pick out the pieces of food with our chopsticks, and dip them into individual bowls of raw egg before eating. Again, many dishes accompanied the delicious meal.

Two days later Su, Yoko and Nobuho's daughter, took us to Tokyo for more sight-seeing. We wanted to see a market, and she took us to an enormous market which was frequented by both Japanese and foreign tourists. In the market, girls in traditional Japanese kimonos were selling green tea; stalls were selling doll-shaped cakes, souvenirs, gifts, parasols and dolls in Japanese costume. A beautiful old temple with curved roofs stood at the end of the market, with a pagoda of many tiers standing alongside it. Su suggested we buy our fortunes, something that is very popular with the Japanese. We pulled a chopstick out of a drum which gave us a number. A chest of tiny drawers stood alongside, and we opened the drawer with the corresponding number. Inside was a pile of identical sheets of paper. Warren and I chose fortunes that were good, but Su's was bad fortune – traditionally this should not be kept or taken home, so Su folded the paper into a strip and tied it onto the branch of a tree with hundreds of others.

My fortune had an asterisk to indicate different types of good fortune that I might have; the Japanese words had also been translated into English. It said '★Any request will be granted you. ★The patient get well soon. ★The lost article will be found. ★The person you wait for appears. ★Build a new house and removal are both well. ★You can start a trip. ★Marriage of any kind, new employment are both well.' Every situation was therefore covered!

Su took us on a train to a fascinating street with wholesale shops selling everything for restaurants. There were uniform shops selling chefs' and waitresses' uniforms, and shops selling display cabinets, baskets, dried flowers, unusual china and earthenware, pots and pans of every size, specialised cooking equipment, restaurant tables with holes, into which specialised cooking stoves could be inserted for customers to cook their own meals, sieves from miniature size up to dustbin lid size, kitchen tools, chairs for restaurants, Chinese bamboo steamers and every type of barbecue. Shops sold stainless steel containers for soup for 1,000 people, moulds and cutters, cutlery and chefs' knives, Chinese and Japanese teapots of all sizes, signs and menus, lanterns, waiters' bill-pads, glasses, lit-up neon signs and painted signs, plastic containers, exquisite lacquer-ware for expensive restaurants, cushions and curtains, electric rice cookers and other electric equipment and, finally, every type of Japanese meal depicted in plastic on plastic plates – we'd seen these plastic meals on display outside the restaurants in the city, so it was interesting to see that the plastic version was much more expensive than the real food! We visited a Tokyo museum to see stunning displays of antique porcelain, fabrics, paintings, drawings, prints and carvings, and as darkness fell we took photos of the streets ablaze with neon lights and advertising signs. We returned home to Yoko's tired and happy.

Yoko and Nobuho wanted to take us to Nikko for the weekend. Nikko is famous in Japan for its spectacular shrines and temples, and we were to stay nearby in the mountains. We drove along the highway; Nobuho's car, like most in Japan, had a satellite navigational system, but at £250 the price was a fraction of the £1,500 that a 'satnav' system cost at that time in England. When reversing his car, there was no need for Nobuho to look round – the satnav screen showed the road behind via a camera on the back of the car. Travelling is very expensive on the highways in Japan, and vehicles frequently have to stop at toll booths to pay to use the road.

As we drove, we noticed that there were many nets set up on tall scaffolding almost the height of electric pylons. These were surrounding the golf ranges, golf being very popular in Japan. There were fields of golden grass growing – this was Japanese rice; not the bright, light green of Indian paddy fields, but very gold, although we understood that in the south of Japan they also grow the green variety. The television had told us that it was 27 °C that day in the south of Japan, although it was only 17°C in the north.

We stopped in a pretty village at a sushi restaurant for lunch, where we sat on cushions on the floor at low tables. Yoko and Nobuho treated us to a superb meal – we had very special sushi and tempura meals, beautifully cooked and stunningly presented. The sushi meals had raw fish, prawns and tofu on rice parcels with hot, fiery wasabi, and the tempura was a selection of aubergine, seaweed, chillis, peppers and asparagus fried in light crispy batter with soy dipping sauce and Japanese pickles.

We drove up a mountainous road with s-bends, and arrived at the Nikko Toshigo shrine, which is a famous warrior's tomb. The ancient buildings were very colourful, often rust red with gold, green and blue, and were intricately carved and gold-leaved. Lovely dark grey curving roofs, made of copper which had darkened with age, were trimmed on the edges with gold with the clover leaf shape of the emblem of the famous warrior. We had to wash our hands with water from bamboo ladles before entering the temple. The buildings were exotic and impressive beyond belief, and were built above and behind each other so that we were surrounded by beautiful roofs towering around us. The roofs overhung the buildings, and the underside was often painted red. Everything was very ornate, and stunning carvings of birds, flowers and people adorned these magnificent buildings. There were crowds of people, almost all Japanese, and we were surprised and delighted to see a traditional Buddhist wedding in progress in one of the small temples. One 17th century building was built only of wood, and had ancient carvings of animals above the doors and windows. Above the door were carved the three wise monkeys (see no evil; hear no evil; speak no evil), which I immediately recognised – a small brass statue of the three wise monkeys had stood on the mantelpiece when I was a child, and it had always fascinated me. I was surprised to discover that this very carving above the door was the one that had popularised the proverb.

We returned to the car and began driving back down the mountain and slowly round the s-bends, when we noticed monkeys sitting on and underneath the barriers at the side of the road. These were Japanese macaques, which are unique to Japan.

We drove through long tunnels cut into the mountains, and I couldn't help but think how awful it would be if there were earth tremors whilst we were inside the tunnels – there had been an earthquake the week before. We stopped to admire a massive waterfall on our way to Kinugawa, where we stayed in a small apartment overlooking a river flowing within a gorge. In the restaurant attached to the apartments, Yoko and Nobuho bought us a fabulous meal of six courses, every course so beautifully presented that we felt we had to take photographs of the food before we ate it!

We later went to the communal bath area. In the cities these baths are apparently mixed, but in most of the country areas there are separate bath areas for men and for women, and everyone bathes naked after showering clean first. There were many different pools – hot, hotter and unbelievably hot, a jacuzzi, an outdoor hot spring pool in the rocks (this area had natural hot springs), a sauna, a steam room and a cold plunge pool. It took a few seconds to acclimatise to the intense heat of the pools and, despite my tanned skin, I looked like a boiled lobster when I got out. The steam room was delicious once I got over the initial shock of walking into a room where steam jetted out of holes in the ceiling; lying naked on a stone sun-lounger, the steam condensed on my skin and ran in cool rivulets down my body. Another pool was just deep enough to lie flat covered with the water, with a stone pillow for my head and a jet of water pummelling on the bottom of each foot – what bliss! Afterwards a shower, using soap, shampoos and conditioner supplied, and into another room where mirrors, hairdryers, body lotions, weighing machines and comfortable chairs ensured a relaxing finish to the Japanese bathing experience. Warren told me afterwards that he had lain for a long time in the outdoor pool, trying to plan how he would build one for us in the garden when we returned home!

We stayed at Yoko's and Nobuho's house for a further two days before setting off cycling. Yoko had persuaded us to change our flight to Bangkok from 30th

October to 5th November, so that she could take us with her for several days to the north of Japan, where she was going to attend a wedding. This would not only be a wonderful opportunity to see another part of Japan, but also a great experience to see a Japanese wedding, so we had agreed to her suggestion, and planned to return to her house after two weeks of cycling.

Yoko and Nobuho were very concerned about us cycling, and Yoko frequently told us to come back at any time if things went wrong, and to telephone her if we had an accident. We were concerned ourselves, though we didn't want to admit this to them, and also after a week of staying with Yoko and Nobuho we had become comfortable. We hadn't cycled now for six weeks, so it was time to start again.

We went to an internet café to e-mail our family and friends before we left. The internet café was going to charge us double, because Warren was standing behind me as I typed on the computer, so he had to go and stand outside until I'd finished. This proved to be standard procedure in Japan, and we found it very strange that they wanted to charge for two people, even though one wasn't using a computer.

Afterwards we went to buy a coffee and, because I always kept a record of what we spent, I wrote the amounts down immediately. We had discovered that it was impossible to understand the receipts at the end of the day – not only could we not read the Japanese script, so didn't know which shop each related to, but the date was written very differently. Today was the 7th October 2003, but the Japanese wrote it as 15-10-07, 15 being the Japanese year since the last emperor's ascension.

★ ★ ★

We eventually set off cycling, having decided to travel east to the coast and then north. Yoko and Nobuho had recommended cycling south to Kyoto, which is a very famous city popular with tourists and with many beautiful things to see. However, Kyoto was 600km (400 miles) along very busy roads, and we knew we wouldn't have enjoyed cycling along roads with so much traffic. We were a little nervous – more so than in any other country, because very few signs are in English, and the Japanese written language is actually a combination of three different scripts – kanji, hiragana and katakana. This was a concern for us in finding our way, finding food and also finding accommodation. Yoko had written a letter in Japanese for us to show someone if we were unable to communicate when we wanted to find bed and breakfast accommodation, but we had a Japanese phrase book and were determined to do our best to learn a few Japanese words.

The sky was very grey as we set off, and it was cool. We would be travelling through busy built-up areas for some time, as we were still within the suburbs of Tokyo. The beautiful ornamental conifer trees in gardens with their gnarled branches were being trimmed into perfect shape by gardeners, so that each branch held a perfect cushion of leaves or pine needles at its end. Men stood on ladders and on platforms on hydraulic arms on the backs of trucks, cutting the branches with hand secateurs. The deciduous trees were just beginning to show their autumn colours, so we hoped that before we left Japan we would see the full splendour of autumn colours. We passed forests of bamboo at the side of the road, 20 to 30 feet high, with such thick feathery plumes of leaves on the tops of the bamboo that the canes bent over the road with the weight.

We came to two major highways, one above the other, both closed in on each side with walls that curved inwards at the top to reduce the noise for the people living nearby. The walls on the lower road stopped at junctions so that the vehicles could turn left or right at the traffic lights, but only windows were in the expressway above, and through the windows we could see vehicles speeding across the junctions. Drivers had to pay to use this faster road. Fortunately a service road also ran alongside this double-decker highway, and we cycled along the pavement out of the way of traffic, as this was allowed in Japan.

We passed a temple with an old Buddhist cemetery surrounding it, and stopped to admire the beautiful gardens, temple and well-kept graves. The wooden-framed Buddhist temple had a handsome green copper roof which curved outwards. Statues of Buddha, large ornamental stone lanterns and flowers stood on the gravestones, and the cemetery, with its ancient gnarled trees, was a beautiful, peaceful place. We noticed 6 feet tall lengths of wood like giant ice lolly sticks with beautiful Japanese script written on them, stacked in special wooden frames by each gravestone. Some were clearly very old, but some were new. We discovered that these were called toba (or sotoba if they were made from stone), and were funerary slats with sacred text. The beautiful script on them was inscribed by the priest with the deceased's name and the name of the person requesting the toba and, through the act of placing the toba on the gravestone, the deceased would attain Buddhahood and the person requesting the toba would secure a long life. The toba was placed on the gravestone at the anniversaries of the deceased's death.

Most days we went into one of the many 7-Eleven or Spar shops to buy food for lunch, and noticed that most of the shelves and fridges were stacked with ready to eat food, some needing only to be microwaved, but others ready to eat cold. The shops heated the food free of charge, and people sat in their cars outside eating their lunch. Machines selling hot and cold drinks stood outside the shop.

The cycling was very slow, because the surface of the pavements was not always good. We frequently had to cross busy roads waiting for pedestrian traffic lights to change to green, and sometimes the width of the pavement was reduced by trees, telegraph poles or plants. However, at least we were safe from the busy traffic by cycling on the path.

We stopped when we saw a Shell sign to buy half a litre of petrol for our cooking stove, in case we found a campsite. The two young lads in red uniform and caps knew two words of English.

'Regular,' said one, when Warren pointed to the green nozzle, and they waved and shouted 'Goodbye,' to us as we left.

'What a delightful experience,' said Warren, as we cycled off. 'If only buying petrol was always so pleasant.' They had been cheerful and laughing as they served us, and incredibly polite, as always in Japan.

We passed waste ground covered with golden rod, its yellow spires of flowers 6 to 8 feet tall, and I saw a shop with the most stunning orchids I'd ever seen, even better than in the floating orchid nurseries in Myanmar.

We lost our way every time we had to cross a river, because the service road ended and we had to find access to the main road above us. At one point we asked two workmen on the other side of a tall wire fence if they could help us – there was no other person in sight. They spoke no English, but pored over our map through the fence for ages. I noticed that the younger one, with his smooth face but new, wispy beard growing only on his chin, had very strange shoes with rubber soles and canvas tops. I had seen identical shoes in a stone-mining museum in Japan, and had been fascinated by the fact that the shoes were divided to give the big toe a space of its own, like the finger of a glove. I hadn't realised that modern workmen wore them, and as the older man moved, I noticed that he wore identical shoes. They gave the impression of cloven hoofs on a human being, and I found it difficult to take my eyes off them, but we saw many more on our travels in Japan. Eventually, being unable to work out which road we should take, the workmen unlocked a gate in the fence, beckoned us through onto their land, through another locked gate which led directly onto a freeway, and stood waving and bowing as we cycled on our way.

It was getting late, so we now had to look for a guesthouse for the first time, and we looked up the word in our dictionary. We stopped at a restaurant to ask – no-one spoke English, but all were very eager to help us, and we eventually understood that there were no hotels ahead of us for 20km, so we should go back 3km to a hotel by the railway station. The restaurant employees came outside and stood waving goodbye to us, after drawing a map to guide us to the hotel. However, within a few hundred yards I saw the English word 'hotel' on a signpost, and we wondered why we had not been directed to this hotel. We followed the sign. Outside the hotel the price of a room was written as 3,850 and 5,250 yen, which sounded very cheap for Japan, so we cycled into the car park which was hidden from the road. The entrance to the car park was covered with a half-length curtain of plastic strips. However, before Warren could go into reception, a woman appeared from the side of the building and called out to us. We couldn't understand what she was saying, but asked her how much a room was. She kept pointing at her watch and saying something in Japanese, and appeared to be trying to stop us going into the hotel. After a while she indicated that she would get someone else to help us. She disappeared round the corner of the building, so Warren decided to go into the reception. As he came out again, the woman reappeared with a man, and she had written prices on a piece of paper. The penny suddenly dropped – I had read about 'Love Hotels' in the guide books for Japan – rooms were hired out for three hours at a time for customers to have a 'rest'. The price for a room in this hotel was 3,850 yen (about £22) but was for three hours only. Love hotels are available after 10pm for overnight guests at a more reasonable rate, but we had no intention of cycling after dark. The couple, who we assumed were caretakers, drew a map giving directions to the Business Hotel at the station, and as we cycled off Warren described the strange reception area of the hotel; there were no people on view and payment for a room was made anonymously through a slot in a darkened kiosk. Photos of different styles of rooms with rotating beds, strange lighting, ceiling mirrors, dungeon-styled rooms and S&M gear were on view for different customers' tastes, and shelves of blue movies stood alongside the kiosk. This tallied with the guide books' description of Love Hotels.

Business Hotels are very respectable, are designed for businessmen who travel and are usually next to the railway station. At 9,975 yen (£57) it was far more than we were used to paying; indeed, it was the most we had ever paid on this trip, but we were tired and hungry. The room was incredibly small but clean and neat, and in a cupboard under the tiny bedside table I found a folding hairdryer, kettle and hotplate, a tray with cups and green tea bags, and a folding reading lamp, each on a different shelf. The bathroom was the smallest I'd ever seen, apart from in a caravan! It was 5 feet by 3 feet, and made entirely of moulded plastic, with the bath and washbasin formed together side-by-side. The bath was thigh-high, but only 3 feet long and narrowing to a wedge shape. Under the basin were holders for a toilet roll and miniature waste bin. The door opened outwards – there was no room for it to open inwards.

When we walked around the town later looking for a restaurant to have our evening meal we saw several more hotels, but each of these showed the price for a three hour 'rest', so there were clearly more Love Hotels in Japan than business hotels.

We liked the idea of the sushi restaurants, where we could sit in the middle of the room while a conveyor belt passed by us with different dishes set out on it. Any dishes eaten were paid for on the way out. However, sushi restaurants are quite expensive, and on this occasion we needed to find somewhere cheaper – the cost of our hotel was more than our usual budget for the whole day. In most of the restaurants even the prices were in Japanese script, so we had no idea of the meals or the prices, so when we found a restaurant which had pictures of meals outside, we decided that it would be safest for our first meal on our own to simply point to a picture! The owner greeted us very excitedly with a lot of bowing, and when he saw us later in a supermarket in the town he acknowledged us with a great deal of laughing and more bowing.

Back at the room afterwards I read parts of 'The Teaching of Buddha' which sat on a shelf – this was obviously the equivalent of our Gideon Bible, and it was in English as well as Japanese. It was interesting to see that Buddhism teaches kindness to others at all times, and had many parables comparable to those in the Christian Bible.

The following day, after falling over each other in the tiny room trying to get ready to leave, we went to the ticket office of the station to enquire about the cost of travelling with our bikes on a train if we decided to cycle one way and travel back to Yoko's house by train. By doing this we could travel further north. We awaited our turn, having pulled ticket number 65 from the machine. Three men sat on seats side by side, each fast asleep with a ticket in his hand. One of them constantly swayed dangerously sideways, and I was convinced he would fall to the floor, but each time he was able to right himself without ever opening his eyes. We were surprised to hear the sound of crickets, and noticed a cage of enormous crickets in the corner of the ticket office. We were concerned that we wouldn't know when our number was due, because the numbers were obviously being called out in Japanese. However, peeping over the shoulder of the man being served, we knew that number 62 was next. Three more numbers were called, with no response from any of the slumbering men on the seat, so our turn came quickly. The railway official spoke no English, and we had considerable problems trying to understand the answers to our questions, but we were finally disappointed to realise that the train journey back to that station would involve complicated changing of trains, and also that our bikes would need to be dismantled and packed into bags – definitely too much of a problem for us.

It was warmer as we cycled out of the town, but the wind was against us. The road was very busy with narrow pavements which disappeared at times, but the scenery became more rural as we travelled. There were many nashi (or Asian) pear orchards in one area that we passed, and warehouse-like shops lined the streets displaying perfect golden apple-shaped nashi pears. We stopped to buy some, and were immediately shown to seats at a table by a constantly bowing lady, who peeled and cored a golden-skinned pear and cut wedges of the pure white crispy flesh for us to taste. They were far crisper, juicier and more delicious than those I'd ever bought in England, and we decided to buy only one, as they were so enormous. However, we noticed that they were only selling in bulk – to one side were piles of 10 kg boxes of perfect fruits, each individual enormous pear encircled with special protective wrapping. We indicated to the lady that we only wanted one, and she showed us a bag of five pears for 500 yen (less than £3). Eventually we were able to make her understand that we couldn't carry so many, so she chose one especially enormous pear the size of a small melon, put it into a bag and gave it to us with a bow.

We bowed in return. 'Ariegato,' (thank you) we said, when she indicated that she didn't want any money, and she stood at the edge of the road to wave goodbye to us.

We passed more nasha pear orchards; the branches were trained to spread like a roof about five feet high, so the pears could easily be picked from below, and the tops of the trees were protected with nets. We also saw persimmon trees bearing the fruits that are often called 'Sharon fruit' in England. These apple-shaped fruits, very popular in Japan, are bright orange when ripe, and have a large flat calyx. Again, the fruits are peeled and sliced for serving, but the flesh is quite dark in colour.

We stopped to use the toilets in a service station, and as always they were beautifully clean and very modern, with heated seats which were bliss on a cold day! The hot air dryers were so fierce that they actually dried our hands, unlike most English versions. The man in charge of the service station chatted to us in Japanese, and we were able to explain, with the aid of maps and our phrase book, where we had cycled. His eyebrows shot up, and he was clearly impressed, and once again we had someone standing on the pavement to wave us goodbye until we were out of sight.

Japan is criss-crossed with electricity pylons, and the towns and roads are a mass of very large cables hanging along and across the streets. Even in the country, we saw pylons joined with cables marching up and over the wooded mountains, and we assumed that the lack of cables underground might be because of the constant danger of earthquakes in Japan, and repairs could be more easily made if cables are kept above ground.

In Japan the lorries were very small, even smaller than in England, which seemed strange after the enormous trucks of Australia. Japan and England, both being relatively small islands, have similar problems with congestion and space. It was fascinating to see in the towns that the taxis had automatically opening car doors, so that when a passenger approached, the door opened without the driver needing to get out of the car.

We passed blocks of flats where every balcony was covered with washing, and quilts hung over the balconies reminding us of duvets hanging on the balconies in Holland. We passed fields of cosmos, a mass of red, pink and white flowers topping pretty green feathery leaves. The area in which we were cycling was now semi-rural, though there was still a lot of traffic, and the railway ran alongside us. There were many new houses built in that area in the Japanese traditional style; they had exquisitely-designed gardens with small Japanese pine trees, large rocks and tall stone lanterns. Some gardens were full of stone benches which held displays of bonsai trees in shallow earthenware dishes, their gnarled trunks and branches making the trees look ancient, but none of them more than a few inches high.

We began to look for a hotel again, but apart from the love hotels in the towns, the word 'hotel' is seldom written in English except in the tourist areas. We memorised the Japanese script for hotel – a three-legged stool with a stick on top; a small capital 'J' with a horizontal line above, and a Roman IV leaning on its side. We asked several people for help, and eventually we found a hotel in a side street. We removed our shoes at the door, and sat to discuss the price of a room. My nose was running, but I knew that a Japanese person would rather sniff all day than be seen blowing his nose into a handkerchief – this is something to be done in private – so I sniffed until I got to the privacy of our room so that I didn't offend the hotel owner. Again we had to pay over £50 for the room for a night. As we were led to our room we noticed lovely Japanese-style rooms off the corridor, but our room was western, which was disappointing. However, our inability to speak any of the language made it impossible for us to ask for a different room. A kettle, cups, teabags and oranges sat on the table. As always, Japanese yukatas (kimono-style dressing gowns) were laid out on the beds, and the television had a slot-machine for coins. On closer inspection we discovered that the back of the slot machine was open, so the 100 yen coin could be constantly re-used! On the bedside table stood a pile of magazines and books full of comic-strip stories, with many pages full of photos of naked women, and for a moment we wondered if we had come to the right sort of hotel . . .

We felt we were very brave that evening, as we searched for a noodles restaurant with no pictures and no English writing. We knew from Yoko's training that a short, dark red curtain hanging above the door of a restaurant indicated a noodle restaurant, which would offer noodle dishes at very reasonable prices. We found such a restaurant and went in.

'Ni ramen,' we said (two noodles), repeating the words that Yoko had taught us.

Sure enough, they understood what we wanted, and the meal was put in front of us within a few minutes. The standard noodle dish is a large bowl with about one litre of clear broth flavoured with misu (sometimes called miso). Misu is a fermented paste made from soya beans and rice, barley or rye, and is used frequently in Japanese cooking, mostly for soup but also in dressings and sauces, or to flavour pickles and grilled food. The soup is full of noodles and vegetables, such as bean sprouts, bamboo shoots, carrots and cabbage, with a slice of tender lean pork floating on the top.

We ate the noodles and vegetables with our chopsticks, slurping loudly in the Japanese manner to show our appreciation of the meal, and drank the broth from the bowl. If we were still hungry we could have asked for tempura (battered pieces of fish, vegetables or meat) or gyoza (the same in a dumpling-like thin pastry which is steamed or fried). Both are served with a soy dipping sauce, and both are delicious.

On our way out of the hotel the next morning, I realised why so many Japanese people shuffle in their mule-style slippers. The slippers supplied are usually too big and would fall off if the feet were raised higher! The owner of the hotel had indicated that we put on a pair of the emerald green plastic slippers as we removed our shoes at the front door. The slippers in every hotel are the same – one size and no left and right, so the slippers were sliding off my feet as I walked, especially as I was wearing socks because it was quite cold that morning. Walking down the two flights of stairs carrying my bike panniers, I nearly fell twice when the slippers fell off my feet and down the stairs. I would have much preferred to have been barefoot, which would have been less dangerous, but I didn't dare remove the slippers for fear of offending the hotel guests.

We went to MacDonald's for breakfast. It was so sad of us, but it was a quick, convenient, cheap and filling meal, and we understood what we were going to get, having asked for a 'sausage egg McMuffin'! MacDonald's in Japan do excellent coffee, with free refills, so we were quite content. At £2.20 each it seemed good value, especially as sometimes in Japan we had paid the same amount for coffee alone. We were amused to see that the man sitting at the table next to us was fast asleep, but concerned to see that a lit cigarette was still in his hand. We had noticed that a very large percentage of the population smoked, and there were seldom areas in restaurants set aside for non-smokers. Even though cigarettes could not be sold to anyone under the age of 20 in Japan, it was obvious that many Japanese teenagers were smokers. They had no problem buying cigarettes because of the vast numbers of vending machines throughout the country.

The wind was strong against us that day and it was very overcast. For most of the day we were cycling on top of a dyke alongside a wide river. Whilst there were mostly tiny fields full of vegetables, there were still a lot of industrial units with massive car parks beside the road below us. A wide river was to our left, and to our right were miles of electricity pylons linked with cables following the line of the river into the distance. On the edge of the river, wild grasses similar to pampas grass grew, and occasionally we saw a grey heron by the water, or a number of white storks surrounding a tractor ploughing a field on our right. Fairly frequently we saw small areas of gravestones in the middle of a field, always approached by a narrow tarmac road, but no other buildings stood nearby, except occasionally an ornate temple or shrine.

The tarmac on our cycle path on the dyke ran out, and we had to cycle onto the road for a while. It was frightening, because the road was narrow but busy, and lorries passed very close to us. We returned to the grass path on the dyke but, with the wind still strong against us, we were averaging only 5 miles per hour.

We stopped at a service station which had rows of machines, from which we chose hot coffees – these were rather sweet, but good and cheap. There was a choice of five different hot coffees, tea or mocha, two iced coffees, iced lemon tea or a variety of soft drinks. The machines gave change, even for notes, so it was never a problem if the correct money wasn't available.

It was fascinating to watch the attendants of the service station running into action as soon as a car arrived. Several of them ran out onto the forecourt, while the driver got out of the car to buy himself a drink. Not only would the car be filled with petrol, but the windows were cleaned and the rubber mats whipped out of the car to be vacuumed. All done with a smile, and in a country where tipping is not the norm and is not expected!

The occasional houses in this rural area were always surrounded by neatly-clipped hedges and trees, and we stopped and sat on a wall opposite one as we ate our packed lunch. An elderly gentleman walked along.

'Konnichi wa,' (good day) we called out.

He replied, hesitated, and went into the house opposite us. Within a few minutes he came out again and trimmed the end of the already perfect hedge, before wandering over to us and sitting on the wall alongside us. We couldn't speak each other's language, but we offered him a biscuit, which he initially refused, then accepted. He sat silently beside us smoking a cigarette, and I indicated the hedge and admired it. With the help of our phrase book, hand signs and a dictionary we conversed a little, and I noticed that he also wore the strange split toe boots that we had previously seen on the workmen, and he also wore a battered conical straw hat.

After taking a photo of all of us we waved goodbye, and we soon arrived in the next town. Several establishments were advertising karaoke, which is incredibly popular in Japan. Karaoke, as the word suggests, originates in Japan; it is even shown on television, and no-one seems to mind that the contestants sing desperately out of tune! In the distance we saw a tall building with Japanese writing on the side. We recognised the symbols for 'hotel' and made our way through the streets to it. I waited outside with the bikes, and when Warren returned he told me the price was even higher than the night before. I shook my head to say 'no', but the receptionist came out and called Warren back in, where they agreed a lower price. We had a beautiful large room with a sofa in the living area, and a very large bathroom. Again, a slot machine was on the side of the television, but it worked without money – except for one channel, that is. The screen on that channel was just a mass of horizontal lines. There was sound, but all we could hear were moans and groans. This was obviously the 'pay-as-you-go-porn-channel'!

As we left our hotel later, we saw that the area was full of people in traditional Japanese costumes, and a large float with a giant masked figure was a few yards down the road, surrounded by adults and children. It was already dark, and many people were carrying burning torches aloft. We hurried along the road to watch the float, and dozens of people in traditional Japanese costume were gently laying the figure down before crossing the level crossing over the railway line to avoid electrocuting themselves on the overhead cables. We took dozens of photos, and it was amusing to see the mixture of old and new. A group of three young teenage girls were beautifully dressed in traditional Japanese kimonos, wearing raised wooden clogs with flip-flop straps and white tabi socks with a split for the big toe; their heads were bent together as they each entered text messages on their mobile phones.

We returned to our hotel room, pleased to have had the opportunity to see the festival. Our beds, as usual, were covered with strange quilts, and our pillows were hard and full of seeds – I woke several times in the night with a numb ear. On other occasions the pillows had been soft, but often with a different filling on one side, which in one hotel had been pieces of cut up plastic straws.

We continued our journey the next day, but unfortunately the weather had turned dull and windy. Many women were working in the fields, and each of them was wearing a quaint floral cotton bonnet which gathered into a deep peak which stood out around the face, completely obscuring the face and protecting it from the sun (except there was none that day!) The bonnet tied at the neck and draped over the shoulders. The women waved as we cycled past.

Often we saw abandoned bikes, many times with missing wheels. At lunchtimes we saw children coming out of school, often on bicycles. The bikes in Japan looked very old-fashioned to us, though Warren assured me that new technology had been used on many, such as belts instead of chains, which were beginning to be used in England by commuters. In Japan the bikes always had a basket and no crossbar, like old-fashioned English ladies' bikes, and had the typical 'sit-up-and-beg' handlebars. The schoolboys wore black or navy suits, the jackets with stand up collars fastened to the neck, sometimes with military-style brass buttons. The boys' uniforms were much more practical than the girls' tiny checked pleated skirts with open jackets, and the very young school children all wore bright yellow caps or sunhats and carried matching yellow umbrellas on rainy days. The fashion for teenage girls seemed to be to wear large, white, baggy, floppy knitted socks, so baggy that they often hung over their shoes. This fashion, especially with their very short skirts, made them look like baby dolls or schoolgirls, even when they were not in school uniform.

The Japanese take education very seriously, and children are expected to work unbelievably hard from a very young age. Attending the right school is considered very important, and students are expected to study through the evenings in order to gain entry to the university of their choice. Failure to gain entry means that one or two more years are spent at school repeating the final years and re-sitting the exams. The pressure on children can be very great, and Japan has a very high rate of child suicide as a result.

The roads were busy, so we tried to travel on smaller roads, but found ourselves either going round in circles or ending up in cul-de-sacs, so we were constantly retracing our steps. We eventually reached the sea, but the grey sand, grey sea, grey sky and stormy winds did nothing to raise our spirits. The cycle path became narrower, and tall weeds encroached on the unused path, whipping at our hands, legs and faces, and I was concerned in case there might be brambles or stinging nettles or the Japanese equivalent.

We arrived at a lake after passing some gorgeous houses and gardens, and cycled along a tarmac path around it. The sun had come out a little, and it was pleasant cycling watching the dozens of men fishing. Virtually every man had at least six fishing rods set up with their lines in the water, and each rod had a radio transmitter on it to set off an alarm if a fish was caught. The fishermen were therefore able to sleep, or relax and drink beer with their friends whilst waiting for the fish to bite. Grey herons lined up alongside the fishermen, occasionally diving into the water to catch fish. On the other side of the tarmac path were fields, and in them women were working, all wearing the same bonnets that we had previously seen.

In this very rural area we saw the word 'hotel' ahead of us. We were tired, but suspicious – the proper hotels we had seen didn't have English wording. As we got closer we saw the price advertised outside as always – 3,700 yen for 3 hours – another love hotel, but this time in the middle of nowhere! Shortly afterwards we found a proper hotel, but it looked very expensive. The cost for a night was over £50, but we felt it would have been at least double the price in England. In the bathroom was everything that we could have needed. Bottles of shampoo, conditioner and soap were lined up on the shelf, though because of my lack of Japanese I was unsure which was which. There were also four bottles of men's toiletries in masculine black bottles. In sealed bags were a fold-up brush, two combs, two toothbrushes and mini toothpastes (these were in every hotel we visited), and two razors, shaving gel and body lotion stood side by side on the shelf. Despite the quality of the hotel, they still didn't accept credit cards.

Dressed in our hotel yukatas, we went to the sento (the public baths) on the sixth floor to enjoy the hot tub, jacuzzi and sauna. We stood uncertainly outside the two entrances, one for men and one for women. We didn't know which was the entrance for men and which for women, and no-one was going in or out to give us a clue. We didn't want to make a mistake, because we would have to strip naked once we were in there! We peeped cautiously round the doors to see if anyone was inside, but both of the sentos were empty. Keeping our fingers crossed that we had chosen the right rooms we each went into a different bathroom. No-one else joined us while we were in there, which was fortunate, but we obviously needed to check our dictionary, so that we could memorise the Japanese words for 'men' and 'women'! Luckily, because we had stayed with Yoko and Nobuho, we knew that we had to shower ourselves clean with the supplied shampoos and soaps whilst we sat on the tiny stools, before getting into the hot communal bath.

When we returned to our room we noticed that the door to the large room opposite ours was open – it was a function room furnished with a long, low table with large white cushions on the floor around it. We heard guests arriving and, as we left our room to go for a meal later, a number of men were already leaving the room opposite. These men approached the step from their room in their stockinged feet, and were looking down at the lines of shoes, laughing, stumbling and leaning on each others' shoulders, obviously unsure which shoes belonged to whom. There were raucous laughs, and the men were falling over, obviously very drunk. Two pretty hostesses in long red skirts and white blouses were handing them shoe-horns to help them put on their shoes, and they smiled at us as we passed. It was only 7pm.

We found another ramen restaurant and sat at a low table with thin cushions on the floor. For 1,600 yen (£9) we had two set meals – fried rice and boiled rice, two big bowls of noodle soup, gyoza (minced pork in dumpling-like pastry, steamed and served with hot English mustard), spring rolls, Japanese pickles and vegetables. Tea or water is always served free of charge, and iced water was always put on the table as soon we arrived.

As we cycled through the small town the following day, we noticed the drain covers on the roads and pavements in Japan – the cast-iron covers had elegant designs of flowers, birds, fish, animals and mountains, ships and light-houses, and they had been enamelled in jewel-like colours. The locals must have thought it very strange if they had noticed us taking photographs of drain covers!

We were once again in a rural area – in the fields alongside the road the rice had just been harvested, and sheaves of rice were hanging upside down on bamboo or wooden poles which were suspended on X-shaped end supports. The rice was wet, because it had rained in the night, and puddles stood in the rice fields. New green shoots were already appearing where the rice had been harvested two inches above the ground, and purple irises were growing in the wet ditches surrounding the field. We passed a heavily-wooded area, but still the telegraph poles with their cables lined the road, the cables tangled up in the trees.

We were now heading towards Mito-shi, where we hoped to spend a couple of days. The road became busier as we approached the city, and we were intrigued to see that cars had been parked on four levels in a metal cage, so we went to investigate. Metal ramps were laid side by side at 90 degrees to the street, so that cars wishing to park could drive onto the ramps from the street. When the ground floor level ramps were full, the cars on their ramps moved sideways and up onto the first floor level one by one, leaving spaces vacant on the ground floor again. Every time a level was filled, the cars moved up another level until all four levels were full. If a car needed to leave, the ramps could move sideways and down until the car was level with the street again, without other cars having to be removed from their ramps – very simple, very clever and very space-saving. The multi-storey car park next door also had two levels of ramps on each floor to give extra storage space for cars, and similar two-storey parking was available for bicycles as well. We had noticed that next to every train station was a large building specifically for parking commuters' bikes, because so many people in Japan cycle. A man is always employed to look after the bikes, and he is so proud of his job that he makes sure that every bike is parked exactly parallel to the next one, with the handlebars all leaning the same way, ensuring a very neat line of bikes!

We found a pleasant hotel by the river where we wanted to stay, but initially they told us that our bikes would have to be left outside in the open. I stood outside looking after the bikes, and I could see through the two sets of tinted glass doors into the smart reception area. When I saw Warren bowing two or three times in gratitude with his hands together, I knew that he had persuaded them to offer a space inside the hotel for our bikes.

The following day was a public holiday in Japan, but we were able to find an internet café open. This was only the second one in Japan that we had found, and in both there was a library for manga as well as an internet café. The Japanese love manga, which is a comic in book form, and the Japanese read more comics than any other nation. Manga books are designed for adults as well as children, can be specifically for women or men only, and can even be educational. Thousands of manga books filled the shelves, and everywhere people were sitting reading these comics, some of which were as thick as telephone directories. Because the Japanese write from right to left and up and down the page, it seemed very strange looking at Japanese books and magazines to see the title page on the back of the book (as we know it)! It was also very strange to see the officer in the post office reading the address on an envelope holding it sideways.

As in the previous internet café, they wouldn't allow Warren to sit with me reading our e-mails without us paying for two people, a problem we had never encountered in any other country, and he wasn't even allowed to sit elsewhere in the building without paying for a ticket to read manga, so Warren had to sit on the ground in the shelter of the doorway, even though it was cold and pouring with rain.

Because we had spent dramatically more than our planned budget since we had been in Japan, in order to save money that evening we decided to cook a meal in our hotel bedroom. Hundreds of instant noodle dishes were available in the shops, as well as other types of ready prepared foods, so it was easy to prepare a reasonably cheap quick meal that evening. The following morning we went to MacDonald's again for breakfast, and the waitress brought us our coffee, chatting cheerfully and backing away bowing so deeply that I thought she must think I was the Queen – how wonderful if we had such polite and cheerful service in England!

As we continued cycling, I noticed that my tyre was going flat (our tenth puncture since we began this trip), so we pulled into a Shell service station to repair it. The men in their smart red uniforms and caps were very interested, and invited us into their small office for a cup of cocoa. We sat around their fire trying to converse, and one asked how old we were. When I wrote the figure '59' for me, one of them got quite excited, pointing at his nose and also at the figure. He was indicating that he, too, was 59. Fortunately we had already learnt that the Japanese point to their nose to indicate themselves, whereas in England we point at our chest. Another confusing gesture is the action to say 'come here', which in Japan is done with the palm raised towards the other person and waggling the fingers up and down, more like a 'goodbye' action. It just goes to show that actions don't always speak louder than words!

The service station attendants gave us a free map of the area, and waved us goodbye. On the map, which was in Japanese, of course, we were surprised and pleased to find campsite symbols. We decided to try to camp, to help eke out our budget. We arrived a short while later at a coastal resort, and as it was now raining heavily we asked the price in several hotels, deciding to leave the camping to another night. The cost of the hotels was two or three times what we had been paying so far, presumably because it was a popular resort. We were directed by locals to a 'cheap' hotel, although it looked inordinately expensive when we arrived – the employees were wearing black suits with bowties, and the large, marbled reception area was dotted with groups of leather chesterfields and coffee tables. The price was 10,500 yen (£60), but there were no credit card facilities. We were cold from cycling in the rain, so decided to take a room despite the high price, but when I used the toilet in our bathroom, and found that the temperature of the toilet seat could be adjusted to suit the individual, I decided that the price was worthwhile and I spent a while sitting there just to thaw out!

It was early afternoon, and we went to the sento to warm up in the hot tub, which was even more bliss. We noticed that on every floor of the hotel there were machines selling not only hot and cold drinks, but also hot food, such as chips and chicken kebabs. In the sento, as well as the usual shampoo, conditioner, liquid soap and moisturiser, was a gritty cleanser made of salt, aloe vera and palm oil (for once the words were in English!), so I glowed with healthy skin by the time I'd finished, especially having spent some time with my feet on the special foot massage machine.

We borrowed hotel umbrellas and set off for an evening meal, not being able to afford the high prices in the hotel restaurant. We paused to exclaim at a vegetable in a small shop that looked exactly like a giant green pear the size of an enormous pumpkin, and we poked it to see if it was real. We eventually realised that it must be a type of pumpkin, because the shop-keeper showed us a packet of dried pumpkin seeds, pointing at the same time to the giant pear.

We found a small restaurant, and made the owners jump as we walked in – they obviously weren't expecting customers on such an awful night. The menu was only in Japanese so we asked for gyoza. No gyoza, we were told in Japanese, but they mentioned tempura. Even better! We nodded enthusiastically and left it to them to bring what they recommended, and a feast appeared. Enormous battered prawns, pieces of fish and different battered vegetables, were all served with a dipping sauce, soup, rice, a dish of meat and vegetables, pickles and a beer each. We sat on the cushions at our low table and held up our beers.

'Campai!' we said in true Japanese toasting fashion. For about £15 in total we had dined like royalty, so were incredibly pleased with ourselves.

The next day we searched for the campsite shown on our map further down the coast. The weather was now warmer and the sun was shining, so this lifted our spirits, especially when we passed a pretty harbour with fishing boats. No signs were in English so we'd memorised the Japanese script for the word campsite – a telegraph pole leaning to the left; a slightly smaller version; a tick with a dash; the word 'cash' in shorthand with a circle on the right, and a final symbol so complex with squares and lines it was impossible for us to memorise!

We eventually found the campsite next to a surfing beach, but it was closed. We knew that most campsites in Japan are open only during July and August, but had hoped that we might be lucky. Barriers were up to prevent cars entering, but these barriers couldn't stop bicycles. We explored the site – there were some pleasant grassy sites for tents, and attractive roofs covered barbecue areas with seats and tables. Best of all, although the toilets had shutters across the entrance, these were not locked and could be easily lifted. There was no electricity in the toilets, but running water was available, and the water at the washing up area was still running. Tap water throughout Japan is safe to use, so we never bought bottled water. We looked at each other and knew what we were going to do …

We went to a shop to buy food to cook that evening, as usual spending a lot of time trying to decide exactly what we were buying. We had previously bought some sweets which had turned out to be fish-flavoured; if we bought pastries we never knew if they were going to be sweet or savoury, and when we bought what we thought was a doughnut we discovered it was a rissole filled with onions! Another time we bought a vacuum pack of what we thought were cooked new potatoes, and they turned out to be a strange doughy mixture. We spent ages trying to decide whether the container we were examining held mayonnaise. It was covered with Japanese writing front and back, but we noticed a line of tiny writing in English.

'Made of finest eggs, oil and vinegar,' it said. As I knew that these were the ingredients for mayonnaise we made a purchase and were right for once!

We spent some time in a coffee shop facing the sea where I wrote my diary. There were several comfortable leather sofas, and we were surprised to see that a number of Japanese customers were fast asleep lying stretched out on these, but we assumed that they were possibly tired after surfing. When it began to get dark at 4.30 we returned to the campsite. Under the roof of the barbecue area we cooked a lovely meal, and enjoyed our first night of camping in Japan, but in the morning after breakfast as we prepared to leave, a car drew up alongside us. We were worried that we were in trouble for camping without permission or without paying, so we smiled as the man got out of his car.

'Konnichi wa,' we said.

He spoke no English and was obviously surprised to see us there, but after a great deal of pointing at watches and indicating the barbecue area, we realised that his only concern was that he had organised a big barbecue for 12 noon, and wanted to make sure that we would have left by that time. We made it clear we were about to leave, and as soon as he left we were on our way.

A hearse went by in the opposite direction, looking incredibly splendid – a normal large black car up to the bottom of the windows, it was gilded ornately to the top of the car, which was topped with a copper gabled roof which had large, gilded birds perched on the top.

We were now travelling along a rural road, and we were happy because the sun was shining. We saw farm workers in a cart and they waved as we passed. They were sifting by hand the sweet potatoes from the fine soil which we had seen everywhere. The soil and potatoes were being lifted from the ground by machine onto a conveyor belt and into the cart. We went through woods where giant bamboos edged the road. The diameter of the bamboo was a full hand span, and it grew 40 to 50 feet tall. Stunning traditionally-built houses with many tiered roofs were bounded by matching roofed garden walls, and the traditional Japanese gardens inside the gates of these big country houses were amazing.

We passed areas that appeared to belong to scrap metal merchants, full of cars and vehicles that looked fairly new and undamaged. The cars were parked side by side almost touching each other, with grass and weeds growing amongst the cars. We discovered later that the reason for the abandoned fairly new cars was because of the stringent and expensive tests that a car in Japan has to have once it is three years old and every two years after that, and then every year once it is nine years old. At a cost of nearly 100,000 yen (£600) for this test, the Japanese are more likely to scrap their car and buy a new one (at half the cost of one in England). So, unlike everywhere else in Asia, old cars are seldom seen on the roads in Japan.

We passed areas full of greenhouses, where vegetables could be grown out of season, and neat, small fields full of sweet potatoes, carrots, onions and rice were on either side. We passed more vast expanses of pink and red cosmos, the cheerful flowers nodding in the sun. We cycled past miles and miles of plastic-covered frames, where tomatoes, cabbages and vegetables that we didn't recognise were growing, and the fields were full of soil as fine as seed compost. At times the prickly shells of sweet chestnuts and their spilled nuts covered the pavements and roads where we cycled, and our wheels split the shells open still further. We cycled along a dyke beside a lake, and laughed when we saw two scarecrows that had been made out of shop window mannequins, standing at the edge of a watery field full of plants. By the side of the road a lady wearing an old-fashioned bonnet sat sorting grains of rice from grass, so I approached her to ask if I could take a photo. She didn't look up, even when I stood very close, so I took her photo anyway.

When we passed a house being constructed in the traditional Japanese style, we felt we had to stop to see it – it was awesome the amount of timber being used for the many tiers of roofs which curved up at the edges, and the complexity of the shapes was unbelievable. Round logs were used as well as sawn timber, and we thought it was possible that these might be left exposed in the interior of the finished house. In contrast, modern Japanese houses are built in exactly the same quick and simple method as in Australia where a wooden frame is built onto a concrete base.

A few days later we woke in our hotel room to glorious sunshine and blue skies, so it was a shock when we left the hotel to find a fierce gale blowing. Fortunately, the wind was behind us this time, so cycling would be easier and we wouldn't end the day with bright red faces and arms as before. We cycled on the wide pavement beside a very busy highway, and were interested to see some of the cars in the car salesrooms that we passed. As well as the normal Japanese cars that we see in England, we were fascinated to see small square cars, many with darkened windows, looking exactly like a child's drawing of Postman Pat's van! Of course, because in Japan the cars drive on the left, the cars all had right hand drive as in England. Interestingly, of the twelve countries that we had visited in the past 16 months, including England, seven of those countries drove on the left – more than we would have imagined.

We were heading towards an area famed for its fishing industry. In a café at lunch time a couple came and sat at the next table and began talking with us. Yoshinori was the first person we had met since leaving Yoko's house who could speak fluent English. His wife, Yukiya, was not so confident, but spoke a little English, and they told us they had just come back from a shopping week in London.

'Buying Wedgwood and Jaeger,' said Yoshinori, nodding to his wife.

'I collect it,' she said, laughing. We spent a long time talking, but had to continue our journey. Yoshinori and Yukiya were disappointed not to be able to 'look after us' they said, but they were on their way north to an appointment.

We were delighted, a short while later, to find a very large supermarket bigger than any we'd seen in Japan before, and we went in to buy food, because we intended to camp that night again if it was possible. Inside it looked like any European supermarket, but it was incredibly noisy. It sounded like a busy outdoor market, because everyone who was filling up shelves or giving away free samples was shouting as loud as they could. There were so many free samples we could have filled ourselves up without buying food! Prices were very reasonable, and we tasted free samples of delicious asparagus and bacon, a meatball in a broth with spring onions, noodles, seaweed, fish, pieces of fruit and sweets. It was fascinating to see some foods with claims on them in English that they were suitable for ages 0 to 100! Even though the whole of the packaging was in Japanese, these words were in English, which we thought very strange.

With our newly bought food strapped onto our bikes we cycled across a long bridge towards a campsite that was marked on our Japanese map. The wind blew us sideways as we crossed the bridge, and when we got to the other side we asked directions to the campsite. An area of grass next to the lighthouse and the beach was apparently free camping, and my heart sank when I saw how exposed and windy it was. However, the toilets were nearby and were spotless, and the now familiar line of hot and cold drinks machines stood nearby. Despite the whistling of the wind, the sound of waves crashing onto the rocks, and the nearby light-house flashing its light, we had a comfortable night after an excellent meal of fresh salmon with potatoes and vegetables cooked by Warren on our small portable stove.

After breakfast in our tent the next morning we set off again, and later found ourselves outside a coffee house in the nearby town. As we parked our bikes to go inside an elderly man approached and spoke in good English, and we chatted for a minute or two. As we drank our coffee he came into the coffee house, and introduced himself as Kiyoshi Yokkaichi. He was 73, though didn't look it – most Japanese are very young-looking – and he told us he worked for the 'City Government' and that he was an important person! He disappeared, coming back with card and scissors, and proceeded to cut out several pictures including a delightful picture of the Choshi light-house and one of Mount Fuji, each one taking only a minute. His grand-daughters arrived and he introduced them to us. He explained that he knew many people in the town, and offered us an hour or two's guided tour without charge. We had reservations, but eventually decided to accept his invitation.

At his suggestion, we parked our bikes in his small garden, and set off with him driving his daughter's car. He took us initially to the fishing docks, where large fishing trawlers were unloading their catch onto lorries, the long silver mackerels spilling out onto the pavement. He asked someone if he could have some fish, and they obviously knew he was someone important, because a minute later two very large plastic baskets of fish were tipped into a giant bin-liner in the boot of his daughter's car, half filling it. Fish spilled out into the boot, but Kiyoshi was delighted.

'There is 20,000 yen worth of fish there,' he said (£114).

However, I couldn't help but wonder what his daughter would say next time she opened the boot of her car – it would surely smell disgusting! On we went, Kiyoshi driving far faster than most Japanese men as he whisked us on a whistle stop tour of Choshi. He stopped the car briefly to point out something, dashed into a shop where he persuaded the assistant to allow us to sample Senbei free of charge and even persuaded her to give us a cup of tea! Senbei were delicious rice biscuits flavoured with soy sauce and shrimp.

We followed him at a trot as he rushed into a tower – he may have been 73, but I was having a job keeping up with him. He waved to the girl at the kiosk and beckoned us through the gates without paying. A lift took us to the top of the tower to admire the view, where he left us for several minutes to give a guided tour to a group of guideless people. Then he whisked us off again and took us to see some caged finches being fed, and after that he asked us if we liked fish. We weren't sure what to answer – did he mean fish to eat or fish to look at in an aquarium? Without waiting for an answer he sprinted into a shop beckoning us to follow, where he asked for samples of fish balls to be given us. The girl indicated the small portions available for tasting, but he persisted, and persuaded her to put two whole balls onto cocktail sticks for us. As we ate them he indicated that we should hurry.

'Quick, eat; quick,' he said, and he stuck four more balls onto sticks while the girl's back was turned, handed them to us and ushered us quickly out of the door.

Off to another tower, where he proudly indicated the notice saying 300 yen entrance price – we hadn't had to pay to visit the roof. He hurried ahead to another floor so we could watch traditional hand-made ropes and belts being made. The man who made them was having a break, but this didn't stop Kiyoshi. The old man was called back from his break at Kiyoshi's request to give us a demonstration of the 600 year old tradition of making beautiful ornate coloured ropes and sashes and belts for traditional kimonos; after the demonstration the old gentleman proudly handed us his business cards. We had already learnt that to show one's respect when handed a business card, one should read it carefully and never put it away without first examining it. Also, one should never write on it as this shows disrespect. I examined the card carefully, but was unsure whether I was holding it upside down or even sideways, which I am sure would have been considered disrespectful, so I held the card carefully inside the palm of my hand so the old gentleman hopefully didn't notice.

Kiyoshi rushed us back to the car, and sped through the side streets. I was concerned to see that the speedometer showed 80 kph as Kiyoshi drove through narrow side streets, but suddenly he swung into the car park of a factory. Here, Kiyoshi explained to us, was the most famous soy sauce factory in Japan, which had been established in 1645. It was Saturday, and the factory was closed, and even Kiyoshi couldn't summon the workers back to the factory to demonstrate soy sauce making to us! However, he was told that we could watch a film explaining how soy sauce was made. We were ushered into an enormous theatre lined with seats, and Kiyoshi told us we were lucky because he had asked for the film to be in English. Not so lucky for the Japanese couple who arrived as the film started, to find it was in a foreign language! There were only five of us in this enormous theatre, and Kiyoshi sat behind us and fell asleep for the 15 minute film, during which we learnt that the soy sauce factory had been established in 1645, and that soy sauce had originated in the 13th century when it was found that the liquid in the bottom of casks which were used to produce miso (fermented soy bean paste, which is part of the Japanese staple diet) had a special flavour of its own. Soy sauce is made from soy beans, wheat and salt. Kiyoshi woke as we all stood up to leave the theatre, and all five of us were handed a complementary bottle of soy sauce. Kiyoshi asked, and got, a second bottle 'for his wife'.

We thought we were now going back to his house for us to collect our bikes, because it had begun to rain very heavily, but Kiyoshi shot across the long bridge and parked in a no parking zone outside the doors of the large supermarket we'd visited the day before. He handed me a tray and tongs.

'Choose which pastries you want,' he said. 'I will pay for them.'

We declined, because he had already been so kind, we told him, so he bought two large packets of the senbai we had enjoyed earlier, which he proudly handed to us. He did, on this occasion, pay for the items that he had picked up!

We got back into the car, and he stopped opposite a hotel. Kiyoshi left us in the car and went across the road to the hotel.

'What's he doing?' Warren asked.

'I don't know,' I replied. 'Perhaps he's trying to get us a good deal at that hotel.'

The hotel, however, looked extremely expensive. It was now pouring with rain as Kiyoshi appeared at the doors of the hotel and beckoned us across the road, so we dashed across the road to the hotel, and followed him through the marble foyer to some sofas, where a waitress immediately appeared with coffees. We offered to pay, but Kiyoshi refused.

'No. I've told you. I know everyone. I don't need to pay for anything.'

Thirty minutes later after drinking the coffees we left, sure enough without paying for the coffee. We stood at the hotel entrance looking out at the torrential rain. Kiyoshi patted his pockets.

'Where are my keys?' he said. 'Oh yes. Oh dear.'

He dashed across the road to the parked car, and Warren and I ran after him. The car was unlocked, the keys were still in the ignition and the engine was still running!

Kiyoshi refused to take us back to our bikes. 'I will get you a good deal at a hotel,' he told us. 'I will introduce you to the manager.'

Now he drove miles through the rain, and he pulled up at a smart Japanese hotel in the country. I was concerned that we'd never find it again on our own, but after a great deal of bowing, nodding of heads and hand-shakes we agreed 8,000 yen for the room, which was less than we had usually paid in Japan, but 13,500 yen (£77) would include evening dinner and breakfast. Although this was well above our budget we felt we had no choice, as there appeared to be no restaurants in the vicinity of the hotel and it was now late in the day. The hotel manager, who spoke a little English, told us anxiously that only Japanese food was available at the hotel, but we assured him that we were very happy with that.

Eventually Kyoshi deposited us back by our bicycles which were now very wet, especially the bags which were not waterproof without the special covers. Kyoshi led us in his car to the edge of the town, pointed us in the right direction, and we cycled as fast as we could through the rain and threatening darkness to the hotel, 8km away, losing our way only once which meant that we had to cycle twice up the same hill. When we arrived we couldn't have been wetter if we had stood fully clothed in the shower.

There were numerous giggles from the reception staff when we arrived, absolutely soaked to the skin with ten soaking wet pannier bags. Three employees of the hotel led us to our room, carrying our dripping bags. One of them spoke a few words of English. This was the first Japanese room we had been given, and it was a very large room empty of furniture except a low table with kettle, teapot and biscuits on it. The room was surrounded by doors, and a quick check in some of these showed that there were cupboards with futons, bed linen and yukatas stored on shelves.

Within minutes we had made a complete mess of the room, putting up numerous clothes lines for our wet clothes and pannier bags, and scattering the contents of the bags around the room to dry out. Everything was soaking wet. We had been told that dinner was 5.30 to 7pm, so intended to go to the sento for a hot bath before dinner. However, we must have misunderstood, because a few minutes later at 5.45, reception phoned to say the meal was ready, so we had to leave the mess and dash down to the restaurant, wearing the hotel's supplied red slippers, which we left with dozens of others outside the dining room door. Large cushions on the floor surrounded long low tables which were set out with a magnificent feast. There were pieces of breaded fish, mackerel, oysters and onions in a mustard sauce, a creamy tofu dish, strong-flavoured pieces of fish in a paste, rice, one enormous prawn that filled a plate, raw tuna, white fish and prawns with grated radish and wasabi, meatballs in broth with spring onions, fresh fruit including pink grapefruit pieces, salad and pots of tea.

The room was full of hotel guests, but we were the only westerners; we were also the only ones not wearing yukatas. Obviously everyone else had had their bath before dinner (as one should in Japan) and had gone to dinner wearing these kimono-like robes. Fortunately we were able to watch the other guests to check how to eat the various dishes, all of which we loved.

As we left the dining room, dozens of red hotel slippers had been turned round and stood waiting in neat pairs by the doorway. It reminded me of the neat lines of bicycles left at the stations in Japan. However, I did wonder if Japanese people suffered with feet ailments, sharing their slippers with so many people.

On our return to our room, we were highly embarrassed to see that the maid had been in the room to lay out the futons on the floor and make our beds, and had tidied our gear as much as she could. However, it was difficult to move around the room without ducking and diving to avoid the dripping wet bags and clothes on the washing lines! The bedroom was lined with sliding doors, but each disclosed a cupboard and no bathroom. We were happy to use the public bath on the ground floor, but would have liked our own toilet. I went to the toilet down the corridor, but had to return for the phrasebook, as the only rooms without numbers had Japanese script that I didn't recognise. The words weren't in our dictionary, so I quietly opened the first door and peeped in – it was obviously the gentlemen's toilet, so it was lucky that no-one was in there! I quickly left and dashed to the second door.

We went to the sento to have a relaxing half hour in the hot tub – we were certainly enjoying the luxury of these communal baths after a day's cycling in the cold, though both of us always ended up with lobster pink skin because of the high temperature of the water! We noticed that Japanese skin was not affected like this. This time several other women joined me – at least I'd picked the right one this time! Again, we hadn't been certain as we couldn't identify the writing on the door! Dressed in my yukata, I bumped into Warren on the stairs as I returned to the bedroom. He whispered that I'd made a faux pas – I had automatically done up my dressing gown right over left, as is normal for women in England. However, this is how the Japanese dress their dead, so I had to quickly rearrange my clothing on the stairs before anyone noticed how disrespectful I had been!

The bedroom that we had been allocated was obviously designed for six people – there were six pairs of red slippers, six yukatas and 6 futons and bedding. There were presumably six men in the room next door – we could hear their voices clearly through the thin wall, one louder and more persistent than the others, so we turned up the air-conditioning to drown their voices and also hoped that the increased air from the vent would dry our bags before morning. As we switched off the air-conditioning the next morning, the sound of communal snoring came through the walls . . .

In the morning there was an announcement over the loud-speaker at 7.45 which we assumed meant that breakfast was ready, so we made our way to the dining room. Again the room was full of hotel guests, which was fortunate because we weren't sure how to eat some of the food, so had to surreptitiously watch to see what other people did. Smoked mackerel, a bowl of soup, rice, black noodles, slices of ham, pickles, shredded vegetables, dried sheets of seaweed and pots of green tea stood on the table. Using our chopsticks we placed rice and pickles on the seaweed, which made a simple form of sushi which was delicious, and after a superb breakfast we were ready to set off again on our bikes.

The phone rang in our room just before we left. It was Kiyoshi again – he was waiting to buy us a cup of coffee in the hotel foyer, he told us. Our hearts sank, because we were keen to start cycling. Down we went, where he showed us a newspaper with an article about himself with his photo. He told us that it showed what an important person he was, and he gave us a photocopy of the article, which he felt sure we would want to keep. It was in Japanese, of course. Cups of coffee arrived, but he also presented us with a jar of instant coffee and a spoon, saying that he hadn't realised how expensive coffee was in Japan. Kiyoshi told us how he had given a lot of fish away to 20 different people, so there were now many local people who owed him favours.

He told us he had come to show us a new local temple which had been closed the day before. He wanted to show it to us before we left Choshi, so we felt obliged to follow him on our bikes to see a splendid temple guarded by two fierce-looking red ogres either side of the newly-opened entrance. There were no parking spaces left, so Kiyoshi parked in front of a gateway.

The temple was very beautiful, and Kiyoshi once again left us to take over as self-appointed guide to a group of people, at the end of which the group politely clapped to show their thanks. He showed us the marble stones with people's names engraved on them, which stated how much they had donated to build the temple. He was amazed that someone had given 30 million yen (£171,000) but had chosen to remain anonymous – he just couldn't understand that someone had given so much but had not wanted their name to be known.

'30 million yen, 30 million yen,' he kept repeating to himself.

He introduced us to two ladies who he knew, and translated their comments.

'You're very lucky to have a guide who speaks such good English,' he translated. There was a lot of ooghing and aahing as he told them of our journey, and he basked in the reflected glory as he told them about us.

'Take one of these,' he said, pointing to a bucket full of folded pieces of paper giving fortunes. We were sure they had to be paid for, and hesitated, but he insisted and handed us one each. Finally we were ready to leave and we went to unlock our bikes. As Kiyoshi got into his car, a Buddhist monk went up to him, obviously telling him that this was not a normal parking place.

Warren said, 'I expect he's telling the monk – do you know who I am?'

Sure enough, Kiyoshi drove over to tell us delightedly that he had been told not to park there.

'I am Kiyoshi Yokkaichi,' he had told the monk, so the monk had bowed respectfully and asked him to park there whenever he liked!

We said our goodbyes, thanking him profusely, and finally we were on our way again, determined to average out the cost of last night's accommodation and meals by camping that night. We eventually found the campsite shown on our map, but it was closed. Several workmen were painting the building, but they didn't speak English. However, we knew that the act of crossing arms or fingers was sign language meaning 'no', 'not available' or 'closed'. This time we couldn't use the campsite illicitly, because the site was busy with workmen.

We passed a community park where boys practised baseball, a very popular sport in Japan, and an elderly lady sprayed the weeds in the park by hand with weed killer. We decided that it would be ideal for camping, especially as there was a public toilet in the park. We sat on a bench watching the game for some time, and as the sun began to set we walked across the field past the baseball players to a quiet corner and began to put up our tent. Nobody was bothered about us, and at 6pm when it was dark and everyone had gone home, we were frightened out of our skins by the community clock playing a tune. The loud-speakers were obviously next to our tent, and woke us again at 7am the next morning. We packed our tent after breakfast, and waved goodbye to the group of elderly people in caps and bonnets playing a game similar to croquet.

Travelling through rural areas the next day we passed a stone merchant with incredibly large and beautiful rocks for sale, each one priced individually. Green or pink stone with a wavy grain and natural holes and pockets for tiny pools or planting was perfect for the Japanese style of garden. However, even though the rocks were undeniably beautiful, at 90,000 to 630,000 yen (£500 to £3,600), they were certainly not cheap, and the largest ones had no price tags. There were even tables and chairs made from solid pieces of polished rock. It was hot again, the weather changing from cool to hot, grey to blue skies, and rain to sun, and we cycled happily along the cycle path which was edged with very tall golden rod, its spikes mingling with the pampas-like grass that grows everywhere in Japan.

It became very hot, and we stopped by some vending drinks machines in the middle of the countryside, because there was a table and some chairs that we could use. We made a cup of tea with our own stove and had our sandwiches, and watched a couple making tall, narrow haystacks in the neighbouring field, into which they appeared to be placing peanut plants, presumably to dry them out.

We arrived at Tomisato, which was labelled a city on our map and looked large, but appeared to have no hotels. Even the police were unable to help us – there were six large love hotels, but no proper hotels, so we had to cycle out of Tomisato towards Narita. There would be plenty of hotels in Narita because it was the nearest city to Tokyo's international airport, but it was even more expensive than usual, because the hotels were obviously built for foreign tourists. For the first time the hotel employees all spoke fluent English, and also for the first time they accepted credit cards!

We gratefully paid for our expensive hotel room by credit card, but were greatly embarrassed when we were called down to reception to be told that 'there was a problem with our credit card'. The hotel manager offered to phone the number on the back of the credit card, and a telephone conversation with our credit card provider in England revealed that they had put a block on our card 'because it was being used in Japan'. The operator at the credit card call centre couldn't explain why security had done this, especially when he could see that in the past 16 months we had also used the card in France, Monaco, Italy, Greece, Turkey, India, Sri Lanka, Myanmar, Thailand, Australia and Hong Kong, as well as England. To ensure it didn't happen again, Warren told them never to put a block on the card again if it was being used in a foreign country. The operator apologised, and said he would put a note on our records to say that we were international travellers, and the next morning our credit card was swiped successfully. The receptionist handed back the credit card to me with both hands outstretched, and I knew that this was a very respectful gesture. We enjoyed ourselves in the next few days addressing each other as 'international traveller' instead of Mary and Warren, and decided that in the future when our occupation was requested on any forms we would write 'international traveller'!

We had only one more night to spend before arriving back at Yoko's, two weeks after leaving her house, and there was a campsite marked on our Shell map. We found it eventually in the middle of a forest. Two park rangers were surprised that we wanted to camp out of season, but they made a telephone call and confirmed that it was acceptable for us to do so. They spoke no English, but Warren was finding that he could usually understand what was being said in Japanese! They led us to a clearing where there were covered barbecues, showed us where to pitch our tent, and unlocked the toilets for us. To Warren's delight they also indicated branches and wood for making fires in one of the barbecue areas, so Warren made a massive fire to deter the mosquitoes – well, that was his excuse, anyway! At 4.30 one of the rangers came to wish us goodnight and said that they were going home – we were alone in the forest.

It began raining at midnight, and although the sound of rain on a tent is a lovely soothing sound, I hoped a) that I wouldn't need to visit the toilet in the night, and b) that the rain would stop before we had to get up. a) was fine, but b) was a big problem. At 7am when we woke it was still pouring with rain, and we discovered that as we had slept, mesmerised by the pitter-patter of rain, the clearing had been filling up with water. The bags in the outer part of the tent were under water, although the inner where we slept was dry. We had to run through the pouring rain to the covered cooking area, where we packed everything into our soaking wet bags. As we left the campsite, the park ranger ran out of his hut, removed his woollen glove to shake hands with us, and wished us good luck. There had been no charge for camping.

This last day of cycling was the worst. It rained hard all day as we cycled through busy roads and across busy junctions, back to the suburbs of Tokyo. However, we had always found that once we were wet we might as well just carry on, and we were determined to get back to Yoko's that day, which was 50km away. The journey was slow, going up and down kerbs, waiting for the numerous traffic lights, and trying to find our way over the rivers. At one point Warren's wheels skidded sideways on a wet metal drain in the road and he crashed to the ground. He was not hurt badly, although a pannier was damaged, but an old lady was very concerned and attempted (completely unsuccessfully because of the weight!) to lift the bike whilst Warren was still lying in a puddle. Every cyclist we saw had an umbrella up, and a group of eight teenage schoolboys cycled in front of us at one point, each protecting themselves from the rain with umbrellas. As we waited at a junction for the lights to change, a woman cycled by with a cigarette in her 'free' hand, as well as an umbrella in the other, and a lorry driver drove by with his manga comic in his hand. We crossed the road and cycled down a service road next to the expressway which was lined with cars and trucks, every driver asleep with his feet on the steering wheel or his seat fully reclined, even though it was the middle of the day. In the cab of a small truck three men were fast asleep side by side.

The rain showed no sign of abating. We were cold and wet through, and I began to long for Yoko's talking bath. The golden rod, which had looked so beautiful yesterday in the sun, was now bent over with the weight of the rain and was looking very sorry for itself. Pyracantha was now thick with red berries – an indication of winter coming – and the branches hung low with the weight.

Finally we could see Yoko's house, but as I cycled up the wet metal-edged ramps in front of her house my tyres slipped sideways, and I fell, bruising my ankle quite badly. It had not been a good day for falling off bikes! Never mind, we were back. Whilst we had been unlucky to have had such bad weather for the time of year in Japan for our cycling trip, the weather had been kind to us on some occasions. We had also had many wonderful experiences and met a lot of incredibly friendly people. Unfortunately the roads in this highly-populated part of Japan were too busy to make cycling easy for us, but another time we might be able to visit the north and south islands of Japan, which are much less populated.

A lovely note from Yoko was attached to a bottle of red wine, welcoming us back, urging us to have a bath to recover, to drink the wine and to eat everything in the house. We did!

★ ★ ★

Our first day back at Yoko and Nobuho's house after cycling was spent drying out our wet tent and washing our clothes. Yoko had a lady who called once a week to clean the house. She also prepared delicious foods to go in the fridge, and she prepared for us a wonderful salad made with mashed pumpkin, wafer-thin slices of Japanese cucumber and mayonnaise with a plate of fried potatoes and bacon. Yoko and Nobuho, like most Japanese professionals, work very hard and very long hours, and tonight both were staying in their apartments in different parts of Tokyo so that they could be at early meetings the next day – to commute to Tokyo from Yoko's house in the rush hour would take 1½ hours. Su, their daughter, spent the evening with us, and we enjoyed a take-away meal of baked eel with rice, which was delicious, and fish marinated with onions, tuna and spinach and soup with tofu.

The following Saturday, Nobuho's brother and sister-in-law, Tomiho and

Yumiko, arrived to meet us. The five of us went for a fabulous Chinese meal at a nearby restaurant, although it was very different from the Chinese food in English restaurants, and afterwards we set off with them all for a night away in the north-west of Japan, a 3 hour drive away. Yoko was working all weekend, taking a group of her students away. (Yoko is a professor of architecture who lectures at Nihon University in Tokyo, and she was taking her students to visit and study buildings). On the way north Nobuho had a phone call and excitedly told us that Yoko wasn't far away, so we stopped at a restaurant; there she was with a group of young students from the university. We were introduced to the students, so there was a lot of bowing and saying 'hello' in Japanese, and we all had a meal together.

We travelled on without Yoko, and to both sides of us and ahead there were ranges of mountains. They were very craggy and spectacular, the most famous being Mount Asama, a very active volcano. The mountains were silhouetted against the pink and orange evening sky. We began to go through the mountains – the tunnels were very long, and as we came out of the last long tunnel, which was over 5km long, the dark mountains ahead were silhouetted against a bright red sky. Only a few minutes later the colour disappeared, and it was dark. We arrived at a large mansion divided into apartments, and Nobuho led the way through the passageways and different floors until we reached his apartment.

After an hour spent in the sento (girls in one and boys in another!), we spent a lovely evening chatting, drinking wine and eating snacks, and Yumiko had brought her delicious home-made umeboshi (pickled plums) and Japanese sauerkraut, so I begged her for the recipes. Eventually we divided the apartment into separate bedrooms with the sliding doors, put our futons on the rush mat covered floor in each room and slept soundly.

The weather was beautiful the next day – blue skies and cumulus clouds looking like cotton wool promised some wonderful photographs. As we were 2,000 metres high, it was much cooler than in Tokyo. In the North Alps a range of eight dormant volcanoes up to 3,000 metres high could be seen, but the South Alps were to the west and out of sight.

Warren and I were surprised to see houses in the villages that looked similar to Swiss chalets as we drove further up the mountain. When we reached a popular skiing area (no snow yet!), we turned to see a stunning view of Mount Fuji, pale silver-grey silhouetted in the distance, its very famous shape easily recognised. Autumn colours were vibrant in this cooler area, and rivers ran down mountains covered with red, orange, yellow and green-leafed trees.

We tasted some strange food called Konjako. I had thought from the pronunciation that we were going to sample cognac, so that was a disappointment! Konjako has a jelly-like consistency and is flavoured with soy or miso. It's made from the large root of a potato-like plant, which takes two years to mature, and is considered a local speciality. It looked like a sweet but had a strange flavour and a chewy texture.

On our way back towards Tokyo, Nobuho told us about when he was driving in England. Having been used to driving at 110km per hour, he thought the English car seemed to be going very fast when the needle reached that speed – it was a while before he realised that the speedometer was showing miles and not kilometres! As we drove past other cars in the dark, I noticed that seven out of ten cars had navigational systems lit up, most of which were large screens built into the dashboard of the car. Probably two or three out of 10 had been added on top of the dashboard after the car was bought. At that time in the UK satellite navigation systems were almost unheard of, because of their incredibly high price.

When we returned home Yoko was there with Yumiko, so we began to prepare food because we were expecting guests. Michiyo, Nobuho's sister, arrived with her husband Kunito and their daughter. Kunito, who had taken us sightseeing in Tokyo and to the sumo wrestling, had brought us a lovely portfolio of the photographs he had taken of us all in Tokyo, so we were thrilled to have these souvenirs of sightseeing in Tokyo.

There were nine of us now, and a long, low table was laid out. We sat on cushions on the floor, and had a lovely, silly evening, laughing and talking, taking group photographs, and eating and drinking beer and sake until it was very late.

Tomiho and Yumiko invited us to their house in Yokohama for two days, after which we were going to meet Kunito and Michiyo for a day's sight-seeing. The following morning we set off with Tomiho and Yumiko to travel 50km south of Tokyo, and it took three hours in heavy traffic. We passed the Bay of Tokyo, which was very built up and industrial. Houses were built incredibly close to each other, and as we approached Yokohama I noticed that there were houses built right to the edge of cliff-like hills, even where the edge of the cliff was steep concrete reinforcing. We had passed through many tolls – a journey of 500km (about 300 miles) in Japan is likely to cost about £50 in tolls. A police car passed us – it was a Nissan Skyline, one of Warren's favourite cars. It looked very smart in black and white, with black Japanese script on the white upper part. A large spoiler, red Ferrari-like lights at the back, and a long red light on the top completed the picture of a very sporty police car.

Tomiho and Yumiko took us to a small nature park near their house. An old farmhouse with the original ancient equipment was open for viewing, and Tomiho and Warren competed with each other playing with the antique children's toys and walking on ancient bamboo stilts. An area had been reserved for growing rice and vegetables, and peanut plants were laid out to dry with the peanuts still attached to the roots. A competition had recently taken place amongst locals to build the best scarecrow – we liked the one which stood over the running water ditch; the water ran up a bamboo pole to the body of the scarecrow, which pulled a string to make the scarecrow's eyes roll and tongue stick out!

It poured with rain the following day, but Yumiko, Warren and I wanted to go to Chinatown in Yokohama for lunch. With umbrellas up we walked ten minutes to the train station, and walked from the train to the Chinatown area. As with all Chinatown areas, there was an impressive entrance archway across the street, and there were entrances on four sides, north, south, east and west. The streets were full of hurrying people with umbrellas. Chinese lanterns hung from the lamp posts, and there were expensive Chinese restaurants, cheap Chinese cafés and shops selling Chinese porcelain, fans, clothes, food and souvenirs. An enormous dragon's head with lit up red eyes had its mouth wide open to form the door to a restaurant, and further down the street was a stunningly beautiful Chinese temple painted ornately in red and gold with dragons mounted on the corners of the turned up roof. We walked inside, and there was a magnificent ceiling covered with paintings of fierce-looking red and gold dragons, and the air was thick with the smoke of burning incense.

We wandered through the streets until we found a suitable restaurant. Our set lunch was a delicious meal with an enormous bowl of soup which provided us with three small bowls each, three different main courses and a dessert of dorayaki, actually a Japanese dessert which is a pancake sandwich filled with sweet bean paste. Accompanied by a large pot of Chinese tea, we paid only 600 yen each (£3.50 pounds), so were very pleased. It made us realise that if one knows where to go, it is possible to eat cheaply in Japan.

We visited several interesting areas, and intended to go to the top of Landmark Tower, the highest building in Yokohama, to see the view. However, as we approached in the pouring rain we saw that above the 40th floor the top part of the building was enshrouded in clouds. There wouldn't be any view that day! As in all the towns, we noticed the evacuation area notices on the lamp-posts, which directed people to safe areas in the event of earthquakes. There were no earthquakes today, thank goodness, but there was plenty of non-stop rain!

We returned to Yumiko's house after a lovely day together. We were in high spirits as we walked in the dark back up the hill from the railway station with the rain bouncing from our umbrellas, and the three of us sang 'Just singing in the rain' at the top of our voices! I expect the neighbours thought that we were practising for the next karaoke competition!

A hot bath revived us, and I marvelled as I laid for ages in Yumiko's bath that Japanese baths never need topping up with hot water, because they are thermostatically-controlled to remain at a pre-set temperature. It suddenly seemed important to get a Japanese bath with all the technology when we returned to England, as well as a Japanese toilet!

Yumiko enjoyed cooking, and she prepared delicious tempura for us and served each of us a beautiful large goblet filled with vegetables of different colours and shapes, all enclosed in light, crispy batter and served with a chilli dipping sauce. The battered vegetables included a clump of three long green beans, a wedge of purple aubergine, a perfectly round mushroom, a floret of white cauliflower, dark green broccoli and a wedge of onion, and these were topped in the goblet with an enormous battered prawn. After our hot baths and lovely food we felt very content. Yumiko offered us some cooked jellyfish to try – it's a Chinese delicacy, and people who know me well would be amazed that I actually tried it. Neither of us liked it well enough to order it in a restaurant, but if you like chewing rubber bands you may well like cooked jellyfish.

The next day Warren and I said our goodbyes to Yumiko and Tomiho and caught the train to a nearby station, where we were to meet Kunito and Michiyo. The day was beautiful, in complete contrast to the torrential rain of the day before. How like England Japan is in many respects – like the English, the Japanese always discuss the weather when they meet because, like us, they have weather that is constantly changing.

Kunito and Michiyo were waiting for us, and as we walked out of the railway station at Kamakura, several Japanese women in traditional kimonos walked ahead. As always, with the kimonos they wore the traditional footwear, which are thonged wooden platform shoes built up on two strips of wood (zori) with white split-toe socks (tabi). They looked so difficult to walk in, and the women were certainly taking very tiny steps.

Young men were waiting for customers with their Japanese rickshaws, two-seater carts that were pulled behind a runner. However, we chose to walk along an avenue of cherry trees set in the middle of the road. At the end of the avenue was a shrine; as always, it was an elegant wooden building with copper-tiled curved roofs upturned at the edges. Young children looked breathtaking in traditional costume, and we discovered that it was a special celebration day for three and seven year old girls and five year old boys. For this special day they visited the shrine in their incredibly expensive, very best, traditional costumes.

Near the shrines fortunes were being sold, and a lady in a white kimono was busy serving young people. As always, the bad luck fortunes were being tied to a wooden frame. Nearby was another frame on which had been tied hand-painted small wooden boards. Personal prayers were written on these, virtually every one (some in English) requesting a good marriage or partner and good health. Nearby a teenage boy and a girl read their fortunes with great concentration, their heads close together. More young children in their lovely clothes were by the shrine, and some were happy to pose for our photographs, especially the pretty girls who were obviously proud of their special kimonos and magnificently-dressed hair. A 5-year old boy, dressed so beautifully that he looked like an angel, ran away from his parents into the middle of a flock of pigeons on the ground, causing chaos as he kicked every one that he could reach.

As Warren quickly pulled out the close-up lens to fit on the camera, broken glass fell out of the bag. The UV filter on the front of the lens had smashed. Whilst this in itself wouldn't have been a big problem, because filters don't cost too much, ground glass had worked its way inside the lens, so the lens would need to be professionally cleaned. We were very upset; we put the lens away, and Kunito promised to take us to Tokyo city centre where the main Canon service centre was situated.

Autumn colours were in the trees, and a temple on a tree-covered island was reflected in the surrounding lake with the red, yellow, green and orange of the leaves. Kunito and Michiyo had brought with them a packed lunch for all of us, so we sat in the sunshine eating sushi and enjoyed the view.

Kunito and Michiyo had planned a route for us to walk, so that we could see some of the different temples and shrines in Kamakura. We began to climb a hill, where pink camellias were flowering and maple trees were beginning to drop their brilliant red leaves. We arrived at a shrine approached by a tunnel through rock, where the tradition was to wash money in a basket in the special waters, and to keep the money to bring more riches. We washed our hands first in the special stone sink, using bamboo ladles to pour water onto our hands, and we duly washed our one yen coins. Maybe I should have washed a note of high value, because I later found another one yen coin on the ground, and wondered whether this was my 100% increase in wealth. As there were 18 yens to one English penny my new-found wealth was not very great!

There were temples and shrines, waterfalls and water features, bells on long tasselled ropes, stone lanterns, a small lake with giant goldfish and carp, and Dogs of Fo guarding the small curved barrel bridge. Dozens of wooden archways formed a tunnel along the steep uphill path out of the shrine, and scores of red-painted wooden archways were erected along a later section of the path as steps led us up a wooded hill to another shrine. This shrine stood in a cool, shady, heavily-wooded area thick with mosses and ferns. Miniature stone shrines stood in the woods, covered with moss and decorated with tiny china foxes representing a popular local god. The path led higher up the hill and it became difficult to negotiate after the heavy rain of the day before. We found ourselves searching for roots and stones to gain foot-holds in the slippery mud, but we reached the top; the path down the other side of the hill faced south, so the ground was dry and easier to negotiate.

The sun was getting lower, so we hurried to our last venue, an area where a giant bronze Buddha sat, towering over the neighbouring buildings. The Buddha had been made in 1252 and was originally gilded and located inside a temple. However, the wooden temple was washed away by a tsunami in 1498, so the Great Buddha appeared sitting in the open air, and this is how he has remained. At a height of 37 feet with a face nearly 8 feet long and eyes over 3 feet wide, it's difficult to believe the weight of 93 tons. The Buddha's eyebrows are just over 4 feet long and his ears, with long ear-lobes, are 6 feet 3 inches long. We were able to go inside the hollow Buddha to see how it had been constructed, which was fascinating.

The Buddha is very beautiful, sitting with hands together and head lowered as if in prayer, and is surrounded by fabulous bronze lanterns and flowers. A Buddhist monk removed the bowl of perfect red apples that had been made as an offering, and conducted a brief ceremony as the sun set. The four of us then walked through the town, admiring the incredibly expensive Japanese lacquer ware in the shops – it cost £2,000 for an intricately designed tray! Small religious statues stood alongside the pavements where we walked, and their heads and shoulders were stacked with small coins that passers-by had made as offerings.

Michiyo produced some cakes, decoratively wrapped in a sheet of paper-thin grained wood and tied with ribbon – it seemed a shame to throw away the wrapping that the baker's shop had supplied! Now we caught the train back to Tokyo, where Kunito and Michiyo took us to the Canon service centre. It had already closed for the day, but as we peered through the glass doors someone came to open the door to let us in. They needed 9 days to deal with the repair, they told us, but we were leaving Japan within a week. They promised to do the work as quickly as possible, returning it to us unrepaired if the job turned out to be a long one. We were impressed with the service and were thankful that, although it was bad luck to have damaged our Canon lens, it was good luck that we had done it in the country where it had been made! (They duly returned the lens within a few days, having cleaned it so that it was as good as new again).

Now Kunito and Michiyo took us to the Izumi Restaurant in the Shinjuko Sumito building. It took 10 seconds to reach the 49th floor, with no feeling of movement apart from a strange sensation in our ears. We cooked our own meal at the table, where we sat enjoying both our food and the stunning view of night-time Tokyo.

We were surprised on our way back to Yoko's house to find that the underground trains were as packed at 10pm as the London rush hour trains, but this was the rush hour – hard-working businessmen go for a drink after finishing work late and were only now returning home. Most people were asleep, and Kunito and Michiyo also fell asleep quickly. The other passengers laughed when

Warren ran over to take their photo; they didn't wake and weren't aware that we had taken photos until we told them later. We arrived back at Yoko's home tired but happy after a very pleasant day. We had one week remaining before we left Japan.

At the weekend, Yoko had a few days off work and was planning to take us to the wedding in the north of Japan. The day before we left, I went by bus alone to the nearby city to go to the internet café. I was fascinated as I travelled on the bus – I watched as people entered the bus, and almost as soon as they sat down they were asleep, their heads nodding or falling sideways onto someone's shoulder (usually a complete stranger!). It was only 10am, and it made no difference if it was a young or old person, male or female – buses and trains are for sleeping on in Japan! I always try very hard not to sleep in trains or buses, because I once missed my station after falling asleep. I was travelling by train from Birmingham to Reading, and fell asleep at Oxford, 30 miles from my stop at Reading. When I woke the train was just leaving Reading, and I was on the way to Portsmouth on the south coast. When I arrived at Portsmouth, I discovered that the next train back to Reading was at 5 o'clock the next morning, so I had to sleep at Portsmouth station, which was very uncomfortable and a bit scary on my own. The return train to Reading stopped at every blade of grass, taking 3½ hours to reach Reading, so I was incredibly tired at work the next day!

★ ★ ★

We set off at 6am on the Saturday with Yoko driving Nobuho's car – bigger and more comfortable than her own, and with a navigational system (always referred to as 'the navigator' by the Japanese). Yoko drove for a couple of hours, and turned off the main highway. The road became mountainous, and we climbed higher and higher up winding roads, and back downhill again – we had crossed the range of mountains that forms the backbone of Japan. Here the colours of the trees were as we had hoped to see – golden, bronze, orange, red, yellow and green trees covered the mountains. The roads were very winding, and often very high; strong fences up to 20 feet high edged the roads to stop rocks falling from above and hitting the road – a particular danger in a country where earth tremors and earthquakes are so common.

We arrived at Ouchi at 9am. Ouchi is a lovely old village with traditional Japanese thatched houses – a living museum. Yoko had last visited Ouchi ten years before, when it had been a very quiet village, but it had since been 'discovered' and was very popular with Japanese tourists – we saw no other westerners there. The car park was busy with cars and coaches, but we found a space.

Originally Ouchi had been an important staging post, just as our home town of Reading was originally an important stop for horse-drawn coaches between London and Bath. At that time restaurants, inns and guesthouses had lined the main street of the village, but when a major highway by-passed Ouchi the village was almost forgotten. Suddenly Ouchi was rediscovered, surprisingly unchanged from that previous era, and the main street with its wooden houses with thatched roofs suddenly became a major tourist attraction. At the end of the street was a massive tree, with bright yellow fan-shaped autumnal leaves – it was a gingko or maidenhair tree. The old shops were fascinating, selling sweets, food, fans, baskets, dried fruits, flowers and souvenirs. Outside the shops hung dried persimmons threaded onto strings, and red and yellow dried chillies hung in bunches alongside orange Chinese lantern seed-pods. An ancient guesthouse, now a museum, had a fire burning in a square hole in the middle of the floor, a black kettle suspended above it. Old tools, skis, snow-shoes, clothes and artefacts were on display.

The street was beginning to fill with Japanese tourists as we walked to a restaurant for lunch. A roaring fire in the middle of the room was cooking small fishes that had been speared onto sticks in 'S' shapes. We removed our shoes and went upstairs; beams were exposed around our low table, and we sat on cushions on the floor eating our exquisite lunch. Warren even had to go on bended knee to pay the cashier on the way out as she was sat on the floor behind a very low desk. As we drove out of Ouchi we were glad we had arrived early – a queue of cars 5km long was now waiting to enter the small car park!

After a short drive we arrived at Aizu-Wakamatsu, Yoko's home town. After visiting the castle, a tall building with many tiered roofs, surrounded by a moat and attractive grounds, we visited Yoko's sister, who owns several sweet shops in the town. The shop was busy, so we sat on the seats surrounding the counters where large, wooden bowls full of beautifully-packaged home-made sweets were displayed. Yoko's sister and brother-in-law served the customers from a raised area behind the L-shaped counter. They had no shoes on, and sat cross-legged packaging people's purchases in pretty bags and wrapping paper. Yoko's sister was a very cheerful person who laughed a lot, and when she had finished serving the customers she took us all to an area behind the shop where we could see a production line – people packing the sweets into cartons ready to be sold. Yoko's sister did demonstrations of sweet-making for tourists, so she now showed us how to make a simple sweet, and we made efforts to copy her to produce one of the most basic sweets that she sells. It was fascinating, and we each left with a present of a clam shell filled with home-made sweets which, as always in Japan, was skilfully wrapped.

Now we had to find the guesthouse which had been booked by Yoko's sister. It was a minshuku or Japanese bed and breakfast, and was very pleasant – we had a large room divided into two by Japanese sliding doors made of wood and paper.

Similar doors (with no lock) divided the room from the main hotel passageway, and on the other side of the room were the same type of sliding doors which led to another passageway and our own private toilet.

A wonderful meal awaited us downstairs after our hot bath – as always, many individual bowls were set before each person. We each had half an aubergine cut into cubes ready to be picked up with chopsticks, and it had been cooked until meltingly tender with a honey glaze. Spinach, wonderfully flavoured with sesame oil and seeds, an enormous prawn decorated with sliced crabsticks and sweetcorn, soup thick with vegetables, kipper cooked in soy sauce, pickles and rice accompanied the meal. Yoko's sister had given us a bottle of sparkling wine, so the meal was another very enjoyable experience.

It was foggy when we woke the next day, and after the usual Japanese breakfast of fish, rice, soup and pickles with green tea we set off towards Tendo. Initially we passed through high mountains, and we noticed that the roads were lined with very high metal louvred fences. The louvres would drop down when snow and blizzards began, to protect the roads from avalanches of snow. There was a lake in the distance partially hidden by the fog, and a volcano ahead of us had a chunk missing from the top – an eruption had blown the top half off the volcano, and the lava had run into a nearby river blocking it, so that lakes had formed, and the river had taken a different course. Great damage had been done, and the landscape was completely changed as a result of the eruption. The volcano was Mount Bandai, and we drove round it along winding roads through trees full of autumn colours.

The fog had dispersed as we parked in the only parking space left when we arrived at the lake, and once again Yoko was amazed how many tourists there were. Warren and I were again the only westerners. Mount Bandai was the highest point in the background of mountains, but had apparently once been almost twice as high. The water of the lake was an incredible petrol blue caused by minerals from the volcano, and apparently there are many hot spas in the area, again because of volcanic activity. Lake Goshikinuma, which means five-coloured lake, was very beautiful and surrounded by deciduous trees. It reminded us very much of English woods, some trees already bare, some gold, red or brown, but already many leaves and pine needles cushioned the ground. At the edge of the lake was a vivid red Japanese maple tree, its tiny crimson leaves transparent in the sunlight.

We were not alone as we walked around the lake, taking a path over stones and rocks, pine needles and leaves, along wooden walkways and up and down natural stone steps, on stepping stones over shallow water, through the trees and past bracken and ferns. The sun filtered through the coloured leaves, and glinted on the extraordinary blue water of the lakes. Despite the people, it was a very peaceful place. After an hour's walk we arrived at the far end of the lake, where we were able to catch a bus back to the car park. We wandered round the shops surrounding the car park and were amazed to see black bear skins, the fur long and lustrous. The vegetable shops were full of familiar and strange vegetables and fruits – the now very familiar and very common Chinese radish, about 15 inches long and often used grated in Japanese dishes, baby purple aubergines, apples at least twice the size of any I've ever seen in England, Nashi pears, persimmons, small Japanese seedless cucumbers, cabbages, Chinese leaves, unfamiliar berries, prickly cucumbers and giant pinky-red tomatoes.

I went to the toilet, and wondered how old people manage to use Asian toilets when their knees become stiff and arthritic, and how they sit on the floor cushions at the table or kneel on the floor in temples to pray. With arthritic fingers, I wondered how they use chopsticks, which need more dexterity than a knife and fork.

We continued on our way, and I noticed that some pine trees were changing colour to golden orange. These were Karamatsu or Japanese Larch trees, deciduous conifers, and on the mountainside their colours looked fabulous. As we travelled further up the mountain, going round the S-bends, the views of other mountain ranges were spectacular. We were over 1,700 metres high, and stopped to take photos. We continued on our journey by car and Yoko commented on a sign.

'Beware of gas,' it said, and Yoko wondered aloud how she could beware of it. Almost immediately there was a terrible smell of sulphur, which continued for quite a long way. Sulphur is a natural gas emitted by volcanoes, and many of the hot springs have this same foul smell.

As we travelled back down the mountain we passed orchards full of Nashi pears, apples and vines. Red apples hung thickly on trees, the branches hanging almost to the ground with the weight, and stalls were selling them by the roadside.

We arrived in Tendo. It was 4pm on a Sunday, and Yoko was going to attend the marriage of one of her students. She had asked special permission if we could come to take photos of the bride and groom, and they had agreed. We waited in the hotel foyer, feeling very scruffy in our travelling clothes, as the foyer gradually filled up with women in kimonos or smart Western dress and black-suited men. By the time Yoko rejoined us, having changed into her smart clothes, there were 500 wedding guests in the hotel foyer. Strangely, every so often one or two hotel guests with wet hair pushed their way through the guests; they were dressed only in their hotel yukatas and slippers, obviously having visited the hotel sento. We noticed that as many as 80% of the wedding guests were middle-aged men, looking very business-like in their black suits and white ties, as though they were about to attend a business conference. They studied their individual printed guest lists carefully to see where they were to sit and whether they recognised other names. Yoko was very proud to see that, as the bridegroom's university tutor, and therefore a very important person, she had been placed at the main table next to the bride and groom.

Warren and I were treated very well, and were shown the massive reception room by the hotel staff. Dozens of maids still scurried around putting exquisitely-wrapped bags filled with presents on each guest's chair. The room was so vast that people at the back would have needed binoculars to see the bride and groom, and the wedding cake was like a tower. It seemed unbelievable that anything so tall could remain upright. I couldn't help but picture the Leaning Tower of Pisa, and hoped that the cake wouldn't end up emulating that very famous building.

The kimonos worn by the ladies were stunning. Made of incredibly expensive hand-embroidered silk, it is apparently an art to put them on. We were introduced to the groom, resplendent in a white brocade kimono, and he asked us to take a photo of him with Yoko. After the guests had filed into the wedding reception room, Warren and I waited outside the massive doors while dozens of waitresses in uniform and wedding attendants in kimonos stood in line until the bride and groom appeared. The bride was wearing a white silk kimono with a large white head-dress, and she apparently later changed into a colourful kimono and then a long, red wedding dress. We were thrilled when the bride and groom stopped in front of us for us to take photos, and no doubt the waitresses and wedding attendants wondered who on earth we were!

We left Yoko at the wedding reception to find our own hotel. Further along the road we passed another wedding group seated for an outside photograph. It was a much smaller wedding, much less formal, and everyone was laughing. The bride wore a colourful kimono, and they allowed us to take photographs. As Warren knelt to take a photo, one guest was heard to say 'international' in English, and everyone laughed. As we walked further down the road we overtook a couple wearing yukatas and zori, the Japanese wooden thonged sandal. Judging by the way they walked in them, these two people were certainly not used to wearing zori! A line of such sandals sat on a shelf in the reception of our very smart hotel when we arrived, and we were amazed to discover that our room, as well as all the other wedding guests' rooms, had been paid for by the groom's father, a prominent business man.

Breakfast the next morning was also included in the hotel bill, and it came in a fabulously beautiful square Japanese lacquer box with a lid which contained four compartments, each with a different Imari bowl. The bowls contained the usual Japanese breakfast, the green vegetables looking especially pretty decorated with yellow and pink flower petals. We also had nori, which are thin, dried seaweed sheets. This time the nori was in one inch wide strips with which we made sushi. We broke small pieces of fish with our chopsticks and placed a bite-sized piece onto the rice in the bowl. Then we placed the seaweed paper over the top of the fish with the chopsticks, and if we carefully pushed the chopsticks either side of the seaweed we could gather up the seaweed encircling the fish and some rice. All we had to do was pop it into our mouths – delicious, especially if first dipped in soy sauce (which we managed to do after a little practice!). We were quite pleased to find that by the time we had finished the breakfast we had mastered the art quite successfully.

We set off again, Yoko filling up with petrol, which we were interested to see cost about two-thirds of the price in England. The sky was full of autumn clouds, which looked like fish scales across the sky. It began to rain slightly, and Yoko commented how surprised she was how few people used umbrellas in England. In Japan, even for a few spots of rain, everyone produces an umbrella. Shops, hotels and restaurants all have special containers for umbrellas, some with locks, or special long narrow plastic bags are provided to fit over the umbrella to stop it dripping in the shop.

Yoko drove us to a temple built high on a mountain. We began to climb the hundreds of steps up the mountainside (I counted 873 plus slopes on the way down!) and we were constantly in deeply shaded woods with autumn colours. Many small temples, gravestones and toba with sacred text were interspersed along the way amongst the ferns, trees and rocks and against mountain walls. Near the souvenir shops stood very tall, majestic cedar trees and small pretty pine trees trimmed into decorative shapes. A huge golden Buddha sat in a temple at the top, and the view looking down was spectacular. Small temples and gnarled trees stood on seemingly unreachable crags outlined against the sheer backdrop, reminding me of Chinese paintings.

At another temple later in the day we were lucky enough to see Japanese people dancing, wearing strange costumes with masks and feathers on their head. An old man beat a drum and others played pipes. A well-preserved 150 year old wooden thatched theatre stood nearby, the actors having just finished a play which had been watched by the audience sitting on banks of tiered grass.

We continued our journey to the east coast, and passed through an avenue of sycamore trees, their leaves vivid red, yellow and green, and giant maple trees with the tiniest of leaves had thick carpets of red leaves beneath them. To our left were ranges of mountains in varying shades of grey, the furthest a pale silver grey outline in the far distance. Rice fields lined the road, and here the rice was drying on individual posts, each sheaf placed horizontally above the other making a spiral shape. We turned left and went in and out of tunnels as we passed under the mountains, and signs constantly warned of raccoons and monkeys in the area. We learnt that the Japanese monkey, the macaque, is happy in colder areas unlike most monkeys, and will even live in areas in north Japan which have bitterly cold winters with deep snow.

As we drove into Kesennuma and found a ryokan, a Japanese inn, it began to rain again. Two rooms were available, and after a bath we were served food on the low table in Yoko's room. It was a feast fit for a photograph and was very expensive food, some of which I had never tasted before. Large bowls of shark's fin soup, a Chinese delicacy, were served. Although the crab in it was delicious I was not keen on the slimy texture of the shark's fin, which we also found very difficult to pick up with chopsticks. Thirteen different plates and bowls each held different dishes. A grilled sole was arranged on a fan-shaped plate, and there was rice, Japanese miso soup, salad, pickles, tempura and cooked squid caught that day. Interestingly, I had never before liked the idea of eating shellfish, so it seems shocking that my first experiences of eating shellfish was eating it raw! Many raw fishes and shellfish made up the main part of the meal – the abalone had a very nice, meaty texture; several oysters had already been removed from their shell and, although I know it's normal even in England to eat them raw, my new-found ability to eat raw fish and shellfish didn't extend to what looked to me like a very slimy-textured meal. There was squid in sauce, octopus, which was surprisingly delicious raw, bonito (a Japanese fish similar to tuna), mackerel and a large raw prawn. The manageress of the hotel knelt on the rush-matted floor and bowed deeply to Yoko, and we were served by a maid.

Our room had no toilet, but there was one only 4 or 5 yards away in the corridor. In our room we had bare or stockinged feet, as we were not allowed to walk even with slippers on the rush mats. As soon as we left the room to go to the toilet, we had to put on the house slippers which were left outside our door, walk five steps to the toilet, where we had to leave the slippers outside and step into the special toilet slippers left inside the toilet (and strangely usually embroidered with the English word 'toilet'!). Leaving the toilet entailed walking backwards out of the toilet slippers in order to step into the other slippers waiting outside, and then we left them five steps later outside the bedroom door! We slept well, but were woken at 6am by the tune of the community clock, which was obviously very close to the hotel.

The last day we travelled south, stopping for a short boat trip in a bay of small islands. Bamboo sticks marked seaweed farms, and there were netted areas where fishermen kept their catch alive until required, because Japanese housewives always insist on very fresh fish. A short while later we arrived back at Yoko's house again.

★ ★ ★

The following day Yoko took us by car to Narita airport in Tokyo – we were leaving Japan and felt very sad to be saying goodbye to our Japanese friends. We had problems when we checked in for our flight to Bangkok, because the check-in assistant asked to see our onward tickets out of Thailand. We explained that we had none, because we intended to cycle south out of Thailand into Malaysia and on to Singapore and Indonesia. We didn't have a plane ticket until we reached Bali, when we would fly to Perth in Western Australia. The assistant said that his computer told him that we couldn't fly to Thailand without an onward ticket, so we showed him our ticket from Bali.

'But how will you get from Bangkok to Bali?' he asked.

'We will cycle through Thailand, Malaysia and Singapore, take a ferry to Java, cycle some more and take another ferry to Bali,' we repeated.

'But how will you get from Bangkok to Bali?' he asked again. He couldn't grasp that there was any mode of travel apart from flying. We explained that we had been to Bangkok before without an onward ticket, and it was easy to buy one there if necessary. We showed him our previous visa, because now he was saying that we had no visa, but in Thailand visas are automatically stamped for 30 days on entry to the country. At this point he told us to go immediately and buy a ticket from Bangkok to Bali, and we could cancel it when we got to Bangkok and get a refund. We refused, and he asked us to return in 30 minutes to speak to a supervisor. She was also concerned. We told her we were obviously going to leave Thailand because we had tickets from Bali to Australia.

'But these are for a year's time,' she said.

'Yes,' said Warren. 'We want to enjoy ourselves.'

She laughed and agreed to let us fly to Bangkok, and we were relieved not to have had to pay excess baggage, especially as our bikes had been weighed as well as our other luggage.

The plane left on time at 7pm, the 3,084 mile (4,972km) journey was uneventful, and we arrived in hot and steamy Bangkok 6½ hours later. It was 30°C, almost midnight and very humid. Fortunately Thailand was two hours behind Japan, so we were just in time to catch the last bus at midnight which would take us to an area where we knew there were plenty of hotels. The bus driver tried to charge us 100 baht for the bikes when he saw us loading them onto the bus, even though the ticket office had already confirmed to us that they would be free. Warren just laughed and ignored his frequent requests for money, so the driver eventually gave up asking.

Our six weeks in Japan was a wonderful experience, made possible and enjoyable by our Japanese friends. Without them we would never have experienced so much or seen so many different places and learnt so many things about Japan. We are indebted to them, and hope to return the favour by welcoming them to our own home in England in the future . . .

CHAPTER 15

BANGKOK

Bangkok, the capital of Thailand, is noisy, polluted, hot, sticky and full of traffic. Many people develop an instant dislike for Bangkok, especially if they arrive during April, May or June, when the weather is especially sticky and floods are likely. Bangkok stands only two metres above sea level, so the city often floods during the monsoon season, when water in the river and canals overflows. Despite this, there is much of interest for the tourist to see in Bangkok and it is the hub of South East Asia for backpackers and travellers. There is cheap accommodation, cheap food, cheap clothes (or anything else the tourist might want to buy) and plenty of night life. However, there are also numerous beautiful temples, canals, the Grand Palace and markets to visit.

After arriving at our hotel in the early hours of the morning, we slept soundly until 10am, despite the loud disco next door. At breakfast (usually a western breakfast in touristy Bangkok of egg, bacon and toast) a punk with pink Mohican spiky hair and numerous face-piercings including a large, silver ball just under his cheekbone was asleep for over an hour at the table next to us. All around in the restaurant were westerners – British, Europeans, Americans and Australians. Bangkok is a major backpackers' destination, and depends heavily on the income that tourists spend.

We wandered around Chaosan Road, popular with backpackers and a bustling area full of shops and stalls. We decided that if we ever flew to Bangkok again we would do so without spare clothes, shoes or a suitcase, because it's possible to buy everything in Bangkok at a fraction of the English price.

After lunch I went to the toilet at the back of the restaurant. There was a sign on the wall. 'Do not put paper in the toilet.' As I couldn't find any toilet paper this was impossible anyway. Later I found a sign outside saying, 'Toilet paper can be bought at the toilet paper box'! Did they sell it by the sheet, I wondered . . .

Now that we weren't so tired, we spent a fairly sleepless night the second night because of the disco noise. We searched for another hotel, because we needed to stay in Bangkok at least a week while we organised visas for Vietnam, Laos and Cambodia. We found a third floor room with a lovely view of temple roofs across the road, each with elegant stag-horn shaped curves at the ends of the roof; the roofs were made up of red, yellow and green fish scale shaped roof tiles set in patterns. The room was large enough for our bikes, though the hotel employees were initially not keen for us to take them into the room and, as always, we had our own shower room and toilet. A notice on the wall showed what a difference a letter can make.

'If guests do damage in hotel room, guests are fine,' the notice read.

We stood at the hotel reception checking out of the first hotel.

'Warren, move the bike away from the lady,' I said, and wondered why Warren grinned.

He explained afterwards. 'She' was no lady – only dressed as one!

It was very difficult planning the next stage of our cycle trip, because visas for Vietnam, Laos and Cambodia only lasted for 3 or 4 weeks from entry into the country, and ran out two months after they had been stamped into the passports. There were also only limited border crossings where visas could be stamped into passports on entry. It looked as though we would have only two months to cycle across Thailand and through each country, which was not long enough. After several hours of planning, phoning embassies, speaking to travel agents and calculating cycle times, we eventually decided that the only way to visit all three countries within the allotted times was to fly to Da Nang in Vietnam, cycle north and then west over the mountain into Laos, and cycle west and south-west across Laos to one of its road borders with Thailand. We could then cycle south through Thailand to the road border with Cambodia, where we were told that we could get a 30 day visa stamped into our passport on entry. Obviously no tourist to Cambodia could miss a visit to Angkor Wat, the site of the famous 1,000 year old temples, so we planned to cycle across Cambodia to Angkor Wat. After visiting the temples, we planned to cycle across Cambodia to the coast, where we hoped to catch a boat to take us back to Thailand again. Passports were always stamped with a 30 day visa on entry to Thailand, and this could be done as many times as we liked, so long as we kept leaving the country and returning again. We bought our flight ticket to Da Nang and left our passports with the travel agent to arrange to have the necessary visas entered into our passports for Vietnam and Laos. We now had a week to spend in Bangkok while we waited for this to be done.

The weather in Bangkok was, and always appears to be, extremely hot and uncomfortable. It was 35°C but unbearably humid. I found myself constantly saying 'I'm sweating', and remembered my teacher in the first year of grammar school scolding me for saying such a thing.

'Mary,' she told me, 'Horses sweat, men perspire, but ladies only glow.' I've never forgotten her saying that, but I certainly didn't feel as though I was glowing in Bangkok, especially when Warren said that anyone going to Bangkok in April would 'sweat like a paedophile in a playground!' It was almost impossible to sleep in such heat, and we found the most comfortable way to sleep was to lie under the fan, covering ourselves with a wet sarong and spraying our faces with a mist of water.

Thai food is wonderful, and we enjoyed the red, yellow or green Thai curries with rice, full of chillies but the heat softened with the flavour of coconut milk, and delicious noodle dishes like Pad Thai. Even in the tourist area in Bangkok a good meal cost us only £1.00. I asked for an iced coffee, which at 30 baht (45p) was delicious and refreshing, so Warren asked for the same. His glass was slightly smaller, but he grinned when he saw that they had given him a glass in the shape of a female body! Rooms were also good value at £4.50 for a double room with bathroom, but air conditioning was more expensive and not very common in the backpacker areas. However, with the high humidity we were beginning to feel that maybe it was necessary.

After watching one of the many big television screens showing videos in the restaurants, we went to bed that night, but Bangkok never sleeps – at least, the part of Bangkok where we were never did. The noise from the street three floors below didn't stop – people shouted, car horns sounded, bells rang (the ice-cream man on his bicycle), music played from radios, motorbikes revved, doors banged (guests in the hotel), car doors slammed, dogs barked and, as the noise began to die down at 4am, a cockerel nearby began to crow, and didn't stop for several hours. By 6am the street cleaners began cleaning the streets, their radios turned up high, and the sun shone brightly into our room through the thin curtains. At that stage we resorted to eye masks (courtesy of British Airways) as well as the ear plugs that we had been wearing all night. We agreed that it was lucky that second-hand English novels were available everywhere in Bangkok – at least we could read if we couldn't sleep at night! The room that we'd found the first time we were in Bangkok had air conditioning but no window – now the lack of a view from a window seemed quite appealing, because there would have been no street noise. In our current hotel there were intercoms on each landing, so from 8am there were raucous voices piercing our ear-drums as the maids called to each other, so we couldn't even sleep late if we'd been kept awake overnight with the noise!

We had an extraordinary e-mail from my brother the next day to say that he had received a parking ticket for the car that we had borrowed from him while we were in England in September. The ticket stated that the car had been parked in a bus lane in Durham. Warren was amazed – he had actually been sitting in the car with the car running, wanting to ask someone the way to a certain street. He asked the parking attendant, who didn't answer Warren's question.

'Move on or I'm going to give you a ticket,' he had said rudely. Warren moved on but still got a ticket. When we thought how helpful people had been all round the world giving us directions, drawing maps, walking with us or even driving slowly so we could follow on our bicycles, we felt sad that our own country could be so different, so unhelpful and even vindictive.

One Sunday we walked through the temple grounds to a restaurant for breakfast. Colourful cockerels looked beautiful as they scratched in the ground, though we hadn't thought them beautiful when they crowed at 4am in the morning! The monks were chanting inside the temple, and we saw two young female monks (we decided that they should be called 'monkesses'!) who had white robes, saffron umbrellas and shaved heads. It was 9am, but very few of the restaurants were open, and the streets for once were quiet and there were very few people around. We walked into the restaurant to find no guests – only two waiters sleeping across the chairs. Obviously in Bangkok most tourists stayed up late and slept in late.

We discovered that my Teva sandals, which I had virtually lived in since we had left England, had split and needed to be replaced. We felt that we had been extremely lucky so many times – bad luck that they had split (and in England would probably be replaced free of charge because it was faulty rubber on the sole of a very expensive sandal), but lucky that it was in Bangkok. For £7.50 in Bangkok we were able to buy identical sandals to my old ones which had cost £65! We were so excited to find such a bargain that we bought two more pairs to send home.

Where else had we been lucky like that? While we were in Australia, Warren's Campagnola gears had broken – bad luck that such an expensive item had broken, but lucky for us it was in Australia. We would never have been able to buy such a component in Asia. After we had replaced the damaged part, we sent the damaged piece to the services department in Australia, who sent a new replacement to England for us. And, of course, we had been lucky to have needed help with our Canon lens while we were in Japan, the country of camera makers.

We visited a nearby temple, Wat Ratchanaddaram, which we understood was a world heritage site. On the site, as with all of the temples, were numerous buildings, each with the typical elegant roofs with fish scale shaped multi-coloured tiles. Sometimes the roofs were cross-shaped, but usually they were stepped in tiers, with gilding and colours on the eaves, the gilding glinting in the sun. However, the oldest temple at Wat Ratchanaddaram was different from these, being built in a square with eight ornate double archways on each side of the square. Above these archways were seven white-painted spires on each side. Above that, as the building went higher and narrower, were four ornate bronze spires on each side which stood out clearly against the white painted building, with a final ornate bronze spire at the very top. The roof was covered with millions of fish scale shaped bronze tiles. Money was being collected to replace the white concrete spires with bronze again, so that the temple could again be as it had been originally, many centuries ago. However, it was very beautiful even as it was, and we walked up the spiral staircase in the centre of the building. Passages radiated off the staircase, and at the end of each passage sat a Buddha image. When we reached the top of the building there was an amazing view of Bangkok, and the sun shone and glinted on the numerous gilded temples throughout Bangkok.

We returned to Khaosan Road, and the smell of fresh pineapple mingling with barbecued chicken and sweet corn hit our nostrils. We looked at some attractive enamelled balls in a box, but they were far too heavy for us to carry on our bikes. The stall-owner, who was deaf and dumb, demonstrated to us that they were stress balls, and tapped into his calculator the price of 140 baht (only £2). We shook our heads and began to leave, so he quickly turned over the calculator to show a printed sign which said 'What is your price?' We laughed with him and shook our heads. A few shops later we decided to buy two good quality rucksacks for a total of 1,450 baht (£22) to send home with the sandals. Warren couldn't resist them at that price. Even though the postage to send them home was more than the cost of the rucksacks, they were still a bargain.

We were spending our time drinking cold drinks or showering, just to keep cool. Thankfully beer was quite cheap at 40 to 50 baht for a 65ml bottle (about 65p to 75p) but wine was relatively expensive. We treated ourselves a few times to a bottle of French table wine which, at 400 baht, was over £6 and 1½ times the price of our hotel room for a night! Despite the fact that red wine was always served cold in Thailand, it was still enjoyable for a change. That day it was especially hot and humid, so we bought a cold beer and went to our room, where we sat on the floor of the large shower with the cool shower gently spraying over us while we drank the cold beer (making sure that the water didn't dilute the beer, of course!). It seemed a good way to cool off, and we did this regularly after that!

Stalls line the streets of Bangkok day and night. As well as wooden souvenirs such as chopsticks, bowls and carved Buddha images in gorgeous woods, there were clothes, CD stalls with music blaring, stalls offering express same day laundry for 25 baht for 1 kilogramme (38p), cocktails for 75p each, baked potatoes, chicken on sticks or barbecued sweetcorn (10 baht), omelettes and rice for 10 baht (15p), freshly squeezed juices, fruits such as papaya, pineapple, mango and melon, peeled and sliced and kept on ice ready to eat, freshly roasted peanuts, second-hand English books, stalls with choices of as many as 80 foods for breakfast, lunch or dinner, toys, shoes and sandals, handbags, cushion covers, sunglasses, hats, hi-fis and bedspreads. Flowers were sold near the temple – enormous lotus buds and yellow flowers made into chains; there were stalls selling

Vietnam
Cycling gardens!

India
young man is dressed to represent one of 29 gods at a local annual festival, all of whom walk bare-footed
through red hot coals at the end of the day

Laos
Monks and other passengers hang on to the top, sides and back of the taxi

Vietnam
Mary cycling towards the Lao border

India
Camels and painted lorries are the preferred form of goods transport in Rajasthan

India
Lorries loaded and ready to go!

India *(left)*
Mary eating her favourite breakfast of Massala Dosa
Vietnam *(right)*
As we left our hotel, the children were waiting to entertain us

India *(left)*
Women are the hod carriers in India
Australia *(right)*
A kookaburra finds a comfortable perch on the back of Mary's bike.

Italy
Mary and Warren rest after the winding, hilly roads; Celle Ligure is in the background

Myanmar
A typical fisherman at Lake Inle before sunrise

India
Outside the tailor's in Kerala – making an excellent job of ironing with an antique iron

Vietnam
Carrying roofing materials, this bicycle is even more loaded than ours

Turkey
Snow in Istanbul; Mary and Warren with the magnificent St Sofia in the background

Cambodia
The barber's business is on the busy pavement of a Phnom Penh street

Laos *(left)*
Four children cycle by, excitedly waving to us
Myanmar *(right)*
A night view of Sule Paya, a 200 year-old Buddhist temple in Yangon

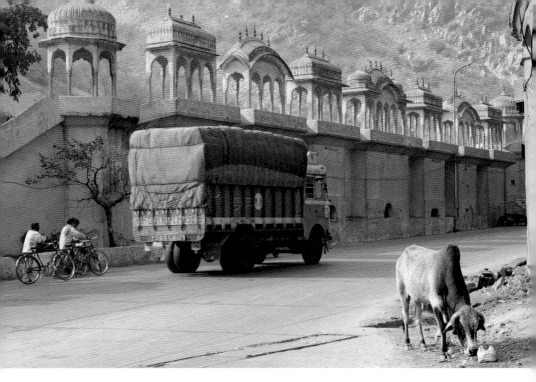

India
A stunning approach to Jaipur, Rajasthan in north India

Australia *(left)*
Warren in his new Ozzie kangaroo leather hat
Laos *(right)*
Village children talk to us through the garden fence

hairpieces, plaited or dreadlocked, or jewellery made of beads, wood and shells. Stalls advertised and showed samples of ID cards, student cards, UK driving licences, press cards, international driving licences – if you've got the money (only 200 baht) you can have the ID. The press cards and student cards were especially popular, because with these anyone could obtain reduced or even free entrance to many of the tourist attractions. Travel agents, cafés, air-conditioned photo and camera shops, classy air-conditioned jewellery shops, restaurants and air-conditioned bars and coffee houses selling superb espresso or iced coffee lined the road behind the stalls, together with banks, exchange booths, ATMs, chemists, internet cafés and tailors. Dogs lay on the pavement blocking the way, and the stalls left only enough room for two people to pass with difficulty between the stalls and the shops.

We took a short journey by air-conditioned taxi to a multi-floor air-conditioned shopping centre with everything anyone could possibly want, so Bangkok really is a shoppers' paradise. Despite the fact that Bangkok is a large Asian city it is clean, and women were constantly sweeping the roads and pavements with besom brooms. They wore face masks and scarves over their hair with conical hats on top to protect them from the dust and exhaust fumes.

We chatted to an Irishman in a café who told us that he was going the next day to a Thai island. We asked him which island it was, but he didn't know the name of it. Was it in the north or the south of Thailand, we asked; was it on the east or the west coast? He didn't know; all he knew was that it would be an 11 hour journey by bus! Hopefully he would know that he had arrived when he got there!

We took a taxi to the Grand Palace, and had a fried rice lunch first in one of the small cafés nearby. The meal cost 65p and was ornately decorated with an exotic purple orchid. On entry to the palace complex we discovered that, although we had worn suitable clothes, flip-flops weren't allowed, so we had to borrow sandals and buy socks from them. We noticed that Thais were exempted the sandals rule, and once again we thought it extraordinary how western countries fall over backwards to treat everyone the same, but how we had constantly found Asian countries to be openly and blatantly discriminating. However, the palace complex was amazing – once inside the main gate we didn't know which way to turn, because everything was so dazzling and spectacular. Within the palace complex are many impressive buildings. Temples were covered with tiny mosaic pieces of gold, blue, red and pieces of mirror; columns rose high with stunning oriental roofs on top covered with the usual red, yellow and green roofs with gilded finials. Many of the gables were covered with gold and vibrant blue exotic designs. Giant statues of demon gate guardians with frightening faces, 20 feet high and studded with colourful jewels, guarded the temples. Other temples were surrounded by Dogs of Fo; spires soared to the sky, the gold glinting in the sunlight; coloured pieces of mirrors surrounded buildings; a bell-shaped golden temple shone brightly; a jade Buddha adorned the main temple; corridors had hand-painted murals on walls, and steps, galleries and terraces were beautifully marbled. Altars with large lotus buds given as offerings were attended by many Thai people; massive columns supporting buildings were covered with jewel-like colours or stunning hand-made tiles, and there were statues of elephants, cows, gods, Thai dancers and Buddha images everywhere. The buildings had fabulous doors and gateways, tall and studded, gilded and coloured, carved and covered with coloured and mirrored mosaics. Gilded roofs one on top of another stood on white buildings as ornate as royal wedding cakes; ornate gilded stupas 40 or 50 feet high were decorated around the base by Thai dancers with demon-like faces, their arms outstretched and upturned hands touching to encircle the stupas. Neat gardens surrounded the Grand Palace Hall, with immaculate grass and neat and perfect Japanese-style trimmed trees. We had a wonderful time, and this was to be our last day in Bangkok.

The next day we caught the bus back to Bangkok airport. The bus was late, so we got to the airport later than intended. Checking had begun at 7am and it was now 7.30; we were worried, because we always liked to arrive early because of the bikes. After checking in they insisted on trying to push our bikes through the x-ray machine on conveyor belts. No-one had ever done this before, and we were worried that the bikes might get stuck but, with Warren running from one end to the other helping to push and pull the bikes, the bikes were successfully x-rayed. Afterwards the girl directed us to the long queue at Cathay Pacific.

'No. We're flying PB Air to Da Nang in Vietnam,' we said.

'Oh, over there then,' she said, and pointed in the opposite direction to a check-in point where one man stood. As we approached, he looked relieved.

'Thank God for that,' he said with an Irish accent. 'I was beginning to think that I was the only passenger. With all the travelling I've done, I've never been the only one in the queue before!'

The girl and young man behind the check-in counter were helpful but unsure what to do with the bikes. He tried to put them on the conveyor belt, but Warren told him they'd jam or fall off when they reached the corner.

'They're usually taken over there through that door,' said Warren, pointing – it was lucky that we'd been through Bangkok airport before.

The lad nodded, removed the bikes and followed Warren's directions.

We made our way later to the departure gate. We could now see why there had been a notice that the check-in closed at 8.30am. The plane left at 9am, and our check-in girl and the young man who had helped with the bikes were now at departure gate number 72 ready to check the tickets! Obviously not too many people were employed by PB Air, but it was rather worrying when the young man disappeared, and later reappeared wearing what Warren swore was a pilot's uniform. He collected some papers and a briefcase from the departure gate, and strode off onto the tarmac and out of sight!

We weren't the only passengers – there were another eight including the Irishman, and we were led to our plane which looked like a large Lear jet. It only seated about 50 people, but it was in very good condition and certainly gave us no concerns as to safety. The journey passed quickly – one hour 45 minutes was very pleasant after the last four flights of 7 hours, 10 hours, 11 hours and 7 hours. We chatted to the Irishman, who told us how he had decided to visit the Bangkok Hilton, the nickname for the infamous Thai prison in Bangkok. He had had problems finding it – no taxi drivers or tourist offices knew where it was, but eventually he had arrived at the prison and had asked if there were any Irish or English inmates he could visit. When told that there was one Irishman and seven Englishmen, he had chosen to chat to the Irishman for half an hour, though he knew nothing about him. The inmate was incredibly grateful – it was the first time he had left his cell for eight months, and he said that conditions were appalling. The first three years had nearly killed him, he said, and he had now been there for seven years, but the Irishman said that he hadn't asked him whether or not he had committed the murder for which he had been imprisoned. For Warren, a former prison officer, it was an interesting story; clearly there were no similarities between English and Thai prisons, and probably no similarities between Thai and English prison officers either.

The plane began to land, and as we descended we could see that the fields surrounding the airport were submerged below yellow water. It was obvious that there had been a lot of rain – it was mid November, so a bit early for the tourist season. We hoped that there wouldn't be too much rain as we cycled through Vietnam.

PB Air had looked after our bikes, but it took us one and a half hours to put them together ready for cycling again. It felt just like India again, as a crowd of taxi drivers stood watching. As soon as we removed the cardboard and bubble-wrap from the bikes, the taxi drivers snatched it up to make comfortable seats on the ground so they could watch us. They spoke English very fluently and far better than anyone we had met in Bangkok, which surprised us.

Eventually we set off with a number of taxi drivers waving until we were out of sight; it was scary on the right side of the road again after so long, but the roads were full of cycles and motorbikes with virtually no cars. At cross-roads it was terrifying – no-one appeared to have right of way, and no-one stopped. They just slowed down and wove in and out of each other from all directions. It reminded me of the motorbike displays that the army give, where each motorbike crosses just missing the other by centimetres. It began to rain; after that the drivers of the motorbikes and cycles were swathed in plastic raincoats or capes billowing out behind them, often with their passengers hunched up behind them under the same coat.

Everyone shouted 'hello' from the pavement as we passed – adults, schoolchildren, and even tiny children – and it felt very similar to being back in India, because everyone was so friendly and welcoming. Children ran forward to speak and wave, asking where we were from as we cycled the short way to the city. We knew that we were going to enjoy Vietnam . . .

CHAPTER 16

VIETNAM

Vietnam is a long, narrow country, slightly larger than Italy, running north to south for over 1,000 miles (1,600km). Because of its length, Vietnam has many different climates, and it can be chilly in Hanoi in the north but tropical in Ho Chi Minh City (Saigon) in the south. The east coast faces the South China Sea, and the south-western tip touches the Gulf of Thailand. Vietnam borders China in the north, Laos in the west and Cambodia in the south-west. 75% of Vietnam is mountainous, although the highest mountains are in the north. Vietnam, together with Laos and Cambodia, forms what is known as Indochina.

The country is very poor – the average annual income is only £150, so to western tourists prices should be very cheap. However, because of foreigner-only prices, Vietnam is not as cheap as India or Indonesia. The Vietnamese are very well-educated compared with other South East Asian countries with a literacy rate of over 80%, and women are accorded the same education as men. A large percentage of Vietnamese speak both English and French (there are many French tourists in Vietnam). Although the Vietnamese Dong is the local currency, the US dollar is very much a second currency, and hotel prices are always quoted and paid for in US dollars.

We found a hotel in Da Nang after cycling from the airport, and were happy to pay US$20 (approximately £15) per night for the luxury room with air conditioning, satellite television and enormous bathroom, even though we knew we could have found cheaper accommodation in the town. We were a bit concerned about the karaoke advertised for the evening (this Japanese past-time had been adopted eagerly by the Vietnamese!), but the hotel assured us that everything would be quiet by 11pm. We decided to stay two nights, even though Da Nang doesn't have a lot to offer to the tourist, just so we could get used to Vietnam before setting off on our bikes. We fell asleep for a couple of hours, tired from the day's travelling, and were extremely hungry when we woke.

We went out for a meal; it was dark, and already the pavements were covered with tiny tables and chairs. This reminded us strongly of our time in Myanmar. A market was still open and lively, with incredible flowers on display – there were more colours of roses than I would have believed possible, and each bud was carefully wrapped in newspaper to protect it, until the opening flower pushed it upwards and off. Women with bicycles wearing pyjama-like suits with short or long sleeves, flip-flops and conical shaped Chinese 'coolie' hats stood chatting; their bicycle baskets were full of fruit and vegetables. Many people sat at the tiny tables eating food from bowls with chopsticks; children played in groups chasing each other, and dogs slept under the tables.

We passed a wine shop with a vast choice of European and New World wines, which cheered us up. We had a look and said that we'd return later after we had eaten.

'What time?' the girl asked. 'I stay open later if necessary.'

We asked the way to a good restaurant, and a young man walked with us to show us the way to a very nice Chinese restaurant. Once again, we were surprised that everyone spoke such good English. On the way back to the hotel we saw a crowd of young children playing outside the hotel. As I took out my camera they screamed and ran forward, jumping up and down excitedly to get into the picture. They came too close for me to take a picture.

'Stand further back – I can't get you in,' I kept saying, and when the camera flashed they jumped and cheered and laughed. It so reminded us of India and the wonderful times we had had there. We went to our room where we watched television, drank our wine and toasted this new country, looking forward to the next day.

At breakfast the next day we were the only guests in the large dining room, and every table except two were laid with white tablecloths and flowers. At the table next to us, two Vietnamese girls sat with their left hands in rubber gloves while they cut red chillies with scissors into shapes which, after a few minutes in iced water, curled open to resemble red ballerina dresses, looking very much like the flowers of the fuschia. Tomato lilies stood on a tray already prepared. A wedding was to take place that afternoon, they told us, and they were preparing the decorations for the food. Breakfast was a surprise – small baguettes, as good as any that we had ever had in France, were served with omelettes or fried eggs and butter and jam. The French bread, we discovered, was made all over Vietnam, so this was something to look forward to at breakfast time. The coffee, however, was terrible, and we never discovered any good coffee the whole of the time that we were in Vietnam. Both cups came filled with black coffee and I asked if I could have milk.

'It's in there,' one of the girls said, and when I stirred there was something thick in the bottom of my cup – condensed milk! Never mind, Lipton's tea, as in every country we'd visited, was available, and Vietnamese tea was also delicious and similar to Chinese tea. After that first breakfast in Vietnam, we always drank tea without milk.

After breakfast we walked to the market, passing a pretty Catholic church. It was Sunday, and hundreds of bikes were parked neatly in rows in the enormous open area in front of the church. The sun shone, and it was very hot and slightly humid, though much cooler than it had been in Bangkok. Bikes and motorbikes whizzed down the road, and we noticed that it was not at all unusual for them to drive on the wrong side of the road – something to be aware of when stepping off the pavement to cross the road.

The smell of flowers filled the air as we approached the market. As well as the roses we'd seen the night before, there were chrysanthemums, gerberas, frangipani, orchids, bird of paradise flowers, and many I didn't recognise. Floral decorations in baskets and on stands were on display, and girls sat snipping stems and leaves to make more. Inside the market were stalls full of fruit, fish, meat, clothes and shoes. On several stalls pink and beige bras lay stacked on top of each other, the conical cups pointing stiffly to the roof – it was decades since I'd seen such awful underwear! Everyone said 'hello', and several times girls grabbed my hand to pull me gently to their stall to show me their wares. People were happy to have photos taken. On the meat stall were boiled pigs' heads, the ears and snout making them very recognisable. Pigs' trotters, cooked and raw, were on every stall, and dark lean meat, similar in colour to venison, looked excellent. There were superb large joints of pork and beef, and women were making mince by chopping the meat over and over again until it was very fine. Fish stalls were full of very fresh fish, and outside were more stalls and shops selling fishing nets, ropes and all types of hardware. We bought several small items, but we didn't like the Vietnamese money. There were 21,000 Dong to £1, and there were no coins, so the notes were grubby and mostly worthless. I had 500 Dong notes in my purse that were worth less than 2½p!

We were hungry, and went into a tiny café to have something to eat. It was late for lunch, and the elderly lady running the café appeared to have finished serving. No-one else was in the café, but she was clearly willing to serve us. She was the first Vietnamese that we had met who spoke no English, but she opened her enormous fridge and pulled out a piece of raw beef on a plate. It looked superb quality, and we nodded enthusiastically; she beckoned to us to sit at a table, as she began to ladle stock into a pan. Within minutes she had brought us a bowl of clear soup, full of noodles, onions, herbs and bean sprouts, and topped with thin slices of the raw beef. The soup was so hot that the beef cooked within seconds in the broth. This was 'pho', a favourite Vietnamese soup served at virtually any time of the day, but especially breakfast, and often served on street stalls. The speed with which the pho was produced belied the amount of work involved to make it. The basic broth is made by boiling beef marrow bones and chicken bones with ginger, spices and onion for hours, after which it's seasoned with fish sauce, sugar, garlic and salt. Rice noodles are added to the soup, with onions, coriander, chives and spring onions. Bean sprouts are often added, or served separately with herbs, chillies and lime wedges. It was delicious, and after we had finished we returned to the street.

Crossing the road was terrifying, especially at cross-roads. We needed to look in four different directions at the same time; no-one ever indicated or slowed down as they approached us, and it was impossible to imagine that the roads could be so full with so many bicycles, mopeds, motor-bikes, scooters and cyclos. Cyclos are Vietnamese bicycle rickshaws; there is one wheel at the back beneath the driver, and two wheels at the front, between which is a seat with space for two very slim passengers. There were virtually no cars at all – if anyone needed a taxi they would take a cyclo or a moto, which simply meant getting onto the back of a motor-bike with one of the locals!

Although our destination was north up the coast, we initially wanted to travel 20 miles south to Hoi An, which we had heard was a lovely town to visit. As we left the next morning we discovered that my back tyre was completely flat, so we had to repair it outside the hotel. Again, it was just as in India or Turkey – Warren was surrounded by eight men and numerous children sitting on their haunches watching him repair it. If one of them was daring enough, he would lean forward and touch the wheel, press the brake, or even ring the bell.

We set off travelling east along a new dual carriageway with three lanes each way, hoping to find a quiet road parallel to the main road. However, we discovered when we got to the South China Sea that it was a cul-de-sac, and we had to turn round and return against the wind to the main road. We joined the throngs of cycles, rickshaws and motorbikes. Lorries occasionally passed, sounding their horns constantly to ensure that the smaller vehicles got out of their way. At one junction two women on a motorbike had had a minor bump, and had fallen off their bike. A man was helping one of the women up from the ground, but the rest of the traffic continued around them in the middle of the road. The lorry wasn't willing to wait; he sounded his very loud horn continuously until the bike was moved out of the way so that he could continue his journey.

Traffic slowed after a while, and we realised that we were in the middle of a funeral procession. Slow motorbikes led the way, each carrying a tall flower similar to a gladiolus stuck to the handlebars. These motorbikes were followed by a decorated van, inside which was an ornate coffin surrounded by men crouching down in the limited space around the coffin. They were throwing pieces of paper out of the open back door, and a long thick 'fuse' of incense was hanging out of the door, the end smoking. We discovered later that it was tradition to throw fake money from the hearse, and we saw packs of such money frequently on market stalls – there was always a choice of Vietnamese Dong or US dollars!

We passed Marble Mountain, a mountain made purely of marble which had been excavated for its valuable stone. Beside the road men were carving amazing eagles, lions, horses, dolphins and other animals out of white, apricot and grey marble. The statues were enormous and very intricately carved, and the sides of the road were lined with pink, white and grey marble coffins, recently carved with designs of lotus buds and flowers.

It began to rain, and despite the fact that we were on a tarmac road, our bikes, bags and legs were becoming covered with grit and sand thrown up with the rain. I was concerned that, if such rain was usual at this time of year, we would have problems later when we reached some of the more rural roads in Vietnam and Laos which might be dirt roads. Everyone had donned plastic raincoats and capes as soon as the rain started, and they cycled or drove their motorbikes with the plastic flapping wildly or filling up like a parachute. As they passed us they often looked hump-backed, because the passenger was hiding from the rain beneath the back of the driver's raincoat.

Occasionally a four-wheel drive vehicle went past in the opposite direction, and these were always driven by a Vietnamese man with a western couple in the back. We could see them pointing at us with shocked looks on their faces. As occasional coach loads of westerners went past there were flashes as the tourists took photographs of us.

A man was on a bicycle pulling 30 feet long lengths of rolled corrugated aluminium for roofing, tied with pieces of string to his bike. In the centre of this long load was a pair of wheels to support the enormous length, and another man on a bike cycled alongside to ensure the load didn't fall off.

Every time we stopped, someone came over to talk to us, always asking where we were from, and chatting in good English. However, when we decided to stop for a cup of tea in a tiny café in the middle of nowhere, we were surprised that they spoke no English at all. We looked up the word for 'tea' and asked for 'tra'. They couldn't understand, however many times we repeated it. We managed to pronounce this one-syllable three-letter word in many different ways, but as Vietnamese is a tonal language, they still couldn't understand us. Apparently, different tones give the same word a totally different meaning, and there can be as many as six different meanings to one word, depending on how it is said. However, after drawing a picture of a teapot all became clear, and we enjoyed two pots of Chinese tea for the grand price of 1,000 Dong (5p)!

By the time we reached Hoi An we might as well have jumped into the sea with all our clothes on, we were so wet. However, we weren't cold, but we were certainly looking forward to a shower and a change of clothes. It was obvious that this was a tourist town, because there were westerners everywhere. The first hotel we approached, a smart balconied building with columns and a garden next to the river, had lovely rooms at very cheap prices (from $7US for a double room with bathroom). However, they insisted that we leave our bikes on the pavement, which we were not willing to do, so we continued our search and ended up at a hotel unfortunately advertised as a state-run Trade Union Hotel. It was, in fact, a beautiful old building built round a courtyard, and we had a large stately room with a 10 feet high ceiling with a massive bathroom with a bath as well as a shower for $9 a night; air conditioning and television was included in the price. By the time we had washed our clothes and ourselves the bath was full of sand and grit.

We set off in the rain to see the town, as we wanted to buy two of the long plastic rain capes that we had seen the locals wearing. Hoi An is a really quaint place, and would obviously be even nicer when the rain stopped. Every stall in the market and every shop had the rain capes that we wanted, so we were able to knock the price down from 95,000 to 35,000 dong (less than £2 each) quite easily, and both the stall-holder and we were happy. For £5 we had a superb 3-course Vietnamese meal each with beer, and returned to our hotel room.

The sun shone the next day, so we were able to see the town in a better light. Hoi An was once a Chinese settlement, so many of the buildings in the town are Chinese in origin, and are quite beautiful even though a large number are in need of repair. Their roofs covered with thick moss and the walls green with damp, the balconied buildings were nevertheless very picturesque. A lovely view from the bridge revealed a mountain in the distance along the river, and a child and two women in coolie hats waved to us from a small boat as they dropped lines into the river in the hope of catching fish. A colourful Chinese temple stood in one street, and in its pretty gardens stood large blue and white bowls holding bonsai trees similar to those we had seen in Japan.

We visited the market, where everyone wanted to guide us to their stall in the hope that we'd buy something. Lovely wooden boxes, inlaid with mother-of-pearl or different coloured woods or carved with dragons, held ten sets of matching chopsticks and chopstick rests. As in India and Turkey, the quality of the fruit and vegetables was superb. Vivid pink dragon-fruit, its white flesh flecked with black seeds, pineapples, small bananas, tiny round lemons and limes similar to those in India, large loose-skinned oranges, beans, cauliflowers, tomatoes, lettuces, cabbages, carrots and onions were stacked neatly on the stalls with fruit and vegetables that we didn't recognise. Everything was there – hardware, fish, plastic and clothes. Often the stall-holders were fast asleep on top of their stalls, or else sitting cross-legged in the middle of the table, almost all of them wearing the typical Vietnamese cone-shaped hats, tied under the chin with silk ribbon.

In one street a line of two dozen cyclos were waiting for the tourists, many of the drivers also fast asleep in their seats. Within a month, when the rain stopped and the weather improved, this town would be full and the cyclos busy. As we walked along, we saw that every other local person on the street was either carrying a load on a yoke over their shoulder with a cane basket at each end, or they had a load on their bike. Sometimes several people were pushing and pulling a cart that was so full that it looked as though it should have been pulled by a bullock.

Wooden boats were moored by the riverside, their owners trying to persuade tourists to go for a boat ride. In one shop we saw women dressed in matching cheongsams (traditional Chinese dresses), all busy doing exquisite embroidery. A man was making bamboo frames for lamp-shades and covering them with stunning jewel-like colours of oriental silk and damask.

After gin and tonics at the happy hour bar, we walked back to the hotel at the end of the day. A woman waved to us as she stood up to her knees in a field of water, surrounded by plants which she was harvesting, and the setting sun glinted on the patches of water around her.

There are over 200 tailors' shops in Hoi An, each of them tiny shops with stacks of wonderful fabrics. Samples of clothes for men and women were on display, and the wonderful evening dresses made in pure silk, Chinese and oriental fabrics were enough to make any woman's mouth water. Unfortunately such clothes were not suitable for cycling, but we decided to have trousers made of strong crease-resistant fabric, and asked for them to just cover the knee. This made them suitable for cycling in a country where bare arms and legs are seldom seen. The quality of the work was excellent, better than in Thailand we were told by other travellers, and we were very pleased at the price as well, having spent £4 pounds for each pair of trousers. After that we decided to have matching tops made, so we felt we were probably the best-dressed foreign cyclists in Vietnam!

We discovered the next day that we certainly weren't the best-dressed cyclists in Vietnam – in the mornings the roads were full of incredibly slim, stunningly beautiful Vietnamese young women cycling in their school uniform. These were the older teenage girls who were still at school. They wore silk trousers, very long and fine in the palest of lilac, which flapped dangerously close to the chains on their bikes. They wore matching lilac dresses which reached the ankles but were split on both sides to the waist. These dresses fitted tightly and had mandarin collars and long narrow sleeves to the wrists. The girls had long shining black hair centrally parted and tied at the back, and perfect teeth gleamed when they smiled. They often wore hats to protect their heads from the sun and long gloves which reminded me of Audrey Hepburn. Warren's disconsolate comment was that girls hadn't looked like that when he was at school!

The next day we cycled to the sea which was only four miles away. It was a pleasant journey with very little traffic. We went down a small lane and found ourselves on the beach, where large coracles made of bamboo were stacked on the beach. Men were sat in their boats mending their fishing nets, and large islands out to sea were shrouded in mist. One of the fishermen came over to talk to us, and explained that each boat, though large, was for one man. We had previously only seen coracles on rivers, and were surprised to see coracles being used in the sea, especially as the large curving waves looked more suitable for a surfboard than a coracle.

On the way back to Hoi An we passed an area of road works and, as in India, many of the labourers were women. They wore masks over their noses and mouths for protection (and we had noticed that many people wore these on their motorbikes and cycles as well), and on top of the scarf over their heads they wore the usual coolie hats. Further down the road we passed a man sat in front of his shack carving perfect barley-twist table legs from mahogany.

When we returned to the hotel we used the internet facilities there, and were very excited to hear that my son, Julian, and his wife, Lucy, were expecting their second baby. Thomas, now 15 months, had been born since we started our journey, so now there was to be a second grandchild born while we were travelling.

Eventually it was time to cycle north back to Da Nang again, and we set off early. The weather was fine and this time we managed to find a very quiet road which ran through tiny villages. Children called 'Hello, hello,' as we passed, and ran after us. A tiny tot, no more than two and a half years old, called 'Hello' from her doorway. I waved to her as I went by, and she immediately returned the wave and called out 'Bye Bye'. I was very impressed! The motor cyclists cycled slowly side by side talking, not only in pairs but even in threes or fours, so the road ahead was often blocked until they moved out of the way. We stopped for a drink of water in the shade of some trees, and a little boy and girl came running out of their nearby house. They seemed too shy to speak, but when we said 'Hello' their faces lit up and they beamed.

We passed cemeteries full of brightly coloured gravestones – pink, red, yellow and blue, now faded in the sunlight. When we approached Marble Mountain for the second time we had to rejoin the main highway, and this time we could examine the statues more closely as it wasn't raining. Six feet high white or grey marble dolphins were leaping out of ornately carved waves; a five feet apricot marble carving of a Chinese mountain was covered with intricately-carved tiny trees, temples, birds and animals, Chinese dogs of Fo, horses and lions; an eight feet high statue of an eagle was carved with wings outstretched, every feather carved in detail in white, grey and apricot marble, the ornately carved claws grasping a captured snake. Marble Mountain stood in the background – a rock in the middle of an otherwise flat area – and I wondered how long Marble Mountain would survive, as the marble was excavated to make these magnificent carvings.

Two young boys on a bicycle drew up alongside and cycled with us.

'Good morning,' they said, 'How are you?' We had a lengthy conversation. 'How old are you?' they asked after a while.

'59,' I said, 'How old are you?'

'I am eleven years old,' they said in unison, cycling off.

Children were coming out of school at lunch time as we cycled into Da Nang, and the roads widened and traffic became heavy again. The children wore long navy blue trousers, white shirts and red narrow silk scarves knotted round their neck like ties, but as well as this school uniform they wore crash helmets, whether they were walking or on bikes. It seemed very sensible in view of the dangerous traffic in the town. We cycled over the busy bridge, and looked for a different hotel this time, finding one with a pleasant room for $9. The receptionist admired our bikes and asked how much they had cost, just as the Indians had always done. As in India we lied and said we didn't know.

'Oh, about US$1,500 I should think,' she said. 'What do you think?' She had turned to an American sitting nearby, who agreed. This was a much closer estimate than the $250 that the Indians usually suggested, but still less than half of the value of each bike.

We went out to have lunch and found a street café, but the owner obviously thought we had lost our way because he began to direct us to a posh restaurant nearby. We said we wanted to eat at his café, and he looked delighted, and brought us free beer to go with the excellent food. In the evening, we were recommended by the hotel to go to Tam's Pub, which we found a few streets away. The position didn't look very promising, because it looked out over a busy roundabout. Two Americans sat drinking beer outside, so we sat and talked to them, and were joined by Tam, the owner.

We discovered from them that a lot of American men who couldn't settle when they went back home to the States after the Vietnam War actually returned to Vietnam where they have married local girls and settled there. There are not many tourists in Da Nang, but there are many Americans who now live there. Tam drew up her chair as we sat with our beer and began to tell us her life story. She was the only Vietnamese girl I ever saw wearing shorts and a vest. Her story was incredible, and I felt that I would like to write a book about her. If only half of her story was true, it was still a fascinating and incredible life that she had led.

She had eight children, seven of them adopted (we met three of them as they helped her in the bar). Every time she found a baby or a child alone who no-one wanted, she adopted it, even though she had very little money of her own. Her brother had been an officer in the South Vietnamese army, and after the War he disappeared for six years. He was eventually found imprisoned in North Vietnam, and was very ill. After a few years he was able to go to the States to live, because the United States allowed men who had been officers in the South Vietnamese army to move to the States.

'He's incredibly happy there,' said Tam. 'He has a really good job in a factory in California making jeans.'

Tam's husband disappeared, leaving her to bring up their only son. She tried to escape Vietnam three times, and when she was caught the third time she was separated from her son and thrown into prison. Eventually she escaped, and over the years had gradually built up a business. When we asked her if she had ever visited her brother in California, she said that she would never be allowed to leave Vietnam unless she married a foreigner.

Vietnamese people, men or women, are very 'touchy feely' people, and constantly touched us on the shoulder, patted us on the arm or knee, or even held our hands. I had often noticed Warren almost gritting his teeth as a male hand persistently touched his knee or his arm! As Tam told us her story, she constantly leaned forward to touch Warren or me on the knee, and we felt very sad to hear her story, though we felt she told it without wanting sympathy or money. She told us how she hated it when she saw some Vietnamese people overcharging tourists, and she believed in giving good value for money because customers would come back again and recommend their friends. In this way she had managed to build up her small business. We certainly had a fantastic meal for very little money at Tam's Pub – her home-made spring rolls were spectacular, and there was an enormous pile of them on the plate. She recommended her pizzas and, although we wouldn't normally have chosen western food, we decided to try them. She proudly placed the pizzas in front of us, and they were the thinnest, crispiest bases piled high with toppings – definitely to be recommended!

The next day we planned to cycle further north up the coast to Lang Co, a place that many Vietnamese people had recommended, though it didn't appear to be on the route for westerners or travellers. Or rather, it was on the main road to Hué, and travellers constantly passed it on the bus from north to south, but it was not mentioned in any of the guide books. Apparently Lang Co had beautiful beaches, so we thought we might spend a few days with sun, sea and sand. The day was very hot, which was unfortunate, because we knew we had a high mountain pass to cycle over, although the locals told us that the views from the top of the mountain were spectacular when the weather was fine.

We were up early the next morning, and by 7am had left the hotel in Da Nang. We had a surprisingly nice breakfast of fried eggs and bread from a local café (just a couple of plastic tables and chairs on the pavement outside someone's shack), while a child with a very melancholy expression stood with a roll in her hand and just looked at us. She never smiled, but had the most enormous dark eyes. We set off on our bikes, and immediately approached a large roundabout. There was no indication of right of way; everyone just piled in as before – he who dares, wins! We found our way to Highway 1 which had three lanes each way, the 'slow' lane full of bikes, cyclos and people pushing large loads.

The traffic was unbelievable; there were lorries, bikes and motorbikes, the lorries and motorbikes sounding their horns constantly. We knew that the deeper the sound of the horn, the bigger the vehicle was behind us! It was almost as if I was operating in slow motion and everything was whizzing past and around me – a bicycle with 20 feet long reinforcing poles sticking out at either end; lorries full of gas bottles; a bicycle with trailer carrying large rusty metal sheets sticking out on either side; a bike piled with cardboard several feet high; cycles with trailers piled high with chopped firewood which looked like mahogany. Motorbikes were parked on the pavement and drove straight onto the road without ever looking, so we always had to watch carefully what was happening on the pavement as well. Cyclos were stacked high with bottled water and soft drinks, tins of cooking oil, boxes of limes and oranges or branches of green bananas. Two men were pushing and pulling a wooden trailer piled high with scrap metal; a woman was washing a baby's bottom on the pavement; an elderly couple pushed a square trolley full of hand-made brushes and brooms; stalls on the edge of the pavement were busy making and selling noodle soup for breakfast; men and women were cleaning the streets; a woman carrying fish in two shallow baskets suspended on a shaped wooden yoke tried to cross the road, the baskets swinging violently as she ran between vehicles; a passenger on a motorbike held a four feet length of tinted glass upright on the seat in front of him, narrowly missing low overhanging branches of trees. Cyclos and bicycles with trailers were carrying four feet cubes of ice from the local ice factory, the water dripping as they cycled. An enormous lorry began to reverse onto the busy road; no-one was helping to direct the lorry, so the traffic was coming to a halt in an untidy crowd and was trying to funnel into the one lane left.

We reached a red traffic light, so slowed down, but noticed that other traffic raced ahead. We had reached a level crossing, and a railway employee laboriously pushed the sliding gate across in front of us. Every motorbike and bike moved forward, so that its front wheel touched the gate, ready for a quick getaway once the gates opened again. The train passed within a minute – it was a very modern looking train compared to those in India because it had windows, but we noticed once it had passed that a man was sat on the outside ledge at the very back of the train, hitching a free lift! Once the train had passed, the railway employee began to open the gate, and as soon as it was open a few inches, dozens of motorbikes shot through the small gap.

We passed a temple being built, a giant marble Buddha already sitting proudly at the unfinished entrance. Suddenly we realised that the bikes and motorbikes had disappeared, and we were alone with the lorries and a few buses – we had passed out of the town. After one hour's cycling we approached another small town, and a range of mountains loomed ahead of us. The tops were clearly outlined against the blue sky, but the lower part of the mountains was obscured by clouds. We had to cross this mountain range.

We stopped for a cup of tea, and I just grabbed my camera in time to take a photo of four young boys on one bicycle, waving as they passed. When the shop owner saw my camera, she asked if I would take a photo of her. Afterwards she asked for 10,000 dong for the pot of Vietnamese tea, which was 10 times the going rate for a tourist price, but as we hadn't agreed a price up front we felt that we had to pay without argument. She was clearly happy when I handed her the note, worth just under 50p, and her sideways knowing look at her friend as she pocketed the money confirmed to us that she had tried it on. This was to be a constant hassle – in the tourist towns the prices were set and were higher than what the locals paid but still reasonable. In more rural areas it seemed that they had heard that foreigners paid a fortune, and they asked for quite ridiculous prices at times. We realised that we always needed to agree the price before we ordered to make sure we had a reasonable deal.

We passed a lake with coracles and giant fishing nets, and the mountains in the background made the view especially beautiful. The road began to climb as it approached the mountain, and soon there were spectacular views of the sand-edged bays far below us, with islands disappearing into the mist across the sea. It was 22km (14 miles) to Lang Co, our destination on the other side of the mountain. It was very hot – indeed, it was the hottest day we'd experienced so far in Vietnam, which was a problem for us cycling uphill. The lorries and buses were chugging up behind us in low gear, their exhaust fumes blasting us with hot smelly diesel fumes as they passed. We could see the road snaking backwards and forwards up the side of the mountain and back down again; lorries were crawling down the other side, one behind the other.

Very few cars passed us, but occasional tourist buses went by, everyone clapping us as they looked out of their air-conditioned windows, and virtually every lorry that passed sounded its horn, or the driver or co-driver hung out of the window giving us the thumbs up sign. It was very motivating, but eventually the incredible heat and humidity, combined with the long, very steep, uphill climb, began to defeat me.

We had heard that machines similar to those used to dig the English Channel tunnel were now being used to tunnel through this mountain below us, and that only the day before the two machines had met in the middle. How I wished we could have cycled through the cool, flat tunnel (although, unless there was a special facility for bikes, tunnels are one of a cyclist's worst nightmares). We understood that the tunnel would be only for larger vehicles, and bicycles and motorbikes would still have to go over the mountain. One of the unexpected problems that had been encountered by the tunnelling team was an underground river which they had to divert. Now we saw evidence of this river – water streamed out of the mountain in different places, and had been 'tapped' by locals, so that hoses pointing upwards sprayed fountains of water, and signs indicated lorry-cleaning services by the enterprising locals. Several times we cycled over to the lay-bys where these hoses were spraying, and stood under the water until we were soaking wet. We also soaked scarves and towels which we wrapped round our necks and heads, and by doing this we managed to cool ourselves a little as we continued, though the intense heat dried our clothes within minutes.

We stopped at a roadside café to have a cool drink, and they tried to charge us double what the tourist towns normally charge. As soon as we questioned the cost, indicating that it was too high, the price dropped to half. They admired the bikes, counting up the gears (27), pressing the tyres, touching the brakes, ringing the bell, and did the thumbs up to us.

We continued, the road signs indicating 10% hills. The heat beat down on us, and the only good thing about the clear sunny day was that we had superb views from the mountain. I was flagging as Warren passed a small waterfall in front of me, and when I reached it I waded into the pool, put my head under the waterfall, and used my cap to throw water over myself. I followed Warren, only to find that round the next corner was the top of the mountain, and a line of cafés and stalls were waiting for customers. We had reached 600 metres in a distance of 10km.

We sat down, although my trousers and shirt were soaking wet, and water was running from my wet hair down my face and leaving a puddle on the floor. It wasn't cold, but I knew that if I didn't dry out before the 10km downhill descent I was going to be very cold and uncomfortable. As we sat having lunch, a cloud crept up over the edge of the mountain and swirled around us, and by the time we left, the way ahead was thick with cloud. We switched on our flashing back lights and set off. The road was an 8% descent the whole way, sweeping backwards and forwards and, being overcast by the low-lying clouds, it was very cool. The 8% hill on the cloud-covered side would have been much more pleasant for cycling up, with a 10% downhill descent in the sun! Occasionally the clouds parted, and we had a glimpse of a long, sandy beach bathed in full sunshine way below us – this was where we hoped to stay.

Suddenly we were out of the clouds and the sun beat down on us again. We were now racing downhill at a very high speed, and the breeze hitting us was as hot as if it came from an oven. We stopped to take a photo of the stunning beach view, and instantly two boys on bikes appeared from nowhere to stand alongside us and tried to sell us maps, cigarette lighters and wallets.

Lang Co was a long beach with one road parallel to the beach. The road was dual carriageway and lined with restaurants. We cycled through the small town without finding any hotels, so we asked in a service station. The coach driver said there was a 5 star resort one kilometre away, but the service station attendant pointed to a new entrance road next to the service station. We had assumed it to be a new development being built – we could see the building in construction at the top – but he told us that accommodation was available there. He assured us that this was the cheaper of the two resorts. We cycled up the new stone roadway edged with a brick pavement. A retaining wall had been built down the centre of the entrance road and was filled with new palm trees and shrubs. A woman showed us dingy rooms with a wall fan, and these were available for $10 a night. We wouldn't have paid more than $5 for such rooms, and shook our heads, so she beckoned us to follow her. We walked across the building site, over sand and rubble, to a row of new attractive, brick-built chalets with gabled tiled roofs, marble steps and terraces. There were five of these new buildings, built in pairs, so that each was a 'semi-detached' one-bedroom apartment with shower room. They stood close to the sea with their own balconies. The room was enormous and bathed in light. The bedroom had a 5 feet bed as well as a 4 feet bed, and an extremely large bathroom with a long marble top in which the washbasin was set. This room was $15, but they agreed to our offer of $12 per night for three nights, and as the price included breakfast we had an even better deal. We looked forward to a relaxing three days of sun, sand and sea. We hadn't yet swum in the South China Sea.

The area around the five buildings where we were staying was surrounded by a building site. New accommodation, a new reception area and a new restaurant were planned, so the resort was eventually going to be very pleasant. We walked across the mounds of sand and rubble to the restaurant close to the sea, and wondered why they hadn't thought to lay the path for the guests. The barman chatted in good English, also spoke fluent French, and made us a superb lunch. We were beginning to think that we'd soon look like spring rolls, we were eating so many, but they were always so delicious in Vietnam. We discovered that this restaurant was used as a half-way house for western tourists on coach trips, who stopped at the restaurant for lunch on the way between Hué and Hoi An, two popular tourist destinations. A South American from Peru was staying overnight, having stopped for lunch, seen the beach, and decided to continue his journey the following day, so that he could enjoy a swim.

The restaurant closed at 5pm, but we continued to sit there drinking our beer. We were amazed that the barman left bottles of spirits and wine behind the bar in a glass fronted case with a very cheap padlock, and several cartons of cigarettes were stacked on a stool behind the open bar.

The road was dark as we went to find a restaurant that evening, and it was obvious that the whole of Lang Co was being developed. There was a new dual carriageway, but no pavements as yet. We had a meal in a small family café that had been recommended, but the unnecessary sounding of very sharp, deep horns as the lorries went by didn't make for a very relaxing meal. Presumably the resort where we stayed would eventually have a decent restaurant that stayed open in the evenings – it would be much more pleasant there away from the road with the view of the sea through the palms.

We had bought a bottle of local Vietnamese wine (rather like the very cheap French wine bought in France by the gallon!), so we drank this back on our balcony as we listened to the waves through the trees. We chatted to two young men in the room next to ours, and they offered us beer. They were the only other guests at the resort apart from the South American, and they were working on the tunnel through the mountain. One of them, a very young-looking Thai, was a hydro-geologist, and had worked in a huge number of different countries, and was due to go to Mozambique to work the following month.

It rained heavily that night and was very overcast and windy in the morning – so much for our swim in the sea! The mountains which overlooked Lang Co had disappeared into the mist. It was very, very windy as we walked the few yards to the sea to dip our feet into the water. The sea was deliciously warm, so would be lovely for swimming if the weather was better. The weather didn't get better as the day progressed, so we went for a walk and found ourselves in the local village. Shops with small quantities of food stood by the dirt road; people were sitting eating, squatting on the edge of the road; a girl was cooking banana fritters in a pan by the side of the road; dogs were sleeping.

Children ran up to us and jumped up and down with excitement if we took a photo. Old people sat in doorways waving to us; a man sat mending a fishing net, a very old man excitedly came up to shake us by the hand, and women and children carried babies. We passed a large church and a temple, and nearby stood coracles close to the water. We were constantly followed by the children, and everyone called out 'hello'. It was obvious that the locals were not used to tourists or foreigners. Scooters went by avoiding puddles, and strange bicycles adapted to carry goods frequently passed us. These vehicles were made from the back half of a bicycle, with a large cage at the front to carry wood or boxes, fruit or scrap metal.

We bought oranges from a girl squatting by a stall, and several people came to watch us purchasing the goods. The oranges had loose green skin, but were deliciously sweet and juicy. Everyone was smiling, and we felt incredibly lucky to be there – the day was overcast, but we were having a wonderful time because everyone was so friendly.

In the evening we walked back along the dark road to the same café as the night before. The lady was clearly quite thrilled to see us, and we imagined how she would tell the neighbours that the foreigners had visited her for a second time. The other restaurants were empty – it was early for the tourist season, but we weren't sure that foreign tourists visited this area. We asked the café owner if she had any wine, and amazingly she produced three bottles. One was labelled red wine, but clearly contained white wine and had been corked with a whisky stopper. She wanted 10,000 dong for it (48p) but we didn't want to risk home-made wine! The second was fortified local red wine for 15,000 dong (71p), or there was an attractive blue and white Chinese porcelain bottle with 'medicinal' wine for 30,000 (£1.42). The bottle was well worth it – it even had a porcelain stopper, but we were not in a position to carry souvenirs on our bikes. We chose the fortified wine, and it was quite pleasant and very similar to the 'port wine' produced and sold in Goa. We asked for everything to be served together this time, and thought she understood, but we still ended up with her superb omelettes as a first course, then spring rolls, which we'd hoped to have as a starter, and after the spring rolls a plate of good home-made chips. Just as he had done the day before, the husband dashed off on his bike and reappeared a few minutes later with a small parcel which he tried to hide from our view as he quickly carried it into the house. We suspected that these were the potatoes to make the chips! The family happily watched television sitting at one of the tables as we ate, the lady laughing when I dropped a chip from my chopsticks. She served them with wedges of lime, salt and pepper and chilli and soy sauce for dipping. The whole meal, including the wine, cost less than £3. We had noticed that when giving money or sometimes when shaking hands, the Vietnamese often touched their right elbow with their left hand to show respect, as they had often done in Myanmar. Also, money was often proffered with two hands, again to show respect, as in Japan.

We were clearly not destined to enjoy the sun, sand and sea in Lang Co, because the next day was just as overcast and windy. When we went for lunch at the restaurant by the sea, two mini buses arrived with western tourists, and we shared a table with two couples from Newcastle. They had bought tickets for £375 each for buses and trains to take them from Saigon to Hanoi along the coastline of Vietnam; the price of the tickets included accommodation. They were staying for 2 or 3 days at each venue, and were thoroughly enjoying everything about Vietnam. For the price paid they had expected poor rooms, so had been pleasantly surprised at the high standard of the hotels where they had stayed. They had been disappointed, however, not to have seen any views from the mountain as they crossed – the mountain had been completed shrouded with cloud on both sides. Now that the cycle ride over the mountain was a few days behind us, we were really glad that the weather had been so good, and we had seen the wonderful views that had been denied to these tourists.

We cycled a short way to the 5 star hotel further along the road to have a look around. At $85 for a room (about £50) the price was phenomenal by Vietnamese standards, but it certainly looked very luxurious and had a lovely restaurant. However, we realised that to someone booking a holiday inclusive of hotels from England, this price would be inflated still further.

The day we were due to leave Lang Co it was pouring with rain, so we decided to stay another day, rather than set off in the rain. It was a good decision, because the rain never abated once during the day, so we walked in our new Vietnamese voluminous plastic rain capes, which kept all but our feet and flip-flops dry. At least it wasn't cold. We found a different café, and had delicious fish and prawn dishes, caught fresh that day. The owner and his brother spoke very little English.

'Where are you from?' they asked.

'England,' we replied.

The restaurant owner excitedly said, 'Ah, Arsenal, Manchester, Liverpool.'

We assumed from this that he was a football supporter.

As we sat there, Warren had his arm along the back of a chair, and was shocked when the restaurant owner stroked his arm. As Warren turned quickly to confront him, the restaurant owner and his brother stroked their own arms and laughed. We both laughed – their arms, like most Vietnamese, were hairless, and they were fascinated by the hair on Warren's arms. Warren lifted his t-shirt, and their eyes bulged at the sight of his hairy chest and stomach! We had noticed that Vietnamese men didn't even have much facial hair – cheeks are usually smooth, and sometimes only one spot on the face grows hair, so that a long string of hair falls from the cheek to below the chin. Often men in Vietnam only had hair on the chin and above the lip, and this was also common in Myanmar and Japan.

The rain caused a power cut, so we sat on the balcony of our room with candles as the afternoon got darker, playing cards and chatting until the power was restored.

The following day it was still windy, but a bit calmer and brighter and no rain – so far! We cycled out of Lang Co travelling north to Hué. Once again I thought what strange combinations of houses they had in Vietnam. There were brand new, very ornate houses on narrow plots between falling down shanty houses. With three floors that had very high ceilings, the new houses looked very tall and narrow. They were rendered and painted green, orange, yellow, or other bright colours, and had fancy cast plaster on the gables at the top facing the street. They had arched windows, fanlights, columns, and balconies with chrome railings which look more suited to bed ends. Some had belfry-like towers or ornate spires, and they usually had high boundary walls or railings and tall wrought-iron gates.

The sky was almost black towards the mountains on our left, and a colourful temple stood out against this dark background. A cow-herd waved as he ushered his cows past in the opposite direction. It was 25°C but felt thundery. Every time we saw the sea on our right or the lagoon on our left, the water was a threatening grey colour reflecting the sky. Red hibiscus flowers covered the bushes in gardens; chickens and their broods pecked in the dirt; women in coolie hats stood talking. Children waved to us from the porches of houses, or ran down the drive to shout 'hello' as we passed. Tables and chairs stood outside houses purporting to be cafés, but we never saw anyone sitting in these places. I bought six tiny bananas for 1,000 dong (less than 5p) and they were sweet and delicious and very similar to the Indian bananas. Everyone stopped talking as I pulled up at the stall, and they refused to let me wait, serving me immediately. Everyone smiled and waved as we left.

We reached a hill; up and up we went, round and round the s-bends, but the road was good with a small hard shoulder for cyclists. Then we were flying down the other side, and were suddenly in a much more rural area. The road was raised from the ground on either side, which was flooded and divided by grass paths to make small rice paddies. We noticed that there were frequent poles along this stretch of road with measurements to show how deep the water was when the road flooded, even though the road was raised several feet above the adjoining fields. There were banana trees and coconut palms, ponds with ducks bobbing in the water, and pigs sniffing in the mud at the edge of the ponds. A water buffalo was knee deep in the water pulling a plough which was guided by a man up to his thighs in the muddy water. Another man stood patiently nearby while his buffalo stood grazing by the roadside. Clouds of colourful dragonflies hovered above us amongst the branches of the trees, and enormous butterflies, black and white or black and shimmering blue or green, fluttered past us. Water buffaloes were grazing in fields standing up to their bellies in water. We passed a broken down bus – three of the passengers were lying under the bus in the shade, their hands behind their heads, as they watched the driver trying to repair it. On the side of the road was a line of wooden coffins, some painted with gold decoration, ready to be sold. Four women shovelled sand into a barrow, while two men stood and watched.

We went through a small town which was busy with children walking and cycling to school. They wore the usual uniform of navy trousers, white shirt and red knotted scarf.

They called out in unison, 'Hello, what is your name? Where are you from? How are you? Good morning.'

We passed the local market, where fruit and vegetables were laid out with women sitting alongside on the ground. Women carried yokes attached to two wide shallow baskets on rope, and the baskets bounced up and down with the spring of the wood as they carried their heavy loads home.

Dogs lay stretched out asleep as we passed each village; tall, dark yellow bamboo grew in tall clumps, and eucalyptus trees with yellow flowers grew alongside. Palm trees were laden with green coconuts, and small papaya trees had large green fruits clinging to the narrow trunks. There were numerous tall haystacks in gardens, some mushroom-shaped where hay had already been taken from the base. We reached another hill, and there was a lovely view of a bay way below us. Back down from the hill there were more rice paddies, and two very young boys with Donald Duck satchels walked hand in hand across the narrow grass path between the flooded fields. Tiny shoots of rice plants recently planted peeped just above the water on either side of them. We passed a tiny one room village hospital. Scaffolding on buildings was the same as in Turkey and India – just any old pieces of wood roughly nailed together! Karaoke signs stood outside bars, and road signs indicated the reducing distance to Hanoi in the north.

A man passed by on the opposite side of the road with four single mattresses tied onto the back of his motorbike – they had been folded in half and stood much higher than him and cantilevered out at the back of his bike. Another motor bike came towards us slowly on the wrong side of the road, swerving to avoid us at the last moment – there were four young men on it. A couple passed us, a girl on a motorbike and a man on a bicycle, and he was holding her motorbike handlebar so that he didn't need to pedal.

As we approached the busy streets of Hué, we were almost immediately approached by a man on a motorbike. He drove alongside us and offered us a room at a hotel. We decided to look at the room, and the owner of the hotel, a Chinese man, was eager to show Warren several different rooms. He showed Warren a room on each of the four floors, rushing from one to the other.

In one of the rooms he pushed open the bathroom door, turning to Warren to say, 'Nice, isn't it?'

'Yes,' said Warren, 'It's very nice,' as he caught the eye of the startled naked girl as she turned – she had been about to turn on the shower.

He followed the owner out of the room, convinced that the owner hadn't even seen the girl, and when Warren saw her later, she was cleaning the corridor. Was she a maid having a shower in one of the rooms without permission? Warren tactfully didn't acknowledge her as he passed. We chose a lovely room for $8 US, and again had a large room which was big enough for our bikes as well; it had air conditioning and an enormous bathroom with bath as well as shower. However, Warren said that he ought to complain, saying that he had assumed that a naked maid came free with every room!

When we went out later we discovered that Hué was much cheaper than Lang Co. Internet cafés were charging 3,000 dong an hour, the cheapest yet (about 15p), and there was a fabulous choice of restaurants. Most of the tourists in Hué were backpackers and travellers, but there were also a couple of very expensive hotels, so we occasionally saw well-dressed tourists in their smart air-conditioned coaches. Warren called them 'sanitised tourists', because they travelled from 5 star hotel to 5 star hotel in their air-conditioned 5 star coaches, so were protected from the heat or any unpleasant smells or sights that might be lurking in that foreign country!

Hué had a big market, and we visited in the hope of buying a watch, Warren having lost his. Most of the time we didn't know what the time was and were not really bothered, but on occasions we needed to know. The first cheap watch we saw was priced at 150,000 dong ($10 or £7.50) and the stall holder refused to reduce the price. As it looked cheap and would probably have cost a maximum of £5 in any English market, we were not willing to pay so much. In any event, the same watch was on every watch stall, and there were dozens of watch stalls, so we eventually found someone willing to sell us the same watch for 40,000 dong.

As we passed each stall the stall-holder called out. 'Madam, buy a hat.' 'Madam, buy tea.' 'Sir, buy cigarettes.'

Eventually we decided we'd seen enough and went to a café to have a cool beer. It was pleasant to have such a wide range of reasonably-priced cafés and restaurants – this was the advantage of destinations which backpackers frequented. Food was excellent and very cheap, and we enjoyed pancakes filled with prawns, egg and bean sprouts with a peanut sauce, delicious stir-fried vegetables in a soy-flavoured sauce, and banana-filled pancakes covered with chocolate sauce.

We rose early one morning to go on a boat trip on the Perfume River to see temples and pagodas a few kilometres away. On the way to the river we stopped at a café to have our usual breakfast of omelettes with French baguettes and Vietnamese tea. Two bikes passed us, each one hidden by dozens of tall house-plants hanging on each side – neither of the men cycling could see properly through the leaves. A man cycled by with dozens of live white geese, their necks protruding from numerous cheap plastic shopping baskets strapped all round the bike.

There were fourteen of us on the boat – a German couple, a French couple, a Dutch couple, two American girls, an Australian couple and a Scottish couple, so we were really international. The Perfume River is wide, and most of the boats on the river were sand-mining boats that were so low in the water with high piles of wet sand that it was amazing that they didn't sink. We were on one of the many dragon boats, which were tired-looking boats with a metal prow in the shape of a dragon's head. A young man piloted the boat, a young girl (probably his sister) pushed the boat out and jumped on, and a very elderly lady who was probably their mother cooked the lunch and told us off every time any one of us went to the small open area at the front. We sat on small plastic chairs in the galley-shaped boat facing each other. There was no safety drill; indeed, there was nothing in the boat in the way of safety equipment.

The boat stopped regularly so we could go and visit the various temples along the river while the Vietnamese family slept in the boat. As in India, entry prices varied depending on whether you were local or a foreigner – 15,000 Dong for locals and 55,000 for foreigners! As we left the boat to visit one temple a man approached the river carrying a packet of Omo and a bag of clothes – it was obviously wash day!

We had lunch on the boat which the women prepared, but I was concerned when I noticed them cooling the cooked noodles in a colander in the river. The noodles were to be served cold, so Warren and I decided to give them a miss! However, we enjoyed the hot rice, the sliced omelette, the freshly cooked beans and tofu fritters instead. The trip ended early when the Vietnamese family refused to take us to a fishing village which had been advertised as part of the itinerary, and the whole group unanimously decided we didn't want to visit another temple. Despite this, it had been a pleasant trip, and a welcome change to chat to so many other travellers as well. English was, of course, the common language.

The following morning we sat in a café by the traffic lights having breakfast, fascinated by the traffic that passed. A cyclo stopped next door with eight 8 feet by 4 feet sheets of thick board similar to MDF. The driver had attached a hook to the foot-rest to stop them sliding off as he cycled, but they were precariously balanced and obviously a very heavy load. Two men carried each sheet with difficulty one at a time into the building. Another cyclo went by with four rusty bicycles laid across it, and a further cyclo had a woman passenger who sat with a treadle sewing machine perched in front of her on the foot-rest – it looked as though she was about to start sewing! One woman's cycle was pulling a long heavy wooden trolley hooked over her back mudguard – these trolleys were usually pushed and pulled by at least two people. The trolley was empty, but every time she went over a small bump in the road the trolley fell off. Another woman sat in a cyclo with a cage of geese at her feet, their heads protruding in every direction. It began to rain, so suddenly everyone was wearing the plastic capes like ours, and several people cycled by with navy blue capes with the Prudential logo on the back.

Later that day we searched for a recommended café, but noticed that there were several cafés with the same name, which was very confusing. We discovered later that once a café was recommended by the guide books, another café opened using the same name and maybe even a third, each one in the hope that they would get the custom meant for the original café! We found the café (or at least, one with the same name!) and were again watching the world go by. It was pouring with rain and beginning to get dark, so every cyclist and motor cyclist who passed wore his cape. Some of the plastic capes had clear windows at the front so that when the cape was thrown over the handlebars of the motor bike it didn't obscure the light. As in the rest of Asia, bicycles in Vietnam never had lights! However, most motorcyclists weren't concerned about obscuring their lights, and as it became darker, the motorbike lights shone blue, green, mauve or pink, depending on the colour of the plastic rain cape that they shone through! Virtually every passenger, either on a bike or motor bike, sat huddled under the driver's cape, but we did see one double-headed cape which we thought was rather clever.

As we sat at the café a young boy tried to sell us roasted peanuts in their shells for 5,000 Dong. I offered 2,000 but he refused and went away, but came back later offering them for 2,000 (10p). I noticed that the locals didn't need to haggle – they got them for 1,000 Dong!

Eventually it was time to leave Hué, and we set off at 7am. This was the best time to see real life in Vietnam and for taking photos of the local people – everyone was carrying large loads of vegetables and fruit, animals or building materials on their bikes or their shoulders. A woman had a cage at the back of her bike exactly the length of the small pig inside it, which lay there squashed against the wire with another pig probably suffocating beneath it. A cyclo pedalled alongside us with six hardwood doors balanced on the front.

I noticed the names over the shop and restaurant doors – Tam Thien, Kim Dinh, Thao Ngoc, Dang Tang, Van Dung, Xi Nang, Ty Tuan, Khan Ly, Bang Suong and Long Hung. There were vast numbers of accents, some above the letters, some below and sometimes more than one on each letter. Of course, not speaking Vietnamese, these words might actually mean 'paint and hardware' or 'sofas reupholstered here' and aren't actual names, but they certainly give a flavour of the language. The Vietnamese language, like Thai, Burmese and Lao, is tonal. The different tones are mid-tone, high-rising tone, low-falling tone, low-rising tone, high-broken tone and low-broken tone. The tone and pronunciation are indicated by the accents. In this way, a two lettered word such as 'ma' can, incredibly, mean 'ghost', 'mother', 'which', 'but', 'tomb', 'horse' or 'rice seedling', depending on how you say it. How can you say a two letter word in so many different ways? No wonder the locals couldn't understand us when we asked for a cup of tea in Vietnamese! Occasionally, as we cycled, a recognisable word could be seen – 'super' at the BP service station or 'karaoke' outside a bar.

We stopped for a cup of tea at a very rural café. The lady spoke no English but understood what we wanted, and we agreed a price up front. We felt quite pleased that we could do this without knowing the language! The only other person in the café was an old woman who talked animatedly to us, but as she was chewing betel nut I could hardly bear to look at her dark red stained mouth and teeth, especially when she smiled. Many of the old women in Vietnam chew betel nut, and they also sometimes smoked cheroots. We took a photo of the old lady, but as soon as we asked her to smile she just stared fixedly at the camera looking very serious, so her red teeth didn't show in the photos.

We passed a section of new dual carriageway as we cycled through a small town, and gardeners were filling the central reservation with plants. Each small plant came in a pretty bamboo basket lined with polythene, but they ripped these off, and broken baskets laid everywhere. There were several war cemeteries along this long straight stretch of road, and we understood that there were a lot of disabled Vietnamese in this area as it had been bombed a lot in the Vietnam War.

We passed a cyclist selling Chinese dumplings – on one side of his bike he had a tall round saucepan with a fire underneath it; steam was coming out of the lid as he cycled along. On the other side of his bike was a glass cabinet displaying the cooked dumplings. As he cycled he rang his bell to tell housewives he was there to sell his food. We passed a barber's shop and someone, presumably the barber, was fast asleep in the barber's chair. In Asia if there's no work to do you don't shuffle papers to look busy – you just go to sleep!

We arrived in Dong Ha and found a hotel on the outskirts. The receptionist spoke German but no English, which was unusual. She initially told us that the hotel was full, but subsequently showed us to a room with two double beds and a living area. The price was far too high, but we eventually agreed a lower price. I had a shower, but the water ran cold halfway through, and I discovered that there was a switch outside the bathroom door to turn on the water heater. There was a knock on the door, and the receptionist explained in German that she was moving us because the water heater was broken in this room. She showed me to another bedroom, much smaller than ours with only single beds and no balcony. This was a concern as we needed somewhere to dry the clothes that we had washed. The room she showed us should have been a much lower price than the first one, but she wouldn't offer a discount. I felt there was something wrong and that perhaps she wanted our room for someone else. I told her in German that I was happy with cold water, and returned to our room. Two minutes later there was another knock at the door – she wanted a chair, she said. I was sat at the dining table in the room writing my diary, but was happy to give her one of the three chairs. She took a chair, but two other hotel employees came in and began to clear the table.

'Was machen Sie?' I asked her, wanting to know what was happening.

'This table is broken,' she replied in German. 'I will give you a better one – a round one.'

I refused, saying we liked the table (which certainly wasn't broken) and she rushed to the next bedroom and ran back with a low coffee table.

'No thank you,' I said firmly in German, and asked them to leave our room.

The following morning, after hot showers (yes, the water heater worked fine), we left the hotel. The door to the next bedroom was open, and two men sat with the low coffee table covered with papers, writing on their laps. If she had been honest about why she wanted us to move rooms, and had offered us a fair lower price for the other room, we would have been willing to move. We had to ask for the breakfast that we'd been promised, and they brought it to us in the reception area of the hotel, where we sat and ate it on our laps.

We intended that day to find a seaside resort we'd been recommended that was further north. We needed to return to Dong Ha because it was at this point that we were going to turn inland to cross over the mountain and into Laos. However, when we returned to Dong Ha, we certainly planned to find a different hotel . . .

★ ★ ★

We wanted to find the pleasant beach area that we'd been told about, so we set off travelling north along the coast, and stopped after a while at a café that was no more than a shack. No-one appeared to be there until we walked through the rooms calling. Two women were asleep in a room behind the café. They didn't understand what we wanted, so one of the women pulled Warren by the arm to the kitchen, where he found some eggs and lifted a frying pan from the wall. With the action of breaking eggs into the pan they understood, and we soon heard the splatter of fierce frying, so guessed our eggs would be well cooked.

We also had Vietnamese tea but in the non-tourist areas the small cups supplied are always left on the table unwashed, just the same as in Myanmar. All the Vietnamese do is pour a drop of tea into the cup, swill it round and throw it onto the floor, before pouring themselves a cup of tea. Afterwards the cup is replaced unwashed on the tray for the next person. We always used our own cups, because of our concern about diseases. As we sat eating our eggs, their mother scratched away in the dirt beneath our table. She'd probably laid the eggs that morning – they were certainly delicious!

The ladies tried to chat to us – one spoke a few words of English and asked if we had children. They understood 'three' when I held up three fingers, but when I held up five fingers to indicate grand-children they were confused. I tried to draw a family tree, but they didn't understand, so out came the photos. They were entranced, thinking my daughters were beautiful and my son handsome, and pointed at Warren and indicated that they were like him. It just wasn't worth the trouble to explain that these were my children from a previous marriage, and they weren't Warren's children, so we just nodded and smiled. The photos were passed around, and they ooghed and aaghed over them, especially those of my grandchildren and especially the baby photos. I explained about the forthcoming sixth grandchild, patting my tummy, and they seemed to understand – or maybe they just thought I was still hungry or, worse still, pregnant! Who knows?

According to the map it wasn't far to the beach resort. Although several people had told us that the hotels were expensive, we thought it would be wonderful to have a bit of luxury for a change. We turned off the main highway, and were now on tarmac that must have been 50 years old, it was so cracked and damaged. Although we were in a very rural area, there were dozens of children walking and cycling, and in the next 10km we saw no less than four large modern schools, so it was obvious that the children were well catered for educationally, and this explained why the children in Vietnam as well as the adults spoke such good English. Sometimes the schoolgirls fell into fits of giggles, because we replied to them when they said hello. We passed a woman who had just bought a wheel barrow, and she had tied the handles to the back of her bicycle, so she could tow it home.

It was a grey, overcast day, and we cycled on and on, regularly asking for directions. We passed rice paddies and temples, forests and villages. The 15km we thought we had to cycle turned into 50km, and we never found any hotels. We eventually realised that we would have to cycle back to Dong Ha, so our few days of luxury in a seaside resort were not to be. We were also incredibly hungry. When we got back to the main road we found a café where they were happy to give us lunch, even though it was late and the tables and chairs had already been stacked away for the afternoon. The man dropped three massive goose eggs into a frying pan and made the most delicious creamy omelette for us to share. Into it he had thrown spring onions, fresh herbs and tomatoes, and he gave us a loaf of bread to eat with it. OK, we were overdosing on eggs that day, but we didn't feel that we had any choice. There were cooked chickens lying on the table, but we didn't know how long they'd been cooked or how long they had been lying there uncovered – clearly the eggs were the safer option!

Further down the road we saw a hump-backed bull pulling a plough, so we stopped to take a photo and the farmer waved to us. Half a mile further on was a water buffalo pulling a plough, so we stopped again. As I took a photo the farmer bent, pulled a lump of mud from the flooded field and threw it at us. Fortunately his aim wasn't good enough, but obviously from this action not all Vietnamese are friendly or want their photos taken! Warren stooped and pretended to let the air out of the tyre of the farmer's bicycle which was on the road, and the farmer went berserk trying to run across the muddy flooded field to get to us. We cycled off laughing.

We passed a family of water buffaloes. Daddy was leading the way along a path, and mummy brought up the rear, nudging her son with her nose whenever he slowed down.

We ended up cycling 92km (58 miles) that day with full bags, only to return to the same town that we'd started in. However, we now found a very nice 2 star hotel for a cheaper price than the previous night's hotel, and it was in the centre of the town. We treated ourselves to some French table wine from a local shop, and sat in our room after our meal having a glass of wine and watching an English film on satellite television.

We went to bed that night praying for a cool, overcast day the next day, because we knew that we had to cycle uphill to 600 metres to get to the border of Laos. No-one listened to my prayers. At 7am it was cool, but there wasn't a cloud in the sky. We were alone as we ate our breakfast in the hotel dining room. As we sat there, one of the staff came into the dining room, took a glass from the display for serving customers, poured a glass of water and drank some, threw the rest onto the terrace floor outside and replaced the glass without washing it! Needless to say, after that we always wiped our cups and cutlery very well before eating – we guessed that this happened in the rural areas, but we were surprised that it should happen in a 2 star hotel!

We set off, buying bread and a bunch of tiny bananas before we left the town to make banana sandwiches for lunch. By 9am it was 23°C and hazy. One tiny cloud hovered above the mountain range that came into sight after 10 miles.

The countryside was now very different from any we'd seen on the coast. It was much more rural than any other area we'd seen in Vietnam, and the mountains were beautiful. Outside the houses, rice and peanuts had been laid out on plastic sheets to dry in the sun. Ahead of us we could see the mountains, with a road zigzagging to the top. We went through a couple of villages and then there were no people at all, just trees and mountains in the distance. The road was going up and down, and ahead of us we could see jagged hills. When we got closer we could see that the hills and small mountains were being blasted. Large rocks were being loaded onto lorries, and in one area stone or marble chippings were piled high by the roadside. The mountain was badly scarred with the blasting, and there would soon be no mountain at all.

There was little traffic on the road, mostly rather old-looking buses or lorries that sped past us stirring up the dust. A bus stopped in front of us, dropping off a passenger, who was handed an old lorry radiator from inside the bus before it set off again. As the buses approached us they sounded their horns to warn that they were about to pass, and because of the mountains surrounding us, the noise echoed all around us.

We were going uphill and down again, and I wondered how we would ever reach 600 metres, the maximum elevation we had to achieve that day. The only consolation was that, after the hot uphill climb, the downhill swoop cooled us down again. We passed several villages of small houses that were no more than shacks. They were built on stilts, the sides made of woven grass, with open holes for doors and windows. The roofs were of corrugated sheets of metal or were thatched. Children called excitedly from their houses or the sides of the road as we passed these villages, and some tried to run alongside to keep up with us. Men carried tools for working in the fields, most of which were rice paddies. Light brown or black and white cows grazed and calves suckled. The cows looked healthy and there were a few dark brown hump-backed cows. There were a large number of dogs and puppies in Vietnam, and most looked in reasonable condition, unlike in India.

We began to follow a wide shallow river. The road wound backwards and forwards, following the route of the river, but it had a good surface. Occasional houses stood by the river, but these were frames on stilts covered with any bit of rag, polythene, or cement sacking that the occupants could find. On our right away from the river the mountain rose steeply, and it was a concern that there were so many rock falls, all of them looking quite recent, and maybe because of the heavy rain we had already experienced.

We were suddenly very excited to see two touring bikes coming towards us, and stopped to chat to the two men riding them. One was Australian and one Dutch, and they had cycled through Laos and Cambodia, doing the same journey that we planned but in reverse. They told us that this was the cloudiest day that they'd seen (there were a few clouds in the sky), whereas for us it was one of the sunniest. They had been on the road for one month, and were very envious when we told them we'd been on the road now for almost 18 months. As we stopped, six or seven small children ran to join us and stood there gazing up at us, saying nothing. As local cyclists arrived at the scene they also stopped, then a man with a scythe who was walking by joined the crowd. More and more children appeared from nowhere. By the time we said goodbye to the two cyclists we were surrounded by 45 children and adults, none of them ever saying a word, nor touching us or the bikes – just standing watching. I turned to look back as we moved away, and all of the locals had dispersed and were walking or cycling off in different directions.

As we continued, the river widened, and groups of houses on stilts stood amongst the tree-covered slopes on the other side. The water bubbled over rocks on the river's downhill descent. An orange and white striped bus passed us – it looked ancient and had a round window in the back. As always, large parcels, bikes and motorbikes were piled high on the top.

We saw families of mountain goats with their kids – every animal we saw in Vietnam seemed to have recently produced offspring. The hills on the other side of the river were densely wooded, but the trees were enshrouded with a large-leaved creeping plant, which made the whole area look really spooky.

We passed a man walking his water buffalo, the buffalo shining from head to toe with a wet coat of mud. Children constantly called 'hello' to us, repeating over and over again, 'hello, hello, hello', their voices gradually receding as we cycled past. Tiny children were often naked and were almost always accompanied by older brothers or sisters. If we stopped to take photos, these country children just stood and looked at us, unlike the boisterous exuberance of the town children, who screamed and jumped up and down in excitement. It was obvious that these children were not used to seeing foreigners.

The road ahead turned left over a bridge across the river, and climbed steeply up and round, backwards and forwards. We reached a high point and stopped to rest, and were amazed to see immediately below us a perfect horse-shoe shape as the river curved round almost in a circle way below us. By now there were quite a few clouds in the sky, but the sun was still beating down on us, and we were getting sunburnt because there was very little shade. The road dropped away to our left, but was sheer rock to our right. There was a road sign warning of rock-blasting 1,000 metres ahead (unusually the sign was in English as well), and I was concerned. Closer examination of the notice showed specific times for blasting – 11am until 1pm. I looked at my watch – it was 1.15pm, so hopefully we were safe!

We arrived at Huong Hoa where we intended staying the night. There were only two guesthouses. The first was filthy with no fan or bathroom and they wanted $10 for a night – the same price we'd paid for our luxury room and bathroom the night before! The second was better, though not good. They also wanted $10 and wouldn't reduce the price. We had little choice; the toilet seat was broken and there was no hot water, but at least this room had good clean mosquito nets over the two double beds. After we had sprayed the rooms with mosquito repellent we found a cockroach on its back in the bathroom – we had found in Kolkata that mosquito spray worked well on cockroaches as well!

We listened to the BBC World Service on our radio and had an early night after a meal in a local café. The next day we had only thirteen miles to cycle before reaching the Laos border. We had found the Vietnamese people warm and friendly, and had thoroughly enjoyed Vietnam. Now we were looking forward to seeing Laos and meeting Lao people.

We were also excited at the thought of our first proper road border crossing on this trip. Despite the fact that we had entered thirteen different countries since we had left England, the only road crossing had been from France to Italy, and that had been an anti-climax as there had been no-one in the kiosk at the border. We had entered Greece and Turkey by ferry, and the rest of the countries by air.

From Huong Hoa the next morning it was downhill again, but there were road-works everywhere and it was very dusty. There were tree-covered mountains as far as the eye could see and quite a few banana plantations. To our right was a wide section of river with small boats, each with a man fishing. We passed a woman with a yoke across her shoulders, but instead of baskets on each end there were cages. In one was a large saucepan with a fire burning under it, and in the other were several pans.

We reached a village – there were groups of people everywhere, and branches of green bananas covered the ground. People were milling around and it was obvious that this was a banana market. People were walking away with poles over their shoulders, and on each end were branches of bananas; motorbikes had special wooden platforms attached to accommodate eight of these enormous branches standing upright. This was Lao Bao, the nearest Vietnamese town to the Laos border. One mile further on we reached the Vietnamese side of the border and had our passports stamped with the date and our Vietnamese visas were cancelled – it was three weeks since we had entered Vietnam. One kilometre further on we reached Laos, where we completed the forms, as always in Asia pulling a hotel address from a guide book to complete on the forms. Immigration forms often requested an address where we planned to stay, and it was not acceptable to say that we didn't know until we got there.

Unlike the two cyclists we'd met the day before, we didn't have to pay a bribe to get our passports stamped, so without any problems we cycled into Laos.

CHAPTER 17

LAOS

Laos is a land-locked country about the size of Great Britain, and is surrounded by China, Myanmar (Burma), Thailand, Cambodia and Vietnam. 70% of the country is covered by mountains or plateaux and 50% is forested. Laos is the poorest country in Indochina; indeed, it is one of the poorest countries in the world, and depends very heavily on foreign aid. 5.4 million people live in Laos, about 8% of Britain's population, so it is sparsely populated, and most Lao people live along the Mekong River valley. This great river runs from China, through Myanmar, Thailand and Cambodia and finally reaches the sea via the famous Mekong River delta in South Vietnam. The Mekong River provides fertile floodplains for agriculture in Laos and is an important means of transportation, but Laos is one of the least developed countries in Asia.

As we left the passport and visa checks in Laos, we were accosted by girls who were trying to sell Kip, the local currency. They had wads of very new-looking notes, which could have been Monopoly money as far as we were concerned – we had no Lao money, and also had no idea what the local currency looked like, so we had no intention of buying it from someone on the road. The cyclists we had met had fortunately told us that there were 10,000 kip to one US dollar, so when one girl offered 8,000 per dollar to Warren, he refused.

'No, 12,000,' he offered.

She laughed and turned to tell her friends, but Warren shrugged. 'You said eight; I said twelve,' he said.

'Nine,' she said.

'No, twelve,' said Warren, as we started to cycle off.

'Ten,' she shouted at our backs as we disappeared down the road.

We knew we would have no problem handing over dollars to anyone in Laos, even in the rural areas. If we paid for anything in dollars, we would receive kip as change, so there was no need to exchange money beforehand. We understood that everyone preferred to be paid in dollars rather than kips, and we had brought

US dollars with us to Indochina for this reason – this was made even more necessary as there were no ATMs in Laos, so we couldn't use our credit cards to get money.

The sky was a lovely bright blue, which reminded us of Australia. The houses now were very similar to the houses on stilts we had seen the day before in Vietnam. Some were more substantial than those we'd seen so far. The children stood on high banks overlooking the road and were calling 'Bye, bye' or 'Money, money'. They didn't call 'hello' as the Vietnamese children had. Most were naked or half naked. Two women stood pounding something in a giant mortar which stood on the ground. They used long thick sticks with rounded ends, pounding with a rhythm one after another, grinding the contents of the mortar. We had seen exactly the same method used in an African village on a previous holiday.

The road initially was very poor and stony, but suddenly was very wide and newly sealed, although there were no markings. Telegraph poles lined the road on one side. The road was straight, going up and down gentle hills. Now we had crossed the mountain we were on a plain, but also the weather had changed dramatically. It was very hot, and we had left behind the rain and cooler weather of Vietnam. Steep banks were at the sides of the road, and groups of houses on stilts stood in areas cleared of trees on these banks. Naked children stood on the very red soil looking down at us. Between the groups of houses was open countryside with trees and mountains in the distance.

It was incredibly hot and the sun beat down on us from the south. There was no shade. I changed into long trousers, because the bottom half of my left leg was burning. We both turned our caps so that the peaks were to the left, shading our left ear and cheek, and we re-applied sunscreen. The brand new road ahead of us was deserted except for a large black sow that was sniffing something on the tarmac. She had such short legs and big belly that her teats dragged on the tarmac. This was a pot-bellied pig, a species that had originated in Vietnam. We hadn't seen any in Vietnam, but were to see many in Laos.

The road went from good to bad to good again – road-works were everywhere, and occasionally we were diverted along very bumpy dirt paths alongside the road, where the bad sections of road were being re-constructed. If a bus or lorry passed, we couldn't see anything ahead or behind, because the dust was so thick. Fortunately there was little traffic. If I needed the toilet I didn't need to look for a bush – this wide new road was so deserted that I could just squat down by the side of the road!

The Lao children were very shy compared to their Vietnamese counterparts, despite the fact that they were shouting 'Money, money' as we passed. They didn't come close when we stopped, and they didn't appear to understand any English, unlike the Vietnamese children. In the 40 miles that we travelled that day we saw numerous children but no schools, whereas in a five mile stretch of road in Vietnam there would be two or three large modern schools. Many of the children we saw carried metal detectors – metal detecting seemed a strange thing to do in a country that still has many unexploded US bombs.

We cycled along another sealed stretch of road. The lane in the opposite direction had been tarred ready for the final layer of tarmac. A set of tarry footprints led across our side of the road, where someone had walked through the tar with bare feet. We heard a strange noise, and discovered that it was a herd of water buffalo with large wooden bells round their necks. They grazed by the roadside alongside cows with metal cowbells, and goats and kids nibbled shrubs beside them.

We found wonderful accommodation for the night in Sepon – a modern house had a small but very comfortable room with a small bathroom with hot water – and all for $2.50 a night! Not only had the kind owner left soap and shampoo in the bathroom, but also a little container full of washing powder and a bucket, so that we could wash our dusty clothes. The owner obviously anticipated an influx of tourists, because he was in the process of building twelve very attractive chalet rooms in two blocks, many of which were going to be air-conditioned, and with modern metal mosquito-screened windows. There didn't appear to be any other accommodation in the town.

Two doors away a young lady had a café, and she produced excellent food for us. We discovered that there was no French bread in Laos, except in the tourist towns, despite the fact that Laos, like Vietnam, had previously been a French colony. In Laos, food is virtually always cooked at the time of ordering, which naturally makes for better taste and less worries about how hygienically the food has been stored. As we sat eating our meal next to the roadside in the town later that evening, an enormous monster of a machine, a grader, went up and down the unlit road grading the surface by scraping it. The dust was awful and the machine made an unbelievable screeching noise as it continued working until 10pm.

The next morning we had to repair a puncture in my tyre before we could start – this was the thirteenth puncture since we had started our trip eighteen months before. Next door to the guest house we were fascinated to see the local service station – it was half of a small wooden shed, left open at the front, which gave sufficient storage space for two 45 gallon petrol drums with hand pumps, and a shelf above held three gallon cans of oil. This was the only type of service station we ever saw until we reached a major town in Laos. Some food shacks also sold petrol in Pepsi and Fanta bottles alongside the genuine articles!

It was a dirt road through Sepon, the road having been rolled ready for sealing. Shacks lined both sides of the road, and these were now open to reveal tiny shops.

Sepon was marked on the map as a fairly substantial town. However as a result of US bombing, the town had been completely destroyed, and now had only a few makeshift houses, apart from our very nice guest house. Ahead of us was a very short stretch of sealed road, along which a man pushed a wheelbarrow with numerous planks of wood 8 feet wide precariously balanced across it. We went over a bridge which had been blocked by a lorry and two ancient looking cars. Piles of sand and rubble filled the gaps between the vehicles. However, we noticed that the obstruction didn't stop two other cyclists and a motorbike, who drove along an already worn path over the pile of sand and onto the road that had been tarred ready to be sealed with tarmac. We followed. No traffic was on this section apart from road-rollers and a few bikes, and the surface was reasonably smooth. The workmen waved as we passed – they weren't concerned that we were on this blocked section of road.

We passed more and more of the small villages of wooden-framed houses on stilts. People waved and children shouted. By now we'd discovered that very few people spoke English, so we had learnt the Lao word 'sabaidi' so that we could call out 'hello'.

The scenery became very much like Africa, with red soil, bush, and the mountains beyond. Some of the fields were so dry that there were deep cracks across them. We passed occasional huts or shacks outside which women worked; even the way these country women were dressed looked African, with checked woven fabric wrapped round their heads like turbans, and similar fabric wrapped round as skirts with blouses on top. Sometimes they carried babies on their backs tied on with woven shawls, and small children ran naked and barefoot. It wouldn't have surprised us to see a herd of elephants under the trees, but there were plenty of water buffalo instead. We occasionally saw white water buffalo, which looked very strange because the red dust had turned their skin a ghostly pink colour.

The road was constantly blocked with branches, piles of rubble or lorries, to stop traffic entering the sections of road being re-constructed. However, there was always space to get a bike through, and it was preferable cycling on the partly made new road than on the bumpy dirt roads that formed the diversions.

I stopped to change into trousers, and two boys came and stood next to us watching fascinated as I did this. Warren looked at their bikes – they had once been reasonable mountain bikes, he told me, but now they had no pedals, no brakes and no tread down the centre of the knobbly tyres. He did the thumbs up to them, however, and they were excited, and one of them set off to race Warren, obviously convinced that he could beat someone cycling with so much baggage. The two of them tore down the deserted, newly sealed road, laughing so much that they nearly fell off their bikes, and eventually the boy admitted defeat and returned to his friend, calling 'Bye, bye' to me as he passed.

At the next small town we found a good hotel with an excellent room for $3 a night. This time we had our own balcony as well as a bathroom with hot water and a room with air conditioning. In practice, we prefer a fan-cooled room to an air-conditioned room unless it is very hot and humid. Asian air-conditioning units can be very noisy, and air-conditioned rooms are usually more expensive than fan-cooled rooms. However, in Vietnam and Laos the temperature at night in December had been a pleasantly cool 20°C, so the ideal was to have a room with mosquito screens, so that we could sleep covered with a blanket with the windows open and no fan or air-conditioning running.

We were finding that Lao prices for rooms were quite a lot cheaper than in Vietnam (this was until we got to the next tourist town in Laos) but, surprisingly for such a poor country, the prices of food in Laos (for tourists anyway) was at least one and a half times the prices in Vietnam. The prices were still cheap, of course, and because of the cheaper accommodation we were finding that it was costing us approximately £13 pounds a day to live in Laos, including beer, whereas it had cost almost £20 a day in Vietnam with beer or wine. This was much cheaper than any other countries we had visited so far apart from India.

Walking round the market later we noticed that most of the women wore skirts made of local fabric woven into a tube, which was wrapped round the waist to make a long wrap-over skirt – these skirts were very similar to those worn by the women in Myanmar. We found a restaurant with a video for karaoke, but fortunately nobody was singing, and our waiter actually spoke a little English. However, there must have been some confusion. We asked for an omelette with tomatoes and onions.

'A vegetable omelette?' he asked.

'Yes,' we said.

Not long afterwards he handed us each a plate with two fried eggs in the middle, surrounded by a ring of sliced cucumber and an outer ring of sliced tomatoes. Having looked forward to an omelette, we were a little disappointed, but a few minutes later the waiter appeared with a plate of chips for each of us. We were really excited – egg and chips! We hadn't had egg and chips for many months. Isn't it amazing how something so ordinary can give so much pleasure?

The next day we had to leave very early, as we knew there was little chance of accommodation for 60 miles, and we usually didn't like to cycle so far. As we left the hotel we noticed that the two four wheel drive cars in the car park both had keys in the ignition, and the van had an open back with a display of tools laid out – we felt this was a good sign that the Lao people must be very honest.

The sky was overcast. I was pleased – someone up there must have been listening to me. So long as it didn't pour with rain I would be happy, because if it was overcast it might be cooler than the last few days.

For the first time the road had markings, and there were signposts galore. It was as though someone had been told to put in as many as they could think of, and within a few yards there were signs advising of crossroads (a dirt road crossing the highway), children, road curving to the left, a speed sign, and a turning to the right (a dirt path). Every bridge and every river (and there were dozens of them) had signposts giving the name of the bridge and the river in a pretty curly script that was obviously Lao but was fortunately also written in letters of the alphabet that we could recognise. There were signs to places large and small, including faraway places like Vientiane (554km) and Pakse (352km) that were not even on this highway. Tiny groups of houses not even big enough to be called villages were now also proudly named on green signs in two languages.

The landscape changed constantly – first of all it was green and lush, then there was arid red soil again. Children aged about 10 were driving motorbikes on the almost empty road. They were driving very well and sensibly. We assumed that they were not legally allowed to, but we'd never seen any policemen. A little boy passed, cycling in the opposite direction. As he passed he waved excitedly to us.

'Hello. How are you? I am very well, thank you,' he shouted, and he flew by on his bicycle without waiting for an answer.

In one village we saw well built houses on stilts. Instead of the rush woven walls they were made of wood and had balconies, window shutters and proper doors – quite substantial and very attractive. Perhaps someone in the village was a good carpenter! The road now was excellent, the surface good, and we were making fast time with a tail wind. We noticed that, although most of the thatched houses on stilts were very basic, one or more in a group of houses always had a television aerial, and it reminded us of the shacks in India that similarly had a satellite dish attached.

Children continued to shout 'Bye, bye' to us, but confusion may have arisen because the Lao word for goodbye is the same as for hello. Occasionally someone called 'hello' or 'good morning', and I was beginning to feel like the Queen, I was waving and smiling so often! The children were no longer shouting 'money, money' at us as we passed. We arrived at an enormous sign that showed that The Government of Japan had paid for Highway 9 to be upgraded, which explained the excellent wide road that we had enjoyed virtually to ourselves.

We were tired, so when we saw a bench in the shade of trees we turned off the road to sit down. A pig sty stood nearby and, judging by the abandoned cigarette packets, it was a popular venue for adults or children to sit and have a smoke. Within minutes four children had appeared, and before long fourteen children were standing watching us, most of them peeping at us from behind the trees. The pig snuffled in the undergrowth nearby, and the children stood quietly at a slight distance, gradually getting braver and coming closer. We shared a packet of biscuits with them and took several photos. When we left I went ahead. I heard Warren calling, and looked back to see him emerging from the trees pushing his bike, followed by a line of fourteen children and looking like the Pied Piper!

When we arrived at our next planned stop for the night we couldn't find the hotel that we had been told was there. We asked various people but no-one spoke English, and a group of people playing boules didn't want to interrupt their game. We eventually discovered that the hotel was closed, but someone had a key, and she led us to a pleasant looking one storey building. Unfortunately when the hotel door was opened, it was obvious that the place had been locked up for a long time, because there was a very musty smell. When the bedroom door was opened, the stench was terrible – the room was empty apart from three single beds with very stained mattresses. The shower room was across the hall, and had a tank of water which had to be scooped up in bowls to be poured over the body; it was obvious the water had stood there for some time, because it was green with algae. There was no other accommodation in the town and, maybe because of this fact, the price named for a bed for the night was extremely high despite the awful condition of the room. However, despite the fact that we'd already cycled over 60 miles in the heat, we decided to continue to Seno, 33km further on. This was the furthest that we had cycled so far in one day, but Warren was good at encouraging me, although I thought he sounded like a midwife.

'Push, Mary, push,' he urged if I began to slow down.

We were both tired, but we were averaging a fast speed despite our tiredness, thanks to the tail wind. By now it was 3.30pm and was 30°C. We had been cycling since 6am.

We approached a town which we assumed to be Seno, but we were confused because there were two towns marked on our map which we hadn't passed. We never actually discovered the name of the town, but there were some very attractive houses – not the over-the-top gaudiness of the new houses in Vietnam, but beautifully-proportioned styles with dormer windows, and balconies with arched hardwood windows and doors. Most of them were very big, obviously built for wealthy Lao people, and we understand that most wealthy people in Laos either work for the Government or else have their own companies.

Our spirits lifted when we saw a guest house which was a small resort of terraced rooms, some with balconies, with pleasant gardens in the centre. It even had its own restaurant near the entrance gates. The room, however, was disappointing. It wasn't bad, but not luxurious as the outside had promised. We would have liked some luxury after our hard day's cycling, because we hoped to stay a couple of days. We had cycled 136km (86 miles), which was the furthest we had done in one day, but we had also managed to clock up our fastest average speed so far as well – 20.3km per hour, or 12.6 miles per hour.

We decided to check out the guest house next door before committing ourselves. A young lad wanted money before showing us the room. He smelt of alcohol and appeared to be drunk, but eventually showed Warren the room. Warren came out laughing loudly – for $4 (the same as the guest house next door) the room had no window, bathroom or fan, and the mattress was on the floor! We returned to the first guest house complex and agreed a reduced rate if we took the room for two days.

There was a list of House Rules in English on the wall of the room:

1. Visitors will not be laundered, cooked in the room, smoked cigarette on the bed and made a noise to another visitors.
2. No sticking naked photo in the room.
3. Don't make anything wrongs of law (narcotic, munitions, politic) and don't take prostitute in room.
4. Visitors will not allowed to meet the outsiders in the room. In case, relation must be permit by the receptionist.

We were to discover that there was a very good reason why one of the above rules had been included . . .

After a quick shower I went to the restaurant in the grounds of the guest house for a bite to eat. Warren was waiting for the plumber to finish fixing the tap back on the washbasin (it had come off in my hand as I turned it), so he said he would join me in a few minutes. The restaurant owner didn't speak any English, and didn't allow me into her kitchen to see the food, which is what normally happens, so I sat with a beer. Two girls came to chat, and one shared her doughnut-like bun with me. They spoke virtually no English but were friendly. Warren arrived and sorted out the restaurant owner – he didn't take 'no' for an answer, and marched into the kitchen, where he managed to get her to understand what we would like to eat. He returned to the table, and the two girls laughed kindly at his face, which was very red from the day's cycling in the sun, and they stroked his red cheeks. One of the girls seemed fascinated by the cleft in his chin, and kept stroking it. They looked at our map and chatted a little, constantly stroking Warren's arm and touching his thigh. Being naïve, I just thought they were being very friendly (bearing in mind how 'touchy feely' the Vietnamese people had been), but they eventually left us, one to stand on the pavement outside the guest house gates, and one to sit with a westerner who had just arrived (the first we'd seen for over a week). Warren laughed at me when I commented on the girls, telling me that they were obviously prostitutes. That explained the girls' clothes – I had been surprised how scantily-clad they were for Lao women, one with tiny shorts and grossly thick platform shoes, and the other with a thin strappy dress slit high at both sides.

We were surprised when one of them served our food, and realised that they worked in the guest house. This was when it clicked – remembering rule number 3 of the House Rules, stating that no prostitute should be taken into the room, we realised that the guest house wanted no outside prostitutes because they had their own in-house service! This appeared to be confirmed by the way the girl with the westerner now had her hand possessively on his thigh, (we discovered later that he was one of the crew that was working on the new highway reconstruction) and the fact that the other girl shortly afterwards walked past the restaurant with a man she had been chatting to on the pavement, and went into one of the guest house rooms with him.

Warren was not well in the night, and had no intention of going anywhere that was more than three feet from a toilet the next day. I left him in bed while I went to have breakfast in the restaurant. All that was available was the traditional breakfast of pho – the noodle soup that we had already experienced in Vietnam. It was delicious with thin pieces of rare beef floating on the top. I was also beginning to get used to the very strange coffee in Laos; it was usually served in a glass which showed two layers, dark brown and cream. The dark brown was Lao coffee, very strong with a slight mocha flavour, and the cream colour was condensed milk, making the coffee very sweet and creamy.

When I returned to the room I felt quite brave that I was flouting House Rule number 1 that said 'guests must not be laundered' and I washed some clothes and hung them from the balcony outside, where they blew in the hot wind and dried in minutes. Afterwards I sat outside on the balcony with a book, to give Warren some peace and quiet so that he could sleep. The restaurant owner came striding across the gardens, and I thought she had come to complain about my washing blowing in the wind. She pointed to the door of our room, and with actions I explained that Warren was sleeping, and to make sure she understood I did vomiting actions (I didn't feel that I could do diarrhoea actions!). To my amazement she strode straight to the open window, pulled back the flapping curtain and leaned right into the room, a maid working nearby running over to join her.

'What are you doing? Go away – he's trying to sleep,' I called out in a theatrical whisper so as not to waken Warren.

They turned to me, grinning, and leaned back through the window again. I rushed over and pulled the window shut, and they sauntered off chatting. Later, Warren told me that the maids had been constantly leaning in and out of the window while I was at breakfast and even coming in and out of the door. He wouldn't have minded, he said, but they kept talking, so that he was constantly disturbed. Fortunately he was covered by a sheet, but presumably the sight of a man with hair on his body was just too much for them to resist, and they had even called the restaurant owner over to have a look as well.

I walked the mile and a half to the town later in the morning, but found it quite disconcerting to be walking on my own; eight people at a table stopped talking and stared at me – no smiles, no waves, no hellos. This was very different from whizzing by on bikes. If I smiled or waved, after a second one waved back and they'd all smile and say 'Sabaidi', but if it was a group of men I didn't want to wave for fear of giving the wrong impression. I really admired the women we had met on our trip who cycled in these countries on their own – Martina from Germany, Helen from California and Jane from Australia. I thought that they were incredibly brave. Backpacking on one's own is not so difficult – backpackers tend to fly or bus from one popular destination to another, and there are always other westerners there, unlike cycling where we had to stay in local accommodation, often where there were no other westerners and where no-one spoke English or had ever seen westerners before.

As I walked, I could smell something good barbecuing, and decided if it was freshly cooked chicken or duck I would have some. As I approached the barbecue, I realised that I didn't recognise any of the cuts of meat – they were all obscure pieces of offal being barbecued, and despite the good smell I decided against meat for lunch.

The only thing that Warren felt he could eat was bread, so I was hoping to find some French bread in this town, but I could find none. I reached the market in the centre of the town. Overcrowded three-wheel bus-taxis were dropping off passengers, and I noticed a man selling ice-cream from the large container on the front of his specially-made bicycle. I stopped dead as I saw that he was scooping ice cream into small pieces of baguettes that had been hollowed open, and I was desperate to ask him where he had bought the bread, but knew that he wouldn't speak English.

I had a drink, bought some plain biscuits for Warren, and began to walk back to the guest house. It was incredibly windy, but the wind was as hot as the Sirocco. A young boy, aged about 10, called out to me in English.

'Hello, how are you; what is your name?' he asked. He had a large growth on the side of his face, and one ear was several inches below the other. When he walked, I noticed his feet were also very deformed, one twice the size of the other and so twisted over that he walked partly on the top of his foot. I tried to converse with him.

'What is your name? How old are you?' I asked, but he had exhausted his supply of English. He smiled and laughed a lot and seemed totally unfazed by his disabilities, and limped away calling to a friend who cycled past.

Warren was better the next day, and we assumed that it had probably been too much sun that had made him ill. We had eaten the same food, but I had been fine. We decided to stay an extra day, as he felt weak after a day with no food. We walked to the town, and dozens of teenage school children were cycling along the road. Four boys, each on a bike, hung onto each other in a long row, the first hanging onto a tractor unit and trailer. They didn't go any faster than the other cyclists, but they did it without effort. One boy had a flat tyre, so he was sat on the back of his friend's bicycle, and towed his empty bike along behind him.

The cycle rickshaw, so common in Vietnam, is almost extinct in Laos, and in its place is the taxi or 'samlor', a three-wheeled motorcycle taxi similar to the tuk-tuk in India. Larger vehicles called 'jumbos' are common in Lao towns. They are designed for four to six passengers sitting opposite each other on bench seats, but in practice carry up to 20 passengers with luggage on the roof, and frequently passengers stand on the platform at the back as well. We saw dozens of both types of vehicles as we walked to the town, and the other main type of vehicle on the road, apart from bicycles, was the tractor unit with trailer – we had last seen such vehicles in Turkey. Whatever the vehicle, it was overloaded with people and goods.

A family of water buffaloes with a calf wandered unconcernedly down the middle of the road, stopping to graze when they found a suitable piece of grass or vegetation. The calf was cream and furry, unlike its parents who had grey elephant-like hide, and we laughed as we watched the family walk slowly across the pedestrian crossing.

We walked around the market, because Asian markets never ceased to fascinate us and were always a wonderful source of photographs of local people. Amazing floral arrangements had been made with pleated leaves and flower buds. We had seen these fixed to fences and in front of Buddha statues, so assumed them to have religious connotations. The beef in the meat section of the market looked fantastic; it was devoid of fat, but the girls had to continually swat flies away. There was a wonderful smell as I passed one stall, which reminded me once again of my childhood – the lady had large polythene bags full of different types of tobacco, and she was constantly stirring the leaves with her hands to enhance the aroma.

We bought two hats with brims to protect our faces and necks from the sun while we cycled, and returned back to our guest house. Later in the afternoon I sat at a stone table in the gardens outside our room writing my diary, and the man in a neighbouring room came and joined me and began to chat. He spoke French, as do many Lao people, but only a little English. Two girls arrived on a motorbike, and the man went into his room, followed by one of the girls. The door shut. The other girl sat at the table with me, and picked a branch of flowers into little sprigs. She spoke no English, except to say her name was Misty (or was it Miss Dee?). After a short time her friend reappeared, and the two girls drove away on their motorbike. The man reappeared and went out in his car. Clearly he wasn't concerned about House Rule Number 3 . . .

We went again to the restaurant, where the restaurant owner was in stitches because Warren asked for fish and did fish swimming actions, snaking his hand backwards and forwards to try to make her understand. She was showing the other customers what he had done, and everyone was laughing. As we were waiting for our meal one of the two girls we had met on the first day arrived, and pulled up her chair close to Warren, and tried to chat. I had to go back to the room for something, and Warren looked at me pleadingly.

'Don't be long,' he said, with a sidelong glance at the girl.

I just laughed.

The meal was superb – fresh fish fried until the skin was crispy but with meltingly moist flesh inside, served with steamed rice and some green vegetables cooked with lots of garlic and served with a soy-based sauce. As always, a small bowl of fish sauce and soy sauce with chopped chillies floating in the sauce was served with the meal. With several large bottles of beer, we paid only 40,000 kip, exactly £3.

We were up very early the next morning to set off cycling again, and as we were eating our breakfast, Warren suddenly jumped up and went to the road with his camera. Seven young Buddhist monks in orange, umber and brown robes were walking in single file along the road with their bowls in their hands in front of them. Two women knelt praying on the pavement, one each side of the road, and as the monks approached the women they stopped and chanted in unison. As each one passed the first woman, she placed some food in their bowl, and they crossed the road to collect food or money in their bowls from their next sponsor.

As we set off cycling at 7am, we saw another 13 young monks walking in single file towards the town, and further up the road we saw another nineteen monks. This was the only time in Vietnam or Laos that we'd seen many monks, though these were all very young, the youngest probably only five years old.

It was a cool 20°C as we set off, and clouds covered the sky. I prayed the clouds would stay but not turn to rain. We turned off Route 9, along which we had been travelling so far in Laos, and turned onto Route 13 cycling south-east to Pakse. Ahead of us the sky began to clear, and patches of blue and turquoise were appearing between the clouds; to our left the sky and clouds were tinged with pink where the sun had just risen.

This road was not newly sealed like the last one, but it had a good surface. A sign on the road indicated that Japan was paying to upgrade all the bridges on Route 13, and we discovered later that Sweden had paid for the road to be reconstructed. We passed numerous tractor units pulling trailers full of people going to work. Sometimes there were so many in the trailers that they had to stand, those on the edge almost falling out onto the road. We were responding to their cries of 'Sabaidi, Good Morning, Hello,' and waving to everyone. The road was easy cycling – this was a plain and almost flat, so we could build up speed despite being blasted by gusts of wind from our left.

Children were parking their bikes under a tree outside a long wooden shack with a roof but no sides. This was a very different school from the many smart modern buildings we'd seen in Vietnam. The children called to us, and invariably the girls burst into high-pitched giggles when we replied. As we waved, even more children ran from their desks to the side of the building to join in the cheers and to wave to us.

We passed a group of houses on stilts, and a little naked girl of about four years old was trying to push her baby brother in a large wooden trailer. As I parked my bike and walked a few yards back along the road with my camera the neighbours cheered, and the mother stood smiling, nodding as I indicated that I would like to take a photograph of her children.

We passed Lak, a small town, and we assumed that water melons were grown in that area, because on either side of the road people sat with mountains of water melons. I wondered how they could make a living with so much competition and so little choice of product. As we cycled out of the town we heard a child screaming in one of the houses, and the father was running down the road towards the house. He ran indoors and within seconds reappeared shouting, with three cows stampeding out of the house in front of him!

We stopped to sit in a small shack café by the side of the road to have a Pepsi. On a table next to the display of Pepsis, beer and soft drinks were Pepsi and Fanta bottles full of petrol, and one litre plastic containers of oil. This was obviously the service station as well! The red dust was blowing everywhere from the gusts of wind, and was settling on everything in the shack including us. We were offered lotus seeds to eat. Apart from its flowers, which are used as offerings to Buddha, the lotus plant is very useful. Petals, stamens and roots have medicinal values, and almost every part of the lotus is edible. The seed pods (similar in shape to the rose on an old-fashioned watering can) are dried and used for flower decorations in England, but in south-east Asia the cone-shaped seed pod is ripped open to reveal a fibrous white flesh packed around a number of seeds. Inside each of these is a type of nut the size of a peanut, which is delicious. The dried seeds are often boiled in syrup to make a popular sweet. The root, cut into thin slices and boiled with pork ribs, makes a delicious soup. The crisp young leaf and the long fleshy stem are also made into different tasty dishes. The large leaf is too tough to eat, but is sometimes used to wrap rice which, when steamed, has the subtle aroma of the leaf.

We cycled on and stopped in the shade of some trees for a drink of water. As we turned to set off again we saw a group of people coming out of the woods on one side of the road. There were about twelve women who all carried large knives, and they were led by a man with a gun over his shoulder. They walked in single file from the woods on one side of the road. I was very nervous; whilst in Vietnam we had been told that earlier that year a western couple on bicycles had been shot in Laos. They had overtaken a bus, unaware that it had been held up by gunmen. The men had sprayed the bus with fire, killing the couple on their bikes as well as a large number of people in the bus. It was obviously a case of being in the wrong place at the wrong time, but the same could apply to us now. We didn't know whether to remain quietly where we were, which would look suspicious if they turned and saw us, or to cycle on as though nothing was amiss. However, at that point the leader with his gun walked into the woods and the women followed. With enormous sighs of relief we cycled as fast as we could until the woods were miles behind us.

We arrived at Paksong, a small town where we planned to stay the night. Two guest houses were opposite each other. The first guest house wanted 35,000 kip, a higher price than anywhere we had paid in Laos. Warren checked it out but said it was a dump with a dark, dingy wash room a long way down the corridor. We tried the other guest house. It was cheaper, and the room was very basic but clean. The owner very proudly showed us the new metal mesh mosquito grills that had been fitted at the windows, and the strip at the bottom of the door. We appreciated this, having often rolled up a towel to block the gap beneath the door, where mosquitoes can easily get in. The floor was concrete but clean. There was a six feet wide bed covered with a faded but clean sheet. There was no top sheet, as was normal in Laos, but we had our own silk sleeping bag liner, so it was no problem. (A silk liner sound luxurious, but silk is lightweight and folds exceptionally small, which made it a perfect piece of equipment for our trip. In really cold weather, the silk liner combined with our down sleeping bags was incredibly warm). A sealed litre bottle of drinking water stood on the table; again, this was the norm in Laos.

The 'shower' room was down the corridor. Again, it had a concrete floor and there was a squat toilet on a raised area at one end. Three large grey clay Ali Baba pots stood three feet high, each filled to the brim with clear, cold water. This was to be used for flushing the toilet and also for showering – for these purposes, two plastic saucepans floated on top of the water.

We showered and decided to relax reading for an hour or two after our lunch. There were cockerels next door making a terrible noise; a pig was squealing nearby; two parrots and two mynah birds in cages near the bedroom were squawking at the tops of their voices, and the man next door was chopping wood.

'I hope this noise stops by bedtime,' I said, 'Or we'll never sleep.' I picked up my book, but within minutes had fallen fast asleep!

We were just ready to go out to have our evening meal when a man arrived, speaking excellent English. He was a teacher at the local school and taught English, and had heard that foreigners had arrived in town. He asked if we would talk to two of his students so that they could practice their English. We didn't have the heart to say we were hungry and wanted to go to eat, so we sat and chatted to them for half an hour. The girl and boy, both fifteen years old, were shy, but had only been learning English for two months. After chatting for half an hour, the girl invited us to her house for a beer, and we walked along the road to a very smart brick-built house. Her mother approached us.

'Sabaidi,' she said, bowing her head with her hands together as in prayer.

'Sabaidi,' we replied, doing the same.

We removed our shoes at the door and were invited to sit on sofas and chairs. Her father was laid on a bare mattress on the floor watching television. The student's two younger sisters joined us, the younger of whom was only 11 years old but was stunningly beautiful. She spoke very good English, and told Warren that she wanted to come with us on our travels.

We shared a bottle of beer. It is a Lao custom that the same glass is used for everyone and is passed round, a little of the drink being poured into the glass for each person. Whilst we were not overly keen to share a glass, it would have offended them deeply if we had refused, so we agreed to have some beer, all of us sipping from the one glass. We were also offered food, but said that we intended to go to a local restaurant, and they recommended one on the edge of the small town. We took group photos, squashed onto the sofa, waved goodbye and made our way up the dark street.

The restaurant was excellent, and we would never have found it without our new friends' recommendation. The music was good and the food superb. We were just finishing when our new friends arrived, and they wanted us to join them at their table. We refused to eat any more as we were full, but sat with them. They had a dish that we'd seen before, which was apparently becoming very popular in Laos. A circular piece of the table was removed and a bucket of hot coals placed in the hole. Over this a domed metal plate with a rim around the edge (it looked a bit like a flying saucer) was placed over the coals. Pork fat was placed at the top of the dome, which melted and ran down lubricating the metal; a combination of meats, fish and shellfish were placed on the top of the metal to cook. Meanwhile the rim was filled with hot water or stock, and glass noodles and vegetables were cooked in this liquid. Everyone helped themselves with chopsticks, putting the food into their own bowls as it cooked, and adding various spicy sauces that were also supplied. It reminded us very much of the Japanese way of cooking and eating. Eventually we said our goodbyes for the second time and left.

I slept soundly, but was woken at 11pm because the cock was crowing. It stopped mid-crow as though someone had nudged him and said 'It's the wrong time,' and I fell asleep again. When I woke again at 4am the cock was crowing again, and Warren had a spare pillow over his head to shut out the noise – he told me that the cock had begun crowing again at 2am. We left at 6am, by which time the parrots were joining in with their squawking, so we were pleased to be leaving early.

As we passed the houses, we noticed that every garden had clay Ali Baba pots, some up to five feet tall. A woman was working a well, and the sky ahead was brightening as the sun rose. Everyone had fires burning in the gardens, and people were either crouched alongside the fires or pans were being heated over them. Dogs and puppies, goats and kids, chickens and chicks, pigs and piglets, water buffaloes and cows and calves, cats and kittens and occasional turkeys were laying or scratching around in the gardens. Splashes of colour were added to the scene as white and vivid pink bougainvillea spilled onto the tin roofs or climbed trees.

We passed two temples being built, the ornate entrance gateways already in place and painted white, green, red and gold. Bells were sounding at another temple and young monks stood outside with their bowls. A line of people were kneeling by the roadside as five monks walked by with their bowls outstretched. We passed a cabinet maker, unbelievably hand-making furniture so that it looked factory-produced. The sky ahead of us was brightening – we were travelling east, and the sun was beginning to rise.

We went over numerous bridges, each one numbered and with plaques to show that Japan had paid for them. A man on a bike followed us for miles, trying to chat, though he spoke no English. If we stopped, so did he, and we began to think he would stay with us when we stopped for accommodation. A salesman passed with his motorbike so full of clothes and pots and pans that we couldn't see him from behind.

We were tired, so when we saw a large tree with grass underneath, we stopped to rest in the shade. We laid down and closed our eyes, but a few minutes later we opened them to see that there was a line of children watching us, standing about fifteen feet away. Very slowly they became braver and came a little closer, some still holding their bicycles, but as Warren got up to get his camera from his bag, they shrieked 'Ooooogh,' and all ran back to the invisible line fifteen feet away. We sat taking portraits of them with the close-up lens, and their mothers watched from a distance in the houses and waved.

As we continued, we passed a cyclist from the Czech Republic going in the opposite direction. He was dressed in proper Lycra cycling gear, and was happy to cycle 200km a day, so was definitely out of our league. He told us that the next guest house was another 40km away, so we knew that we would have to cycle over 100km again that day. Eventually we reached the village with the guest house, and met a German who was staying there while he worked in the area. He had lived and worked in Laos for seven years as a water and sanitation engineer, and said that he wouldn't like to return to his home in East Germany, as he didn't like it since re-unification. The German laughed when we said that it was very hot cycling.

'It's cold now,' he replied. 'This is winter!'

Well, yes – we had planned the trip so that we would be cycling at the coolest time possible, so we had done well there, but it was still hot for cycling.

A calendar hung on the wall of the hall of the guest house, showing Lao women on each page. We commented to him that the girls were nowhere near as attractive as most Lao women we had seen, but that they were all very fair-skinned. We wondered if it was the same in Laos as in India, where the fairest people are considered the most beautiful, regardless of actual looks. He told us this was exactly the situation, and he agreed with us that the normal darker skin of Lao women was far more beautiful. The Lao people were always amazed that he and his western friends, who could have their pick of Lao women, always chose what the Lao people considered to be the ugly ones! In Asia, the lighter the skin the more attractive a person is deemed to be. This reflects the way it was in England 100 years ago, when a fair skin indicated upper class – the peasants who worked in the fields had dark skin from being out in the sun all day. Nowadays in England, it is the people with the money who can afford to go abroad for their holidays who show off their wealth with a healthy tan!

Later, looking for sunscreen for ourselves in the market, we noticed that Vaseline Intensive Care lotion had in it 'whitening UV protection', and also available was 'White Lady bleaching cream'. White was apparently beautiful! After our evening meal we returned to our room at 7.30pm. On the floor of the hall one of the guest-house employees was lying on a rug under a mosquito net, fully clothed and snoring loudly.

The next day we saw bright green rice fields for the first time in Laos – the others had been bone dry and full of stubble. We stopped for a coffee at a tiny stall because we saw French baguettes on the table – we were approaching Pakse, where we would have no problem getting bread for the first time in Laos. The bread was yesterday's, but we didn't mind. As we drank our coffee, the girl pulled a black-feathered chicken from a bowl of water next to us, and effortlessly plucked it in front of us by rubbing the skin. Behind her on two shelves was a strange assortment of goods for sale – condensed milk, Ponds face cream, Nivea cream, motor oil, Omo washing powder, cigarettes, instant noodles, bicycle inner tubes, soap, soy sauce, fish sauce, toilet rolls, washing up liquid and coils of rope.

Ahead of us on the road was a range of mountains, and my heart sank when I saw them. Thankfully, though, the road curved to the left, so we went round the mountains keeping them on our right. As we drew near to Pakse we heard more and more people speaking English – this was to be the first town in Laos where we were likely to see tourists. Higher craggy mountains appeared a long way off to our left, silhouetted grey against the sky, some topped with clouds. This range of mountains is almost 2,000 metres high. We stopped for a drink at the Lao version of a transport café, and chatted to one of the other three customers, who spoke some English. The girl who had served us brought us half a pineapple, cut into chunks, as well as the cold drinks that we ordered. It was juicy, sweet and delicious, and she never charged us for it.

We began to pass large houses with wrought iron gates that were so ornate that they wouldn't have looked out of place outside Buckingham Palace. We passed a complex of temples, and soon after that shops and restaurants heralded the approach to Pakse. As we entered the town we saw that there were a number of attractive old French colonial buildings, and in Pakse we would have our first sight of the Mekong River.

Accommodation was much more expensive than we had previously paid in Laos – we had to pay $10 a night, but we found a French colonial building which had been built in 1929, and was now converted to a guest house with extra rooms built in the grounds. Our room was pleasant with beautiful rosewood floorboards, and there was plenty of room for our bikes and a desk where I could sit to write my diary. In the centre of the courtyard was a pleasant seating area with a bamboo roof and open sides, and the floor was covered with old, hand-painted floor tiles. A pretty kitten was fast asleep in the most comfortable of the chairs.

It was strange as we walked around the town to see westerners again – many French, but also English, American, Dutch, German and Australian travellers. In Pakse a popular form of taxi transport is the motorbike with a sidecar with space for two people squashed side by side with an arched cover over the top. Underneath the feet is a long flat board protruding forward and behind, so that plenty of goods can also be carried. We hadn't seen this form of transport elsewhere in Laos.

Pakse is a pleasant, relaxing small town, and we stayed there for a few days. Breakfast was especially good, though at $2 it was comparatively expensive. We had fried eggs, French bread, butter and the best strawberry jam since leaving home, coffee and tea, followed by a plate of fresh papaya and pineapple.

We used the internet café to catch up on our e-mails. The cafés were very expensive in Laos – £2.70 per hour, compared with 14p per hour in Vietnam, but this was the first place since we had entered Laos that we had been able to e-mail anyone. We heard on the BBC World Service that Saddam Hussein had been captured, and heard Tony Blair giving a speech. We thought that his way of speaking was very strange, hesitating after every few words (as though listening to someone telling him what words to say next). We had never noticed this before – it sounded very unnatural and reminded us of how George Bush gave his speeches . . .

From Pakse we planned to travel west towards the Thai border, but before leaving Laos we wanted to visit Wat Phou, the ruins of a 12th Century Angkor-period temple and palace buildings. We set off to cycle the 25 miles south to Champasak, the nearest village to Wat Phou. The traffic in Pakse as we left was the busiest we had experienced so far in Laos, but still nothing compared with the Vietnamese roads. On the way out of the town, Warren went into a bank to exchange some US$100 banknotes for smaller denominations, and he said that it didn't look like a bank as we knew it – behind the counter, which had no security doors, stood a large table stacked high with US dollars.

We turned off towards the new bridge over the River Mekong, so that we could take the quiet road shown on our map that travelled along the east side of the river. The bridge had a notice on it with the Lao and Japanese flags displayed and the name of the bridge – the Lao-Nippon Bridge. It was obvious why the bridge had been so named, and we were impressed as we crossed the bridge to find it was exactly one mile wide. The turning left to the road following the river never materialised, and we cycled five miles before deciding to retrace our route over the bridge and took the main road south.

After 20 miles we reached a junction where a number of westerners were waiting for a bus. They were going to Four Thousand Islands, a pretty stretch of river 100km further south, just before the Cambodian border. We wouldn't have time to visit this section of the Mekong River, as it was not possible to cross the border at that point. Because of the visa restrictions we didn't have time to go so far out of our way. Several of the tourists had been waiting for the boat to take them down-river, but the boats were notoriously unreliable and had not arrived the day before, and by 11.30am had not arrived that day either. The boats were supposed to arrive at that junction at 10am each day, but apparently if there were insufficient passengers to make it worthwhile at Pakse, the boat didn't bother to leave!

We stopped at the junction for a cold drink, and were amused to see that when the local jumbo (taxi bus) arrived, dozens of screaming women rushed at the bus waving bunches of turnip-like root vegetables trying to sell them. It was nice to know that even the locals could be hassled sometimes! We tried some of these vegetables – they are peeled and eaten raw, and have a texture similar to radish, but have a pleasant, slightly sweet taste.

Another 5 miles further on, we arrived at the Mekong River. The road disappeared into soft, sandy soil as we descended down to the river edge, and a young man immediately offered us a ferry. We didn't know the going rate, but we had to cross, so just accepted the fare (75p for the two of us) and had to wheel our bicycles up an unsteady plank onto more planks which were lashed across two canoes. This was our ferry! We couldn't sit down and there didn't seem room for both of us, but a motorbike joined us, so we all stood squashed together as the young man started up the lawn-mower engine which was tied onto the back of the canoes, and we set off across the Mekong. We watched as the local bus drove onto another ferry – three slightly bigger boats were lashed together with planks to accommodate two buses! I definitely wouldn't have felt safe inside a bus on such a ferry.

The River Mekong was over a mile wide at this point, and it was very beautiful with mountains in the distance and islands to our right. We made it across with no mishaps, and were immediately accosted as we pushed our bikes up the slope on the other side by someone offering us accommodation for 15,000 kip per night (just over £1). We agreed to look at the room, and followed the man on his motorbike.

At the back of a small restaurant the owner, who never stopped laughing, had built five rooms in a row, each with a private bathroom at the back of it, and another five rooms and bathrooms backed onto these. They were what we would describe as 'rustic'. Built of wood on the outer walls, with inner walls and ceilings made of wooden frames covered with woven rushes, the rooms were very dark – the walls were dark brown and the floor was concrete. We had a six feet wide bed, a bedside table, and a fan in the ceiling. There was just room for our bikes as well. The concrete-floored bathroom was enormous with a squat toilet on a raised concrete platform at one end. Alongside stood a plastic dustbin filled with water for flushing the toilet. At the other end of the room was a washbasin fixed to the wall, and a tap and shower were in the centre of the room. There was no plumbing beneath the washbasin – the water simply ran onto the floor below it and made its way to the other end of the bathroom to the drain. Despite this description, it was actually quite pleasant, and many of the rooms were filled during the day, as the owner collected passengers from the ferry. It was the cheapest room so far, and certainly not the worst. In the garden behind the rooms were tables and chairs made from a local hardwood, placed under the shade of trees overlooking the Mekong River – a lovely place to have our breakfast. The owner's wife cooked delightful food, so we were very content with our accommodation.

We chatted to two other travellers who were staying at the same place – Aike from Belgium and Donnchadh (Gaelic for Duncan) from Ireland – and went for a meal with them that evening. Fish with chilli and coconut milk served with sticky rice was my choice, and afterwards I was persuaded to try the bananas in Lao-Lao, the local spirit. Four bananas arrived. They had been fried in butter and sugar, Lao-Lao was poured over and the plate was brought flaming to the table.

They were delicious, though I had a headache the next morning. I asked for the recipe to make Lao-Lao – here it is:

'First cook rice by steaming it in a large drum. Then take the cooked rice and wash it in the nearest river. Return the rice to a large drum and add alcohol powder [yeast]. Cover with plastic and let mixture ferment for seven days. One week later add water, re-cover mixture and stand one more week. Finally build a good hot fire under the drum and place a bowl on top filled with cold water. This will distill the Lao-Lao and the clear liquid will drain from a pipe in the bottom of the drum into your Lao-Lao bottle.' We wondered if Lao-Lao would taste the same using Thames River water as it did with Mekong River water?

The four of us cycled to Wat Phou the following morning, Aike and Donnchadh hiring two ancient bikes from the hotel owner. The ruins of two impressive 12th century palace buildings stood either side of a path. Carved lintels over the doorways and turned stone spindles on the windows were especially fascinating. Beyond the palaces were very steep stone steps climbing the mountain, flanked on either side by Frangipani trees, the national tree of Laos. Frangipani flowers were scattered like confetti all the way up, the unbelievably waxy-looking flowers looking almost too beautiful to be real. The steps were very narrow, in places only wide enough for the tip of the toe, but incredibly steep. As we climbed the steps we turned frequently to admire the view, which was framed by the avenue of Frangipani trees. The Mekong River flowed across the scene in the far distance, and below us stood the ruins of the ancient palace buildings. We reached an ancient temple, which had originally been Hindu but was now Buddhist, and it stood in the shade of the trees with the sheer cliff of the mountain rising behind it. The view from this sanctuary was magnificent. We sat for a long time in the shade talking, and eventually returned down the steps to the heat again. Before leaving we watched women and children digging in holes by some water, and discovered that they were searching for frogs to eat.

We stayed a second night in Champasak before returning to Pakse. Once again we had to catch a ferry, and this time it was cheaper. As we docked, two women who had been serving food from a large saucepan collected the dishes discarded by customers. Any meat still in the dishes was scraped back into the large pot of noodle soup ready for the next customers. Maybe it was best sometimes that we didn't see what went into the food . . .

We passed a house with colourful fences – they had been made from a large sheet of rubber after flip-flop soles had been cut out. The sheets of holey rubber were nailed to fence posts to stop piglets from escaping onto the road. Alongside, plant pots had been made from the tails of bombs. The bomb shells stood on their fins with colourful flowers cascading out of the tops. Obviously this family was keen on recycling.

We returned to our previous guest house in Pakse, and I sat in the cool tiled area with a pot of Lao tea while Warren raised the handlebars on my bicycle to try to relieve the pain on my hands and wrists. The next day we would be setting off towards Thailand; we had spent two weeks in Laos. Now we had 322 miles to cycle in Thailand before reaching the Cambodian border. We would be celebrating Christmas on our bicycles . . .

CHAPTER 18

THAILAND

Thailand is a large country about the size of France. It is 2000km long from north to south and, because of its long coastline along the Indian Ocean and the Gulf of Thailand, has many beaches and islands. It is bordered on the west by Myanmar (Burma), and the Mekong River forms much of the border on the east with Laos and Cambodia. The north of Thailand has mountains and fertile valleys, and a range of mountains runs down the west, dividing Thailand from Myanmar. The southern part of Thailand, which borders Malaysia, is predominantly rain-forest.

We left Pakse at 7am to cycle to the Thai border. On the outskirts of Pakse we saw a café that was open – at least, we thought it must be a café because two chairs and a table sat outside a house and next to the table was a gas bottle with a wok on it! It was amazing the difference two miles made. We were only down the road from the centre of Pakse, a town that was very tourist-orientated, but the owner of this café spoke no English and couldn't understand what we wanted. No problem – we bought some bread from a nearby stall and with actions we explained that we wanted some fried eggs, so we could make fried egg sandwiches. A kettle of delicious Lao tea already stood freshly made on the table. The café owner was initially taken aback at the sight of a US$1 note, but after consultation with a friend was happy to accept it. We bought bananas from her to use up our kip, the local currency, because we knew we would need no more – Thailand was a very short distance away.

We crossed the Lao–Nippon Bridge once more. At the next village we passed a market. A woman had just bought a dozen chickens and carried six in each hand, all tied by the feet and feebly flapping their wings as they were carried upside down to her motorbike. Two men were tying dozens of live chickens and ducks onto the top of a three-wheel taxi (a samlar). The white heads of the ducks stuck out of the top of black and brown chicken plumage, but many of the chickens were tied by their feet and hanging down the side. Another similarly-full taxi passed us a few minutes later in the opposite direction, with people sitting underneath the ducks and chickens.

Warren noticed a problem with his wheel, and stopped to examine it. He was immediately surrounded by numerous children and several adults, so I was busy taking photographs. Eventually he found that the aluminium wheel rim had split, a very serious problem, so we hoped that we could make it to Thailand where a replacement might be available. It certainly wouldn't be possible to buy a replacement in Laos.

It was 29 miles to the border, and we arrived at 10am. The Laos-Thailand border was chaotic. As at the Vietnam-Laos border, there were no signs to indicate where to go, but we managed to get our Lao visa cancelled and moved on to the Thai immigration office. Ahead of us was an even more chaotic area where a new section of road was being built alongside a row of small shops. Amid the chaos it would have been possible to have cycled straight into Thailand without seeing immigration, though we would have eventually had a problem on leaving the country again, without the relevant visa stamped into our passports.

Once we were through immigration, we went for a cup of tea at one of the small cafés lining the street, and were immediately approached by a Thai man who introduced himself as Mr Pong. He spoke good English, and invited us to come and stay at his house. He produced a visitors' book, and there were kind things written by many different people about him – he had given food and a room to all of them for no charge. Whether he was genuine or not we had no idea, but in any event we wanted to cycle further that day, so we couldn't take up his offer of accommodation.

It was a shock as we set off again to realise that we had to cross to the left side of the road to cycle. This was the third time we had entered Thailand on our bicycles, and this time we needed to cycle through a non-tourist area in order to reach Cambodia. The road was good, and the terrain was up and down hills – very different from the plains of Laos. We passed twelve Buddhist monks walking in single file in the middle of nowhere. They were dressed in brown and dark orange robes, and were carrying backpacks. At the side of the roads women were making brooms and rakes, and their wares were displayed for sale. Some brushes were made of soft grasses, some made of stiff twigs. There were bamboo rakes and soft brushes on very long bamboo poles, designed to reach high corners.

It began to get very windy, and unfortunately the wind was against us. It was hard cycling down the hills against the wind, let alone up. The Thai flags which were displayed from many shops were ripping in the wind. We stopped at the side of the road in a village to have a drink of water. There was a loud metallic banging noise, and we noticed a section of corrugated iron about to be ripped off a nearby roof by the wind, so we moved on quickly. We could see clouds of red dust coming down the road towards us, having been blown from the side dirt roads. We just had to shut our eyes before it hit us, stinging our legs as it went past. As we approached the town, we saw that coloured banners fixed to the street lights ready for the New Year festivities had been ripped to shreds in the wind.

In the town we found a hotel next to the 7-Eleven shop. The hotel room was basic and a little shabby but very cheap, so we booked a room for the night. As we wandered round the town it seemed to us very westernised after Laos and Vietnam, even though it wasn't a tourist town. There were supermarkets with good choices of food, banks with ATMs (there had been none in Laos, although Vietnam had a few), shops selling cakes and pastries, shops with wine and an internet café. Delicious food was being made on street stalls, including toast being made over hot coals. We queued to buy sweet eggy pancakes called roti, made by a man on a street stall. He took tiny balls of pastry and threw them around like pizza dough until they were the size of tea plates. Then they were thrown onto the hot griddle, where he turned in the edges to make them square. A raw egg was dropped onto each one, the pancakes rose, and he turned them back and forth, adding cubes of butter. The rotis were drizzled with condensed milk and sugar and were delicious, though not for someone on a diet! The wind continued to blow, and once it got dark the temperature dropped below 20°C. We felt very cold, and realised how we'd become used to high temperatures.

Not as many people spoke English as we had anticipated. We mustn't expect them to – after all, we are the foreigners, and we always try to learn as much of the language as we can. However, we had imagined that Thailand, clearly a country with far more money than Laos and Vietnam, would have a high number of English-speaking locals. The tonal languages of Thailand and Indochina are very difficult to master for the foreigner, but with sign language and our efforts at speaking we usually managed quite well. After a meal that evening we went to buy more rotis, and a customer who spoke a little English insisted on treating us after chatting for a while in the queue as we waited our turn.

The next morning we set off again. It was 20°C as we cycled off, but we noticed that the locals on motorbikes and backs of trucks and even people walking were wearing balaclavas with slits only for eyes. Some even had only two holes for the eyes in their balaclavas, which looked quite sinister. We remembered that the Indians had worn these because they felt the cold when the temperature dropped as low as 20°C, and we found constantly in Thailand that people wrapped up in sweaters, thick jackets and woolly hats, even in the middle of the day. Shops were full of balaclavas and warm clothes. Even the dogs were dressed in t-shirts to keep them warm, and they remained dressed like this for the whole of the day, even when the temperature reached almost 30°C. No doubt they would have thought the British most uncaring if they had seen unclothed dogs in England when the temperature dropped close to freezing.

The tractor units and trailers that we had seen near the border with Laos had now almost entirely disappeared, and expensive cars such as Opel, Mercedes, BMW, Toyota and even a Porsche were on the road. There was a lay-by with 15 lorries in it, some articulated and some with trailers, and the drivers were sat at tables in a transport café. The tables were covered with empty beer bottles, even though it was still only 8.30am. We were glad that they were going in the opposite direction, though we found that the Thai drivers were very courteous drivers.

We passed rows of stupas displayed for sale. There were marble ones inlaid with mirrors, all-mirror ones and ones painted white, red and gold, or green and gold. We stopped for tea, and were pleased when the owner of the café understood when we asked for 'nm char'. Two glasses of Chinese tea arrived, and she chatted with only a very few words of English. She offered us the use of her toilet, and proudly showed me through her house to an enormous shower room with a western toilet. However, when I asked her how much we owed her, she shook her head.

'Oh, no. Welcome Thailand,' she said, and wouldn't take any money. We were very touched.

We continued cycling on a dual carriageway most of the way, and arrived at Ubon Ratchathani, a large city. Now we saw a large new shopping centre and big Esso service stations. KFC and MacDonalds were advertised, and we saw a large Tesco supermarket for the first time since leaving England. We were stupidly excited – we hadn't seen large shops for so long, and couldn't resist visiting Tesco's after booking into a hotel. Here we experienced our first sign of Christmas since the black dwarf we had seen dressed in a Father Christmas outfit in India the year before! Palm trees were decorated with Christmas lights, and there were signs in several shop windows saying 'Happy Christmas'. There were Christmas decorations and Christmas jingles playing, and the shop assistants were wearing Father Christmas hats. I wondered if they understood the significance of Christmas, bearing in mind that 95% of Thais are Buddhist, but it was interesting for us to see. (We were told later by English friends living in Thailand that many Thais believe that Father Christmas was crucified on Christmas Day – maybe it's our fault, in the Christian world, for concentrating so much on Father Christmas rather than the true meaning of Christmas).

In a nearby book shop there were shop assistants dressed as wizards to promote a new Harry Potter book – how distant Vietnam and Laos suddenly seemed. This town was nowhere near any tourist route, but the shops were amazing, and the streets and car parks were full of very expensive cars. However, once again, we found very few people who spoke English.

With the help of a local tuk-tuk driver we were able to find an excellent bicycle shop a few kilometres outside of the town. We took Warren's bicycle with us, but the tuk-tuk was so rusty that there seemed a danger that the bottom of the floor might part company with the sides and the bicycle would fall through! The bicycle shop was owned by a family who were very keen on cycle-touring, and Warren was embarrassed at how cheap the very good quality bike parts were. We were actually able to pay by credit card as well, which was a novel experience after so long! We had cups of tea with the shop owner, while our tuk-tuk driver slept in his vehicle outside.

We found a local café to have rice and fried eggs for breakfast each day, and made friends with the people who worked there. An old Chinese man served us each time we went in, and he tried to teach us Thai words. Each day we were able to add another word to our vocabulary, but we weren't sure if we were learning Thai with a Chinese accent! He told us that he had come from Peking, as it had been called when he lived there, though Peking had been known as Beijing since the 1980s.

We went for a walk to the other end of the town to see a complex of temples that we had passed on the way into the town. The temples were surrounded by trees in their walled gardens, and each of the buildings was painted cream with rust-coloured tiered roofs with the usual golden stag-horn finials. On the gables were elegant carvings and paintings of Thai people in gold, pale blue and rust. The temple doors were ornately carved from solid teak. The atmosphere of the temple and surrounding area was very tranquil and relaxing. There were many stalls set out on the pavement alongside the temple, and we noticed that the locals had tapped into the overhead electric cables and had nailed electric sockets to the temple walls for the use of the stall-holders. I wondered what happened when it rained . . .

That evening the wind dropped, and we felt it was warm enough to sit outside to eat in a pleasant garden restaurant. As we sat enjoying our meal, a man suddenly appeared over the top of a small tree between the restaurant and the road, and into view came the elephant that he was riding. It was a surprise in such a big city, but the restaurant customers ran to buy pieces of sugar cane from the owner, so that they could feed the elephant.

Once Warren's bike had been repaired, we left Ubon to continue towards Cambodia. The locals were busy setting up stalls and fairground rides in the town ready for the New Year festivities. We found it a real joy to cycle in Thailand – there had been such a lack of any traffic at all in Laos that we'd almost forgotten the constant sounding of horns in Vietnam. The only time we heard horns in Thailand was when the driver wanted to catch our attention to wave to us. The Thais were very courteous drivers, and would let us in if we needed to cross lanes or junctions, which was certainly very different from our experiences in most countries.

We began to experience the same problem that we'd had in Japan – although in Thailand signs are occasionally in English, mostly they're in Thai script, which was impossible for us to decipher, so that at each junction we had to stop and check the directions before continuing. The seconds clicked down on traffic lights to indicate how long before the red light would change to green. We found it a little unnerving as we waited, because we were surrounded at traffic lights by motor bikes. We noticed as we passed a service station that it was just over 17 baht (25p) for the most expensive petrol, so driving was cheap in Thailand! It was five miles before we were away from the towns, and there were large expanses of paddy fields as far as the eye could see, unlike the small divided fields that we'd seen in Vietnam and Laos. Cows and water buffalo grazed in the fields of rice stubble.

We had chosen to travel along a fairly major road which followed the route of the railway line, because we felt it most likely that there would be hotels in towns with railway stations. This was not a tourist area, so hotels were not likely to be plentiful unless the towns were large. People were continually waving to us from their cars, or doing the 'thumbs up' sign to us. A lorry going in the opposite direction sounded his horn as he approached. I looked up at the driver – all I could see was the palm of a hand raised in a wave close to the heavily tinted windscreen, and the gleam of white teeth in a perfect smile, just like the grin of the Cheshire Cat in 'Alice in Wonderland'!

We were travelling west parallel to the northern border of Cambodia, before turning south-west towards Aranya Prathet, a popular border crossing where we could cross into Cambodia, paying for a visa on entry. The wind had, unfortunately, dropped, so we had no tail wind to help us. There were frequent open bus shelters along the roads, which were ideal places to stop and rest in the shade. Often people were having a picnic lunch or a sleep on the benches in the shade of the roof. We stopped in one, and a man stopped his four wheel drive twin cab to talk to us in English. He was a school teacher at the local school, and wanted to wish us a happy Christmas and new year. He went on his way after recommending a hotel in the next town, where we had a very nice, carpeted, air-conditioned room for 490 baht (just over £7). We were enjoying some high standards in Thailand.

In Thailand the night markets are famous – as soon as it became dark (at 6pm every night of the year) the stalls would open, and food could be bought very cheaply. The choice in the night markets was amazing. Thai curries and rice were ladled into separate plastic bags and tied ready for carrying home or to the plastic communal tables dotted around the market. For 15 baht (about 25p) we could have a delicious Thai curry and rice each. Not everything on the stalls was recognisable. The chicken legs looked quite good – they were definitely chicken legs because they still had the feet on, but feet alone could also be bought, skewered onto a stick. We weren't sure what to do with them – suck them or chew them? Several stalls had deep fried insects – small black beetles, very large locusts and what looked suspiciously like cockroaches. We understood that they were very crunchy, but weren't willing to try them, and I wondered how the stall-holders spent their day catching the food. Fish was on many of the stalls, usually whole and fried or barbecued with a crunchy oatmeal coating.

As we left our hotel room at 6am the next morning, the lift doors opened to allow us into the hotel foyer. We were amazed to hear very loud music, and in the hotel car park were about fifty people doing aerobics. They looked extremely uncoordinated, but every so often they all cheered – not much fun for anyone wanting to sleep in after 6am! It was Christmas Eve, and our coldest morning so far. The temperature had dropped to 15°C, and it was misty. We were very cold initially, but this may have been because we were still wearing shorts and sandals rather than putting on thicker clothes. As we cycled, we saw the sun rise beyond the haystacks standing in the fields of stubble – a red ball rising above the mist over the fields.

We passed Buddhist temples, and monks were walking in single file along the road, collecting food from the local people in their bowls. There were ponds everywhere, most of them shaded by trees. The water was dark and muddy, but the surface was usually covered with bronze circular leaves, and vivid pink water-lilies flowered in superb contrast several inches above the water. Cows and water buffalo grazed in the paddy fields, small birds often sitting on their backs.

We stopped at lunch time for something to eat. We had discovered that wherever we were in Thailand, however basic the café, they could always provide 'khao phat'. This is unfortunately pronounced 'cow pat', but at least that made it easier to remember. Khao phat is rice fried with various vegetables, usually a little grated carrot, some green vegetable and onion, with egg, and sometimes small pieces of meat. Tomato was often added, and it was virtually always decorated with cucumber. Soy sauce with chopped Thai chillies was always served with it, and we would pour this over the rice either with or without the chillies, depending on how spicy we wanted it to be. It was a very cheap and delicious meal for lunch time.

As the day wore on it was getting very hot, and we had to wear gloves to protect the backs of our hands from being burnt, so we were glad to arrive at our destination, the next large town. We couldn't find the hotel we had chosen from our guide book, so asked two policemen. They didn't know where it was either, so phoned someone on their mobile phone. Then one of them jumped onto his motorbike and indicated for us to follow, so we had a police escort to the door of the hotel.

Because it was Christmas Eve, and my mother's birthday, we later tried to phone home. This is an easy thing to do in Bangkok, because all internet cafés there have international phones, but we now discovered that in non-tourist towns the only place to phone internationally is at the Post Office. The Post Office was now closed, so we had to wait until the next day – Christmas Day. On a television in the café where we ate, we saw that Father Christmas was on the news. He was driving a buffalo-drawn cart with Santa's little helper holding up a parasol to protect him from the sun. The newscaster wore a Father Christmas hat, and they played 'Jingle Bells'!

The next morning was Christmas Day. The only present we'd bought each other was a new wheel rim each, and we had wrapped them in inner tubes and tyres and had pretty silver spokes put on them to make them sparkly! We had had some long days of cycling, having cycled over 170km in the last two days. Today we had an easy cycle ride of just over 50km before we could relax and enjoy Christmas Day.

A lorry went by – the open back was full of children aged about 9 years old. They looked surprised to see us as they passed, but when we waved they all cheered and grinned and waved and shouted, and continued to do so until they were out of sight round a bend, their cheers still echoing down the road.

We stopped at a stall to buy cans of iced coffee – in Thailand there are pleasant cafés en route, far more civilised than Laos or Vietnam, and the cafés had fridges to keep drinks cool instead of containers of ice. At the side of the café we saw two splendid cocks fighting, their owner proudly watching them. I'd never before seen cocks with their neck feathers up – they looked like Elizabethans with ruffs round their necks. Cock-fighting is very popular in Thailand, and the cockerels that we saw everywhere were stunning – their feathers were gold and green, or glossy green, black and rust, and their magnificent arching tail feathers swept down to the ground.

We passed a village with a large pond in front of the houses. The pond was full of bright pink water lilies, which were enhanced by the white ducks with red circular patches round their eyes. For many miles we cycled along stretches of straight roads which were surrounded by rice paddies full of golden stubble as far as the eye could see on either side. The fields were dotted with trees, but there was no sign of life and no houses. This was different from Laos and Vietnam, where people worked the fields surrounding their houses.

We later discovered that during the bad recession in the 1990s in Thailand, banks had repossessed land belonging to farmers. Because the bank doesn't want to farm the land, but just wants to make a profit at the right time, the farmland stands unused in many areas of Thailand.

An open-backed bus-taxi went by full of women going to market. When they saw us they screamed, and all did the thumbs up with both hands, and they waved with both hands until they were out of sight. We were now approaching Buri Ram, another town, and eventually found a hotel. As it was Christmas day we chose the most expensive room in the hotel to treat ourselves. It cost us 400 baht, which is less than £6. It was very large and on the ground floor, which was ideal for the bikes, and had air conditioning and hot water.

We had some chicken and rice (Christmas lunch?), though we often avoided meat in non-tourist parts of south-east Asia. The Asians have a tendency to chop everything up complete with bones, and the meat is often very dark. We were never quite sure which part of the chicken was being used . . .

We bought a box from the post office and sent 22 films back to England via the Thai courier service, which we had discovered was very reliable. We had been saving up our films from Vietnam and Laos, because we had been told that the post from both of those countries was unreliable. At the same time we sent home items that we no longer needed, including road maps which showed our cycling route. We telephoned my mother to wish her a happy 85th birthday. She was thrilled to hear from us and was getting ready to spend Christmas day with my brother and his family. Afterwards we phoned Warren's parents and brothers and my children in England to wish them all a happy Christmas. Dialling a total of 34 digits for each number was time-consuming, especially as the lines to UK were constantly engaged, presumably with every British person in Thailand phoning home to speak to their families!

We found a pleasant restaurant, and met a few westerners there. This wasn't a tourist town, and the only westerners we met were men accompanied by Thai women, who were taking their new boyfriends home to meet their parents. As we sat in the bar I had an unexpected Christmas treat. A man came in selling pieces of sugar cane. I paid 50 baht to feed them to the baby elephant that he had brought with him. The elephant was very greedy, his trunk searching me for more sugar cane as soon as he'd put each piece of cane into his mouth, and the hot air from his trunk blew over me as he did so. It was a little scary but also a lovely experience.

We stayed at the hotel a further night, so that on Boxing Day we didn't have to cycle, but we set off again the day after that. It was just after 6am as we set off, and wasn't as cold as it had previously been – maybe 18° or 19°C. We stopped at a stall for breakfast. The woman's pretty 6-year old young daughter stood cuddling a fat, fluffy puppy. I took a photo of her, and as the camera flashed she and her mother laughed. The little girl put her hands together as in prayer, the tips of her fingers up to her forehead, and did a little bobbing curtsey to say thank you. I wished that I had had the camera ready to take a second photo.

We had a tail wind, so made good progress, and as we approached Nang Rong we were surprised to see a sign for 'B&B' in English. We hadn't seen such a sign since we had left England. We found a lovely room there, and the owner was a very nice Thai man who spoke excellent English. He told us that he had travelled a lot and had worked in England in the 70s. We couldn't believe it when he told us that he had worked in Reading, my home town! What a small world! Most of the travellers stayed there for six months at a time, teaching English to Thai children in the local schools, so they paid only $3 per day for accommodation and food. He was trying to find English students, because most of his students were Swiss and German. He was concerned that they were teaching Thai children English with a foreign accent!

His guest house had a garden where we could relax with a drink, and he later took us to the night market in his car where we were able to buy a very cheap meal and take it back to eat in the garden. At the owner's recommendation we tried pumpkin custard, a Thai dessert made by steaming a hollowed-out small pumpkin which had been filled with egg custard made with coconut milk. Large wedges of cold pumpkin custard are sold in the market for 10 baht, and it tastes absolutely delicious. It was a recipe that we intended to try back home. Warren also loved the chillies that had been barbecued until they were charred black, and ate loads of them. However, he complained of a burning sensation the following day – enough said!

A newcomer arrived – a Frenchman who lived in Thailand and who was at that time studying Buddhism. He had previously lived in India studying Hinduism, and wrote books on religions. We chatted for ages and he gave us recommendations of places to visit, places to stay and people to contact if we needed guides. He said that he could live in Thailand on 20,000 baht a month (less than £300), which included the rent for a large house, a full-time driver, a cook, a housemaid and food for everyone!

The guesthouse owner's wife cooked us the best breakfast ever, which we ate on the covered area outside. The table tops were made of highly varnished thick slices of tree trunk with the bark still attached, and the stools were made of similar smaller chunks of trees. After eggs and toast, with the best marmalade I had tasted since we left England, we had delicious fresh fruit salad full of tropical fruits in fresh, clear coconut milk. On top of the fruit were delicious chunks of gelatinous coconut, the unripe coconut that we had first tasted in Goa.

We stayed a further day at the B&B, and cycled 40km to a nearby temple set in a historical park. It was pleasant to be cycling without our heavy bags. We were amused to pass a sign with incorrect spelling, which once again showed how a letter or two can change the whole meaning of a word or sentence.

'City Limit – Produce Speed.'

The main part of the journey was flat, but because the temple was set high on a hill, we had to cycle up a seriously steep hill for the last few miles. The first sight of Prasat Meung Tam Hindu monument was impressive. Built during the 12th century, the temple is dedicated to the Hindu god, Shiva. A long stone path lined on both sides with stone columns topped with stone lotus buds leads to a bridge, and the five-headed naga, a mythical snake, forms the rails over the bridge. Beyond the bridge, 52 steep steps climb to the very top of the hill. The temple was in amazing condition considering its age, and the views from the top of the hill were magnificent, even though it was hazy. The temple was very similar in style and age to one we had seen in Laos, and we knew that we would see even more when we reached Cambodia, the home of Angkor temples.

We continued our journey the following day, and we set off to cycle only 40km to a village where we had been told there was accommodation - after that there was no more accommodation for 100km. This meant that the second day we would have a long cycle ride ahead of us. When we arrived at the village where the hotel was supposed to be we couldn't find it, though everyone kept pointing us down the road towards a lake. We eventually found a deserted, very ramshackle-looking holiday complex, set amongst some trees by a lake. We wandered up and down, but there appeared to be no-one there. The car park area was full of weeds, so it looked as though no-one had stayed there for some time. However, there was some washing hanging on a line, which presumably meant that someone was around. It was rather worrying, however, when we noticed how dirty the washing was. Peeping through the windows, it was obvious that someone was living in one of the rooms, but judging from the condition of the room it could have been a tramp.

We waited for a while, reluctant to set off again knowing that the next town was so far away. After 30 minutes we were suddenly aware that we were being watched, and turned to see a man standing in a doorway. We walked over to him, and told him that we wanted a room for the night. He appeared to understand, because he fetched a key and showed us to a very basic, rather dirty room with no window, which had a bathroom with cold water only. There was air-conditioning, but it was very noisy, and sounded as though it might not last the night. The cost of the room was exorbitantly high and he wouldn't reduce it – he obviously knew that we had no other choice. We had doubts whether he actually owned or managed this resort, but we knew it was another 100km to alternative accommodation. We also felt concerned that we appeared to be the only people staying there, in the middle of nowhere, and our concerns were further strengthened when we found that the key wouldn't lock the door – it simply turned in the keyhole. By this time the owner of the resort (if that was who he was!) had disappeared, so we were unable to ask if we could be moved to another room. We tried the doors to the other rooms, but they were all locked. However, we discovered that our key opened every door to every other room, but none of them were furnished. We were quite alarmed at this stage – any other sane person with half a brain would have left, despite the fact that we had paid for the room. However, having geared ourselves to a short cycle ride, neither of us wanted to set off for another 100km so late in the day.

There were loads of mosquitoes in our room and plenty more could get in through cracks in the ceiling and under the door, but unfortunately there was nowhere we could hang the mosquito net. Outside our room Warren found some pieces of wood amongst the piles of rubbish. He wedged thin slivers of wood into cracks in the wall and ceiling, and twisted pieces of wire onto them. To these points he attached our mosquito net. We sprayed the room with mosquito spray, turned on the air conditioning, took all of our valuables with us because we couldn't lock the door, and cycled to the village to find somewhere to have a meal. We were lucky to find a cheap café, and returned to the resort in the dark.

We pushed our bikes past the gates and into the car park, but had to stop to switch on our torches. It was pitch black; there were no lights, stars or moon to light our way. We felt very nervous, flashing our torches at the bushes and trees to check if anyone was there, and we both had the horrible feeling once again that we were being watched. As we approached our room, we heard a terrible clattering noise, which we realised was the air conditioning unit. We knew that it would be impossible to sleep with such a noise, so we had to turn it off, so we could now expect a very hot, uncomfortable night. We used a plank that we had found in the grounds to wedge shut the door, leant our bikes against the plank, opened the door to the bathroom in the hope of getting some fresh air into the windowless room, and went to bed.

We both slept badly; we woke several times, certain that we could hear someone outside, but without a window to peep through we had no idea who or what was there, and there was no way either of us intended going out of the room until morning.

In the middle of the night I woke from a fitful sleep when I heard a loud bang.

'What was that?' I shouted.

'It's ok – it was me. Don't worry,' replied Warren, so I relaxed and tried to sleep again.

Having dozed off, I was suddenly awakened by a blood-curdling scream, and Warren leapt out of bed and switched on the light. My heart was beating so hard that it felt that it would jump out of my chest. We both felt certain that it had been a man screaming, and although we tried to persuade ourselves that it might have been an animal, we weren't able to convince ourselves. It was 3am – another three hours before daylight. We pulled out our very sharp kitchen knives and laid them by the bed. We didn't even want to switch the light off, but we needed to try to sleep. However, neither of us could sleep any more, despite knowing that we had a long cycle ride ahead of us within a few hours.

We were so desperate to get away from that strange place that by 5am we were dressed and had quietly packed our cycle bags ready to leave. We were very nervous, and for some reason I was concerned that the gates to the entrance might be locked. We opened the door to our room very quietly. It was still pitch black outside, and deathly quiet with no breeze. We were scared to switch on our torches or bicycle lights in case we drew attention to ourselves, but after a quick flash of the torch to indicate the way we ran across the uneven car park pushing our bikes as quietly as we could. With relief we saw that the gates were open, so we flew through, mounted our bikes and, with the cycle lights now shining to show us the way, cycled up the hill like bats out of hell until we were back on the main road.

It wasn't until now that Warren told me what the bang had been in the middle of the night. He had obviously been very concerned about the security of our room in that strange resort in the middle of nowhere, because he had had a dream that someone had broken into the room. Warren dreamt that he had leapt up from the bed and hit the man on the chin – the noise I had heard was his fist hitting the wall! How extraordinary that Warren, who had never hit anyone in his life, had acted out a dream like that. When I saw the graze on his hand, I was also obviously worried that he might continue having such dreams – I didn't want him to think I was the intruder in his dream next time! Fortunately for both of us, Warren never had such a dream again.

The sun rose quickly just after 6am. An old man cycled in the opposite direction. His saddle was so low that his knees were close to his chin. He smiled a very gummy smile and waved to us. Everything suddenly seemed very normal again. We must have climbed a lot the previous day without realising it, because we had a very long descent initially, the bikes speeding along with very little help from us.

We stopped regularly for water and a rest in one of the bus shelters if there was no café. A man with his water buffalo grazing tried to chat to us. He had a catapult in his hand which was rather disconcerting, but catapults are used to fire stones to control the direction of the animals. A motorbike went by in the opposite direction, four young men on it shouting and waving 'hello'. The fields now were full of sugar cane on one side and hemp on the other, and lorries were loaded with sugar cane that had been harvested.

Warren suddenly swerved and shouted for me to stop. He had seen a large black scorpion crossing the road in front of his bike, and he chased it across the road to try to take a photo of it. He kept throwing a guide book alongside it, so that the book would give an indication of the size of the scorpion in the photo, but the scorpion refused to stop, although it didn't move fast. Warren got his photo, but the scorpion never made it across the road – a passing bus went over the top of it, throwing it up into the air, but the scorpion continued valiantly on until a motorbike on the hard shoulder hit it, bringing the scorpion's life to an untimely end.

There were forests of eucalyptus trees and large fields of hemp and sugar cane. It was a long, hot journey. We stopped for pad thai, and I was so thirsty that I drank two cans of iced coffee in two gulps and one litre of very cold water. We arrived at Aranya Prathet at 1pm, so we'd made good time, but when I got off my bike my legs and arms were shaking. We'd done 64 miles in 4¾ hours, an average of 13.46 mph, our best ever, and a very good speed with such heavily-laden bikes. We felt that we were getting used to the long, hot days.

We were now only 6km from the Cambodian border, but booked into a very smart hotel paying the highest price so far (900 baht plus 7% VAT, about £14). We thought we deserved a bit of luxury, especially after the night before, but the room would have cost more than ten times as much in an English hotel. We even had a meal there that evening, treating ourselves to a very European peppered steak and a bottle of wine.

The next day was New Year's Eve, and we planned to wait until the New Year before entering Cambodia. We tried to buy some more US dollars, because we knew we would need them in Cambodia, and we wanted to make sure that we had plenty. We had previously tried to get them in Ubon, but the banks told us that they could only buy dollars and not sell them. Here in Aranya Prathet we thought it would be easy – we were only 6km from the Cambodian border, and in Cambodia the US dollar is used more than the local currency, the Riel. We were sent from bank to bank, but although every bank had the buying and selling price listed, no-one would sell us dollars. We even saw a customer selling dollars as we approached the counter in one bank, but when we asked to buy some were told they had none! One bank explained that they always sent dollars to head office and were not able to sell them to us. We were very confused – we had had no problem buying dollars in Bangkok. What was going on? Didn't the banks want to make a profit? It was as though there was some sort of conspiracy. At the last bank we tried, a young man suggested in a whisper that we should go to a local electrical shop to ask 'if they could help'. We took his advice.

At the electrical shop we were asked if we had Thai baht to buy dollars, and they insisted on seeing the money before beckoning us through to the back of the shop, where dollars were counted out onto a table and exchanged for baht. We received the same exchange rate that had been displayed in the bank, so we weren't getting a bad deal. It turned out that we had received an even better deal when we counted the money again back at the hotel, because we had been given too many notes! We never found out exactly why we needed to go to such lengths to obtain dollars, but knew that Thailand was very keen that all of South East Asia adopted one currency – the baht. We wondered if the banks had been told not to sell dollars in an attempt to keep only baht in circulation.

We bought a couple of bottles of wine to see in the New Year and, because of the time difference, we toasted ourselves and everyone back home seven hours before them. We watched Lord of the Rings on our satellite television in our posh hotel bedroom and then fell asleep – it was 2004 in Thailand and would soon be 2004 back home in England, although the Buddhist year was still 2547 until 13th April.

In the morning we sat in the air-conditioned coffee room of the hotel reading the Bangkok Post, which is written in English. It was the first time we had read a newspaper for months. I thought it amusing to see the weather forecast for the local areas – 'cold, minimum of 18°C; cool – minimum of 23°C'. We wondered how they would describe the conditions in England, or even Moscow or Zurich which showed minus temperatures!

We wandered round the market, and bought three small pineapples, peeled and ready to eat, for 10 baht (about 15p). They were so sweet and juicy that we ended up having to go and wash ourselves afterwards. In front of the fish stalls were washing-up bowls full of flapping fish. Three had jumped out of the bowls, and one was unbelievably making its way down the road, 'walking' on a pair of fins three stalls away! I wondered how long it could survive out of the water, and wished it luck.

We needed to buy sewing thread to do some repairs, and I eventually found a shop that sold a well-known make available in England. At 10 baht (15p) it cost about a tenth of the English price, and we thought that if manufacturers were able to make a profit in Thailand, the profit margin back home must be phenomenal!

A truck drove slowly past. In the back sat a giant golden Buddha and alongside was a Buddhist monk in orange robes. The truck stopped frequently, so that locals could hand food and gifts to the monk. Several Thai people called out 'Happy New Year' to us as we passed, but we saw very few other westerners.

The next day we set off for the Cambodian border. On the Thai side of the border was an enormous market, many people having just set up their stalls. The border was chaotic to say the least. I have never seen so many people at a border – there were literally thousands of Cambodian people walking through to Thailand, many of them with baskets on yokes across their shoulders, obviously hoping to sell cheap goods in Thailand. Queues of Cambodians lined up pushing home-made wooden carts. The carts were either empty, because they hoped to fill up with Thai goods that were unavailable in Cambodia, or they were stacked high with cheap Cambodian goods to sell in Thailand. We understood that the Cambodians had no problem in getting day visas, but that goods were smuggled quite openly between the two countries.

Initially we had to queue to have our passports stamped to show that we were leaving Thailand, and then we went to join the long queue to wait for immigration. We must have looked out of place, because we were pulled out of the queue by a Cambodian official, and were directed to a short queue marked 'Alien Passports'. I felt as though I should have been standing alongside a spaceship instead of a bicycle. Our passports were stamped very quickly with the necessary visas and we began to cycle along the tarmac road into Cambodia.

Incredibly the first few buildings that we passed were large casinos - Cambodia receives a lot of revenue from the casinos which are frequented by the Thais, gambling being illegal in Thailand. The road alongside these casinos was newly sealed and in good condition.

Suddenly and dramatically, however, the condition of the road changed. We found ourselves cycling along a busy, very crowded dirt road that was utter chaos. We were cycling on the right hand side of the road once more, with dirt on the side of the road instead of pavements. We were reminded of India again – dirt, stones, traffic, noise, horns sounding, people rushing, dust. We cycled amongst it all. There were ancient lorries belching black exhaust fumes, and there were trucks with people packed like sardines in the open back, the drivers speeding like 'little boy racers'. We had been warned that the roads in Cambodia were bad, but had never imagined how bad. We didn't know it at the time, but the roads in the next few days were gradually going to get worse and worse, so that for the first time on this trip we would wish that we hadn't entered a country ...

CHAPTER 19

CAMBODIA

Cambodia is about half the size of Italy or Japan, and is bordered on the west, north, east and south-east by Thailand, Laos and Vietnam. Its main geographical features are the Mekong River which runs from north to south, and the massive Tonle Sap Lake (the Great Lake), one of the world's richest sources of freshwater fish. Most of the country is low-lying, but in the south-west and north-east are highlands, some of which are remote and forested. The coastline on the south-western border faces the Gulf of Thailand. Decades of wars have caused Cambodia's economy to be in very poor shape. Cambodia is one of the poorest countries in Asia and, like Laos, depends heavily on foreign aid. Tourism, however, is beginning to boom, and the ancient temples of Angkor Wat have made Cambodia a popular country to visit.

As we cycled away from the border we realised just how bad the roads were going to be for cycling. Initially the ancient sealed road was covered with large raised lumps, as though a cement lorry had driven along the road spilling its load. It was like cycling over rumble strips, but it went on for several miles. There were too many bumps to avoid, so we were just thrown about as we cycled over them. I had to grip the handlebars so tightly that it caused more pain than usual in my hands and wrists. After that there were holes in the road – no, they were craters. Sometimes they were so big we had to cycle on the wrong side of the road to go round them – a dangerous thing to do, because the pick-up trucks full of dozens of people drove at top speed with horns blaring at us, despite the holes in the road. At times we were convinced that they were deliberately going as close to us as they dared. We couldn't imagine how the people in the back of the trucks stayed in the vehicle, especially those sitting on the edge, and sometimes there was even a passenger sitting on the bonnet clinging on for dear life! If we heard two horns sounding behind us it meant that two of these pick-up trucks were racing each other, so it was necessary for us to throw ourselves into a crater, or onto the dirt at the side of the road to avoid being run over. The lorries went slowly, but the numerous pick-up trucks, which were the local form of taxi, were constantly overtaking the lorries. We could see clouds of dust ahead where they were rushing along the dirt at the side of the road to avoid pot-holes. In some sections of the road the tarmac had completely disintegrated, and deep furrows in the road had been filled with sharp rubble which we had to negotiate slowly.

We had been warned that once we got to Cambodia we should never walk off the road, because it was possible that we could stand on an unexploded mine – this was a country still full of land-mines. We knew, therefore, that Cambodia was a potentially dangerous country in which to cycle, and that even if we needed to relieve ourselves we shouldn't attempt to find a bush to hide behind. However, at the moment it appeared to us that there were more dangers lurking on the main highway than at the side of the road!

It seemed extraordinary that in Laos we had cycled for miles on our own with no traffic on wide, new, perfect roads, paid for by foreign aid, but here a very busy main road was in total decay. Amazingly, this road was the main tourist route from Bangkok in Thailand to Siem Riep, the nearest town to the ancient Angkor Wat temples, which were the most popular tourist attraction in Cambodia. Although Cambodia receives a lot of foreign aid, it didn't appear to be receiving help to upgrade the roads, even though tourism was the main trade of the future, and tourists obviously needed to be able to travel around the country.

Cars, trucks and lorries swerved around pot-holes and trenches, and bounced up and down as they went over piles of packed dirt and gravel. The red dust was a constant problem, as was the obnoxious smell of exhaust fumes from poorly-maintained vehicles. We noticed that nine out of ten of the vehicles and motorbikes had no registration plates and, judging by the way the locals were driving, it appeared that no qualifications were needed to drive on the roads of Cambodia either.

There were giant fields of rice on either side of the road. People were working in the fields, often with canopies set up to give them shade. The terrain was dead flat. As we passed villages, we noticed frequent official painted signs with flags, which were for the 'Cambodian People's Party'. In the villages every stall and shop had plastic containers, including Pepsi bottles, of petrol and oil. One had a piece of cardboard propped up, on which was written 'ESSO'. Large galvanised funnels stood alongside the bottles, so that the contents of the Pepsi bottles could be poured into the tanks of vehicles. Shacks, many on short stilts, lined the roads in the villages, and ponds were full of vivid pink water-lilies. Rice was laid out on plastic sheets to dry alongside banana trees and coconut palms.

Children shouted 'hello' to us, but we had to simply shout 'hello' back without looking round or waving – it was important to keep our hands firmly on the handlebars and our eyes fixed on the section of road immediately ahead of us.

Lorries went by with much of the bodywork missing. The engines and radiators were exposed, and the drivers were sitting in the open with nothing around them – no windscreen, no doors, and no proper seat.

We were travelling due east, and we were cycling against the wind as well as battling with the difficult road surface. Pigs were being transported on the back of motorbikes, sometimes in bamboo cages, but usually just strapped in pairs across the back of the motorbikes – they were always laid on their backs with their feet in the air and their heads hanging down. At first I thought the pigs were dead, because they stayed very quiet in that position, but occasionally they squealed or wriggled their feet, so I knew they were alive. I wondered how many pigs arrived at their destination with their backs broken because of the terrible road. Many motorbikes were also carrying live chickens, and they always had a pole extending out on both sides so that dozens of chickens could be hung upside down on the poles, their feet tied together. This still left space for one or two passengers on the motorbike.

It was hot, dusty and very hard going, but eventually we had cycled 35 miles to a town where we knew there was accommodation, and we stopped first at a restaurant to have some lunch. We were surprised to see that the menu was priced in Thai baht and US dollars, but there was no mention of the Cambodian riel. We were just in time – as we sat down, a tourist bus arrived. This was apparently one of the stops for tourist buses from Siem Reap to the border, and travellers of all nationalities piled out to order lunch. There was little choice, and we ordered fried rice and a cool drink, after which we booked into a hotel where we had a large but basic room for $5US a night. Choice of food that night was again very limited in this small town, and we were surprised that we were still paying for everything in Thai baht and hadn't yet seen any Cambodian money. We went to bed early after another meal of rice, hoping that the next day's cycling would improve. It was 7.30pm, and already the employees of the small hotel had settled into their collapsible beds scattered around the building.

We had breakfast the next morning in the town – yes, more rice! As we cycled out of the town we realised that this was the end of the 'sealed' road. We were now on a dirt road worse than any farm track in Europe, with ruts and holes, bumps, piles of loose soil, and sharp rocks sticking out of hard patches of dirt. We were covered almost immediately with a layer of red dust, and the going was bone-shaking and slow. Fortunately there was less traffic than the day before, but the cars and trucks that did go by sped past, leaving us in a cloud of dust, choking and unable to see.

The sun rose to our right as we travelled north-east. There were large areas of water and massive fields of rice on either side. There were no hills, but numerous small bridges where the water crossed the road. Three wooden carts pulled by hump-backed cows passed on the other side of the road, the carts full of harvested rice. Men on bikes and in trucks wore lengths of checked fabric wound round their heads like turbans. These scarves were very common in Cambodia. Women often wore them over the top of large-brimmed hats and draped across their faces.

We could see for miles because of the flat terrain, so there was no need to stop to admire the countryside. This was fortunate, as we needed all our concentration to negotiate the poor road. We had travelled on unmapped tracks in the bush in Africa that were better than this road, but it was shown as a main road on the Cambodian map. As we continued we had to be careful not to cycle into a pile of loose dirt at the bottom of a hole or at the side of the road, because this would bring the bikes to an abrupt halt, slewing the tyres sideways and throwing us off. Our tyres were smooth ones, designed for sealed roads, and until now we had never felt the need for thick knobbly mountain-bike tyres, which slow the bike down on a sealed road.

Ahead of us we could hear loud banging and wondered what it was. We discovered that it was the first of many bridges that we had to cross made of a metal frame. We had to cycle over flat metal plates laid loosely down. It looked temporary but we suspected that it was a permanent fixture. The metal plates were warped and uneven, and moved beneath the vehicles making the loud noise we'd heard. Later bridges had enormous sections of metal completely missing, and damaged pieces of sharp, twisted metal stuck up into the air. We were concerned that even the weight of a bicycle would cause the plates to move or drop, but lorries went slowly across and trucks full of passengers raced across with no concern. One bridge had a pile of dirt covering the damaged metal, but lengths of jagged, ripped metal protruded out of the soil, which was packed hard into piles making it difficult to manoeuvre around them. Later there were two or three wooden bridges, each of them with whole planks missing, so we usually decided it was safest to get off our bikes and walk across these bridges.

The cycling was very slow and painful. Which route should we take? – the very bumpy up and down bit, the very stony bit, or the bit that looks smoother, but could be loose soil that stops the bike dead throwing us off? There was no shade – just flat fields on either side of us – and the only trees we saw were in the villages that we occasionally passed through. It was very much hotter that day, because the wind had dropped, and the temperature rose to 35°C in the shade. However, we weren't in the shade, and when we applied sunscreen to our burning skin, the dust stuck even more to our bodies.

We could hear ahead of us the sound of hammering, and passed a village where they were carving giant Buddha images and other statues from local red stone. As they sanded the statues with electric sanders to make them smooth, the red dust was indistinguishable from the dust rising from the road as the cars and lorries passed.

The road was so bad we wondered if we had taken the wrong road, but after a couple of hours several tourist buses had passed, so we guessed that the road must be the correct one. As we stood waiting for a bus to cross a bridge, the tourists in their air-conditioned bus gave us a round of applause, but later buses went by with the curtains pulled – they weren't even looking out of the window any more. The trees, shrubs and plants at the sides of the road were dying or already dead, suffocated under a thick coat of red dust. I wondered if the Cambodian people living alongside that road suffered in the same way.

We had to stop to repair a puncture. There was no sign of glass or a nail, so we assumed that a sharp stone had pierced the inner tube. As usual, once we stopped to do the repair, we were surrounded by a crowd of men watching as Warren worked. They were incredibly impressed with the speed in which he repaired the puncture (plenty of practice!), and were fascinated by the bikes.

That day's journey was again only 30 miles, but on this terrain it seemed like 100 miles. We were making very slow progress, and were relieved at last to be approaching the village where we hoped to stop. Warren was ahead, and when I reached him he was surrounded by a group of schoolboys. They spoke very good English, and at Warren's request they were teaching him some Cambodian.

'No,' said an 11-year-old to Warren. 'Watch my lips,' and he patiently repeated the words. Warren repeated them until the boys were happy with his pronunciation. The crowd was growing, and by this time there were a dozen boys, all keen to practice their English or teach us Cambodian.

Two miles further on, we found the only guesthouse in the village. The room was very dirty, had a dark, dingy bathroom, and was small, but the owner still wanted US$5 and refused to reduce the price. We had no choice unless we wanted to cycle a further 35 miles, so we insisted on the room being cleaned before we moved in, and had a meal once more of fried rice. There was an alternative of chicken soup, but when she lifted the lid off the pot and I saw a whole chicken submerged in clear liquid, its claws sticking up out of the stock, I decided I would rather have fried rice once again.

In Cambodia there are no fridges in the cafés and restaurants (apart from in the expensive tourist hotels), but only insulated chests in which the cans are stacked with ice. This means that drinks are slightly cool if you're lucky, and warm if you're not. We walked around the village searching for a cold beer, and as we approached one stall a young plump girl called out in excellent English. We sat down and drank the beer, and she joined us at the table to chat. Her English was astonishingly good, and she told us that her father paid for her to have private lessons. She was nine years old. Her father spoke virtually no English, but when we complimented him on his clever daughter, he beamed – she was obviously his pride and joy, and he knew the value of being able to speak good English to the tourists.

A tourist bus stopped outside the café – this was a toilet stop on the tourist route – and pandemonium reigned as children rushed forward trying to sell bracelets and other souvenirs, and asking for foreign coins, a lucrative hobby. One young boy sat next to me.

'How do you do,' he said politely. 'Where are you from? How old are you?' He tried to sell me a £1 coin that an English tourist had given him. He wanted 7,000 riel.

'It's only worth 6,000 riel,' I said, so he offered it to me at that price.

Once he realized I wasn't interested in English money and was not part of the travelling party, he dashed off to catch one of them before they left. His English was excellent; he was 14 years old.

The sun had just set as we crossed the road to return to our guesthouse. We looked along the road where we had cycled. A vehicle was approaching with lights on, a strange red foggy haze around it as it drove along the dirt road – there was no breeze tonight to disperse the dust. When we went into our room we discovered that the bathroom floor was covered with several inches of dark brown water. As there had been none on the floor when we left, we knew that it had come up through the hole in the floor where the water from the shower drained away. As I didn't want to wade through the water to reach the raised squat toilet at the furthest end of the bathroom, I called the owner of the guesthouse who was just getting into bed. He grudgingly sorted out the problem with a very long bamboo pole, blaming us when he found a plastic shampoo sachet in the drainage hole, even though it wasn't ours.

As we took the bikes out of the room the next morning we found that I had another puncture, this time in my front tyre – two in one day! Having to repair this delayed our departure, but as we set off we thought that the road didn't look as bad as before. We were wrong – although there weren't so many pot-holes, there was a lot of loose soil, which for cyclists is very dangerous and something I dreaded. We were skidding all over the place as we hit these patches, impossible to distinguish from solid soil until we cycled over them. There was a wind from the east again, which made progress even slower, but at least it helped to cool us a little, and kept the temperature down to 30°C.

At one stage the centre of the road had piles of sharp rubble along it, presumably put there ready to fill the holes. The piles had obviously been there some time, judging from the worn paths going around the piles, forcing lorries to go on the wrong side of the road against oncoming traffic. Warren was trying to negotiate one section when a motorbike with three people on it went straight towards him. It was not going fast, and Warren expected it to stop, but it ran straight into him, bruising his leg and ripping off the pannier bags on one side. Warren's fall was cushioned because he fell onto the three people, who were still on their motorbike. They didn't understand English, but they certainly understood that he was annoyed when he kicked their bike and shouted at them.

We stopped to watch four locals emptying one pond into another to catch fish. Two young men and two young women worked in pairs. One couple stood either side of the first pond holding ropes with a bucket tied in the middle. They swung the bucket into the water, and emptied it into another pond over which a net was being held by the second couple; this would catch any fish that they scooped up. They worked with an amazing rhythm, but stopped to stare and smile at us once they saw us. We beckoned for them to continue, so we could take a photo, and we set off again, calling 'bye bye' as we went. None of us could wave – they had their hands full, and we daren't take our hands off the handlebars either.

Then the inevitable happened – in order to avoid a sharp rock protruding from the dirt road, I swerved into a pile of loose dirt; my wheels slewed sideways and I was thrown off my bike onto gravel. My arm and elbow were badly grazed, but the pedal of my bike had been forced agonisingly into the front of my shin, and a dark blue swelling the size of half a cricket ball had appeared within seconds. It was quite frightening, as I could literally feel the skin stretching over the swelling, and it was incredibly painful. (It was four years before the bruise finally disappeared!) As anyone can imagine, I was definitely wishing that I was anywhere except Cambodia, and we were both regretting that we had chosen this route, but we had no choice but to continue, now even more slowly than before.

In the next village I stopped to take a sip of water, and was immediately surrounded by dozens of half-clad children, several carrying puppies, who ran to greet me. They were happy and eager to have their photos taken, but couldn't understand when I tried to get them to move closer together so I could get them all into the one photo. A woman ran from the other side of the road to push her young daughter into the group, to make sure that she was in the photo as well.

Further down the road we were interested to see harvested rice being processed in a threshing machine. The rice was being shovelled into the machine to separate the grains from the stalks. The stalks were shot into the air, making a pile at the side of the machine, and these were kept for animal fodder. Women with buckets were collecting the green grains of rice and carrying them to a large plastic sheet, where they were spread out to dry in the sun. Children were kept busy chasing away puppies and chickens, which constantly walked through the pile of rice.

An American on a motorbike passed us going in the opposite direction, and he stopped to talk to us, amazed that anyone was foolish enough to cycle on such a road. He had lived in Cambodia for seven years, but returned regularly to his home town in Alaska for three months every year. He was studying the temple ruins in the country. He told us that, despite its bad condition, the road was 100 times better than it had been. Until recently there had been holes big enough for cars to literally disappear into, and vehicles had previously needed to drive through the paddy fields to avoid bad sections of road! We commented on the taxi pick-up trucks with the dozens of passengers, and the fact that they always passed by so close, even travelling on the wrong side of the road to do so. He told us that this was the norm – a game to these drivers, most of whom were not qualified to drive. He warned us to be very careful – if a Cambodian hit anyone, he told us, the driver and passengers just disappeared as fast as they could and would even abandon their vehicle if necessary. The police were never of help either, and he warned us to be even more alert on the narrower newly sealed roads, because the locals drove on the well-sealed roads even faster. This only added to the concerns that we already had about cycling in Cambodia.

After 13 miles of hell that day we were on a sealed road again – many times better than before, but still a very poor road in bad condition. In places the tarmac had sunk to reveal craters full of sharp stones, and the surface of the better sections was very rough and uneven.

The scenery became greener as we approached Siem Reap, and trees lining the road gave us intermittent welcome shade. Siem Reap was a surprise. We knew it was a boom town because of its proximity to the Angkor Wat temples, but we were surprised to see dozens of very large, new, very beautiful and obviously expensive hotels lining the road, many still in the course of construction. Almost all of them had the word 'Angkor' in the name, which we imagined might cause a lot of confusion (Casa Angkor, Princess Angkor, Angkor Star, Ankoriana and The Grand d'Angkor, made famous because Charlie Chaplin had stayed there in the 1930s, when he had visited the Angkor temples by elephant).

We found the guesthouse that had been recommended to us, and at $4 it was cheaper than the last two nights, and infinitely nicer. We had an immaculately clean room and bathroom, and there was a yard outside with a pleasant thatched raised area with hammocks, low tables and cushions for relaxing, and another terracotta-tiled paved area with tables and chairs for eating. Despite the fact that Siem Reap was a tourist town with many travellers wanting accommodation, there were so many guest-houses and hotels that competition was stiff, and there were plenty of bargains.

We showered and had a meal and handed over our dust-covered clothes for laundering. We pushed the bikes into the room, and this was when we found another puncture on my bike – the third in two days! I fell asleep instantly, though it was early afternoon, woke to have a superb meal with a bottle of wine in one of the very pleasant restaurants in the town, and slept soundly through the night as well.

We spent the next day wandering round Siem Reap – how different it was from the rest of Cambodia! Smart restaurants, new supermarkets, shops, markets, bars and cafés were everywhere. We discovered that everything in Siem Reap was priced in US dollars; the labels on the supermarket shelves were even in dollars and cents, but when dollars were handed over, change was given in dollars but the cents were converted to riel, so two different currencies were handed back to us in change! The only time that a shop quoted the price in the local currency was if the price was lower than a dollar. This was different from Laos and Vietnam, where only the price of hotels was quoted in dollars. However, because Laos and Cambodia have no ATMs, it is absolutely necessary for tourists to take supplies of US dollars to pay for hotels, food and souvenirs.

We discovered that the shops were full of well-known guide books at very cheap prices. If a guide book was marked as US$22, it could be bought for US$3 in Siem Reap. When we examined the books we discovered that they were fakes – the pages had been photocopied and put inside identical covers. Most of the copies were fairly good, but on occasions a really poor copy was on sale, where it was very obvious that the pages had been photocopied. We were amazed that they were able to get away with this, but assumed that the publishers were aware what was happening. Many bargains were to be had; we bought some good quality outdoor clothes that would have been very expensive in England but had been made in Cambodia, and were therefore very cheap.

Warren went to arrange transport for us for that afternoon and the next day, as we wanted to visit the Angkor Wat temples, several kilometres away. Most people go by moto, which means sitting on the back of a local motorbike, but because I have a fear of motorbikes I couldn't do this. Warren booked a tuk-tuk, which in Cambodia is a motorbike with an articulated two-wheel trailer on the back for two passengers to sit side by side. A roof gives protection from the sun.

That afternoon the tuk-tuk took us to visit an unofficial land-mine museum near Siem Reap which had been recommended to us. The owner, Aki Ra, who thought he was 27 at that time but wasn't absolutely certain of his age, had been brought up by the Khmer Rouge after they had killed his parents when he was 5 years old. He had been accustomed to seeing people killed and tortured as punishments for 'crimes' such as stealing scraps from the pig swill because they were starving, and thought that this was how everyone lived. One of Aki Ra's earliest memories was of seeing a line of 150 people being marched along. They were professional people who were considered to be the enemy, and were being taken to the infamous killing fields.

He was taught by the Khmer Rouge how to lay mines, fire guns and rocket launchers, and make simple bombs. He was given his first gun at the age of ten. It was an AK47, and the gun was difficult for him to handle as it was almost the same size as he was. At the age of 13 his village was overthrown by the Vietnamese, and he was given two options – join the Vietnamese or be killed, so not much of a choice! He was then conscripted into the Vietnamese army and he fought against the Khmer Rouge until 1990. When the Vietnamese troops were pulled out of Cambodia, he joined the Cambodian army. He was 17 by that time, and for the first time he was given a formal education. (He now speaks English, French and Japanese). In 1993 the UN had peace-keeping forces in the area, and he volunteered to work for them helping to clear mines that had been laid over the years by various fighting forces. For the first time in his life he and his friends saw electricity, toilets, roads, cars and concrete houses. When the UN put a film on a huge cinema screen, people ran away when they saw the tanks coming on the screen, because they thought they were real.

He has built up his land-mine museum to make people aware of the horror of the landmine, and is now able to help the thousands of people in Cambodia who have been disabled by landmines. Initially his museum was very popular, but the authorities began to harass him, saying that it presented a negative picture of Cambodia. He was even put into prison several times. The reason for the harassment became apparent when another war museum was opened in the area – there was no room for two war museums in Siem Reap, and the second one was being run by a Government official. Aki Ra continues, because he doesn't charge an entrance fee, so technically it isn't a museum that he runs. Aki Ra depends solely on donations to continue his work. He now works solely for the people of Cambodia, and goes regularly into the rural areas to help clear the remaining mines and to educate the farmers about landmines which they may still find on their land. Numerous children who have been disabled by landmines have been taken in and brought up by Aki Ra, and he and his wife have educated them and taught them trades so they don't need to beg.

It's estimated that there are still 3 million unexploded landmines and bombs lying on or under the ground in Cambodia, now mostly in the rural areas. The one thing you don't do in Cambodia is walk off a well-worn track, even if you're desperate for a wee – better to lose your dignity than a limb or your life. The rainy season sometimes buries these mines deeper, brings them to the surface or moves them, so the process of locating and removing landmines is likely to continue in Cambodia for many years.

We were then taken in the tuk-tuk to Angkor Wat to see the sunset. The price of a daily ticket to Angkor Wat includes being able to go to one of the temples the afternoon before to see the sun setting. Angkor Wat is the largest of the Angkor temples – a very large, breathtaking temple in amazingly good condition. Unlike most of the temples at Angkor, it was not abandoned to the elements for centuries, so is better preserved than the others. Built in the 12th century, it has a wide stone causeway across a vast moat, which leads to one of the entrances in the square outer wall of the temple. Inside are buildings, pools, towers with domes, carvings, sculptures and bas-reliefs. Incredibly steep steps lead to the top of the temples; the reason for the steep steps is because it is considered that it should be no easy task to reach the kingdom of the gods, but such steps have claimed their victims, in recent years as well as in history.

Every tourist visiting Cambodia must see the temples of Angkor. The temples were built between the 9th and 14th centuries, and are considered architectural wonders of the world. The kings of the mighty Khmer empire ruled from Angkor, but only the walls of the city and the temples remain, because only gods were allowed to dwell in structures made of brick and stone. The houses, palaces and public buildings built of wood have long since disappeared.

Over the centuries there were reports from explorers of a walled city of temples in Cambodia, and in the late 19th century a French explorer published a book with descriptions and sketches of the temple city, and expeditions were sent to Angkor to produce detailed sketches, photographs and plans of the temples. Angkor Wat had been restored in the 16th century and was a Buddhist shrine, but the other temples had been left to the elements and the jungle for centuries. The first restoration began in the 1930s, but most was carried out in the 1960s. War in Cambodia interrupted restoration work, so the jungle grew back again. Unfortunately, the fighting that took place in and around Angkor Wat added considerably to the damage of the temples, especially to the statues which were often vandalized and were used as target practice by soldiers. In 1992 Angkor was classed as a World Heritage site, so the buildings are now protected.

Angkor is the place to go for people interested in ancient history and architecture, but every year the crowds of tourists become bigger. We were able to take hundreds of photos without too many tourists in the way, although Buddhist monks in orange robes were always welcome to walk into the picture when we clicked the camera. However, Angkor Wat is likely to become more and more crowded as the years go by, so we considered ourselves lucky to visit it at a time when it was not too busy.

The following morning we were back at Angkor Wat at 5.30am to watch the sun rise behind the three ornate towers of the temple. I have a fear of heights so chose not to climb up the unbelievably steep steps to the top of the temple, but left Warren to do that while I explored the surrounding cloisters and small buildings, bas-reliefs, sculptures and carvings. I found a small deserted temple raised high above the ground on steep steps which was one of my favourite places.

Because of the cost ($40 for the two of us for one day), we chose to spend only one day at the temples, so we were there from sunrise to sunset. It was a long, hot day, but food, drink and souvenir stalls were everywhere; the roads were mostly sealed and there were plenty of excellent new toilet facilities. I was amused to see a sign in the toilet cubicle, which requested that the locals should not squat on these western toilets with their feet on the seat!

In our tuk-tuk we could speed between temples, which were spread over a massive area. We chose a few of the 100 plus temples to visit, and marvelled at each one. Every temple was different, each with its own style and something special to see. The Bayon, a very special place and one of our favourites, has 216 gigantic carved faces gently smiling down from four sides of each of the high towers. At any one time we could see several faces around us, some full-face, some in profile, looking down from a height. Each face is made from ten or more large blocks of stone, probably weighing a ton each.

The Baphuon has a superb 200 metre causeway raised on hundreds of pillars. As everyone walked along the top, Warren and I found a way to get underneath to take photos of the sun shining through the pillars holding up the causeway.

The magnificent Terrace of Elephants is a 350 metre long viewing stand which used to be used for public ceremonies. Carved stone elephants parade along the front of it with carved lions and other animals.

Angkor Thom is the walled city, 10 square kilometres in size. At the height of its period it had one million inhabitants, at a time when London's population was 50,000, which shows how important a place it was. Massive gateways 20 metres high are topped by giant stone faces set in the wall, and are approached by causeways across moats with rows of 54 stone gods on one side and 54 stone demons on the other, each row forming a balustrade to the sides of the bridge. There are five such entrances.

Preah Khan is a maze of vaulted corridors, and four impressive walkways approach the gates of the temple. At Neak Pean a large elegant square pool, unfortunately no longer holding water, is entered by steps surrounding it; it is surrounded by four similar smaller pools, and was once used for ritual purification. The smaller pools were filled from the main pool via ornamental spouts in the shapes of the heads of an elephant, a horse, a lion and a human. At Eastern Mebon, perfectly-carved life-size elephants guard each corner of the temple, and at Banteay Kdei the four entrances are guarded by garuda, which are mythical creatures, half-bird and half-man.

Ta Prohm is probably the most photographed and popular temple because, unlike the other temples at Angkor, it has been left as it was discovered. Trees with monstrous roots encircle the stonework of walls and buildings, and have slowly pulled apart the stones over the centuries; sometimes only the tentacle-like roots of the trees now hold the walls together. Crumbling towers amidst the shade of giant banyan trees made us aware of how exciting it must have been when the explorers hacked their way through the jungle to discover these amazing temples. Moss, creeping plants and lichen adorn the stonework, but we could still see the fine carvings beneath, and many of the corridors and doorways were blocked by piles of carved stone. Many others of the temples had these giant trees in their midst, the massive buttresses and roots of the trees strangling the walls of buildings, but at Ta Prohm the jungle is all around, and monkeys swung through the trees and ran across the ground, despite the tourists walking around. Ta Prohm is probably the most famous and most recognised because of its eerie qualities and photogenic atmosphere, and it is instantly familiar because it has been used as the setting for many films, the most well known being Tomb Raider.

At each of the temples we visited, we marvelled at the delicate carvings, amazed that they were still so sharp and detailed after 10 centuries, and were incredulous that the one ton blocks of sandstone had been carried over 50km from the quarries. There were superb causeways, statues of animals, humans and mythical creatures (the best yet to see in Phnom Penh National Museum), the unbelievable bas-reliefs covering vast walls depicting stories of battles and myths, the closed courtyards and cloisters, the vaulted ceilings and galleries, the massive towers, the city walls, the turned stone vertical spindles that decorated the window openings, the wide moats and the monumental gateways. All painted a vivid picture of amazing pomp, grandeur and splendour from a long-ago era. We couldn't stop taking photos, and took over 400 photos that day.

As sunset approached, we climbed a steep hill with hordes of other people to Phnom Bakeng, and those unwilling or unable to climb could pay for a ride up the hill on an elephant. We watched the sun set from the top of the hill, and were incredibly happy that we had visited Angkor. The pain of the three days of cycling receded into the background – not forgotten, but now past. We returned to our guesthouse knowing that we had seen something very special.

We stayed in Siem Reap for several days after we had visited the temples, doing very little apart from enjoying the choice of excellent restaurants; it was a delight to enjoy wonderful food at different restaurants after travelling through Laos and Cambodia. We also spent time reading and relaxing in the hammocks in the gardens of our guesthouse and chatting to the other travellers. My bruised, swollen leg was still very painful, and I wanted to rest it as long as possible before starting cycling again. However, as there were so many beggars in Siem Reap with missing legs or arms, their injuries having been sustained by exploding mines, I felt a fraud complaining because of a bruise that now extended from foot to knee.

Because of the problems we had encountered with the condition of the roads and the dangerous driving of the locals, we knew that we wanted to cycle as little as possible in Cambodia, and I was also concerned whether I could cycle far with my injured leg. We therefore decided to take the boat across the Great Lake to the capital of Phnom Penh instead of cycling.

We set off early one morning to catch the boat. The taxi bus, which was to pick us up from our hotel at 5.45am, didn't arrive until 6.30am, and there were light drops of rain falling as it arrived. The mini bus was already full and so was the roof rack, but the driver shinned up the side of the bus in his bare feet, and Warren passed the bikes to him. He strapped them on top of a pile of rucksacks and car tyres, so at least they were well-cushioned. We somehow managed to fit into the bus, and began the 20 minute journey to the lake. The sealed road changed into a dirt and stone road after a short while. We had passed some pleasant villages, but the further we went the worse the local accommodation looked. The road became narrower and narrower as we approached the lake, and the bus was eventually winding in and out of people, bikes and parked vehicles. Rundown shacks on stilts were on both sides of us, and the water was also on both sides of this approach, which was now only a track. We had to go quite a long way along this track, because it was the dry season.

The Tonle Sap Lake (the Great Lake) is joined to the Mekong River at Phnom Penh by a 100km canal. During the wet season, from mid-May to early October, the level of the Mekong rises. The water backs up the river and the canal into Tonle Sap Lake. The lake swells at this time from 2,500 square kilometres to an incredible 13,000 square kilometres, flooding the surrounding plains and forests. When the dry season begins, the river reverses its flow and drains the lake back into the Mekong River again.

The dirt road we were now travelling on disappeared during the wet season, and the houses on stilts stood in the water. The port moves with the water, but apparently the worst time to take the boat is in May, when the lake has receded so much that there's a large area of dried mud to cross; the first rains make the mud as slippery as ice. It was now 12th January.

The closer we got to the boat, the more squalid became the surroundings. The whole of the track in front of the shacks was heaving with people. The people had to part to allow the bus through, its horn sounding constantly as it slowly made its way to the end of the track. Litter was everywhere, mostly plastic bags, and pigs snuffled through the debris, obviously hoping to find a morsel of food. Tiny children sat naked in the dirt, and older children played at the edge of the water. Most people seemed to be hurrying along, carrying goods, pushing carts with goods, driving motorbikes loaded with goods, but there were many women who just sat in their doorways, their eyes vacant. Despite the fact that the fishing industry in Tonle Sap supports one million people in Cambodia, the air of the place was of terrible poverty. There were obviously far too many people trying to make a living in that small area.

When we alighted from the bus we were besieged by people. Children were pulling our clothes and looking up with begging eyes; women carrying trays full of bread called out to us.

'Madam, madam, sir, sir. Cheese sandwich?' Their calls didn't stop until we were completely out of sight. Fortunately most of the travellers on the bus had not yet had breakfast, so at least the passengers were able to give them their custom.

As we had our bikes and 10 bags to collect, Warren and I were the last to walk the few yards across dirt and rubble to a narrow, steep gangway plank, along which we had to carefully negotiate our way with our loaded bikes. We were directed to a long narrow boat with a walkway about 18" wide around it. There was no railing on the outside. Several passengers sat on the narrow roof, which was the equivalent of sitting on a train or bus roof. There were no seats left inside, so we had to sit on the metal gangway steps. This wouldn't have been so bad if the boat had been cheap, but we had paid $46 between us, which was more than 10 days accommodation in Siem Reap!

The boat set off, being pulled for the first section through the shallow waters. At one stage we were stuck on a sandbank, and the tug had to pull us clear; once we were in deeper water, the boat picked up a little speed leaving the tug behind. We passed fishermen laying nets, a few isolated houses on stilts, and then we were on the open lake and the boat picked up speed, the water spraying high on both sides, and the boat bumping painfully through the waves. The crew closed the door behind me, because a massive wave of water rushed in behind my back, completely swamping the man sitting behind me. Now I had to sit leaning forward, because the door followed the line of the boat, leaning inwards. It wasn't long before the men on top of the boat came down to join us in the tiny hallway area, so we were unbelievably crowded. However, it had obviously been very cold and uncomfortable on the roof. The sky was still grey, threatening rain, and there was a high wind which was producing substantial waves. The boat was moving very fast, bumping hard on the waves. There were now many of us squashed into a tiny area, some sitting on plastic stools, some on the floor. We travelled like this, feeling pretty miserable, whilst other passengers (who had arrived earlier but had paid the same price as us) slept in their seats inside the air-conditioned cabin for the next few hours. It was as though we were on the open sea – nothing was within sight in any direction on this massive lake, except the horizon and occasional distant fishing boats.

We approached a narrower section of the lake, the waves disappeared and floating vegetation was visible on both sides. As the boat entered the channel joining the Mekong and Tonle Sap some of the passengers, refreshed from their sleep in the cabin, came out to clamber over us to get outside to take photographs. The crew allowed those of us without seats to go into the cabin to sit down, and we were annoyed when we found that some girls were sleeping across two seats each, so there should have been some free seats. However, where Warren had been sitting, facing straight down the gangway of the cabin, he had noticed that the whole boat twisted frighteningly as it banged the waves, so on reflection we had probably been safer near the exit. We sat down, and for the last stretch of the four hour boat journey to Phnom Penh we dozed, utterly exhausted.

Complete chaos reigned once we docked, with passengers literally climbing over each other and the luggage area at the back of the boat to fetch their bags. The crew stood blocking the way, offering to help if they were paid money. They wanted $2 to help Warren to carry the bikes off the boat, but as we never like other people handling the bikes anyway, we refused. It was amazing that no-one had been knocked off the narrow walkway round the boat, because there was no room for anyone to pass.

Crowds of taxi-drivers swamped us as we walked up the steps to the quayside, many with placards announcing which hotels or guesthouses they represented. By the time we had put our bags on our bikes the quayside was deserted except for one man, who offered to lead us to a hotel. His main reason for the recommendation was that the hotel offered free beer from 7.30 to 8pm, but we agreed to follow him on his motorbike through the streets. We were surprised and pleased that Phnom Penh was not as busy as we had expected, as we normally don't like cycling in big cities.

Phnom Penh had been the capital of Cambodia since the 15th century after the decline of Angkor, and it was considered an important position for sea trade with China. In the 19th century, the French took control of Cambodia, but independence in 1953 ended French control. In 1975 Phnom Penh surrendered to the Khmer Rouge after years of fighting, after which the entire population of the city and surrounding towns, including the sick, elderly and disabled, were forced to go to the countryside to work in the fields for 12 to 15 hours a day. Anyone who disobeyed faced immediate execution. The Khmer Rouge, under Pol Pot, wanted to turn Cambodia into an agrarian concentration camp worked by peasants. Professionals, teachers, doctors, skilled workers, monks and artists were considered the enemy, and these were the people removed, imprisoned, tortured and executed in the killing fields. Phnom Penh became deserted, and fell into total disrepair, even ruin, over the next few years.

With tourism now on the increase in Cambodia, Phnom Penh is now a mixture of old and new. The beautiful old Royal Palace and Museum buildings contrast with modern new hotels. Unfortunately, many of the elegant old French colonial buildings are now in a terrible state of disrepair. One still had the old sign over the gateway – Cambodian Red Cross. Obviously once an elegant cream-painted building, the tall shuttered windows were now empty holes, and most of the tiles of the now warped roof were missing. Some of these old French buildings are still in use, but on most of them the rich cream painted rendering is badly stained with serious damp and moss, the panelled doors are falling off their hinges, and the roofs and verandahs are in bad repair. The very few French colonial houses that have been renovated, such as two buildings used by UNESCO and an insurance company, looked beautiful.

Wide boulevards lined with trees and kept clean by constantly sweeping cleaning women in uniforms, contrasted with unkempt side streets of dirt with pot-holes filled with bricks and rubble. In these side streets piles of rotting rubbish were heaped at the roadsides, and homeless people slept amongst the piles of coconut shells, fruit peelings, rusty tins and bags of rubbish.

The motorbike driver leading us arrived at the hotel he had recommended, and I looked after the bikes while Warren went to look at the room. Another motorbike driver, one of the many local taxis, was fast asleep laid across the top of his motorbike, his feet on the handlebars, and the motorbike propped up on its stand at the side of the noisy street. Two of the hotel employees chatted to me, both extolling the virtues of the hotel, but majoring on the fact that from 7.30pm until 8pm the beer was free. They explained that the beer was not limited – we could order jugs of beer, ordering the last one at one minute to eight, in order to maximize the quantity of free beer that we could have. I began to realise that it was likely that there'd be hordes of drunken tourists around the hotel because of the free beer, but Warren returned to say that the available rooms were very shabby, they were on the sixth floor, and there was no lift. Because we would have to carry 10 heavy bags up the stairs, this made the decision easy for us, and we cycled off to find another hotel.

We found another one near the Royal Palace, and were happy with the position in a quiet side road. There was no free beer, but the cheaper room was on the ground floor, which meant that our bikes could be wheeled straight into the room complete with bags. As before in Cambodia, this air-conditioned room was padded with no window, but at least that meant it was quiet! The other strange thing we noticed was that on the other side of this road there were garages on the ground floor with apartments built above them. Televisions, beds and armchairs furnished these ground floor garages, and people clearly lived and slept in these large 'rooms'. However, at night-time the car was driven in to join them, and locked behind the double doors! In the mornings when the car was reversed out, the occupants also pushed out a large metal cage on wheels; into this cage the women hung their washing, which was padlocked whilst it stood on the pavement during the daylight hours.

We found an excellent café the next morning for breakfast. It was a bakery, run by a Khmer family who had lived for 12 years in New Zealand running a similar business. They had returned to Phnom Penh to live, and in the pleasant air-conditioned surroundings of the bakery restaurant, mouth-watering cakes, sweet and savoury pastries, different breads and rolls were on display under glass counters. Every item was clearly labelled to explain what it was – apfel strudels, sausage rolls, lemon tarts, chocolate brownies, cheese and bacon baps, profiteroles and cream buns lay side by side looking incredibly foreign to us and temptingly delicious. The fact that the café also served superb coffee made it a very popular meeting-place for westerners. In the corner of the café was the usual shrine – a miniature red and gold temple adorned with lights, decorations and mosaic mirrors. Miniature Buddha images sat looking out of the temple, and incense sticks stood upright in a small bowl of sand. A cup of coffee and a cake on a plate sat in front of the shrine as offerings. Often we saw fruit – a pineapple, a bunch of bananas or a papaya. Sometimes a handful of cigarettes were laid in front of the shrine, or opened beer cans. I often wondered if the cans were full, half full or empty, and what happened to the fruit, the cigarettes and other offerings afterwards?

As we sat having our breakfast, we watched a man who had set up a very tattered old barber's chair on the dirt pavement across the road. Judging from the state of the chair, he had found it on a rubbish tip. He had propped a mirror up on the wall in front of the chair, and beside it on a nail hung a bag with his equipment for shaving or cutting hair. Most of the time he sat in the chair himself, often asleep, but occasionally a passing motorbike stopped, and the driver seated himself in the chair to be shaved or have his hair cut. It reminded us so vividly of India.

We set off to explore the city. Despite the fact that the traffic was not as bad as we had expected it to be, it was still frightening to cross the road on foot – very similar to Vietnam. The American we had met on the road to Siem Reap had warned us that, when crossing the road on foot or driving a vehicle, you should never make eye contact with anyone else. If an accident occurs in Cambodia, even if it wasn't your fault, you could be blamed if it was considered that you had seen the other person. You have to have guts, just step off the pavement and cross, letting traffic weave around you as you go – a difficult concept for a westerner, especially on roads that are several lanes wide. To make matters worse, although in Cambodia the traffic drives on the right, when a motorbike or car or even a bus wants to turn left, the driver turns onto the left side of the road, forcing oncoming traffic to go onto the wrong side of the road around him, and he continues on the wrong side of the road until there's an opening that will allow the vehicle to turn left. This means that you need eyes in the back of your head as well as in the front (though don't let them see that you can see them!), and it also meant that when cycling, vehicles were overtaking us on both sides and in opposite directions.

A cyclo passed us full to overflowing with green bananas. The driver sat in his usual high position behind the seat for the passenger, but his feet weren't turning the pedals. A motorbike drove alongside him, and the motorbike driver kept his foot on the cyclo, pushing it along. A motorbike went by in the very busy rush hour traffic with a small trailer loaded so high around and behind him with plastic containers that it was the size and shape of a Luton van. Tuk-tuks passed us, water dripping on the ground as they passed. They always carried a plastic container of water with a tube attached, so that water dripped out of the tube onto the engine to cool it. A motorbike went by with three Buddhist monks on the back as passengers; they sat side-saddle in opposite directions with flip-flops dangling unconcernedly from their toes a few inches from the ground.

One morning I rose early and walked to the Mekong River to take photos of the sunrise. Men were just beginning to stir from their sleep in their cyclos, which they had covered with pieces of polythene in case it rained during the night. The area in front of the Royal Palace was teeming with local people. There was no sign of any tourists. Hundreds of individual food stalls were set up supplying locals with breakfast; an elephant was being fed giant bunches of bananas on the street; women were arranging lotus buds into bunches ready to sell for offerings; fishing boats were still out on the river; children were defecating in the river, and dogs were lying under the tables in the hope of a dropped morsel of food. One-legged beggars put out their hands as I passed, and Buddhist monks went by in twos and threes carrying their alms bowls in one hand and raised lemon-coloured umbrellas in the other, even though the sun was not yet hot. The sun rose, a perfect orange ball, and I returned to the guesthouse to have breakfast.

Because Phnom Penh has plenty of western tourists, there is an abundance of good restaurants, so once again we enjoyed a good choice of food. Unfortunately, Cambodia is much more expensive than Vietnam, Thailand or Laos – a 650ml bottle of beer cost the equivalent of more than £1, compared to 70p in Thailand, 28p in Vietnam and 50p in Laos. French table wine was available, but at extortionate prices, so we reserved wine for special occasions. Whisky seemed to be the alcoholic drink that was always cheap in comparison, as it had been in India. At least ice was safe to add to drinks in Cambodia, because many years before the French had set up special factories for ice-making.

We found a restaurant that had been set up to help the children of Phnom Penh. As well as all profits going to the children, the children were trained as chefs and waiters in the restaurant. The food was excellent, the atmosphere superb, and the restaurant was always full. Everyone was pleased to be able to do something constructive to help the locals, rather than just handing over money to beggars. Also in the city were establishments to train the blind and disabled, and massage centres had been set up in the tourist areas called 'Seeing Hands', where every masseur or masseuse was blind.

We stayed a few days in Phnom Penh, but made the decision that we didn't want to visit the Killing Fields or the museum in Phnom Penh that had been a place of imprisonment and torture. The manager of our guesthouse had been surprised that we hadn't visited these tourist places, saying that most tourists wanted to see them. Mass graves are in the prison grounds, and there are dozens of rooms with photos floor to ceiling of everyone who 'passed through' the prison, sometimes showing photos of them before and after torture. The guide-books said a visit was a depressing experience, but we knew that we would find it terribly upsetting. 17,000 of the men, women and children in the prison had been taken to the killing fields. We read that more than 8,000 skulls, arranged by sex and age, were on display there behind glass, after the remains had been exhumed from some of the mass graves. We couldn't imagine why anyone would want to visit such a display, and I imagined that it must be unbearable for relatives of anyone who died in the killing fields to know that such a display existed.

We decided to continue our journey by bus to the south coast, even though we were told that the state of the road was good. There were two roads to the south coast – the old one and the new one. The old one was more likely to have accommodation, but we were told that the road surface was as bad as the one we had already cycled on in Cambodia – there was no way we wanted to experience such a road again, especially as I was still suffering with my bruised leg. We were told that the new road had a good surface, but that it was a very dangerous road, with maniacs speeding and overtaking each other, with constant accidents. We really didn't want to spend three days cycling along such a road, especially as we were told that there was very little accommodation along that route. The bus was the only other option.

We cycled to the bus station early one morning, and the bus driver opened up the underneath of the bus for us to put in the bikes. It was an open hole with a spare tyre and the cap for refuelling. We could see the road beneath. After Warren had crawled in to put the bikes in on their sides, he was covered in dirt and grease – his head, arms and clothes. The front wheels of the bikes had been removed and were placed in another compartment with some bags under the bus. We were concerned about the bikes, and would happily have paid full fare for each bike if they would have allowed them inside the bus, but apparently every bus that left Phnom Penh to Sihanoukville, a seaside resort on the south coast, was full. We added our bags to the pile that blocked the emergency exit inside the bus, and the bus set off, stopping half a minute later to refuel at a service station, which probably ensured that our bikes were now covered with diesel.

Our decision to travel by bus was justified as we travelled along. The scenery was boring with very little to see; we saw no hotels or guest houses en route, and vehicles constantly overtook each other dangerously on the single carriageway road, their horns blaring; we constantly cringed as we saw cars racing towards the bus, seemingly determined to commit suicide.

We arrived in Sihanoukville on time four hours later, but the bus stopped every few hundred yards so that locals could alight outside their homes. We watched the door to the baggage compartment below our window being opened, and several bags and our front wheels were removed every time and placed in the middle of the road, while the passenger pulled out his bags from the back of the compartment. We eventually arrived at the bus station, managed to put the bikes together again, much to the enjoyment of a crowd of teenagers, and cycled off to Serendipity Beach to find a room close to the beach.

We had been told by so many Cambodians how wonderful the beach was at Sihanoukville, that we were very disappointed when we saw it. A narrow crescent of sand, disappointingly with quite a lot of rubbish on it, was lined with old-fashioned deckchairs and small tables. These chairs and tables belonged to the many cafés along the beach. A stiff breeze made the beach comfortably cool, but it was so strong that reading a book or menu was a struggle. The water looked clear and safe, and islands could be seen just off the end of the crescent. Trees lined the beach, but it was very busy. There were children everywhere – they carried sarongs for sale or had large flat baskets full of fruit on their heads – even the youngest of children could efficiently peel and chop tropical fruits to prepare a delicious fruit salad for the tourists. Some children carried crisps and biscuits in baskets on their heads, and others wandered round the beach collecting empty cans or bottles in large plastic bags – they hovered around the tourists, waiting for the last of the beer to be poured, hoping to get the empty cans. The children were very confident and loved to chat in their excellent English, but it was disconcerting that, for the first time ever, children stood watching us eat, and if we left anything on our plates they asked if they could have it – a piece of baguette, some left over salad, or a few chips. These children lived on the streets, and made a living as well as they could, but most were aged only about 10 years old. I noticed with concern that pretty girls, aged only 12 or 13, surrounded the single western men, stroking their arms and sitting on the edges of their chairs. Cows walked onto the beach, and for a moment I thought I was back in India. However, I think for beautiful beaches we had already been spoiled by seeing those wonderful ones in India, Sri Lanka and Australia.

We went on a boat trip to a nearby island. We were able to snorkel over the reef in the shallow clear waters, but we were warned not to touch the long-spined urchins on the sea bed. This was the first time that Warren and I had worn swimsuits since Australia, so we looked like piebald ponies with our very dark tanned legs and arms and white bodies. It was wonderful just to lie on the beach with only three other couples and the sound of the waves. We had a barbecue on the beach, the crew having cooked fish, meat and baked potatoes for us while we were swimming. After a very relaxing afternoon of reading, swimming and chatting, we returned on the boat while the organiser, a New Zealander, prepared a dessert of fresh fruit salad for us.

We chatted in the bar that evening with Suzanna, an Australian girl, and she told us about her experience of getting to Sihanoukville; it made us realise how much easier it was just to travel by bicycle. She had gone to Phnom Penh the day before she travelled to Sihanoukville to buy a bus ticket to ensure that she booked a seat near the front of the bus. She arrived at the bus stop the next day half an hour early, but because she wanted to get off the bus before the terminus, she asked that her bag went into the baggage compartment last (obviously none of the locals had considered that idea on our bus!). By the time she got on the bus, having watched that her bag was put in last, the bus was full, and a Buddhist monk was sitting in her seat. (In practice, although we all had tickets with seat numbers on, these numbers are disregarded by the locals). The monk would not have even paid for a ticket, but the bus driver refused to let her past and refused to ask him to move, but indicated a very narrow seat next to the driver. She was unhappy with this seat for a four hour journey, but eventually agreed to sit there – too late! Someone had been sold a last minute ticket and had pushed their way past her and was now sitting in it. She would have to catch the next bus several hours later, she was told. She got off the bus, but before she could collect her bag the bus had set off, with Suzanna running alongside to attract the driver's attention. He grudgingly stopped, opened the compartment, threw her bag onto the ground in the middle of the road and continued his journey.

She got her money back from the bus company and now decided to take a shared taxi rather than wait for the next bus. Knowing how over-crowded the local taxis usually were, she agreed to pay the taxi-driver four times the normal price in order to be one of only three people on the back seat. A westerner and an elderly Cambodian lady joined her in the back and they set off, the taxi soon stopping for a man with two children aged about 10 and 12 years old. The man sat on the front passenger seat with his two children on his lap. The taxi stopped again for a westerner, but when offered the hand-brake between the two front seats, the westerner shook his head. The taxi-driver didn't want to lose a fare, and knew he couldn't put any more people in the back because Suzanna had paid extra, so he dragged the Cambodian woman out of the back, put her on the hand-brake, and the westerner had a comfortable seat in the back. They continued for a short while, the taxi now well overloaded. In the boot of the car were sacks of rice, a box of car spare parts, a crate of noisy roosters, and the luggage from everyone in the car. The boot lid wouldn't shut, and constantly banged up and down. Suzanna couldn't believe it when the taxi stopped for another passenger, and the man now wanting a lift was carrying two live ducks, tied together and being carried upside down by their feet. She told the driver there were too many people, but the taxi driver spoke very soothingly to her.

'Don't worry – I am an experienced driver,' he said, and with that he took the ducks, stuffed them down a narrow gap in the boot as you would a towel or a sweater, and got back into the driving seat with the eighth passenger on his lap!

So now there were only three people in the back, as agreed, but five passengers in the front! Suzanna said that she had read in the guide books, as we had, that Cambodian drivers were 'visually-challenged psychopaths', and she hadn't been able to understand this, having only experienced the driving in the towns. Warren and I, on the other hand, had already had our three days of experience of the Cambodian roads. Now she understood – the driver, along with every other driver on the road, was on a mission to overtake everything, regardless of whether something was overtaking in the opposite direction or not. They were shooting past vehicles with inches to spare before the vehicles from the opposite direction hit them. Suzanna was carrying two cow bells that she'd bought as souvenirs, and the clanging of these bells combined with the frantic noise of the roosters, the muffled quacks of the ducks in the boot and the banging of the car boot lid accompanied them for the whole journey!

We had some very nice meals while we were in Sihanoukville, especially fresh fish caught locally, but some of the standards were quite laughable. A meal was brought to Warren with a baked potato on the plate.

'I ordered chips,' said Warren.

'What? You don't want this?' asked the waiter, picking up the potato. When Warren repeated that he had ordered chips, the waiter carried the potato back to the kitchen in his hand! The next day I had barbecued fish and a baked potato, but I discovered that the potato was not fully cooked. I told the waiter the potato was still hard, so he leaned across the table and squeezed it with his fingers.

Without thinking, I immediately slapped the back of his hand hard and said indignantly, 'Well, I certainly don't want that one now!' The waiter leapt back several feet in fright.

'You want to change your meal?' he asked.

As Warren and I often said, it was probably best that we didn't know what happened in the kitchens ... Interestingly, we had noticed that in Thailand and all of the countries in Indochina none of the locals ate rice with chopsticks, as we attempt to do in Thai restaurants back home. A spoon and fork is supplied for rice, although noodles are usually eaten with chopsticks. A spoon and chopsticks are supplied together if noodle soup is ordered.

We considered going on a boat trip – it took tourists by boat to a nearby National Park, and after a half hour's walk through the jungle the tourists visited a local village. This sounded very interesting, but then we heard bad reports from several westerners who had done this trip. They said that the Cambodians who were leading the tourists had tried to leave rubbish on the beach after the lunchtime barbecue. The westerners wouldn't allow them, insisting that the rubbish (mostly water bottles and cans) should be put into a bag and removed. As they walked through the jungle to the village, they noticed that the Cambodians were throwing the bottles one by one into the bushes as they walked. When they got to the local village in the jungle which was alongside a lake, the westerners wondered why they had bothered. It could have been so idyllic, except that the ground around and under the thatched houses on stilts and in front of the lake was completely covered with rubbish, and the smell was atrocious. We decided not to bother with that rather expensive trip.

We found a smart restaurant run by English people, and treated ourselves one evening to fillet steak. I had blue cheese sauce with mine – blue cheese sauce! I hadn't tasted blue cheese since France. I asked the owner if they had a problem getting blue cheese, and was told that it was available in Phnom Penh, together with smoked ham and Feta cheese. They couldn't get the locals to eat it because of the bad smell, the owner said. We thought that this was extraordinary considering that the locals eat durian, a local fruit with a smell like rotting flesh – it's green and spiky on the outside, with a delicious soft milky flesh that smells so disgusting that no-one is allowed to take durian into hotels – definitely, like blue cheese, an acquired taste. However, despite the fact that we thoroughly enjoyed our western meal, we were enjoying Cambodian, or Khmer, food as well. Luk-Lak was our favourite local dish – cubes or slices of beef stir-fried and served in a delicious brown sauce on rice and usually topped with a fried egg. Fish Amok was another delicious Cambodian speciality, which was a fish curry made with coconut milk.

A group of local businessmen sat at the next table to us, and were chatting to the owner of the restaurant. The owner was explaining how he wanted to extend the premises, but had not been able to obtain permission.

'How much did you pay?' asked one of the business men. We knew he meant as a bribe, not to have the work done.

'Not much,' replied the restaurant owner.

'Leave it to me. I'll sort something out for you,' said the businessman. No doubt a bigger bribe would solve the problem . . .

The week became very busy, because Chinese New Year was being celebrated – locals were dressed as Chinese dragons dancing round poles. It was 22nd January 2004, the year of the monkey, and as I was born in the year of the monkey it seemed a good excuse to celebrate with a bottle of wine! The weekend afterwards was incredibly busy on the beach. The part of the beach that the westerners frequented was kept fairly clean, some of the restaurants meticulously keeping the area around their restaurants clean and tidy. However, when we walked further along the beach, where it was busy with locals, it was unbelievable how much rubbish had been left on the beach and under the tables and chairs in the beach restaurants.

We saw local families arriving on motorbikes. Just as a baby automatically grips a finger put within its palm straight after birth, as soon as a Cambodian baby can sit or stand it will grip the handlebars of its father's motorbike, so that it can be transported sitting or standing on the fuel tank in front of the driver, who might often be its 10 or 12 year old brother or sister, with another two or three of the family behind the driver.

We sat chatting to an Australian girl in one of the beach bars one evening. She disappeared to the loo, returning to say, 'Thank the French for the bread and the western toilets here.'

'Western toilets?' I replied in an astonished voice. 'There are more Asian toilets in France than there are in Asia.'

A pretty girl who was standing next to us with her husband turned and laughed, saying she'd thought the same as soon as French toilets had been mentioned.

'We're on our way to live in Australia,' she said, indicating the Australian man beside her. She was English and they were recently married. 'I'm going to meet my mother-in-law for the first time,' she said, with the nails of both hands to her teeth in mock terror.

She told us that they had packed everything they wanted to take to Australia into a 100 cubic feet box. There couldn't have been much room after her husband had packed his five bicycles, so Warren and he had lots to talk about. Instead of wedding presents, friends and family had given them money in different currencies, because they intended to take six months to follow their box of belongings to Australia. They had already travelled through Russia and China.

As we walked back to our guesthouse, a very new moon was hanging in the sky – a perfect smile, exactly like the one we'd seen in Goa just over a year before. It just didn't seem possible that it was 19 months since we had first set off with our bikes from Dover to Calais. We had been able to buy a special 60 day visa from the Thai embassy in Phnom Penh, and in two days time we planned to catch the boat to take us to the border of Thailand. We would have 60 days to cycle in

Thailand before having to arrange for more visas, so were looking forward to the wonderful beaches and islands that we'd heard about . . .

The road from Sihanoukville in Cambodia to Thailand was apparently very scenic, going up and down over hills and valleys. However, we had been told that the road was dirt all the way, and we'd had enough of Cambodian dirt roads. There was also no accommodation en route, and there were four rivers to cross by ferry. It therefore seemed sensible to take the only alternative route, which was by sea.

The four hour ferry ran from Sihanoukville to Krong Koh Kong, still in Cambodia but only 10km from the border with Thailand. We weren't going to make the same mistake as we had taking the last ferry, arriving last and having no seat, so we were the first to arrive one and a half hours before the boat set off, and took the best seats. It was a larger boat than before, and we understood from the guide books that no-one was allowed on the roof on this trip. The reason for this was that the boat was a river boat and, as such, was not really suitable for travelling on the open sea (despite the fact that that was where it was going!). The waves could therefore be especially dangerous for anyone sitting on the roof.

Despite the rules, by the time the boat set off there were almost as many people on the roof as inside the cabin, which was now full. Metal steps went up onto the 18" wide 'deck' on both sides, but luggage was piled on one side blocking one of the two exits, and a Cambodian woman clambered over the rucksacks and settled down to sleep on top of them. The rest of everyone's luggage was on top of the boat with the other passengers, and at the last minute rows of men marched onto the boat with full sacks on their shoulders, which were stacked at the front of the boat. There were sacks of vegetables, bananas and rice, obviously destined for markets, shops and restaurants.

After a couple of hours the boat pulled into a port. None of us (the westerners) knew where we were, and there was no mention on the ticket that there would be a stop, but the locals obviously knew about it because some of them disembarked, and girls came onto the boat to sell food. Even more luggage was stacked on the front of the boat before we set off. Two more hours passed, and we approached Krong Ko Kong. The quayside was so full of locals waiting to offer motorbike rides or rides in trucks that it seemed certain that somebody would be pushed over the edge in the crush. When we got outside the cabin, there was no gangway set up, and we had to jump over a wide gap onto the quayside several feet higher than the boat. None of the locals helped. The scene was just utter noisy chaos as they all shouted at the top of their voices.

'Ma'am, ma'am, mo' bi'? Mo'bi?' they shouted, offering us a moto, the name for the Cambodian motor bike taxi.

'Thailand? Thailand?' shouted those hoping to take us the 10km trip to the Thai border.

I was frightened that I would be pushed backwards into the water between the quayside and the boat, but Warren pulled me through the shouting crowds. Even when we said 'No' to them they followed through the crowds, offering hotel accommodation, taxi or moto. They just wouldn't listen to us when we told them that we knew where we wanted to stay (we had checked the guide books) and that we had transport. It was incredibly frightening. I noticed one westerner standing on top of one of the trucks, his camera clicking away as he pointed it at the chaotic crowds.

'This is fantastic,' he shouted. 'No-one back home would believe such pandemonium if they didn't see the photos!'

By the time Warren had fought his way through the crowd with our two bikes and 10 bags, we were the last to leave, but still they wouldn't leave us alone. We were surrounded by the last dozen or so locals who were desperate for business. We knew we had only a few yards to cycle to a hotel round the corner, but they were riding their motorbikes slowly alongside us, still offering to take us elsewhere (to make commission on the introduction). They accompanied us to the entrance of the hotel. We passed two Frenchmen, walking along the road to the same hotel, and seven motorbikes surrounded them, driving at walking pace. The moto drivers were obviously hoping to tell the hotel owner that they had brought the tourists to his hotel – any commission would be added to the hotel bill and be paid by the tourist, just as in India. The two Frenchmen were the only guests at the hotel apart from us until ten minutes later, when several motorbikes arrived with passengers from the boat. It appears that they had been driven along the more expensive 'tourist route'!

The prices of the hotel and on every menu and in every shop in the town were in Thai baht, despite the fact that we were still in Cambodia. Dollars were also acceptable. We wanted to use up our remaining local currency, but when we asked a restaurant owner at breakfast the next morning how much the bill was in Cambodian riel, he looked horrified. He obviously didn't want any of the local currency . . .

CHAPTER 20

THAILAND AGAIN

We set off for Thailand, cycling over the new bridge which had been built by the Thai military. It was 1.9km long, and after another 8km we were at the Thai border. As always, the border was chaos, with no signs to point anyone in the right direction, but eventually we had our Cambodian visas cancelled, and a new Thai stamp in our passports. On the Cambodian side of the border was a tiny white-painted hut, not even as big as the average garden shed, with a sign under the corrugated roof saying 'Customs and Excise'. The whole building leaned precariously to one side, and a uniformed man sat outside the empty building – was he too scared to sit inside? He was presumably waiting for custom.

We planned to cycle hugging the coastline round the Gulf of Thailand, and we knew that we had to spend several days in busy traffic as we passed south of Bangkok. After that we would begin to travel south down the east coast of Thailand which faced the Gulf of Thailand, where we hoped to visit some of the beautiful Thai islands. Our plans after that were to cross over to the west coast and travel south to Malaysia.

We were now cycling on the left again. As soon as we entered Thailand, the road went up and down like a switchback. After a period of not cycling in Cambodia, we found it hard work; the day was overcast, but the temperature was 30° and humid, despite the fact that this was one of the coolest months of the year. We wondered how we would manage cycling in south-east Asia and Indonesia until the end of August, when we had a flight booked from Bali to Perth in Western Australia. It was now 30th January, 2004.

We passed a sign announcing the narrowest part of Thailand, so we took a photograph of ourselves and our bicycles with the sign in the background. At that point, Thailand is a narrow strip only a few hundred metres wide between the sea and the Cambodian border on the top of the hill to our right. We turned off when we saw a sign to a beach resort. The price was incredibly expensive for Thailand

– 500 baht, nearly £7 – but we had an air-conditioned chalet on the beach with palm trees, which looked out over Ko Chang, an island in the distance. We were the only people staying in the resort. We walked along the beach, and in the shade of the palm trees several men were making a boat by hand. The hardwood rib-cage was hand-carved, and planks of hardwood were being fitted to it with wooden pegs. We watched the sun set behind Ko Chang, and we saw no other people on the beach or in the resort until the evening, when a man arrived by motorbike with his girl-friend. He waded into the sea-water lake behind the chalets with a powerful torch on his head. The water was less than knee-deep, and he carried a thin bamboo stick. The end of it was split into 5 or 6 prongs, and he used this to spear shrimps, rarely missing. Within half an hour he had filled a bucket hanging from his shoulder, and he and his girl-friend disappeared back down the track on his motorbike.

In the night it rained heavily, so when we set off in the morning it was cooler than usual. We passed fields where tables were set up in rows, the tops covered with mesh. Tiny fish had been laid out to dry on these trestle tables, and the workers waved as we passed. Further on the colour of the fish changed from silver to pink, and as we slowed and drew closer we could see that these were flattened squid, graded into sizes. A transvestite (or lady boy, as they are called in Thailand) approached and called out 'hello' in a falsetto voice. He was wearing a white lacy negligee, which looked quite bizarre – he hadn't yet put on his wig or makeup.

We found again that very few people spoke English; this was not a tourist area, but we were beginning to feel more comfortable with some Thai words, and when we said 'Thao rai?' ('How much?'), we were quite pleased that we could usually understand the reply. We arrived at Trat, an unprepossessing large town which sees a number of tourists, but only because passengers need to change buses in Trat on their way from Bangkok to Cambodia.

The night market was the main place for eating; dozens of stalls sold food, each one selling different dishes. There were barbecued corns on the cob, pieces of meat on sticks, balls of meat on sticks, ready-prepared fruit to take away, ready-made Thai curries, prawns, hard-boiled eggs, sausages, cooked ducks and large pork joints, squid, crabs, octopus, prawns, fish, tuna steaks, noodles, rice, pancakes, fried rice and parcels of food cooked in banana leaves. Some stalls sold only sweets and puddings; some had fish and meat ready to cook, but most meals were ready-cooked and being sold for 15p to 30p per portion. The hot food was ladled into polythene bags to take away or to be eaten at the plastic tables and chairs in the middle of the market.

Because of the Avian 'flu that was so prevalent in Thailand at that time, most chickens had been removed from sale, although eggs were still available. We didn't know where the eggs came from. Sorry, we know where eggs come from, but if the chickens had been slaughtered where had they come from? The Thai papers mentioned that the 'flu was probably spreading because owners were smuggling their beloved fighting cocks outside of the 'red' areas. The owners would receive no compensation for a fighting cock that had to be slaughtered because of the 'flu, but because of its considerable value to the owner they were willing to take risks.

Judging from the vast number of stalls, and the enormous number of locals buying food, very few Thais cooked food at home. We saw only three other westerners. One stall-holder had cleverly written up a sign saying 'English menu', so we were able to choose from 40 different dishes, and ate prawn tempura and crispy pork with Chinese broccoli in oyster sauce, which was delicious. At 40 baht each they were probably the most expensive meals in the market, but at 53p a bargain for us! With a large bottle of icy cold beer costing another 40 baht we were well pleased, and we walked back to the hotel with some fresh pineapple cubes on sticks, which we ate after dipping each cube into delicious pink chilli sugar (sugar and red chilli crushed together with a pestle and mortar).

The next day we went to the market at lunch time, but were disappointed to find it was closed. Women wearing orange fluorescent vests, hats made of bamboo, and scarves covering their hair, neck and shoulders, were cleaning the rubbish. We noticed that KFC was in the town and still open, despite the chicken crisis – hopefully their meat was imported. The indoor market was open, where stalls were full of whole pigs' heads, dark as though smoked. The heads were flat, having had the bones removed, but the ears and snout were still intact with holes where the eyes had once been. Stalls were full of household goods, even selling toilet paper, a commodity not used by most Thais. I found it amusing to see the make of one – 'Sit and Smile'.

We found a quiet bar down a back street – it was empty, and a girl sat behind the tall counter, only the top of her head showing. We looked over the counter – she was breast-feeding her baby. Warren asked in Thai for a beer and two glasses, but was disappointed that he didn't know how to say 'whenever you're ready'.

After we had left Trat, we cycled past stalls stood at the side of the road selling hats in different shapes made of bamboo and grasses which had been varnished. We went through areas of cultivated bamboo, and also saw (and smelt) more of the drying fish on trestles. After just over 40km we arrived at a ferry, where we planned to cross to the island of Ko Chang, a mountainous island with several waterfalls and rainforest. The ferry was an open boat, which was fortunate, because the large four wheel drive vehicles kept their engines running, so that the drivers could sleep or read in their air-conditioned boxes – fine for them, but not for those of us on deck, spending half an hour breathing in exhaust fumes.

Ko Chang is the second largest island in Thailand, although it's only 24km by

15km. It's very mountainous for such a small island, its highest point being 744 metres. The island is green, the mountains are covered with jungle, and the whole of the west coast is lined with beaches. It forms one of a group of 47 islands that have been awarded National Park status, due to the pristine rain forests and marine life. During the rainy season there are impressive waterfalls inland, and activities for tourists include hill trekking, elephant jungle-trekking, sailing, kayaking and water sports, and the area is a major diving centre for diving and snorkelling.

Once off the ferry we had to negotiate a steep mountain to get to the west coast on the other side of the island where the beaches were. The gradient of the mountain was impossible to cycle, and in the heat I found it almost impossible even to push the bikes. Where there were bends the road seemed to be almost vertical and very dangerous. Trucks passed us with tourists hanging out of the back, but even they crawled up the hill. We regretted not hiring a truck to take our bikes. At one point two motorbikes passed us towing a man in a wheelchair. They were approaching the top of the hill, and we wondered how they would stop him going too fast down the other side? We reached the summit, and we sped down the hill at full speed, the brakes making the wheels so hot that they couldn't be touched when we stopped. There was no sign of the wheelchair, so we assumed that he had safely negotiated the downhill stretch of the road.

We arrived at one resort, but I was disgusted by the standard of the beach huts for the price. For 350 baht there was a bamboo windowless room on stilts 2 metres square. The walls and the thatched ceiling didn't meet, so mosquitoes could come and go as they pleased. A double mattress on the floor virtually filled the room, and a mosquito net was the only other feature. For 500 baht a similar room had a tiny concrete room attached with shower and squat toilet. There were more mosquitoes sitting on the mosquito net than I'd ever seen in my life before, and I decided to look elsewhere, especially when they told me that air-conditioned units were available for 2,000 baht (£27, extremely expensive for a room in Thailand). Further down the road were solidly built chalets on stilts behind a restaurant, each with a verandah with a table and four chairs. Inside was fairly dismal, but a palace compared with the other resort. An iron bedstead with mattress was the only furniture, but there was room for our bikes, and the three windows had mosquito screens. A broken door led to the large tiled bathroom which was permanently wet because the shower leaked, but there was plenty of cool water for showers, and we certainly needed them after cycling over the mountain! The price was 350 baht. We discovered later that food in the attached restaurant was excellent, so we were pleased with our choice, and we spent a few days relaxing in Ko Chang. We sat on our verandah each evening with cold beers, the jungle-clad mountain soaring almost vertically behind us, and a constant sea breeze keeping the high temperatures comfortable. Because Ko Chang was geared to tourists, there were good restaurants and bars on or close to the beach.

The room didn't include the usual towels, glasses, soap or bottled water that we had become accustomed to in Thai hotels, but we had our own mosquito net and settled under that with our silk sleeping bag liner as a sheet. It rained in the night, so we were pleased to be in a solid chalet and not in a bamboo hut which might leak.

A group of Thais moved into the chalet next to us, and we saw 10 of them coming out of the room onto the verandah at breakfast time – they obviously had a bargain by dividing the cost of the room between ten adults! The cost of accommodation in Thailand was always per room, not per person. We later met a hotel owner who refused to let rooms to Thais because they always overfilled the rooms in this way, causing a lot of extra cleaning work.

After a few days of relaxation we set off cycling again, having caught the ferry back to the mainland. We found ourselves amongst plantations of rubber trees, their trunks cut with diagonal lines, the white rubber solution running down the grooves into the half coconut shells strapped to the trunks. Nearby fields were full of new rubber trees, still very small with only a few leaves. Beneath the new trees, lines of pineapples had been planted, many of them with deep pink and green spiky leaves, with the rarer red pineapple fruit beginning to emerge above the clumps of leaves. Once the trees became established with a canopy of leaves casting shade on the ground, the rubber trees would no longer be under-planted with fruit. Hemp grew in many fields, and we passed a number of small garden nurseries. Everything was very green and lush, and we entered an area full of fruit trees. The trees were heavily laden with mangoes, the fruits set off by the luxuriant glossy green foliage. The fruits were pale green, dark green, apricot or yellow, and I noticed that they were on stalks so long that the mangoes appeared to be hanging from the branches on long lengths of green string.

Two small trucks passed us, laden to overflowing with pineapples, and the air was thick with the delicious scent of the fruit long after the trucks had disappeared into the distance. On either side of the road giant jackfruits were hanging close to the trunks of the jackfruit trees, their knobbly green skin encasing the golden segments of rubbery fruit. Sometimes the fruit hung so low it rested on the ground. The fruit of the jackfruit, the largest tree-growing fruit in the world, can weigh up to 36 kg. Even a tree only 10 cm across can have these huge fruits growing on it. Durian fruit was also growing on trees, smaller and pricklier than the jackfruit, but much prized for its tasty but foul-smelling fruit. There were many other fruits and nuts we didn't recognize and, of course, there were the common fruits – the untidy banana plant with its extraordinary large purple flower at the end of the bunch of bananas, the stem turned 180° with the weight of the fruit, so that the bananas grew 'upside down'. Once the bananas ripen and have been harvested, the shoot bearing the fruit has to be cut right out, so that new shoots emerge from the ground, otherwise the plant dies back. There were papayas, with their delicious orange flesh encased in large green-skinned fruits, clustered around the bare skinny stem of the tree, and the coconut palms, tall and resplendent, with bunches of large green-skinned coconuts hanging high above the ground.

We arrived at Chanthaburi and were pleased to find a smart new hotel by the river. Our room and bathroom, for the same price as the previous day in Ko Chang, was very pleasant, clean and air-conditioned with good quality furniture and an elegant cut-glass lamp by the television. We were on the fourth floor, and had a balcony with arched roof overlooking the river. In the hotel gardens was a restaurant on decking by the river. We decided to stay a couple of days.

The day we left the chef hadn't turned up, so we didn't get breakfast at the hotel. We turned off the main road, hoping to stay close to the beaches. We passed a large poster announcing 'Happy New Year 2547' in Thai and English. 2547 is the Buddhist year, well ahead of the Christian one.

We stopped at a café and asked for a coffee. The owner spoke a little English.

'Do you speak Thailand?' he asked, because we had spoken in Thai.

He pulled up a chair to our table and chatted, practising his few words of English. It was rather a concern to me to find I was beginning to like the strange coffee that the Thais made, adding both dried milk and condensed milk to the instant coffee mix, and they always served a glass of Chinese tea alongside as well at no extra cost.

We had turned off the main road, hoping to keep as close to the sea on our left as possible. We found a deserted beach resort, where the cheapest rooms were 750 baht – horribly expensive. We asked at a smart hotel further on, and were amazed to be told that rooms ranged from 1,100 to 4,000 baht. We were hoping to find something for 200 baht! We eventually found another resort where we were able to get the price reduced to 600, but it seemed strange to be the only people in the resort and on the beach. We had hoped that these out-of-the-way places, away from western tourists, would be cheap, but we were finding exactly the opposite. Obviously a room on the beach will usually be more expensive than in a town, but the last few days were stretching our budget badly.

We continued the next day, passing over bridges below which were houses on stilts leaning over the river bank. Locals sat on the decks and in the fishing boats, and waved to us as we passed. We kept losing our way, because we were away from the main road, but very few people spoke English, and the signs were in Thai script. We stood by the roadside poring over our map, when a truck with three men stopped to help us. One of them spoke English.

'Turn right, then after 7km turn right again, then left,' he said in fluent English.

We set off, and so did they – at 12 mph behind us. After 5 miles I stopped to take a photo of a temple, and they tumbled out of the truck again, repeated the directions, and left us.

We stopped at a small café for a cold drink. The owner was asleep stretched out on a bench, so we helped ourselves to drinks from the fridge, opened them, took straws, and sat down. He woke before we had finished and came over to us with his hands in prayer gesture.

'Sawasdee,' he said, so we said and did the same. At only 10p for two bottles of Coke, we were hopeful that cheaper days were coming, or maybe he just hadn't realised that it was usual to charge westerners higher prices than the locals!

We arrived at the junction to the main road, where traffic sped by on six lanes on both sides. However, there was a wide hard shoulder where we could cycle safely, and the road surfaces were usually very good in Thailand. The only problem was that the motorbikes (and sometimes the cars) drove on the hard shoulder going the wrong way in order to get to a turning just down the road, which was very disconcerting. It was very hot on the road, over 30°C, but it wasn't far to Klaeng, where we found a very cheap local hotel. At last, a hotel for 200 baht! In this town there were only the local small cafés with pre-prepared food. We were amused to see outside one of them a small truck laden down with giant blocks of ice. The back axle was almost flat on the ground with the wheels literally splaying out; the doors were all missing, and the seats were falling apart. Thai vehicles went from one extreme to another – there were vehicles like this one, falling apart, and also expensive four wheel drive cars; there were Indian-style painted lorries with one seat but no doors, but also modern trucks with tinted windows.

On the way out of the town the next morning we passed a Chinese temple, one of many we had seen in the area. They were always painted in red and gold, blue and green, with dragons peering round the buildings, their long talons clinging to the colourfully painted columns at the entrance.

A dog was sniffing by the grass verge, and jumped dramatically as I passed. He hadn't heard me coming, and tried to run off fast, but his feet couldn't get a purchase on the loose dirt, and for a few seconds he ran on the spot before his front feet reached the grass and he shot away. I cycled on laughing out loud at the dog's cartoon-like actions. There were many dogs in Thailand, and a lot of them were fairly aggressive to us, barking and chasing us as we cycled by. However, by that time I had perfected a loud growl, which so far had worked wonderfully, the dogs turning tail and running away. Unfortunately a lot of these half wild dogs were mangy and in very poor condition – indeed, we saw numerous dogs with no fur at all, their bare skin looking quite horrible. On the other hand, many Thai people keep dogs, and these were usually in very good condition.

We passed a few garden nurseries, where pots stood with bougainvillea bushes. Each plant had several branches of a different colour – red, pink, white, purple, yellow and orange. Even more impressive were the bougainvilleas that had been trained up a coiled wire, the top a stunning topiary of a dragon's head – the whole plant was a purple flowering dragon, and we had seen such displays in the entrances of hotels.

We arrived in Rayong, a large town with international shops and restaurants like MacDonalds, a Tesco store, KFC and Pizza Company, all grouped in one area. The rest of the town had the usual cheap cafés. We could find only one hotel, and were surprised that we had to pay 600 baht in such a non-tourist town, but the room was very luxurious.

Walking around the town it was obvious that Valentines' Day was approaching. Everywhere were shops and stalls full of red Valentines Day presents – fluffy red heart-shaped cushions edged with white, with 'I love you' written on the cushion in English, but occasionally in Thai. Large red heart-shaped balloons, soft toys holding red hearts, artificial red roses galore, red cut-out cupids hanging on strings, heart-shaped clocks, and heart-shaped boxes of sweets or artificial flowers. The florists were busy making enormous Valentine's displays with real red roses and bouquets with red bows and ribbons.

We had been having a problem finding food that suited us in the non-tourist areas. Every meal seemed to be made with so many chillies that our mouths were burnt at the first bite. In the tourist areas we had had sensational food, which we now suspected was 'tamed' by the Thai cooks by adding fewer chillies than usual especially for the westerners. Certainly Thai food was very much hotter than Indian food. We had seen a western-looking restaurant as we cycled into the town, so walked a mile back through the streets to find it, but walking along the pavements in Thai towns is difficult. Although the pavements were about 15 feet wide, there were steps up and down in odd places and broken concrete drain covers, protruding lumps of concrete and pipes waiting to trip up the unwary, or obstacles in the way. We had to wind our way through tables and chairs with people sat eating, past open fires heating giant pots, step over tools and pieces of vehicles as mechanics spilled out of the workshop onto the pavement repairing vehicles, and through piles of goods from the shops – fridges, washing machines, baskets of vegetables, shelves stacked with goods and stalls with food. The kerbs were very high – over a foot high in most places – and unofficial ramps made of concrete enabled motorbikes to drive onto the pavement to park and make more obstacles for us to circumnavigate. Sometimes a wooden hut filled the pavement, so we had to step onto the busy road to walk around it. We passed a stall on which were wooden handles, or so we thought, most of them looking quite old. However, on closer inspection we realised that they were carved wooden penises, but we didn't know what they were for. We found out later that these phallic symbols are considered good luck, and are worn by boys and men on a waist string under their clothes. They can apparently increase gambling luck, attract women, give protection, cure illnesses, bring prosperity and presumably bring all types of luck to whoever has one!

We passed the hospital, on top of which was a long neon sign with constantly running advertisements in Thai. We wondered what it could be advertising, and spent a few minutes making suggestions.

'If anyone wants a cataract operation, there's been a cancellation today,' said Warren.

'Good news,' I retorted. 'Only two people died on the operating table this month.'

'Haemorrhoids clinic on Mondays – standing room only,' Warren responded.

'This week only,' I added, 'Breast implants – buy one, get one half price.'

'Prosthetics department now closed, because it was costing an arm and a leg,' was Warren's reply.

'Special offer on hip replacements this week,' I suggested, warming to the theme. 'Two hip operations for the price of one.'

'Broken legs set while you wait,' said Warren, not to be outdone.

'In view of the time of year, there should be a special offer for Valentine's Day – heart operations half price,' was my final reply.

We found the restaurant, and decided to splash out on a bottle of wine, and asked for red. The bottle brought to the table was ice cold, and we asked if they had a warm one. We knew this was confusing for the Thais, because red wine is usually served cold in Thailand, even though the label on the bottle clearly suggests serving it at room temperature. Next they brought us a bottle of white wine which was warm! We decided to go for white, but now had the problem of explaining we wanted cold white wine! It took a while, and we were just about to ask for beer instead, when a cold bottle of white wine arrived, complete with ice bucket. The meal and the wine were delicious.

On we travelled, passing the Department of Anti-Trafficking for Women and Girls as we left the town. The roads were still very busy, but now there were plenty of modern service stations with toilets, and there were shops such as 7-Eleven to supply us with coffee or snacks. We were travelling north, so the north-east wind was often against us, but we would soon turn west to go south of Bangkok and after that we would turn south to cycle down the main peninsular of Thailand.

Alongside the road locals were sitting under umbrellas with stalls, obviously selling something. As we approached, we were surprised to see that for sale on every stall were polythene bags of coloured noodles – pink, peach, yellow and pale green. The noodles looked like bags of knitting wool! Further on we approached

Hat Jomtien, which was south of the well-known resort of Pattaya. Pattaya is famous for sun, sand, sea and sex, and specialises in sleazy bars; as that type of resort was not our scene, we decided to stay in Hat Jomtien which the guide books told us was quieter.

We found it to be one of the busiest places we had so far visited, with the beach on one side of the road and hotels and guesthouses on the other. It was very expensive, and even more so because it was the weekend. As we booked into a hotel, the receptionist wrote the date – 14/2/47.

'It's Valentine's Day,' she announced. She stroked my hand with her fingers and put her hand alongside mine.

'Like Thailand,' she said, meaning that my hands were as brown as hers. This was despite me often wearing cycling gloves in an attempt to protect my hands from the sun!

As we left the hotel a little later we found the pavements lined with people and police were driving slowly along the road. For the next five minutes it was impossible to cross the road as hundreds of motorbikes roared past, accompanied by the occasional policeman on a motorbike. Many of the bikes had handle bars that were very high, so the riders drove with their hands in the air on the bars, and other bikes had long elongated front forks. Huge Honda Goldwings went by with padded leather seats like armchairs, and many of the riders wore bandanas which made them look like gypsies. There were westerners as well as Thais; the road was awash with black and chrome, and it looked like a scene from the film, 'Easy Rider'.

We had already discovered that complaints are something that the Thais don't know how to handle, just the same as in India. The following day I chose a dish from an English written menu in a restaurant – it was a yellow curry with potatoes and tofu. I'm not particularly keen on tofu but love potatoes in curry, but when the meal came there was no potato. I called the waiter, and told him there should be potatoes in it.

'No,' he said positively.

'Yes,' I replied. 'The menu said potatoes.'

He looked confused for a moment. 'No potatoes today,' he suddenly said, and began to walk away.

I called after him, 'I chose yellow curry because it said potatoes were in it.'

He didn't know what to do or what to say. At this moment the owner arrived, took the plate from the table and handed it to the waiter.

'One minute, please,' he said to me, and turned to say something in Thai to the waiter.

My rice on its separate dish got colder and colder until several minutes later I got my meal back. Warren had now finished his meal. The meal handed back to me was now cold, except for the hot potatoes in it! Obviously somewhere they had managed to find the potatoes. The moral of the story is, when in Asia eat what you've been given and be grateful for it!

We cycled through Pattaya the next day. A small pick-up truck passed us pulling four trailers, three carrying jet skis and the fourth carrying a speedboat. We knew we were now going to have several days of very busy traffic as we edged our way as close to the coast as we could, going just south of Bangkok. It was 10 miles before the very busy resort was behind us, but we were encouraged as motorbike drivers and policemen gave us the thumbs up as we cycled by. The hard shoulder disappeared after 30 miles, and the road was incredibly busy as the large trucks whooshed past us, one after another. We found another road parallel to the main road, which we assumed was the old road. The surface was terrible, so it was slow going, but at least we were safe from the busy traffic. We turned onto another road, which passed small villages. It was still very busy. There were saltpans in this area, and some backwaters with the giant Chinese fishing nets that we had seen and photographed in Kerala, south India. Apart from that, the road was incredibly boring, dusty, hot and busy, and there were more dead dogs by the side of the road than we had ever seen anywhere. To make matters worse, Warren then had a puncture, which we spent 30 minutes repairing in the shade of a bus shelter. In such heat the worst part of a puncture for Warren is pumping the tyre back up to 90 psi, so he was really fed up when he had a second puncture less than an hour later. In fact, in the next four days we were to have six punctures, mostly from the broken glass at the side of the road.

Several men sat in the bus shelter watching Warren repair the puncture, and offering 'help' which was usually only a hindrance. On this occasion, the only way Warren could find the hole in the inner tube was to put it into a nearby muddy puddle. The men fingered the tyres and tutted and shook their heads. How could we explain that these tyres were supposed to be slick, and were not worn and bald, as they thought? Our tyres were designed to be used on sealed roads, taking us faster along such roads than knobbly tyres, which would require much more effort.

We spent hours on the road that day; it was the worst road so far in Thailand, with no hard shoulder, parked cars, motorbikes overtaking parked cars on the wrong side of the road and coming towards us, roaring lorries and busy traffic. We arrived at the next town, Chonburi, shattered, dirty and with headaches. We had to cycle for several miles around the town before we found the hotel that we had been directed to by some motorbike drivers. It looked a very cheap hotel, so we were amazed when they told us the price – 690 baht, nearly £10. Warren went to look at the room, and returned to say it was horrible, dirty and dingy, and there were no blankets or top sheets on the beds. He whispered to me that he thought it was a Love Hotel (remember these from Japan?), and as we cycled off he described the rooms. Each room he passed had the door open, and every room had a similar chair, which looked like a gynaecologist's chair with stirrups. The walls were mirrored, and the rooms were dark and dingy, as though to cover up the dirt – it was certainly not soft, romantic lighting. In the room he had been shown, a pile of videos sat next to a video recorder at the end of the bed. There were plenty of cars parked outside many of the rooms, so we assumed that the hotel would also be quite noisy with the guests coming and going . . .

For 690 baht we could stay in a luxury hotel, and a bit of luxury was what we now needed. Every time we asked someone if there was a hotel, we were directed further on, until we had cycled another 10 miles. Unfortunately, we were also going in the opposite direction to the one we wanted to travel. Another motorbike driver directed us to The Star Inn, which was a short distance away. We couldn't find it, but everyone had heard of it and pointed in one direction or another. Eventually we went down a side street and saw five illuminated stars, so assumed it was the Star Inn – the name was in Thai script, so we couldn't read it. We cycled towards the building, but a girl at the end of a long drive beckoned us. As we approached on our bikes, we saw that rooms were built in rows with car parking spaces in front. She directed us to the next row, where another girl directed us further, and a third girl directed us into a car parking space in front of a room. Large plastic curtains were pulled down to hide cars already parked in front of other rooms, and my heart sank as I recognized the similarity with the Japanese Love Hotels – we'd found another one! We checked the price – 300 baht for three hours, or 600 baht for the night.

We set off once again, and only a few hundred yards further down the main road found a lovely hotel, where they welcomed us with the Thai prayer gesture, and the bellboy showed us to our room on the fourth floor – a balcony, air conditioning, satellite television, carpets, a bathroom with hot water and fluffy towels, a fridge full of cold drinks, and a 7 feet wide bed made up with crisp white cotton sheets – bliss! It was the same price as the first Love Hotel, so we couldn't understand why anyone would go to these dingy hotels. We had spent 2½ hours looking for a hotel so, despite the high price of the hotel, we cycled to the local Tesco supermarket and bought ourselves a bottle of wine, which we drank in our room while watching television. We felt we deserved it after such a day.

We left our luxury hotel in Chonburi at first light in the morning, but stopped almost immediately when we saw a pavement stall selling toast. The Thai girl on the stall called to us in excellent English, and asked us where we were from.

'England,' we replied.

'Where in England?' she asked, 'My husband is from England. We live in Bristol.'

That explained the good English. They were visiting Thailand for two months, she told us. She was the first English-speaking Thai that we'd met for days, so we chatted for a while as she prepared our breakfast. Warren had rice with minced pork and chilli with a fried egg on top, but I chose the Thai-style toast, barbecued with butter and sugar on it. The total cost was 27p, and as we sat on the steps of a shop eating our breakfast, she brought over to us two beer mugs full of hot white liquid.

'I'd like you to try this,' she said. 'It's made of yellow beans and is very good for the body.' Well, we needed that alright, and it tasted milky and delicious, so after our cheap but delicious breakfast we set off.

Within half a kilometre we had reached a very busy traffic junction, completely unlike any junction back home. There were five lanes on both sides of all four roads approaching the cross roads. Traffic was piling up waiting to turn right once the road was clear. A policeman was trying, not very successfully, to direct traffic. Crowds of pedestrians stood on the pavements and the islands in the middle of the roads, waiting for a safe time to cross. It was terrifying as the traffic roared past – lorries, buses, motorbikes and cycles, with only inches between them and us waiting in the centre of the junction. There was only a matter of seconds in which we could all shoot across the road to safety, so we dashed across the road before the traffic bore down on us from the left again.

The traffic was very heavy and, although there was a hard shoulder, the taxi-buses were continually pulling onto the hard shoulder in front of us to pick up or set down passengers. People were going to work, most of them to the Toyota and Honda factories nearby, all dressed in identical shirts and trousers. Now we were only 15km south of the centre of Bangkok, which explained why there was so much traffic.

We reached a town and realised that we didn't know if we were on the correct road, but no-one was able to help us. We therefore cycled by compass, travelling west all the time, knowing that we should eventually reach the river which we had to cross. The traffic became more and more congested, until ahead of us we could see a man directing traffic, first to the right, then to the left, and then straight ahead. We went straight on as directed, cycling up a metal ramp, and suddenly and surprisingly found ourselves on a large rusting ferry boat with three lanes of traffic on it – we had reached the river! A tug nudged the ferry out onto the wide river almost instantly, and we began to cross the wide river. We noticed that several other ferries were crossing at the same time. Halfway across, other ferries passed us in the opposite direction, each ferry boat managing to dodge the others, and another tug nudged us into a bay and we were disembarking again. As cyclists we had nothing to pay.

Although we had found the river we knew that we were lost, so Warren approached some policemen outside a police station. Although they spoke no

English, they were enjoying being helpful, drawing maps and waving their arms to explain directions and, because we were unable to understand what they were saying, one of them drove off in front of us on his motorbike and led us for the next 5km through the heavy traffic. He left us, directing us onto a massive road with four lanes in each direction. Strangely, there was another road alongside this freeway, again with four lanes in each direction, just beyond a small wall to our left. Beyond these further eight lanes were shops and houses. We were bowling along in the slowest lane of the freeway at 18 mph with the wind behind us, feeling quite safe because there were so many lanes for the other traffic to use, when Warren shouted that we had to move to the pavement as he had a puncture. This was easier said than done, because we had to lift our very heavily-laden bicycles over the small wall, and cross eight lanes of fast-moving traffic. We eventually made it safely to the pavement, where we repaired the puncture with the usual audience of locals watching us.

After 35 miles we approached Samut Sakhon, and were amazed to see monkeys at the side of the road. There was a wide dirty ditch full of water and rubbish, beyond it a large concrete pipe and beyond that were palm trees. Locals were feeding the monkeys, who had crossed the water and were climbing the small trees by the road, often jumping into the water and swimming. There were whole families including tiny babies, but we kept well away from them. We noticed one man feeding the monkeys, but as soon as his food ran out one of the monkeys became very aggressive and attacked him. The man backed off quickly and shot away on his motorbike.

We continued into the town to find a hotel. We were amused later that evening to read the English translation of the restaurant menu. We had the choice of steamed ducks' feet with pork stomach, mixed salad with hot hogs' entrails, assorted pork intestine soup, fried fish stomachs or soup with fish stomachs. This reminded us of the menus that we'd seen translated in Turkey, and we found it difficult to imagine what some of these meals actually were.

The journey continued in a similar way the next day on busy roads, and the only interesting thing that we saw were some saltpans. The whole area was divided into large squares, each shallow square filled with sea water. Some of the squares were filled with piles of salt, waiting to be transported elsewhere, and there were windmills, each with six triangular sails made of woven grass. These mills were attached to pumps and were used to pump water into different pans. On the other side of the road, a mountain of salt was being moved manually. Men and women were each carrying two shallow bamboo baskets on yokes on their shoulders, and they filled these baskets with salt and walked to another area to deposit it. There it was being put into bags, and countless stalls and shops were selling bags of very large-grained unrefined sea salt along the side of the road.

When we arrived in the next town we had to ask a policeman where the hotel was, and it took a long time to find, because the word 'hotel' was not written anywhere in English. It reminded us of searching for hotels in Japan, and having to learn the foreign script. We eventually found what we thought was a hotel, though there was no sign of any kind. For once it was very cheap, and we were able to wheel our bicycles straight into the large room which was on the ground floor. However, a little later a large cockroach ran across the floor and out under the door, immediately followed by his family and friends – one of the problems with ground floor rooms!

We went out to explore, and found an enormous market along the railway line. The railway line formed a path through the centre of the market, so presumably no train was expected. We treated ourselves to spring rolls, stuffed pancakes and waffles from various stalls. After eating rotis covered with condensed milk and sugar sauce, we were in a terrible mess! I thought about buying a tea towel from a nearby stall to clean ourselves, but two kittens slept so soundly on the top of the pile despite the noise in the market, that I didn't like to disturb them.

The next day we left the hotel early to cycle 37 miles to Phetchaburi. A line of policemen stood to attention in their skin-tight shirts and trousers, being given orders for the day before setting off on their motorbikes. We turned onto the main road again; we were now travelling south-east, having 'turned the corner', but amazingly the wind had changed from north-east so was still against us – the words 'Sod's Law' sprang to mind! Along the hard shoulder of the dual-carriageway 10 orange-robed Buddhist monks walked in line. Every one of them had bare feet, and I was amazed that they were able to walk and stand without problems on the coarse gravel paths at the sides of the roads.

This day we each had a puncture, so we were getting pretty fed up with having to stop in the heat to repair the tubes, but we still made good time. As we entered Phetchaburi, a monkey ran across the four-lane road in front of us, climbed up a pole and sat on the sunblind over a shop window, watching us. As we left our hotel a short while later, monkeys were playing along the pavement, running up telegraph poles and street lights and swinging on the electricity cables. They sat close to cafés, hoping for food to be dropped, and they raced the dogs for any scraps. There were dozens of them of all sizes, but we kept well away knowing how aggressive they could be.

We found a restaurant overlooking the river, and sat by the window.

'Is that a crocodile?' asked Warren, pointing out of the window.

'No,' I said. 'It looks like a log.'

At that moment the log, which turned out to be a six feet long monitor lizard (sometimes called an iguana), dived under the water, and another one on the river bank crawled into the water to join it. We spent a fascinating hour watching these prehistoric-looking reptiles.

At the night market that evening Warren decided to try the seafood omelettes, and for 25p he had a crispy omelette filled with mussels and other seafood, served with stir-fried greens and bean sprouts. For 12p we had a large bag full of vegetable tempura with a chilli dipping sauce. There was chicken on the menu, but we decided not to have any – we didn't fancy the sticks of 'chicken tails' (as the owner called them), which were four parsons' noses on a stick for a few pence. We tried many of the different meals. Sometimes we ate as we walked around the market, sometimes we sat at the tables, and many local people chatted to us. As we left, we saw marinated mackerel being put onto a barbecue, something we fancied for next time, so we asked what it was called, and were surprised to find that the Thai word for mackerel was Saba, the same as in Japan.

The street lights were on in Phetchaburi as we walked back to our hotel. These lights were spectacular – on the top of very tall dark green columns stood gilded mythical birds, their wings outspread. From each bird's beak hung a strawberry-shaped frosted glass light with a gilded top. We returned to our hotel and listened to The World Service, and heard that Avian 'flu had spread to cats – a leopard and several domestic cats had been infected. Did this mean we couldn't even eat cats now? . . . (Only joking!)

As we left the hotel early the next morning, the road was empty apart from the monkeys and dogs. The dogs were barking at the monkeys and chasing them, but the monkeys were much too fast, and could run up the telegraph poles or street lights to avoid the dogs at their tails. Monkeys rummaged in the dustbins, clattered along the corrugated iron roof of a walkway before swinging up into the trees, and swung between telegraph poles along the electric cables. Hanging from the electricity cables, the monkeys appeared to be teasing the dogs as they threw pieces of rubbish at them.

After a number of miles along the hard shoulder, we had to swerve to avoid a dead snake. We'd seen many dead snakes on the roadside in Thailand, some pretty big, but never one that big – it was about 5 or 6 inches in diameter. We thought it likely that no-one would believe us so, although it seemed a bit macabre to do so, we took a photo. We didn't want people thinking we were telling fishermen's tales, and from the photo we could later identify what type of snake it was.

Now the road was beginning to be a bit more interesting, with agriculture on either side of the road instead of industry, and we were making fast progress. We were pleased to arrive early in Cha-Am, a beach resort which seemed to be a mirror image of Hat Jomtien on the other side of the Gulf of Thailand. On one side of the road were hotels, guesthouses, restaurants and shops, and on the other side of the road was a narrow strip of sand full of deckchairs, many of them sitting in the shade of the trees on the beach. We found a brand new hotel, pretentiously calling itself a 'resort', which had a charming restaurant facing the beach. Here they served excellent breakfasts and, even better news, excellent coffee! Best of all, the accommodation was very reasonably priced, so we decided to stay a few days to recover from the busy roads of the last few days.

Bicycles for two, three or even four people were available to rent in the town, and as it was a weekend the road was full of them. Six or seven people, including children, sat on the four-seater bicycles, squashed into the very narrow sections between the handlebars and saddles. There were some westerners in the town, but it was obvious that this was more a tourist town for the locals, who could drive from Bangkok very quickly for a day or a weekend away. The 'resort' where we stayed had several very pleasant brand new two-storey houses behind the hotel, which had two double bedrooms, a living room, kitchen and bathroom. For 1,500 baht (£20) per night this was a lot of money by Thai standards, but at 13,000 baht for a month (about £6 a night) they were incredibly good value, especially for westerners.

At the side of the hotel was a small road, along which was a kitchen which supplied food to the people on the beach. We often saw a motorbike drive past the hotel, the driver holding a plate or even a tray on the palm of his hand as he drove across the road and onto the sand. If he wanted to deliver a 'cook-your-own' meal, where food was fried in the centre of a shaped metal plate over a fire and vegetables boiled around it, the driver took a passenger who sat backwards holding the barbecue on the back of the motorbike with various foods around it on a tray. As they drove past we noticed that the barbecue was already lit and the water was boiling and bubbling in the metal container!

We went a second time to a small local café, because the food served the first time had been so good. The owner was clearly delighted to see us arrive a second time in his restaurant, jumping up from a chair as we arrived.

'Sawasdee-Ka,' he said, doing a little bow with the prayer gesture. There was a breeze, which brought the temperature down to a pleasant 28°C. After cooking our meal, the owner went across the road to the beach with a metal detector, but because of the breeze he obviously felt cold, so pulled a woollen balaclava over the top of his cap. Only his eyes showed through the slit. (Balaclavas are sold in all the local markets, stalls and shops, but usually only in the non-tourist towns – in the tourist areas they sell bikinis and shorts!).

The young staff members in our hotel were very pleasant and cheerful, and often shared with us the different local fruits that they were continually eating. We were therefore able to try quite a few strange fruits that we had never eaten before.

The maid was cleaning our room, and wanted to practise her English.

'Yua peecham?' she asked.

'Pardon?' I said.

She repeated it. Oh, how I hate not being able to understand – sometimes it can be so embarrassing. She repeated it a third time, this time very slowly.

'You appee Cha-Am?'

Was I happy in Cha-Am? 'Yes,' I said. 'It's very nice.' She beamed as though I'd paid her a personal compliment . . .

We couldn't stay in Cha-Am for ever, though, and we knew that only 25km down the road was another beach resort, so we packed our bags and set off after four days. We turned onto the main road, and were surprised to see that the beach was clear of the hundreds of deck chairs that constantly littered it. We discovered that there was a law which stated that the beach should be cleared every Wednesday! We left the town, noticing that on our right was a range of mountains in the west. This was the mountain range that divides Myanmar and Thailand, and we would have the mountain range to our right for many miles as we travelled south.

Hua Hin used to be a fishing village, but was made popular many decades ago because the King decided to build a summer palace close to the village. There are dozens of piers made of wood, which were once used for drying fish. The old fishing village has now disappeared, so the piers have been converted into guesthouses, with rooms built on top of them.

As we cycled into Hua Hin we could see that this was a much larger tourist town, and there were many westerners. There were Indian restaurants, Italian restaurants and Chinese restaurants as well as Thai restaurants, supermarkets and many shops. Outside the restaurants enormous prawns, lobsters, crabs and fish were displayed every evening on ice to entice the western customers to choose a fish dish in the restaurant.

There were many tailors' shops, and the window displays were full of elegant, beautifully-cut evening dresses for ladies and smart suits for men. Prices were from £30 for a made-to-measure man's suit or from £25 for a stunning long evening gown made of fabulous silk fabric. There were shops full of exquisite handbags, shoes, sandals and boots made of snakeskin, crocodile skin or even stingray, which had a hard, slightly knobbly surface. Notices in the windows of the shops and restaurants announced 'Wir sprechen Deutsch', so we knew that there would be many Germans in the town. The book exchanges had very few English books, only Scandinavian or German, and the town appeared to be full of blond giants. We discovered that most of the tourists were from Sweden, Germany or Finland.

We booked into a guesthouse which was actually a pier built out over the sea with wooden rooms on either side of a central corridor. We had a room big enough for our bikes, as well as a bathroom, satellite television and a fridge. Outside each room on the wooden pier was a table and two chairs, and at the end of the pier was an area laid out with sun loungers, tables and chairs, so that guests could sit having a drink looking out over the sea. As the tide came in at night, the water lapped beneath the pier; we could hear the sound of the shallow water swishing around below us, which helped to lull us to sleep. We could look out onto the beach and the sea, and small local fishing boats were moored next to our jetty. Beyond the boats in this tiny bay was a Chinese temple on a small rocky peninsular, and just beyond the temple was the Hilton Hotel, where people with much more money than us stayed. However, both our guesthouse and the Hilton Hotel had the same view, except we had the advantage of charming colourful fishing boats in the foreground. We discovered later that the Hilton Hotel was trying to purchase the land where our guesthouse stood.

We met Wyn and Ulla in Hua Hin, two Australian ladies in their sixties, who were spending four months cycling in South East Asia. As they had cycled north from Singapore, and planned to cycle in Vietnam, Laos and Cambodia – in other words, doing the same journey as us but in reverse – we were able to help each other by exchanging notes on good places to stay and visit.

We went to the night market, which spread over several streets. We had intended to buy a cheap meal, but one stall had a fabulous selection of fresh fish, mostly red snappers, and giant tiger prawns crawled across them, trying to escape. I chose a whole red snapper – it was 120 baht for a large one, deep fried with red curry sauce and vegetables. It was noticeable that, now we were in a tourist area, the amount of chillies in the curry was reduced to an acceptable level for westerners, so for less than £2 I had a delicious meal, although by Thai standards it was very expensive – it was also the most expensive meal in the night market.

It was fascinating to watch the Thais cooking – everything was done at such a fast pace, and it was an entertainment to watch them. Close to our table three large woks were constantly on the go, as well as a barbecue. The main chef, wearing shorts and a t-shirt, looked quite masculine, but the next time we visited the street market he was wearing a tarty red dress. Everything was happening in fast motion, with two chefs throwing whole fish into deep fat in a wok and stir-frying vegetables in another wok; spices were being thrown into the mixture, so that the sharp acrid smell caught our throats for an instant; stir-fried rice was being thrown up and down in the wok; sauce was thrown in with handfuls of sugar, pinches of salt, ladles full of stock, and flames flew six feet into the air around the woks, the heat hitting us three tables away. Waitresses were preparing fish and tiger prawns so quickly it was impossible to see the blade of the knife, steamed rice was scooped fast out of the electric rice steamer, pressed into moulds and turned out onto plates, which were dashed to the tables. Prepared vegetables were sitting separately in plastic containers, which the chefs grabbed in handfuls to throw into the woks, and a girl was preparing and chopping vegetables as fast as she could to top up these containers.

Because this was a tourist area, the night market stalls had English translations on the placards and menus. One stall had a sign saying 'Asda Price – Bloody Good – Luvly Jubbly'! There were stalls selling stir-fried noodles, fried mussels, seafood, hot coffee, hot tea, Ovaltine and cocoa, and pancake rotis were listed with every possible filling. There were stalls with spices and herbs, or stalls making fresh fruit or vegetable juices to order – coconut, mango, tomato, watermelon, cantaloupe melon, pineapple, banana, orange, guava, carrot, lemon or strawberry. Stalls sold silk scarves, cushion covers, bangles and jewellery, wind chimes, toys, t-shirts, underwear, flip-flops, wallets and bags, shells, clothes, sunglasses, hats, carved wooden ornaments and Buddha images, CDs at ridiculous prices and flowers arranged into chains for offerings to Buddha.

As we returned to our guesthouse, a tourist posed by a display of fresh fish while her husband took a photo.

'Spot the old trout,' whispered Warren, and I was laughing so much that the owner of a tailor's shop trying to entice me into his shop couldn't get any sense out of me.

I woke early in the morning and peeped out of the curtains. A red sky was silhouetting the fishing boats in the water below our pier, so I jumped out of bed to take a photo, and then returned to bed for another hour or two. It was 6.30am – if we had been cycling we would have been setting off by now.

As you can imagine, washing our clothes was a daily chore on our journeys, as we tended to wash our cycling clothes and put them back on in the morning. Apart from the campsites in Europe and Australia, we always had to hand wash everything. In Asia laundry is cheap, but we always worried that things might go missing, so preferred to do it ourselves. If there was a bucket everything was fine, and we carried a universal plug for washbasins (if there was one!), but as these plugs fitted on the hole rather than fitting tightly into it, we usually lost the soapy, sudsy water once we started swishing the clothes in the water. So Warren, always inventing and making useful things (usually from scraps he found at the side of the road!), invented a stay-in plug that couldn't be dislodged and fitted all sizes of holes including flat holes on the floors of showers. I was impressed, and Warren stood grinning proudly at his prototype. However, I felt that there was no fortune to be made from making and selling wash basin plugs!

We spent a day on a Thai Cookery Course, because we wanted to recreate the dishes we had tasted once we returned home. We accompanied our tutor to the market, which was interesting, because we could ask about the fruits and vegetables that we didn't recognise. Ratthreeya, our tutor, bought shelled coconuts, which were put into a machine to be grated, and the grated meat was put into another machine twice to press out all the juice. Approximately 2 kg of coconut meat became a litre of coconut milk, and this was put into a polythene bag and sealed with a rubber band. Back at her home, we watched Ratthreeya making different recipes, after which we copied what she had done. We made red and green curry pastes, which she insisted we continue to pound long after we thought the paste was ready, and with the paste we made the most delicious green curry soup with vegetables, prawns and fish. This would normally have been made with chicken, but chicken was off the menu at that time because of Avian flu. We learnt how to make Tom-Yam soup, probably one of the most famous dishes in Thai cuisine; our chilli-flavoured soup had three prawns so enormous that they hung over the edge of the bowls. We were getting very full, having eaten everything we had made, and between each recipe plates of mango, pineapple, or flavoured sweet rice were put on the table for us to eat. We made a delicious Thai dessert, and also a fish soufflé that was steamed in a box; we learnt how to make the box from banana leaves, and took the box of fish soufflé back to our room to eat later. We were eager to try these recipes again once we got back to England.

Despite the fact that we had bought a 60 day visa for Thailand, we could see this wouldn't be long enough if we continued at the same pace so decided, after looking at maps and calculating distances, that we would travel the next section to Surat Thani by bus, train or car. We wanted to stay at beaches further south and the next 500km was less interesting; at Surat Thani we could catch a ferry to some lovely islands. We spent a very frustrating day trying to organise transport. We approached a large taxi to ask the cost.

'4,000 baht,' he said.

We declined, but he shouted after us as we walked away.

'3,000 baht.'

We went to enquire about hire cars. It was 1,200 baht for a pick-up truck, plus fuel and a drop-off charge in another city. We asked an open-backed taxi, and after checking a map for the distance (nearly 500km), he quoted 2,500 baht. We checked two other car hire companies. The first recommended we drop off the car in a city 400km away from our destination, as they didn't have a drop-off point in Surat Thani. The second didn't have suitable vehicles available, but the cost would have been even higher. We went to the train station where, after queuing for some time, we discovered that the only train that would carry bicycles was at 11pm, arriving at 5am, so we would be waiting all day and evening before catching the train, and when we arrived we would have to wait for daylight before cycling 18km to Surat Thani. We were quoted 820 baht for sleepers and space for bicycles. Despite the fact that I am usually travel sick on buses, we made enquiries at the bus station, but the price for the journey was the same as the train, and they refused to take our bikes.

We decided to accept the cheaper taxi, but when we returned to him he added another 2,000 baht to the price, so we refused. We returned to the first car hire company and were now so desperate that we agreed to hire a car, even when she told us it was now 2,675 instead of 1,200 baht. When the car was dropped off to us at 6pm as agreed the next day, we were told there had been a mistake, and it was 2,675 plus the original quote of 1,200 baht! We tore up the agreement and said we would catch the train. After walking across the town to the train station again, we were quoted a much higher price than before, and were now told that they couldn't confirm that our bikes would be accepted on the train until 3 hours before the train arrived. This was useless, and we were beginning to despair, but as we left the station the car hire representative was standing waiting for us, saying that she had spoken to her manager and they would honour the second quote of 2,675 baht. We had to walk a mile to her office, she leading on her motorbike, and it was 8.30pm before we finally returned to our guesthouse, completely exhausted, with the pick-up truck. We both agreed how simple it was to travel by bicycle, just getting up in the morning and getting onto our bikes!

We set off early the next morning with our bicycles and ten bags in the back of the pick-up truck, while we sat in the air-conditioned 4-seater cab. The road was good, mostly a dual-carriageway with two lanes each way, but it was disconcerting to be speeding along overtaking, when suddenly a motorbike would appear from the bottom of the deep ditch in the central reservation and continue past us going the wrong way on the narrow central reservation – we discovered that it was usual for motorbikes to cross from the other side of the road via the central grassy ditch, rather than wait for an official turning point. In the same way, cars often drove along the hard shoulder at the side of the road in the wrong direction, rather than drive a few kilometres to an official u-turning point, so it was quite frightening at times to have traffic passing on both sides going in the wrong direction!

Every so often there were dozens, maybe hundreds, of stalls lining the road, every one selling the same goods as the one next to it. We couldn't understand this – we had seen it throughout Thailand. In one area they all sold weather-vanes and windmills. 20km further on, they all sold bananas. Another 30km and everyone had the same cakes in boxes, followed by stalls with hats and baskets made of cane, and further on were brooms and brushes. It seemed as though it would be considered an unfair advantage to try to sell something different!

We passed Prachuap Khiri Khan, where Thailand is only 10km wide from the mountainous Myanmar border in the west to the Gulf of Thailand in the east. After this point, Thailand widens again, but still we had the mountains to our right defining the Myanmar border. As we sped along the dual carriageway, we could see a gold Buddha's head above the trees and, as we approached, we could see the enormous seated golden statue of Buddha towering over the surrounding buildings, trees and road. We passed a giant painted concrete peacock, its legs straddling the entrance to one of the many temples.

We wanted to visit three of an archipelago of 80 islands off the east coast of Thailand. We would take the ferry from Surat Thani to well-known Koh Samui, which has an airport and is quite touristy; then we would take another ferry to Koh Phan-Gnan, a much quieter island, and after that a ferry to Koh Tao, a very small island visited mainly by divers. From Koh Tao we would complete the loop by taking a ferry to Chumphon, back up the east coast of Thailand and ideally placed for us to cycle across to the border with Myanmar to renew our Thai visas.

Although usually quieter than its touristy neighbour, Koh Phan-Gnan is famous, or infamous, for its full moon parties at Had Rin Beach, when thousands of party lovers turn up to dance, drink and smoke the night away – as many as 12,000 would invade that part of the island for the full moon. As the full moon was due within the next few days, we wanted to stay well clear of that island until the party-goers had left again. Prices of accommodation and food rocketed in the area at full moon.

The mountains eventually disappeared as we turned towards Surat Thani, where sad-looking mangy dogs slept on the pavements and roads. Despite the cost of the car rental and fuel, it had actually been cheaper for us to travel by car than by bicycle, because on a bike the 500km would have taken about a week to travel, with accommodation on each of the nights. Now we were in Surat Thani we found that the only ferry from the town was the slow overnight ferry at 11pm. The only other alternative was to travel another 70km to a shorter ferry the following day. We decided to take the overnight ferry, but we were a little concerned when we saw the boat, which was wooden and rather sad-looking. With three decks, the lowest one was the engine room, the middle one was stacked with motorbikes, bags of vegetables, and all sorts of luggage including our bikes, and the top one was the sleeping area. The floors of the two lower decks were wooden and varnished, but unless you were 5 feet high or less (1.5 metres) you had to stoop, otherwise your head hit the ceiling. The top floor was lined with windows on both sides, and on the floor were two long strips of wood, which enclosed a line of 40 narrow mattresses on either side of the boat, the end ones sloping somewhat. Each mattress had a clean sheet and small pillow, and we were surprised to discover that Thais slept on one side and westerners on the other. The Thai side was full, but fortunately as there were fewer westerners we had more room. It all looked surprisingly clean and neat, despite the close proximity of the mattresses to each other, and I hoped that I wouldn't get someone very fat next to me, spilling over onto my mattress! Instead, my neighbour was a young girl with masses of Titian-red curly hair, which blew in the breeze from the window and fan, so that if I turned in the night, I had a face-full of her hair as it wafted onto my pillow.

The boat left 10 minutes early, the main lights were doused immediately, and we chugged away from the harbour. This slow boat to China, sorry Koh Samui, took 6 hours to travel the 76km (47 miles). We slept well and arrived on time at 5am. We cycled through the deserted streets, and by 5.30 we were booked into a very nice hotel, and were in our room in time to see the sun rise from behind the mountains at the back of the hotel. The tops of a clump of very tall palms were silhouetted against the red sky, whilst their trunks were partially shrouded in the morning mist. We slept again until mid-day, and rose ready to start exploring the island, which we knew was full of beautiful white sandy beaches and coconut palms . . .

Warren had lost his 'dong' some time ago, so was pleased to discover a welding shop behind our hotel in Nathon, the port in Koh Samui. Personally, I thought it was sufficient for a bicycle bell to go 'ding', but Warren wanted the dong back as well. He walked into the welding shop, waking them from their sleep in their hammocks. He showed the welder the inside of the bell, pointing with finger and thumb to signify a gun, and making a ray-gun sound. The welder gave the thumbs up sign to show he understood, and knelt to do the work. After a flash of arc-light he handed the base of the bell back to Warren, who replaced the top dome and rang the bell – ding dong! Warren beamed and gave the thumbs up, and the welder probably realised for the first time what he had repaired.

'Thao rai?' asked Warren, wanting to know how much to pay.

'No charge,' said the welder in perfect English.

Later that evening we saw two women walking towards us, obviously dressed for a night out. After they passed, Warren whispered, 'The one in the yellow sequinned dress was the welder!'

Koh Samui has a road encircling the island, so we decided to cycle around it. It was 7th March, Warren's birthday. We passed some very expensive five star resorts (US$2,000 per night, so obviously not for backpackers!) set in coconut palm groves on hills overlooking the bays. We arrived at Lamai Beach where we stayed a night, and found a narrow strip of sand with some pleasant restaurants and bungalow 'resorts'. Outside most resorts were advertisements for boat trips to Koh Pha-Ngan for the full moon party that night, and also day trips for the 'visa run' to Myanmar, where tourists and foreign residents could renew their Thai visas by stepping out of Thailand for a minute and back in again. (This can be done as many times as needed with no limit, so it's lucky that Thailand is surrounded by so many countries. We discovered later that foreigners permanently residing in Thailand also had to do it every three months, even if they were married to a Thai).

The next day was very overcast again, but was also hot and humid. We didn't have far to cycle, but there were hills which were not shown on our maps. When we left Lamai at 9.30am, the roads were empty in the resort, and the restaurants and shops were closed and shuttered. Koh Samui is very much a tourist island, so obviously the tourists were late risers. Having been used to cafés being open at 6.30am in non-tourist towns where we could have an early breakfast, we found this quite strange. We stopped at two designated viewpoints on the way, but because of strong south-easterly winds, the sea had very big waves, and we weren't able to see the clear shallow blue-green seas that we had anticipated.

We arrived at Chaweng, and knew immediately that we weren't going to like it. It's the main resort on Koh Samui, and was full of hotels, guest houses, bungalow resorts, tourist shops, MacDonalds, Pizza Hut, bars and restaurants. On Koh Samui, prices for accommodation and food were comparatively high for Thailand, but this resort was even more expensive. As we sat on the verandah of our bungalow, we heard the sound of a loud engine approaching, and automatically ducked as an aeroplane flew very low over our bungalow with a thundering roar. The airport is very close to Chaweng Beach, but fortunately the planes stop flying at night. However, we were still disturbed at night by drunken singing as westerners passed our bungalow in the early hours of the morning. The overcast sky decided to let loose the rains, just as we moved into our bungalow, and within minutes the roads were flooded and the electricity was cut off until an hour later (just like India, we thought!).

A friend back home had suggested we contact English friends of hers who lived in Koh Samui, so we phoned Wendy and Roger and arranged to meet for a drink. Many drinks later, we all walked down the very loud side streets, because they wanted to show us the sights. Here we saw the 'lady boys' or 'Katoey' beckoning people into their bars; they were all incredibly beautiful – more beautiful than the girls, we thought. After this we needed another drink, so we went to Wendy and Roger's favourite beachside restaurant, where we sat in deckchairs on the dark, pleasantly breezy beach having another drink. It was arranged that we would cycle to their house the next day, where they had invited us to stay for as long as we wanted.

After struggling up the hills the next day on our bikes (too many drinks the night before, we realised!), we arrived at the furthest north-eastern corner of the island. This was a small quiet peninsular away from the main road around the island, and Wendy and Roger's house stood high on a hill, facing a bay in one direction and Koh Pha-Ngan across the sea in another. A kidney-shaped pool went round one corner of the house, the water overflowing over the edge, which was level with the tops of coconut palms and looked out across the sea. Roger and Wendy had been having some building work done, and Roger had been forced to remove the hammocks from the terrace, because he kept finding the workmen asleep in them. However, he now put them back up so that we could use them.

The best part of the day was late in the afternoon before the sun set. Every day just before 6pm, Roger would suddenly say, 'How about a gin and tonic, everyone?'

'Oh, what a lovely idea,' Wendy always replied, as though it was the first time she had ever heard him say it.

We sat or stood in the pool cooling off with our gins and tonics, bottles of beer and bowls of crisps and nuts on the edge of the pool, watching the sun set across the sea. The stars appeared, and eventually we all got out of the water with wrinkly fingers. After a shower, we sat each evening on the high terrace eating, drinking and talking with the many friends who constantly arrived to enjoy Wendy and Roger's incredibly generous hospitality.

One story that Roger told us was when his dog accidentally bit off his finger. Wendy interrupted the story at this point to scream.

'And I had to pick it up!'

Roger was rushed to the hospital where the doctor did a very good job sewing back his finger, and told Roger that he hadn't had any practice of sewing on fingers.

'What do you normally sew on, then?' asked Roger.

'Penises,' replied the doctor, and went on to explain that Thai women were well-known for chopping off their husbands' private parts if they found that their husbands had been unfaithful. The doctors had had such success in sewing on penises that apparently now the Thai women rushed to the blender with the detached member to ensure that there was no way it could be sewn back on. We were all cringing at the thought, the men clutching their crutches in horror, and the women aghast at such misuse of kitchen equipment!

After three days of doing very little apart from having a wonderful time, we said our goodbyes to Wendy and Roger, and cycled on across the north coast of the island and back to Nathon. On the way we chatted to a local Thai man on a motorbike. He had a chained monkey on his platform sidecar, and he explained how monkeys are trained in Koh Samui to run up the coconut palms and pick coconuts. Coconuts are the main source of income for the island after tourism.

At Nathon we were given contradicting advice from every ferry ticket agency – we had to continue another 9km to another ferry, said one; we had to return 15km back the way we'd come, said another. Finally we were told there was no longer a car ferry to or from Koh Pha-Ngan, and the express boats wouldn't take our bikes. We were stuck – how could we continue? We'd never before had a problem putting bikes on any boat. We decided to bluff it, and I went to buy tickets for the express boat that was due in five minutes.

I handed her the money and said, 'We have bicycles – no problem? OK?'

She muttered something in Thai to a man outside, but handed me my change saying nothing and charging nothing extra. I took this as acceptance of our bikes. We cycled along the jetty and up the gangplank to the waiting boat, where the crew indicated where the bikes should go without any questions.

The boat sped away, full of travellers, all of whom were smoking, all of whom were tattooed, most of whom looked as though they could do with a decent meal and wash, and none of whom appeared to be aged over 23. One hour later we approached Koh Pha-Ngan. The weather had now calmed down – we understood that the wind, grey skies and rain we had experienced on Koh Samui had been the tail end of a typhoon from The Phillipines. Now, for the first time, we could see stripes of jade and aquamarine water, and ahead of us the jungle-covered mountains of Koh Pha-Ngan. Between the turquoise of the sea and the dark green of the island it looked as though an artist had painted a pure white line to separate the two – this was the white sandy beach that surrounded the island.

Two young Thai men jumped off the boat before the gangplank was set down, and as they walked along the jetty they shouted to everyone.

'Welcome to Paradi'.'

The ferry was met by dozens of local taxis – pick-up trucks with seats in the back – but we booked into a room at a local guesthouse for the night. After some research, we decided to go to one of the two beaches in a bay called Ao Thong Nai Pan on the north-eastern side of the island. However, locals told us that the road through the jungle and over the mountain was unsuitable even for motorbikes, and a large-scale map on the wall of a restaurant showed the road wiggling backwards and forwards like a varicose vein across the island. We therefore hired a pick-up truck taxi, put the bikes in the back, and left the next morning. We were glad to have done so – the concrete road soon gave way to a dirt road, recently improved by filling some of the ruts with soil and stones so that vehicles could now move beyond first gear. However, sections were still very bad and it would have been impossible for us to have negotiated these roads with their loose surfaces, deep ruts and very steep ascents and descents. Warren thought the route would have been very challenging for a serious mountain cyclist training for a competition, but was certainly not possible for us with our touring bikes with heavy panniers. As it was, only four wheel drive vehicles could negotiate this road.

We travelled through jungle, so the road was often in shade, and many palm trees lined the winding roller coaster road. Occasionally we could glimpse the sea far below us. After 17km we arrived at our chosen bungalow resort on the other side of the island, set in the palm trees on the edge of the beach. Fortunately there was a vacant bungalow - we hadn't pre-booked accommodation, knowing that something would be available. The wooden bungalows on stilts were set in lovely gardens, and each had a verandah with table, chairs and hammock. Tall palm trees towered over lush tropical plants, with white sandy paths winding between the plants and pools to the steps of the bungalows. Apricot-coloured amaryllis, yellow trumpets and white arum lilies peeped between lush bamboos, pink, white and green striped leaves, banana plants and ferns, and purple bougainvillea cascaded over the roofs of some of the bungalows. Small statues stood amongst the plants.

A pretty wooden bar with tiered thatched roof was set next to the beach but in the shade of the trees and plants. From the bar we could see the beach through an archway of palm fronds. Scattered in the gardens, set into alcoves and leafy pockets, were raised hardwood platforms with thatched roofs, where we could sit on carpets and piles of cushions on the floor, relaxing with a drink or snack.

Tables and chairs were dotted around the gardens in the shade, some on the white sandy beach, looking out onto the shallow blue and green sea of the bay. The bay was almost enclosed with rocky and tree-covered headlands on both sides, and jungle covered the hills surrounding the bay. Within the bay were twin beaches, divided by another rocky headland (a steep 20 minute hike over the headland for anyone feeling energetic). Our beach was a perfect crescent of pure white sand, a wide beach with a very shallow pool of water in the sand, left by the receding tide. Every day the same dog ran excitedly round in circles in this pool, his tail waving hysterically as his nose dived into the water chasing tiny fish marooned in the pool.

Beautiful longboats were moored in the shallow water of the bay. These traditional fishing boats were still used for fishing, but were now used more profitably for taking tourists to different parts of the island. Sometimes the locals sat early in the morning with their fishing nets spread across the beach, and many of the restaurant staff joined in with needle, thread and scissors, to help make the necessary repairs. When a fishing boat returned from a trip, there was great excitement as the locals rushed to the boats with baskets to help unload the catch.

Restaurants, a couple of shops and bungalow resorts lined the beach, all set back so that the view of the beach (thankfully devoid of sun loungers) was unspoilt. When we went into the sea, which was an incredible range of turquoises, aquamarines and jades, the water was so warm it was like walking into a bath, but the shallowness of the water meant that even after wading a long distance out, we were still only thigh deep in water. The water was perfectly clear, so we could see the sand at the bottom and the occasional shell. The whole bay was as still as a millpond, with only the slightest ripple of waves lapping onto the beach. One of my favourite activities was lazily lying in the shallow water at the edge of the beach, elbows sinking in the soft sand, watching tiny fish swimming in the few inches of clear water around me. Even better, I liked floating on my back in the very still, warm water, which was so relaxing with the sun on my face that I could fall asleep, confident that there were only a few inches of water beneath me. Warren occasionally struck out towards the other beach if he felt like a more energetic swim.

The sun reflected through the water making rippled patterns of light and shade on the sand below, and bounced back up onto the elegant longboats, where patterns of light danced along the dark varnished sides of the boats. Warren and I sat on the beach in the shade, or lay in hammocks between palm trees, reading.

We walked along the beach, constantly saying, 'Isn't this beautiful?' 'What a lovely, peaceful place,' or 'This is just heaven.' This was indeed paradise!

After the sun had set behind the mountain, fairy lights and paraffin lamps were switched on to light up the trees and the restaurants along the beach. We were often the only ones in the restaurants in the evenings, and even in the daytime it was rare to see other tourists on the beach before 11am.

In our resort, soft music drifted gently through loudspeakers hidden in the foliage, and at night subtle lighting was set in pretty terracotta pots with cut-out shapes, lighting the paths through the gardens. Small oil lamps and candles made the seating areas attractive places to relax. We were told that an artist owned the resort, and could imagine how he had enjoyed designing the gardens. For 400 baht (£5.50) for a bungalow per night, we were paying more than other bungalows on the beach, but thought the resort well worth the extra money.

We ate exquisite food in the restaurants, and because we were a captive audience we accepted that food would be more expensive than in mainland Thailand. However, we could both have a lovely meal with cold beer for less than £5, the price of beer now being over £1 for a 650ml bottle.

We hired a plastic sit-on double kayak one day, and paddled to our twin beach and around the bay. We stayed close to the coast, where giant boulders lined the water near the headland. Hundreds of crabs ran sideways ahead of us, clearly disturbed from their sunbathing, and a five feet monitor lizard with short, bandy legs and a tail as long as its body ambled slowly across the top of a nearby boulder, only a few feet away from us. On one isolated stretch of the bay that we passed, half-finished bungalows clung to boulders and cliffs, and Buddhist monks in orange robes sat on the rocks in twos and threes. As we left the entrance to the bay, the sea became choppy, which emphasised the way our bay was protected from the elements. On the headland were three bungalows set one above the other on the giant boulders. Hammocks were strung up on the verandahs, and there was a restaurant close by to serve these very isolated bungalows. We returned to our resort after our exertions, and lay on the cushions in the seating area of our resort with a beer, chatting to fellow guests.

One day we booked a longboat for a boat trip. Only one other couple joined us as we waded through the shallow water and hauled ourselves into the boat, which tipped dramatically as each person did this. On the prows of these boats are multi-coloured ribbons and flowers, and a car diesel engine pivots at the back, operating a propeller at the end of a 6 feet pole. To manoeuvre the boat, the propeller has to be pushed from side to side, and the throttle is activated by pulling a piece of string. The boats are long and elegant, made of varnished hardwood with colourful stripes along the sides.

The boat sped through the waves spraying us, but we were glad of the refreshing shower. We arrived at Koh Maa, a tiny island off the north coast of Koh Pha-Ngan. Several other boats had already dropped anchor, as this was a popular spot for snorkelling and diving. Wearing snorkels and goggles, we dropped over the side of the boat into the clear water and drifted around on the surface looking down at the magical world below us. Although the fish were not as large as those we had seen on the Great Barrier Reef, there were many of them and they were in startlingly vivid colours. Dozens of colourful small striped fish surrounded us and came eye to eye with us through our goggles. Large purple anemones clung to rocks, and there were many types of hard coral. Considering we had only paid 300 baht each (£4), we thought the snorkelling was amazingly good value, but the trip was not over yet.

The longboat set off to Bottle Beach, a small pretty cove with a few bungalows along its lovely white sandy beach. Bottle Beach is only accessible by sea, unless one was willing to hike with a guide over the jungle-clad mountain from the nearest dirt road. The four of us had a leisurely meal in one of the restaurants, tasting delicious Massaman curry for the first time. Then we set off again, this time to Than Sadat Beach. Here bungalows clung one above the other to the side of boulder cliffs, long stilts supporting them at the front, and rickety walkways being the only access from the beach. On the beach were more restaurants and bungalows, but Warren and I walked past them with our two companions and into the jungle for a 1km uphill walk to a waterfall. It was possible to walk up the stepped boulders of the river at this time of year because the water was not yet in full flow, but a path through the jungle made for easier walking, and was shaded from the fierce sun. We sat on the boulders at the top of the waterfall, resting and enjoying the peace and quiet. The four of us were the only ones there; it was heaven.

It was time to return to our beach, having enjoyed over five hours visiting other parts of the island. Despite the beautiful bays and beaches we'd seen, we still thought 'ours' the best, and will definitely one day return for a relaxing holiday again, staying at the same place if possible.

On the sixth morning we woke at 8.30am. Whereas we were usually woken by pencil-thin shafts of light shining through the gaps between the wooden walls and floorboards, this morning there were none. Instead, there was the almost forgotten sound of rain falling – heavy rain. We scrambled out of our mosquito net and went onto the verandah, where we laid in hammocks listening to and watching the rain. The temperature dropped to a much cooler 26°C, and I was sure the plants must have been smiling! There was no need today for the resort employees to hose the gardens. It was like being in deep jungle, with water dripping noisily off giant leaves, puddling in crevices in the plants, and running in rivulets down branches and trunks to the ground. A short time later the rain stopped, the sun came out, and birds and cicadas sang their hearts out in the trees.

We spent a couple more days on our paradise beach. On two mornings as we sat having breakfast, we watched one of the local fishermen sitting on his haunches on a white surfboard, using a length of wood to paddle from his boat moored at sea to the beach. The first morning he carried a car battery behind him on the surfboard, the board tipping dangerously with the weight, but the second morning he had a large basket full of goods with a small dog sat on the top.

It was sadly time for us to leave. We wanted to stay longer, but our visas were running out. We had walked barefoot for eight days, because everything we needed was along the beach – restaurants, bars, internet cafés (though admittedly the most expensive yet) and a couple of shops. At the weekend most bungalows had apparently been full, but still the beach was quiet with plenty of solitude for anyone who wanted it. With its very foreign name, Thong Yai Pan Nai, we thought the beach should be renamed – perhaps to Paradise or Heaven, I suggested, but Warren's suggested name was The Dog's Bollocks!

We left Koh Pha-Ngan and, one and a half hours later, our ferry was approaching Koh Tao, a much smaller island. Koh Tao is popular for diving, and there is only one long stretch of narrow beach close to the village where the ferry lands. There are very few roads on this tiny isolated island. Giant boulders were strewn along the coast, and thatched bungalows clung to these in small groups overlooking the sea, especially if there was a small piece of sand nearby. We found a bungalow not far from the ferry, set in gardens that were noisy only from the sound of cicadas. Massive boulders the size of a 3-storey house were scattered in the gardens. They reminded me of the giant pink granite boulders scattered along the northern coast of Brittany, where houses are built into the boulders, so that walls of the house are actually part of the granite boulders.

Our bungalow had walls of varnished woven grass on wooden frames, and a thatched roof. In the morning the walls glowed with a luminous reddish-gold light where the sun hit the outside of the walls. The attached bathroom had a pebble floor with four round stepping stones. Possibly someone had thought it artistic but, because there were gaps between the walls and the thatched roof, the bathroom was a haven for spiders, cockroaches, geckos and something big that scrabbled in the corner each night and moved the pebbles. Every time I went to the loo I peered in carefully first before stepping in – if there was a spider (or something worse!) on the white porcelain of the toilet I was definitely not going to use it!

We decided to book a boat trip that circumnavigated the island, stopping at various points for snorkelling. Once again we were amazed by the underwater world that was immediately apparent through the clear water. We swam through shoals of fish which were unperturbed by us. I was fascinated to see a colourful rock, which looked as though someone had thrown a handful of jewels onto it, and on closer inspection discovered that the 'jewels' were types of anemone in the shape of tiny pointed bottle brushes, in bright purple, turquoise, golden yellow, orange, red, green and white. When we waved our hands close to them, the miniature brush shapes disappeared, leaving a single spot of colour on the rock. There were larger anemones swaying backwards and forwards with the waves, and these were purple, turquoise, vivid blue, and green. When we snorkelled over sandy areas, large black and silver sea slugs lay unmoving on the bottom. Even larger were the navy blue ones with corrugated edges down their sides. Very spiny black sea urchins sat on rocks in groups, but best of all were the fish in every colour of the rainbow. My favourites were the tiny vivid electric blue fish, no more than one inch long, but swimming in small shoals and standing out in the crowds despite their small size.

Finally we visited Koh Nangyuan, not one island but actually three islands joined by two permanent spits of white coral sand. Postcards showed these three tiny islands with stunning empty beaches, but unfortunately when we saw them the numbers of tourists sunbathing on the sand spits spoilt the view. No-one was allowed on the island before 8am or after 6pm unless they were staying at the one resort which was inordinately expensive, so obviously at sunrise or sunset the islands must have been especially beautiful with very few people around.

It was time to move on again, and we booked a ferry to Chumphon on the mainland's east coast, ready to make the visa run to Myanmar on the west coast of Thailand. When it was time to board the boat our hearts sank, because we had to push and carry our bikes and ten heavy bags along a floating jetty, which was in a terrible state of disrepair and was tipping precariously towards the sea. I was worried that we and the bikes would disappear through a rotten floor board, and we didn't dare lean on any of the railings or posts, as many were loose. After negotiating the jetty, we had to carry our bikes down twelve steps onto a narrow unfixed plank perched on the sides of a fishing boat, up and over obstacles across the boat, up onto the edge of the boat and across into the next boat. We had some fairly unwilling help from the crew and, as I was the last person to embark, the boat set off the minute my foot was on the boat.

Three hours later we arrived at Chumphon. It was now 2pm, the temperature had soared to 36°C and it was very humid, so we were very surprised and pleased when we realised that the ferry ticket included free transport to the town, 10km away. We had planned to cycle, and hadn't been looking forward to a cycle ride in the heat of the afternoon. Only a short while later we had booked into a hotel, where we had a room five times more luxurious than the last one (and with satellite television), and it was half the price we had paid the day before – we were back in a non-tourist area! Now all we had to do was cycle over the mountain range to Ranong . . .

Because the temperature was now so much higher, we started getting up early again in order to cycle as soon as it was light. We left Chumphong at 6am the next morning. It was not quite light at that time, and was only 24°C, beautifully cool for cycling. We had to travel west across Thailand and expected to be travelling over a mountain pass. However, the mountain never materialized – obviously the man designing the map had allowed himself to get carried away painting in mountain ranges. The road was a fairly busy single carriageway with a wide shoulder for bikes and motorbikes, but it was a pretty road, winding through very green countryside with rubber plantations, coconut palms and forest-covered hills. We travelled along the undulating road, passing many garden nurseries where rows of tiny rubber trees and coconut palms stood in rows, and giant brown glazed pots were decorated with dragons. Each of the isolated houses that we passed were fronted with hedges of bougainvillaea – gold, apricot, cerise, white, cream, orange, purple, lilac, scarlet, crimson, salmon and pink, all mixed together in a gloriously violent clash of colours.

Trucks and motorbikes went by with monkeys as passengers. As the vehicles passed us the monkeys grinned at us, hanging by one hand as they leant out of the vehicle. Or were they snarling? – How does one tell? In one area we couldn't understand why polystyrene boxes and insulated buckets stood outside every house, until we saw the 'iceman' coming – he drove a truck full of ice-cubes covered with a tarpaulin. At the end of every drive he jumped out, filled the boxes or buckets with ice cubes, sounded his horn and continued on his way.

We had been travelling west across Thailand, and had turned south, following the road that ran parallel with the border between Thailand and Myanmar. At one point a muddy river lined with coconut palms was only 100 metres away from us. This river formed the border, and a sign said 'The Union of Myanmar – 100m' and pointed to a small ferry, unfortunately not for the use of westerners. Children shouted 'hello', people waved and cars sounded their horns along the way – something that only ever happened in the non-tourist areas. After 60km of cycling, we booked into a bungalow, and later went to a nearby restaurant for some food. The owner spoke some English and welcomed us to his table.

'You are the cyclists staying at the bungalow,' he said.

Obviously word had got round in this out-of-the-way place. His son handed us a menu, helpfully translated into English as well as Thai. Banana Flame Bay was on the menu, as well as Chicken Gordon Blue and Crabseset (Crepe Suzette). There were no prices. We had a chicken and chilli dish – chicken was now back on the menus, so either Avian flu was not affecting that part of Thailand or the virus had been eradicated – the third option didn't bear thinking about! With the chicken we had an enormous plate of stir-fried vegetables in oyster sauce, a heaped dish of fried, spicy cashew nuts, two bowls of soup, two bowls of steamed rice, one banana flambé, two 650ml bottles of beer and a bottle of 7-Up. We couldn't believe it when we were presented with a bill for just over £3, especially as it had been one of the nicest complete meals that we had had in Thailand.

The next day we were up early again. We were cycling fast down a hill passing a driveway entrance, when three dogs came bounding out, barking furiously at us. I picked up speed in an effort to shake off the big yellow dog that was snapping at my heels and pannier bags. I had no time to reach for my dog-dazer, but shouted and growled at the dog in the hope of scaring it off as my legs went faster and faster trying to get away. However, the dog kept pace with me, snapping at me and growling - it was obviously determined to catch me. Suddenly from behind I heard the unmistakeable noise of a dog yelping in agony followed by a loud crash. I slowed and stopped, forgetting in that moment the big yellow dog that had been snapping at my heels. However, he was no longer interested in me now that I wasn't cycling. I heard a dog yelping in the woods on the other side of the road. When I turned to see what had happened, I saw Warren lying on his back in the middle of the road, not moving. His bike and pannier bags were strewn across the road. I cycled back quickly, agonizing over how badly hurt he might be. Three Thai women came out of a nearby house, and the yellow dog trotted up to them and sat next to them, as though to say, 'What a nice dog I am – none of this is anything to do with me.' The women just stood and watched us.

Warren wasn't moving and his eyes were closed. Blood was oozing from a bad graze on his shoulder. My heart sank as I knelt on the ground and took his hand. As I called his name his eyes opened, and I helped him to sit up. His shoulder and elbow were badly grazed, and his knee and hands were bruised. He kept looking at his hands and feeling his limbs. Nothing felt broken, he told me, and he turned around and saw his bike.

'Oh no, oh no,' he said, all injuries now forgotten, as he leapt up to check his bike.

I had to make him sit down again, and persuaded him to deal with the bike later. I collected the bags from the road, and a passing motor cyclist stopped to see if he could help. There was no sign of the two black dogs, one of whom had caused Warren's accident. As Warren had cycled behind me, the black dog had run straight out in front of Warren's front wheel, and he had been unable to avoid it. It was a big dog and was knocked on its side by the wheel, but the heavily-laden bike going fast down a hill couldn't stop quickly, and the dog had been pushed along the road before the bike collapsed with Warren on it.

The three Thai women smiled and laughed, which is the normal reaction for Thais to show in such circumstances. This made me lose my temper, and I shouted at them pointing at the yellow dog by their side and making actions to show that it should be shot. They obviously couldn't understand exactly what I was saying, but probably got my drift. Their reaction was unacceptable to me, a westerner, but equally my reaction was unacceptable to them as Asians — emotions and anger should never be shown in Asia. The women disappeared into their house and the yellow dog followed them.

The handlebars of Warren's bike pointed in the wrong direction, and the wheel was buckled. The racks for the bags were twisted. Warren pulled out his tool kit and straightened the bike as well as he could. However, the front fork was twisted, which was really bad news, although not so badly that the bike couldn't be cycled. The buckled wheel could be straightened out properly once we found a decent cycle shop.

We set off again, going very slowly, and stopped fairly soon for breakfast. We were very concerned about the graze on Warren's shoulder, because in high humidity infection can soon set in. When the lad serving us breakfast saw the graze he was just as concerned, and returned with cotton wool and tincture to treat it, which was very kind. He spoke no English, so I did a silly pantomime, barking like a dog, making a dashing movement with my hand, hitting myself to show the crash, and a falling down action, also pointing to the bike. Everyone in the café understood from my actions what had happened, and were all very sympathetic.

We continued on our way — the road was very pretty, with yellow blossom trees with racemes of yellow flowers which reminded me of Laburnam. One large tree was losing its flowers; petals drifted down like large yellow snowflakes, covering the ground beneath in a thick yellow carpet. Other trees in blossom had purple candles of flowers, like a cross between lilac and the flowers of the Horse Chestnut tree. We passed a stall selling drinks, and a little girl jumped up and down excitedly.

'Farang, farang,' she shouted to her mother — foreigners!

We waved and called out 'Sawasdi-ka', and she ran into the road to wave as we went by.

This road, which we had thought would be fairly flat because it travelled beside the river, went up and down and round and round, and culminated in a very steep hill with a waterfall pouring down one side. The west coast of Thailand near Ranong is very green and there are many waterfalls, because the mountains in the area hold the monsoon rains longer, and it therefore has the highest average rainfall in Thailand. Once we reached the top we were able to free-wheel fast down the other side to cool off, and shortly afterwards we arrived in Ranong, where we found a hotel with a room on the ground floor – once again, easy for us to wheel in the bicycles.

Ranong was a rather depressing town, with a few slightly western cafés but not many hotels. We assumed that it was only on the travellers' maps because of its proximity to Myanmar and therefore its suitability for a visa run, but few westerners ever stayed there.

Now we had reached Ranong, we had to renew our Thai visas. We went to find a sawngthaew, a pick-up truck converted to a taxi for 10 plus people. Bench seats are fitted along each side behind the driver, and a metal roof gives shade from the sun. A step at the back enables extra passengers to stand, hanging on for dear life to a rail across the roof.

'How much to the Andaman Club pier?' we asked.

'100 baht each,' he replied.

We laughed at this 'farang' price, so he agreed to the normal 20 baht fare, and we set off. The taxi drove up over a mountain and down again to a pier by the sea, 8km away. Here we were led to a luxury immigration office (apparently run by a luxury hotel), where Thai officers stamped our passports to show we were leaving the country. We were the only foreigners; everyone else was going to the luxury 5-star hotel on a Burmese island in the estuary, where they could have a day out in the casino. Because casinos are illegal in Thailand, there appears to be at least one casino on the other side of every border.

We climbed into an air-conditioned catamaran and, 25 minutes later, docked at the pier of the hotel complex. Here we had to go past metal detectors and place our bags on the same type of conveyor belt/x-ray machine that airports have. Our passports were stamped with a 3-day Myanmar visa, and we were charged 500 baht each (less than £7) for the return boat trip and visa. We were the only ones who wished to return immediately on the boat to Thailand, where we once again went to the immigration office and had our passports stamped with the automatic 30 day Thai visa.

And that, according to the guide books, is the simple but expensive way to renew a Thai visa at Ranong. We discovered that virtually all other travellers took what they thought was the cheap way – a taxi to a different pier, where they had to collect paperwork and walk 1km to the port. There they paid 300 or 400 baht for a longboat, with no protection against the sun or the sea spraying into the open boat. Half an hour later they arrived at a shack on stilts on an island where they had to pay 300 baht (or US$5) for a 3-day visa, get back onto the boat again to the Myanmar mainland to get the Burmese visa stamped into their passports. Back to Thailand on the longboat again, and another 1km walk back to immigration to get the 30 day Thai visa stamped in their passports. The final cost for the 'cheap' way was 600 or 700 baht – not a very good deal!

Another sawngthaew took us back to our hotel, and stopped to pick up five Thai people en route. As they climbed in, a dog followed them. The passengers tried to push it out, but it dug in its heels and wouldn't move from under the seat. Two other people later got off, the dog decided to leave as well, and calmly trotted off down a side street as though he knew exactly where he was going – and he never paid his 20 baht either!

That night it seemed to be getting hotter – at 3.30am I got up to get some water, and found that it was still 30°C, even under the fan. We decided that in future when we could afford it we would book air-conditioned rooms instead of fan rooms – it was the end of March, and the tourist season was coming to an end.

When we set off cycling at 6.15, it was 25°C and comfortably cool. There were a lot of clouds, so I hoped the day would be overcast, but by 7.30 the sun was up and the clouds had disappeared. It was already 30°C again. We stopped for breakfast at a roadside café. On the tables were large Nescafé jars full of exquisite flowers – salmon-coloured buds similar to globe artichokes opened out to large dahlia-like flowers with petals still tightly closed in the centre. The petals were edged with white, and looked like wax. Extraordinarily, they felt like wax as well, and looked too beautiful and perfect to be real. I took a photo of them and the lad who served us, seeing my interest, beckoned me through the café and out into a long garden full of lush tropical flowers and plants.

'Beautiful flowers,' he said, pointing down to circles of tall leaves; at the base of these leaves, the salmon-coloured flowers sprouted through the ground. Their stems were thick and fleshy and without leaves. I took more photos and thanked him for showing me, and I was delighted after breakfast when he presented me with a perfect flower just opening on a long stem. We discovered later that these flowers are called 'dahla' by the locals, and that they grow in southern Thailand. Petals can be pulled off and dipped in batter and fried to make tempura.

The scenery was again quite beautiful; the road was undulating with a range of high mountains to our left and sometimes ahead of us. It was always a relief when the road turned to go round the mountains rather than over them. Every time I slowed down going up a hill my glasses steamed up in the humid heat, and I couldn't see. There was also no refreshing breeze to cool us as we flew down the hills; instead we were bombarded with an oven-hot airstream. There were just too many of those dreaded signs showing a lorry going up an incline, which warned lorries to get into low gear. We passed several mosques, because this area has a large population of Muslims, but most of the mosques were very small, serving only small, isolated villages. It was also noticeable in such Muslim areas that there were cows in the villages, rather than the pigs that we had seen in the Buddhist areas.

A short while later Warren had a puncture, so this held us up while we repaired it, and the day got hotter. We set off again, but I realised that Warren was out of sight behind me, so I waited for a while in the shade for him. The road was winding, so I couldn't see far down the road, but as I stood looking back a lorry came round the corner. As it passed, the passenger hung out of the window shouting to me in Thai and pointing urgently back along the road. I was terrified – I immediately thought Warren must have had another accident, and I turned my bike and pedalled furiously back the way I had come. After half a mile I still hadn't seen him, but as I turned the next bend I saw him pushing his bike. His face was like thunder – he had another puncture! He had walked half a mile, because the puncture repair kit was in my bag, so he was cross with me as well. We repaired the puncture in a bus shelter, but after Warren had finally pumped the tyre back up to 90 psi, he found that the valve on the inner tube had broken, so that the air escaped again. He had to start again, replacing the tube with a new one. He was not a happy bunny ...

We finally arrived in a village called Kapoe, very hot and tired and ready for a shower and rest. Apart from a few shops and buildings, there appeared to be only an enormous police college. We stopped to ask two policemen where there was a hotel, and were horrified when they told us that the nearest hotel was another 50km further on. In despair I parked my bike against a tree and sat down on the grass to drink some water. The policemen returned to their car and were using mobile phones, but shortly afterwards another policeman came out from the police station, and asked if he could help. His English was quite good, so we assumed that the other policemen had called him to come and talk to us. As soon as he realised our predicament, he offered us the use of his police house. He told us that he only used it three or four times a month when he was working late, otherwise he returned home, 50km away, to his family. We accepted his offer gratefully, and followed him to a row of plain terraced houses at the side of the police college.

His house was very basic to say the least, with one very dark room downstairs with a concrete floor and walls, furnished with a single bed, a table and a stool. The only decoration on the walls were three large posters of the King – no, not Elvis, but the King of Thailand, every Thai's national hero. Although the King is now in his 70s, most of the posters displayed showed him as a man in his 30s, and many photos and posters of the royal family displayed in people's homes showed the young King with his very young family.

Next to an ancient empty refrigerator was a rice cooker standing on a wooden box, and this was used for boiling water to make coffee or tea. At the back of the room was a concrete-walled 'shower' room, which contained a squat toilet and a concrete tank full of water for sluicing yourself as you stood on the concrete floor. The only tap was outside, which was attached to a hose coming through the window to fill the concrete tank. A second smaller tank was for filling jugs of water to flush the toilet. Although the house was fairly grim, we were still incredibly thankful to our policeman friend for offering us the accommodation. Dozens of his neighbours stood at the front door looking in, surprised to see westerners in the house, but they were very friendly and welcoming. Children peeped round their parents' legs, initially too shy to say hello to us.

He left, but after a while returned to the house, and we were glad to see that he removed his gun, which he had left on the table. He also took a riot helmet from a shelf, gave us some containers of instant coffee, sugar and dried milk, and said goodbye. We found that upstairs there were two unfurnished, unused rooms with the doors missing. We opened the shutters upstairs to let a breeze in, laid our own camping mattresses on the floor, and covered them with our own mosquito net. After a meal at the only restaurant still open after 6pm, we returned to the house and actually had a very good night's sleep. The only sound that disturbed us was the now familiar raucous call of the large forest gecko – 'Uh-oh! Uh-oh!' – and the call of the Tokay gecko, whose similar loud call sounds like 'Okay! Okay!' We hadn't ever seen these geckos, and understood that they were highly secretive and seldom seen nocturnal creatures. However, we were told by a friend that the large forest gecko is brown with white spots and very green eyes and can grow up to 37cm, and the Tokay gecko is slightly smaller, is turquoise blue with orange or red spots, and is very aggressive.

The next day we set off, after filling our new friend's empty fridge with a selection of soft drinks and beers to say 'thank you'. The scenery was much the same as the previous days, until we passed an area where there was a strong smell of apples. We slowed our bikes and looked around, and noticed that the trees on both sides were cashew nut trees. I found it fascinating to see how cashew nuts grow. They begin to form at the end of a branch with a green outer coating. They form the well-known kidney shape, hanging in the shape of a 'C', and a swelling appears above the nut. This swelling gradually forms a fruit which looks very much like a small bell-shaped sweet pepper, which can be red, yellow or green. The fruit has a cross-shaped hollow underneath in which the cashew nut nestles, so the fruit and its nut look exactly like a bell complete with its clanger. As the fruit ripens, the outer covering of the nut becomes hard and brown. We had often seen the fruit on the market stalls – the fruit is hollow like a pepper, and has a pleasant taste of apples, hence the strong smell of apples in the air as we had passed the cashew nut orchard. We thought it unsurprising that cashew nuts are expensive, because there didn't seem to be many nuts on each tree, and they would obviously be labour-intensive to harvest.

One morning, as we left our hotel when it was still dark at 6am, we had a lovely surprise as we passed the local temple. A large tree outside the temple was lit with dozens of fluorescent tubes which were painted in stripes of many colours. The tubes were suspended vertically from the branches like giant luminescent bean pods. We passed places with strange names like Ban Bang Man, Ban Bang Dong and Ban Bang Hwa. We were now seeing more mosques than Buddhist temples, and often saw Muslim women walking and driving motorbikes, their eyes peeping out from slits in their black burqas, or their hair covered with a hijab or scarf. A lorry passed with giant blocks of ice, the melting cold water pouring onto the road and splashing us as it passed.

The scenery on the west coast was beautiful – the prettiest road since our long-ago journey to the southern-most tip of India. This area is very lush and green with rubber plantations on one side and olive palm plantations on the other. These two crops are usually associated with Malaysia, but as Malaysia was now only 700km (434 miles) away, it was hardly surprising that there were similar crops in that part of Thailand.

Tall rubber trees stood in neat straight lines with diagonal cuts on their trunks. Because latex oozes from injuries and cuts as a milky sap from a rubber tree, each night a new diagonal cut is made in the bark, causing a new flow of latex to run towards the collection cup. The cut is made on only half of the trunk one day; the next day another cut is made below it, and another and another, until a large diamond has been cut out on one side of the trunk. Not until those cuts in the bark have healed are cuts made on the other side of the tree. Half coconut shells are attached to the trunk to collect the latex or liquid rubber, and this is poured into blue plastic containers the size and shape of old-fashioned milk churns. We passed such containers full of the white liquid, sitting on the road at the end of drives. We watched the driver of a pick-up truck weigh the churns on ancient kitchen scales, and pour the thick white creamy-textured liquid from the churns into an enormous tank filling the back of the truck. The liquid rubber is then taken to a factory for central processing. The coagulated rubber is rolled in old-fashioned mangles to remove the water, and fresh or smoked sheets of raw rubber are hung out to dry in the sun. We often saw the white or brown mats of rubber hanging on lines to dry, looking like lines full of washing. Apparently 90% of rubber production now comes from plantations of rubber trees in South East Asia.

We saw occasional jackfruit trees with their giant fruits, coconut palms and banana trees were common, and everything was backed by the majestic lushly-vegetated mountains, which were capped with clouds. Although we hadn't seen water buffalo since Myanmar, now there were many again. People were friendly and calling to us. A motorbike with sidecar went past, the whole family shouting and cheering and waving to us – mother, father and one child were on the bike, and seven other children of various sizes and ages stood and sat in the sidecar.

We arrived at a non-tourist town, where we stocked up with toiletries and other necessities. We had learnt not to buy such things in the tourist areas, where prices were heavily inflated. For instance, a bar of Imperial Leather soap was 12 baht, compared to 30 baht in a tourist town, and 100 paracetamol in a non-tourist area was the same price as 10 paracetamol in the tourist towns! We had noticed since leaving Ranong that many local people were wearing thanakha sun protection on their faces, and this is an influence from nearby Myanmar, where everyone wears it painted in white or cream designs on the cheeks.

We approached Bang Niang which was a small seaside resort, so decided to stay for a while as it seemed pleasant and was fairly quiet. Parked alongside the massage parlour was a yellow van, which had a section at the side that lifted up to produce a canopy, and the bottom dropped down to form three steps. These steps led up to an ATM machine set into the side of the van. Presumably this van was used because there was not yet a bank in the resort, and we thought it a clever idea. We found a bungalow set amongst coconut palms on the beach for 500 baht (about £7) per night – for 'bungalow', which is how the Thais always advertise their accommodation, read 'room with bathroom built on stilts, often with a verandah, most often built of wood and with a thatched roof.' Occasionally, but for a much higher price, the bungalows were built of stone with a tiled roof, which were more insect-proof. There was a wonderful breeze from the sea, and we could hear the waves from our bungalow. There were several very good restaurants selling local fish dishes, so we were looking forward to having a few relaxing days, lying in the hammock, reading, swimming and generally doing nothing much at all.

The first evening we had just had prawn cocktails made with the most amazing tiger prawns for a starter. Thunder rumbled in the distance, and large drops of rain began to fall. We were sat in the open, and to begin with everyone ignored the rain, but as the rain became heavier one by one everyone picked up their plates and moved. The waitress put our bowls onto a tray, and led us along a path. By the time we reached a covered area a few yards away, our clothes were soaking wet with the deluge. We sat on cushions on the floor next to low tables; sheets of rain fell, instantly flooding the path alongside us with several inches of water. The waitresses giggled as they ran between the kitchen and the covered area with umbrellas, but the wind had also picked up and just blew the umbrellas out of their hands. Rain began to drip through the thatched roof, which was designed to provide shelter from sun, not rain, and as streams of water began to run down the light fittings, we knew it was only minutes before we would be plunged into darkness. We were also concerned about our belongings back in our bungalow, and wondered if the thatched roof would leak, so we paid our bill as soon as we had eaten our blue-spotted sea bass, and ran hell for leather through the torrential rain along the beach, which was well-lit by the constant flashes of lightning.

As well as a thatched roof, our bungalow also had a ceiling of woven grass which we hoped would hold back the rain, and so far everything inside the bungalow was dry. After drying ourselves, we sat on the dark verandah wrapped in towels watching the storm over the sea, as dramatic bolts of lightning connected the sea and the sky. Thunder rumbled all around us. Finally the storm appeared to be abating, so we crawled into our giant mosquito net, which made the six feet wide bed look like a four poster bed, and were able to sleep without the worry of rain pouring through our ceiling.

In the morning I woke first, and walked barefoot out of the bungalow onto the beach; the sea was only 15 metres away. Several coconuts had dropped to the ground in the night, so I looked warily up as I walked, avoiding walking underneath any bunches of coconuts high up in the palms. I stepped into the shallow waves; the tide was just receding, but even at high tide there was a strip of sand stretching off into the distance as far as I could see in either direction. On the high tide line was a sprinkling of delicate shells in mauves, reds, pinks, yellows, oranges and whites, and pieces of coral worn smooth from the battering of the waves. The shells were striped and swirled and occasionally spotted, and the insides of many were lined with smooth mother-of-pearl. It was 9am, but apart from a girl jogging and another westerner walking his two friendly golden retrievers, there was no-one else on the beach. We later discovered that mostly German tourists and ex-pats stayed in Bang Niang – we never saw anyone else from Britain in that resort.

While we stayed in Bang Niang the thunder rumbled every afternoon, and it usually rained during the night for a short time. We went swimming. The water temperature was 30°C, so we couldn't feel the difference from the air temperature – just how I like it!

I woke at 5.30am one morning; I thought it seemed very light outside, but it was too early for sunrise. I peeped out of the curtains, and the sight took my breath away, so I wrapped a sarong around me and walked out onto the verandah. The clouds had disappeared, although there was still a faint rumble of thunder in the distance. Above the horizon in the west, where I had last seen the sun setting, an enormous white ball hung low in the sky. A pathway of ivory light shone on the becalmed sea from the horizon, widening until it reached the beach in front of our bungalow. Everything was very still; the only sound was a swishing noise as the gentle waves touched the sand a few yards away. I had never seen such a spectacular full moon before, and within half an hour the sun was beginning to rise in the opposite direction. The rising red sun reflected on the clouds in the west, so that pink clouds surrounded the moon, which had not yet disappeared over the horizon. It was a truly magnificent moment.

Cocks were crowing as we left Bang Niang several days later on our bicycles, making our way up and down the hills – we had noticed that there were plenty of chickens in the villages again, so hoped the Avian Flu had been wiped out. As usual, for breakfast on the road we wanted to find a stall or café to fry eggs for us, either to go on rice or to put into bread. (Bread was usually only available at 7-Eleven shops, which were in the large towns or in the tourist areas).

'Khay-daaw?' we asked the first café owner, hoping that we would be able to buy some fried eggs to eat with boiled rice.

'No have,' she replied, and the next café gave us the same response.

We decided to have whatever was on offer at the next stall. Every stall or café tends to have one or two ready-prepared dishes, and they were always busy filling polythene bags with individual take-away portions for their customers. Judging from the large number of people who queued for take-away breakfasts at these stalls every morning, very few Thais even prepared their own breakfasts!

At the next café they were selling turmeric-coloured rice, plain noodles and chunks of cooked chicken, all of which were cold and stood uncovered. We felt that a piping hot dish would be safer, but the only hot dish was a rice dish that looked like porridge with chunks of cooked pork in it. This was a traditional Thai breakfast. We asked for one portion, and the large bowlful came liberally sprinkled with fresh herbs, spices and soy sauce. The rice was delicious, but the meat was pigs' kidneys – something I couldn't eat. Warren finished the bowl, declaring the kidneys tender and delicious, so for 10 baht (14p) we had had enough to keep us going for a while.

We stopped one night in Khao Lak, where we found a small resort which had very basic rooms, but had the most amazing restaurant. That evening we sat surrounded by water as we ate our meal – the tables and chairs were on a wooden platform which was built on stilts and protruded out into the sea within a small bay. It was incredibly peaceful and quite idyllic.

It was now less than 40 miles before we reached Phuket. Phuket is the most well-known tourist destination in Thailand, and is Thailand's biggest island (55km by 20km). It is joined to the mainland by a bridge, although most visitors arrive via the island's international airport. Although the interior is green with rice paddies, rubber plantations, cashew nut trees, pineapple and coconut plantations, the tourists are attracted to the sandy bays and the blue-green seas.

Because we had heard of the concentrated areas of hotels, guesthouses, sleazy girlie bars, tourist shops, restaurants, travel agents and dive shops in Phuket, we had decided initially to avoid Phuket altogether. However, we could see from the map that by doing so we were committing ourselves to a very long day of cycling before reaching accommodation, so we decided to enter Phuket via its bridge in the north, and try to find somewhere quiet to stay. We could see from the guide books that there were resorts charging up to US$8,200 per night for a villa or pavilion complete with maid and cook, where the staff ratio to guests was 3.5 to 1, but these were the ultimate – no doubt we could find something to suit our budget . . .

We arrived at the bridge which crosses a stretch of sea no wider than a big river, after which there's a long stretch of mangrove swamps on either side of the dual carriageway. We stopped after a few miles for a cold drink at a shop, which was quite fortuitous, because we were approached by a man called Oh. He gave us a leaflet with directions to a nearby camping ground with two bungalows. Oh told us that the camping ground was situated by a very quiet beach next to his shrimp farm, so we decided to take a look. We turned off the main road and onto a dirt track; ahead of us was a herd of buffalo, glowering at us beneath their menacing-looking large horns. However, they were more scared of us than we were of them, and quickly shot off the track in both directions as we approached, the baby buffaloes running fast to keep up with their parents.

At 500 baht (£7) we thought the bungalow was quite expensive. It was large and very clean with a decent bathroom, but apart from mattresses on the varnished wooden floor it was completely unfurnished. We also discovered later that electricity was only available from 6pm (when it became dark) until the early hours of the morning. A camp fire was set up, and apparently they had sing-songs with Oh playing the guitar when there were more guests. As it was now well out of season we were the only guests, and by the end of April, only three weeks away, the camping ground would be closed.

A wooded area of young casuarina pine trees ran down a shallow slope to the beach, 15 metres away. In the season (November to March), tents were set up in the shade of these trees. At this time of year it was unthinkable to sleep in a tent – we needed a fan, or preferably air conditioning! The beach was 17km long, lined with casuarinas, mangroves and wild pineapple trees (Pandanus), with the occasional coconut palm. The sea was ideal for swimming, because it shelved down fairly gently, and diving is popular in the area, because further out to sea the water is crystal clear. We walked along the beach, but were disappointed that the beach hadn't been kept very clean. However, once the tide went out there was a wide section of beach that had been cleaned by the sea – as far as the eye could see, there was no-one in sight in either direction and no footprints even on the sand except our own footprints behind us.

We stayed for three days. As the campsite was very isolated we ate our meals at the campsite restaurant, where food was cooked by Tim, Oh's wife. She also had a helper, Doo, who spoke no English. We sat in a special outdoor room, surrounded by walls of mosquito screens, so that flies and mosquitoes couldn't get in, but the breeze could. It was amusing at night to see the pale geckos running up the outside of the screen catching insects, and the campsite cats running up the 10 feet high screens chasing the geckos, although they never succeeded in catching any. At breakfast time, the herd of buffaloes often passed by, grazing right up to the room. However, if they looked in and caught our eyes, they turned tail and ran, starting a stampede!

Oh was very proud of his shrimp farm, and eagerly offered to show us round. In covered concrete tanks he grew shrimps from eggs laid by enormous tiger prawn mothers in the mangrove swamps. Tiger prawns live in 40 metres of water, but move to the mangroves to lay their eggs. The water in the covered tanks was kept at 33°C without heat, because they were set in a polythene-covered frame like a large green-house. At 20 days old, when the shrimps were fully formed, about one centimetre long and as thin as a line drawn with a pencil, they were ready to be sold to different types of shrimp farmers, who had special outdoor pools. We had seen many of these when we were cycling – large shallow oblong pools covering acres of ground, each with paddles at intervals which churned the water to oxygenate it, which is vital for the shrimps' survival and growth.

We did very little for the three days at Oh and Tim's camping ground, apart from swimming, reading and walking. We walked a mile or two along the beach, but the only signs of life were the sand crabs, which chased the waves as they receded into the sea, and ran back again as the waves tumbled back onto the sand. Apparently sea turtles normally visited this beach, usually between the months of December and February, but for some reason they hadn't been seen that year. Many people, including those doing projects on the sea turtle, stayed at the campsite at that time. Judging by the photos that we were shown of the crowds of people surrounding the magnificent turtles, we felt it likely that the turtles had got fed up with the crowds and had decided to find another beach . . .

On the third day our peace was shattered when 12 people arrived, and large canvas tents were set up under the casuarina pine trees. They were English and Thai, and were part of a project for rehabilitating gibbons. We were kept awake that night, because they were still talking loudly in the early hours of the morning. By 7am the next morning we had moved on; we cycled south to see if we could find anywhere else interesting on the island.

We travelled along the dual carriageway and passed a golf course with stunning lakes. There were rubber plantations, pineapple plantations and coconut groves. There were beautiful mosques, including an elegant one at Hat Surin which was white with onion-shaped domes that were covered with tiles in all shades of green. Ahead of us was a very steep hill, the end of a mountain range, which we had to cross to get to the bay we had decided to visit. When we arrived at Kamala Beach we found prices were quite high but, with the help of a guide book, we found a hotel with very good rooms at reasonable rates. For the same price as the previous nights at the camping ground, we now had a large ground floor room with a terrace with table and chairs. The beach was on the other side of the low terrace wall. There was air-conditioning (what bliss!), satellite television, a fridge with a mini bar, and a bathroom with two showers, one with hot water which was very unusual. Bed linen and towels were changed every day, toilet paper was supplied without charge (yes, quite often they did charge!), and the floors were washed every day. When we were told that the price also included breakfast, we were dumbfounded. We had somehow managed to find a very good value hotel, even though this was a popular beach resort in Phuket.

The beach was lined with trees and restaurants; behind the restaurants ran a river parallel to the sea, which joined the sea further along, effectively cutting off one end of the beach at high tide. An extremely rickety hand-made bridge crossed part of the river, collapsing into the water at one end at high tide. As the tide went out, the sea made interesting shapes around sandbanks, creating pools and rivers in the wide crescent of beach. Once again, though, we noticed that the beach wasn't as clean as it could have been.

Although a pleasant breeze blew from the sea in the afternoons, the temperature was soaring every day to 37°C. April is the hottest month in Thailand, and after April it begins to rain. We watched television, and were surprised to see that Bangkok had the highest temperature in Asia at 39°C. In South America the highest temperature of 33° was in Rio de Janeiro; in Australia, it was 33° in Darwin; in North America the hottest place was Miami at 31°; in New Delhi in India the temperature reached 38°, and the hottest temperature in Africa was Cairo at 34°. We appeared to be in one of the hottest places in the world!

Each afternoon at 5pm we walked to one of the restaurants on the beach for a beer while we watched the sun set. We had to pass three very small bars, and in every one of these were eight Thai girls, each of them perched cross-legged on a high stool with a mirror held up in front of her face. They were applying lipstick, smoothing eye-brows, brushing on blusher and patting their hair. When we returned an hour or so later, they were all there still doing exactly the same. This was the same every single day, but we noticed that if a western man went into one of these bars during the evening, he was instantly surrounded by four or five girls at his table.

On 13th April 2004 it was the new year – the Buddhist one, that is. This was the third time in four months that we had celebrated the new year! First of all there had been the Christian one, then the Chinese one and now the Buddhist one. Having been in Myanmar, another Buddhist country, in April of 2003, we knew what was going to happen. For the new year (a three day public holiday for the Thais), the Thais celebrate the Water Festival, which means that buckets of water are thrown over anyone who passes. Whilst we didn't mind being sprayed by the odd water pistol, a bucket of water in the face is not very nice even in very hot weather. Also, we often carried cameras and books, which could be damaged by water.

When we woke on 13th April we heard the screams outside, and saw the soaking wet tiled entrance of the hotel, now covered with wet towels to soak up the puddles on the floor. Outside the hotel entrance was a group of young men waiting with bowls of water to throw at anyone who ventured outside. We went for breakfast on the rooftop restaurant of the hotel, and later sat on our verandah overlooking the beach and read books. We also had lunch at the hotel and, because we knew that no-one was allowed to throw water after sunset, at 6.30pm we were safe to go to a beach-side restaurant for a drink and a meal. Fortunately in Phuket we discovered that the water-throwing festivities only lasted for one day, whereas in the north it was five days!

To continue cycling south, we first had to go north again the way we had come and back over the bridge. At that point we had to turn north-east and then east following the coast. After two or three days cycling we would be cycling south again, having followed the coastline round the bay. As we cycled over the bridge out of Phuket a red sun was rising above the trees, reflecting in the sea. We turned north-east and followed the coast around Phang-Nga Bay (pronounced 'pangar'). Two monks in saffron robes walked along the road collecting alms. Two dogs followed them, hoping to receive a bite to eat, and a sad-looking third dog with a missing leg gamely tried to keep up with them.

We stopped for breakfast en route and ordered food. As we sat waiting for our meal, we saw the chef picking up our fried eggs in her hand to transfer them to plates. Her assistant stood alongside, opening the stiff top of the soy sauce bottle with her teeth. A minute later both the eggs and the sauce arrived at our table.

We had no shade from the trees as we cycled. Whilst cycling we had a self-made breeze, but if we stopped in the sun we could immediately feel our skin burning. The dense shade in the mature rubber plantations looked very welcoming. At one stage the sealed road had been rubber-coated, where a truck had over-turned and deposited its large tank of liquid latex onto the road. The empty damaged tank lay in a nearby ditch.

We passed a temple with a wonderful tall fence with mythical birds and people topping every spike. The two magnificent entrances were flanked by life-sized concrete painted elephants. Further along the road was hot steaming evidence that real elephants were nearby, and we soon passed a village where a number of baby elephants were being trained to carry people. Unfortunately there was no sign of the mothers of these tiny elephants, nor did the baby elephants look very healthy.

Now the scenery was changing dramatically, and to our right we could see oddly-shaped hills, some round-topped, some conical, some leaning, some tall and square, some with overhanging tops. There were many stacks, hills and rocks hundreds of feet tall, but all of them had sheer vertical or near-vertical sides, making dramatic profiles. Plants and trees grew on the tops and even down the sides of many of the vertical cliffs, but where the rock was bare we could see the stripes of the limestone. Stalactites hung from overhanging sections, almost joining the stalagmites which had formed beneath them, and caves were clearly visible in many of the stacks. We cycled into Phang-Nga town, which was dwarfed and surrounded by these hills.

Ao Phang-Nga (Phang-Nga Bay) is a marine National Park, and is famous for its limestone cliffs, mangrove forests and karst caves. Fault movements on the mainland pushed massive chunks of limestone above the ground, forming the hills and stacks we had already seen. In the bay itself, 40 islands with massive vertical cliffs were formed, as well as caves which feature prehistoric art.

We booked a boat trip to visit Ao Phang-Nga, and a German couple were the only other tourists on the boat. The German girl was pretty, but I found it difficult when speaking to her to take my eyes off her facial piercings. As well as large silver studs at the side of each nostril, she had two silver rings, one looping in and out of each nostril, and each joined by a chain. Under her bottom lip was a silver spike more than one centimetre long, which pointed downwards until she smiled, when it jutted straight out of her chin. I couldn't help wondering how her boyfriend kissed her – carefully, I suspected!

We climbed into the long-tailed boat, and travelled along tidal channels that wove in and out of the massive mangrove forests. These channels are used by the fishermen as aquatic highways, and smaller channels led off the main ones. We saw several water monitor lizards, thinking initially that they were crocodiles. They can grow up to 2.2 metres in length, almost as long as the famous Komodo dragons of Indonesia.

The mangroves were dense; the tangled roots arched down into the sea and were reflected upside down in the water, making strange geometric patterns. Birds flew out of the branches of the mangroves as we approached, leaving the glossy bright green leaves quivering. Limestone islands and rocks towered out of the mangrove forests, many of them studded with caves. The limestone cliffs rose vertically out of the sea, striped and patterned in shades of white to darkest grey, beige to brown, and palest apricot to rust, making the rock look as though it had been draped in folds of striped fabric.

The boat left the mangroves and entered the open bay, which was scattered with islands of all shapes and sizes. We approached one, and could see that the sea flowed into a cave, the entrance of which was a mass of stalactites forming a curtain of rock hanging above the water. The boat manoeuvred carefully into the cave to avoid the stalactites, and as we looked up into the shadows we could see and hear something. We assumed that there were bats above us, but swifts began to swoop around the upper parts of the cave, and we realised that this was one of the caves where the swifts build their nests from saliva. Locals risk life and limb climbing to the top of these vast caves to collect the birds' nests, because they are so highly valued. These delicate nests are sold at a great profit to make the famous and very expensive Chinese delicacy, birds' nest soup. Warren and I wondered if people drinking this soup realised that it was made of bird spit!

The boat continued through the cave and came out the other side of the rock, again under an overhang of stalactites A floating shop went past us, the sun shining through the bottles stacked on the shelves, and we approached a Muslim floating fishing village. The whole village was built on stilts in the sea alongside a vertical limestone cliff, and as well as a mosque with a golden onion-shaped dome, the village had a school, a health clinic and a market. We docked at one of the many jetties to visit the village, but tourism had spoilt it. Now the local people only wanted to sell souvenirs, food and drink at highly inflated prices, and the original atmosphere of a fishing village had disappeared. Because it was a Muslim village, alcohol, dogs and pigs were completely banned.

Our journey by boat continued. Very few of the islands or giant rocks had shorelines – most rose straight out of the sea, rising vertically for hundreds of feet. Now we approached Khao Phing-Kan, an island made of rock that has split into two rocks which are leaning on each other. Although it's a very small island, it has another tiny island in one of its bays. Originally called Ko Tapu, this island is now rather sadly called James Bond Island, because it once featured in the film, 'The Man with the Golden Gun'. This island, though tiny in diameter, is massive in height. Tapu is Thai for 'nail', and the island, or stack, looks like a giant nail or spike driven into the shallow sea. Its base is much narrower than its top, making it look as though it could topple at any moment into the bay. Stunted trees and vegetation cling to crevices around the stack, and the small flat area at the top is covered with gnarled trees.

We disembarked to explore the island. There were tourists, but not too many because it was the end of the tourist season. Inside a cave bats were hanging upside down, and there were natural 'windows' looking out to sea with bars at the windows – these bars were columns that had been formed when stalactites and stalagmites had met. Alongside the cave was a rock which had clearly split into two, showing a glorious pattern of stripes within the rock. The rock towered above the trees and leant at a precarious angle against its partner. Trees grew above us in the rocks, and the roots emerged through holes and cracks in the rocks, and hung in curtains from overhanging rocks, mingling with stalactites.

An official notice in Thai and English explained how the island had been formed. The English translation said 'Khao Phing Kan was occurred from the crack and slide of rock due to gravity fault as the base of rock was scoured out by the torrent making the upper rock in which the weight was huge sliding down in the form of leaning on.' So now we knew!

We felt that the island was spoilt by the row of stalls selling tourist souvenirs. Next to a notice requesting people not to damage the ecology, the stall-holders sold beautiful shells and pieces of coral that should have been left in the sea, and scorpions, butterflies and beetles were encased in plastic ready to hang on someone's wall.

Our boat continued its journey, taking us past many more islands. The stalactites and stalagmites covered the sides of the cliffs, looking like wax from a candle in a draught. The boat drew alongside one of the cliffs, so that we could admire the prehistoric cave paintings. Human figures, fish, crabs, shrimps, elephants, birds, bats, boats and fishing equipment all featured in the simple paintings, and we returned to the mainland having been enthralled and impressed with the extraordinary beauty of Phang-Nga Bay.

That evening in an outdoor restaurant, a drunk beggar arrived. He was the first beggar we had ever seen in Thailand. He annoyed several people, and eventually arrived at our table as the waitress was giving us our bill. The beggar put his hand out to Warren right under his nose.

Warren turned to the beggar and said, 'Mai-ao karp.'

The beggar retreated quickly looking taken aback, and the waitress looked at Warren full of admiration, and laughingly said something we didn't understand – she spoke no English. She turned and spoke to her fellow waitresses, nodding at the beggar who was now making his way hurriedly along the pavement away from the restaurant. They all looked very impressed as well, and applauded Warren. Our English friends in Koh Samui had told us it meant 'Go away', but now we'd used it for the first time with such outstanding results, we wondered just how strong the wording was in Thai! The words were not in our Thai phrase book, but unfortunately the only words in phrase books are usually phrases such as 'Pleased to meet you', 'Here is my business card', and 'Please excuse me', rather than the more useful phrases like 'Go away', 'Leave me alone', or 'No, I don't want my photo taken with this poor emaciated baby elephant chained to a tree.' The most common phrase that we have ever needed is 'What is that?' Surprisingly, it has never been in any of our phrase books.

We left our hotel early the next morning, just in time to see ten tiny Buddhist monks, aged between 5 and 10, walking in single file down the road followed by an adult monk. It was 6am, and still completely dark, but by 6.10am it would be fully light – it never ceased to amaze us how quickly it changes from light to dark and vice versa in Asia. We had a choice of two roads to our next destination, Krabi. One was the old road, which the guide book described as winding and pretty. We'd taken detours many times on this trip when the signpost said 'scenic route', and had discovered that for 'scenic' or 'pretty', read 'hilly'. Often there hadn't even been any views on a scenic route – just hills with trees blocking any possible views. We therefore decided on the new road, especially when we discovered that it was 5km shorter than the old road.

We had gone a short way and asked directions of a motor-cyclist, after which we turned left. He very kindly followed us to explain that he meant left after one kilometre (or one kilo, as they say in Thailand). We thanked him, and he shot off in a different direction. The sun began to rise from behind one of the vertical-sided hills, and the limestone hills around us were lit with a pink glow. Sheer cliffs loomed above us, and there were still many of the limestone hills as we entered Ao Luk, a small town sitting in a dip completely surrounded by steep-sided hills and giant rocks that loomed over the buildings. One of the hills had a massive cave going through the centre of it, over 100 feet up, and we understood that the area had many caves popular with tourists.

There was a large National Park in Ao Luk, so we decided to visit it. We were impressed to see very tall rainforest trees in the shade of enormous lime-stone cliffs, again covered with stalactites and stalagmites. These cliffs gave permanent shade to magnificent specimens of rainforest trees with vast buttresses, strangling fig vines and tall palm trees. They also gave us welcoming shade on that very hot day, but we could glimpse the sun peeping through the canopy high above us.

Unfortunately a concrete path had been laid through the forest, and we felt that a natural path would have been more suitable environmentally, but it was obvious from damage to plants and worn paths through the undergrowth that people had not respected this forest. We could hear loud shouts and people calling to each other, and the path opened out into an idyllic spot where a river ran out of a high cave entrance, its top adorned with thick stalactites. However, the beautiful blue-green pool in the shade below the waterfall, surrounded by huge trees, was unfortunately full of local Thai people swimming, their clothes, shoes and towels draped over the buttresses of rainforest trees and hanging from branches. The water dropped in tiers down a waterfall, each rock on the steps of the waterfall hollowed out with centuries of rushing water, so that mini-pools had been formed out of every rock. Every mini-pool and every part of the waterfalls and the large pool was full of Thai people shouting and calling to each other, and children and adults climbed up and down the beautiful waterfalls. We felt sad that such an idyllic spot was allowed to be spoilt in such a way by the National Park authorities. Young men climbed the ancient trees, probably 500 years old, using the branches as springboards to dive-bomb into the pools. Around the pools the ground had been cleared of leaves and branches to make room for concrete tables and chairs and picnic areas for the swimmers. This was also sad, because we had been told in Australia that in rainforest environments, the leaves, branches, dead logs, and other natural debris should remain where they fall to allow nature to take its natural course. The setting was unbelievably beautiful, but should have been peaceful and serene. Maybe it would have been quieter if we hadn't arrived on a Sunday, but we felt that the beauty of that ancient rain forest had been desecrated.

We walked on, following the concrete path. Now we were alone – no-one was interested in the trees and plants. Extraordinary roots from enormous trees wove in and out of the ground; a tiny squirrel with a stripe down its back jumped from leaf to giant leaf and disappeared into the undergrowth. Concrete steps led upwards, and as we followed the steps we came to a narrow slit-like entrance to a deep cave in the rock. At the end of this narrow high cave sat a Buddha image, lit by rays of sun shining through an opening in the cave's roof, high above us. The Buddha was surrounded by stalactites and stalagmites. As we left the forest the heat of the day hit us again, and we cycled on to Krabi.

We now had one week left on our Thai visas, so once again we needed to renew our visas. We had decided to pay 500 baht each to extend our visas by another 10 days. That would enable us to make our way to Malaysia without panic. However, when we went to the Immigration office in Krabi, we discovered that the fee for such a visa extension had been increased to 1,900 baht each (£26). We now had four options – we could cycle like mad to the border before our visa ran out, involving some long, hot days of cycling; we could pay the 1,900 baht each and cycle to Malaysia at a more relaxed speed; we could catch two buses from Krabi to the border to get a free 30 day visa on re-entering the country so that we could spend relaxing days at South Thailand's beaches (the journey was more than five hours each way by bus, so not a pleasant day, but at a cost of less than 500 baht), or we could overstay our visa and pay fines at the border. We chose to spend a day on buses to Malaysia and back to Krabi, so that we could relax on the beaches ...

One of the reasons that we had decided to get another 30 day visa for Thailand, was because we needed to 'use up' time before reaching Western Australia. Our plans were to cycle south through Malaysia to Singapore, where we would get a ferry to Indonesia. Indonesia had always been somewhere I especially wanted to visit, and every island is so different that we were looking forward to travelling to several islands on our journey east towards Bali. From Bali we had already booked Qantas flights, so we would fly to Perth in Western Australia, hopefully in time for the magnificent displays of wild spring-time flowers. However, the beginning of spring in Australia is September, and we didn't want to arrive in Perth earlier than that as it would still be relatively cool. When we discovered that Indonesia had changed their visa rules, so we could only stay 30 days in Indonesia instead of the 60 days we had hoped for, we realised that we needed to adjust our plans, otherwise we would be arriving in Perth in the winter.

We had a few options. If we arrived in Australia in the winter, we could fly from Perth to Darwin or Broome in northern Australia for a few weeks, where the temperature would be much hotter. However, internal flights in Australia are expensive, and we were concerned about our budget. Another option that we considered was to fly to The Philippines for a few weeks, but we discovered that the weather there was unbearably hot and humid at that time and the typhoon season was approaching. We could spend time in Malaysia and Singapore, but they are more expensive than Thailand, so it made sense budget-wise to spend any extra time in Thailand. Once again we had found it impossible to plan our route so that we could visit each country at the best time – we now planned to stay longer in Thailand, despite the fact that the tourist season was finishing, and it was becoming unbearably hot.

We had been keen to visit south east Thailand, where we had been told that the scenery was magnificent and there were superb mosques, the area being Muslim. However, problems were breaking out in the area. We read in the Bangkok Post that some Buddhist monks had been hacked to death, and fighting had broken out between Muslim extremists and the Security Forces. Although tourists were not in any way targeted, we felt it was sensible to avoid the area, so we decided to cycle down the west coast of Southern Thailand, as close to the coast as possible, visiting the beaches on the Andaman Sea. Whilst the whole of southern Thailand is predominantly Muslim, there didn't seem to be any problems in the west. Despite these problems, I feel at this stage that we should add that in our experience the Muslim people in every country had always been very friendly, generous and honest, and we had especially enjoyed the Muslim countries and Muslim areas through which we had travelled.

Our second visa run in Thailand went better than we had expected. We were crammed into a mini bus for the four hour journey, but at least it was air-conditioned. At Hat Yai, the largest city before Malaysia, we had to change to a local bus or take a taxi. The local bus was cheap, but would drop us off at the border and leave us to find our own way through the Thai and Malaysian immigration offices. The taxi would wait for us at immigration and guide us – it was also air-conditioned, so we decided to splash out and go by taxi. For 500 baht (about £7) the taxi took an hour each way to drive 60km, accompanying us to the Thai immigration office, where they stamped us out of the country. It was another kilometre before we reached the Malaysian border, but our taxi driver was happy to take us. We entered Malaysia, where our passports were stamped with an automatic 3 month visa to stay in Malaysia. However, we weren't going to stay at the moment, so travelled a short taxi journey to another office, where we had our passports stamped out of Malaysia. There was a one kilometre drive back to Thailand, where we were given a new 30 day visa on entering Thailand – this was the sixth time we had entered Thailand in one year! We certainly would have preferred to have paid for a 3 month or 6 month visa, but it just isn't possible in Thailand. Back at Hat Yai we had a short time before the mini bus returned to Krabi, so at our request the taxi driver took us to some bike shops. We were able at last to get some Kevlar inserts, which are strips of man-made fibre to be inserted between tyres and inner tubes. Police wear bulletproof vests made of Kevlar, so with our kevlar inserts we hoped to reduce the number of punctures in the future, although the Kevlar would add weight to our bikes. We had had 30 punctures between us since we began our journey, 13 of which had been in the last few weeks in Thailand.

Thirteen hours after leaving Krabi we were back again. We decided to stay a few days before cycling to Malaysia via the coastline, avoiding the main roads and the mountain pass that we had travelled in the mini bus.

One evening in Krabi, Warren saw a young man carrying a strange bag, which we recognised immediately as a 'bar-bag'. We carry the same bags ourselves – square bags with a metal rod that clips onto the front of the handlebars of a bike. Precious items, such as money, passports and cameras are carried in these bags, which are unclipped as soon as we leave our bikes, and shoulder straps are added for carrying. The young man was Singaporean, and was cycling (with sponsors) from London to New Zealand. Two other men joined him, another Singaporean and a Malaysian who works and lives in Singapore. We spent an enjoyable evening together, and promised to get in touch as soon as we reached Singapore. One of them was finishing his trip there, and he offered us accommodation and a gin sling once we arrived in Singapore – an offer not to be refused!

Because we had a room with a fan, we were finding ourselves standing under the shower two or three times a night and, without drying ourselves, returning to bed to lie under the fan to cool off. Even better, we sometimes soaked a sarong which we laid over ourselves, so that the fan and the wet fabric cooled us down. We realised that we were going to have to spend more of our budget on air-conditioned rooms, so that at least we could always have a good night's sleep.

We cycled a short trip to the coast, because we'd heard there were some beautiful islands and beaches to visit. Ao Nang was surprisingly full of westerners, who all arrived in ancient sawngthaews (pick-up trucks converted to taxis for 10 plus people). The sides and backs of the sawngthaews were open, backpackers stood on the back steps hanging onto the rails, and their backpacks were piled up on top on the roof rack. Many Thais arrived for day trips, but they came in incredibly smart, modern double-decker coaches, artistically painted with pictures of underwater scenes, mountains or flowers. These coaches were air-conditioned and the enormous tinted windows had curtains.

In Ao Nang we found The Irish Rover Pub selling draught Guinness, and I was tempted inside by the board on the street which said 'Shepherds Pie with mixed fresh vegetables and lashings of gravy'. After almost two years of travelling, the thought of such a dish was too much to resist! Whereas most Thai restaurants are closed by 7.30 or 8pm, or even 6pm in non-tourist towns, this pub began to get crowded at 7.30. It became quite noisy, and an English middle-aged couple sitting on a large table nearby were loudly extolling the virtues of Australia to four young backpackers, and complaining that New Zealand had been cold, even in the hottest month of February. They went on and on, grumbling that they had been unable to find accommodation, and had sometimes had to travel hundreds of kilometres just to find somewhere to stay.

'We'd 'ad enuff,' the wife said loudly. 'We cu' ar losses an' 'anded the 'ire car back a week early. We lost ar money but we flew back to Sydney. Mind, we fort the scenery in Noo Zealand was boo'iful though.'

It was a long time since we'd heard the accent. On our other side two Brummies were complaining to each other that the sausages in their sausage casserole were the wrong sort. Why was everyone complaining? This pub served real European sausages, not the pink plastic boiled sausages normally available in Thailand. Had they got Lincolnshire sausages instead of Cumberland? We returned to our quiet, air-conditioned room and had a glass of wine while we watched an English film on television.

Ao Nang had a pleasant beach, but it was full of long-tailed boats which were local water taxis waiting to take tourists to any of the neighbouring islands or beaches, making Ao Nang a very convenient centre. Phi Phi Island (pronounced 'Pee Pee') was a very popular tourist destination 42 kilometres away in the middle of the bay, and tourists were taken there by express boat. Although we had been told that Phi Phi Island had very beautiful beaches, we were also told that it was very touristy, so we preferred to visit the smaller islands or beaches.

We took the boat to Phranang Cave Beach, and long-tailed boats and speedboats criss-crossed the sea on their way to different islands, passing the limestone stacks in the bay. A cave at the end of the sandy beach has a legend that in the 3rd century BC an Indian princess drowned in a storm as her ship foundered nearby. The legend has it that her spirit inhabits the cave near the wreck, and she is able to grant favours to anyone who comes to pay respect. The requests of local fishermen were usually to catch plenty of fish, and as thanks for such plentiful catches they placed carved phallic symbols in the cave. There are huge mounds of these phallic symbols just inside the entrance to the cave, some painted, some natural wood, some golden, but one fisherman must have caught Moby Dick to have left a tree trunk carved into a six foot phallus!

We walked across the peninsula towards another beach, passing through shady woods. Fascinating openings in the rocks led to caves inside the hills, and roots from trees high above protruded through the roofs of caves and rooted into the ground, forming curtains and barriers. Once again, almost all of the surfaces of the limestone rocks, inside the caves and outside on the cliffs, were covered with stalactites. There were even beaches of golden sand with overhanging limestone rocks adorned with curtains of stalactites.

We visited Diamond Cave. This cave had a subtly-lit walkway to guide the way, and we were enthralled to see a golden 'waterfall' of sparkling quartz inside the cave. The limestone formations in this cave were spectacular, but the best thing of all was that we were the only ones there. There were cathedral-like domes, hollow stone tubes like organ pipes which resonated deeply when tapped, sheets of wavy thin stalactites stretching up to the top of the cavern, and rocks shaped like ferns and trees. Bats hung upside down high above us. Mythology said that this was the Indian sea princess' Grand Palace, while the other cave with the phallic symbols was her spirit's summer palace.

The sky was changing from blue to grey late afternoon when we caught another boat back. It was only a ten minute ride to our beach, but as we approached the beach the dark grey skies let loose a torrent of rain, so that the dash from boat to shelter made us as wet as if we'd swum back. We walked up the hill to our hotel – there was no point in hurrying as we couldn't get any wetter, and our belongings were safely stowed away in a waterproof bag. The hill running down to the beach was like a raging torrent as we tried to cross, and as we stepped into the road up to our ankles in warm rushing water, one of my flip-flops was ripped off and shot back down the hill. I ran down the road, half hopping, with Warren laughing too much to be able to help me. I had to crawl on my stomach in the water to reach my flip-flop, because it had become wedged under a parked car. We walked the rest of the way back to our hotel barefoot, laughing when hot rain gushed off the roofs onto us.

One day at mid-day it began to get dark, and thunder rumbled in the distance. This was unusual – although it had rained late afternoon on most days, it had never rained that early in the day. As always before the storms, the wind suddenly began to blow. The wind always pre-empted the storms, and indicated a change of pressure and a different weather system approaching. We always knew it would be only moments before the rain began, at which stage the winds dropped again. We stood on the road near the beach, and the sand was being picked up and was painfully hitting our arms and legs. The sky became darker and darker. Until a few minutes before locals had been trying to persuade tourists to take water taxis, but as the fierce winds whipped up the waves, the empty long-tailed boats suddenly left the beach and rushed en masse to the next beach north, presumably to a more sheltered bay. The clouds were scudding across the sky at high speed, and palm trees were bent nearly double in the wind. Hats were flying across the road, and everyone dashed away from the palm trees, which were shedding dead fronds and coconuts. The temperature suddenly dropped 2° or 3°C. We dashed to our favourite coffee shop, where we were welcomed and given iced water, because there was already a power cut and the coffee-making machine wasn't working without electricity. Thunder cracked loudly overhead, lightning lit up the now black skies and the rain began. Within minutes it was falling so hard that we couldn't see across the road and drains were blocking, so that floodwater was rising fast towards the steps of the shops. We settled down to wait for the rain to stop. One and a half hours later the deluge abated. The sun came out, and very quickly dried the roads and pavements. Only puddles remained to remind us that it had rained.

Although the rain had finished, gigantic waves began to crash onto the beach, and one of the long-tailed boats returning tourists from another beach overturned as it approached the sand, tipping the passengers and their belongings into the sea, and crushing the metal-framed canopy which is designed to give shade to the passengers. Fortunately no-one was hurt, but no doubt a few cameras had been ruined, and the boat-owner would certainly have had no insurance. We had already noticed that these boats were very unstable, especially if passengers were not evenly distributed, and the owner of a long-tailed boat often asked a passenger to move a few inches to left or right to balance the boat correctly. It doesn't help the stability that there is a heavy diesel engine driving the propeller which is mounted high up on the stern of the boat. We noticed that the only people helping the boat owner to right the boat and retrieve the broken engine were the backpackers – none of the locals waded into the waves to help.

After an enjoyable few days at Ao Nang we moved on again. As we cycled, a terrible noise approached us from behind, and an old bus belching exhaust fumes passed us. There was a terrible scraping noise as it passed, and it was obvious that some part of the bus was dragging on the road, but because of the dense exhaust fumes we couldn't see what it was. A few hundred yards further on the bus stopped in the middle of the road, and began reversing towards us, weaving all over the road. The driver clearly couldn't see us behind him, so we cycled onto the wrong side of the road to safety. We watched as the driver jumped out of the bus, picked up the rear door of the bus which was now lying in the road, threw it through the open doorway, and continued noisily on his way!

As we cycled along a quiet road, we disturbed a 3 feet monitor lizard on the dirt at the side of the road. It ambled into the long grass and disappeared as we passed. The same day we saw two dead baby monkeys at different places at the side of the road. We were cycling through villages. In one of them, three little boys at the first house shouted 'Hello, hello, hello, hello,' jumping up and down excitedly. Further up the road children looked to see what the commotion was, and they shouted in the same way as we passed, and so it went on through the whole village. We felt like royalty passing through!

We cycled from the mainland across a bridge onto an island, and had to catch a ferry onto another island – the ferry crossing was no wider than a river. This island was Koh Lanta Noi (north Koh Lanta) and was of no interest to tourists, because it was surrounded by mangroves instead of beaches. However, one more short ferry from the south of that island took us to the north of Koh Lanta Yai (South Koh Lanta). The whole of the west coast is beach, but as it was now May and past the tourist season, most of the hotels, guesthouses, bars, restaurants, cafés and shops had closed down. We were lucky to find a bungalow resort that was still open, and we chose an air-conditioned brick-built bungalow in the gardens of this resort, which fronted onto the beach. An open-air restaurant served food and drink all day, and we had the 4km beach to ourselves for most of the time.

As Koh Lanta was a tourist area there was an internet café there, so we went in to e-mail friends and family. This was the first time we had been able to contact anyone for a while, so it was a terrible shock to find e-mails from my brother, John, to say that my mother had been rushed into hospital, having had a heart attack. Initially the doctors had said that she wouldn't survive the night, but she was sitting up having a cup of tea at 11 o'clock the next morning. John's e-mails indicated that she was progressing well and was in very good spirits. My mother wrote a letter to us, which John copied onto an e-mail and sent to us. In it Mum said she was feeling very well, and on no account should we come home, because she didn't want to spoil our travelling. She even went so far as to say that she would refuse to see us if we did return! Whilst I knew my mother would be pleased to see us if we returned, I also knew that she would be very upset that we had changed our plans because of her. After phone calls with my brother, e-mails from my son and messages from my mother, we decided not to return to England immediately. However, we planned to stay a while in Koh Lanta where we could keep in touch – not every town we visited had internet cafés or even international phones.

The bay in Koh Lanta is quite pretty, with a wooded headland at each end. At this time of year the cloud formations were quite spectacular; in the high season there wouldn't have been any of these clouds, but it was the clouds that were now making the most amazing sunsets that we'd seen in Thailand. We found a very pleasant beach bar, where we sat every evening with gin and tonics – a real luxury for us! On the first evening, we looked out across the bay – to our right was the tree-covered headland at the end of the bay, now a black silhouette against the sky. On the horizon, a number of limestone islands were now grey silhouettes, and the sun was setting between the two largest of these islands. In the sky above the islands, it was as though an artist had painted bold strokes of luminous pink, orange and mauve on top of the turquoise of the sky. Below these colours were narrow banks of cotton-wool clouds, which were constantly changing colour as the sun sank to the horizon.

Every evening, once the sun began to set all the local dogs came onto the sand, where they liked to lie in the evenings. They sat in a line facing the sea as though they were watching the sun set, and it was quite amusing to see their silhouettes outlined against the pink sea. One of the dogs adopted us, but this may have been because Warren gave it some crusts of bread, which it wolfed down and enjoyed as if they'd been pork chops! Whenever we went back to our cottage in the grounds of the resort, the dog was waiting for us, lying across the door in the hope that we would let him in once the door was opened. Possibly the cool draught from the air conditioning coming under the door was also a bonus for him.

One morning we sat on the sundeck of the resort where we were staying, which overlooked the beach. It was breakfast time, and we were having our first coffee of the day. We looked out to sea, and as we watched we were excited to see a tornado on the horizon. A bank of white clouds above the horizon had a dark flat base, and from the base of those clouds was a vertical black line slightly funnelled at the top. Where the black line joined the horizon it was surrounded by a hazy area, which was the water being sucked up into the funnel. As we watched and took photos, the black line of the tornado curved sideways at the top but was still attached to the cloud, although the base stayed in the same spot. It curved and twisted more and more, then the whole area beneath the clouds darkened, and the line faded into the dark sky. The sky became shaded in vertical stripes, which indicated a lot of rain in that area. The bright white sails of a yacht glinted in the sun as the yacht gradually edged in front of this dark area, and the tiny white triangles were distinctly outlined against the dark sky beyond it. The storm was probably miles out to sea, and during the ten minutes that we had been watching the tornado, there had been sun and blue skies further along the horizon, and it was sunny and calm where we sat by the beach.

Later in the day we walked a mile to the end of the beach. On the way back we saw a pair of eagles soaring over the beach above us, and gliding around the small casuarina pine trees at the edge of the beach. At times they were almost motionless, hanging in the sky above the trees, their wing-tips quivering. Their heads were bent down searching for prey, and we watched them for a long time. They were magnificent – they had white heads and necks with brown bodies and wings. The tips of their wings were dark, and the wing tip feathers were like out-stretched fingers. The sun was shining on them, and they were perfectly silhouetted against the bright blue sky and white clouds. With their massive wings slowly rising up and down, they looked like animated drop-leaf tables. We had never before had such a superb close-up view of eagles in flight, and we saw this pair of eagles on a few occasions during our stay in Koh Lanta.

One day we were surprised to see three western girls arriving on the beach in their bikinis, and going into the sea for a swim. It was unusual to see other people apart from us on the four kilometre curving beach. Warren was tempted to run full pelt down the beach to them, shouting frantically, 'Get out of the water! Get out of the water!' and pointing dramatically at the sea behind them, but I managed to dissuade him. I wasn't sure that the joke would work without the Jaws music in the background!

Every day we phoned my brother, and I sent long e-mails which John printed daily and read to Mum. However, I wanted to send a proper hand-written letter to my mother, so we set off on our bikes. We couldn't find the Post Office, and had to ask several people who kept pointing up the road or down the road, and eventually we tracked it down. It was well hidden in a deserted shopping precinct. The good news was that the sign on the door said 'Open'. The bad news was that although the door was unlocked and we could push it open, there was no sign of anyone in the small post office.

'Saswadi-ka,' we called, but there was no response.

We checked outside again. The sign on the window said 'Open 8.30am – 4.30pm'. Inside was a desk instead of a counter, and it was a bit disconcerting that small piles of letters and envelopes were scattered on the concrete floor around the desk, as though someone had been sorting them before abandoning them. I wondered how safe my letter would be if left at the post office. A large folder was lying on the desk with sheets of postage stamps protruding, and no doubt the drawer that acted as a till wasn't locked. A handbag was lying on top of a filing cabinet at the back of the room.

Warren went in search of someone, anyone. All of the shops, restaurants, cafés and bars around the post office in the precinct were closed until November, but eventually Warren found someone in a nearby restaurant who said that the post office was closed for lunch.

Warren said, 'No, the door's open,' but the local just kept repeating the same words.

'No, closed lunch.'

We stood outside the post office wondering what to do and when to return, or whether to just post the letter in a post box with plenty of stamps. A man wearing a T-shirt with a post office logo came up to us.

'What do you want?' he asked. This sounds abrupt, but it's the way all Asians talk, and no offence is meant. Often someone will call, 'You, you,' if they want to talk to you, and a request for something in a shop or restaurant in Thailand is often abruptly answered by 'No have.' Also, anyone who has ever been to a Chinese restaurant in London's Chinatown will have been approached by a waiter saying, 'What you want?' Anyway, I digress – we told the Post Office employee we wanted to send a letter to England.

'Closed for lunch,' he said.

I found it really strange that he'd bothered to leave his table in the restaurant to come to tell us, and was not willing to help us, when clearly from the sign in the window he should not have closed the post office for lunch anyway! We'd never known a Thai have a lunch break before – it's the norm to go into a shop and find several people sat on the floor eating noodles at lunch time.

The following day we went back to the post office to send a small package. It was rather worrying that the post office employee said that he didn't have any stamps, especially as I had seen sheets of them in the folder the day before. He promised that he would put some stamps on later, took our money and laid the package behind him. The more we thought about it, the more worried we were that our package might not be sent. The guidebooks warn that tourists in Asia should always watch the stamps being franked, to ensure that they cannot be removed and used again. The stamps on a large parcel could be worth more than the employee's salary. Five hours later we decided to return to ask for our package back. There were still no stamps on it, and a different man said that he planned to take it to the town the next day to put stamps on it! He seemed to have no qualms in handing over the package to us, even though he had never seen us before. I think I should add that this strange experience in no way reflects the Thai post service generally. The post office employees are usually very helpful and efficient, and the Thai postal service is normally excellent – even the regular postcards sent to my mother usually arrived in England within a week.

We left the post office and went to the internet café to send another long newsy e-mail to my brother for my mother to read. My mother was writing letters to me, which John copied onto e-mails and sent to us. The internet café was a strange combination of different shops. It was a long narrow shop and, like all shops in Thailand the front wall to the street was a roller shutter which, when lifted, exposed the whole shop to the street. Down one side was a long counter – this was the pharmacy. Down the other side was a shorter counter, behind which a girl advertised tours. It wasn't exactly a travel agent, but that sort of thing. At the back of the shop, still opposite the pharmacy counter, were four computers – this was the internet café.

We were sat at our computer for a while, when we noticed that we were completely alone in the shop, and continued to be alone for over an hour. This amazed us, because on the pharmacy counter were dozens of large plastic jars of frequently requested medication. Each jar contained 1,000 tablets of paracetamol or other similar drugs. I stood examining the labels for some time. The other medication – boxed tubes, tablets, pills and ointments – were stacked neatly behind unlocked glass doors under the long glass counter and on the wall behind the counter of this well stocked pharmacy. In all the times we used that internet café, we never saw a pharmacist or anyone serving, although we once saw a girl sat there preparing morning glory leaves on the counter for her lunchtime stir-fry! We had previously visited other chemists in Thailand, and had often had to wait up to five minutes in the empty shop before someone came running from across the street or a neighbouring shop. How different from the security that we have to adopt in England!

Talking about internet cafés, we had some frustrating, though amusing experiences in them. In Koh Lanta the charge was usually 2 baht a minute, but we found one at 70 baht per hour. However, once we had finished, usually after one hour plus, they just didn't know how to calculate the amount due. After tapping completely irrelevant and obscure figures into a calculator for a minute or so they announced a price – any price. This price seldom matched the figure shown on the calculator. One girl just couldn't work it out, threw down the calculator in disgust and walked off without telling us the price on one occasion. When they told us the price we often disagreed.

'No, it should be …. Baht,' we said, because we had already calculated it ourselves, and they would get terribly flustered and tap away again. We tried to show them how to calculate the figure, but they were really just not interested. The two girls running the internet café in Koh Lanta usually spent their time on the computers, chatting to boys on the internet chat-room. Perhaps they should have spent some of that time learning the two times table or something useful! Even where the price was 2 baht a minute, a calculator was used to calculate the price. Another day in the same internet café a tourist went to pay and complained that the computer had crashed and she'd lost something she was typing.

'Oh yes,' the girl said, taking her money. 'We often have problems with that computer!'

In the shops it was the same problem with calculations; if we handed over a 100 baht note for a 75 baht purchase, they tapped into a calculator to see how much change to give us! Sometimes we felt like slapping them round the head and saying, 'Surely you can do better than that?' However, I'm not sure that young British shop employees would do any better without their computerised tills!

In the resort where we were staying they had what we thought was a good, simple system if we wanted our room cleaned. All we had to do was to put the key to our room in a special box in reception. We did. Three hours later we returned and asked for the key.

'No have,' said the girl behind the desk. 'Ask cleaner.'

We searched the grounds until we found her – she was asleep in a chair on someone's verandah, her trolley of cleaning materials blocking the path.

'No have,' she said, when we asked for the key, and settled back to sleep again. A repeat of this performance finally produced the key – the cleaner still had it in her trolley, and our room hadn't yet been cleaned.

Going into one of the local shops, we wanted to enquire about the price of something. The assistant sat on a chair, asleep with her head on a table. We woke her and asked the price. She half raised her head, named the price, and went back to sleep! However, we thought this preferable to being followed and hassled as we walked around the shops, which is something that seldom happens in Thailand.

One day we walked two miles along the beach to the other end of the bay. Outside the bars and restaurants that had closed down, bamboo chairs were laying on their sides on the sand, damaged where the high tide had battered them. At the end of the bay we reached a very expensive resort. It was unfortunate that on either side of this resort were two areas used by local fishermen. Although the moored long-tailed fishing boats looked picturesque in the bay, the beach in front of these two areas was simply a dumping ground. Broken glass beer bottles embedded in the sand were the most dangerous obstacles, but piles of plastic and glass bottles, pieces of fabric and broken plastic, polythene bags, single flip-flops, chunks of polystyrene, half coconut shells, piles of empty oyster and mussel shells, rusty tins, plastic oil cans, plastic straws, abandoned pieces of rope and fishing nets amongst and between the lobster pots and piles of nets all ensured that the area looked like the local rubbish tip. Unfortunately, although Thailand has large numbers of beautiful beaches, there doesn't appear to be the proper infrastructure to ensure that the beaches are kept beautiful. Although a few people make an effort and most tourist beaches are kept reasonably clean, this is only because they know that the tourists expect it.

One day I pushed my bike through the garden of the resort on my way to the shops. In front of me on the path was a large yellow and brown locust. I pushed the bike around it, but in its fright it jumped sideways and clung upright to one of the spokes of the wheel. Surprisingly I couldn't prise it off, so I had to set off cycling and hope that when it let go it wouldn't fly into my face!

We noticed that at the weekends Thais came to stay at the resort, large numbers of them sharing one double room, because the charge is for the room and not per person. We don't know where they went during the day when it was very hot, because we only ever saw them on the beach at sunrise or at sunset, and remembered that this was also the case in India.

It was still incredibly hot, the temperature never going below 25°C at night and up to 35°C during the day. The humidity was incredibly high, making these temperatures very difficult to bear. Now that it was May the rain, wind and storms could be expected to increase and virtually all of the resorts would soon close down. Only the larger resorts were open all year, but from 1st May to 31st October the cost of a room or cottage was half the normal price. There was an expensive resort next to ours, but the food was so good at our resort (and at a fraction of the price at the expensive resort), that the tourists staying there used to come to eat in our resort's restaurant. This was lucky for us, because we appeared to be the only people staying in the resort after a few days, so we had plenty of other westerners to chat to during the evenings. Also, because he wasn't busy, the chef agreed that I could watch him making the Massaman curry that we especially liked. I was able to make notes of the recipe, so that we could make the curry when we got back to England.

My mother's health had improved daily and she was enjoying the company of the other ladies in the ward. The doctors were very pleased with her, and she was due to be moved the next day to a convalescent ward, ready for her return home. We had been in Koh Lanta for 10 days, so we now felt comfortable moving on to the next town, travelling south towards Malaysia. We knew that there would be two nights in towns with no internet cafés or international phones before we reached Trang, a very large town.

We set off on our bicycles at 6am, but Warren had to return with our adopted dog. He wouldn't stop following us, and we were concerned that we might never get rid of him. On the way to Koh Lanta we had followed the car ferry signs for five miles along a dirt road, but we had since discovered that there was a special ferry for motorbikes which avoided this detour. There was a long-tailed boat waiting – the ferry was a normal long-tailed boat with the prow of the boat cut off to form a blunt front for vehicular access. Boards had been laid across the boat to form a deck, but it was quite high and, knowing the long-tailed boats' tendency to tip, we felt quite nervous. A two feet wide gangplank formed a nerve-wracking wobbly access onto the boat, but I had noticed that motorbikes normally drove straight on and sat astride their bikes, which stood side by side in pairs on the narrow boat.

Fortunately we were the only passengers on that boat, and we pushed the bikes on and laid them down. Warren asked the price.

'40 baht,' said the ferryman.

'No, 20 baht,' said Warren.

'OK,' the ferryman replied.

As the boat set off, I hurriedly kneeled on the planks, hanging on to the sides. The boat rocked from side to side in the waves, and I was very nervous. It was fortunate that the crossing was only 8 minutes long, so by 6.30am we were on the next island.

We passed the mangroves, and occasionally we saw a very mature tree with a massive trunk. Such trees are always revered in Asia, and are often encircled with yards of fabric or ribbons, usually red or pink. Shrines are set up around these trees, and offerings and garlands decorate the shrines.

We stopped for breakfast. The café looked fine from the road, but as we got close we could see the tables were covered – and I mean covered – with flies. The owner came over with a dirty cloth and slapped the top of the table with it, causing a cloud of flies to rise into the air, only to hover and immediately resume their previous positions on the table. Flies sat on the previously cooked food, which stood on the serving counter. We felt safe, however, with the fried eggs we ordered. A wok full of oil was heated by a foot long flame, and four eggs were dropped into the very hot oil and deep-fried. They were the crispiest fried eggs I'd ever had, but as we put them into the bread we had provided the yolks burst, so we ended up making a real mess of ourselves!

We cycled along roads lined with trees covered with scarlet flowers and large black seedpods. It was as though the road ahead was lit with flames, and when I examined the flowers closely each individual flower about one inch across was like a miniature iris, but with 12 very long delicate stamens. Sometimes the trees had similar yellow flowers, and there were also the Laburnam-like trees that we had seen before and striking purple-flowered jacaranda trees. The grass verges next to the road were full of petunia-like purple trumpets, and also clover-pink flowers like tiny round pink bottle brushes.

Often in southern Thailand there are massive plantations on either side of the road. These are the oil palms. Whereas the common coconut palm has a tall, slim, elegant slightly ridged trunk with a burst of palm fronds high up in the sky, the olive palm grows in a different way. It starts life as a clump of graceful fronds close to the ground, and as it grows taller the lower fronds die off, forming a very rough jagged trunk, even if the fronds are neatly trimmed away. Dirt collects in these rough pockets, forming perfect havens for seeds to germinate, so all sorts of plants cling to the trunks of these trees, ferns being the most common. They grow all the way up the trunk, making it look like it has green shaggy hair that needs cutting. The ferns thrive in the shade of the plantations, and termite mounds also lean against the trunks. The trees have yellow-red fruits like olives, and these fruits are processed to make very creamy oil, not dissimilar to coconut oil. This is made into body oil, creams, soap, margarine, vegetable butter and even lubricants.

We passed a lorry that had broken down, and the usual broken branches of trees had been placed in the road and were sticking out of the driver's window to warn approaching traffic of the obstruction – no red triangles in that part of the world! A motorcyclist passed, one hand holding on to a stack of 10 plastic garden chairs on the passenger seat behind him.

Because of lack of accommodation, we cycled to Trang in two days instead of three, so the second day was a very long, hot day of cycling for us. As we approached this big town, we could see mountains beyond it. These were part of a mountain range that runs down the centre of Thailand. In the town, we passed a secondary school. The children in their school uniform were just coming out of school. Literally hundreds of motorbikes belonging to the children lined the lane that approached the school, and stalls were set up outside the school gates, cooking barbecued chicken, banana fritters and pork satay to tempt the children as they left school. Motorbike taxis were also waiting in the street outside the school.

We booked into a hotel, feeling very hot and tired from the journey, and went to the internet café. There were two e-mails, one with very good news and one with very bad news. Julian had e-mailed to say that he and Lucy now had a baby girl, Amy, my new grand-daughter. However, there was an e-mail from my niece asking me to ring, because Mum had suffered a relapse after having another heart attack the night before. On the phone my niece told us that once again the doctors had been surprised how well she had recovered, but that she was still weak. I now felt guilty that we had continued our travelling, although Mum had been in good spirits and was recovering well when we left Koh Lanta. However, there was no way now that we wanted to continue cycling, and we went and booked the first available flights back home. Fortunately Trang has a very small airport, so we could fly to Bangkok and from there back to Heathrow. We booked the first flights available which were the next morning; we had spent four months in Thailand.

We spent the evening preparing the bikes for the flight by covering them with protective cardboard, and jettisoning as much of our belongings as we could, wanting to reduce the weight to avoid excess baggage. The maid was thrilled when we told her that she could keep these items, and put her hands in prayer up to her face to say thank you.

In the morning we went again to the internet café. It took an age for the internet to connect. My brother, John, had sent an e-mail, so I clicked to open it. After what seemed an age the message was open in front of me. It was the worst of news, and my eyes could only focus on the first words, 'I am sorry to have to tell you like this, but Mum died . . .' The rest was a blur. Warren stood behind me reading the message, and put his hand on my shoulder. I couldn't move; I couldn't speak. I stared at the words, my heart heavy, as tears poured down my cheeks. Warren pushed a tissue into my hand, and as I turned to him I saw that he was also crying.

What can I say? – 'if only' are such futile words. Mum had been proud of us and had been interested in what we were doing, and she was a generous person who wanted us to continue our journey. Her visitors had looked forward to hearing from her where we were and what we had been doing, and she had enjoyed showing them the latest postcards from us, which we had sent to her every week of our journey. Whilst we had been away on our journey, she had learnt to type long letters to us on the computer, which John pasted into e-mails to send us – quite an achievement for an 85-year-old lady. I was very proud of her, and am glad that I told her so. We later heard that on the day before she died, Mum had the nurses in stitches with amusing stories.

We were taken by minibus taxi to Trang airport. The airport is modern but very small. Thai Airlines fly only one plane a day to Bangkok and two planes on Fridays. No other airline uses the airport, so it is probably closed for much of the time. Our baggage went through without any hitches, and we were finally sat on the plane awaiting take-off. As our plane taxied slowly towards the runway, we noticed about a dozen airport staff – baggage-handlers, check-in girls, security staff – stood in a line outside the airport building, waving goodbye to the plane. We'd never seen such a thing before, and wondered if it was the entire staff of the small airport, waiting for the plane to leave so that they could close the airport. I felt a lump in my throat and tears in my eyes as I waved back to them, and as I turned to Warren I saw that he, too, had tears in his eyes. For the time being our journey was finished, but we were terribly sad to be returning to England under such circumstances. We planned to go back – sooner or later – to continue our journey, but for now our future plans were uncertain.

In 23 months we had cycled 8,944 miles (14,297km) through 15 countries; we had been on numerous flights with our bicycles (each one with our fingers crossed, hoping that we wouldn't be charged excess baggage). We had taken over 30 ferries, some where we stood on raft-like contraptions with our bikes, some where we got wet, one where we had to carry our bikes to the boat as we waded through water, and some on luxury liner-like ferries with restaurants.

We had met wonderful people in every country, we'd made many new friends, and we had been lucky to see the way people really live in areas seldom visited by tourists. We had learnt a lot, and one important thing we'd learnt was that we should be very grateful to have been born in England. Whilst it's wonderful to visit foreign countries, some of them would not be pleasant to live in permanently. Compared to many people in the world, everyone in England is rich. None of us have to bring up our families literally on the pavement, or wonder where the next crust of bread (or bowl of rice) is coming from. We have comfortable homes, we are educated, and we can get medical treatment if we are ill. We take far too much for granted, and are often quick to complain about our lot. Warren and I hope that we have learnt to appreciate many of the things we used to take for granted. We may now be poorer if we look at our bank balance, but we consider that we are much richer for everything that we have experienced on our journey. I hope we don't forget this lesson that we have learnt. Our cycling journey had lasted for two years, and was the most amazing experience of our lives.

We returned to England in the middle of May, and how beautiful it was at that time of year. There were blue skies and the sun was shining; the fields were full of golden rape; bluebells and primroses were flowering in the woods; grass verges were full of wild flowers; there were green rolling hills and birds singing; Laburnam, May and Lilac trees were in blossom; blue-tits played in the branches and robins hopped in the gardens. I couldn't help but think how much my mother would have loved to have seen it. We had travelled the world; it had been the best time of our lives, but we had returned to this beautiful country – we have so much to be thankful for.

Dreams are for living, and Warren and I have lived our dream . . .

RECIPES FROM OUR TRAVELS

The following recipes have been given to us by some of the people that we have met on our travels. Most of the recipes are 'cheat's' recipes, but I don't apologise for that. If a recipe is simple and quick to make, but tastes delicious, why should anyone apologise?

GREECE

SAGANAKI
Serves 4

Saganaki is a delicious fried cheese starter popular throughout Greece. The Greeks usually use Kasseri, Kefalotiri or Graviera cheeses, but Feta cheese can be used (though it isn't as hard a cheese).

454g Kasseri, Kefalotiri or Graviera
Cornflour
1 egg, beaten with 1 teaspoon cornflour
3 tbsp melted butter (ideally clarified)
Juice of half a lemon and 4 wedges to serve
2 – 3 tablespoons brandy, heated until lukewarm (optional)

Cut the cheese into four ½" thick slices.

Dredge the cheese in cornflour until lightly coated. If using feta cheese, place cheese in the freezer for about 30 minutes before frying.

When ready to serve, dip the cheese in the egg mix, and heat the clarified butter in a large non stick frying pan.

Gently heat the brandy (if using) in a separate pan.

When the butter is very hot, fry the cheese slices on both sides until lightly browned.

Pour the brandy over the cheese and ignite it. Douse the flames by sprinkling over the lemon juice.

Place the cheese on warm serving plates and serve immediately with lemon wedges.

A Greek salad and bread would be delicious side dishes to make this starter into a more substantial meal.

Note:

- Kasseri is sheep's or goat's cheese, which is sharp, salty and hard (similar to Cheddar).
- Gravieri is a hard cheese made from cow's milk and has a delicate taste.
- Kefalotiri is made from ewe's or goat's milk and is hard, salty and piquant.

TURKEY

LENTIL SOUP
Serves 8

Lentil soup was available in every café and restaurant that we visited throughout Turkey. Each café had its own recipe, but all of them had that unmistakable middle-Eastern flavour of cumin and mint. This recipe serves 8, but the recipe can be halved or alternatively any left-over soup freezes well in individual portions in freezer bags

250g red lentils
1 large onion, finely chopped
1 tin chopped tomatoes
2 cloves garlic, crushed
1½ litres vegetable or chicken stock (preferably fresh)
Olive oil
1½ dessertspoons cumin
1 level tablespoon freshly chopped mint
salt and black pepper
a pinch of dried red chilli flakes
Lemon juice (optional)

Chop onions and garlic, and gently fry them without browning in olive oil until soft. Add the cumin and chopped tomatoes, stock and lentils and bring to a boil.

Add the mint, chilli flakes and some pepper.

Cook on medium heat for at least 30-40 minutes, but preferably for an hour, until the lentils are soft and the mixture has become creamy.

Taste and add salt (never add salt at the beginning of cooking to lentils, as the lentils will remain hard). Also add more mint, cumin, chilli or pepper if required. Purée the soup with a stick blender or in a processor or blender.

aste again. You may like to add a squeeze of lemon juice if you feel the soup needs it. If the soup is too thick, add a little water.

Serve with chunks of fresh bread.

INDIA

GOBI MANCHURIAN
Serves 6

Originally a Chinese recipe, Gobi Manchurian has been adopted by the Indians and is now available throughout most of India. It was originally available as street food, but is now offered in most restaurants as a delicious starter, and is often served at Indian weddings. The dish is usually served quite dry as a starter, each piece of cauliflower speared with a cocktail stick, in which case you will only need half the amount of sauce shown here. However, it is also delicious served as a side dish, in which case serve it with all of the sauce.

1 medium cauliflower broken into bite-sized florettes
1 tablespoon milk

BATTER:
2 teaspoons ginger, finely chopped
2 teaspoons garlic, finely chopped
1 teaspoon red chilli powder
60g plain flour
4 tablespoons cornflour
Pinch of salt
Approximately 80ml water
Oil for deep frying

SAUCE:
2 teaspoons ginger, finely chopped
2 teaspoons garlic, finely chopped
2 dry red chillies, finely chopped
5 spring onions, very finely sliced
350ml water
1½ tablespoon dark soy sauce
1 tablespoon sweet chilli sauce
1 tablespoon tomato ketchup
1 tablespoon cornflour + 60ml cold water

Boil the florettes in plenty of water and 1 tablespoon milk until almost tender.

Drain and pat dry on a clean cloth.

Mix batter ingredients with water gradually, until the batter is thick enough to stick to the florettes. Tip the florettes into the batter and stir to ensure all are coated. Deep fry the florettes in hot oil a few at a time, turning them to ensure that they are golden all over. Set aside.

Add 60ml of water to 1 tablespoon cornflour and stir to dissolve. Put to one side.

Fry ginger, garlic and crushed red chilli for a minute. Add a pinch of salt and the spring onions. Stir fry for a minute. Add the water and bring to a boil. Gradually add the cornflour and water to the sauce and stir continuously until it resumes boiling and thickens. Continue to stir for a minute whilst boiling until the sauce becomes transparent.

Stir in the soy sauce, tomato ketchup and chilli sauce. Then add the cooked cauliflower florettes. Gently stir until the sauce has coated the florettes. Serve piping hot on a plate with a toothpick in each florette if serving as a starter. If serving as a side dish, pour into a serving dish with all of the sauce.

MYANMAR

GREEN TOMATO SALAD
Serves 2

Until tasting this Burmese salad, I hadn't realized that green tomatoes could be eaten raw, and I couldn't believe how delicious this salad was. Once again, the restaurant owner kindly demonstrated how to make this recipe so that I could make it myself when I returned to England.

2 large green tomatoes
1 medium red onion
Large pinch of salt and sugar
2 tablespoons of peanuts (unsalted)
Vegetable oil

To make peanut oil, roughly chop or crush half of the peanuts, and very gently cook them in the vegetable oil over low heat. Turn off the heat and allow the flavour of the peanuts to penetrate the oil. Strain the oil, discarding the peanuts.

Cut the tomatoes in half through the stem end, and cut each half into very thin slices. Put them into a bowl.

Finely slice the red onion, and add the slices to the tomatoes.

Finely chop the rest of the peanuts, and add them to the tomatoes and onions with a large pinch of salt and sugar.

Finally, pour over a little of the peanut oil. Mix well and serve.

AUSTRALIA

MARIE'S SALMON PATTIES
Serves 4 (makes 8 patties)

A wonderful store cupboard recipe, these delicious patties are even simpler to make than fish cakes, and are delicious hot (with salad and new potatoes) or cold (with potato salad). They can also be made much smaller, making them suitable for a cold buffet. Red salmon tastes better than pink, and red onion is better than white, but just use whatever you have in your store cupboard!

418g tin of salmon, drained and bones removed
1 medium very finely-diced onion
2 medium eggs, beaten
3 flat tablespoons flour (any sort)
1 heaped tablespoon finely chopped fresh parsley (optional)
3 tbsp oil for cooking
Salt and pepper

Mix together the salmon, onion, eggs, parsley and season to taste. Gradually add the flour until the mixture is a fairly sloppy consistency. (You may not need to add all of the flour).

Heat the oil in a frying pan and drop dollops (a slightly heaped tablespoon) into the oil. Don't worry about making the patties into neat shapes like fish cakes – they're supposed to look rustic! Press down with a spatula or fish slice to flatten slightly, and when browned on one side flip over to brown the other side.

I like them served hot with lemon wedges, new potatoes, salad and the following sauce:

CRÈME PESTO SAUCE:

2 heaped tablespoons crème fraiche
1 heaped dessertspoon pesto sauce

Mix together until blended.

If I serve the salmon patties cold, I like them with this easy potato salad:

POTATO SALAD:
Serves 2

300g tin of new potatoes, drained and finely sliced
1 heaped tablespoon crème fraiche or plain yogurt (the crème fraiche
makes a creamier dressing)
1 heaped tablespoon tartare sauce
Finely chopped chives or spring onions (optional)

Mix everything together, making sure the potatoes are coated with the sauce.

AUSTRALIA

KIRSTY'S MEXICAN STARTER
Serves 8

I wondered what Kirsty was doing when she began spreading refried beans on a plate, but the finished recipe was a delicious starter to share with friends. You may feel initially that it looks as though you're spreading cat food onto a plate but stick with it – everyone we've served this to has enjoyed it! I use a china flan dish to serve this, or you can use a dinner plate. The following quantities are approximate.

A tin of refried beans
200g mayonnaise (full fat, light or whatever you want)
Mild chilli powder, taco or similar seasoning (sprinkle thickly over the mayo)
200g sour cream or crème fraîche
1 very finely chopped green pepper
2 very ripe mashed avocados (mash with a fork on a plate first)
3 finely chopped tomatoes (remove seeds first)
225g grated cheddar cheese
Very finely sliced spring onions (green part only)

Tortilla chips to serve (any flavour)

Spread a layer of each of the above ingredients in turn into the dish or plate, starting with the refried beans, then a layer of mayonnaise. Sprinkle the mayonnaise liberally with mild chilli powder (or similar), continuing with each ingredient. Make sure that you spread each layer to cover the whole plate or dish, finally topping with the grated cheese and enough sliced spring onions to look decorative.

Serve as a dip with tortilla chips. Enjoy!

THAILAND

QUICK MASSAMAN CURRY
Serves 4

Massaman curry is a popular dish in Southern Thailand. Massaman is a Muslim-influenced curry and is a delicious blend of Thai and Indian. This recipe was demonstrated to me by the chef of a restaurant in Thailand. Having made it many times since we returned to England, we can confirm that this recipe tastes just like the Massaman Curry we had in restaurants in Thailand. If you can't get Massaman or red curry paste, substitute Rogan Josh curry paste – it still tastes good! The chef cooked the chicken breast from frozen – he kept portions in bags in the freezer, each portion being sufficient for one serving.

2 raw chicken breasts (approx. 400g) chopped into bite-sized pieces
1 heaped tablespoon Massaman or red curry paste
5 medium waxy potatoes (approx. 600g uncooked) cooked and cut into bite-sized pieces
100g salted peanuts, roughly chopped (You can substitute cashew nuts for peanuts if you wish, though peanuts are far more common in Massaman curries in Thailand.)
2 medium onions (approx. 280g) chopped into chunky pieces and separated
1 heaped tablespoon of peanut butter
2 tins coconut milk
2 slightly heaped dessertspoons sugar
1 chicken or vegetable stock cube, crumbled

Steamed or boiled Thai rice to serve

Drop the chicken pieces into boiling water (can be cooked from frozen if wished) – the chicken will only take a minute to poach.

Meanwhile put the curry paste into a large saucepan and cover with the coconut milk. Heat gently until dissolved. Add the sugar and the onions.

Bring to the boil and simmer until the onions are softened but still have a 'bite'. Add the chicken and the rest of the ingredients into the curry, and simmer for a few minutes for the flavours to amalgamate.

The consistency should be quite runny (like soup). Add some water if it's too thick. Taste and add more seasoning if necessary, though the salt in the peanuts and stock cube will probably be sufficient.

Serve in a bowl with a portion of steamed or boiled rice on the side.

(The Thais always press the rice into a bowl or mould, and tip carefully out onto the plate. Thais add spoonfuls of the curry to the rice to eat it, but if you prefer to tip the rice into the curry then that's fine).

AUTHOR'S FOOTNOTE

On Boxing Day, 26th December, 2004, 6 months after we had returned to England, we were horrified to watch on television the devastation and loss of life caused by the tsunami which struck Asia. Over 225,000 people died in eleven different countries leaving millions homeless. So many of the areas hit were places that we knew and loved – places that we had visited on our trip.

• In Sri Lanka a train was travelling from Colombo to Hikkaduwa when the tsunami rushed 60 feet inland and swept the train with its eight carriages and 1,500 passengers off the rails, leaving the railroad a pile of twisted metal; over 1,000 passengers on the train died. We had cycled along this very route in Sri Lanka to Hikkaduwa alongside the railway line.

• At Mirrisa, Sri Lanka, where we stayed in two properties that backed onto the beautiful crescent beach, the giant waves swept over the beach, across the gardens and through the houses, carrying everything in its way.

• In Kanyakumari, the holy town at the southernmost point in India that we visited, the tsunami hit the tiny island 400 metres offshore as people waited for the ancient rusty ferry to take them back to the mainland. Over 800 people died in Kanyakumari, but more than 8,000 people died in the state of Tamil Nadu.

• In Mamallapurum, in Tamil Nadu in east India, the huge ancient granite statues on the beach survived (as they had probably done before with previous tsunamis), although whole settlements were swept away by the giant waves. We had stayed several days in this resort.

• When the tsunami hit Ranong in Thailand, where we went by boat to Myanmar on a visa run, the waves were higher than the many schools that it hit, drowning children and teachers.

• Phuket was badly hit, and we wondered what had happened to Oh, who ran the shrimp farm in north Phuket, and his lovely wife, Tim, who cooked us such delicious meals. Their shrimp farm adjoined the camping ground where we stayed, where tents could be set up under the trees which led down the slope to the beach. What horrors did the backpackers have to endure as the massive waves hit them as they slept zipped inside their tents under the trees on Boxing Day morning?

• The beach resort of Kamala Beach in Phuket was devastated by the massive waves and was full of western tourists. The beach was littered with bodies after the waves receded. This is the resort where our ground floor room and terrace overlooked the beach, only 10 feet away.

• Bang Niang in Thailand was where we stayed on the beach in a thatched bungalow on stilts, and where we watched the lightning from our bungalow on the beach and saw the full moon light a path across the sea to our door. The area close to Bang Niang beach is quite flat, and as a result the tsunami waves penetrated three kilometres inland, demolishing the area.

• Bodies were floating in the street at nearby Khao Lak, and this was one of the worst hit areas in Thailand – over 5,000 people died there that day. This was where we stayed at a small resort next to the sea, with the restaurant actually built over the water on a wooden jetty. I wondered how many tourists would have been sat having their breakfast there as the tsunami hit.

• In Ao Phang Nga, where we went by boat to see the limestone islands and caves, kayakers were trapped in the limestone caves and drowned, and the village was flooded.

• Koh Lanta, where we stayed while my mother was in hospital, was hit by the tsunami, though it was luckily partially protected by a big sand bar. I wonder what happened to the bungalow resort where we stayed, because the open air restaurant and gardens were next to the beach with no wall to protect them from the enormous waves.

• A friend of ours who was in Yangon, Myanmar at the time of the tsunami, told us that she had felt a three minute earthquake, although there was no damage in that area. On her return to Bangkok en route for England she met dozens of backpackers who had lost their friends in the disaster.

And then tragedy struck once again – in May 2008 Cyclone Nargis raged through southern Myanmar's Ayeyarwady Delta, leaving a trail of flattened villages and broken lives. Over 138,000 were reported dead or missing, thousands were injured and millions were left homeless. Most of the dead, injured and homeless lived in the city of Yangon, where Warren and I had stayed, and in the low-lying rice-growing delta area of the Ayeyarwady (or Irrawaddy) river – the river along which Warren and I had travelled by boat from Mandalay to Bagan, the ancient Burmese city of ancient temples.

BICYCLE SPECIFICATIONS

For those of you interested in the specifications of our bikes, Warren has provided me with the following details

Frames	Handbuilt by framebuilder, Dave Yates of Gateshead. Made from Reynolds 525 crome-moly to take 26" wheels.
	The wheels and bicycles were built by Rikki Pankhurst of AW Cycles of Caversham, Reading.
Gears	Campagnola Athena racing triple groupset (2 chain rings changed to extend the lower gearing).
Wheels	Azonic Pyramid rims with Sap spokes.
Brakes	Shimano Deore XT V-brakes.
Handle bars	Drop handle bars.
Saddles	Brookes professional leather saddles.
Seat posts	Suspension seat posts.
Pedals	MKS platform with MT Zefal toe clip
Lights	Lumotec Halogen stand light/Nordlicht generator (front lights) and Cateye LED (back).
Mudguards	SKS mudguards.
Racks	Blackburn carrier racks (front and rear) and Klickfix top bag holder.

Panniers	Karrimore Iberian panniers and top bag with separate waterproof covers (*initially bright red, the bags had faded to silvery pink by the end of our trip!*)
Locks	Abus Granit bike locks and cable.
Pump	Zefal HP2.
Spares	2 spare spokes 1 spare gear cable 1 spare brake cable 2 spare inner tubes Puncture repair kit